Holding UNPOL to Account

International Humanitarian Law Series

VOLUME 50

The International Humanitarian Law Series is a series of monographs and edited volumes which aims to promote scholarly analysis and discussion of both the theory and practice of the international legal regulation of armed conflict.

The series explores substantive issues of International Humanitarian Law including,

- protection for victims of armed conflict and regulation of the means and methods of warfare
- questions of application of the various legal regimes for the conduct of armed conflict
- issues relating to the implementation of International Humanitarian Law obligations
- national and international approaches to the enforcement of the law and
- the interactions between International Humanitarian Law and other related areas of international law such as Human Rights, Refugee Law, Arms Control and Disarmament Law, and International Criminal Law.

The titles published in this series are listed at *brill.com/ihul*

Holding UNPOL to Account

Individual Criminal Accountability of United Nations Police Personnel

By

Ai Kihara-Hunt

BRILL
NIJHOFF

LEIDEN | BOSTON

Cover illustration: Peacekeepers of the United Nations Interim Force in Lebanon (UNIFIL) stand next to their folded flags during a handover ceremony from Italian Major-General Luciano Portolano to Irish Major-General Michael Beary of the command of Lebanon's U.N. peacekeeping forces at the United Nations headquarters in Naqoura, southern Lebanon, July 19, 2016. REUTERS/Ali Hashisho TPX IMAGES OF THE DAY.

Library of Congress Cataloging-in-Publication Data

Names: Kihara-Hunt, Ai, author.
Title: Holding UNPOL to account : individual criminal accountability of United Nations police personnel / by Ai Kihara-Hunt.
Description: Leiden ; Boston : Brill Nijhoff, 2017. | Series: International humanitarian law series ; VOLUME 50 | Based on author's thesis (doctoral - University of Essex, School of Law, 2015) issued under title: Individual criminal accountability of UN police personnel. | Includes bibliographical references and index.
Identifiers: LCCN 2016058677 (print) | LCCN 2016059779 (ebook) | ISBN 9789004328808 (hardback : alk. paper) | ISBN 9789004328815 (E-book)
Subjects: LCSH: International police. | United Nations--Peacekeeping forces. | United Nations--Privileges and immunities | Police misconduct. | War crimes.
Classification: LCC KZ6374 .K545 2017 (print) | LCC KZ6374 (ebook) | DDC 341.7/2--dc23
LC record available at https://lccn.loc.gov/2016058677

Typeface for the Latin, Greek, and Cyrillic scripts: "Brill". See and download: brill.com/brill-typeface.

ISSN 1389-6776
ISBN 978-90-04-32880-8 (hardback)
ISBN 978-90-04-32881-5 (e-book)

This book is printed on acid-free paper and produced in a sustainable manner.

Contents

Foreword IX
Acknowledgements XI
List of Cases XII
List of Treaties XIX
Acronyms XXI

1 **Introduction** 1
1 The Issue 1
2 The Evolution of UN Peace Operations 3
3 The Scope of This Work 5
4 Issues Outside the Scope of This Work 8
5 Structure 10
6 Definitions and Clarifications 11
7 Conclusion 13

2 **UN Police in Peace Operations** 15
1 The Evolution of the Functions of the UN Police in UN Peace Operations 16
1-1 *The Creation of the Institution of the UN Police* 17
1-2 *Post-cold War* 22
1-3 *From Monitoring to Reform* 27
1-4 *Multi-dimensional Policing* 28
1-5 *Executive Policing* 31
1-6 *Formed Police Units* 32
1-7 *A Holistic 'rule of law' Approach* 34
2 The Growth in Size of the UN Police 38
3 Ensuring the Deployment of the Required Types of Personnel 42
3-1 *Expertise Required of UN Police Officers* 42
3-2 *Personal Qualities Required* 50
3-3 *The UN's Efforts in Securing Adherence to the Required Criteria* 52
4 Conclusion 62

3 **Evidence of the Commission of Crimes by UN Police** 65
1 Findings Regarding Particularized Allegations 69
Misconduct Entries over Time 71
Nature of Alleged Crimes 88

Nationality of Suspects 91
Prosecution 92
2 Possible Patterns of Criminal Conduct 95
2-1 *Evidence of the Scale of Wrongdoing* 97
2-2 *Nature of Alleged Criminal Offences* 104
2-3 *Analysis in Relation to the Sending State* 107
2-4 *Possible Reasons for the Patterns* 110
3 Evidence of Prosecution 114
4 Conclusion 117

4 Current UN Machinery for Collecting Information Regarding Alleged Crimes for Domestic Criminal Proceedings 119
1 Benchmarks 120
Benchmark 1 120
Benchmark 2 120
Benchmark 3 122
Benchmark 4 123
2 Evolution of the Approach to, and the Mechanisms for, Dealing with Criminal Misconduct 123
3 Analysis of the Mechanisms' Performance 134
Benchmark 1 134
Benchmark 2 158
Benchmark 3 172
Benchmark 4 178

5 Criminal Jurisdiction under International and National Law 188
1 Introduction 188
2 Criminal Laws to Which the UN Police are Subject 191
2-1 *The Host State's Criminal Law* 191
2-2 *The Sending State's Criminal Law* 202
3 International Law Governing Jurisdiction 202
3-1 *Host State Jurisdiction* 204
3-2 *The Sending State's Jurisdiction* 206
3-3 *Exercise of Criminal Jurisdiction by Other States* 208
4 National Laws Dealing with Jurisdiction 212
4-1 *The Host State* 213
4-2 *Sending States* 213
4-3 *The National Laws Governing the Jurisdiction of Other States* 223
4-4 *Competing Bases of National Jurisdiction* 226
5 Conclusion 227

6 **Immunity as a Potential Legal Barrier** 230

1 The Law of Immunity 231

1-1 *The Rationale for Immunity* 231

1-2 *Sources* 234

1-3 *Status of UN Police Personnel in Terms of Immunity* 239

1-4 *Scope of Immunities for UN Police Personnel* 246

1-5 *Determining the Scope of Immunity, and When it May be Waived* 263

2 Application of Immunity in Practice 272

2-1 *Inappropriate Assertions of Immunity* 275

2-2 *Inappropriate Use of Waiver* 277

3 Conclusion 279

3-1 *Theory* 279

3-2 *Practice* 282

7 **Is There an Obligation to Investigate and Prosecute?** 287

1 IHRL Monitoring Mechanisms 288

2 A State's Obligation to Investigate and Prosecute UN Police Officers, in Relation to Serious Crimes 290

2-1 *Existence of the Obligation in General* 291

2-2 *Two Ways in which the Obligation to Investigate and Prosecute Arises* 294

2-3 *Does it Matter Which Substantive Right is at Issue?* 299

3 Scope of the Obligation 301

3-1 *Obligation to Investigate* 301

3-2 *Obligation to Prosecute and Punish* 307

4 The Obligation of the Host State to Investigate and Prosecute 311

5 The Sending State's Obligation 315

6 Special Circumstances Pertaining to Formed Police Units (FPUs) 317

7 Does Immunity have any Impact on a State's Obligation to Prosecute? 323

8 Does the UN have an Obligation to Investigate and Prosecute Crimes Committed by UN Police Officers? 325

8-1 *Applicability of IHRL to the UN* 326

8-2 *Content of the UN's Obligations* 331

9 Conclusion 338

8 **Conclusion** 341

Bibliography 353

Index 429

Foreword

The United Nations Secretary-General in late October 2016 fired the Military Force Commander of the United Nations Mission in South Sudan following a devastating report showing how UN troops refused to respond to desperate calls for help from trapped UN colleagues, some of whom were then raped and assaulted by South Sudanese government troops. Earlier in 2016 the Secretary-General fired his Special Representative in the Central African Republic after an independent commission found that senior UN officials in the mission had failed to take appropriate action after learning that French troops deployed in a separate mission had traded food for sexual favors from juveniles. And in 2010, UN peacekeepers from Nepal brought cholera to Haiti when they deployed there as part of the UN Mission. This was several months after the earthquake. Haiti had not had a cholera outbreak in over 100 years and epidemiological studies conducted by the Yale Medical School and other experts showed conclusively that the cholera strain found in Haiti originated in western Nepal, precisely where the Nepali peacekeepers had been stationed before coming to Haiti. Over 10,000 Haitians have died from the disease which is still rampant and spreading even further following Hurricane Matthew. The UN initially denied responsibility and rejected any suggestion of being obliged to compensate the victims.

To say that the UN has a major problem with holding its peacekeepers: military, police and civilians, accountable for their behavior while in Mission would be an understatement. It is exactly this problem that Ai Kihara-Hunt has plunged into with great rigor and thoroughness in her study, *Holding UNPOL to Account: Individual Criminal Accountability of UN Police Personnel*. While focusing on the police component of UN peace operations, Ms. Kihara-Hunt identifies the main challenges common to the entire enterprise: the UN's reluctance to hold itself to the same standards it demands of the host nation and indeed of all Member-States. Specifically, this study shows that a lack of political will inhibits serious investigations from occurring, let alone prosecutions.

There is a large transparency deficit where just obtaining basic information on alleged criminal behavior by UN police is extremely difficult to find. Ms. Kihara-Hunt calls for the UN to be much more transparent in handling these cases. Again, this is another core value that the UN often demands of others but seems most reluctant to apply to its own acts.

This all leads to an absence of accountability for criminal behavior by UN police. This is especially destructive since UNPOL, as the study notes, have even more contact with the local population than their UN military colleagues do and UNPOL have a broad mandate to promote proper behavior by the local police through training, mentoring and assessing. As part of their mission in most UN peace operations, UN Police correctly emphasize the importance of accountability in police reform projects to combat impunity. If crimes or misconduct committed by the local police go unpunished the population understandably will have little faith in their police. Yet here are the UN police effectively enjoying a status that puts them above the law. This is not a good recipe for enhancing respect for human rights or building the rule of law, two core goals of UNPOL in peace operations.

Ms. Kihara-Hunt's study meticulously examines thousands of cases from dozens of countries and she has created a much-needed data-base from the information available, something the UN has never done. Her research shows that the UN has a major problem that cannot remain hidden any longer. While the study identifies hurdles that exist to investigate and prosecute, such as the difficulty of gathering evidence, presenting testimony from witnesses and, in some cases, issues of immunity arise, the main problem lies elsewhere. The UNPOL officer's sending state lacks the political will to prosecute these cases. This is not a surprise since unfortunately many states who offer police for deployment to UN peace operations themselves fail to hold their police accountable for crimes and misdeeds committed at home. So it is highly unlikely that these states would prosecute officers for acts committed far from home in some foreign country.

The study reveals that the types of crimes most often committed by UN Police occur while they are off-duty and bespeak a lack of integrity. This is a crucial finding since one of the two main criteria the UN supposedly applies when evaluating candidates for deployment along with their core competence is their integrity. That so many police officers who are chosen for deployment lack the requisite integrity shows that the UN must change how it evaluates candidates.

Ms. Kihara-Hunt urges the UN to make these changes because not only will it prevent criminal behavior and lead to greater respect for the rule of law but also because the UN's legitimacy is at stake. If the UN cannot live up to its own values, then there is little chance that the host-country beneficiaries of UN peace operations will adopt them. The way forward is much clearer thanks to Ai Kihara-Hunt's work. Now the question is will the UN, under the leadership of a new Secretary-General, have the political will and courage to do what is necessary.

William G. O'Neill
Brooklyn, NY

Acknowledgements

This book was initially written as a doctoral thesis under the supervision of Professor Françoise Hampson and Mr. Scott Sheeran. I am much obliged to them in completing the foundation of this book.

I am extremely grateful for the dedication and effort of Professor Françoise Hampson and Ms. Felicity Szesnat in leading me to shape this work into the current form.

I would also like to thank a number of senior UN personnel for their keen interest and kind guidance they have offered me during the course of my research.

Most importantly, I would like to express my gratitude to my family, Werner and Aiko Jane, for their extensive emotional and technical support throughout the time of my research.

List of Cases

Accordance with International Law of the Unilateral Declaration of Independence in Respect of Kosovo (Declaration of Simma J) [2010] ICJ Rep 478

Affaire Gentilhomme, Schaff-Benhadji and Zerouki v France App nos 48205/99, 48207/99 and 48209/99 (ECtHR, 14 May 2002)

Ahmet Özkan and Others v UK App no 21689/93, (ECtHR, 6 April 2004)

Akpinar and Altun v Turkey ECHR 2007-III

Aksoy v Turkey ECHR 1996-VI

Al-Adsani v UK ECHR 2001-XI

Al-Jedda v UK [2011] ECHR 1092

Al-Skeini and Others v UK [2011] ECHR 1093

Ali Medjnoune v Algeria 9 Selected Decisions of the Human Rights Committee 182

Angelova and Iliev v Bulgaria ECHR 2007-IX

Applicability of Article VI, Section 22, of the Convention on the Privileges and Immunities of the United Nations (Advisory Opinion) [1989] ICJ Rep 177

Applicability of Article VI, Section 22, of the Convention on the Privileges and Immunities of the United Nations (Written Statement Submitted on behalf of the Secretary-General of the United Nations) [1989] ICJ Rep 173

Armed Activities on the Territory of the Congo (DRC v Uganda) [2005] ICJ Rep 168

Arrest Warrant of 11 April 2000 (DRC v Belgium) (Diss Op Van den Wyngaert) [2002] ICJ Rep 137

Arrest Warrant of 11 April 2000 (DRC v Belgium) (Judgment) [2002] ICJ Rep 3

Arrest Warrant of 11 April 2000 (DRC v Belgium) (Sep Op Guillaume P) [2002] ICJ Rep 35

Arrest Warrant of 11 April 2000 (DRC v Belgium) (Sep Op Higgins, Koojimans and Buergenthal) [2002] ICJ Rep 63

Assanidze v Georgia ECHR 2004-II

Banković and Others v Belgium and Others (Admissibility) ECHR 2001-XII

Bazorkina v Russia ECHR 2006-I

Behrami and Behrami v France and Sarmati v France, Germany and Norway (Admissibility) App nos 71412/01, 78166/01 (ECtHR, 2 May 2007)

Beker v Turkey App no 27866/03 (ECtHR, 24 March 2009)

Bekos v Greece App no 15250/02 (ECtHR, 13 December 2005)

Bilbija et al (2006) AP-953/05 (Constitutional Court of Bosnia and Herzegovina, in the Appeal of Milorad Bilbija et al, 8 July 2006)

Blake v Guatemala Inter-Am Ct HR Series C No 36 (24 January 1998)

Boery v Ghaddafi Cour de Cassation [2001] 125 ILR 490

Bogdan Subotić (2005) AP-696/04 (The Constitutional Court of Bosnia and Herzegovina, 23 September 2005)

Bouterse v Public Prosecutor Court of Appeal of Amsterdam (Gerechtshof Amsterdam) 20 November 2000

Bulacio v Argentina Inter-Am Ct HR Series C No 100 (18 September 2003)

Caballero Delgado and Santana v Colombia Inter-Am Ct HR Series C No 22 (8 December 1995)

Çakıcı v Turkey [1999] ECHR 43

Calvelli and Ciglio v Italy ECHR 2002-I

Case concerning Application of the Convention on the Prevention and Punishment of the Crime of Genocide (Bosnia and Herzegovina v Serbia and Montenegro) (Judgment of 26 February 2007) [2007] ICJ Rep 43 (ICJ)

Case concerning Barcelona Traction, Light and Power Co Ltd (Belgium v Spain) (New Application: 1962) (Second phase) [1970] ICJ Rep 3

Case concerning Military and Paramilitary Activities in and against Nicaragua (Nicaragua v US) (Merits) [1986] ICJ Rep 12

Certain Questions of Mutual Assistance in Criminal Matters (Djibouti v France) (Judgment) [2008] ICJ Rep 172

Corfu Channels case (UK v Albania) (Merits) [1949] ICJ Rep 4

Cynthia Brzak and Nasr Ishak v The United Nations, Kofi Annan, Wendy Chambering, Ruud Lubbers, et al (Certiorari – Summary Dispositions) Order list 562 US 09-1481

Cynthia Brzak and Nasr Ishak v The United Nations, Kofi Annan, Wendy Chambering, Ruud Lubbers, et al Docket No. 08-2799-cv 597 F 3d 107 (2010)

Cynthia Brzak and Nasr Ishak v The United Nations, Kofi Annan, Wendy Chambering, Ruud Lubbers, et al 551 F Supp 2d 313 (SDNY 2008)

Cyprus v Turkey ECHR 2001-IV

Difference Relating to Immunity from Legal Process of a Special Rapporteur of the Commission on Human Rights (Advisory Opinion) [1999] ICJ Rep 62

Difference Relating to Immunity from Legal Process of a Special Rapporteur of the Commission on Human Rights (Diss Op Koroma) [1999] ICJ Rpt 111

Difference Relating to Immunity from Legal Process of a Special Rapporteur of the Commission on Human Rights (Written Statement submitted on behalf of the Secretary-General of the United Nations) (ICJ 2 October 1999), <http://wwwicj-cijorg/docket/files/100/8658pdf>, accessed 30 November 2011

Dink v Turkey App no 2668/07 (ECtHR, 14 September 2010)

Dodov v Bulgaria ECHR 2008

Durand v Peru Inter-Am Ct HR Series C No 68 (16 August 2000)

Eduardo Bleier v Uruguay 1 Selected Decisions of the Human Rights Committee 109

Almeida de Quinteros v Uruguay 2 Selected Decisions of the Human Rights Committee 138

Edwards v UK Series A No 247 B

El Hassy v Lybia Communication no 1422/2005 (Human Rights Committee, 24 October 2007)
El Moctar v Secretary-General of the United Nations Case no UNDT/NBI/2011/011, Judgment no UNDT/2012/113, (UNDT, 24 July 2012)
Ergi v Turkey ECHR 1998-IV
Etienne Tête v France Series A No 54
Eugenia Lazăr v Romania App no 32146/05 (ECtHR, 16 February 2010)
Ferrini v Germany [2004] Italian Court of Cassation, Decision No 5044/2004, 128 ILR 658
Finucame v UK ECHR 2003-VIII
Gajić v Germany (Admissibility) App no 31446/02 (ECtHR, 28 August 2007)
Genie-Lacayo v Nicaragua Inter-Am Ct HR Series C No 30 (29 January 1997)
Georgia v Russia (II) (Admissibility) App no 38263/08 (ECtHR, 19 December 2011)
Godinez-Cruz v Honduras (Merits) Inter-Am Ct HR Series C No 5 (20 January 1989)
H C M A v The Netherlands 3 Selected Decisions of the Human Rights Committee 19
Gongadze v Ukraine App no 34056/02 (ECtHR, 8 November 2005)
Guiliani and Gaggio v Italy ECHR-2011
Gül v Turkey App no 22676/93 (ECtHR, 14 December 2000)
Güleç v Turkey ECHR 1998-IV
Hassan Abbousedra v Lybia Communication no 1751/2008 (Human Rights Committee, 25 October 2010)
HRH Prince Abdul Aziz Bin Fahd Bin Abdul Aziz v Mrs Janan George Harb [2015] EWCA Civ 481
Hugh Jordan v UK ECHR 2001-III
Ilaşcu and Others v Moldova and Russia ECHR 2004-VII
Ilhan v Turkey ECHR 2000-VII
Imakayeva v Russia ECHR 2006-XIII
Interpretation of the Agreement of 25 March 1951 between the WHO and Egypt (Advisory Opinion) [1980] ICJ Rep 73
Isayeva v Russia App no 57950/00 (ECtHR, 6 July 2005)
Jaloud v the Netherlands [2014] ECHR 1292
Jankauskas v Lithuania App no 59304/00 (ECtHR, 16 December 2003)
Joaquín David Herrera Rubio v Colombia 2 Selected Decisions of the Human Rights Committee 192
Jones v Ministry of Interior Al-Mamlaka Al-Arabiya AS Saudiya (the Kingdom of Saudi Arabia) [2006] UKHL 26
Jones and Others v UK ECHR 2014
José Vicente and Amado Villafañe Chaparro, Dioselina Torres Crespo, Hermes Enrique Torres Solis and Vicencio Chaparro Izquierdo v Colombia 6 Selected Decisions of the Human Rights Committee 135

Jurisdictional Immunities of the State (*Germany v Italy: Greece intervening*) (Diss Op Trindade) [2012] ICJ Rep 179
Jurisdictional Immunities of the State (*Germany v Italy: Greece intervening*) (Judgement) [2012] ICJ Rep 99
Kalogeropoulou and Others v Greece and Germany (Admissibility) EHCR 2002-X
Kasumaj v Greece (Admissibility) App no 6974/05 (ECtHR, 5 July 2007)
Kaya v Turkey ECHR 1998-I
Kelly and Others v UK App no 30054/96 (ECtHR, 4 May 2001)
Kemal Kiliç v Turkey ECHR 2000-III
Khilal Avadanov v Azerbaijan Communication no 1633/2007 (Human Rights Committee, 25 October 2010)
Kurt v Turkey ECHR 1998-III
L C B v UK ECHR 1998-III 1403
La Palmeras v Colombia Inter-Am Ct HR Series C No 90 (6 December 2001)
Legal Consequences of the Construction of a Wall in the Occupied Palestinian Territory (Advisory Opinion) [2004] ICJ Rep 316
Legal Status of Eastern Greenland Case (*Denmark v Norway*) (Judgment) PCIJ Rep Series A/B, No 53, 48
Loayza-Tamayo v Peru Inter-Am Ct HR Series C No42 (27 November 1998)
Loizidou v Turkey Series A No 310
Lotus (*France v Turkey*) (Judgment) PCIJ Rep Series A No 10
M C v Bulgaria ECHR 2003-XII
M G B and S P v Trinidad and Tobago 3 Selected Decisions of the Human Rights Committee 36
M & Co v Germany Series A No 64
Mahmut Kaya v Turkey ECHR 2000-III
Marcellana and Gumanoy v The Philippines Communication no 1560/2007 (Human Rights Committee, 30 October 2008)
Maria da Penha Maia Fernandes v Brazil 12.051 Inter-Am Com HR Series L No 54/01
Özgür Gündem v Turkey ECHR 2000-III
Marija and Dragana Novakovic, on behalf of their son, Zoran Novakovic (deceased) v Serbia Communication no 1556/2007 (Human Rights Committee, 21 October 2010)
Matthews v UK [1999] ECHR 12
McCann and Others v UK Series A No 324
McKerr v UK ECHR 2001-III
McShane v UK App no 43290/98 (ECtHR 28 May 2002)
Mehmet Şentürk and Bekir Şentürk v Turkey App no 13423/09 (ECtHR, 9 April 2013)
Menesheva v Russia App no 59261/00 (ECtHR, 9 March 2006)
Menson and Others v UK ECHR 2003-V

Messaouda Kimouche v Algeria Communication no 1328/2004 (Human Rights Committee, 10 July 2007)

Mikayil Mammadov v Azerbaijan App no 4762/05 (ECtHR, 17 December 2009)

Mojsiewiew v Poland App no 11818/02 (ECtHR, 24 March 2009)

Mothers of Srebrenica Association v State of the Netherlands Case no 10/04437 EV/AS (Supreme Court of the Netherlands, 13 April 2012), English translation available at: <http://wwwrechtspraaknl/Organisatie/Hoge-Raad/Supreme-court/Summaries-of-some-important-rulings-of-the-Supreme-Court/Pages/Ruling-Dutch-Supreme-Court-Mothers-of-Srebrenicaaspx> Accessed 1 January 2015

Nguyen-Kropp Postica v Secretary-General of the United Nations Cases no UNDT/NY/2010/107; UNDT/NY/2011/004 Judgment no UNDT/2013/176 (UNDT, 20 December 2013)

North Sea Continental Shelf case (Federal Republic of Germany v Denmark/The Netherlands) [1969] ICJ Rep 3

Nuclear Tests Case (Australia v France) (Merits) [1974] ICJ Rep 253

Nuhanovic v The State of the Netherlands Case no 265618 HA ZA 06-1672 (Court of Appeal in the Hague, 5 July 2011) English translation available at <http://zoekenrechtspraaknl> Accessed 29 December 2014

Nuhanovic v The State of the Netherlands Case no 265615/HA ZA 06-1671 (DC Hague, 10 September 2008) English translation available at <http://zoekenrechtspraaknl> Accessed 29 December 2014

Nydia Erika Bautista de Arellana v Colombia 6 Selected Decisions of the Human Rights Commitee 103

Ognyanova v Bulgaria App no 46317/99 (ECtHR, 23 February 2006)

Öğur v Turkey ECHR 1999-III

Öneryildiz v Turkey ECHR 2004-XII

Osman and Osman v UK ECHR 1998-VIII

Osmanoglu v Turkey App no 48804/99 (ECtHR, 24 January 2008)

Paniagua-Morales v Guatemala Inter-Am Ct HR Series C No 37 (8 March 1998)

Paul and Audrey Edwards v UK ECHR 2002-II

Powell v UK ECHR 2000-V

Prisacariu v Secretary-General of the United Nations Case no UNDT/NY/2012/023, Judgment No UNDT/2014/045 (UNDT, 23 April 2014)

Prosecutor v Akeyasu (Decision on the Motion to Subpoena a Witness) ICTR-96-4-T (19 November 1997)

Prosecutor v Braškić (Decision of Trial Chamber I on Protective Measures of General Phillippe Morillon, Witness of the Trial Chamber) IT-95-14-T (12 May 1999) [2]

Prosecutor v Braškić (Judgment on the request of Croatia for review of the decision of the Trial Chamber II of 18 July 1997) IT-95-14-A (29 October 1997)

Prosecutor v Brima et al (Decision on Prosecution Appeal Against Decision on Oral Application for Witness TF1-150 to Testify Without Being Compelled to Answer Questions on Grounds of Confidentiality) SCSL-2004-16-AR73 (26 May 2006)
Prosecutor v Brima et al (Diss Op Donerty on the Prosecution's Oral Application for Leave to Be Granted to Witness TF1-150 to Testify Without Being Compelled to Answer Any Questions on Grounds of Confidentiality) SCSL-04-16-T, TC II (22 September 2005)
Prosecutor v Brima et al (Sep and Conc Op Robertson, Decision on Prosecution Appeal against Decision on Oral Application for Witness TF1-150 to Testify Without Being Compelled to Answer Questions on Groudns of Confidentiality) SCSL-04-16, AC (26 May 2006)
Prosecutor v Furundzija (Trial Judgement) ICTY-95-17/1-T (10 December 1998)
Questions relating to the Obligation to Prosecute or Extradite (*Belgium v Senegal*) [2012] ICJ Rpt 422
R (*on the application of Al-Jedda*) (*FC*) *v Secretary of State for Defence* (Sep Op Bingham LJ) [2007] UKHL 58
R A V N v Argentina 3 Selected Decisions of the Human Rights Committee 20
Rafael Mojica v Dominican Republic 5 Selected Decisions of the Human Rights Committee 70
Ramsahai and Others v the Netherlands [2007] ECHR 393
Reavey v UK App no 34640/04 (ECtHR, 27 November 2007)
Regina v Bow Street Metropolitan Stipendary Magistrate, ex parte Pinochet [1999] UKHL 17, [2000] 1 AC 147
Reparation for Injuries Suffered in the Service of the United Nations (Advisory Opinion) [1949] ICJ Rep 174
Rosario Celis Laureano v Peru 6 Selected Decisions of the Human Rights Committee 63
S E v Argentina 3 Selected Decisions of the Human Rights Committee 41
Salman v Turkey ECHR 2000-VII
Shaip Canhasi v UNMIK Case no 004/08 (The Human Rights Advisory Panel, 15 July 2008)
Shanaghan v UK App no 37715/97 (ECtHR, 4 August 2001)
Shefqet Maliqi, against the United Nations Mission in Kosovo (*UNMIK*) Registration no 361/01, (the Kosovo Ombudsperson, 13 March 2002)
Silih v Slovenia ECHR 2009
Solomou and Others v Turkey App no 36832/97 (ECtHR, 24 June 2008)
Standard Chartered Bank v ITC and Others [1987] 1 WLR 641, 648 (Bingham J)
Sundara Arachchige Lalith Rajapakse v Sri Lanka Communication no 1250/2004 (Human Rights Committee, 14 July 2006)
Svetlana Jočić v UNMIK Case no 34/09 (Human Rights Advisory Panel, 23 April 2013)

Tanis and Others v Turkey ECHR 2005-VIII
Tanli v Turkey ECHR 2001-III
Tanrikulu v Turkey ECHR 1999-IV
The Legality of the Threat or Use of Nuclear Weapons (Advisory Opinion) [1996] ICJ Rep 238
The Legality of the Threat or Use of Nuclear Weapons (Declaration of Bedjaoui P) [1996] ICJ Rep 268
The State of the Netherlands (Ministry of Defence and Ministry of Foreign Affairs) v Hasan Nuhanovic Case no 12/03324 LZ/TT (Judgement of 6 September 2013) Supreme Court of the Netherlands, English translation available at: <http://wwwrechtspraaknl/Organisatie/Hoge-Raad/OverDeHogeRaad/publicaties/Documents/12%2003324pdf> Accessed 10 March 2015
Tradesman v Colombia Inter-Am Ct HR Series C No 109 (5 July 2004)
US v Coplon et al US Dist Ct SDNY 10 May 1949, 84 F Supp 472 (SDNY 1949)
Nottebohm case (Lichtenstein v Guatemala) (Second phase) (Judgment of 6 April 1955) [1955] ICJ Rep 4
US v Melekh US Dist Ct SDNY, 28 November 1960, 190 F Supp 67 (SDNY 1960)
Attorney-General v Eichmann (Israel Sup Ct 1962), 36 Int'l L Rep 277, 1968 (English translation)
US v Rey 663 F 2d 1086 DNM (2009)
Vadivel Sathasivam and Parathesi Saraswathi v Sri Lanka Communication no 1436/2005 (Human Rights Committee, 8 July 2008)
Varnava and Others v Turkey ECHR 2009
Velásquez Rodríguez v Honduras Inter-Am Ct HR Series C No 4 (29 July 1988)
Westchester County v William Ranollo New Rochelle City Ct, 8 November 1946, 187 Misc 777; 67 NYS 2d 31 (City Ct of New York, New Rochelle 1946); (1946) 13 ILR 168-171
Wong Sun et al v US 371 US 471 (1963), 83 S Ct 407; 9 L Ed 2d 441; 1963 US LEXIS 2431
X and Y v The Netherlands Series A No 91
Yaşa v Turkey ECHR 1998-VI
Yasoda Sharma v Nepal Communication no 1469/2006 (Human Rights Committee, 6 November 2008)
Yousuf v Samantar 699 F 3rd 763 (4th Circuit)
Zheikov v Russia Communication No 889/1999 (Human Rights Committee, 17 March 2006)

List of Treaties

Agreement between the Government of Sudan and the United Nations concerning the Status of the United Nations Mission in Sudan, (adopted and entered into force 28 December 2005), 2005 UN Jurid YB 44

American Convention on Human Rights (adopted 22 November 1969, entered into force 18 July 1978) 1144 UNTS 123

Convention against Torture and Other Cruel, Inhuman or Degrading Treatment or Punishment (adopted 10 December 1984, entered into force 26 June 1987) 1465 UNTS 85

Convention on the High Seas (adopted 29 April 1958, entered into force 30 September 1962) 450 UNTS 11

Convention on the Privileges and Immunities of the United Nations (adopted 13 February 1946, entered into force 17 September 1946) 1 UNTS 15

Convention on the Safety of United Nations and Associated Personnel (adopted on 9 December 1994, entered into force on 15 January 1999) 2051 UNTS 363

Geneva Convention for the Amelioration of the Condition of the Wounded and Sick in Armed Forces in the Field of August 12, 1949 (adopted 8 December 1949, entered into force 21 October 1950) 75 UNTS 30

Geneva Convention for the Amelioration of the Condition of the Wounded, Sick and Shipwrecked Members of the Armed Forces at Sea of August 12, 1949 (adopted 8 December 1949, entered into force 21 October 1950) 75 UNTS 84

Geneva Convention Relative to the Protection of Civilian Population in Time of War of August 12, 1949 (adopted 8 December 1949, entered into force 21 October 1950) 75 UNTS 286

Geneva Convention Relative to the Treatment of Prisoners of War of August 12, 1949 (adopted 8 December 1949, entered into force 21 October 1950) 75 UNTS 134

Convention for the Protection of Human Rights and Fundamental Freedoms (European Convention on Human Rights, as amended) (ECHR) 213 UNTS 222

International Covenant on Economic, Social and Cultural Rights (adopted 16 December 1966, entered into force 3 January 1976), 993 UNTS 3

International Covenant on Civil and Political Rights (adopted 16 December 1966, entered into force 23 March 1977), 999 UNTS 171

Protocol Additional to the Geneva Conventions of 12 August 1949, and Relating to the Protection of Victims of International Armed Conflicts (Protocol I) 1979 UNTS 4

Rome Statute of the International Criminal Court (17 July 1998, entered in force 1 June 2002) 2187 UNTS 90

The Charter of the United Nations (adopted 26 June 1945, entered into force 24 October 1945) 1 UNTS XVI

Vienna Convention on Consular Relations (adopted 24 April 1963, entered into force 19 March 1967), 1 UNTS 596

Vienna Convention on Diplomatic Relations (adopted 18 April 1961, entered into force on 24 April 1964) 500 UNTS 95

Acronyms

ANP	Angolan National Police
ARIO	the Articles on the Responsibility of International Organizations
ASG	Assistant Secretary-General
BoI	Board of Inquiry
CAT	Committee against Torture
CDT	Conduct and Discipline Team
CDU	Conduct and Discipline Unit
CEDAW	Committee on the Elimination of Discrimination against Women
CERD	Committee on the Elimination of Racial Discrimination
CESCR	Committee on Economic, Social and Cultural Rights
CIVPOL	Civilian Police
CMW	Committee on Migrant Workers
COE	Contingent-Owned Equipment
CRC	Committee on the Rights of the Child
CRPD	Committee on the Rights of Persons with Disabilities
DFS	Department of Field Support
DPKO	Department of Peacekeeping Operations
DRC	Democratic Republic of the Congo
DSS	Department of Safety and Security
ECHR	European Convention on Human Rights
ECtHR	European Court of Human Rights
ECOMOG	Economic Community of West African States' cease-fire monitoring group
FPU	Formed Police Unit
Frente POLISARIO	Frente Popular para la Liberación de Saguia el-Hamra y de Río de Oro
GA	General Assembly
HRC	Human Rights Committee
IACHR	Inter-American Commission on Human Rights
IACtHR	Inter-American Court of Human Rights
ICCPR	International Covenant on Civil and Political Rights
ICESCR	International Covenant on Economic, Social and Cultural Rights
ICL	International Criminal Law
ID	Identification
ICJ	International Court of Justice
HRAP	Human Rights Advisory Panel
IHL	International Humanitarian Law

IHRL	International Human Rights Law
ILC	International Law Commission
IPO	Individual Police Officer
IPTF	International Police Task Force
KFOR	Kosovo Force
KLA	the Kosovo Liberation Army
MINUGUA	United Nations Verification Mission in Guatemala
MINURCAT	United Nations Mission in the Central African Republic and Chad
MINURSO	United Nations Mission for the Referendum in Western Sahara
MINUSCA	United Nations Multidimensional Integrated Stabilization Mission in the Central African Republic
MINUSMA	United Nations Multidimensional Integrated Stabilization Mission in Mali
MINUSTAH	United Nations Stabilization Mission in Haiti
MIPONUH	United Nations Civilian Police Mission in Haiti
MONUC	UN Organization Mission in the Democratic Republic of the Congo
MONUSCO	United Nations Organization Stabilization Mission in the Democratic Republic of the Congo
MoU	Memorandum of Understanding
MSU	Multinational Specialized Unit
NATO	North Atlantic Treaty Organization
NGO	Non-Governmental Organization
OHCHR	the Office of the High Commissioner for Human Rights
OHRM	Office of Human Resources Management
OIOS	Office of the Internal Oversight Services
OLA	the Office of Legal Affairs
ONUB	United Nations Operation in Burundi
ONUC	United Nations Operation in Congo
ONUMOZ	United Nations Operation in Mozambique
ONUSAL	United Nations Observer Mission in El Salvador
OROLSI	Office of the Rule of Law and Security Institutions
PCC	Police Contributing Country
PhP	Personal History Form
PMSS	Personnel and Management Support Services
PN	National Police
PNC	*Policia Nacional Civil*
PO	Peace Operation
POC	Protection of Civilians

PSO	Peace Support Operation
RRU	Rapid Response Unit
SAAT	Selection Assessment and Assistance Team
SAT	Selection Assistance Team
SEA	Sexual exploitation and abuse
SFOR	Stabilization Force
SG	Secretary-General
SOP	Standard Operating Procedure
SPC	Standing Police Capacity
SPU	Special Police Unit
SRSG	Special Representative of the Secretary-General
SWAPO	South West Africa People's Organization
SWAPOL	Swaziland for Positive Living
TCC	Troop Contributing Country
UDHR	Universal Declaration of Human Rights
UN	United Nations
UNAMA	United Nations Assistance Mission in Afghanistan
UNAMI	United Nations Assistance Mission in Iraq
UNAMID	African Union-United Nations Hybrid Operation in Darfur
UNAMIR	UN Assistance Mission in Rwanda
UNAMSIL	United Nations Mission in Sierra Leone
UNAVEM I	United Nations Angola Verification Mission I
UNAVEM II	United Nations Angola Verification Mission II
UNAVEM III	United Nations Angola Verification Mission III
UNEF I	First United Nations Emergency Force
UNFICYP	United Nations Peacekeeping Force in Cyprus
UNIFSA	United Nations Organization Interim Security Force for Abyei
UNITA	União Nacional para a Independência Total de Angola
UNITAF	Unified Task Force
UNMEE	UN Mission in Ethiopia and Eritrea
UNMIBH	United Nations Mission in Bosnia and Herzegovina
UNMIH	United Nations Mission in Haiti
UNMIK	United Nations Mission in Kosovo
UNMIL	United Nations Mission in Liberia
UNMIS	United Nations Mission in Sudan
UNMISET	United Nations Mission of Support in East Timor
UNMISS	United Nations Mission in the Republic of South Sudan
UNMIT	United Nations Integrated Mission in Timor-Leste
UNMOGIP	United Nations Military Observer Groupin India and Pakistan
UNMOT	UN Mission of Observers in Tajikistan

UNOCI	United Nations Operation in Cote d'Ivoire
UNOMIG	UN Observer Mission in Georgia
UNOMUR	UN Observer Mission in Rwanda-Uganda
UNOSOM II	United Nations Operation in Somalia II
UNPROFOR	United Nations Protection Force
UNSAS	Standby Arrangements System
UNSF	UN Security Force in West New Guinea
UNTAC	United Nations Transitional Authority in Cambodia
UNTAES	UN Transitional Authority in Eastern Slavonia, Baranja and Western Sirmium
UNTAET	United Nations Transitional Administration in East Timor
UNTAG	United Nations Transition Assistance Group
UNTSO	United Nations Truce Supervision Organization
USG	Under Secretary-General

CHAPTER 1

Introduction

1 The Issue

Since the 1990s, reports of serious misconduct by personnel engaged in United Nations (UN) Peace Operations have begun to come to light. In particular, allegations of sexual offences and human trafficking have attracted the public's attention.[1] These allegations have been made against various categories of UN personnel, including the UN police. One would expect criminal proceedings to be brought against the alleged offenders. However, there is little evidence that this is happening. This may be simply a lack of publicly available information about any such proceedings,[2] or it may indicate that proceedings are not being brought at all. This calls into question the efficacy of the legal and practical framework for ensuring criminal accountability. That a lack of accountability is perceived as being problematic is clear from the fact that the UN General Assembly has discussed measures to ensure the individual criminal accountability of civilian members of UN Peace Operations, including the UN police.[3]

Whilst these problems are not unique to the UN police, there are three reasons why this work focuses exclusively on the criminal accountability of the UN police. First, although accountability issues have been discussed at length

---

1 See Chapter 3, Sections 1 and 2-2-1.

2 See Chapter 3, Section 3.

3 UNGA, 'Ensuring the Accountability of United Nations Staff and Experts on Mission with Respect to Criminal Acts Committed in Peacekeeping Operations' (16 August 2006) UN Doc. A/60/980, (hereinafter '2006 Legal Experts Report'); UNGA, 'Criminal Accountability of United Nations Officials and Experts on Mission' (11 September 2007) UN Doc. A/62/329, (hereinafter '2007 Secretariat Note'); UNGA, 'Report of the Ad Hoc Committee on Criminal Accountability of United Nations Officials and Experts on Mission' (15 April 2008) UN Doc. A/63/54, (hereinafter '2008 Ad Hoc Committee Report'); UNGA, 'Comprehensive Report on All Processes Involved in the Investigation and Prosecution of Crimes Committed against Deployed United Nations Peacekeepers' (9 December 2011) UN Doc. A/66/598, (hereinafter 'Report on Investigation'). For all discussions held by the Sixth Committee of the General Assembly since 2006, see UNGA Sixth Committee, '69th Session: Criminal Accountability of United Nations Officials and Experts on Mission (Agenda Item 75)' (2014) <http://www.un.org/en/ga/sixth/69/criminal_accountability.shtml> accessed 30 November 2014; UNGA Sixth Committee, 'Seventieth session: Criminal Accountability of United Nations Officials and Experts on Mission (Agenda Item 80)' (2015) <http://www.un.org/en/ga/sixth/70/criminal_accountability.shtml> accessed 19 September 2016.

 | DOI 10.1163/9789004328815_002

elsewhere in relation to members of military contingents, they have not been addressed in relation to the UN police.[4] Second, whilst it is clear which States have criminal jurisdiction over members of the armed forces, it is not so clear in relation to the UN police.[5] Third, as will be shown, because of the evolution of their functions, the UN police play a more public role than before.[6] Thus, there may be a significant impact on public trust in the police if criminal conduct by the UN police remains unaddressed.

For these reasons, it is very important that the criminal accountability of the UN police be effectively addressed, over and above the general principle of accountability in normal societies. As will be shown,[7] this has become more important as Peace Operations and the functions required of the UN police have evolved over time. The UN police are being called on not only to monitor the local police, but also increasingly to carry out actual policing tasks, and to build or rebuild national rule of law institutions. It is thus extremely important that crimes committed by the UN police are addressed in an effective manner, as, during missions, it is the UN police who are in a position to inculcate the concept of criminal accountability in local communities, including creating trust in the concept and function of a police force.[8] If criminal behaviour committed by the UN police were to be appropriately addressed, and if the local people were aware of these proceedings and sanctions, they may learn that accountability is taken seriously and may then act as a 'watchdog' for their own police forces.

---

4 Marten Zwanenburg, *Accountability of Peace Support Operations* (Martinus Nijhoff Publishers 2005), (hereinafter 'Accountability of PSO'); Guglielmo Verdirame, 'UN Accountability for Human Rights Violations in Post-Conflict Situations' in Nigel D White and Dirk Klaasen (eds), *The UN, Human Rights and Post-Conflict Situations* (Manchester University Press 2005), (hereinafter 'UN Accountability for Human Rights Violations'); Andrew Ladley, 'Peacekeeper Abuse, Immunity and Impunity: The Need for Effective Criminal and Civil Accountability on International Peace Operations' (2005) 1 *Politics and Ethics Review* 81; Guglielmo Verdirame, *The UN and Human Rights: Who Guards the Guardians?* (Cambridge University Press 2011), (hereinafter 'Who Guards the Guardians'); Sarah Elizabeth Mendelson, *Barracks and Brothels: Peacekeepers and Human Trafficking in the Balkans* (CSIS 2005); Elizabeth F Defeis, 'UN Peacekeepers and Sexual Abuse and Exploitation: An End to Impunity' (2008) 7 *Washington University Global Study Law Review* 185; Alexandra R Harrington, 'Victims of Peace: Current Abuse Allegations Against UN Peacekeepers and the Role of Law in Preventing Them in the Future' (2005) 12 *ILSA Journal of International & Comparative Law* 125.

5 In the case of members of armed forces, their sending States have exclusive criminal jurisdiction over any crimes they commit. See Chapter 5, Section 2.

6 See Section 2.

7 See Chapter 2, Section 1.

8 See Section 2. See also Chapter 2, Section 1.

In an ideal world, one would seek to eliminate all criminal conduct by UN police, but this is not a realistic goal. Instead, the emphasis arguably should be on deterring UN police from committing crimes. Ensuring that a proper investigation is conducted where an individual member of the UN police is alleged to have committed a crime, and bringing criminal proceedings leading to an appropriate sanction where such an allegation is proven, would show that accountability is taken seriously by the UN. It would also act as a deterrent to other UN police members.[9]

Whilst all forms of punishment may be seen as having a deterrent effect on the future commission of crimes, the fact that criminal proceedings take place in public, as well as the nature of the penalties that may be imposed, may well increase this effect. As the International Court of Justice (ICJ) ruled in relation to genocide:

> One of the most effective ways of preventing criminal acts, in general, is to provide penalties for persons committing such acts, and to impose those penalties effectively on those who commit the acts one is trying to prevent.[10]

In order to understand the incidence of criminal behaviour by the UN police and the machinery that has been developed to address it, an appreciation of the dramatic evolution of Peace Operations and, more specifically, the role played in these Operations by the UN police, is required.

2 The Evolution of UN Peace Operations

Understanding the context in which the UN police have undertaken operations is fundamental to understanding the evolution of UN Peace Operations themselves. There is nothing in the UN Charter which explicitly authorizes or establishes Peace Operations.[11] Instead, they have evolved on an *ad hoc*

9 See Section 3.

10 *Case concerning Application of the Convention on the Prevention and Punishment of the Crime of Genocide (Bosnia and Herzegovina v Serbia and Montenegro)* (Judgment of 26 February 2007) [2007] ICJ Rep 43 (ICJ), para. 426.

11 Over time, the UN has used different terms to describe different types of Peace Operations, including 'Peacekeeping Operations', 'Peace Operations', 'Peace Enforcement', and 'Peace Support Operations'. See UN GA and UN SC, 'An Agenda for Peace: Preventive Diplomacy, Peacemaking and Peace-keeping' (17 June 1992) UN Doc. A/47/277-S/24111, (hereinafter 'Agenda for Peace'); UN GA and UN SC, 'Supplement to an Agenda for Peace:

basis.[12] Early Peace Operations were established following the end of inter-State conflicts, where it was mainly a matter of making sure that hostilities between States did not re-ignite. Originally, the parties concerned were required to give their consent to an Operation. Initially, the UN police played only a small role in these operations. Over time, the UN began deploying police alongside its military contingents.[13] However, at that stage, it was not clear whether the UN considered the role of the police as being distinct from that of the military.

The end of the Cold War led to many more Peace Operations being established. The mandates for all these Operations were created by the UN Security Council.[14] These mandates were broader and more wide-ranging than those of earlier Operations, because they were dealing with a very different kind of a situation. From this point onwards, UN police were often deployed in situations of internal rather than international armed conflict. Generally, these were situations in which either fighting was still continuing, or where the cessation of hostilities was very fragile. In some instances, either the Operation as a whole, or the mandate of the force concerned, had been imposed by the UN under a Chapter VII resolution. In many cases, the State being assisted by the UN was extremely weak, and was either failing, or had already failed.[15]

Amongst these Peace Operations, two were unique, in that the UN became, in effect, the government of the State concerned. This was the case with both the United Nations Interim Administration Mission in Kosovo (UNMIK), and the UN Transitional Administration in East Timor (UNTAET). In these missions, the UN did not simply work alongside the local government. Rather, it was the only governmental authority. As a result, the UN police constituted the sole police force.

Position Paper of the Secretary-General on the Occasion of the Fiftieth Anniversary of the United Nations' (January) UN Doc. A/50/60-S/1995/1, (hereinafter 'Supplement to Agenda for Peace'); UNGA/SC, 'Report of the Panel on United Nations Peace Operations' (21 August 2000) UN Doc. A/55/305-S/2000/809, (hereinafter 'Brahimi Report'); UN DPKO/DFS, 'United Nations Peacekeeping Operations: Principles and Guidelines' (January 2008) UN Doc. –, (hereinafter 'Capstone').

12 The UN police were established in 1948, and have since evolved out of necessity to fill the gap left by the idea of a standing UN Force, as provided for in The Charter of the United Nations (adopted 26 June 1945, entered into force 24 October 1945) 1 UNTS XVI, Article 43 (hereinafter 'UN Charter').

13 This took place from around 1960, until the end of the Cold War. See Chapter 2, Section 1-1.

14 Only one mandate was created by the UN General Assembly before 1990. See Section 2.

15 For example, Somalia. For the background to this mission, see UN DPKO, 'Somalia: United Nations Operation in Somalia I' <http://www.un.org/en/peacekeeping/missions/past/unosomi.htm> accessed 2 January 2015.

Since the turn of this century, Peace Operations have focused more on establishing the rule of law, and not solely on ensuring there are no hostilities. By doing so, the UN is trying to restore faith in the machinery that delivers the rule of law, accountability and security. In some States, the UN is attempting to build the rule of law for the first time, based on an acknowledgement that establishing peace and stability are reliant on this taking place.[16] The role of the police is vital to this process. If, in the process of attempting to inculcate the values of good governance, the rule of law, and accountability, there were to be a mismatch between these values and the way in which UN personnel behave, it would in all likelihood have a seriously adverse effect on the UN. In other words, it is not so much the fact that UN police commit crimes, but that these crimes go unpunished that harms the UN.[17] This harm could manifest in two ways: first, the UN may become less effective if the population loses confidence in the values that it is trying to inculcate; and, second, the UN may lose legitimacy through not living up to these values itself.

This work is limited to considering the criminal accountability of UN police members in relation to serious crimes.[18] Criminal law is an expression of a community's condemnation of certain types of conduct, which carries with it the possibility of punishment by the State.[19] Disciplinary penalties do not have the same connotation as criminal sanctions. For these reasons, this work will focus solely on individual criminal accountability.

3 The Scope of This Work

This work thus focuses on crimes committed by members of the UN police, whether deployed as Individual Police Officers (IPOs) or in Formed Police Units (FPUs).[20] Presumably, the UN's aim is to ensure that where members of the UN police commit serious crimes, they are called to account by the relevant criminal justice system. In light of this, this work attempts to assess whether,

---

16 UN SC, 'Report of the Secretary-General on the Rule of Law and Transitional Justice in Conflict and Post-Conflict Societies' (23 August 2004) UN Doc. S/2004/616.

17 Note that the Secretary-General reported in this regard that, '[...] if the rule of law means anything at all, it means that no one, including peacekeepers, is above the law'. Ibid, para. 33.

18 See Section 4.

19 William Wilson, *Criminal Law: Doctrine and Theory* (2nd edn, Pearson Education 2003), p.4.

20 On the different forms of deployment, see Chapter 2, Sections 1–6 and 3-3-1.

in practice, serious criminal behaviour goes unpunished and, if so, why that is the case.

Because this research aims to suggest pragmatic remedies to address any identified shortcomings, it is necessarily underpinned by an examination of the current context. The first part of this work entails an examination of the nature and scale of the problems. The data used to conduct this analysis consists of allegations of crimes committed by personnel associated with UN Peace Operations, collected by the author from publicly available information sources.[21] The main source of information was material available on the internet. Most of the information was found on the websites of: (1) the UN, its Peace Operations and UN agencies, (2) host State and sending State governments, (3) NGO reports, and (4) media articles. UN sources and NGO reports are treated separately for several reasons: one is that information derived from UN sources only contains those allegations that in fact ended up in a form of complaint to the UN, while NGO sources can contain other, broader information regarding allegations; another is the uneven number and types of reports by the UN, in particular after offices were established to deal with misconduct;[22] and yet another is that the contents of the information provided by these two sources may differ.[23] The analysis focuses not only on the way in which complaints are responded to, but also the need to address situations in which crimes have been committed, but no official allegations have been made. Thus, the scope of this work is not limited solely to allegations brought to the attention of the UN, but also includes criminal behaviour that goes unreported. The trigger for an entry in the author's data was an allegation of criminal conduct. In each case, there was an attempt to identify whether administrative or criminal proceedings had ensued, and whether any information was available regarding the ultimate outcome of these proceedings. In cases in which an allegation was brought before the Court, court records were sought. The information was

---

21 These data are referred to throughout this work as the author's data. Part of the data concerning allegations before 2005 was collected by the author, in conjunction with 68 volunteer researchers coordinated by the author, in a previous study for a working paper for the former Sub-Commission for Human Rights. UN ECOSOC, 'Working Paper on the Accountability of International Personnel Taking Part in Peace Support Operations Submitted by Françoise Hampson' (7 July 2005) UN Doc. E/CN.4/Sub.2/2005/42. The creation of the database, its modification, and the collection of information since 2005 have been carried out by the author.

22 See Chapter 4, Section 2.

23 For example, it is possible that the UN reports more on allegations that are properly responded to.

corroborated, where possible, with other sources.[24] Measures taken to prevent the commission of crimes are touched upon wherever they arise, even though prevention is not the focus of this work.

The second part is the evaluation of the effectiveness of the machinery which currently exists to ensure the criminal accountability of UN police members. This evaluation may make it possible to identify the source of any problems arising in this regard. These may be legal, practical or political problems, including the lack of political will.

Traditionally, only States can exercise criminal jurisdiction in relation to criminal acts alleged to have been committed by individual UN police members.[25] Although the UN has the authority to bring disciplinary proceedings, it has no authority to bring criminal proceedings. However, given that the UN police are part of the UN structure, it is likely that allegations will be brought to the attention of the UN in the first instance. It is therefore necessary to consider the role that the UN system can play in relation to the instituting of criminal proceedings by the host or sending States.[26] As members of the UN police belong to the UN, this may raise very specific issues in relation to the exercise of criminal accountability. There may be a claim that acts of UN personnel are subject to immunity from prosecution. Therefore, when considering barriers

---

24 Allegations and offences dealt with in the author's data are those that meet the definition of *crimes* for the purposes of this work. See Section 6 for this definition. The allegations are not necessarily substantiated. All the allegations in the author's data concern *crimes* by people who are, or have been, involved in Peace Operations, and are not limited to UN police. This category is considered in a broad sense, ranging from members of armed forces, to UN police officers, UN international civil servants, other international components, and other foreign and local personnel. This is done in order to make possible a meaningful comparison between different categories of personnel or different types of crimes. Where the information from two sources appears similar, but is not identical, the two pieces of information are treated as two separate cases. There may thus be more than one entry in the author's data which is actually dealing with a single allegation. For each alleged case, information was sought about the name of the alleged perpetrator, the name of the victim (where appropriate), the date(s) of the event, the kind of offence, a description of the offence, the person or section to which the act or omission of misconduct was first reported, case details, immunities claimed or waived, details of any criminal, disciplinary or administrative proceedings carried out in response to the allegation, the nationality and status of the alleged perpetrator, the nationality and status of the alleged victim, and the source of the information.

25 Where one is dealing with an international or hybrid court, the sovereign State must have accepted the transfer of authority to that court.

26 See Chapter 4.

to prosecution, it is necessary to consider the operation of the immunity system, both in theory and in practice.

If it is found that legal and practical barriers do not sufficiently explain all the problems identified, it is possible that the problem is that there is insufficient political will on the part of States to pursue criminal accountability. This work seeks arguments under international law to encourage States that are otherwise unwilling to address the issue to bring criminal prosecutions and, separately, arguments which support the UN in its attempts to enable prosecution by States.

It is acknowledged that the machinery in place to address criminal behaviour on the part of UN police members has evolved dramatically since its inception. In 2005, the publication of a UN report which established a strategy to eliminate sexual exploitation and abuse (known as the 'Zeid Report') had an important impact on this machinery.[27] In order to present an accurate picture of the issues surrounding this machinery, and to analyze its efficacy, this research deals primarily with the period running from 1990 until late 2015. More specifically, with regard to data relating to alleged wrongdoing, the cut-off date in this regard is 31 December 2014. With regard to the UN system for dealing with alleged misconduct, the period covered is from the beginning of Peace Operations to the end of 2015.

4 Issues Outside the Scope of This Work

As already noted, this work focuses on the individual criminal accountability of UN police members. However, given that there are many closely related issues, it is important to identify which issues fall outside the scope of this work.

Based on the assumption that serious crimes cannot be fully accounted for through disciplinary sanctions, this work excludes disciplinary accountability. Disciplinary accountability is defined, for these purposes, as disciplinary or administrative sanctions, and the proceedings through which these are imposed. However, since it is possible that these proceedings deal with disciplinary offences which are also criminal in nature, some steps taken during these

---

27 UNGA, 'A Comprehensive Strategy to Eliminate Future Sexual Exploitation and Abuse in United Nations Peacekeeping Operations' (24 March 2005) UN Doc. A/59/710, (hereinafter 'Zeid Report'). Prince Zeid, who was appointed as a Special Advisor on SEA in Peace Operations, examined the nature and extent of SEA problems, analyzed existing mechanisms for dealing with SEA allegations in Peace Operations, and sought ways to eliminate future incidents. Ibid, p. 1.

proceedings may be discussed where they are, or can be, used in subsequent criminal proceedings.

It is possible that victims of some crimes may seek civil redress independently of any criminal prosecution of the wrongdoer. However, it may not be possible to seek civil redress from an individual UN police officer if the act is carried out in relation to his official functions.[28] Even if it is possible to lodge a civil claim, a consideration of the civil liability of individual UN police personnel for criminal acts is outside the scope of this work.

It is also possible that the UN's legal responsibility as an employer may be questioned in relation to its employees' wrongdoing. As a result, the issue of the vicarious liability of the UN arises, particularly if the conduct occurred in the course of discharging their functions.[29] For example, if UN police members are alleged to have engaged in the indiscriminate shooting of civilian demonstrators whom the police were supposed to control, and to have caused fatal or serious injuries in the process, there may be a question as to whether the UN is responsible. In some cases, victims may seek to bring civil claims against the UN.[30] This issue falls outside the scope of this work.

Separately, there may be circumstances in which the UN's civil liability for its own acts in relation to the criminal conduct is scrutinized. These may include instances where the UN condones or covers up criminal conduct committed by the UN police, or is perceived to do so. This issue falls outside the scope of this work.

In the case of incidents such as traffic accidents, the UN may offer a voluntary payment to the victim. These are *ex gratia* payments, which do not amount to an admission of responsibility on the part of the UN. They are made on a discretionary basis,[31] although it is not clear how decisions are reached in this regard. However, this practice does not come within the scope of this work.

As far as sending States are concerned, UN police members are not State agents.[32] Therefore, the issue of State responsibility for the acts of State agents

---

28 See Chapter 5, Section 2-4.

29 Françoise Hampson and Ai Kihara-Hunt, 'The Accountability of Personnel Associated with Peacekeeping Operations' in Chiyuki Aoi, Cedric De Coning and Ramesh Thakur (eds), *Unintended Consequences of Peacekeeping* (UNU 2007), pp. 204–205, (hereinafter 'PKO Personnel Accountability').

30 Such claims are normally handled through a Civil Claims Unit. Ibid, pp. 204–205.

31 UN, 'Secretary-General's Bulletin on the Financial Regulations and Rules of the United Nations' (9 May 2003) UN Doc. ST/SGB/2003/7, Regulation 5.11, Rule 105.12.

32 See Chapter 7, introductory section.

does not arise.[33] The sending State's responsibility for the conduct of its own UN police officers is not discussed in this work.

5 Structure

This work begins by presenting a detailed overview of the problems encountered in ensuring that the UN police are held to account for any crimes they commit. Chapter 2 examines the evolution of the functions of the UN police as an institution, and the evolution of the roles that they play in Peace Operations. It then analyzes how the UN ensures that the required expertise is delivered, so that these functions can be effectively fulfilled. It also considers the way in which situations into which the UN police are deployed, and the revised functions they are called on to perform, might lead to an increase in the risk of criminal behaviour. Chapter 3 identifies the nature and scale of the problem created by criminal behaviour by members of the UN police and, based on this information, explores whether any pattern emerges relating to criminal wrongdoing. The information used is derived from the author's data.[34] The chapter also considers, within the limits of the available information, the question of the prosecution of suspects.

Chapter 4 considers the effectiveness of the various mechanisms currently used for addressing criminal conduct by the UN police. In particular, it focuses on the way in which the UN generates evidence that can be used by a State in criminal proceedings. The initial focus is on the UN's own mechanisms, but the chapter also examines the way in which the UN relates to the host and sending States in attempting to ensure that they bring criminal proceedings against individual UN police members.

The next two chapters consider whether there are any legal obstacles to bringing criminal proceedings against members of the UN police and, if so, what these are. Chapter 5 examines whether there are any restrictions on the exercise of criminal jurisdiction by the relevant States. Chapter 6 considers whether a State, in attempting to exercise jurisdiction, may be confronted by the argument that the acts in question are protected from judicial scrutiny by UN immunity. The issue of immunity is therefore examined both in theory and in practice.

---

33 However, in exceptional circumstances, the conduct of FPUs may be attributed to their sending States. See Chapter 2, Section 1-6, and Chapter 7, Section 6.

34 See Section 3, above.

By the end of Chapter 6, a determination may be made as to what extent any problems affecting the effectiveness of the existing machinery are attributable to practical matters or legal concerns. Insofar as these concerns do not explain the problems identified, another possibility is that there may be a lack of political will in this regard. However, a consideration of the role, if any, played by political will in this process is outside the scope of this work. Nevertheless, a question arises as to whether it is possible to construct arguments based on other areas of law in order to put pressure on an otherwise unwilling State to bring criminal proceedings. The obvious source for such arguments is international human rights law (IHRL). Chapter 7 therefore considers whether arguments can be made under IHRL that a State has a legal obligation to act. Leaving aside any legal obligation, given that the effectiveness and legitimacy of UN operations are at stake, it is reasonable to expect that the UN should do all it can do to encourage States to launch criminal proceedings. Any potential obligations on the part of the UN in this regard, and the practical implications of any such obligations, are also discussed in Chapter 7.

Chapter 8 sets out the conclusions reached in this work, and makes specific proposals for addressing the problems identified, where feasible.

6 Definitions and Clarifications

Some terms and concepts used in this work require definition at the outset.

First, for the purposes of this work, *Peace Operations* include all Operations created by or endorsed by the UN, with the exception of enforcement actions or operations based on a collective right to self-defence. Operations created by the UN are those holding a mandate under Chapter VI or Chapter VII of the UN Charter. They are established either by the Security Council or, in exceptional cases, by the General Assembly.[35] They include traditional peacekeeping and peace enforcement operations. Sometimes the term 'Peace Support Operations (PSOs)' is used to refer to some of these operations, but this term excludes traditional peacekeeping.[36] These operations may or may not include

35 To date, there has been only one such operation, UNEF I. UN DPKO, 'First United Nations Emergency Force: UNEF I (November 1956–June 1967)' <http://www.un.org/en/peacekeeping/missions/past/unefi.htm> accessed 30 November 2014.

36 For example, the UN used this term in relation to the UN Mission in Sudan (UNMIS). UNSC Res 1547 (11 June 2004) UN Doc. S/RES/1547, op. paras. 1, 3, 5. See also Alex J Bellamy, Paul Williams and Stuart Griffin, *Understanding Peacekeeping* (1st edn, Polity Press 2004), pp. 165–185; UN ECOSOC, Sub-Commission Paper, (hereinafter 'Sub-Commission Paper').

a military component. Also included are operations authorized by another organization which are subsequently endorsed by the UN, such as the Kosovo Force (KFOR) in Kosovo, and the Economic Community of West African States' cease-fire monitoring group (ECOMOG) operation in Liberia. These are only considered if they fall into the general categories of peacekeeping, peace enforcement or peace support operations.[37]

Second, as noted earlier, those *crimes* referred to in this work are limited to *serious crimes*. These are crimes which attract the possibility of a sentence of imprisonment in virtually every State. Examples of such crimes include murder, rape, and sexual abuse.[38] *Crimes* therefore exclude acts such as minor traffic offences, which normally only attract fines. However, States' national laws may vary as to what constitutes criminal conduct, and there is no universal definition of each crime.[39] Therefore, for an act or omission to be termed a *crime* in this work, it is not necessary for the conduct to be categorized in the same way, or to have the same scope, in every jurisdiction.

Third, *allegations* and *substantiated allegations* need to be defined. An *allegation* refers to information that indicates that a criminal offence has been committed. This can take the form of a complaint made to the UN or another body, or information reported by external sources including the media. An *allegation* is therefore not substantiated by the outcome of any kind of investigation, whether it be criminal, administrative or disciplinary. However, a complaint that does not appear to have been made in good faith and where it is not corroborated by other sources, is not dealt with in this work. *Substantiated allegations* are those allegations into which an investigation has been conducted, often by the UN or States, and where the investigation's findings have corroborated the complaint.

Fourth, *UN police personnel* include all individuals who have either been selected and seconded by a State to the UN, or who have been directly selected

37 This definition is based on an earlier study. See Hampson and Kihara-Hunt, 'PKO Personnel Accountability', pp. 195–196. Note that this definition differs from that of 'Peace Operations' in the 2015 report of the High-Level Independent Panel on United Nations Peace Operations, in that the latter includes other UN entities such as the Secretary-General's special envoys, mediators, and regional preventive diplomacy offices. UNGA/SC, 'Uniting Our Strength for Peace – Politics, Partnerships and People – Report of the High-Level Independent Panel on United Nations Peace Operations' (16 June 2015) UN Doc. A/70/95-S/2015/446.

38 This list is not exhaustive. For example, depending on the facts and circumstances of the case, certain cases of theft, abuse, physical assault and certain forms of trafficking offences are also included.

39 UNGA, 2006 Legal Experts Report, para. 19.

and recruited by the UN,[40] and who are deployed to a Peace Operation to deliver a service as part of the international police presence in the mission. They may be deployed either as IPOs, or collectively as FPUs.[41] They are required to be, and normally are, serving or recently retired police officers in their home States.[42] However, this work also includes those who do not fall into this category, where they are nevertheless deployed as part of the international police body. Some may be employed by private companies hired by States to select, train and deploy police to international missions, such as the American members of the UN police.[43] The UN previously referred to the international police deployed in Peace Operations as 'CIVPOL',[44] but has re-named this 'UNPOL'.[45] This work includes both CIVPOL and UNPOL within the category of UN police.

Fifth, the terms *host* and *sending* State must be defined. The *host State* is the State in whose territory the Peace Operation takes place, although some operations may be based in two or more host States.[46] The term *sending State* denotes a State that contributes members to the UN police. The sending State does this by selecting, training, and seconding police officers to the UN. In cases where the UN recruits police directly, technically there is no sending State, as the State of nationality is not involved in this process.[47] In these instances, the term *sending State* will nevertheless still be used to indicate the State of nationality of the UN police concerned. However, in the main, the sending State is normally the State of nationality of the police officer concerned.[48]

7 Conclusion

As this chapter has demonstrated, ensuring that UN police members are held to account for crimes they commit would have a significant impact both on the

40 On different modes of selection, see Chapter 2, Section 3-3-1.

41 On different modes of deployment, see Chapter 2, Section 3-3-1.

42 On the criteria for selection, see Chapter 2, Section 3.

43 See Chapter 2, Section 3-3-1.

44 The term 'Civilian Police', which is the origin of the term CIVPOL, began to be used when the UN Peacekeeping Force in Cyprus (UNFICYP) was operational. See Chapter 2, Section 1-1.

45 This name was changed in 2005. See Chapter 2, Section 1-7.

46 For example, United Nations Truce Supervision Organization (UNTSO), the United Nations Military Observer Group in India and Pakistan (UNMOGIP), the First United Nations Emergency Force (UNEF I), and the United Nations Mission in Ethiopia and Eritrea (UNMEE) had two host States.

47 See Chapter 2, Section 3-3-1.

48 See Chapter 2, Section 3-1.

effectiveness and the legitimacy of UN operations. Crimes alleged to have been committed by the UN police and others, and the apparent lack of a response to these allegations, appears to be generating a range of problems. It is significant that this issue is being discussed by the UN and its Member States in the General Assembly.[49] It is possible that there are genuine obstacles, both legal and practical, standing in the way of States which are willing to bring criminal proceedings. However, there could also be political unwillingness on the part of States to bring such proceedings. This work addresses the efficacy of every stage of this process, from the point at which the alleged criminal act is committed, to the prosecution, whether successful or not, of the alleged wrongdoer. Where a State potentially has a primary obligation to do something, but does not act accordingly, an issue arises regarding the responsibility of the UN to take measures to deal with the situation. Where the UN fails to take any action in the face of the non-prosecution of members of the UN police suspected of criminal behaviour, it may be necessary to distinguish between situations where the UN simply fails to act, and those, if any, in which the UN covers up the non-prosecution. Part of the problem is the lack of publicly available information regarding actions taken, or not taken, by the UN. This is related to the general problem of a lack of transparency on the part of the UN.

The first step is thus to establish an accurate picture of the issue. This requires an examination of the UN police and their position within UN Peace Operations. Therefore, Chapter 2 analyzes the evolution of the institutional functions and roles that the UN police play in UN Peace Operations, and the expertise they require in order to fulfil these functions and roles.

49 See Section 1.

CHAPTER 2

UN Police in Peace Operations

The previous chapter suggested that criminal behaviour committed by the UN police has a significant impact on the UN's legitimacy and effectiveness. This chapter considers some of the issues which may affect both the rate at which the UN police commit crimes, and the types of crimes they commit. These issues arguably include: (1) whether the increasing number of functions the UN police are called on to perform leads to an increase in the number and types of crimes they commit; (2) whether the environments in which the UN police operate, which are likely to be volatile and violent, affect the number and kind of crimes committed; (3) whether the increasing numbers of UN police officers deployed has a bearing on the rate and type of crimes they commit; and (4) whether a lack of certain skills and qualities on the part of UN police officers affects the number and type of crimes committed by them. These four issues are expanded on below.

First, the type of functions which the UN police are called on to perform, and how these have evolved, must be examined, in order to see if this has any bearing on the crimes they commit. If, increasingly, different demands are being made of the UN police, different mechanisms may be necessary to deal with these demands. It has already been suggested that the proper delivery of criminal accountability of UN police is vital to the success of a mission,[1] but if they are engaging in functions that require more contact with the local population, their behaviour will be more visible to this population. Delivering different functions may mean that they have more opportunities to engage in criminal behaviour which is either directly[2] or indirectly[3] related to these functions. Separately, if a crime is committed for which no-one is prosecuted, the population is likely to be more aware of the lack of criminal accountability. This makes it all the more important that criminal accountability be properly addressed. This is not only critical for the accomplishment of the mission, but also to establishing respect for rule of law institutions in the host State.

1 Chapter 1, Section 1.

2 For example, if, in early missions, the UN police did not engage in crowd control, but do now, there is the added possibility that they may use excessive force in order to control a crowd.

3 For example, if these broader functions mean that the UN police are driving more in order to carry out their duties, this may give rise to more criminal behaviour in the form of driving offences.

 | DOI 10.1163/9789004328815_003

Second, the evolution of their functions may be linked to the different contexts in which the UN police operate. If some functions appear to be linked to a higher incidence of criminal behaviour, it may not be so much these functions that are triggering more criminal conduct, but rather the field environment. Thus, it is necessary to examine the context in which the UN police are called on to operate.

Third, whether there has been an increase in the number of UN police officers requires consideration. One way to determine whether the manner in which the functions of the UN police have evolved is indicative of the police's increased importance, is to analyze any change in the size of the UN police force. If the number of UN police officers has increased, and especially if it has grown disproportionately in relation to the other mission components, this may indicate additional importance being attached to this force. The deployment of a larger number of officers means that the UN police are more visible to the local population, both in terms of their behaviour and any consequences they face if they commit crimes. The size of the UN police force also matters with respect to the possibility of a co-relationship between the size of the police presence and the scale of their criminal wrongdoing.

Lastly, whether UN police officers are selected with reference to the functions that they are required to exercise must be considered. If there are changes in the functions and roles of the UN police, the expertise required of them will also change. If, for example, the UN police were not required to control a violent crowd in earlier missions, but are required to do so in current missions, ensuring the deployment of UN police officers with the appropriate skill set and equipment may reduce the risk that they will use excessive force in delivering this new function. Thus, it is necessary to probe the way in which the UN is ensuring that the appropriate skill set is delivered through its control over the selection and training of UN police officers. In relation to the incidence of criminal conduct, expertise-oriented selection and training in particular skills is only relevant in relation to crimes that are committed in the performance of their duty. For example, whether or not a UN police officer rapes someone in his private accommodation whilst off-duty is not affected by whether he is equipped with a specific skill set. There may also be other elements that contribute to mitigating the likelihood of criminal behavior.

1 The Evolution of the Functions of the UN Police in UN Peace Operations

The transformation of the situations in which Peace Operations are deployed has resulted in an evolution of the functions of the UN police. The reasons for the creation and expansion of the UN police, and the evolution of their functions, are analyzed insofar as this may have impacted on criminal behaviour by UN police officers, and the machinery developed to address this behaviour.

1-1 *The Creation of the Institution of the UN Police*

UN police were not originally involved in Peace Operations. This is not surprising, as early Peace Operations were established in generally benign environments after inter-State conflicts had ended.[4] Thus, there were no major law and order problems.[5] Police participated in Peace Operations for the first time

---

4 This was with an exception of the UN Operation in the Congo (ONUC).

5 The first 'Peacekeeping Operation' was the UN Truce Supervision Organization (UNTSO). UN DPKO, 'UNTSO United Nations Truce Supervision Organization' <http://www.un.org/en/peacekeeping/missions/untso/> accessed 3 August 2014. It was established in 1948 to monitor the truce in Palestine following the partition of Palestine, which took place in order to resolve the Arab-Israeli dispute. UN, *The Blue Helmets: A Review of United Nations Peace-Keeping* (3 edn, UN 1996) p. 17. Similarly, a UN Military Observer Group in India and Pakistan (UNMOGIP) was established in the following year to observe the ceasefire between these two States. UNSC Res 39 (14 January 1948) UN Doc. S/RES/39; UNSC Res 47 (21 April 1948) UN Doc. S/RES/47. These two operations included unarmed military observers with a limited mandate to monitor the ceasefire between States. Established in 1956, the UN Emergency Force (UNEF I) was the first peacekeeping operation to include armed military personnel. UN DPKO, 'First United Nations Emergency Force: UNEF I (November 1956–June 1967)' <http://www.un.org/en/peacekeeping/missions/past/unefi.htm> accessed 30 November 2014. It worked as a buffer between Israel and Egypt. In addition, some policing functions were delivered by a Swedish special civil section. However, it was very clear from the beginning that the arrangement was temporary. Erwin A Schmidl, *Police in Peace Operations* (Militärwiss Büro des Bundesministeriums für Landesverteidigung, Informationen zur Sicherheitspolitik, Issue 10, 1998), p. 8, (hereinafter 'Police in PO'). UNEF I had a wider mandate than the two earlier operations, assisting in the maintenance of law and order and the prevention of the recurrence of conflict. Law and order functions were assumed by the military on a temporary basis, and came within the military role of assisting civilians. Robert B Oakley, Michael J Dziedzic and Eliot M Goldberg (eds), *Policing the New World Disorder: Peace Operations and Public Security* (NDU Press 1998), p. 17, (hereinafter 'Policing Disorder'). These two types of operations were subsequently conceptualized, largely by the then Secretary-General Hammarskjöld, under the heading of 'preventive diplomacy'. Alex J Bellamy and Paul D Williams, *Understanding Peacekeeping* (2nd edn, Polity 2010), pp. 83–84, (hereinafter 'Understanding Peacekeeping'). They became the 'peacekeeping' blueprint. UN, *The Blue Helmets: A Review of United Nations Peacekeeping*, vol 5 (UN 1990), p. 8, (hereinafter '1990 Blue Helmets'). The three principles that Hammarskjöld listed after the completion of UNEF I were: the consent of the host State, impartiality, and prohibition of the use of force except in self-defence. UNGA, 'Summary Study of the Experience Derived from the Establishment and Operation of the Force: Report of the Secretary-General' (9 October 1958) UN Doc. A/3943, (hereinafter 'Summary Study'). (Hammarskjöld included another principle in his report: that of the

in 1960, in the UN Operation in Congo (ONUC). Unlike previous missions, there was a complete break-down of law and order institutions in the Congo, and this mission was mandated to restore law and order.[6] As a result, small police contingents were deployed as part of a larger group of 'law and order' institutions.[7]

---

non-inclusion of Permanent Members of the Security Council – but this principle was not seen as being as important as other three, as the nature and circumstances of operations changed after the Cold War.) These three principles became the 'peacekeeping principles'. During early operations, the host States were mostly capable of running their own internal affairs, including law and order functions. These functions were thus limited within the Peace Operations. These Operations were conducted by military personnel, and not by police. It was also observed that, generally speaking, the mission areas had no local population, and there were virtually no law and order problems, except for occasional needs, in particular in Gaza. Oakley, Dziedzic and Goldberg, *Policing Disorder*, p. 17. Nevertheless, the idea of policing in Peace Operations existed from the very early days of the UN. In 1948, the former Secretary-General Lie proposed that the General Assembly should establish a UN police service of at least 800 personnel, but the idea was rejected after consideration. UN DPKO, 'Brief History' [2011] *UN Police Magazine* 6, p. 6.

6 UNSC Res 145 (22 July 1960) UN Doc. UNSC/RES/145.

7 The Secretary-General's report on the establishment of ONUC explained the process of deploying contingents, 'including police units'. UNSC, 'First Report by the Secretary-General on the Implementation of Security Council Resolution S/4387 of 14 July 1960' (18 July 1960) UN Doc. S/4389, p. 10. The discussion was focused more on which contributing States the UN would accept offers from, and not on whether they were military or police. The records do not clearly indicate who initiated the move to establish the first Ghanaian police contingent. Schmidl, *Police in PO*, p. 8. There is also no reference to ONUC in meeting records, speeches made or reports by the Secretary-General, which are available in the UN archive. Amongst those, see UNSC, 'Note Verbale Dated 5 August 1960 from the Permanent Representative of Ghana Addressed to the Secretary-General' (6 August 1960) UN Doc. S/4420; First Report by the Secretary-General in UNSC, 'Security Council Official Records, 15th Year: 873rd Meeting, 13/14 July 1960' (1 January 1960) UN Doc. S/PV.873, paras. 18–29; UNSC, 'Cable Dated 60/07/12 from the President of the Republic of the Congo and Supreme Commander of the National Army and the Prime minister and Minister of National Defence Addressed to the Secretary-General of the United Nations' (13 July 1960) UN Doc. S/4382, on the information on the exchange of communications between the Congo and the Secretary-General, where the Congo requested technical assistance with administration, particularly in the area of security administration and, separately, military assistance from the UN; UNSC, 'Second Report by the Secretary-General on the Implementation of Security Council Resolutions S/4387 of 14 July 1960 and S/4405 of 22 July 1960' (6 August 1960) UN Doc. S/4417 and UNSC, 'Second Report by the Secretary-General on the Implementation of Security Council Resolutions S/4387 of 14 July 1960 and S/4405 of 22 July 1960 – Addendum No 5' (11 August 1960) UN Doc. S/4417/Add.5, where the Secretary-General explained his plan for assistance to the Congo as technical assistance plus some other forms of assistance at the higher civilian administration level; UNSC, 'Second Report by the Secretary-General on the Implementation of Security Council Resolutions S/4387 of 14 July 1960 and S/4405 of 22 July 1960 – Addendum No 10' (20 August 1960)

The UN police assisted the military, and came under military command.[8] In ONUC, the police were tasked with a mixture of roles, including training, and contributing directly to public security.[9] There were three operations in which the UN police were deployed before the end of the Cold War: ONUC, the UN Security Force in West New Guinea (UNSF), and the UN Peacekeeping Force in Cyprus (UNFICYP). There was no coherent evolution of UN police functions as, in each operation, these functions were determined on an *ad hoc* basis. A feature of early police operations was that there was no clear distinction between military and police tasks,[10] except that the police were mainly concerned with maintaining civil order.[11] Although the military was also used for riot control, it was observed that they were neither trained nor equipped for that role.[12]

UN Doc. S/4417/Add.10 on the deployment, referring to Ghanaian contingents without mentioning the police; three related resolutions UNSC Res 4387 (14 July 1960) UN Doc. S/4387, UNSC Res 4405 (1960) UN Doc. S/4405 and UNSC 4426 (9 August 1960) UN Doc. S/4426. It appears from the record that these police units were seen as part of the mission component, driven by appeals and corresponding offers for national contingents. One noticeable point gleaned from meeting records was that Ghana, together with some other African States, urged the UN to take measures against Belgian troops in Katanga province. Ghana was very keen to offer its military for immediate deployment as part of ONUC. It wrote to the Secretary-General, stating that it would send its troops to work under the central government of the Congo if its offer was not immediately accepted. UNSC, Note Verbale Dated 5 August 1960 from the Permanent Representative of Ghana Addressed to the Secretary-General.

8 In ONUC, the first Ghanaian police contingents were under military command, and the subsequent Nigerian police component was technically outside the ONUC structure. Following a request from Nigeria, it was placed within the technical assistance team that was offered to the Congo in parallel with ONUC activities. This arrangement was made through a tri-party agreement between the UN, Nigeria and the Congo. Schmidl, *Police in PO*, p. 9.

9 The UN police functions included assisting local police with law enforcement matters, training them, and developing the institution of the police in the host State. Annika S Hansen, *Policing the Peace: The Rise of United Nations Formed Police Units* (ZIF Center for International Peace Operations-Policy Briefing vol 2, 2011), p. 1, (hereinafter 'Policing the Peace'). They were also engaged in guarding key installations and conducting patrols. UN DPKO, 'Brief History', pp. 6–7.

10 Annika S Hansen, *From Congo to Kosovo: Civilian Police in Peace Operations* (Oxford University Press for the International Institute for Strategic Studies 2002), p. 17, (hereinafter 'From Congo'). It does not appear that there was a serious discussion about the functions that ONUC police companies were to deliver. William J Durch, *United Nations Police Evolution, Present Capacity and Future Tasks* (The Henry L Stimson Center, Discussion Paper, 2010), p. 2, (hereinafter 'UNPOL Evolution'). Nothing appears in the meeting records of the Security Council either. See above n. 5 and 7.

11 Oakley, Dziedzic and Goldberg, *Policing Disorder*, p. 17.

12 Ibid, p. 17.

The UN police were recognized as an independent entity when they were deployed outside the military command in UNFICYP. In order to respond to communal tensions,[13] it was considered necessary to have a police component[14] to reinforce the local law enforcement institutions,[15] and not merely to assist the military.[16] The UN police monitored and supervised local police, assisted with investigations, and carried out other law enforcement tasks in relation to matters with inter-communal aspects.[17] At this point, the term 'Civilian Police' appeared and, since then, all UN police have been non-military.[18]

13 Following the independence of the Republic of Cyprus in 1960, the tensions between Greek and Turkish Cypriots continued, with the situation becoming violent in 1963. The mission was called on to prevent the recurrence of fighting between the two communities, and to contribute to the restoration of law and order, and the return to normal conditions.

14 The UN police operated as national units, with each contingent assigned to a district. Although they were deployed as national units, they were not delivering the same functions as the national units which had been deployed as Formed Police Units since 1999. On Formed Police Units, see Section 1-6. They worked as individual police experts who assisted the local police force in specialized areas. They did not work as cohesive units to react to situations that potentially involved a higher risk, nor were they specifically assigned to the guarding of personnel or installations that needed special protection.

15 It was decided that a small detachment of around 30 officers was necessary to reinforce the local law enforcement institutions. Oakley, Dziedzic and Goldberg, *Policing Disorder*, p. 18.

16 In response to the situation in 1964, when U Thant's Special Representative suggested including a military police element in the new force, U Thant's military advisor opposed the idea on the basis that military police normally only function in support of the military. Ibid, p. 18. In fact, military police normally conduct policing functions in cases against military personnel only. There may be some exceptions, such as Egypt and Indonesia, whose military police also plays gendarme-like roles. Schmidl, *Police in PO*, p. 10. The Force Commander suggested including a civilian police component outside the military command. Oakley, Dziedzic and Goldberg, *Policing Disorder*, p. 18. The suggestion was incorporated into the plan of the mission.

17 UN DPKO, 'UNFICYP Background' <http://www.un.org/en/peacekeeping/missions/unficyp/background.shtml> accessed 24 August 2014. '[I]ncidents where Greek or Turkish Cypriots are involved with the opposite community' and cases of missing persons were directly investigated by the UN police. Oakley, Dziedzic and Goldberg, *Policing Disorder*, p. 17. However, the UN police in UNFICYP did not bring investigated cases to prosecution. Bellamy and Williams, *Understanding Peacekeeping*, p. 379.

18 At this stage, police matters were dealt with within the military component of the UN Department of Peacekeeping Operations. Later in 1993, a Civilian Police Unit was formed. UN DPKO, 'UNPOL' <http://www.un.org/en/peacekeeping/sites/police/division.shtml> accessed 12 December 2014.

It appears to be no coincidence that the delivery of these early functions by the UN police appeared to face no major challenges. One reason is that the benign environment allowed them to deliver their functions without much resistance from the local police.[19] Another reason is that they were generally placed within the less intrusive 'Capacity Building' operations.[20] The modest nature

19 For example, see the reception of the UN police by the local population, as described by several police officers who served as UN police in UNFICYP. In Gerald Hesztera, *30 Jahre Polizei – Kontingente im UN – Einsatz* (BMI 1994), pp. 10–18, cited in Oakley, Dziedzic and Goldberg, *Policing Disorder*, p. 34. However, the environment in ONUC was an exception.

20 'Capacity Building' operations can be divided into two different types: 'advising and supporting operations', which take the least intrusive approach and provide technical assistance or strategic support to build the capacity of the local police; and 'training and mentoring', in which the international police are directly involved in the delivery of capacity building measures. Thaddeus Lin and Patrick Law, 'Objective-Based Policing Typology' (The Oceanic Conference on International Studies, 2–4 July 2008), p. 17, (hereinafter 'Policing Typology'). This is with the possible exception of the second Peace Operation that had a police component: the UN Security Force (UNSF). In 1962, the UNSF was deployed primarily as a military component in West New Guinea during the handover of the territory from the Netherlands to Indonesia. Oakley, Dziedzic and Goldberg, *Policing Disorder*, p. 17. It had a dual role of observing the compliance of the parties with provisional agreements pending the transfer of authority from the Netherlands to the UN transitional administration (UNTEA), and acting as a temporary internal security force during UNTEA's mandate (UN DPKO, 'Brief History', pp. 7–8.), supplementing the existing Papuan police (as stipulated in Article VIII of the Indonesian-Netherlands agreement). The UNSF was initially planned as being an exclusively military operation, but for the role of the chief of police. UN, *Annual Report of the Secretary General on the Work of the Organization 16 June 1962–15 June 1963* (UN 1963), p. 36. The plan was to rely on existing administrative and police structures, both local Papuan and Dutch, regarding law enforcement. However, due to the early departure of Dutch officers and the lack of capacity of the Papuan police, the UN needed to deploy police from the Philippines on a temporary basis. Oakley, Dziedzic and Goldberg, *Policing Disorder*, p. 18. It was considered necessary for policing functions to be delivered by civilian police, and not by the military. It was thought that the military would react in a military manner to situations not amounting to large-scale civil disorder, which would not be an adequate substitute for having police stations throughout the country. Ibid, p. 18. This was the first time that the UN hired police to carry out law enforcement tasks instead of assisting or training the local police. The UN perceived this as an unusual example of the UN police taking up law enforcement tasks themselves, and this did not happen again during the next four decades. UN DPKO, 'Brief History', p. 8. However, that perception is debatable as, in some subsequent missions, the UN police also conducted law enforcement tasks alongside the local police (for example, in UNFICYP). It may be more correctly stated that it was unique, in that the UN police took a lead on law enforcement tasks, assisted by a few local counterparts. A British police officer was put in charge of the Papuan police (Oakley, Dziedzic and Goldberg, *Policing*

of early operations was due to the strict adherence to the principle of consent, which meant that there was no need to resort to a Chapter VII mandate.[21]

1-2 *Post-cold War*

The dramatic changes wrought by the end of the Cold War may have had several different implications for the issue at hand.[22] After it ended, the UN intervened in more non-international armed conflicts than international armed conflicts.[23] This meant that the environment in the host State was often volatile, characterized by continuing fighting and dysfunctional governmental institutions.[24] The policing and judicial institutions were often severely

---

Disorder, p. 18), but this may have been due to the particular circumstances of the transfer of authority of a territory from one State to another in the process of decolonization.

21 Hammarskjöld called these 'Chapter Six-and-half' operations. UNGA, Summary Study.

22 None of the Peace Operations established between 1967 and 1988 had a police component. This was mainly because the effectiveness of the Security Council was severely undermined by the Cold War. Bellamy and Williams, *Understanding Peacekeeping*, p. 88. Only three operations, with limited mandates, were established between 1970 and 1987. Political fallout in ONUC, due to the conflicting political interests of the US and the Soviet Union, resulted in a financial crisis, which had a negative impact on the Operation. Ibid, pp. 85–87. In 1967, Egypt withdrew its consent for UNEF I and, based on the principle of the consent of the host State, the mission had to be withdrawn. This controversial termination of the mission created a loss of faith in the effectiveness of UN intervention. Marten Zwanenburg, *Accountability of Peace Support Operations* (Martinus Nijhoff Publishers 2005), p. 14.

23 This was related to the emergence of many claims to self-determination based on ethnicity, religion, culture and language. This arose from the fact that many small and newly emerged States had lost their backing by Cold War superpowers. Bellamy and Williams criticize the argument that the ethnic rivalries and 'roguish' behaviour previously held in check by the superpowers exploded into civil war. They argue that, in fact, the majority of the conflicts into which Peace Operations were deployed between 1988 and 1993 addressed conflicts that predated 1988. According to them, it is more appropriate to state that this period saw the conclusion of many civil wars that had been provoked and sustained by the Cold War's ideological struggle. With the withdrawal of the patronage of the superpowers, local clients faced difficulties in maintaining their 'fighting effort'. Bellamy and Williams, *Understanding Peacekeeping*, pp. 94–95.

24 For example, in UNAVEM II, the fighting parties lacked commitment to the peace process, and the fighting continued during the mission. Ibid, pp. 104–111. Likewise, UNPROFOR was deployed into a situation of on-going hostilities. Boutros Boutros-Ghali, 'Introduction' in UN (ed), *The United Nations and Cambodia, 1991–1995* (UN, 1995), Section 600. Other examples are: Somalia, former Yugoslavia, Liberia, Haiti, Zaire, and Albania. Michael J Dziedzic, 'Policing the New World Disorder: Addressing Gaps in Public Security during Peace Operations' in Max G Manwaring and John T Fishel (eds), *Toward Responsibility in*

impaired. Infrastructure was frequently destroyed, and populations displaced. Hostilities often took place outside the traditional battlefield, directly affecting civilians, and resulting in heavy civilian casualties.

The UN approach to Peace Operations also changed.[25] This included an increase in the number of such operations that were established.[26] Dramatic changes also took place in relation to the concept of Peace Operations. The mandates not only monitored the *status quo*, but also included work on good governance in an attempt to create and sustain peace.[27] The UN also began undertaking more comprehensive and complex tasks.[28] New operations were multifunctional, with political, humanitarian, social and economic components alongside that of the military.[29] At this point, the UN started relying on the powers laid down in Chapter VII of the UN Charter,[30] marking a clear departure from the original absolute requirement of consent.[31] In subsequent

---

the New World Disorder – Challenges and Lessons of Peace Operations (Frank Cass 1998), p. 134, (hereinafter 'Addressing Gaps'). This was recognized by the UN, which stated that, '[p]eace-keeping today can involve constant danger'. UN GA and UN SC, 'Supplement to an Agenda for Peace: Position Paper of the Secretary-General on the Occasion of the Fiftieth Anniversary of the United Nations' (January) UN Doc. A/50/60-S/1995/1, Section 15, (hereinafter 'Supplement to Agenda for Peace').

25 At this point (1992), the Secretary-General established a department dedicated to peacekeeping: the Department of Peacekeeping Operations (DPKO). UN DPKO, 'Department of Peacekeeping Operations' <https://www.un.org/en/peacekeeping/about/dpko/> accessed 7 August 2014.

26 More operations were authorized during these five years than during the previous four decades put together. Bellamy and Williams, *Understanding Peacekeeping*, pp. 93–94.

27 This move was backed by the optimism of and confidence in the UN of powerful States. Ibid, pp. 93–94.

28 Ibid, pp. 93–94.

29 The new and transformed operations are often called 'new types of operations' or 'robust peacekeeping', in contrast to earlier 'traditional peacekeeping'. The optimism is reflected in the *Agenda for Peace*, which called for different methods to respond to issues of international peace and security, including peacemaking and peacekeeping. The latter was backed by new and increased demands for peacekeeping, emphasizing the need for the UN's involvement in the actual implementation of peace settlements and for a flexible response. UN GA and UN SC, Supplement to Agenda for Peace, paras. 44–50.

30 The UN Iran-Iraq Military Observer Group (UNIIMOG), deployed in 1988, was the first mission to be based on a specific reference to Articles 39 and 40 of the UN Charter.

31 UNGA, Summary Study. The concept of the non-use of force was interpreted more widely than before, allowing the use of force for the defence of the mandate. Secretary-General Boutros-Ghali took the position that broader rules of engagement could be called on in order for peacekeepers to react to the use of force against them, and to use force to forestall an escalation in violence. UN GA and UN SC, Supplement to Agenda for Peace, p. 120.

operations, the consent of the host State was sometimes either obtained through pressure, or was not granted. In some situations, there were many national actors involved, but it was not clear which actors' consent mattered.[32]

The UN police faced a difficult working environment, not only because of the fragility in the host State, but also because the indigenous police, with whom they were supposed to work, were often involved in the original conflict.[33] In addition, post-conflict societies are often characterized by a surge in crime, which places an additional burden on both the national police, and the UN police assisting them. [34] These difficult working environments may have had an adverse impact on the behaviour of the UN police.[35]

Around this time, instead of working alongside military contingents, the UN police were given a distinct role of their own.[36] This made it easier for the local

32 For example, UNAMEM II was deployed into situations where the consent and cooperation of fighting parties vacillated. Somalia is another host State where the lack of meaningful consent of national actors caused severe difficulties to the mission. Bellamy and Williams, *Understanding Peacekeeping*, pp. 104–111, 196–197. Missions that depart from the principle of consent of the host States are called Peace Enforcement Operations. 'Peace Enforcement is generally considered to be synonymous with activities sanctioned under Chapter VII of the UN Charter'. Ibid, p. 214. The reliance on Chapter VII had the biggest influence on the military, but there was a ripple effect on the UN police.

33 In such situations, the indigenous police forces did not willingly act as counterparts to the UN police. For a discussion of the lack of cooperation by indigenous police, see Sections 1–3 and 1–4.

34 Therefore, the law and order requirements of the host State may differ from that of peaceful societies. Hansen, *From Congo*, pp. 88–89.

35 For the actual rate of alleged criminal conduct by the UN police, see Chapter 3, Section 2-2.

36 For example, the UN Transition Assistance Group (UNTAG, 1989–1990), which had a mandate to supervise the ceasefire between Namibia's South West Africa People's Organization (SWAPO) and South African forces, and to assist in the electoral process and the country's transition to independence, created the first ever Police Commissioner to lead the police component directly under the Special Representative of the Secretary-General (SRSG). During the following five years, missions with increasing mandates and police components were established in Western Sahara (UN Mission for the Referendum in Western Sahara [MINURSO], 1991-current), Angola (UN Angola Verification Mission [UNAVEM II], 1991–1995), El Salvador (UN Observer Mission in El Salvador [ONUSAL], 1991–1995), Cambodia (UN Transitional Authority in Cambodia [UNTAC], 1992–1993), Mozambique (UN Operation in Mozambique [ONUMOZ], 1992–1994), Former Yugoslavia (UN Protection Force [UNPROFOR], 1992–1995), Somalia (UN Operation in Somalia [UNOSOM II], 1993–1995), Rwanda (UN Assistance Mission in Rwanda [UNAMIR], 1993–1996), and Haiti (UN Mission in Haiti [UNMIH], 1993–1996). Bellamy and Williams, *Understanding Peacekeeping*, pp. 237–242. In part, the deployment of police was promoted because they were a cheaper and lower-profile option for sending States at the time. Although they

population to identify which acts were carried out by police, and which acts were carried out by military contingents.

In the immediate aftermath of the Cold War, there were only minor changes in the functions of the UN police. In operations established between 1988 and 1991 (the UN Transition Assistance Group [UNTAG],[37] UN Mission for the Referendum in Western Sahara [MINURSO][38] and the UN Angola Verification Mission II [UNAVEM II]),[39] the UN police essentially carried out monitoring functions.[40] In these operations, the UN police were not involved in conducting

---

are not cheaper per person, sending States can second a handful of police officers, whilst an equivalent military contribution would consist of hundreds of soldiers. Renata Dwan, *Executive Policing: Enforcing the Law in Peace Operations* (Oxford University Press 2002), p. 70, (hereinafter 'Executive Policing').

37 UNTAG was established in 1989 to assist the SRSG to ensure the independence of Namibia through UN-led free and fair elections, and to deliver a number of other functions. UN DPKO, 'Namibia – UNTAG' <http://www.un.org/en/peacekeeping/missions/past/untagFT.htm> accessed 27 June 2013.

38 MINURSO was established in 1991 following the settlement by Morocco and the *Frente Popular para la Liberación de Saguia el-Hamra y de Río de Oro* (Frente POLISARIO). The mission is on-going, and is mandated to prepare a referendum in which the people of Western Sahara choose between independence and integration with Morocco. UN DPKO, 'MINURSO – United Nations Mission for the Referendum in Western Sahara' <http://www.un.org/en/peacekeeping/missions/minurso/> accessed 8 December 2014.

39 UNAVEM II was established 1991 to verify the arrangements agreed to by the Angolan Government and the *União Nacional para a Independência Total de Angola* (UNITA), for monitoring the ceasefire and the activities of the indigenous police during this time, and to monitor elections in accordance with the Peace Accords. UN DPKO, 'Angola – United Nations Angola Verification Mission II' <http://www.un.org/en/peacekeeping/missions/past/Unavem2/Unavem2.htm> accessed 8 December 2014.

40 Lin and Law describe traditional operations as the 'deployment of unarmed police officers to monitor and oversee implementation of police reform and/or relevant aspects of peace agreement', Lin and Law, 'Policing Typology', p. 13. On monitoring missions, see also: Joshua G Smith, Victoria K Holt and William J Durch, *Enhancing United Nations Capacity to Support Post-Conflict Policing and Rule of Law* (Henry L Stimson Center, 2010), p. 17, (hereinafter 'Enhancing Capacity'); Bellamy and Williams, *Understanding Peacekeeping*, p. 390. The subject of monitoring may vary in this type of police function, such as: the verification that the local police forces' actions are consistent with the terms of peace agreements; monitoring the local police's compliance with human rights norms; and the verification of important processes, e.g. disarmament, demobilization and elections. Lin and Law, 'Policing Typology', p. 13. In UNTAG, the UN police accompanied and monitored the conduct of the national police during patrols, political gatherings and investigations. Their focus was to ensure impartial law enforcement by the national police but in reality, that meant following the South Africa-controlled Southwest African Police (SWAPOL)

law and order functions, nor were they involved in capacity-building functions, as they did not play a direct role in training and reforming the host State's police service. These early operations also differed from those taking place later, in that they lacked the authority to enforce the law, and were limited to monitoring, recording and reporting infringements.[41]

The UN appears not to have made a distinction between the earliest operations, which essentially carried out capacity-building functions, and those taking place around the end of the Cold War, which carried out monitoring functions. The tasks of the UN police were conceptualized as 'SMART':

- Supporting human rights;
- Monitoring local policing;
- Advising the local police on best practice;
- Reporting on incidents to the UN;
- Training local police on best practice and human rights.[42]

It appears that this concept was based on pre-1991 UN police operations.[43] UN police operations before 1990, and those in the early 1990s, had in common the fact that the UN police were not as visible to the local population as they would have been had they been involved in actual policing. Thus, their behaviour was

---

patrols in an attempt to reduce police intimidation of the local population. Durch, *UNPOL Evolution*, p. 5. MINURSO had only six UN police officers to oversee the 'safe passage of flights facilitating family visits between refugees and their families'. Lin and Law, 'Policing Typology', p. 14. In UNAVEM II, UN police were tasked with validating the national monitoring team's work on the verification of impartiality of the Angolan National Police (ANP); and monitoring and verifying the impartiality of ANP in their work. UN DPKO, 'Angola – UNAVEM II Facts and Figures' <http://www.un.org/en/peacekeeping/missions/past/Unavem2/UnavemIIF.html> accessed 22 August 2014. The ONUMOZ police, although established in 1992, also had a monitoring mandate. They had the task of monitoring 'all police activities in the country' to determine whether they were in compliance with the General Peace Agreement. James L Woods, 'Mozambique: The CIVPOL Operation' in Robert B Oakley, Michael J Dziedzic and Eliot M Goldberg (eds), *Policing the New World Disorder: Peace Operations and Public Security* (DIANE Publishing 1998), p. 153.

41 Lin and Law, 'Policing Typology', p. 14.

42 The 'SMART' concept featured in the training booklet for UN police personnel, and was developed by the Department of Peacekeeping Operations (DPKO) and the UN Centre for Human Rights in 1995. Halvor Hartz, 'CIVPOL: The UN Instrument for Police Reform' (1999) 6 *International Peacekeeping* 27, p. 31, (hereinafter 'CIVPOL').

43 The concept, for example, does not appear to sit comfortably with the UN police conducting arrests and detentions, as it had in UNTAC since 1993. See Section 1-3.

not as critical to the success of the local police as it would have been had they been building or reforming the indigenous police force.

1-3 *From Monitoring to Reform*

The change in the functions carried out by the UN police in the mid-1990s was significant because it may have changed the impact of their behaviour. Their engagement in different kinds of tasks may also have had an impact on their behaviour. The UN Transitional Authority in Cambodia (UNTAC) provided the first turning point. UNTAC's aim was to 'supervise and control' local police forces, among other State institutions.[44] The training of local police became an explicit part of UN police tasks.[45] More importantly, the environment surrounding the UNTAC police revealed the limitations of the SMART framework.[46] For example, initially, they were not authorized to carry out arrests and detentions, but in order to respond to the law and order problems in the host State, they needed that authority.[47] Another example is that the mandate lacked any provision for reforming the local police forces.[48] This became problematic, particularly when faced with a lack of cooperation by the local police.[49] Because the UNTAC police were heavily involved in advising the local police, their behaviour could be witnessed and copied by local police. The

44 UNTAC learnt lessons from UNTAG, but the UN police in UNTAC were authorized to do more than those in UNTAG. Hansen, *From Congo*, p. 18. Lee Kim, M Cheryl and Mark Metrikas, 'Holding a Fragile Peace: The Military and Civilian Components of UNTAC' in M Doyle, I Johnstone and Robert C Orr (eds), *Keeping the Peace: Multidimensional UN Operations in Cambodia and El Salvador* (Cambridge University Press 1997), p. 108, (hereinafter 'Holding Peace').

45 In earlier missions, the UN police were tasked with assisting or working alongside the local police in restoring law and order (ONUC), or undertaking investigations into intercommunal matters (UNFICYP). However, UNTAC had an explicit training mandate.

46 Bellamy and Williams, *Understanding Peacekeeping*, p. 379.

47 In January 1993, UNTAC was authorized to arrest and detain criminal suspects. However, this did not result in the prosecution of major human rights violations, mainly because of the restrictive interpretation of the mandate. Mats Berdal and Michael Leifer, 'Cambodia' (1991) 1994 *The New Interventionism* 25, p. 45.

48 Kim, Cheryl and Metrikas, 'Holding Peace', p. 108. See also Hansen, *From Congo*, p. 18. The resistance met by the UN police when attempting to monitor local police forces in UNTAC also raised the question as to whether civilian police should be armed. Ibid, p. 19.

49 Cambodia's police were unwilling to maintain law and order in an impartial manner, or to allow UNTAC police to monitor their conduct. There were also problems encountered due to the unwillingness of SWAPOL to cooperate with the UNTAG mission. Hansen, *From Congo*, p. 19. This usually derived from the lack of consent by fighting parties, and the fragility of any peace agreements. See also Section 1-2, above. Ibid, pp. 18–19.

mandate's effectiveness thus depended on the behaviour of UN police personnel to a greater extent than heretofore.[50]

This was magnified when police reform eventually became a central function of the UN police in the UN Observer Mission in El Salvador (ONUSAL). One of the ONUSAL police's functions was to select and train a new police force.[51] The UN Mission in Haiti (UNMIH) was also tasked with military and police reform. This period thus involved a shift from simply monitoring and supporting the local police, to having a wider role.[52]

1-4 *Multi-dimensional Policing*

Within a few years, the UN police began to be tasked with a much wider range of responsibilities and, most significantly, to carry out some law enforcement tasks themselves, including investigations, searches, arrests, detention, and crowd and riot control.[53] The UN police also engaged more directly in delivering capacity-building activities, with the aim of reforming domestic police behaviour through training and mentoring.[54] This corresponds with the new multi-functional Peace Operations model, which has the establishment and maintenance (or reform) of public security and local law enforcement capacity as its central aim.[55] The institutional acknowledgement of the pivotal role played by the UN police resulted in the creation of the Civilian Police Unit in the Department of Peacekeeping Operations (DPKO) in 1993.[56]

The International Police Task Force (IPTF), which formed a major part of the United Nations Mission in Bosnia and Herzegovina (UNMIBH), can be seen as

50 Ibid, p. 19.

51 The UN police were tasked with selecting and training the new *Policia Nacional Civil* (PNC). The former police force was left in place until the new one became functional. The UN police also monitored the compliance of the old National Police (PN) with human rights standards. Ibid, pp. 20–21.

52 Bethan K Greener, 'The Rise of Policing in Peace Operations' (2011) 18 *International Peacekeeping* 183, pp. 185–186, (hereinafter 'The Rise of Policing'). See also Hansen, *From Congo* p. 20.

53 Other tasks involved mentoring, advising and training local police forces, and building institutional capacity through restructuring, reforming and rebuilding national police forces. Bellamy and Williams, *Understanding Peacekeeping*, p. 379.

54 This is in contrast with the earlier, more modest model of capacity-building presented in Section 1-1. Lin and Law, 'Policing Typology', p. 17.

55 Multi-dimensional operations are defined as those to 'help establish and maintain public security and to reform, restructure and/or rebuild indigenous law enforcement capacity'. Smith, Holt and Durch, *Enhancing Capacity*, p. 19.

56 The Civilian Police Unit was tasked with planning and coordinating all matters in relation to the activities of the UN police. Hansen, *From Congo*, p. 21.

a turning point.[57] Two main functions of the UN police became more apparent as a result of this operation.[58] The first function was that of actual policing, including investigation, arrest and detention, assisting in bringing prosecutions, and road management. The UN police constituted the only police presence during the transition period.[59] The second function was the simultaneous training of the new local police force, and assisting in the building of a new justice system.[60] Its significance lies in the fact that the UN police became involved for the first time in developing a democratic and multi-ethnic local police force by selecting, vetting and training the local police.[61] Since the IPTF, these dual functions have been pursued in subsequent police operations.[62]

At first sight, one would assume that there would be an increase in the number of criminal acts committed. Separately, where the police were involved in carrying out actual policing duties, the local population would be witness as to how they were performing. If they were involved in the commission of serious crimes, the local population would see that. Any criminal behaviour on the part of the UN police would thus have had a direct impact on the local population. If the UN police engaged in training the local police, those being trained would also be aware that the UN police had committed crimes, even if these were not committed in the course of their duties. This would have set a bad example, and would have had a severely adverse effect on the cultivation of respect for the rule of law, including accountability.

These changes appear to have derived from the UN's recognition that ensuring peace and stability requires prioritizing the establishment of the rule of law.[63] In turn, the rule of law requires that the reformed or newly-established local police force be held accountable for their conduct. It is expected that this

---

57 It was established in 1995. UN DPKO, 'UNMIBH' <http://www.un.org/en/peacekeeping/missions/past/unmibh/> accessed 16 August 2014.

58 Bellamy and Williams, *Understanding Peacekeeping*, pp. 380–381.

59 Carrying out such a wide range of policing tasks is sometimes called 'executive policing'. For example, Bellamy and Williams considers the IPTF as conducting 'executive policing'. Ibid, pp. 379–380. Other authors consider 'executive policing' in more limited circumstance. See Section 1-5.

60 Ibid, pp. 379–380.

61 UN DPKO, *UN Police Magazine* (6 edn, 2011), p. 13.

62 Among them were UN Organization Mission in the Democratic Republic of the Congo (MONUC) and UN Mission in the Sudan (UNMIS). Bellamy and Williams, *Understanding Peacekeeping*, p. 392.

63 UN GA and UN SC, 'An Agenda for Peace: Preventive Diplomacy, Peacemaking and Peacekeeping' (17 June 1992) UN Doc. A/47/277 – S/24111, para. 57, (hereinafter 'Agenda for Peace').

will affect the content of the capacity-building which is provided by the UN police. It would have a negative impact on the effectiveness and legitimacy of the UN police's work if the very UN police officers responsible for inculcating the accountability of the police force were not themselves held accountable for their behaviour.

The UN's review of its approach after the catastrophes in the military operations in the mid-1990s had an effect on the mode of operation of the UN police. In Angola, partly due to severely limited resources, UNAVEM II failed to disarm ex-fighters and stop the fighting that claimed up to 300,000 lives.[64] Similar events occurred elsewhere, most notably the genocide in Rwanda in 1994,[65] and the mass killings of civilians in the UN 'safe area' in Srebrenica in 1995.[66] One key cause appears to be a mismatch between ambitious goals and limited principles, mandates and resources.[67] These catastrophes primarily concerned the military, but they had a ripple effect on the UN police's operational planning. Around this time, a debate arose as to whether the UN police in general should be armed.[68] This probably resulted from the recognition of the severe challenges faced by the UN in maintaining public safety and order.[69]

---

64 In order to oversee the demobilization of ex-fighters and to monitor elections, UNAVEM II was provided with 350 military observers, 90 police observers and 400 civilian election monitors.

65 About one million people were killed in the genocide.

66 About 7,600 Bosnian men and boys were killed in Srebrenica.

67 Bellamy and Williams, *Understanding Peacekeeping*, p. 104. This failure was recognized by the Secretary-General Boutros-Ghali on multiple occasions. '[...] the vast increase in field deployment has to be supported by an overburdened Headquarters staff that resource constraints have held at levels appropriate to an earlier, far less demanding, time. Meanwhile, there is continuing damage to the credibility of the Security Council and of the Organization as a whole when the Council adopts decisions that cannot be carried out because the necessary troops are not forthcoming'. UN GA and UN SC, Supplement to Agenda for Peace: Section 99. '[T]he Organization has come to realize that a mix of peacekeeping and enforcement is not the answer to a lack of consent and cooperation by the parties to the conflict'. Boutros-Ghali, 'Introduction', Section 600.

68 Hansen, *From Congo*, p. 59. Early deployments of small groups of armed UN police took place in 1992–95, when contingents from Spanish *Guardia Civil* and the Argentinian *Gendarmeria Nacionale* were deployed in Haiti and El Salvador, respectively. In Haiti, the US Military Police and special forces worked closely with civilian police (the Haitian National Police) on joint patrols, and provided support at police stations. In contrast to later deployments, these police units were integrated into the international police or military force without having separately defined functions. Dwan, *Executive Policing*, p. 71.

69 The link between the need to provide public safety and order and the desirability of arming the UN police can be seen, for example, in the following report: UNSC, 'Report of the

Subsequently, in the UN Civilian Police Mission in Haiti (MIPONUH), a formed unit of armed UN police were deployed as a Special Police Unit (SPU) in order to deliver specific tasks, mainly that of assisting mission personnel, and protecting mission property.[70] The UN's re-evaluation of its approach to interventions gave birth to a more flexible model, that of UN Peace Support Operations. However, this did not result in any major changes in UN police functions.[71]

1-5 *Executive Policing*

The context in which the UN police were deployed changed fundamentally in 1999 with the birth of 'executive policing'.[72] 'Executive policing' is where the power and practice of law enforcement within a particular territory derives from the assumption that the UN is the sovereign authority in that territory.[73] Two such operations – one in Kosovo and another in East Timor – were established in the same year with full authority over all aspects of civil administration.[74] As part of the administration, the UN police carried out all policing

---

Secretary-General Pursuant to Paragraph 10 of Security Council Resolution 1244 (1999)' (12 June 1999) UN Doc. S/1999/672, para. 9.

70 They were deployed in December 1997. The SPU was justified on the following basis: '[a]s the resources available to the Haitian National Police remain insufficient and the countries contributing the majority of the civilian police element are not prepared to deploy their personnel without appropriate security backing'. UN, 'Report of the Secretary-General on the United Nations Transition Mission in Haiti', UN Doc S/1997/832/Add.1, 20 November 1997, paras. 7, 8.

71 Peace Support Operations were designed to undertake a variety of civilian and military tasks, ranging from the maintenance of law and order to the mentoring of security forces, infrastructure reconstruction and national reconciliation. The peace support model allows flexibility for the actors involved, based on the idea that the mission should have the space to adapt its posture between peacekeeping and peace enforcement, depending on the parties' compliance. Peter Nadin, 'Peace Support: A New Concept for UN Peacekeeping?' (*United Nations University*, 29 May 2013) <http://unu.edu/publications/articles/peace-support-a-new-concept-for-un-peacekeeping.html> accessed 22 August 2014. See also Bellamy and Williams, *Understanding Peacekeeping*, pp. 279–284.

72 Hansen, *From Congo*, p. 25.

73 Dwan, *Executive Policing*, p. 1. This is different in Multi-dimensional Operations like the IPTF, where the authority of the UN police to conduct policing tasks derives from the consent of the host government. Therefore, the local authority can withdraw or modify the authority to arrest, detain and carry arms. Smith, Holt and Durch, *Enhancing Capacity*, p. 21.

74 UNMIK was established alongside the Kosovo Force (KFOR), following the intervention by the North Atlantic Treaty Organization (NATO) in the conflict between the government and the Kosovo Liberation Army (KLA). Tasks included: maintaining law and order, protecting human rights, distributing humanitarian aid, reconstructing infrastructure,

tasks themselves. This included: carrying out investigations, making arrests and detaining people, controlling traffic, conducting patrols (including borders patrols), gathering and analyzing criminal intelligence and forensic evidence, and managing and administering the police as an institution.[75] It is possible that some of these functions provided more of an opportunity for criminal behaviour by the UN police than others. Carrying out policing tasks meant that the UN police needed to engage with local communities to familiarize themselves with their needs.[76] This meant that police officers had more daily contact with local communities than ever before. Thus, their behaviour was more visible to the local community than it had previously been.

The UN police were also part of the effort to build or re-build local institutions, including the local police. They built up the local police by selecting, vetting, training, transferring skills, supervising and mentoring them. In doing so, the UN police were required to act as role models.[77] Therefore, their behaviour was vital, not only to the effectiveness and legitimacy of the UN missions,[78] but also for the effect they had on the local institutions they were building.

1-6 *Formed Police Units*

A new type of UN police unit was introduced when executive policing mandates were brought in, that of FPUs.[79] An FPU is a cohesive national unit of 140 police officers,[80] which is given specific tasks requiring a formed response and involving a higher security risk.[81] FPUs emerged partly to fill the perceived 'security gap' between the police and the military.[82] This gap became apparent

---

developing democratic institutions, and ensuring the return of refugees and the displaced. UNSC Res 1244 (10 June 1999) UN Doc. S/RES/1244. UNTAET was established to provide governmental functions during the transitional period, and to build State institutions to lead East Timor to independence from Indonesia. UNSC Res 1272 (25 October 1999) UN Doc. S/RES/1272. There have been no further UN transitional administrations since these two operations ended.

75 Hansen, *From Congo*, p. 28. It is important to note that the UN police have been carrying out policing tasks in other missions. See Sections 1–2, 1–3 and 1–4.

76 Ibid, p. 59.

77 See Chapter 1, Section 2.

78 See Chapter 1, Section 7.

79 UNMIK was the first mission in which FPUs were deployed alongside other UN police. UN DPKO, 'Formed Police Units' <http://www.un.org/en/peacekeeping/sites/police/units.shtml> accessed 30 June 2011, (hereinafter 'Formed Police Units').

80 An FPU may number from 120 to 140 police officers. Hansen, *Policing the Peace*, p. 2.

81 UN DPKO/DFS, 'Formed Police Units in United Nations Peacekeeping Operations' (1 March 2010) UN Doc. Ref.2009.32, para. 12, (hereinafter 'Formed Police Units in PKO').

82 Hansen, *Policing the Peace*, p. 2. In other words, the introduction of FPUs was based on the recognition that some functions could not be delivered effectively either by the military

in multi-dimensional operations, in which local environments were characterized by fragile public security. The FPUs' strength lies in the fact that they are armed, better and more heavily equipped,[83] and able to act as a cohesive unit, giving them a 'heightened robustness'.[84] As such, they specialize in the harder edge of policing, such as riot control, protection roles, countering organized crime, counter-insurgency, border-patrols, and intelligence collection.[85] FPU officers undertake tasks distinct from those carried out by individual UN police officers deployed on an individual basis (IPOs),[86] as FPUs generally lack the powers to arrest people or engage in law and order tasks.[87]

It is important to note that FPUs are distinct from earlier deployments of national police units. Hansen described ONUC police as the first FPU, and the deployment of FPUs in UNMIK and later missions as a 'return' to the first model.[88] However, ONUC police were not deployed in response to identified needs, nor were they a distinct component within the mission.[89] In fact, the

---

or by a collection of individual police officers (IPOs, who were individually recruited). IPOs were not equipped to respond to volatile situations, and they were not recruited to provide a rapid response to heightened security situations. On the other hand, deploying military units to control large civilian crowds ran the risk of escalating the violence. By the late 1990s, FPUs were regarded as a strategic asset, specifically designed to fill a perceived gap between the ability of the military and the unarmed police monitors to deal with situations such as serious challenges to law and order, or the non-compliance with peace agreements. Dwan, *Executive Policing*, p. 71. See also Dziedzic, 'Addressing Gaps', pp. 144–145. It appears that the UN made a conscious decision to deploy a group of police officers equipped with the appropriate skills, who were able to deliver specific functions. The dilemma is that, whilst the proper use of FPUs can address the security gap, deploying FPUs in an environment where the point is to demilitarize police and to nurture public trust in police may turn out to be counterproductive. Hansen, *From Congo*, pp. 70–72. See also Alice Hills, 'The Inherent Limits of Military Forces in Policing Peace Operations' (2001) 8 *International Peacekeeping* 79 pp. 92ff; Greener, 'The Rise of Policing', p. 188.

83 Hansen, *Policing the Peace*, p. 2.

84 UN DPKO/DFS, Formed Police Units in PKO, para. 12.

85 Ibid, para. 8; UN DPKO, 'Formed Police Units' <http://www.un.org/en/peacekeeping/sites/police/units.shtml>. See also Michael Dziedzic and Christine Stark, *Bridging the Public Security Gap* (United States Institute of Peace Briefing, June, 2006), (hereinafter 'Bridging Security Gap').

86 On IPOs, see Section 3-3-1.

87 Hansen, *Policing the Peace*, p. 2.

88 Ibid, p. 1.

89 These arrangements and, in particular, their status in the mission were made on an *ad hoc* basis. Ghanaian and Nigerian police appear to have been deployed through different arrangements, and their legal statuses differed. The Ghanaian police appear to have been considered the same as a military contingent, while Nigerian police functioned as

SPU deployed in Haiti[90] was much closer to the FPU model, in that they are both formed national units and undertake only specific tasks. However, the functions of FPUs are more defined and distinct from the SPU. FPUs have a different mode of deployment, which is based on an agreement between the UN and the sending State,[91] while the SPU was still a group of IPOs.

In Kosovo, in fact, there were two kinds of FPUs. One was the SPU within the UNMIK police. The SPU was intended to contribute to protecting UN staff, providing operational support and back-up to other UN police units, dealing with threats to public order, and assisting the emerging Kosovo Police Service with crowd control.[92] The other unit was the Multinational Specialized Unit (MSU), which was deployed under the Kosovo Force (KFOR) command. The MSU was charged with law enforcement tasks, in particular, gathering intelligence on organized crime, and responding to civil disturbances.[93] UNTAET also had an FPU component called the Rapid Response Unit (RRU). They dealt with major security threats and large-scale disturbances.[94]

1-7 *A Holistic 'rule of law' Approach*

Along with the steady increase in the demand for UN Peace Operations,[95] a 21st century development appears to be the recognition of, and explicit focus

technical assistance personnel through a tri-party agreement, outside the mission. See Section 1-1.

90 See Section 1-5.

91 See Section 3-3-1.

92 UN DPKO, 'Guidelines for Governments Contributing Special Police Units to UNMIK' (1999) UN Doc. –, p. 9. See also UNGA, 'Report of the Secretary-General on the United Nations Interim Administration Mission in Kosovo' (12 July 1999) UN Doc. S/1999/779; UNSC, Report of the Secretary-General Pursuant to Paragraph 10 of Security Council Resolution 1244 (1999), para. 9 (b), which set out that the SPU was assigned to undertake public order functions, including crowd control and area security, as well as other special police functions.

93 In fact, the MSU in KFOR followed the same model as the Stabilization Force (SFOR) in Bosnia and Herzegovina. The MSU in SFOR was tasked with the protection of returnees and elected officials. They also conducted patrols, and were available to assist the IPTF in preserving public order, on request. Dwan, *Executive Policing*, pp. 71–72.

94 Ibid, p. 72.

95 The increase was both in the number and size of operations. To date (December 2014), sixteen operations have been established since 2000. Those operations were mostly mandated with a wide range of tasks, except for two traditional monitoring operations: UN Mission in Ethiopia and Eritrea (UNMEE) and United Nations Supervision Mission in Syria (UNSMIS). The number of uniformed personnel, military and police together, more than doubled in size since June 2000. UN DPKO, 'Peacekeeping Fact Sheet Archive' <http://www.un.org/en/peacekeeping/resources/statistics/factsheet_archive.shtml> accessed 28 February 2015, (hereinafter 'Peacekeeping Fact Sheet Archive').

on, the rule of law.[96] In 2000, a high-level panel on UN Peace Operations, appointed by the Secretary-General, recommended that the UN police and other elements should take a holistic approach to upholding the rule of law and respect for human rights.[97] It was acknowledged that the police play a central role in Peace Operations, and recommendations were made that the UN police should focus on restructuring, training and reforming local police forces.[98] The UN considers the 'rule of law' to be a:

> [...] principle of governance in which all persons, institutions and entities [...] are accountable to laws that are publicly promulgated, equally enforced and independently adjudicated, and which are consistent with international human rights norms and standards.[99]

The UN has increasingly recognized the 'rule of law' as the key to developing lasting peace,[100] and that the judiciary, the penal system and respect for human rights are important components of the rule of law.[101] In these circumstances, the behaviour of individual UN police officers is likely to have a much longer-term impact on the effectiveness and legitimacy of the UN than ever before.[102]

96 Bellamy and Williams, *Understanding Peacekeeping*, p. 380.

97 The panel was set up by the Secretary-General to review the UN's activities on peace and security. UN, 'Identical letters dated 21 August 2000 from the Secretary-General to the President of the General Assembly and the President of the Security Council', in UN Doc. A/55/305–S/2000/809, 21 August 2000, p. 1. The Panel's report is referred to as the 'Brahimi Report', named after the chairman of the panel. UNGA and UNSC, 'Report of the Panel on United Nations Peace Operations' (21 August 2000) UN Doc. A/55/305–S/2000/809, (hereinafter 'Brahimi Report').

98 Ibid, paras. 39, 119.

99 UNSC, 'The Rule of Law and Transitional Justice in Conflict and Post-Conflict Societies', UN Doc S/2004/616, Section 6.

100 The link between peace and the rule of law was first recognized by UNGA and UNSC, Supplement to Agenda for Peace, para. 59. This highlighted 'the obvious link'. The Brahimi Report also emphasized the importance of the rule of law to the Peace Operations, and made recommendations to improve the UN's capacity to deliver it. UNGA and UNSC, Brahimi Report, paras. 29–47. The Security Council resolution on the UN police has reiterated that the rule of law is necessary for developing a sustainable peace. UNSC Res 2185 (20 November 2014) UN Doc. S/RES/2185, preamble, pp. 1–2.

101 The Brahimi Report recommended having specialists in those areas, as well as in other relevant areas, in order to create a 'rule of law' team. UNGA and UNSC, Brahimi Report, para. 10(e).

102 See Chapter 1, Section 1 for the importance of this issue.

Since 2001, all Peace Operations have been given an explicit mandate to engage in rule of law and policing activities.[103] The UN police have increasingly engaged in the 'three Rs' – reform, restructuring and rebuilding.[104] This is entrenched within a broader rule of law approach that incorporates reform in the judicial and corrections sectors.[105] This transformation can clearly be seen in successive missions deployed in the same places. In Haiti, earlier missions (UNMIH[106] and MIPONUH[107]) focused on policing, and not on the sustainable reform of the police. Later, the UN Stabilization Mission in Haiti (MINUSTAH) was given a broader mandate to support the establishment of the rule of law, including the reform of judicial and corrections systems.[108]

---

103 W G O'Neil, 'UN Peacekeeping Operations and Rule of Law Programs' in A Hurwitz (ed), *Civil War and the Rule of Law* (Lynne Rienner 2008), p. 95. The four operations that have been established since (UN Mission in the Republic of South Sudan – UNMISS-, UN Interim Security Force for Abyei – UNISFA, UN Multidimensional Integrated Stabilization Mission in Mali – MINUSMA –, and UN Multidimensional Integrated Stabilization Mission in the Central African Republic – MINUSCA) also have an explicit rule of law and policing mandate. UNSC Res 1996 (8 July 2011) UN Doc. S/RES/1996, para. 3(c); UNSC Res 1990 (27 June 2011) UN Doc. S/RES/1990, para. 2(e)(f); UNSC Res 2100 (25 April 2013) UN Doc. S/RES/2100, para. 16(a)(iii); UNSC Res 2149 (10 April 2014) UN Doc. S/RES/2149, para. 30(f).

104 For example, the UN Mission in Liberia (UNMIL) was established in 2003 with a mandate for reforming the police, judicial and corrections institutions. In 2003, it created a Legal and Judicial System Support Division and a Corrections Advisory Unit within the Mission. The UN Mission of Support in East Timor (UNMISET) and the UN Operation in Cote d'Ivoire (UNOCI) had police and judicial reform as part of their mandates, and the UN Stabilization Mission in Haiti (MINUSTAH), the UN Operation in Burundi (ONUB), the UN Mission in the Sudan (UNMIS), the UN Integrated Mission in Timor-Leste (UNMIT), the African Union-United Nations Hybrid Operation in Darfur (UNAMID), the UN Mission in the Central African Republic and Chad (MINURCAT), and the UN Organization Stabilization Mission in the Democratic Republic of the Congo (MONUSCO) were established between 2002 and 2010 with police, judicial and corrections reform mandates. However, it appears that these ambitious mandates have not been supported by sufficient resources. Durch, *UNPOL Evolution*, pp. 39–40; UNSC Res 1925 (28 May 2010) UN Doc. S/RES/1925; Greener, 'The Rise of Policing' p. 186; William J Durch and Michelle Ket, *Police in UN Peacekeeping: Improving Selection, Recruitment, and Deployment* (Providing for Peacekeepning, 2013), pp. 9, 186 (hereinafter 'Police in UN Peacekeeping'); Hansen, *From Congo*, p. 9.

105 Bellamy and Williams, *Understanding Peacekeeping*, p. 395.

106 See Section 1-3.

107 See Section 1-4.

108 J G Smith, Victoria K Holt and William J Durch, *Enhancing United Nations Capacity for Post-Conflict Police Operations* (The Henry L Stimson Center, 2007), p. 35, (hereinafter 'Enhancing UN Capacity').

In response to their rapidly growing importance and increasing functions, the institutional framework of the UN police has also been adapted. In the DPKO, the Police Unit was upgraded to a Police Division in 2000. In 2005, the official name of the UN police was changed from Civilian Police (CIVPOL) to UN Police (UNPOL), following the decision that the name CIVPOL did not reflect the fact that more than half of the UN police were armed.[109] In 2007, when the Office of the Rule of Law and Security Institutions (OROLSI) was established in order for there to be a more coherent and coordinated approach across various related components, the Police Division was placed within it. The Standing Police Capacity (SPC) also became operational in 2007.[110] In 2015, the Security Council supported the holding of annual heads of police components' meetings.[111] This indicates that the UN has a vision for establishing a firm place for the UN police in future Peace Operations.[112]

As the UN itself recognizes, the tasks required of the UN police have become far more intertwined with the aim of Peace Operations.[113] The Secretary-General stated that the work of the UN police is indispensable in establishing long-term law and order. He emphasized that the focus on police reform has shifted from merely 'mentoring and monitoring national forces', to 'building capacity through training [and] advising' and, more importantly, 'leading by example'.[114] If the UN police officers are there to lead by example, any crimes

109 See Section 2 for figures.

110 This follows the 2004 recommendation, by the High-Level Panel commissioned by the Secretary-General, that a stand-by force of senior police officers and managers for UN peace operations be created to improve the UN's ability to swiftly deploy a police presence in the field. UNGA, 'A More Secure World: Our Shared Responsibility – Report of the High-level Panel on Threats, Challenges and Change' (2 December 2004) UN Doc. A/59/565, para. 223. The creation of the SPC with an initial strength of 25 police officers was approved in 2006, and became operational in October 2007. Since its establishment, the SPC has provided capacity for new operations, as well as assistance to existing missions. UN DPKO, *UN Police Magazine*, p. 15. As of June 2015, the SPC had an authorized strength of 40 personnel. UN OIOS, 'Evaluation Report – Programme evaluation of the Standing Police Capacity of the Police Division, DPKO' (12 June 2015) UN Doc. IED-14-002, paras. 6–7.

111 UNSC Res 2185, para. 31.

112 The Brahimi Report also oversaw the demand that the number of UN police officers should remain high. UNGA and UNSC, Brahimi Report, para. 119.

113 UNPOL, 'Professionalising United Nations Police in Peacekeeping, Vision for the Police Division and United Nations Police in Peacekeeping, Vision in Brief', September 2010; UNGA, 'Report of the Secretary General on the United Nations Police' (15 December 2011) UN Doc. A/66/615, para. 6, (hereinafter 'SG Report on UN Police').

114 Message from Ban Ki-Moon, UN DPKO, *UN Police Magazine* (2nd edn, UN June 2007), p. 1. See Chapter 1, Section 1.

committed by them, whether or not these are related to their official work, would have a significant impact on the UN mission. Addressing accountability for criminal conduct committed by UN police officers, then, should be a significant priority for the UN.[115]

2 The Growth in Size of the UN Police

The evolution of the functions of the UN police may be reflected in the shift in size of the UN police force, both in absolute terms and in comparison to that of the military. Size may be indicative of whether they have acquired more functions and, separately, whether these functions are being seen as more important. There is also a question of visibility. If there are more UN police, the local population is likely to be both more aware of their behaviour, and of whether they are held accountable if they commit a crime. Whether the UN police's expansion in size has anything to do with the rate of reported crimes, either on its own or when taken together with their functions, also needs to be considered.

Until the end of the Cold War, the UN police force was very small, consisting of fewer than 1,000 officers globally.[116] Around the end of the Cold War, the UN police rapidly began being deployed in greater numbers per mission. UNTAG is a good example: it had an authorized strength of 360 in 1978; 500 in January 1989;[117] 1,500 in August 1989; and 2,000 in September 1989.[118] This increase

---

115 See Chapter 1, Section 7.

116 In 1960, the very first police contingent was deployed in ONUC. There were some 30 Ghanaian officers, who were replaced by a 400-strong Nigerian police contingent. Durch, *UNPOL Evolution*. The Nigerian police contingent was technically not within the mission, and was a small annex to the 19,828 personnel who were posted at the peak deployment. UN DPKO, 'Republic of the Congo – ONUC Facts and Figures' <http://www.un.org/en/peacekeeping/missions/past/onucF.html> accessed 10 August 2014. UNFICYP had 173 UN police officers in June 1964. UN DPKO, 'UNFICYP Fact Sheet' <http://www.unficyp.org/nqcontent.cfm?a_id=1593> accessed 2 January 2015.

117 See UNSC, 'Further Report of the Secretary-General Concerning the Implementation of Security Council Resolutions 435 (1978) and 439 (1978) Concerning the Question of Namibia' (23 January 1989) UN Doc. S/20412, para. 42, (hereinafter 'Further Report on Namibia').

118 UNSC, 'Letter Dated 26 May 1989 from the President of the Security Council Addressed to the Secretary-General' (26 May 1989) UN Doc. S/20658; UNSC, 'Letter Dated 28 September 1989 from the President of the Security Council Addressed to the Secretary-General' (28 September 1989) UN Doc. S/20872; UNSC Res 640 (29 August 1989) UN Doc. S/RES/640; UNSC Res 643 (31 October 1989) UN Doc. S/RES/643; Hansen, *From Congo*, p. 17.

was more than simply proportional to the growth in the total number of UN personnel.[119]

Even in operations with a military focus, a larger number of police were deployed.[120] For operations with more comprehensive mandates, there were even bigger police components. For example, UNTAC was authorized to deploy 3,500 UN police, together with 15,547 military contingent personnel and 893 military observers at its peak.[121] For operations with a focus on the rule of law, the UN police had considerable strength. ONUMOZ had 1,444 UN police personnel, compared to 6,625 troops and military support personnel, and 354 military observers.[122]

---

119 It should be noted that the strength of military personnel was set more flexibly than that of the police. The Secretary-General proposed that there should be a maximum of 7,500 military personnel. However, initially 1,500 personnel should be deployed, with the possibility of deploying more personnel up to that maximum should this be warranted by the situation on the ground. On the other hand, as regards police personnel, the Secretary-General proposed that he should set the precise number of these personnel, which could change in response to the precise need on the ground. See UNSC, Further Report on Namibia, paras. 42–46; UNSC, 'Explanatory Statement by the Secretary-General Concerning his Further Report (S/20412) Concerning the Implementation of Security Council Resolutions 435 (1978) and 439 (1978) Concerning the Question of Namibia' (9 February 1989) UN Doc. S/20457, para. 4; UNSC, 'Report of the Secretary-General on the Implementation of Security Council Resolution 640 (1989) Concerning the Question of Namibia' (6 October 1989) UN Doc. S/20883, paras. 16–21, 22–27.

120 UNPROFOR had '38,599 military personnel, including 684 military observers, and 803 civilian police' in March 1995. UN DPKO, 'Former Yugoslavia – UNPROFOR' <http://www.un.org/en/peacekeeping/missions/past/unprof_p.htm> accessed 10 August 2014. UNOSOM II was initially authorized to deploy up to 28,000 military and 2,800 UN police personnel. UN DPKO, 'Somalia – UNOSOM II Facts and Figures' <http://www.un.org/en/peacekeeping/missions/past/unosom2facts.html> accessed 22 August 2014. UNAVEM III had 7,000 military and 360 police. UN DPKO, 'Angola – UNAVEM III' <http://www.un.org/Depts/DPKO/Missions/unavem_f.htm> accessed 22 August 2014.

121 The maximum deployment was in June 1993 with 15,991 military personnel, inclusive of contingent personnel and observers, and 3,359 UN police. UN DPKO, 'Cambodia – UNTAC Facts and Figures' <http://www.un.org/en/peacekeeping/missions/past/untacfacts.html> accessed 10 August 2014. Initially, UNMIH had 700 military and 567 UN police, which was expanded to 6,000 military and 900 UN police in 1995. UN DPKO, 'Haiti Facts and Figures' <http://www.un.org/en/peacekeeping/missions/past/unmihfacts.html> accessed 10 August 2014.

122 UN DPKO, 'Mozambique – ONUMOZ Facts and Figures' <http://www.un.org/en/peacekeeping/missions/past/onumozF.html> accessed 10 August 2014. Note also that UNMIBH (including IPTF) initially had an authorized strength of 1,721 police monitors. This was expanded to 2,057 in November 1997. UNSC Res 1035 (21 December 1995) UN Doc. S/RES/

UN police were deployed in the largest numbers in executive policing operations.[123] UNMIK was initially authorized to have 4,718 UN police officers, the biggest force to date.[124] Similarly, UNTAET had a maximum strength of 1,640 UN police officers.[125]

Operations since 2000 have seen a further increase in the number of the UN police deployed. It has become normal to have a police component with more than 1,000 officers.[126] The comparative size of the UN police has also grown, the police: military ratio frequently being one: four or five.[127] In MINUSTAH, the ratio reached one: two.[128] Amongst current operations, UNAMID deserves a special mention. In this first joint operation with the African Union, 6,432 UN police officers, the largest number ever, were authorized for deployment. The police: military ratio was one: three.[129]

1035 (1995). UN DPKO, 'Bosnia and Herzegovina – UNMIBH Facts and Figures' <http://www.un.org/en/peacekeeping/missions/past/unmibh/facts.html> accessed 10 August 2014. Military assistance was provided by NATO forces (SFOR).

123 Bellamy and Williams, *Understanding Peacekeeping*, p. 394.

124 UN DPKO, 'UNMIK Facts and Figures' <http://www.un.org/en/peacekeeping/missions/unmik/facts.shtml> accessed 10 August 2014. Military assistance was provided by NATO's KFOR.

125 Together with 9,150 military personnel. UN DPKO, 'East Timor – UNTAET Facts and Figures' <http://www.un.org/en/peacekeeping/missions/past/etimor/UntaetF.htm> accessed 10 August 2014.

126 UNMISET was authorized to have 1,250 UN police. UN DPKO, 'East Timor – UNMISET – Facts and Figures' <http://www.un.org/en/peacekeeping/missions/past/unmiset/facts.html> accessed 16 August 2014. UNMIL was authorized to have 1,115 UN police. UN DPKO, 'UNMIL Facts and Figures' <http://www.un.org/en/peacekeeping/missions/unmil/facts.shtml> accessed 16 August 2014. UNOCI had 1,366 UN police at its peak on 31 June 2014. UN DPKO, 'UNOCI Facts and Figures' <http://www.un.org/en/peacekeeping/missions/unoci/facts.shtml> accessed 16 August 2014. MINUSTAH was authorized to have 4,391 UN police officers. UN DPKO, 'MINUSTAH Facts and Figures' <http://www.un.org/en/peacekeeping/missions/minustah/facts.shtml> accessed 16 August 2014, (hereinafter 'MINUSTAH Facts and Figures'). UNMIT had 1,608 UN police. UN DPKO, 'UNMIT Facts and Figures' <http://www.un.org/en/peacekeeping/missions/past/unmit/facts.shtml> accessed 16 August 2014.

127 UNMISET's ratio of UN police to military was 1:4; UNMIL 1:4.5; and UNOCI 1:5.2 (30 June 2014). Ibid.

128 UN DPKO, 'MINUSTAH Facts and Figures' <http://www.un.org/en/peacekeeping/missions/minustah/facts.shtml>.

129 UN DPKO, 'UNAMID Facts and Figures' <http://www.un.org/en/peacekeeping/missions/unamid/facts.shtml> accessed 16 August 2014.

Overall, the global size of the UN police force has grown from 35 in 1988,[130] to 4,613 in January 2000,[131] to 7,300 in August 2006, and to its peak of 14,669 in 2010.[132] As of December 2015, there were 13,858 UN police officers.[133]

The UN police are the fastest growing component in Peace Operations. As the UN Police Advisor acknowledged, this growth in numbers comes together with an increased demand for the integration of the rule of law, in particular reforms and institution-building, in Peace Operations.[134] The growth in size is influenced by the evolution of the functions of the UN police. It appears that some newer functions, such as the actual carrying out of policing tasks and reforms, restructuring and rebuilding, require larger UN police components.

The rapid increase in FPUs is responsible for a large part of the increase in the number of UN police.[135] Sixteen years after the creation of FPUs, 9,470 police officers were deployed as FPUs, constituting about 68 percent of the total UN police personnel.[136] This is significant, given that FPU personnel are only assigned specific functions. This may indicate that the nature of FPU functions requires significant numbers, or that the environments in which FPUs are deployed require significant numbers, or both. It may also be related to their mode of deployment, which will be discussed in the following section.[137]

---

130 See Section 1-1.

131 This was alongside 1,320 Military Observers and 12,710 military troops. UN DPKO, 'Troop and Police Contributors' <http://www.un.org/en/peacekeeping/resources/statistics/contributors.shtml> accessed 18 February 2016, (hereinafter 'Troop and Police Contributors').

132 UN DPKO, 'Fact Sheet archive' <http://www.un.org/en/peacekeeping/resources/statistics/factsheet_archive.shtml>. At its peak, 14,669 UN police officers were deployed, while its authorized strength was 17,616. UN DPKO, 'History of United Nations Police' <http://www.un.org/en/peacekeeping/sites/police/history.shtml> accessed 19 September 2016.

133 As of 31 December 2015, 4,388 IPOs and 9,470 FPU officers, totaling 13,858 UN police officers, were deployed in missions. This number includes the two IPOs deployed in the UN Assistance Mission in Iraq (UNAMI). Data available at UN DPKO, 'Troop and Police Contributors' <http://www.un.org/en/peacekeeping/resources/statistics/contributors.shtml>.

134 UNPOL, 'Professionalising United Nations Police in Peacekeeping, Vision for the Police Division and United Nations Police in Peacekeeping, Vision in brief', September 2010.

135 Hansen, *Policing the Peace*, p. 1.

136 Data taken from UN DPKO, 'Troop and Police Contributors' <http://www.un.org/en/peacekeeping/resources/statistics/contributors.shtml>.

137 See Section 3.

3 Ensuring the Deployment of the Required Types of Personnel

In order for the UN to minimize the likelihood of criminal behaviour by UN police personnel, it needs to ensure that it has the appropriate people. This requirement has two aspects.

One is that they need to be equipped with the specific expertise necessary to deliver their functions properly. Their incapacity may cause unintended criminal behaviour. For example, if FPU officers have no expertise in controlling a violent crowd, they may be more likely to resort to lethal force in a situation where it is unnecessary. This requirement is only relevant to crimes that are committed in the exercise of their functions.

Another requirement is that UN police officers have the right personal qualities. This relates to their behaviour, and the policing cultures they come from. Accordingly, this requirement is relevant to all crimes, regardless of any link to the functions of the UN police.

The following section first identifies the expertise and personal qualities required of UN police personnel and, second, examines how the UN attempts to meet this requirement.

3-1 *Expertise Required of UN Police Officers*

No Requirement

It is unsurprising that no particular expertise was formally required of UN police officers early on, because their deployment was *ad hoc*,[138] and their functions were unclear.[139] It was up to each sending State to select officers for deployment.[140] The general thinking was that 'a policeman is a policeman is a policeman'.[141] Insofar as the deployment of the UN police was not widespread, and was infrequent, this arrangement did not pose a serious problem.

General Minimum Requirements

Two problems relating to UN police surfaced after they became a standard element in Peace Operations. The first was that many UN police officers did not appear to be properly qualified. The second was the incidence of misconduct committed by individual UN police officers during the course of their

138 Hansen, *From Congo* p. 50.

139 See Section 1-1.

140 On the mode of deployment, see Section 2-2-2 below.

141 Hansen, *From Congo* pp. 54–55.

deployment.[142] UNTAC was the first mission for which the UN specified recruitment standards.[143] At a minimum, they were required to have a command of the mission language (often English),[144] the ability to operate four-wheel drive vehicles, and five years' policing experience.[145]

It is interesting that the UN appears to be more concerned that UN police officers have policing experience, than simply knowledge of policing.[146] A 1997 document specified that they must be 'a sworn member of the police force'.[147] This appears to exclude voluntary police officers, and reserve police officers who serve in some police forces on an irregular basis. It was also clarified that even where an officer was a sworn member of a police force, that officer should not be included if he did not have policing experience, unless he was specifically selected by the UN.[148] Later, it was also stipulated that the required five-year period should exclude any time spent being trained.[149] Arguably, monitoring roles could have been played by someone with theoretical knowledge, but without practical experience. This would not be the case with actual policing duties, and even less so when mentoring, reforming, rebuilding or restructuring the local police.

142 When problems occurred with low quality staff and incidents such as the misconduct by some UN police officers surfaced in Cambodia, the UN defined minimum standards for the selection of international staff. Ibid, p. 19; Hartz, 'CIVPOL', p. 39.

143 Hansen, *From Congo* p. 50.

144 The language requirement has become more important, as UN police must communicate with their local counterparts in order to carry out their functions. UNITAR and IPS, *The United Nations Transitional Authority in Cambodia* (*UNTAC: Debriefing and Lessons: Report and Recommendations of the International Conference, Singapore, August 1994*) (Nassrine Azimi ed, Martinus Nijhoff Publishers 1995), p. 17.

145 Hansen, *From Congo*, p. 50. Two more minimum requirements were added in 2007: first, the age limit was set between 25 and 62, with an explicit preference for under 55s; and second, basic computer skills were required. UN DPKO, 'Guidelines for United Nations Police Officers on Assignment with Peacekeeping Operations' UN Doc. DPKO/PD/2006/00135, paras. 44, 52.

146 Hansen argues that, '[e]xperience provides a policeman [...] with the flexibility and discretion to deal with the types of extraordinary situations that are common in a war-torn society'. Hansen, *From Congo*, pp. 51–52.

147 UN DPKO, *Selection Standard and Training Guidelines for UNCIVPOL* (UN 1997), p. 2, (hereinafter '1997 Selection Standard').

148 Ibid, p. 8.

149 UN, *Guidelines for United Nations Police Officers on Assignment with Peacekeeping Operations* (UN Doc DPKO/PD/2006/00135, 29 June 2007), para. 45, (hereinafter '2007 Guidelines').

The UN also stipulated that those who had retired from the police within the previous five years would be eligible.[150] Being retired for more than five years may have meant that the person would have been out of touch with the necessary skills. This seems to indicate that what the UN is seeking is not so much the existing institutional link between the individual officer and the sending State,[151] but rather that the officer concerned has the necessary policing skills.

Requiring that UN police personnel have policing experience indicates that the UN recognizes policing as an expertise.[152] This experience is considered to be the most important criterion for delivering the functions of the UN police. The Guidelines state that 'personnel assigned to their national police and other law enforcement agencies' may be accepted.[153] This may be a reference to States which have both State and Federal police, in an attempt to ensure that both types are eligible to be UN Police officers.[154]

Evidence shows that people other than police officers occasionally join a mission.[155] Some States, most notably the US, recruit personnel through contracting companies.[156] American UN police are private contractors, and not police officers, at least for such time as they work for a UN Peace Operation. Although it was claimed that a large number were retired police officers,[157] there were also claims that at least some were over 66 years old,[158] or had never

150 UN DPKO, *1997 Selection Standard*, p. 7; UN, *2007 Guidelines*, para. 45.

151 This differs from the military, where retired military officers are not eligible to join in a military troop in UN Peace Operations. This may have implications regarding jurisdiction. See Chapter 5, Sections 2–2, 3–2, and 4–2.

152 Policing is considered to be a professional skill for the purpose of determining their immunity status. See Chapter 6, Section 1-3.

153 UN, *2007 Guidelines*, para. 45.

154 For example, the US and Canada, where each State has its own police force, which is separate from the Federal police.

155 Colum Lynch, 'Misconduct, Corruption by US Police Mar Bosnian Mission' *Washington Post* (Washington, 29 May 2001) <http://www.balkanpeace.org/index.php?index=article&articleid=11668> accessed 12 August 2014.

156 They are employed through DynCorp, a defense contractor hired by the State Department to handle all recruitment of US police personnel for international missions. In 2008, the US had about 2,000 people working on international policing missions, all of whom were private contractors. Bellamy and Williams, *Understanding Peacekeeping*, p. 384; Hansen, *From Congo*; p. 51; Lynch, 'Misconduct, Corruption by US Police Mar Bosnian Mission'. It is suggested that the standards for and the process of recruitment of American UN police officers is *ad hoc*. Dziedzic, 'Addressing Gaps', p. 139.

157 Hansen, *From Congo*, p. 48.

158 Lynch, 'Misconduct, Corruption by US Police Mar Bosnian Mission'.

been police officers.[159] This matters for two reasons. One is that the requirement that UN police personnel be serving or recently retired police officers is an important way of ensuring that the necessary expertise is delivered. The other is that, in addition to the laws, regulations and codes that apply to ordinary nationals abroad, police officers are normally subject to additional laws, regulations and codes. The implications of a UN police officer not being a national police officer will be discussed later.[160]

It is reported that the three basic requirements are often not met. A majority of candidates for the UNMIL police were apparently unable to drive, and could not speak the mission language.[161] Many UNPROFOR police officers reportedly had the same problems,[162] as well as no knowledge of basic monitoring skills.[163] In Sierra Leone, a review of the UN police was critical of the lack of experience of some UN police officers.[164] Language can be an obvious challenge for police officers, given that many different States, using many different languages, are now contributing police officers.[165] There have been a number of Police Commissioners and senior police officers who acknowledged that the quality of police personnel was a major problem.[166]

---

159 Ibid. See also Hansen, *From Congo* pp. 57–58, where she claims that DynCorp selection is resulting in too many unqualified and unsuitable officers being selected.

160 See Chapter 5, Section 4-2-3.

161 Durch and Ket, *Police in UN Peacekeeping*, p. 80.

162 48% of incoming monitors did not speak English, according to a 1992 quality review. Halvor A Hartz, 'Experiences from UNPROFOR – UNCIVPOL' in Wolfgang Biermann and Martin Vadset (eds), *UN Peacekeeping in Trouble: Lessons Learned from the Former Yugoslavia* (Ashgate 1998), p. 311.

163 43% of the UN police were not able to handle a motor vehicle. Ibid, p. 311. If UN police have problems with driving skills, it would not be surprising if there were more motoring offences. See Chapter 3, Section 2-2-2.

164 It assessed that some UN police officers had less professional experience and competence than the local police, to whom they were supposed to provide advice. J G Smith, Victoria K Holt and William J Durch, *From Timor-Leste to Darfur: New Initiatives for Enhancing UN Civilian Policing Capacity* (The Henry L Stimson Center, Future of Peace Operations Programe Issue Brief, August 2007, 2007), p. 6, (hereinafter 'From Timor-Leste to Darfur').

165 As of 31 July 2014, 87 States are contributing police to UN Peace Operations. UN DPKO, Monthly Summary Contributions <http://www.un.org/en/peacekeeping/contributors/2014/jul14_1.pdf> accessed 14 August 2014.

166 Ali Mahmoud, 'UN Operation in Mozambique (ONUMOZ)' in Nassrine Azimi (ed), *The Role and Functions of Civilian Police in United Nations Peace-Keeping Operations: Debriefing and Lessons* (Kluwer Law International 1996), pp. 44, 49–50, in relation to UN police personnel deployed in the ONUMOZ; Selwyn Mettle, 'Operation in Somalia (UNOSOM)' in Nassrime Azimi (ed), *The Role and Functions of Civilian Police in United Nations Peace-Keeping*

It is acknowledged that there are multiple reasons for the difficulties experienced in securing good quality UN police personnel. First, police officers joining UN Peace Operations are generally not a standing reserve force waiting to be deployed.[167] If deployed to a UN Peace Operation, they may not easily be replaced at home. This makes sending States hesitant to deploy their most qualified officers abroad.[168] They also either do not specialize in, or are not trained in, international policing.[169] These factors, when taken together, mean an almost permanent shortfall of available officers. This has resulted in some unqualified, inexperienced or underperforming officers being deployed.[170]

Operations: Debriefing and Lessons (Kluwer Law International 1996), p. 56; Carlos Abad Ruiz, 'Role and Functions of the Civilian Police in Human Rights Verification Missions' in Nassrine Azimi (ed), *The Role and Functions of Civilian Police in United Nations Peace-Keeping Operations* (Kluwer Law International 1996), p. 89, (hereinafter 'Roles and Functions'), in relation to the UN police personnel deployed in the MINUGUA; Muhammad Anwarul Iqbal, 'An Overview of the CIVPOL Operations in Angola (UNAVEM)' in Nassrin Azimi (ed), *The Role and Functions of Civilian Police in United Nations Peace-Keeping Operations: Debriefing and Lessons* (Kluwer Law International 1996), p. 98, on the same in relation to the UNAVEM mission; Kjell Johansen, 'Civilian Police in Former Yugoslavia (UNPROFOR)' in Nassrine Azimi (ed), *The Role and Functions of Civilian Police in United Nations Peace-Keeping Operations: Debriefing and Lessons* (Kluwer International 1996), p. 119, identified the same problem in relation to UN police in UNPROFOR; Klaas C Roos, 'Debriefing of Civilian Police Components: UN Transitional Authority in Cambodia (UNTAC)' in Nassrine Azimi (ed), *The Role and Functions of Civilian Police in United Nations Peace-Keeping Operations: Debriefing and Lessons* (Kluwer Law International 1996), p. 123, (hereinafter 'UNTAC Debriefing'), and Kar Chye Oh, 'Singapore Civilian Police Contingent in UNTAC: Observations and Lessons Learned' in Nassire Azimi (ed), *The Role and Functions of Civilian Police in United Nations Peace-Keeping Operations: Debriefing and Lessons* (Kluwer International 1996), p. 137, (hereinafter 'Singaporeans in UNTAC'), both stated the same in relation to UNTAC police; Alex Morrison, 'Methodology, Contents and Structure of UN Civilian Police Training Programmes' in Nassrin Azimi (ed), *The Role and Functions of Civilian Police in United Nations Peace-Keeping Operations: Debriefing and Lessons* (Kluwer Law International 1996), p. 145, questioned the quality of UN police personnel in general. It was also claimed that UN police were the most problematic issue in Peace Operations at that time. Government of Canada, *Toward a Rapid Reaction Capability for the United Nations* (Prepared for the 50th session of the UNGA, September 1995, 1995).

167 Hansen, *From Congo*, p. 48; Dziedzic, 'Addressing Gaps', p. 137.

168 Greener, 'The Rise of Policing', p. 188.

169 Dziedzic, 'Addressing Gaps', p. 137.

170 Nina M Serafino, *Policing in Peacekeeping and Related Stability Operations: Problems and Proposed Solutions* (Library of Congress, CRS Report for Congress, 30 March 2004), p. 14. Because the pressure to recruit sufficient numbers of personnel is so great, efforts to control the quality of personnel have to be set aside at times. Hansen, *From Congo* p. 51.

A dilemma arises in attempting to balance these two needs: that of being able to deploy a certain number of UN police personnel rapidly,[171] and that of being able to ensure their quality. Procedural issues in securing compliance with the required standards will be discussed later.[172]

Additional General Criteria

Additional criteria focus on operational skills. First, investigation and reporting skills were required in the mid-1990s.[173] This appears to correspond to the needs generated by monitoring operations.[174] Second, more policing and practical skills were listed as desirable in 1997.[175] It may be that the UN Secretariat realized the importance of making operational skills an explicit requirement. This may have been particularly important because of the very different policing cultures in sending States. A former Police Commissioner stated that, '[p]olice forces of the world sometimes only have the name 'Police' in common'.[176] However, possibly influenced by the difficulties in securing police personnel who met these requirements, they were subsequently reduced. By 2007, only a handful of required skills remained: interviewing techniques, negotiation, mediation and conflict resolution skills, and first aid.[177] Previous

---

171 Mobilizing the UN police is time-consuming, and the UN constantly lacks UN police personnel. Dziedzic, 'Addressing Gaps', p. 137. See also Hansen, *From Congo*, p. 60. For example, it took UNTAC eight months to reach full deployment. UNITAR and IPS, *UNTAC debriefing*, p. 17.

172 See Section 3-3.

173 The 1995 Police Handbook contained additional criteria. Among them were the requirements that police officers '[h]ave the appropriate operational skills' for the post, and '[b]e capable of conducting analytical investigations into alleged incidents, and of compiling and submitting factual and impartial recommendations'. UN, *United Nations Civilian Police Handbook* (UN 1995), p. 24, (hereinafter '1995 Handbook').

174 As discussed in Section 1-2, by 1995, the UN police were delivering many more functions, but there may have been a delay in reflecting the need for these in the list of required skills.

175 The 1997 selection guidelines set out the desirable skills in the form of a long 'wish-list'. They ranged from knowledge of their national laws, legal system and codes of conduct, to basic but specific policing skills, including crime scene skills, patrols, traffic control, report writing and interviewing techniques, to negotiation and conflict resolution skills, to practical skills, including being able to operate communications equipment and knowledge of radio procedures, first aid and map-reading. UN DPKO, *1997 Selection Standard*, p. 9.

176 Hartz, 'Experiences from UNPROFOR', p. 312.

177 Knowledge of land navigation and global positioning systems has replaced map-reading skills. UN, *2007 Guidelines*, para. 53. The current desired skills are identical to the ones set out in 2007. UN DPKO, 'UN Police Division Minimum Recruitment Requirements'

mission experience with a UN Peace Operation was explicitly mentioned.[178] This may suggest that the UN recognized that international policing is different from domestic policing.

Specific Expertise Requirements

In the early missions, the need to specify the required kinds of policing expertise was not recognized.[179] The lack of specification, beyond general policing skills, caused problems.[180] Early missions focused on advising and monitoring,[181] but it was observed that police officers deployed for monitoring purposes were not trained in monitoring.[182]

With the dramatic increase in the variety of tasks required of UN police, the need for specific expertise began to be recognized in the late 1990s. The UN began specifying these requirements, which included: traffic management, monitoring, criminal investigation, training, managing or administration, the number of years of professional experience, and the desired ranks for specific missions.[183] A recent example is that the UN sought UN police officers for UNOCI to:

> [...] assist in building the capacity of the Ivorian law enforcement agencies in such specialized areas as crowd control, community policing, judicial policing, communication, criminal investigation, sexual and gender based violence, organized crime and border management.[184]

Filling positions requiring specific expertise has been even more challenging than securing the requisite numbers of officers. In particular, specialized

---

<http://www.un.org/en/peacekeeping/sites/police/requirements.shtml> accessed 12 Aug. 2014, (hereinafter 'Minimum Requirement').

178 UN, *1995 Handbook*; UN DPKO, *1997 Selection Standard*; UN, *2007 Guidelines*.

179 See above, Section 3-1, entitled '*no requirement*'.

180 Hansen, *From Congo*, p. 53. In UNTAC, the level of required police experience was too general, as there were substantial differences among various national police forces. UNITAR and IPS, *UNTAC debriefing*, p. 17.

181 See Section 2-1-1.

182 Hartz, 'Experiences from UNPROFOR', p. 312. UNTAES suffered from a severe shortage of police with training experience. Hansen, *From Congo*, p. 53.

183 UN DPKO, *1997 Selection Standard*, p. 11. For example, for a group of UN police in Bosnia, the UN asked States to provide those who had the necessary specific skills and ranks. Dziedzic, 'Addressing Gaps', p. 140; Hansen, *From Congo*, pp. 54–55.

184 UNSC, 'Special Report of the Secretary-General on the United Nations Operation in Côte d'Ivoire' (29 March 2012) UN Doc. S/2012/186, para. 65.

policing capabilities, such as forensic specialists or police trainers, are also in heavy demand at home.[185] For example, despite the fact that 'police development' was intended to be a major part of UNTAET and UNMISET, none of the 1,270 UNTAET officers were recruited to be trainers or institution-building experts, while none of the 150 UNMISET police advisers had development or capacity-building expertise.[186] Frequent rotation of UN police personnel also poses a challenge, as experience can be lost.[187] The needs in the field are not well understood by UN headquarters or sending States, which exacerbates the problem.[188]

One recent significant change is that the ability to use firearms has been added as a general requirement for all UN police personnel. Until around 2010, proficiency in firearms use was only required in relation to missions in which police were armed, or was limited to those positions requiring the use of firearms.[189] However, the most recent criteria include the mandatory command of firearms, and all police personnel must be tested in this regard.[190] This could be a reflection of the new environments in which UN Peace Operations operate,[191] but considering that there are still traditional monitoring-type operations,[192]

185 Greener, 'The Rise of Policing', p. 188. UNGA, SG Report on UN Police, paras. 51–55. Hansen adds narcotics and organized crime as a specialization in high demand. Hansen, *From Congo*, p. 55.

186 Ludovic Hood, 'Missed Opportunities: The United Nations, Police Service and Defence Force Development in Timor Leste, 1999–2004' (2006) 8 *Civil Wars* 143, pp. 146, 149.

187 Hansen, *From Congo*, p. 55. This also put UN police officers at a disadvantage vis-à-vis the local police officers whom they were supposed to monitor, because the UN police continuously changed their personnel, whilst the local police officers remained the same. Hartz, 'Experiences from UNPROFOR' p. 315.

188 Hansen, *From Congo*, p. 55.

189 The 1997 Selection Guidelines required UN police personnel to have a 'detailed knowledge of the use proficiency, care and control of personal issue firearms', but only in relation to missions in which police are armed. UN DPKO, *1997 Selection Standard*, p. 9. Likewise, there was no general requirement regarding the use of firearms in 2007. The Guidelines only stated that the UN police were only authorized to use firearms in some missions, and that they should 'preferably' receive UN Selection Assistance team clearance to do so. UN DPKO, 2007 Guidelines, para. 50.

190 UN DPKO, 'Minimum Requirement' <http://www.un.org/en/peacekeeping/sites/police/requirements.shtml>. However, senior UN officials advised on multiple occasions that a command of firearms is only required of those who are deployed to armed positions. E-mail communications with a senior UN official, November 2014; communications with two senior UN officials, July 2016.

191 See Sections 1–2, 1–3, 1–4, 1–5, 1–6, and 1–7.

192 For example, UNFICYP.

it is difficult to explain why all UN police personnel require this skill. It is hard to imagine that all police personnel who normally operate unarmed at home are capable of, or are comfortable with, using firearms. It is also difficult to imagine that it is the UN's intention to exclude those officers from unarmed monitoring missions.

Requirements for FPU Personnel

It has been clearly established that FPU personnel must have a particular form of expertise. Responding to heightened security situations requires disciplined group action.[193] This in turn requires more than just a group of police officers capable of using firearms. The demand was for a group of police officers who have a similar approach to dealing with situations which require significant numbers of officers. Although officers within an FPU may never have worked together,[194] they should come from the same legal and policing culture, and be trained to respond to a situation in the same way. In addition, as members of an armed police unit, they obviously need to be able to use firearms, but they also need to be 'trained in and have the flexibility to use either less-than-lethal or lethal force, as circumstances dictate'.[195] On the other hand, as they work in a national unit, they are not operating in a setting which requires them to communicate on a daily basis with the local population to the same extent as individual officers.[196] In 2012, the requirement for FPU officers was lowered to two years of experience,[197] and the requirement that they have a command of the mission language has been dropped for ordinary FPU members. Only half of senior FPU officials are required to have a command of the mission language, whilst other senior officers must have a command of English.[198]

3-2 *Personal Qualities Required*

Equally, or arguably more importantly, the UN needs to ensure that UN police officers have particular personal qualities, such as integrity, as they are

---

193 Dziedzic and Stark, *Bridging Security Gap.*

194 Currently, the UN requests that a unit exist for at least six months prior to its deployment. UN DPKO/DFS, 'Formed Police Units in United Nations Peacekeeping Operations' (1 March 2010) UN Doc. Ref. 2009. 32, para. 97.

195 Dziedzic and Stark, *Bridging Security Gap.*

196 However, because the FPU are heavily armed, there may be a more dramatic impact on the local population if they conduct their duties in an inappropriate manner. See Section 3-2.

197 UN DPKO, 'Standing Operating Procedures: Assessment of Operational Capability of Formed Police Units for Service in United Nations Peacekeeping Operations' UN Doc. Ref.2012.11, para. 14, (hereinafter '2012 FPU SOP').

198 Ibid, para. 21.

increasingly operating as role models.[199] Some personal qualities have been included in the requirement and selection criteria for UN police personnel. These relate to mental and physical health, personal and professional integrity, and other personal qualities.[200] Over time, these requirements have not changed much, and have focused on good judgement, an objective attitude, polite manners, self-discipline, inter-cultural skills, and leadership.[201] This appears to indicate that UN police officers are expected to use their discretion to solve difficult problems, interact with colleagues and communities with different cultural backgrounds, and work in difficult conditions.

There is also an exclusion criterion. Those officers who have been convicted of a crime are excluded from becoming UN police officers. This is one of the ways in which the UN seeks to uphold professional integrity amongst UN police personnel. However, therein lies a paradox. In sending States which struggle to hold their police to account, a clean criminal record may not mean that a police officer has never committed a crime. Instead, in these States, crimes committed by police officers may either not be addressed at all, or may be addressed only within the police disciplinary system.

By 2007, the UN added a further criterion for disqualifying police candidates. No police officer against whom any disciplinary charge has ever been upheld, or who is under investigation, or who is being prosecuted for any disciplinary or criminal offence (except for minor traffic offences) can join the UN police (for this purpose, driving while intoxicated, or dangerous or careless driving, are not considered minor traffic offences).[202] There are two issues to consider with this approach. One is the same as the question of a record of criminal conviction, as described above. The other is related to the variety of disciplinary offences in different police forces. For example, disciplinary offences can include disobeying superior orders, or leaving a post without prior approval. In terms of ensuring professional integrity, such offences are arguably insufficiently serious to disqualify a police candidate. Moreover, a candidate may be working in an authoritarian or undemocratic police force, for example, one in which superior orders are given that do not conform to human rights standards.[203]

199 See Section 1-7.

200 UN, *1995 Handbook*, pp. 22–24; UN DPKO, *1997 Selection Standard*, pp. 8–9; UN DPKO, 'Minimum Requirement' <http://www.un.org/en/peacekeeping/sites/police/requirements.shtml>.

201 UN DPKO, 'Minimum Requirement' <http://www.un.org/en/peacekeeping/sites/police/requirements.shtml>.

202 UN, *2007 Guidelines*, para. 61b.

203 'Experience has shown that police from non-democratic countries often do not measure up to the standards set by the UN CivPol Unit'. Hansen, *From Congo*, p. 52. See also Gino

If a candidate disobeys an order to commit a human rights violation, such an offence should not disqualify him from serving as a UN police officer.

The 2012 development relating to exclusionary criteria is interesting. The requirements for IPOs have remained the same.[204] However, the exclusion criteria for FPU personnel have been modified to include investigation, prosecution or conviction for criminal offences, violations of human rights law (IHRL) or international humanitarian law (IHL), as well as serious misconduct in previous UN missions.[205] The UN has dropped disciplinary offences from the exclusion criteria, but only for FPU personnel.

A particularly important issue is the quality of personnel in FPUs. A number of UN police personnel come from States in which democratic standards are not upheld.[206] It creates a problem if these officers conduct themselves on a mission as they would back home, but it is arguably even more problematic in relation to FPUs, as 'they are more heavily armed, play a more confrontational role and can therefore have a greater destabilizing effect'.[207]

3-3 *The UN's Efforts in Securing Adherence to the Required Criteria*

Due to the increasingly vital role that the UN police play,[208] one would expect the UN to strengthen its measures to control the quality of the UN police personnel, both through obtaining the necessary expertise, and through excluding those with questionable integrity. This expectation necessitates an examination of the procedural guarantees put in place prior to the deployment of UN police.

3-3-1 Selection

Currently, there are two different categories of UN police personnel, and three different ways for a police officer to join the UN police.

Costa, 'The United Nations and the Reform of the Police in El Salvador' in Nassrin Azimi (ed), *The Role and Functions of Civilian Police in United Nations Peace-Keeping Operations: Debriefing and Lessons* (Kluwer Law International 1996), p. 80.

204 UN DPKO, 'Standing Operating Procedure: Assessment of Individual Police Officers for Service in United Nations Peacekeeping Operations and Special Political Missions' UN Doc. Ref 2011/18. However, a senior UN official testified that the UN also requires IPOs not to have been involved in criminal offences, IHRL or IHL violations, or serious misconduct during previous UN mission assignments. Communication with a senior UN official, July 2016.

205 UN DPKO, 2012 FPU SOP, para. 25b.

206 See Chapter 6, Section 3-2. See also Greener, 'The Rise of Policing', p. 190.

207 Hansen, *From Congo*, p. 72. However, FPU personnel are expected to have less communication with the local population on a day-to-day basis. See Section 3-1, under '*Requirements for FPU personnel*'.

208 See Section 1.

Individual Police Officers (IPOs)

The first category of UN police personnel is that of IPOs. IPOs include all UN police officers, except FPU officers. The newly formed Specialized Police Teams (SPTs, a group of experts in a particular area of policing) are therefore also included in this category. In principle, IPOs are selected and seconded by sending States.[209] In the planning phase, the UN Police Division may informally consult with member States.[210] The sending States are then required to select and nominate police officers with the required skills and profiles.[211] There may also be offers from some sending States to match stand-by personnel through an established system called the Peacekeeping Capability Readiness System (PCRS).[212] Thus, sending States play a central role in the selection of personnel. It appears that the UN was not involved in the nomination and selection process at all until the early 1990s.[213] By 1997, the UN Secretariat, which assisted

209 UN DPKO, 2007 Guidelines, para. 13. On SPTs, see, for example, UNSC Res 2185, preamble, p. 2.

210 UN DPKO, 2007 Guidelines, para. 60. As of 2015, these consultations are carried out by the Strategic Force Generation and Capability Planning Cell. UNGA/SC, 'Report of the Secretary-General on the Future of the United Nations Peace Operations: Implementation of the Receommendations of the High-Level Indepdent Panel on Peace Operations' (2 September 2015) UN Doc. A/70/357–S/2015/682, para. 86, (hereinafter 'SG Response to High Panel Report').

211 UN DPKO, *1997 Selection Standard*, p. 11.

212 This new system replaced the UN Standby Arrangements System (UNSAS) in July 2015. The UNSAS framework was developed in 1994 in order to deploy peacekeeping units more rapidly. Using the UNSAS framework, the UN has concluded various Memoranda of Understanding. Through this UNSAS system, sending States could declare stand-by resources, whether these are military formations, military personnel, civilian personnel, or materials or equipment, prior to these being solicited by the UN for a specific mission. Thorsten Stodiek, 'International Police Forces in Peace Operations' in Harvey Langholtz, Boris Kondoch and Alan Wells (eds), *International Peacekeeping: The Yearbook of International Peace Operations*, vol 9 (Koninklijke Brill N V 2004), p. 98. Some States have also made domestic arrangements for the rapid deployment of their police officers to overseas missions. (Such arrangements include: making a roster of officers, preparing a pool of reserve officers, and training them. See for example, arrangements made in Australia, New Zealand, Nigeria and China, in Greener, 'The Rise of Policing', p. 185.) The new PCRS framework is far more standardized and comprehensive. Under it, sending States must provide information on the status and results of the vetting of military and police contingents, as well as the evaluation and operational readiness of offered contingents. The PCRS framework is managed by the Strategic Force Generation and Capability Planning Cell in the DPKO. UN, 'UN Force Link' <https://cc.unlb.org/default.aspx> accessed 18 September 2016. UNGA/SC, SG Response to 2015 High Panel, para. 86.

213 In earlier operations, sending States selected their police personnel on an *ad hoc* basis, and the UN simply accepted them. Hansen, *From Congo*, p. 48. See also Durch and Ket,

in the selection of officers at the request of sending States prior to their deployment, had established a selection assistance team.[214] In 2005, this was called the Selection Assistance Team (SAT), but, in 2012, it was renamed the Selection Assessment and Assistance Team (SAAT).[215] In the beginning, the selection process, including the necessary tests, was essentially left to the States concerned.[216] Over time, the selection assistance team has become more involved in the actual assessment of candidates. The roles and procedures followed by this team have become more institutionalized. While the SAT's assessment focused on the minimum requirements, the SAAT has widened these criteria to include the general suitability of the IPOs for the positions that they are nominated to fill.[217] This represents significant progress. However, the SAAT assessment is still very focused on the minimum standards,[218] and it appears

Police in UN Peacekeeping p. 22, which claims that quality control dated back to the mid-1990s at least.

214 UN DPKO, *1997 Selection Standard*, p. 11.

215 UNPOL, 'Towards a New UN Police: Revised Procedures for Assessment of Individual Police Officers' (2013) <http://www.womenspolicenetwork.org/wp-content/uploads/2013/08/II.1.B-Importance-of-new-assessment-procedure.pdf> accessed 10 December 2014, p. 4, (hereinafter '2013 Revised Procedures').

216 UN DPKO, *1997 Selection Standard*, p. 11. For example, the Handbook emphasizes that '[a]ll tests would be administered in the home country and all related costs will be borne by the Government of the home country concerned', p. 11, para. 5.

217 UNPOL, '2013 Revised Procedures' (2013) <http://www.womenspolicenetwork.org/wp-content/uploads/2013/08/II.1.B-Importance-of-new-assessment-procedure.pdf>, p. 4. With the involvement of the SAAT, the sending States pre-select the candidates, and provide the team with a list of these candidates (their names, gender, dates of birth, valid identification (ID) numbers and their date of entry into the police service). UNPOL, 'UN Selection Assistance and Assessment Team (SAAT)' (2013) <www.womenspolicenetwork.org/wp-content/uploads/2013/04/UN-SAAT.pdf> accessed 15 December 2014, p. 2, (hereinafter 'UN SAAT'). Under the SAT, the list contained only the candidates' names, dates of birth, their ranks and police ID numbers. UNPOL, '2013 Revised Procedures' (2013) <http://www.womenspolicenetwork.org/wp-content/uploads/2013/08/II.1.B-Importance-of-new-assessment-procedure.pdf>, p. 8. The tests administered by SAT and SAAT deal with language, driving and firearms skills. These tests are carried out in addition to interviews. Interviews by SAT were conducted only to assess oral language skills, but in the case of SAAT interviews, other criteria, including professional experience and understanding the UN's core values and computer skills, are also to be assessed. Ibid, pp. 5–6.

218 See, for example, UNPOL, 'UN SAAT' (2013) <www.womenspolicenetwork.org/wp-content/uploads/2013/04/UN-SAAT.pdf>, p. 1, where it claims that SAAT teams assist with tests in language, firearms and driving skills.

that, ambitiously, all the criteria are assessed in a short interview.[219] Above all, the involvement of assessment teams in the selection process is not mandatory. In 2010, it was reported that about 45 out of 100 sending States requested visits by the team,[220] and in 2011, SAATs made 29 visits covering 45 countries.[221] Apparently, they assessed 16,644 police candidates all together. Considering the number of candidates to be screened against the very specialized expertise demanded of the UN police, it is difficult to imagine that a thorough and accurate assessment of each candidate is possible.[222] Yet SAAT tests screened out 70 percent of police candidates in 2011.[223] This appears to indicate the difficulty inherent in maintaining a minimum standard of personnel, rather than an indication that the UN demands high standards. Since 2012, assessment has become mandatory, but can be done after deployment. An internal policy stipulates that there should be pre-deployment phone interviews in these cases,[224] but considering the volume of UN police candidates and the practice pre-2012, it is difficult to imagine that phone interviews were conducted for half of all IPOs.[225] Moreover, if IPOs are subject to assessment after their deployment, sending them back would be more difficult than not deploying them in the first place.

In relation to the exclusion criteria, when the sending States prepare their lists of pre-selected police officers for assignment to Peace Operations,[226] they have been required since at least 2005 to declare in writing that none of their

---

219 Interviews are supposed to take twenty minutes for each candidate. UNPOL, '2013 Revised Procedures' (2013) <http://www.womenspolicenetwork.org/wp-content/uploads/2013/08/II.1.B-Importance-of-new-assessment-procedure.pdf>, p. 6.

220 UNPOL, 'UN SAAT' (2013) <www.womenspolicenetwork.org/wp-content/uploads/2013/04/UN-SAAT.pdf>, p. 2.

221 William J Durch and Madeline L England, *Enhancing United Nations Capacity to Support Post-Conflict Policing and Rule of Law: Revised and Updated* (Stimson Centre Report No 63 Rev 1, 2010), p. 46, (hereinafter 'Enhancing Capacity Revised'); UN DPKO, 'Recruitment: Member States' [2012] *UN Police Magazine* 22, p. 22, (hereinafter 'Member States').

222 Durch and Ket, *Police in UN Peacekeeping*, p. 22.

223 Durch and England, *Enhancing Capacity Revised*, p. 46; UN DPKO, *UNPOL Magazine* (9 edn, UN July 2012), p. 22.

224 UN DPKO, 2012 SOP, paras. 27, 30, 69.

225 If 16,644 police candidates were assessed in their sending States in 2011, there would still be thousands of others, in 45 out of 100 countries, who were not interviewed by phone (Durch and England, *Enhancing Capacity Revised*, p. 46; UN DPKO, 'Member States', p. 22). Besides, at the time the 2007 Guidelines were adopted, it was clear that not all the candidates were interviewed. UN DPKO, 2007 Guidelines, para. 62.

226 There is no equivalent in the 1997 Selection standard. See UN DPKO, *1997 Selection Standard.*

pre-selected candidates are under investigation, facing prosecution or have had charges laid against them for any criminal, human rights or disciplinary offences. Since 2012, individual police officers have been required to make an additional mandatory declaration.[227] However, the UN assessment teams do not check whether these declarations have been truthfully made.[228] In theory, the DPKO, in particular the Police Division, can check each candidate's background for any misconduct in previous missions and beyond, 'within DPKO records'.[229] However, the DPKO has only maintained records of misconduct for previous missions since the recording system was put in place in the mid-2000s.[230] In addition, it does not have access to the records of candidates' performances back home. When dealing with tens of thousands of police candidates, it is difficult to expect that the UN will in fact check individual candidates' backgrounds. The only realistic possibility is a background check of their possible involvement in gross human rights violations. A new human rights screening policy has been developed by the Office of the High Commissioner for Human Rights (OHCHR) and the DPKO, which allows OHCHR to screen candidates' names against its records of human rights violators.[231]

In considering the selection and deployment process, it may be worth noting that there has been a significant change in the kind of States sending police officers to the UN. In the 1990s, Western and North American States provided a large number of UN police personnel. Over time and, since 2000 in particular, South Asian and African States have become the main sending States.[232] Currently, those States sending the greatest numbers of both UN police and

227 UNPOL, '2013 Revised Procedures' (2013) <http://www.womenspolicenetwork.org/wp-content/uploads/2013/08/II.1.B-Importance-of-new-assessment-procedure.pdf>, p. 5.

228 See UNPOL, 'UN SAAT' (2013) <www.womenspolicenetwork.org/wp-content/uploads/2013/04/UN-SAAT.pdf>, and UNPOL, '2013 Revised Procedures' (2013) <http://www.womenspolicenetwork.org/wp-content/uploads/2013/08/II.1.B-Importance-of-new-assessment-procedure.pdf>, neither of which mention checking this record.

229 UN, *2007 Guidelines*, paras. 69–70.

230 See Chapter 4, Section 3-2 for information on the UN's misconduct tracking system.

231 UN, 'Human Rights Secreening of United Nations Personnel' (11 December 2012) UN Doc. (on file with author).

232 UN DPKO, 'Troop and Police Contributors' <http://www.un.org/en/peacekeeping/resources/statistics/contributors.shtml>. The 2015 High-Level Independent Panel on United Nations Peace Operations described this trend as 'the decline in contributions from many high-capability countries'. UNGA/SC, 'Uniting Our Strength for Peace – Politics, Partnerships and People – Report of the High-Level Independent Panel on United Nations Peace Operations' (16 June 2015) UN Doc. A/70/95-S/2015/446, para. 198, (hereinafter '2015 High Panel Report').

military contingents are also those States which have been criticized for their reluctance to hold their security forces to account.[233] Some of those States which used to send high numbers of personnel to the UN in the 1990s have reduced these numbers. This may partly be because they are now sending their police officers to places such as Afghanistan and Iraq, through bilateral or regional agreements.[234] It is also claimed that Western States stopped sending their police officers to UN missions because these officers had become frustrated by working alongside less capable police officers.[235] To address this problem, it was suggested that police officers with the same nationality should be deployed together.[236] This suggestion was rejected, and may have resulted in some States sending significantly reduced numbers of police officers to the UN. The reductions by certain States may have implications for the kinds of policing cultures UN police officers now come from.[237]

In addition to recruitment based on the sending States' pre-selection, a small number of IPOs are selected through individual applications made directly to the UN.[238] Police candidates who go through this process are selected through the UN's assessment of their profiles, experiences and skills based on the information provided by them in their Personal History Forms (PHPs) and interviews.[239] This process is much more thorough when compared to the sending governments' selection process, as the UN has an opportunity to assess detailed accounts of each position the candidate has held. In the PHP, candidates are required to divulge whether they have ever been:

233 See Chapter 6, Section 3-2.

234 Durch, *UNPOL Evolution*, p. 10.

235 Ruiz, 'Roles and Functions', p. 89.

236 Oh, 'Singaporeans in UNTAC', p. 138. UNTAET deployed police officers from two States to work in the same area to see if the operation would proceed more smoothly. Communication with a senior UN personnel, January 2006. Having a large number of sending States was also problematic in coordinating work. Jürgen Reimann, 'Debriefing on CIVPOL Experiences: United Nations Mission for the Referendum in Western Sahara (MINURSO)' in Nassrine Azimi (ed), *The Role and Functions of Civilian Police in United Nations Peace-Keeping Operations: Debriefing and Lessons* (Kluwer International 1996), p. 110; Roos, 'UNTAC Debriefing', p. 124.

237 It may demonstrate that UN police personnel may come from 'countries not necessarily associated with strong traditions of democratic, human-rights-based policing'. Greener, 'The Rise of Policing', p. 190. See Chapter 6, Section 3-2 for a discussion of their human rights performance.

238 These persons are called 'contracted' officers. UN DPKO, 'Getting Involved' <http://www.un.org/en/peacekeeping/sites/police/recruitment.shtml> accessed 10 January 2015. In earlier missions, all UN police officers were seconded. See Section 1-1.

239 UN, *2007 Guidelines*, para. 42.

> [...] arrested, indicted, or summoned into court as a defendant in criminal proceedings, or convicted, fined or imprisoned for the violation of any law (excluding minor traffic violations).[240]

This question is presumably used for excluding police candidates with insufficient professional integrity. The issues raised above (in relation to the disqualification of candidates pre-selected by the sending States) apply equally to this process.[241]

It is also worth pointing out that, not having found specific specialists in adequate numbers amongst the seconded police personnel they receive, some Peace Operations have added civilian posts to perform specific functions, such as police officers, project managers, procurement specialists and civil engineers.[242]

Formed Police Units

Arrangements for FPUs differ from that of IPOs. Here, sending States provide a group of police personnel as a unit. Their selection and deployment procedures are the same as for military contingents, under what is called a Contingent-Owned Equipment (COE) system.[243] Under this system, the UN enters into a legally binding agreement, a Memorandum of Understanding (MoU), with each sending State.[244] The MoU stipulates that it is the sending State's responsibility to ensure that the personnel it provides:

> [...] meet the standards established by the United Nations for service with [the United Nations peacekeeping mission], inter alia, with respect to rank, experience, physical fitness, specialization and knowledge of languages.[245]

---

240 Question number 32 of the PHP. The PHP form is available as an annex to the UN DPKO, 2007 Guidelines.

241 In addition, according to the senior UN official, sending States are obliged to attest to individual declarations made by their police officers. Personal Communication with a senior UN official, November 2014.

242 Durch, *UNPOL Evolution*, p. 31.

243 For the historical development of COE system for the military, see Bruce Oswald, *Documents on the Law of UN Peace Operations* (Oxford University Press 2010), p. 51, (hereinafter 'Documents').

244 For more details of MoUs, see Chapter 5, Section 2-1-1.

245 UN, 'Model Memorandum of Understanding between the United Nations and [participating State] contributing resources to [the United Nations Peacekeeping Operation]' UN Doc. A/C.5/60/26, annex AAnnex 4, para. 4; UN, 'Model Memorandum of Understanding

In 2012, the UN put in place an additional assessment procedure,[246] but this serves only to confirm the identity of individual candidates.[247]

In terms of records of criminal offences, violations of IHRL and IHL, and serious misconduct in a previous UN mission, two attestations are now required: one by the sending States for all FPU personnel, and the other by the individual officers themselves.[248] This policy requires that the assessment team 'verify' these attestations during their visits,[249] but considering the time-frame and the number of personnel, it is likely to mean that no action is taken other than checking if these forms have been signed and submitted. If the UN wished to check the human rights background of each FPU officer, it should require each police officer to submit details of their previous work at the very least. That would enable the UN to check this information against its information on human rights violations, even though this would not save any time on the selection process.[250]

---

between the United Nations and the xxx Contributing Resources to the xxxx' UN Doc. (on file with author), (hereinafter 'FPU MoU').

246 The teams are called Formed Police Assessment Teams (FPATs), and are composed of certified instructors, who are staff members of the Police Division, and other serving UN police officers, prior to their deployment. UN DPKO, 2012 FPU SOP, paras. 7, 38–45.

247 Ibid, para. 63. Certain officers in FPUs, such as the FPU Commander, the Deputy Commander, the Platoon Commanders and the Section Commanders, as well as the Operations Officer, the Liaison Officer, the Logistics Officer and the Duty Officers, are also subject to operational interviews, examination of their curriculum vitae and language tests. Ibid, paras. 63, 64, 70. In the procedure currently in place, driving and weapons tests are only held for those who are authorized to drive or use weapons. Ibid, paras. 74–80, 81–91.

248 Ibid, para. 51 and Annex D; para. 52 and Annex E.

249 Ibid, para. 52b.

250 In this regard, it may be worth noting that military personnel and battalions deployed in UN missions have been implicated for their involvement in human rights violations. They include Nepal's Bhairabnath Battalion led by Lt. Col. Raju Basnet deployed in Burundi in 2005; Major Niranjan Basnet deployed in Chad in 2009, who was repatriated to Nepal in December 2009; and Lt. Col. Kumar Lama, who was arrested in the UK in January 2013 and faced trial, based on universal jurisdiction, on torture charges while on leave from UNMISS where he served as a Military Observer. Amnesty International, 'Nepal: Bar Human Rights Violators from UN Peacekeeping Missions' (17 December 2009) <http://www.amnesty.org.au/news/comments/22304/> accessed 2 April 2015; Advocacy Forum – Nepal, *Vetting in Nepal: Challenges and Issues* (July 2014, 2014), pp. 36–42; Owen Bowcott, 'Nepalese Colonel Faces Torture Trial in UK' *The Guardian* (London, 27 February 2015) <http://www.theguardian.com/law/2015/feb/27/nepalese-colonel-faces-torture-trial-in-uk> accessed 2 April 2015.

Resorting to FPUs has improved the situation on one front, that is, the speed of deployment. As FPUs consist of many officers, it is easier to fill the required number of police slots immediately.[251] It may also be that they do not require much training in order to ensure the unit works as a cohesive entity, although they may require mission-specific training. The UN claims that they are 'self-sufficient and rapidly deployable'.[252]

This leads to a consideration of possible reasons underlying the recent heavy reliance on FPUs. One is that the standard of quality control has been lowered for the sake of the speed of deployment.[253] As FPUs are deployed as a unit, not only has the required level of expertise been lowered,[254] but also fewer quality control checks are conducted. This may mean that the process is less thorough. Recruiting police officers on an individual basis would require enlisting more than 10,000 police officers globally in recent years.[255]

Another possible reason is financial. As the UN's payment/reimbursement schemes for IPOs and FPUs differ, deploying the same number of FPU personnel costs half of what it costs to deploy IPOs.[256] For sending States, this acts as an incentive, as they receive reimbursements for FPU members at the same rate as for military contingents, as well as payments for the wear and tear of equipment.[257]

This raises an important question: is the UN using FPU personnel for positions for which they are not designed? While acknowledging that there is an increased need for FPU-type functions, the use of FPUs cannot be seen as a

---

251 Durch, *UNPOL Evolution*, p. 36. However, Hansen claims that FPUs are as difficult to recruit as IPOs, as they also usually form part of the daily public security structures back home. The possible exception is Italy, as Italy has a massive and intricate network of security forces, 120,000 of which are *Carabinieri*. Hansen, *From Congo*, p. 72.

252 UN DPKO, 'Formed Police Units' <http://www.un.org/en/peacekeeping/sites/police/units.shtml>.

253 Hansen, *From Congo*, p. 52. See also Chuck Call and Michael Barnett, 'Looking for a Few Good Cops: Peacekeeping, Peacebuilding and CIVPOL' (1999) 6 *International Peacekeeping* 43, p. 51.

254 See Section 3-1, above.

255 It was observed that the labour-intensive recruitment process for IPOs caused 'fragmented police missions'. Smith, Holt and Durch, *Enhancing UN Capacity*, p. 2. Bellamy and Williams consider this task 'almost impossible'. Bellamy and Williams, *Understanding Peacekeeping*, p. 396.

256 The UN pays a mission subsistence allowance (MSA) to individual officers under the IPO scheme at a rate of between 2,500 and 4,200 US dollars, whilst paying a standard cost reimbursement to the sending States at a rate of 1,400 US dollars per officer per month in case of FPU personnel. Smith, Holt and Durch, *From Timor-Leste to Darfur*, p. 4.

257 Durch, *UNPOL Evolution*, p. 36.

solution to filling IPO positions, as FPUs have distinct functions. Over-reliance on FPUs would cause problems, not least the unnecessary militarization of the police.[258]

3-3-2 Training

Training is another means by which the UN can ensure the necessary expertise among UN police personnel. There are two main stages of training. First, the UN requires sending States to ensure their officers have the necessary expertise, including the provision of training.[259] Since at least the mid-1990s, the UN has provided guidance on the content of generic pre-deployment training.[260] More recently, the UN has also started providing more precise modules and training materials in an attempt to standardize training.[261] These provide more information of the type of policing required in Peace Operations, the applicable laws and codes of conduct,[262] as well as assisting the sending States to conduct training.[263] Second, the UN also provides training on the deployment of UN police in the host States, mainly on mission-specific content,[264] and any applicable codes and policies.[265] Some missions conducted training after police officers were deployed to their duty stations, but the constant in-theatre needs proved to be too immediate to call officers back for training.[266] One fundamental point regarding training is that policing in UN Peace Operations requires not only very specialized skills, but also the right kind of policing

258 Hansen, *From Congo*, p. 60.

259 UN, *2007 Guidelines*, para. 56.

260 The Guidance dealt with monitoring, human rights, first aid, safety and some mission-specific content. UN DPKO, *1997 Selection Standard*, pp. 12–27.

261 This was because the content of training varied widely as between sending States. Hansen, *From Congo*, p. 57.

262 The content of the required training would take at least two weeks to deliver. See UN DPKO, 'Training Standards for Police – Experts on Mission', <http://pbpu.unlb.org/PBPS/Library/Training%20Standards%20for%20police%20-%20Experts%20on%20Mission.pdf> Accessed 3 December 2014.

263 UN DPKO, 'Training Support Services for Member States' <http://www.peacekeepingbest-practices.unlb.org/PBPS/Pages/Public/PeaceKeepingTraining.aspx?page=support&menukey=_12_4; training Support Services for Member States> Accessed 14 February 2015; UN DPKO, 'Training Support Services for Member States', <http://www.peacekeeping-bestpractices.unlb.org/PBPS/Pages/Public/PeaceKeepingTraining.aspx?page=support&menukey=_12_4> Accessed 6 November 2014. See also Hansen, *From Congo*, p. 52. In 2009, the UN Police Division developed pre-deployment training curricula that were sent out to member States. Greener, 'The Rise of Policing', p. 190.

264 Hansen, *From Congo*, p. 52.

265 UN DPKO, *1997 Selection Standard*, pp. 27–36.

266 Hansen, *From Congo*, pp. 59–60.

culture.[267] A few weeks of training cannot be expected to bring about the required expertise. Nonetheless, it may be a useful means for informing the UN police about the mission-specific operational settings, as well as any relevant policies and codes, including those dealing with prohibited behaviour.

4 Conclusion

This chapter shows that, as an institution, the UN police have rapidly acquired additional functions. They have also gained more importance in UN Peace Operations, as these missions have shifted focus. The functions of the UN police have been transformed from monitoring and advising indigenous police forces, to carrying out policing themselves, to reforming, rebuilding and restructuring the local police forces and judicial systems. In particular, the UN police have played a central role since the focus of Peace Operations has shifted to the rule of law. Accordingly, UN police officers have become much more influential in relation to the behaviour of the local police, as well as future rule of law institutions in the host State. The significant increase in the scope of the functions the UN police must carry out is also demonstrated by the UN polices' increase in size. They have become the fastest-growing component of Peace Operations, going from only a few dozen personnel to over 13,000 officers.[268] This has gone hand-in-hand with dramatic changes in the environments into which they are deployed.

As their functions have evolved, so too has the relationship between the UN police and the host population. Recent policing involves a much closer relationship with the host population.[269] In a host society that has experienced a fragile rule of law, insecurity, and law enforcement actors who are detached from the community, re-building national institutions and providing training is not enough. Often it is much more challenging to gain the trust of the local population, to whom the UN police are increasingly visible. The UN is expected to provide role models for democratic, impartial and professional policing. Misconduct by a UN police officer has a serious and negative impact, and can thus undermine the effectiveness and legitimacy of a UN operation.[270]

267 See Section 3-2.

268 See Section 2.

269 See Section 1. Note also that policing involves a deeper relationship with the host population than do military operations in general. Bellamy and Williams, *Understanding Peacekeeping*, p. 384.

270 '[T]he success of "a few good cops" are overshadowed by the ineptness and misconduct of others. They remain a critical factor hampering the effectiveness of UN police'. Hansen, *From Congo*, p. 48.

Problems of misconduct do not remain just that. Rather, they significantly impede an operation's ability to fulfill its mandate.[271] It is also important to remember that once the opportunity to gain the trust of the local police and population is lost, it is difficult to regain it. This may be the case particularly in respect of a population which has suffered from a lack of police professionalism and integrity before the UN police were deployed.

It is therefore vitally important that the UN ensures that the quality of its police personnel is kept to the required standard. In many situations, the UN needs to be able to rapidly deploy a sizeable number of police personnel. If all such personnel are properly trained prior to deployment, this would not be problem. In practice, however, the UN has to spend time and effort providing training for officers, and pairing less competent officers with those who are better qualified for the job. These problems prevent rapid deployment.[272]

Since the quality of personnel is so important, one would expect that the UN would not only require sending States to select officers with the required expertise and qualities, but also that the UN would check that this is the case. In this regard, an increasing effort is being made by the UN, but the above analysis shows that this check is not thorough. It also raises the possibility that the UN may be resorting to FPUs more frequently than its functional needs require.[273] If that is the case, it suggests that the quality control of UN police personnel is not a sufficiently high priority. Thus, the most important challenge for the UN is to recruit an adequate number of suitably qualified personnel.[274]

The UN is faced with a genuine dilemma: if it is to carry out the mandates established by the Security Council, it requires a significant number of UN police officers. However, it is difficult for the UN to recruit sufficient numbers of personnel. There appear to be limitations both with regard to the actual number of personnel being made available by States, and in relation to range of States from which they come. If, in order to minimize the risk of criminal wrongdoing, and to protect the effectiveness and legitimacy of the mission, the UN were to insist on the necessary expertise and personal qualities, there is a risk that it would not obtain the numbers of personnel required. The UN has recently acknowledged this issue publicly, and has initiated reforms to address it.[275]

---

271 Bellamy and Williams, p. 384. See also Hansen, *From Congo*, p. 50, where she claims that the most severe consequence of not securing the necessary quality of personnel is 'a loss of credibility, respect and confidence among the local police force and the population'.

272 Hansen, *From Congo*, pp. 50, 55.

273 See Section 3-3-1.

274 Hansen, *From Congo*, p. 48; UNGA, SG Report on UN Police, para. 51; UNGA/SC, 2015 High Panel Report, para. 161.

275 UNGA/SC, 2015 High Panel Report, paras. 158, 161; UNGA, SG Report on UN Police, paras. 51–65; UNGA/SC, SG Response to 2015 High Panel, paras. 85–90.

This chapter has established that the institutional policing functions within Peace Operations have changed dramatically and how, as well as how the environments in which they are deployed have also undergone significant changes. Before looking at how the members of the UN police can be called to account for criminal behaviour, and whether there are any barriers to this, it is necessary to consider if there is any evidence of criminal wrongdoing by UN police personnel.

CHAPTER 3

Evidence of the Commission of Crimes by UN Police

Against the backdrop of the functional importance of the UN police, and the increasingly public role that they play, this chapter examines whether there is any evidence of UN police officers committing serious crimes and, if so, whether there is evidence which suggests that they are called to account for these crimes.

The first problem faced in attempting to research issues relating to crimes committed by UN mission personnel, including the UN police, and the extent to which they are individually called to account for their acts, is the significant lack of information. This also has a considerably adverse effect on the UN's own ability to address the issue of the criminal accountability of its personnel.

It is submitted that the UN should do two things: the first is to collect information in a systematic way, so that the UN itself has an accurate and comprehensive picture of the problems it faces. As suggested in the previous chapter,[1] any failure on the part of the UN to address the criminal accountability of its personnel in Peace Operations would severely undermine the effectiveness and legitimacy of its missions. Having a picture of the nature and extent of the problems is a necessary step in tackling the issue of accountability. If it wishes to maximize its use of resources in order to pursue its mission effectively, it must be able to identify anything that undermines this aim. The information collected should be in a suitable form, and should be appropriately disaggregated, so that it is useful for combating impunity.[2] This would enable the UN to ascertain the relationship between each of these variables and the misconduct in question. In order for the data to be comprehensive, the collection of information should be triggered by the alleged commission of criminal misconduct,

1 See Chapter 1, Sections 1 and 7.

2 Possible categories might be: the type of misconduct committed, the category of personnel the suspect falls into, the nationality of the suspect, the mission in which the misconduct was committed, and whether or not the act was committed in the performance of the officer's official functions. In particular, if it is argued that the complexity of new UN police functions and/or the increased challenges of the situations in which they find themselves have contributed to increased rates of criminal behaviour, one would expect a higher proportion of the crimes to be committed in the course of official functions in such missions.

 | DOI 10.1163/9789004328815_004

and not a complaint about such behaviour. Clearly, where the information does not reach the UN, it is difficult for the organization to record it. Nevertheless, the need for a comprehensive picture requires the UN to be proactive in seeking out relevant information. Reliance on the submission of a complaint as the trigger would not meet the UN's needs. There is only one entity that is able to collect comprehensive data regarding misconduct, and that is the UN. If the UN were to hold accurate and comprehensive data, this would enable it to identify which crimes are most prevalent, and to concentrate on deterring the commission of these crimes. If the data were to reveal any trends regarding which nationalities were responsible for the most allegations of misconduct, this would also be useful in terms of planning which States to approach to send personnel.

The second action the UN should take is to make this information available to the public. Currently, the only available information concerns the total number of allegations made annually, which is disaggregated into the category of personnel committing alleged crimes, the type of misconduct committed, and the mission in which the act was committed.[3] However, this information is both insufficient and is not the right kind of information which is required for obtaining an accurate overall picture of the problems. As a result, the author needed to look elsewhere for information.[4]

It is in the UN's interest to make this information public. First, this will improve the transparency of the organization. As the UN is attempting to inculcate in the host State values that increase the prospect of sustainable peace, including good governance,[5] it should recognize that transparency is a vital part of this process. Therefore, making sufficient information public is beneficial in its own right. Second, by making information available to the public, the UN can equip the public to pursue issues of criminal accountability. For example, if it is the case that the UN police from certain sending States are committing crimes at a disproportionately high rate, and if that information is available to the public, it may enable them to place pressure on those States to address the criminal accountability of those officers, or to advocate for police officers from

3 See Chapter 3, introductory section; Chapter 4, Sections 3-2 and 3-5. In 2015, the UN published the nationality of alleged wrongdoers in relation to sexual exploitation and abuse cases in its report. UNGA, 'Report of the Secretary-General on the Special Measures for Protection from Sexual Exploitation and Sexual Abuse' (13 February 2015) UN Doc. A/69/779, (hereinafter '2015 SEA Report').

4 See later section on the author's data, Section 1.

5 See Chapter 1, Section 2; Chapter 2, Section 1.

States with better systems of accountability. Both of these would give impetus to addressing criminal accountability. One might wonder if this would lead to sending States indicating that they would not send any more personnel to Peace Operations if the information regarding the suspects' nationalities were to be made public.[6] Separately, the UN may fear that sending States could withhold personnel.[7] However, it is uncertain whether many sending States would be deterred from sending their police officers to serve in UN missions, considering the economic interest that may be involved in the arrangement.[8]

It is necessary to state at the outset that there is no way of knowing what proportion of misconduct is officially complained of, and what proportion of complaints is officially recorded. In the type of situations in which Peace Operations are established, there may be multiple obstacles to laying a complaint. There are difficulties in relation to physically making a complaint, including difficulties in travelling to the point where complaints can be made, in particular where victims are based in remote places, or where effective communication is hampered by language difficulties.[9] In countries where many languages are used by different groups of people, this language barrier multiplies. In addition, there may be cultural or historical difficulties. Local people may lack trust in accountability mechanisms, in particular where they have not experienced reliable accountability mechanisms in recent history.[10] For a population which may have come through a violent conflict with virtually no rule of law, the lodging of a complaint will be very unfamiliar and difficult.[11] There may also

---

6 Information suggests that some large contributors have expressed concerns about their countries being named for the abuse of a few officers. Michael Fleshman, *Tough UN Line on Peacekeeper Abuses* (Africa Survival, April 2005, 2005).

7 For further details, Chapter 4, Section 3-5.

8 See Chapter 2, Section 3-3-1 for their selection procedure.

9 Françoise Hampson and Ai Kihara-Hunt, 'The Accountability of Personnel Associated with Peacekeeping Operations' in Chiyuki Aoi, Cedric De Coning and Ramesh Thakur (eds), *Unintended Consequences of Peacekeeping* (UNU 2007), p. 205.

10 Ibid, p. 205. Victims may seek economic gain by cooperating with investigations. Local girls (victims of SEA) refused to cooperate when they were informed that they would not be paid for information. See also UNGA, 'Report of the Office of Internal Oversight Services on its Investigation into Allegations of Sexual Exploitation and Abuse in the Ituri Region (Bunia) in the United Nations Organization Mission in the Democratic Republic of the Congo' (5 April 2007) UN Doc. A/61/841, para. 13, where more reasons for non-cooperation are provided.

11 Sarah Martin, *Must Boys be Boys? Ending Sexual Exploitation and Abuse in UN Peacekeeping Missions* (Refugees International, October 2005), p. 3.

be a cultural reluctance to report some types of crimes, for example, those of a sexual nature.[12] This chapter is concerned only with those allegations which have generated complaints.

In order to make a comparison between the scale of criminal misconduct committed by national police and the extent to which these allegations are addressed in a stable society, it is useful to cite the rate of both alleged and substantiated crimes committed in such a society. If a comparison between the rate of alleged crimes committed by the UN police and that of a normal society were to reveal a lower rate for the former, the problem is unlikely be the behaviour of the UN police. However, if the rate of allegations against the UN police were to be higher but the rate of conviction lower, the problem would be what is done about the allegations. As an example of such a society, the rate of allegations made against the England and Wales police forces will be cited. It has been reported that at least 6,740 allegations of potentially criminal behaviour were made against police officers in these places in a one-year period,[13] which amounts to a rate of 525.1 allegations per 10,000 police personnel. 179 instances of criminal conduct appeared to have been substantiated against members of these police forces in the three years leading up to mid-2013.[14] Taking into

---

12 John Van Kesteren, Pat Maythew and Paul Nieuwbeert, 'Criminal Victimization in Seventeen Industrialised Countries: Key Findings from the 2000 International Crime Survey', The Hague: Scientific Research and Development Centre, 2000.

13 Serious non-sexual assault, sexual assault and assault are counted as an allegation of potentially criminal behaviour. Other categories, such as the breach of the Police and Criminal Evidence Act, could also entail criminal conduct, but because it is not clear what proportion of breaches of the Act was criminal, it was not counted. Independent Police Complaints Commission, *Police Complaints: Statistics 2011/12* (IPCC Research and Statistics Series: Paper 25, 2012), p. 17.

14 Tom Payne, 'Brothel-Running, Child Abuse Images, and Selling Firearms Among Nearly 200 Crimes Committed by Police in Last Three Years' *Independent* (16 January 2014) <http://www.independent.co.uk/news/uk/crime/sex-drugs-and-evenin-all-the-police-officers-that-break-the-law-9065376.html> accessed 1 January 2015. Apparently this was in addition to the 477 officers who were fired for misconduct, the 52 officers who were demoted, and the hundreds more who were reprimanded or fined. Reports showed that 1,849 sanctions were imposed on police officers for misconduct in England and Wales in one year (2007/8 financial year), and that the following year, 1,388 sanctions were imposed on them for misconduct. Independent Police Complaints Commission, *Misconduct Sanctions Imposed on Officers 2007/08* (2008); Independent Police Complaints Commission, *Misconduct Sanctions Imposed on Officers 2008/9* (2009).

account the number of police officers,[15] the rate of substantiated criminal conduct per 10,000 police officers per year was 4.6.

1 Findings Regarding Particularized Allegations

In order to evaluate the scale and seriousness of the problem, the author gathered data on particularized allegations of serious crimes committed by Peace Operations personnel between 1948 and 2014. Information was gathered from official UN reports, reports from sending States, reports by non-governmental organizations (NGOs), and the media. In order to distinguish this data from any other datasets, it will be referred to as the 'author's data'. The trigger for the inclusion of information in the author's data was an allegation of criminal conduct. In each case, there was an attempt to identify the content of the allegation, whether administrative or criminal proceedings had ensued, and what the ultimate outcome of the proceedings was. This was done even if the suspected perpetrator was not identified.[16] One problem needs to be acknowledged at the outset. While effort has been made to identify what constitutes a serious crime for the purposes of this work,[17] this largely depends on the domestic laws of the host and sending States. For example, without precise information as to the alleged victim's age, the content of the host State's national laws, and those of the suspect's sending State, it is impossible to determine whether consensual sexual intercourse with a fifteen-year old constitutes a crime.[18] To that extent, it is possible that the author's data contains offences that are merely disciplinary. The data currently has 545 entries against all categories of Peace Operations personnel,[19] providing a picture of particularized allegations of criminal conduct.

---

15 The number was given as 128,351 officers as of September 2013. Alan Travis, 'Police Numbers Fall by Further 3,488 Officers' *The Guardian* (London) <http://www.theguardian.com/uk-news/2014/jan/29/police-numbers-fall-by-3488-officers> accessed 21 August 2014.

16 See Chapter 1, Section 3, for further details on the methodology used in the collection of the author's data.

17 See Chapter 1, Section 6.

18 The difficulty is exacerbated because the UN does not reveal the suspect's nationality. See Chapter 4, Section 3-5.

19 This includes UN civilian staff, including UN Volunteers, members of national contingents, Military Observers, UN police personnel, consultants and contractors working for

The difficulties inherent in collecting reliable data cannot be overstated. Data collection cannot be systematic, as there is no reason to believe that each UN mission has been evenly reported on. Some types of criminal conduct may have been more widely reported than others. There may also have been a period during which the media and other sources were paying special attention to a specific mission or crime. Sometimes, the situation in a particular sending State may lead to more attention being paid to a mission in which its military contingent is active. Misconduct by police officers from some States may be unevenly reported, either due to the States' own diligence or to public scandals. It is possible that the collection of allegations has not been systematic or comprehensive within the UN.[20] Both UN and State reports may be more focused on the allegations over which action was taken, rather than those where no action was taken. This is especially true since 2000, as the UN has begun reporting on the actions it has taken with regard to select cases.[21] For these reasons, the information collected for the author's data is expected to represent a small proportion of the total allegations made. In addition, a lot of criminal behaviour may not result in complaints.[22] Taking into account the level of awareness of the local population of what should be reported, and how it should be reported,[23] as well as the power relations that may exist between UN police officers and victims, or between the UN and the local population in general, the percentage of reporting may be even lower than in other societies.[24] It may also be the case that the UN's attempts to investigate misconduct face resistance on the part of the suspect's colleagues and commanders. For example, the UN's

---

UN Peace Operations, and the UN's implementing partners, such as NGOs working in humanitarian assistance.

20 On the mechanism to collect information of wrongdoing by members of the UN police, see Chapter 4, Section 3-1.

21 There are two sets of data made available to public. General information on the number of allegations and investigations is provided by the Conduct and Discipline Unit (CDU). The Office of the Internal Oversight Services (OIOS) provides information on select cases, giving some case details. For more details, see Section 2.

22 For example, Chile noted in the discussion at the General Assembly that they were not convinced that the registered number of allegations reflected the true extent of the problem. UNGA Sixth Committee, 'Summary Record of the 8th Meeting, Held at Headquarters, New York, on Friday, 12 October 2012, at 10 a.m.' (5 December 2012) UN Doc. A/C.6/67/SR.8, para. 67. On the issues of the UN's internal mechanism to receive complaints, see Chapter 4, Section 3-1.

23 On the issue of awareness, see Chapter 4, Section 3-1-1 (a).

24 It is also possible that complaints are made to other institutions, entities or groups. In that case, complaints may not reach the UN police.

investigatory body, the Office of the Internal Oversight Services (OIOS), reported that some UN police officers attempted to obstruct an investigation into the sexual abuse of a minor, as well as two separate allegations of sexual exploitation and abuse, all of which were reportedly committed by police officers from the same sending State.[25]

Misconduct Entries over Time

Up until 1990, only one case of misconduct, that of UNIFIL military personnel in 1979, was located by the author.[26] The next cases date from the early 1990s, and relate to the UN Observer Mission in El Salvador (ONUSAL), and the UN Transitional Authority in Cambodia (UNTAC). It is remarkable that the two operations had such different levels of reports of criminal conduct. Only one allegation was recorded for ONUSAL, that of illegal drugs trafficking by a UN police officer.[27] In comparison, in UNTAC, there were 30 entries of allegations of criminal conduct: six against UN police personnel, and 18 against members of military contingents. The status of the remaining suspects was not identified.[28]

---

25 UNGA, 'Report of the Office of Internal Oversight Services on Peacekeeping Operations' (1 March 2011) UN Doc. A/65/271 (Part II), (hereinafter '2011 OIOS Report'), para. 98.

26 A military member of UNIFIL force was accused of smuggling explosives into Israel to support the PLA. The accused was tried at the District Court of Haifa, Israel. UN, 'District Court of Haifa, The Government of Israel against Papa Coli Ben Dista Saar: Judgement of 10 May 1979: Question of the Jurisdiction of an Israeli Court Regarding a Member of a National Contingent within UNIFIL, Accused of Smuggling Explosives into Israeli Territory – Claim of Immunity from Territorial Jurisdiction – Question Whether the Accused Could be Considered as a Member of a Foreign Military Force Present in Israel with the Consent and Permission of the State – Extent of the Immunity of Jurisdiction of Members of Such Forces in the Absence of a Specific Agreement on the Matter between the Host State and the Country of the Military Forces Origin – Question Whether the Accused Could be Considered as Enjoying Immunity from Jurisdiction as a Member of a United Nations Force' (1979) 1979 UN Jurid YB 205.

27 Tor Tanke Holm and Espen Barth Eide (eds), *Peacebuilding and Police Reform* (Frank Cass 2000), p. 51.

28 Note that some of the information sources have incomplete references. This is because part of the information was taken from the working paper prepared for the former Sub-Commission on Human Rights, which had a different standard for citing sources. UN ECOSOC, 'Working Paper on the Accountability of International Personnel Taking Part in Peace Support Operations Submitted by Françoise Hampson' (7 July 2005) UN Doc. E/CN.4/Sub.2/2005/42. Holm and Eide, *Peacebuilding and Police Reform*, p. 51; Janet E Heininger, *Peacekeeping in Transition: The United Nations in Cambodia* (Twentieth Century Fund Press 1994); UNITAR and IPS, *The United Nations Transitional Authority in Cambodia (UNTAC: Debriefing and Lessons: Report and Recommendations of the International*

This indicates that, in UNTAC, there was a higher rate of reported crimes per 10,000 officers for UN police personnel than for military personnel.[29]

Thereafter, there was a sudden increase in the author's data of particularized accounts of allegations in relation to the missions in the Balkans. In the United Nations Mission in Bosnia and Herzegovina (UNMIBH), 26 allegations appear in the author's data, 18 of which were against UN police members.[30]

Conference, Singapore, August 1994) (Nassrine Azimi ed, Martinus Nijhoff Publishers 1995); 'An Open Letter to Yasushi Akashi' *The Phnom Penh Post* (Phnom Penh, 22 August 2014) <http://www.phnompenhpost.com/national/open-letter-yasushi-akashi> accessed 25 August 2015; *USA Survival* <www.usasurvival.org/ck052804.shtml>; *The Gazette* (*Montreal*) (25 April 1997); *The Associated Press* (6 December 1993); Angela Mackay, 'Sex and the Peacekeeping Soldier: The New UN Resolution' (*Peace News*, June–August 2001) <http://peacenews.info/node/3602/sex-and-peacekeeping-soldier-new-un-resolution> accessed 22 August 2014; Machel Graça, *The Impact of War on Children* (Orient Blackswan 2001); B Byrne R Marcus and T Powers-Steves, (Report No3); *Washington Post* (29 October 1993); *The Times* (27 August 1993); *Associated Press* (13 December 1993); Trevor Findlay, *Cambodia: The Legacy and Lessons of UNTAC* (Oxford University Press 1995), pp. 46, 151; *South China Morning Post* (*Hong Kong*) (Hong Kong, 28 December 1992) <www.scmp.com/>; *The Associated Press* (24 November 2004); *Inter-Press Service* (24 July 1995) <www.ips.org>; Correspondence, 'Behaviour of UNTAC Troops in Cambodia and Thailand, Lieutenant General John Sanderson' *Sanderson Papers, MS 359, Box 31, Folder 181* (29 June 1992); Heininger, *Peacekeeping in Transition: The United Nations in Cambodia*, p. 76; Judy Ledgerwood, *UN Peacekeeping Missions: The Lessons from Cambodia* (PN 1994); Sandra Whitworth, *Men, Militarism and UN Peacekeeping: A Gendered Analysis* (Lynn Rienner 2004), pp. 64–71.

29 This rate corresponds to 17.3 allegations per 10,000 UN police personnel in comparison to 11.3 allegations per 10,000 military personnel, and 0 allegations per 10,000 civilian personnel. The rate was obtained by ratio calculation. The data used for the number of police and military personnel are the number of maximum deployed personnel provided by the DPKO: military personnel 15,991; UN police personnel 3,359, as of June 1993. The number of personnel was taken from UN DPKO, 'Cambodia – UNTAC Facts and Figures' <http://www.un.org/en/peacekeeping/missions/past/untacfacts.html> accessed 10 August 2014.

30 Magin McKenna, 'Sins of the Peacekeepers' (*Sunday Herald*, 30 June 2002) <http://www.sundayherald.com/25914> accessed 30 August 2005; Human Rights Watch, *Hopes Betrayed – Trafficking of Women and Girls To Post-Conflict Bosnia and Herzegovina for Forced Prostitution* (November 2002, vol 14, no 9 (D), 2002); 'M2 Presswire' <http://www.m2.com/m2/web/page.php/home> accessed 5 September 2005; UNGA, 'Investigation into Allegations of Fraud at the United Nations Mission in Bosnia and Herzegovina' (20 December 1999) UN Doc. A/54/683; Sarah Mendelson, 'US–Russian Military Relations: Between Friend and Foe' (2001) 25 *Washington Quartery* 161; UNGA, 'Report of the Office of Internal Oversight Services' (19 September 2001) UN Doc. A/56/381, para. 75; UNGA, 'Report of the Office of Internal Oversight Services' (11 September 2003) UN Doc. A/58/364; 'A police officer and divorced mother of three, Kathryn Bolkovac was looking for a fresh start when

In the UN Protection Force (UNPROFOR), seven allegations are listed, six of which were against military personnel, whilst the remaining entry concerned a civilian staff member.[31] Additionally, five entries were for a mission in Bosnia and Herzegovina, three of which involved military personnel, whilst two involved UN police personnel.[32] A noticeable trend in the data in relation to UNMIBH and UNPROFOR is that allegations against UN police were made at a much higher rate than those against their military counterparts.[33]

---

she signed up as a UN peacekeeper in Bosnia' *The Guardian Weekend* (London, 22 January 2011) 19; Colum Lynch, 'Misconduct, Corruption by US Police Mar Bosnian Mission' *Washington Post* (Washington, 29 May 2001) <http://www.balkanpeace.org/index.php?index=article&articleid=11668> accessed 12 August 2014.

31 Declan Walsh and Nicola Byrne, 'UN Peacekeepers Criticized' *The Scotsman* (22 December 2002) <https://www.globalpolicy.org/component/content/article/199/40816.html> accessed 22 August 2014; 'Canadian troops did not visit Serb brothels Federal official says' *The Vancouver Sun* (Vancouver, 2 November 1993); Dennis Bernstein, 'Answers needed to charges of UN misconduct in Bosnia' *Pacific News Service* (6 April 1993) <http://politicsforum.org/forum/viewtopic.php?f=42&t=31398> accessed 5 September 2005; 'Canadian Armed Forces: Peacekeepers Brief Performance sheet' <http://www.geocities.com/famous_bosniaks/english/general_lewis_mackenzie.html> accessed 3 August 2005; Manfred Gerstenfeld, 'The UN's Own Abuses' *Jerusalem Post* (Jerusalem, 30 August 2001) <http://www.jpost.com/editions/2001/08/30/opinion/opinion.33735.html> accessed 20 July 2005; 'B-info' (27 October 1993) <www.b-info.com/places/macedonia/republic/news/93-10/93-10-27.mic> accessed 15 September 2005; William Norman Grigg, 'Beasts in Blue Berets' (*The New American*, 1997) <http://whatreallyhappened.com/RANCHO/POLITICS/UN/peace.html> accessed 28 August 2015; US Senate, 'Debate in US senate' (*The Library of Congress*, 05 November 1993) <http://thomas.loc.gov/cgi-bin/query/z?r103:S05NO3-1112> accessed 29 August 2005.

32 Walsh and Byrne, 'UN Peacekeepers Criticized'; 'UN Peacekeeper Accused of Assaulting Congo Girl' (*Paksearch*, January 2002) <http://www.pakseach.com/br2002/jan/3/un%20peacekeeper%20accused%20of%20assaulting%20congo%20girl.htm> accessed 29 August 2005; Kelly Patricia O'Meara, 'US: DynCorp Disgrace' (*Insight Magazine*, 14 January 2002) <http://www.corpwatch.org/article.php?id=11119> accessed 22 August 2014; Declan Walsh, 'Peacekeeper Jailed for Porn Films' *Scotsman* (23 January 2003) <http://www.peacewomen.org/un/pkwatch/News/03/Irishpeacekeeper.html> accessed 28 August 2006.

33 All together, the rate is 70.2 allegations per 10,000 UN police personnel, compared to 2.4 allegations against 10,000 military personnel. The number of personnel was taken from UN DPKO, 'Bosnia and Herzegovina – UNMIBH Facts and Figures' <http://www.un.org/en/peacekeeping/missions/past/unmibh/facts.html> accessed 10 August 2014 and UN DPKO, 'Former Yugoslavia – UNPROFOR' <http://www.un.org/en/peacekeeping/missions/past/unprof_p.htm> accessed 10 August 2014. Note that UNMIBH did not have a military component. Instead, the NATO-led Stabilization Force (SFOR) provided military functions alongside the UNMIBH, and had around 32,000 personnel. 14 allegations appear

Reports of criminal misconduct by military contingents surfaced in a few other Peace Operations around the mid-1990s,[34] but there were no reports of misconduct by UN police personnel. No allegations appear in the author's data in relation to missions in Angola, although there were three sizable missions there.[35]

---

in the author's data against SFOR personnel. Human Rights Watch, *Hopes Betrayed*; McKenna, 'Sins of the Peacekeepers' (*Sunday Herald*, 30 June 2002) <http://www.sundayherald.com/25914>; O'Meara, 'DynCorp Disgrace' (*Insight Magazine*, 14 January 2002) <http://www.corpwatch.org/article.php?id=11119>. This gives 4.4 allegations per 10,000 personnel over a period of 8 years. The number of NATO personnel was taken from NATO, 'NATO Ends SFOR Mission' (2 December 2004) <http://www.nato.int/docu/update/2004/12-December/e1202a.htm> accessed 22 August 2014.

34 The author's data had two entries on alleged criminal misconduct by military contingent personnel in the UN Operation in Mozambique (ONUMOZ); twenty against US-led military operation Unified Task Force (UNITAF) in Somalia; five entries on allegations against personnel working for UN Verification Mission in Guatemala (MINUGUA). Human Rights Watch, 'Mozambique' <http://www.hrw.org/reports/1995/WR95/AFRICA-06.htm> accessed 28 August 2006; UNGA, 'Promotion and Protection of the rights of Children – Impact of Armed Conflict on Children' (26 August 1996) UN Doc. A/51/306; Thalif Deen, 'Rights: UN Targets Sexual Exploitation by Peacekeepers' *Inter Press Service* (25 July 2002) <http://www.ipsnews.net/2002/07/rights-un-targets-sexual-exploitation-by-peacekeepers/> accessed 28 August 2015;, 'Canadian Armed Forces: Peacekeepers Brief Performance sheet' <http://www.geocities.com/famous_bosniaks/english/general_lewis_mackenzie.html>; Rakiya Omaar and Alexander De Waal, *Somalia: Human Rights Abuses by the United Nations Forces* (African Rights, 1993); Rakiya Omaar and Alexander De Waal, *Somalia: Operation Restore Hope: A Preliminary Assessment* (African Rights 1993); Keith Jones, 'International Workers Bulletin: Canadian Government Defends Military over Atrocities in Somalia' (*World Socialist Website*, 28 July 1997) <http://www.wsws.org/public_html/iwb7-28/canada.htm> accessed 22 August 2006; Agostinho Zacarias, *The United Nations and International Peacekeeping* (Tauris Academic Studies 1996); William J Durch, *UN Peacekeeping, American Politics, and the Uncivil Wars of the 1990s* (Macmillan 1997); Human Rights Watch, *Somalia: Beyond the Warlords; the Need for a Verdict on Human Rights Abuses* (7 March 1993, vol 2, 1993); Gerstenfeld, 'The UN's Own Abuses'; Jean-Paul Brodeur, 'C & C' (2002) <http://conflits.org/article.php3?id_article=496> accessed 2 September 2005; Richard Wilson, 'Violent Truths: the Politics of Memory in Guatemala' <http://www.c-r.org/accord/guat/accord2/wilson.shtml> accessed 22 August 2005; UN MINUGUA, 'Press Release' (28 May 1997) accessed 22 August 2005; UN MINUGUA, 'Press Release' (25 June 1998) accessed 20 August 2005; UN MINUGUA, 'Press Release' (7 August 1997) accessed 22 August 2005; UN MINUGUA, 'Press Release' (4 June 1997) accessed 22 August 2005.

35 United Nations Angola Verification Mission I (UNAVEM I, 1989–1991); United Nations Angola Verification Mission II (UNAVEM II, 1991–1995); United Nations Angola Verification Mission III (UNAVEM III, 1995–1997). UNAVEM I had 70 military observers and additional international and local civilian staff at its peak; UNAVEM II had the maximum authorized strength of 350 military observers, 126 UN police, 220 international civilian staff, 145 local staff (October 1994 – February 1995). There were separately 400 electoral observers

Unlike in other missions, in the UN Mission in Kosovo (UNMIK) and the UN Transitional Administration in East Timor (UNTAET), the UN was the government, and could itself bring criminal proceedings in the host States.[36] These Transitional Administrations faced many more allegations as compared to other operations at that time. In UNMIK, 43 allegations appear in the author's data, 26 of which involved UN police personnel.[37]

---

during the polling period. UNAVEM III had total of 4,220 military personnel, comprising 283 military observers, 3,649 troops and 288 UN police as of 30 June 1997. UN DPKO, 'Angola – UNAVEM I Facts and Figures' <http://www.un.org/depts/DPKO/Missions/unavem1/UnavemIF.html> accessed 22 August 2014; UN DPKO, 'Angola – UNAVEM II Facts and Figures' <http://www.un.org/en/peacekeeping/missions/past/Unavem2/UnavemIIF.html> accessed 22 August 2014; UN DPKO, 'Angola – UNAVEM III' <http://www.un.org/Depts/DPKO/Missions/unavem_f.htm> accessed 22 August 2014.

36 See Chapter 1, Section 2; Chapter 2, Section 1-5.

37 UNICEF, *Trafficking in Human Beings in Southeastern Europe* (June 2002, 2002); US Office, 'US Office Pristina' <http://www.usofficepristina.rpo.at/hrkos2.htm> accessed 22 August 2005; OSCE Mission in Kosovo, *Kosovo Review of the Criminal Justice System, September 2001–February 2002 – Themes: Independence of the Judiciary, Detention, Mental Health Issues* (Department of Human Rights and Rule of Law, 2002); Amnesty International, 'News' <http://news.amnesty.org/library/index/engeur700052002?open&of=eng-2eu> accessed 23 August 2005; UNMIK, 'UNMIK Online' (May 2004) <http://www.unmikonline.org/pub/focuskos/may04/focuskchron.htm> accessed 23 August 2006; UN, 'Kosovo News' <http://www.un.org/peace/kosovo/news/kosovo2.htm> accessed 23 August 2006; JJ, 'Home Planet' <http://home.planet.nl/~kempe103/> accessed 23 August 2005; OSCE Mission in Kosovo, *Kosovo Review of the Criminal Justice System – Themes: Legal Representation, Detention, Trafficking & Sexually Related Crimes, Municipal & Minor Offence Courts* (Department of Human Rights and Rule of Law, October 2001); UN Wire, (20 April 2004) <http://unwire.org/UNWire/20040420/Current_Print.asp> accessed 26 August 2005; Amnesty International, *Kosovo (Serbia and Montenegro): So Does It Mean That We Have the Rights? – Protecting the Human Rights of Women and Girls Trafficked for Forced Prostitution in Kosovo* (EUR 70/010/2004, 2004); UN ECOSOC, Sub-Commission Paper; UN, 'Probe Closed of Police Officers Connected to Deadly Shootings in Kosovo' (19 May 2004) <http://www.un.org/apps/news/story.asp?NewsID=10794&Cr=kosovo&Cr1=&Kw1=unmik&Kw2=misconduct&Kw3=> accessed 26 August 2006; Human Rights Watch, 'EU Should Ensure International Mission is Accountable' (10 March 2008) <https://www.hrw.org/news/2008/03/09/kosovo-eu-should-ensure-international-mission-accountable> accessed 29 August 2015; Amnesty International, *Kosovo (Serbia) The UN in Kosovo – a Legacy of Impunity* (EUR70/015/2006 November 2006); 'Peacekeepers Die in Clash over Iraq' *The Telegraph* (19 April 2004) <http://www.telegraph.co.uk/news/main.jhtml?xml=/news/2004/04/19/wkos19.xml> accessed 25 August 2006; UNMIK, 'UNMIK Online' (13 August 2001) <http://www.unmikonline.org/press/2001/trans/tr130801.html> accessed 24 August 2005; OSCE Mission in Kosovo, *Kosovo: A Review of the Criminal Justice System 1 September 2000–28 February 2001* (Department of Human Rights and Rule of Law, 2001); UNGA, 'Report on the Activities of the Office of Internal Oversight on Peacekeeping Operations for the Period from 1 January to 31 December 2012' (12 Mar 2013) UN Doc.

In UNTAET, 17 allegations can be found, including three against UN police personnel.[38]

A/67/297(Part II); UNGA, 'Report of the Office of Internal Oversight Services for the Period from 1 July 2001 to 30 June 2002' (4 Oct 2002) UN Doc. A/57/451; UNGA, 'Report on the Activities of the Internal Oversight Services' (11 Sept 2003) UN Doc. A/58/364; UNGA, 'Report of the Office of Internal Oversight Services' (27 October 2004) UN Doc. A/59/359; UNGA, 'Report of the Secretary-General on the Activities of the Office of Internal Oversight Services' (9 September 2005) UN Doc. A/60/346; UNGA, 'Report on the Activities of the Office of Internal Oversight Services for the period from 1 January to 31 December 2007' (25 February 2008) UN Doc. A/62/281 (Part II); UN, 'Report on the Activities of the Office of Internal Oversight Services for the Period from 1 July 2008 to 30 June 2009' (26 August 2009) UN Doc. A/64/326 (Part I)/Add.1; UNGA, 'Report of the Office of Internal Oversight Services on Peacekeeping Operations' (23 February 2010) UN Doc. A/64/326 (Part II), (hereinafter '2010 OIOS PKO Report'); Colum Lynch, 'UN Faces More Accusations of Sexual Misconduct' *Washington Post* (13 March 2005) <http://www.washingtonpost.com/wp-dyn/articles/A30286-2005Mar12.html> accessed 25 August 2015; 'Kosovo UN Troops "Fuel Sex Trade"' *BBC* (London, 6 May 2004) <http://news.bbc.co.uk/2/hi/europe/3686173.stm> accessed 27 August 2015. 13 cases were laid against civilian personnel, including two UN Volunteers. This amounts to 57.5 allegations per 10,000 UN police personnel, which is more than double the rate for civilian personnel, which is 28.4 allegations per 10,000 personnel. KFOR, the NATO-led force that worked alongside UNMIK, has 20 allegations listed against its personnel in the author's data. The rate of allegations against KFOR personnel is 4.0 per 10,000 personnel. For KFOR's strength, see NATO, 'NATO's Role in Kosovo' (10 June 2010) <http://web.archive.org/web/20100611233430/http://www.nato.int/cps/en/natolive/topics_48818.htm> accessed 28 August 2015. For KFOR allegations, see UNICEF, *Trafficking in Human Beings in Southeastern Europe*; 'US Servicemen Beat Kosovo Civilians' *BBC* (16 September 2000) <http://news.bbc.co.uk/2/hi/americas/927323.stm> accessed 8 August 2008; Biniam Tekle, 'UN Peacekeeping Watch – Learning from Others' Experiences: Human Rights Violations Committed by Peacekeepers' *Dehai News* (9 May 2004) <http://www.dehai.org/archives/dehai_news_archive/0163.html> accessed 8 August 2008; *CNN* (19 September 2000) <http://www.cnn.com/2000/us/09/19/ussoldiers.kosovo.ap/> accessed 8 September 2006; *Der Spiegel* (1 February) <http://www.balkanpeace.org/hed/archive/feb01/hed2555.shtml> accessed 21 August 2007; JJ, 'Home Planet' <http://home.planet.nl/~kempe103/>; Amnesty International, *The Apparent Lack of Accountability of International Peace-Keeping Forces in Kosovo and Bosnia-Hercegovina* (EUR 05/002/2004, 31 March 2004, 2004); Amnesty International, *Serbia and Montenegro (Kosovo): The Legacy of Past Human Rights Abuses* (EUR 70/009/2004, 31 March 2004, 2004); Amnesty International, *Kosovo (Serbia and Montenegro): So Does It Mean That We Have the Rights? – Protecting the Human Rights of Women and Girls Trafficked for Forced Prostitution in Kosovo*; 'Kosovo Peacekeepers Accused of Theft' *BBC* (26 June 2000) <http://news.bbc.co.uk/1/hi/world/europe/806408> accessed 2 August 2007; 'Kosovo UN Troops "Fuel Sex Trade"'.

38 Judicial System Monitoring Programme, 'JSMP' (6 November 2002) <http://66.102.9.104/search?q=cache:0Vvw99PcDQIJ:www.jsmp.minihub.org/News/Summary%25201

Other Operations launched around this time were the UN Mission in Sierra Leone (UNAMSIL), the UN Mission in Ethiopia and Eritrea (UNMEE), and the UN Organization Mission in the Democratic Republic of the Congo (MONUC). UNMEE had a modest monitoring mandate, while UNAMSIL and MONUC had more wide-reaching ones.[39] It is remarkable that, for the first two missions,

---

-8%2520November.pdf+rape+Police+Jordan&hl=ja> accessed 28 July 2005; ABC, 'Allegations against Jordanian Peacekeepers' (*AM Archive*, 25 June 2001) <http://www.abc.net.au/am/stories/s317953.htm> accessed 28 August 2015; Amnesty International, *East Timor: Justice Past Present and Future* (ASA 57/001/2001, 27 July 2001); AFLANZ, 'Armed Forces Law Association of New Zealand' <http://www.aflanz.org/news.htm> accessed 2 September 2005; UNTAET, 'Media Release: Jordanian Civilian Police Indicted on Rape Charges' (24 August 2001) <http://www.un.org/en/peacekeeping/missions/past/etimor/DB/db240801.htm> accessed 28 August 2015; East Timor Action Network (ETAN), 'UN Policeman Charged with Rape in East Timor' (19–25 August 2001) <http://www.etan.org/et2001c/August/19-25/24unpolc.htm> accessed 3 September 2005; UNTAET, 'Media Release' (6 August 2001) <http://www.un.org/peace/etimor/DB/db060801.htm> accessed 29 August 2005; UNTAET, 'Media Release' (3 August 2001) <http://www.un.org/peace/etimor/DB/db030801.htm> accessed 25 July 2005; Frederick Rawski, 'To Waive or Not to Waive: Immunity and Accountability in UN Peacekeeping Operations' (2002) 18 *Connecticut journal of international law* 103; Hitoshi Wada, 'Houjin Dansei-ni UNTAET ga Syazai Wakai Seiritsu Hutou Taiho Meguru Teiso Jiken' (*Asia Kisya Club,*, 1 February 2002) <http://apc.cup.com/?no=93.1.0.0.33.0.0.0.0.0.> accessed 3 September 2005; 'Sexual Assault Inquiry into Peace Troops' *The Australian* (26 June 2001); UN, 'Police Officers Suspected of Rape Will Enjoy No Immunity UN Official Says' (6 July 2001) <http://www.un.org/peace/etimor/news/01jul06.htm> accessed 22 August 2005; UN, 'Police Officer Serving with UN Mission in East Timor Charged with Rape' (24 August 2001) <http://www.un.org/peace/etimor/news/01aug24.htm> accessed 22 August 2005; UNTAET, 'Media Release' (6 July 2001) <http://www.un.org/peace/etimor/DB/db060701.htm> accessed 22 August 2005; UNTAET, 'Media Release' (10 August 2001) <http://www.un.org/peace/etimor/DB/db100801.htm> accessed 23 August 2005; East Timor Action Network (ETAN), 'UN Peacekeepers in Timor Face Possible Sex Charges' (3 August 2001) <http://www.etan.org/et2001c/August/01-4/03unpeac.htm> accessed 24 August 2005; 'UN Peacekeeper Charged with Rape' *BBC* (London, 24 August 2001) <http://news.bbc.co.uk/2/hi/asia-pacific/1508473.stm> accessed 25 August 2006; UNGA, Report on the Activities of the Internal Oversight Services; UNGA, 'Report on the Activities of the Office of Internal Oversight' (23 February 2007) UN Doc. A/61/264(Part II); Mark Dodd, 'Hushed Rape of Timor' *The Weekend Australian* (26 March 2005) <http://www.etan.org/et2005/march/20/26hushed.htm> accessed 25 August 2005; 'UN Peacekeepers in Timor Face Possible Sex Charges' *Reuters* (3 August 2001); 'UN Takes Step to Prevent Sex Abuse in East Timor' *ABC PM* (30 August 2006) <http://www.abc.net.au/pm/content/2006/s1728448.htm> accessed 28 August 2015. Six cases involved military contingent members, whilst five involved civilian personnel. This makes the ratio of 18.3, 6.6, 20.1 allegations per 10, 000 police, military, and civilian personnel respectively in UNTAET.

39 See Chapter 2, Sections 1-2, 1-3 and 1-4.

no allegations were entered against UN police personnel, probably partly reflecting the small size of the UN police components.[40] In MONUC, the size of UN police component was much bigger,[41] the police functions and the mission mandate were ambitious, and the environment was characterized with violence.[42] There were 98 entries against all categories of MONUC personnel, including five against UN police personnel.[43] One observation is that missions

---

40 The maximum strength of the UN police components for the two missions was 87 and 214 respectively.

41 MONUC stood at 1,229 on 30 June 2007.

42 See Chapter 2, Section 1-4.

43 Cahal Milmo, 'UN Troops Buy Sex from Teenage Refugees in Congo Camp' *The Independent* (25 May 2005) <http://www.africaspeaks.com/reasoning/index.php?topic=1834.0;wap2> accessed 29 August 2015; IRIN, 'DRC' (*Peacewomen*, 11 January 2004) <www.peacewomen.org/un/pkwatch/press.html#drc> accessed 25 August 2005; Kate Holt, 'DR Congo's Shameful Sex Secret' *BBC* (03 June 2004) <http://news.bbc.co.uk/go/pr/fr/-/2/hi/africa/3769469.stm> accessed 25 August 2006; William Wallis, 'UN Staff in Congo Face Child Sex Claims' (*Peacewomen*, 17 May 2004) <www.peacewomen.org/un/pkwatch/news/04/sexclaims.html> accessed 25 August 2006; Peacewomen, 'Sexual Abuse in Congo' (2004) <www.peacewomen.org/un/pkwatch/news/04/sexabusecongo.html> accessed 26 August 2005; David Lewis, 'Sexual Abuse in Congo' *Reuters* (10 May 2004) <www.peacewomen.org/un/pkwatch/news/04/sexabusecongo.html> accessed 26 August 2006; UN Wire, (27 May 2004) <http://www.unwire.org/unwire/20040527/449_24314.asp> accessed 25 August 2005; Rodrique Ngowi, 'CNews' (*CANOE*, 11 May 2004) <http://cnews.canoe.ca/cnews/world/2004/05/11/455562-ap.html> accessed 24 August 2005;, 'Peacekeeper accused' (*Paksearch*, January 2002) <http://www.pakseach.com/br2002/jan/3/un%20peacekeeper%20accused%20of%20assaulting%20congo%20girl.htm>; William Wallis, 'UN Staff in Congo Face Child Sex Claims' *Financial Times* (Nairobi, 15 May 2004) <http://www.freerepublic.com/focus/f-news/1137380/posts> accessed 14 November 2014; UN, 'Member of UN Mission in DR of Congo Accused of Sexual Abuse Sent Home for Trial' (26 May 2004) <http://www.un.org/apps/news/story.asp?NewsID=10882&Cr=congo> accessed 26 August 2006; 'Seven UN Uruguayan Peacekeepers Probed for Stealing Sacred Objects in DRCongo' *BBC* (London, 12 September 2003); Clarin, 'Acusan a Cascos Azules de Uruguay por Torturas en Africa' (21 September 2003) <http://old.clarin.com/diario/2003/09/21/i-02201.htm> accessed 15 August 2006; Jehan Khaleeli, 'Addressing the Sexual Misconduct by Peacekeepers' (*Refugees International*, 23 September 2004) <http://www.globalpolicy.org/security/peacekpg/general/2004/0923misconduct.htm>; 'UN Soldiers Arrested in DR Congo' *BBC* (London, 13 February 2005) <http://www.news.bbc.co.uk/1/hi/world/africa/4262743.stm> accessed 24 August 2005; 'Morroco Soldiers Face Sexual Abuse Charge' *CNN* (13 February 2005) <http://www.cnn.com/2005/WORLD/africa/02/13/morroco.abuse.reut/> accessed 26 August 2006; 'UN Troops Held Over Sex Crimes' *CNN* (15 February 2005) <http://www.cnn.com/2005/WORLD/africa/02/15/un.congo.peacekeepers/> accessed 25 August 2006; Scoop, 'UN-Arrest of 6 Peacekeepers for Sexual Abuse' (16 February 2005) <http://www.scoop.co.nz/stories/WO0502/S00429

.htm> accessed 23 August 2006; 'Peacekeepers Held for Sex Crimes' *CBS News* (15 February 2005) <http://www.cbsnews.com/stories/2005/02/15/world/main674173.shtml> accessed 15 August 2006; 'Briefing Deboutcongolais' <http://www.deboutcongolais.info/weblogs/briefing> accessed 15 August 2006; 'News from Africa: War and Peace' (January 2002) <http://www.newsfromafrica.org/newsfromafrica/articles/art_614.html> accessed 14 August 2006; Peacewomen, 'Peacewomen' <www.peacewomen.org/> accessed 25 August 2005; UN OHCHR, *Africa Quarterly Report*; Xinhua, 'English News' <www.xinhuanet.com/english/> accessed 28 August 2006; 'Great Lakes: Focus on Sexual Misconduct by UN Personnel' *Irinnews* (23 July 2004) <http://www.irinnews.org/report.asp?ReportID=42343&SelectRegion=Africa&SelectCountry=GREAT%20LAKES> accessed 25 August 2015; 'Global Policy Forum' <www.globalpolicy.org> accessed 25 August 2006; Survival International, <www.survival-international.org/> accessed 15 August 2006; 'Heritiers de la Justice' <www.heritiers.org/> accessed 15 August 2006; Norwegian Refugee Council, <www.nrc.no/engindex.htm> accessed 18 August 2006; MONUC, 'MONUC News' <http://www.monuc.org/news.aspx?newsID=9167> accessed 15 August 2006; FOK, 'Lawsuit against the UN and Other International Organizations' (5 May 2006) <http://www.un-follies.blogspot.com/> accessed 29 August 2015; 'Jaque Grinberg – an Apology' *The Independent* (28 April 2005) <http://www.independent.co.uk/news/world/politics/jaque-grinberg--an-apology-6147266.html> accessed 15 August 2006; Kate Holt and Sarah Hughes, 'Sex and the UN: When Peacemakers Become Predators' *Independent* (11 January 2005) <http://www.independent.co.uk/news/world/africa/sex-and-the-un-when-peacemakers-become-predators-6155183.html> accessed 5 January 2015; UNGA, 'Report of the Secretary-General on Special Measures for Protection from Sexual Exploitation and Sexual Abuse' (15 June 2007) UN Doc. A/61/957; UNGA, 'Report of the Special Rapporteur on Violence against Women, its Causes and Consequences, Yakin Ertürk, Mission to the DRC' (28 February 2008) UN Doc. A/HRC/7/6/Add.4; 'Probe into MONUC Gold, Arms Trafficking "Well Advanced"' *IRIN* (25 May 2007) <http://www.irinnews.org/Report.aspx?ReportId=72373> accessed 15 August 2006; James Munyaneza, 'Rwanda Insists on Probe into MONUC Misconduct' (*Allafrica*, 15 July 2007) <http://allafrica.com/stories/200707161302.html> accessed 15 August 2008; UNGA, 2011 OIOS PKO Report; 'Burundi: UN Peacekeepers Suspended for Sexual Misconduct' *IRIN* (21 December 2004) <http://list.web.net/archives/women-peace-and-security/2004-December/001261.html> accessed 15 July 2006; 'UN Suspends Soldiers in Burundi Over Sex Abuse' *Afrol News* (17 December 2004) <http://www.afrol.com/articles/15055> accessed 25 August 2015; 'UN Acts to Halt Abuses' *BBC* (18 October 2005) <http://news.bbc.co.uk/2/hi/americas/4354934.stm> accessed 24 August 2007; Peacewomen, 'UN Sex Abuse Sackings in Burundi' (July 2005) <www.peacewomen.org/news/Burundi/July05/UNSexAbuse.htm> accessed 22 July 2006; UNGA, OIOS Report 2004; UNGA, Report on the Activities of the Office of Internal Oversight; UNGA, 'Report of the Office of Internal Oversight Services on Peacekeeping Operations' (23 February 2009) UN Doc. A/63/302 (Part II); UNGA, 2010 OIOS PKO Report; UNGA, 'Report of the Office of Internal Oversight Services – Part One' (15 August 2006) UN Doc. A/61/264 (Part I), (hereinafter 'OIOS 2006 Report'); UNGA, OIOS 2008 Report, (hereinafter 'OIOS 2008 Report'); UN, 'Press Conference on Peacekeeping Misconduct Allegations' (25 July 2007) <http://www.un.org/press/en/2007/070725_Lute.doc.htm> accessed 22 August 2008; Kate Holt

with a high number of allegations against UN police personnel also faced more allegations against military contingent personnel.[44]

---

and Sarah Hughes, 'Sex and Death in the Heart of Africa' *The Independent* (25 May 2004) <http://www.independent.co.uk/news/world/africa/sex-and-death-in-the-heart-of-africa-6169265.html> accessed 14 August 2008; Wallis, 'UN Staff in Congo Face Child Sex Claims'; Fleshman, *Tough UN Line on Peacekeeper Abuses*; 'Peacekeepers "Abusing Children"' *BBC* (London, 27 May 2008) <http://news.bbc.co.uk/2/hi/7420798.stm> accessed 2 May 2010; Joseph Loconte, 'The UN Sex Scandal' *The Magazine* (3 January 2005) <http://www.weeklystandard.com/Content/Public/Articles/000/000/005/081zxelz.asp> accessed 15 August 2012; 'UN Soldiers Arrested for Alleged Sexual Abuse' *China Daily* (16 February 2005) <http://china.org.cn/english/international/120416.htm> accessed 16 May 2007; Colum Lynch, 'UN Says Its Workers Abuse Women in Congo' *Wathington Post* (27 November 2004) <http://www.washingtonpost.com/wp-dyn/articles/A15363-2004Nov26.html> accessed 22 July 2007; Jonathan Clayton and James Bone, 'Sex Scandal in Congo Threatens to Engulf UN's Peacekeepers' *The Times* (23 December 2004) <http://www.thetimes.co.uk/tto/news/world/article1975210.ece> accessed 15 July 2006; Martin Plaut, 'UN Troops "Traded Gold for Guns"' *BBC* (23 May 2007) <http://news.bbc.co.uk/2/hi/africa/6681457.stm> accessed 22 August 2008; 'Push to Make Dads of "Peacekeeper Babies" Pay' *The Weekend Australian* (26 May 2005); UN News Center, 'UN Probe Finds Peacekeepers in DR Congo Used Excessive Force' (11 June 2007) <http://www.un.org/apps/news/story.asp?NewsID=22862> accessed 22 August 2008; Colum Lynch, 'UN Sexual Abuse Alleged in Congo' *The Washington Post* (16 December 2004) <http://www.washingtonpost.com/wp-dyn/articles/A3145-2004Dec15.html> accessed 24 August 2007; UNGA, 'Investigation by the Office of Internal Oversight Services into Allegations of Sexual Exploitation and Abuse in the United Nations Organization Mission in the Democratic Republic of the Congo' (5 January 2005) UN Doc. A/59/661; Peacewomen, 'Nigeria Recalls UN Peacekeepers' (19 September 2005) <http://www.isn.ethz.ch/news/sw/details.cfm?id=12877> accessed 2 September 2007; 'UN Peace Missions in Fraud Probe' *BBC* (19 December 2007) <http://news.bbc.co.uk/2/hi/africa/7151558.stm> accessed 20 August 2009; 'Three Army Officers Facing Rape Allegations' *Tha Indian News* (18 March 2008) <http://www.thaindian.com/newsportal/lifestyle/three-army-officers-facing-rape-allegations_10028631.html> accessed 5 September 2010; UN Radio, 'UN Is Investigating Allegations of Peacekeepers Trafficking in Arms and Gold in the Democratic Republic of the Congo' (23 May 2007) <http://www.un.org/radio/detail/7017.html> accessed 10 August 2010; MONUC, 'Press Release: United Nations Investigates Allegations of Gold Trafficking in Ituri' (23 May 2007) <http://www.monuc.org/News.aspx?newsID=14640> accessed 22 April 2009. For MONUC, the number of allegations per 10,000 personnel is 40.7. The number of personnel was taken from UN DPKO, 'MONUC Facts and Figures' <http://www.un.org/en/peacekeeping/missions/past/monuc/facts.shtml> accessed 29 August 2015.

44 In order to provide some comparison, the allegations against military contingent personnel for UNAMSIL, UNMEE and MONUC were 8, 10 and 72 respectively. This translates into 4.6, 25.4 and 38.6 entries per 10,000 respectively. For UNAMSIL allegations, see: UNGA, 'Investigation into Sexual Exploitation of Refugees by Aid Workers in West Africa'

(11 October 2002) UN Doc. A/57/465 (hereinafter 'OIOS West Africa Report'); Nancy Ely-Raphel, 'The UN and the Sex Slave Trade in Bosnia: Isolated Case or Larger Problem in the UN system' (*US Government, Office to Monitor and Combat Trafficking*, 24 April 2002) <http://www.state.gov/p/io/rls/rm/2002/9777.htm> accessed 20 July 2007; Julia Stuart, 'Dark Side of Peacekeeping' *The Independent* (10 July 2003) <http://www.peacewomen.org/news/SierraLeone/newsarchive03/darksidepk.html> accessed 10 September 2006; UN OCHA, 'Humanitarian Situation Report – Sierra Leone, February 01–28 2002' UN Doc.; Amnesty International, *Asia Pacific Report* (2003); South Asia Human Rights Documentation Centre, *Human Rights Features* (Volume 6(3), 31 March–6 April 2003, 2003); Human Rights Watch, *'We'll Kill You If You Cry' – Sexual Violence in Sierra Leone Conflict* (Vol 15, No 1 (A) – January 2003, 2003); 'Child Refugee Sex Scandal' *BBC* (26 February 2002) <http://news.bbc.co.uk/2/hi/africa/1842512.stm> accessed 15 July 2005; 'Aid-for-Sex Children Speak Out' *BBC* (27 February 2002) <http://news.bbc.co.uk/2/hi/africa/1843930.stm> accessed 28 August 2015; 'African Refugees Condemn Sex Abuses' *BBC* (London, 28 February 2002) <http://news.bbc.co.uk/2/hi/africa/1847483.stm> accessed 15 August 2015; 'Sex-for-Aid Under UN Spotlight' *BBC* (8 March 2002) <http://news.bbc.co.uk/2/hi/africa/1861763.stm> accessed 20 August 2015; 'Britons in Sex-for-Aid Scandal' *BBC* (18 March 2002) <http://news.bbc.co.uk/2/hi/africa/1878063.stm> accessed 12 August 2015; Peacewomen, 'Nigeria Recalls UN Peacekeepers' (19 September 2005) <http://www.isn.ethz.ch/news/sw/details.cfm?id=12877>. For UNMEE allegations, see: Walsh, 'Peacekeeper Jailed for Porn Films'; Walsh and Byrne, 'UN Peacekeepers Criticized'; Matthias Muindi, 'Sex scandal threatens UN peace mission' (*Peacelink*, September 2001) accessed 22 August 2005; 'UNMEE to Investigate Misconduct of Peacekeepers' (*Intellnet*, 1 March 2001) <http://www.intellnet.org/news/2001/03/01/3048-1.phtml> accessed 1 February 2006; UN Wire, 'UN to Investigate Alledged Sex Abuse by Peacekeepers' (2 March 2001) <http://www.unwire.org/unwire/20010302/13293_story.asp> accessed 10 October 2005; 'UN Sends Porn Peacekeeper Home' *Breaking News* (20 December 2002) <http://archives.tcm.ie/breakingnews/2002/12/20/story81564.asp>; Roberto Bonzio, 'Establising an International Framework for the Elimination of Trafficking in Persons Especially Women and Children' *Reuters* (28 August 2001) <http://www.protectionproject.org/human_rights/countryreport/ethiopia.htm> accessed 29 August 2005; IRIN-HOA, *Horn of Africa IRIN-HOA* (Weekly Round-up #53, 1–7 September 2001, 2001); Alex Last, 'Porn Scandal Rocks Eritrean Peace Force' *BBC* (Asmara, 20 December 2002) <http://news.bbc.co.uk/2/hi/africa/2595003.stm> accessed 3 August 2006; University of Lille, 'UNMEE' <http://www.univ-lille1.fr/pfeda/ethiop/docs01/0831unmee.htm> accessed 30 July 2005; UNMEE, 'UN Mission in Ethiopia to Probe Misconduct Charges against Former Peacekeeper' (*Reliefweb*, 28 Feb 2001) <http://www.reliefweb.int/w/rwb.nsf/0/5ee44b3a66b9466685256a01006bfdf0?opendocument> accessed 22 August 2006; UN, 'Press Statement on Establishment of Board of Inquiry on Allegations of Misconduct' (5 September 2001) <http://www.un.org/depts/dpko/unmee/st050901.htm> accessed 22 August 2006; European Parliament, 'Sitting on Thursday 4 Oct 2001' (4 October 2001) <http://www3.europarl.eu.int/omk/omnsapir.so/debatsl5?file=20011004en&langue=en&questid=h-0745_01&level=annex_quest_doc> accessed 31 August 2006; 'Horn-Eritrea-Italy: Eritrean Govt Probing Allegations of Child Prostitution Ring' *AFP* (30 August 2001) <http://www.aegis.com/news/afp/2001/

One interesting overall trend illustrated by the author's data is that the number of reports of specific criminal incidents in each mission has decreased slowly since UNTAC.[45]

---

af010883.html> accessed 10 August 2005; UN News Centre, 'UN Mission Expresses Shock That Eritrea Alledges Old and New Offenses' (10 May 2004); 'UN to Probe Alleged Sexual Abuse by Danish Peacekeepers' *AP* (28 February 2001); Ray Murphy, 'Sexual Misconduct by Peacekeeping Personnel' in Ray Murphy and Katarina Mansson (eds), *Peace Operations and Huma Rights* (Routledge 2008); 'Eritrea Arrests UN Staff' *Reuters* (2006) <http://www/redorbit.com/news/international/639859/eritrea_arrests_un_staff_on_people_smuggling_charge/index.html> accessed 10 September 2008; 'Eritrea Expels Five UN Staff Over Espionage' *AFP* (5 September 2006) <http://www.reliefweb.int/node/434798> accessed 26 August 2008; UN OIOS, 'Office of Internal Oversight Services: Annual Reports' <http://www.un.org/Depts/oios/pages/annual_reports.html> accessed 22 December 2014; UNGA, Report on the Activities of the Office of Internal Oversight; UNGA, OIOS 2008 Report; UNGA, 2009 OIOS PKO Report; 'Eritrea Arrests UN Staff on People Smuggling Charge' *Reuters* (31 August 2006) <http://www.redorbit.com/news/international/639859/eritrea_arrests_un_staff_on_people_smuggling_charge/index.html> accessed 2 September 2007; Walsh, 'Peacekeeper Jailed for Porn Films'; Martin, *Must Boys be Boys*; UNMEE, 'SG Annan Responds to Eritrean Allegations against UNMEE' (May 2004) <http://www.unmeeonline.org/index.php?option=com_content&task=view&id=935&Itemid=53> accessed 15 July 2008; UNMEE Military Officers, 'Military Officers Raise Questions on Force Commander' (*UN Forum*, 15 December 2005) <http://www.unforum.com/UNheadlines290.htm> accessed 29 August 2015; UNMEE, 'Statement on Allegations against UNMEE Staff' (25 September 2006) <http://www.unmeeonline.org/index.php?option=com_content&task=view&id=419&Itemid=53> accessed 26 August 2015; IRIN, 'Eritrea: UN Protests at Staff Expulsions' (*Reliefweb*, 7 September 2006) <http://www.reliefweb.int/rw/rwb.nsf/db900sid/LSGZ-6TED8W?OpenDocument&query=unmee> accessed 29 August 2015; UN, 'UN News: As Eritrea Decides to Expel 5 UN Personnel, Annan Decries "Pattern of Hostility"' (6 September 2006) <http://www.un.org/apps/news/story.asp?NewsID=19735&Cr=eritrea&Cr1=#> accessed 20 August 2015; 'Eritrea Expels Five UN Staff over Episonage' *AFP* (5 September 2006) <http://www.reliefweb.int/rw/rwb.nsf/db900sid/HMYT-6TCR4P?OpenDocument&query=unmee> accessed 20 August 2015; UN, 'UN Spokesperson's Noon Briefing' (21 March 2007) <http://www.un.org/News/briefings/docs/2007/db070321.doc.htm> accessed 20 August 2008. For MONUC allegations, see above, n.43. The numbers of personnel were taken from UN DPKO, 'Sierra Leone – UNAMSIL – Facts and Figures' <http://www.un.org/en/peacekeeping/missions/past/unamsil/facts.html> accessed 29 August 2015; UN DPKO, 'Ethiopia and Eritrea – UNMEE – Facts and Figures' <http://www.un.org/en/peacekeeping/missions/past/unmee/facts.html> accessed 29 August 2015; UN DPKO, 'MONUC Facts and Figures' <http://www.un.org/en/peacekeeping/missions/past/monuc/facts.shtml>.

45 Taking the length of each mission into account, the author's data show that UNTAC (1992–1993) had 11.5 allegations per 10,000 UN police personnel per 12 months. The figures mostly decreased over time. In missions in Bosnia, the rate of allegations was 10.0;

Since 2000, the scale of allegations of criminal misconduct may have been influenced by a new source of information. Two different UN institutions began centralizing information on misconduct by all personnel categories. Since the mid-2000s, it has also begun to make this information partially available to the public.[46] What is apparent is that allegations continue to be reported, both against the UN police and military personnel. According to the author's data, there were more allegations per head against UN police members than against military members.[47] The rate of allegations in proportion to the size of

---

UNMIK recorded 3.7; UNTAET 7.0; and MONUC 3.8. In comparison, for military contingent members, the allegations per 10,000 personnel per 12 months showed the following shift: UNTAC 7.5; UNPROFOR 0.4 and SFOR 0.6 (compared to UN police figures for Bosnian missions); UNAMSIL 0.7; KFOR 0.3; UNTAET 2.5; UNMEE 3.2 and MONUC 3.6.

46 See Section 1.

47 UNMIL had 8 entries against UN police personnel, a rate of 71.7 allegations per 10,000 personnel. Military personnel had 12 allegations made against them, making the rate 8.0 per 10,000 personnel. Civilian personnel had 6 allegations lodged against them. The rate for civilian personnel was 40.2 per 10,000 personnel. Likewise, in UNOCI, allegations made against UN police, military contingent personnel, civilian staff were 0, 8, and 6 respectively, making the rate per 10,000 personnel 0, 10.1 and 46.4. MINUSTAH had 11, 18 and 5 entries against UN police, military and civilians respectively. This was at a rate of 25.1, 20.1 and 28.2 per 10,000 UN police, military and civilian personnel respectively. In ONUB, no allegation was made against UN police personnel, but 1 allegation was made against civilian personnel, whilst 7 allegations were made against military personnel. This meant the rate of allegations per 10,000 military personnel was 13.0 and the rate of allegations per 10,000 civilian personnel was 11.1. UNMIS had 1, 4 and 6 allegations against UN police, military and civilian personnel respectively, making the rate per 10,000 personnel 14.2, 4.3 and 14.0. UNMIT had 3 allegations laid against UN police, and 2 allegations against civilian personnel. This is at the rate of 18.6 and 16.0 entries per 10,000 police and civilian personnel. UNMIT did not have a military component. The new UN system has had a distorting effect on the data, as more information has become available. Thus, the figures cited must be understood in this context. For UNMIL allegations, see Sarah Martin, 'Sexual Exploitation in Liberia: Are the Conditions Ripe for Another Scandal?' (*Refugees International*, 20 April 2004) <http://www.refugeesinternational.org/cgi-bin/ri/bulletin> accessed 22 September 2008; Wellington Geevon-Smith, 'The Grand Gedeh: Advocacy Group Expresses Concerns About Sexual Exploitation by Aid Staff' (17 March) <http://www.grandgedeh.com/gg-en0504.htm> accessed 22 August 2010; 'Over Allegations of Abusing Duty Free Privilege: Unmil Boss Demands Evidence Or Apology' *All Africa* (26 February 2004) <http://allafrica.com/stories/200402270636.html> accessed 29 August 2015; 'Liberia: Gambian Peacekeepers Flog Lawmaker' *All Africa* (17 May 2004) <http://allafrica.com/stories/200405170740.html> accessed 30 August 2015; 'Sexual Exploitation in Liberia: Are the Conditions Ripe for Another Scandal?' (SOS, 20 August 2004) <http://www.sos-sexisme.org/English/Sexual_Exploitation.htm> accessed 30 August 2015; UNGA, 2010 OIOS

PKO Report; UNGA, 'Peacekeeping operations, Report of the Office of Internal Oversight Services' (1 March 2011) UN Doc. A/65/271 (Part II); UNGA, 'Report of the Office of the Internal Oversight Services on the Activities of the Office of Internal Oversight Services on Peace Operations for the Period 1 January to 31 December 2013' (25 February 2014) UN Doc. A/68/337 (Part II); UNGA, OIOS Report 2013; UNGA, OIOS 2001 Report; UNGA, Report on the Activities of the Office of Internal Oversight; UNGA, OIOS 2008 Report; UNGA, 2009 OIOS PKO Report; UNGA, 2010 OIOS PKO Report; Peacewomen, 'Liberia: UNMIL Investigating Alleged Sexual Misconduct by Peacekeepers in Four Incidents' (3 May 2005) <http://www.peacewomen.org/un/pkwatch/News/05/UNMILinvestigating.html> accessed 22 August 2008; US State Government, *US State Government Report: Liberia – Country Reports on Human Rights Practices, Released by the Bureau of Democracy, HR and Labor* (6 March 2007, 2007); Owen Bowcott, 'Report Reveals Shame of UN Peacekeepers' *The Guardian* (London, 25 March 2005) <http://www.guardian.co.uk/world/2005/mar/25/unitednations> accessed 30 November 2014; Lynch, 'UN Faces More Accusations of Sexual Misconduct'; 'UN Says Scores Of Peacekeepers Ousted for Abuse' *Washington Post* (1 December 2006) <http://www.washingtonpost.com/wp-dyn/content/article/2006/11/30/AR2006113001388.html> accessed 20 August 2009; Sarah Lyall, 'Aid Workers Are Said to Abuse Girls' *The New York Times* (9 May 2006) <http://www.nytimes.com/2006/05/09/world/africa/09liberia.html?_r=0> accessed 29 August 2009; 'Child Refugee Sex Scandal'; 'Aid-for-Sex Children Speak Out'; 'African Refugees Condemn Sex Abuses'; Save the Children, *From Camp to Community: Liberia Study on Exploitation of Children* (2006); UNMIL, 'Press Release' (7 June 2006) <www.un.org/Depts/dpko/missions/unmil/pr7june.pdf> accessed 20 August 2008. For UNOCI allegations, see Abel Doualy, *Fraternite Matin* <http://fratmat.net/content/detail.php?cid=185T4Y955V1> accessed 19 August 2008; UNOCI, 'Press Release' (31 October 2004) <http://www.un.org/french/peace/peace/cu_mission/onuci/pr83.pdf> accessed 20 August 2006; UNGA, 2014 OIOS PKO Report; UNGA, 2011 OIOS PKO Report; UNGA, 2010 OIOS PKO Report; UNGA, 2009 OIOS PKO Report; UNGA, OIOS 2008 Report; UN, 'Press Conference on Peacekeeping Misconduct Allegations' (25 July 2007) <http://www.un.org/press/en/2007/070725_Lute.doc.htm>; 'Peacekeepers "Abusing Children"'; Laura Burke, 'UN Peacekeepers Traded Food For Sex' (*The World Post-WikiLeaks*, 9 January 2011) <http://www.huffingtonpost.com/2011/09/01/wikileaks-un-peacekeepers_n_944917.html> accessed 12 August 2015; UN News Center, 'UN Will Not Turn "Blind Eye" to Peacekeepers' Misconduct, Vows UN Official' (25 July 2007) <http://www.un.org/apps/news/story.asp?NewsID=23333> accessed 22 August 2009. For MINUSTAH allegations, see *The Globe and Mail* <http://www.haiti-news.com/article.php3?id_article=2876> accessed 29 August 2008; 'UN Peacekeepers Sweep into Violent Haitian Shanty Town' (*ReliefWeb*, 14 December 2004) <http://www.reliefweb.int/w/rwb.nsf/6686f45896f15dbc852567ae00530132/bf3b6ea11a76e78f85256f6a0076ee82?OpenDocument> accessed 22 July 2008; UNGA, OIOS 2008 Report; UNGA, 2011 OIOS PKO Report; UN, *Panel Discussion: Sexual exploitation and Abuse in Conflict and Post-Conflict Situations* (Available at <http://wwwunmultimediaorg/tv/webcast/2011/10/panel-discussion-sexual-exploitation-and-abuse-in-conflict-and-post-conflict-situationshtml> accessed 10 January 2015, 2011); UN, 'Spokesperson's Daily Highlights' (23 January 2012) <http://un.mofat.go.kr/webmodule/htsboard/template/read/legengreadboard.jsp?typeID=16&boardid=10470&seqno=671694&c=&t=&pag

enum=1&tableName=TYPE_ENGLEGATIO&pc=&dc=&wc=&lu=&vu=&iu=&du=> accessed 30 August 2015; Institute for Justice and Democracy in Haiti, 'Soldiers in Uruguay Released from Charges of Sexual Assault in Haiti' (*Canada Haiti Action Network*, 9 January 2012) <http://www.canadahaitiaction.ca/content/soldiers-uruguay-released-charges-sexual-assault-haiti> accessed 30 August 2015; 'Uruguay Apologises' *BBC* (7 September 2011) <http://www.bbc.co.uk/news/world-latin-america-14817191> accessed 30 August 2015; Ben and Alexis, 'Ben and Lexi: Regarding MINUSTAH' (29 July 2011) <http://blexi.blogspot.it/2011/07/regarding-minustah.html> accessed 30 August 2015; UNGA, 2014 OIOS PKO Report; UNGA, OIOS Report 2013; UNGA, 2011 OIOS PKO Report; UNGA, 2009 OIOS PKO Report; UNGA, OIOS 2008 Report; 'S Lanka Troops "Abused Haitians"' *BBC* (2 November 2007) <http://news.bbc.co.uk/2/hi/south_asia/7075866.stm> accessed 15 September 2009; 'UN Sends Home Sri Lankan Peacekeepers on Sex Misconduct Charges' *DPA News* (2 November 2007) <http://www.digitaljournal.com/article/244922> accessed 15 August 2010; Reed Lingsay, 'UN Effort Dogged by Sex Claims Peacekeepers Based in Haiti the Latest Accused of Abuse' *San Francisco Chronicle* (22 December 2006) <http://www.sfgate.com/cgi-bin/article.cgi?f=/c/a/2006/12/22/MNGRLN47IA1.DTL> accessed 28 August 2009; UN News Center, 'Haiti – Three UN Peacekeepers Repatriated for Sexual Abuse' (13 March 2012) <http://www.un.org/apps/news/story.asp?NewsID=41538#.VUJL-mZzdWo> accessed 2 August 2014; Lynch, 'UN Faces More Accusations of Sexual Misconduct'; Mark Weisbrot, 'Is This Minustah's "Abu Ghraib Moment" in Haiti?' *The Guardian* (3 September 2011) <http://www.theguardian.com/commentisfree/cifamerica/2011/sep/03/minustah-un-haiti-abuse> accessed 2 September 2014; 'Sri Lanka to Probe UN Sex Claims' *BBC* (3 November 2007) <http://news.bbc.co.uk/2/hi/south_asia/7076284.stm> accessed 11 August 2012; 'S Lanka Troops "Abused Haitians"'; 'UN Says Scores Of Peacekeepers Ousted for Abuse'; 'Uruguay Marines Charged over Haiti Abuse' *BBC* (24 September 2012) <http://www.bbc.com/news/world-latin-america-19708878> accessed 1 August 2014; 'Millennials Writing for Social Change: MINUSTAH Soldiers: Personae Non Gratae' (5 February 2015) <https://w4socialchange2015.wordpress.com/2015/02/05/minustah-soldiers-personae-non-gratae/> accessed 30 March 2015; Refugees International, 'Haiti: Sexual Exploitation by Peacekeepers Likely to Be a Problem' (7 March 2005) <www.refworld.org/docid/47a6eeb40.html> accessed 3 September 2014; 'UN Wants Charges against Sri Lanka Troops for Misconduct in Haiti' *Tamil Week* (30 March 2008) <http://tamilweek.com/news-features/archives/1243> accessed 3 July 2010; 'UN Investigating Allegation of Rape in Haiti by Three UN Pakistani Peacekeepers' *Reuters* (23 Feburuary 2005) <http://www2.webster.edu/~corbetre/haiti-archive-new/msg24640.html> accessed 25 July 2008; 'UN Peacekeepers in Haiti Cleared or Rape' *Jamaica Observer* (25 February 2005) <http://www.jamaicaobserver.com/news/html/20050224T200000-0500_75738_OBS_UN_PEACEKEEPERS_IN_HAITI_CLEARED_OF_RAPE.asp> accessed 2 September 2008; Ezili Danto, 'Statement of Haitian Mother of Five, Raped and Sodomized by Jordanian Soldier "Peacekeeping" in Haiti' (28 November 2005) <http://www.margueritelaurent.com/campaigns/campaignone/testimonies/jordanrape.html> accessed 22 August 2008; 'UN Haiti Troops Accused of Rape' *BBC* (30 November 2006) <http://www.bbc.co.uk/carribian/news/story/2006/11/061130_unrapehaiti.shtml> accessed 30 August 2008; Luis Andres Henao, 'Uruguay Apologizes over Alleged Rape by UN Peacekeepers' *Reuters* (6 September 2011)

<http://www.reuters.com/article/2011/09/07/us-haiti-uruguay-un-idUSTRE78603I20110907> accessed 20 August 2014; 'Pakistan UN Peacekeeping Role at Risk after 3 Punished in Haiti Sexual Abuse Case' *The Express Tribune* (14 March 2012) <http://tribune.com.pk/story/349652/pakistan-risks-un-peacekeeping-role-after-3-found-guilty-of-sexual-abuse-in-haiti/> accessed 12 August 2015; 'UN in Haiti Accused of Second Massacre' (*Haiti Information Project*, 21 January 2007) <http://www.haitiaction.net/News/HIP/1_21_7/1_21_7.html> accessed 30 August 2015; 'US Embassy in Haiti Acknowledges Excessive Force by UN' (*Haiti Information Project*, 24 January 2007) <http://www.haitiaction.net/News/HIP/1_23_7/1_23_7.html> accessed 29 August 2015; 'Haiti: Poor Residents of Capital Describe a State of Siege' *Inter Press Service* (28 February 2007) <http://www.ipsnews.net/2007/02/haiti-poor-residents-of-capital-describe-a-state-of-siege/> accessed 29 August 2015. For ONUB allegations, see 'Burundi: UN Mission Sets Up Units to Check Sexual Abuse' *IRIN* (15 November 2004) <http://www.globalpolicy.org/security/peacekpg/general/2004/1115checkabuse.htm> accessed 9 July 2008; ONUB, 'Press Release: Heeding Annan's Zero-Tolerance on Sex Abuse, UN Suspends Two Solders in Burundi' (17 December 2004) <http://www.un.org/Depts/dpko/missions/onub/pr45e.pdf> accessed 10 August 2008; UNGA, OIOS 2008 Report; Reliefweb, 'Four Ethiopian Peacekeepers Suspected of Sex Crimes in Burundi' (10 March 2005) <http://www.reliefweb.int/rw/rwb.nsf/db900sid/RMOI-6AD37F?OpenDocument&query=onub%20sexual> accessed 30 August 2008; 'UN Sex Abuse Sackings in Burundi' *BBC* (19 July 2005) <http://news.bbc.co.uk/2/hi/africa/4697465.stm> accessed 25 August 2008; UN News Center, 'Heeding Annan's Zero-Tolerance on Sex Abuse, UN Suspends Two Soldiers in Burundi' (17 December 2004) <http://www.un.org/apps/news/story.asp?NewsID=12853&Cr=sex&Cr1> accessed 7 September 2008. For UNMIS allegations, see UNGA, OIOS Report 2013; UNGA, 2011 OIOS PKO Report; UNGA, 2010 OIOS PKO Report; UNGA, 2009 OIOS PKO Report; UNGA, OIOS 2008 Report; UNGA, Report on the Activities of the Office of Internal Oversight; 'Human Development: UNMIS Spokesperson: No Evidence that Supports Akhir Lahza Allegations' *Sudan Vision Daily* (19 May 2007) <http://www.sudanvisiondaily.com/modules.php?name=News&file=article&sid=21319> accessed 7 July 2008; 'Justice Minister Investigates UNMIS Rape Allegations' *Sudan Vision Daily* (13 September 2007) <http://www.sudanvisiondaily.com/modules.php?name=News&file=article&sid=25518> accessed 9 September 2010; 'UN to Probe Sudan Sex Abuse Claim' *BBC* (3 January 2007) <http://news.bbc.co.uk/2/hi/africa/6226829.stm> accessed 10 September 2009; Kate Holt and Sarah Hughes, 'UN Staff Accused of Raping Children in Sudan' *The Telegraph* (2 Jan 2007) <http://www.telegraph.co.uk/news/worldnews/1538476/UN-staff-accused-of-raping-children-in-Sudan.html> accessed 10 October 2012. For UNMIT allegations, see UNGA, 2014 OIOS PKO Report; UNGA, 2011 OIOS PKO Report; 'Peacekeeper Kills E Timor Refugee' *BBC* (23 February 2007) <http://news.bbc.co.uk/2/hi/asia-pacific/6388741.stm> accessed 1 August 2010; UNMIT, 'UNMIT Human Rights and Transitional Justice Section Report: Report on Human Rights Developments in Timor Leste, August 2006 – August 2007' UN Doc. on file with author; Lindsay Murdoch, 'UN Under Fire for Turning a Blind Eye to Peacekeepers Misconduct' *The Sydney Morning Herald* (7 May 2007) <http://www.smh.com.au/news/world/un-under-fire-for-turning-a-blind-eye-to-peacekeepers-misconduct/2007/05/06/1178390145310.html> accessed 30 August 2015.

personnel was lower in missions established in the new century, compared to earlier missions.[48]

According to the author's data, some missions had a higher rate of allegations than other missions. Since 2005, allegations against UN police personnel have been entered as follows: eleven in the UN Stabilization Mission in Haiti (MINUSTAH), seven in the UN Mission in Liberia (UNMIL), four in MONUC, two in UNMIK,[49] two in MONUSCO, one in the UN Mission in Sudan (UNMIS) and three in the United Nations Integrated Mission in Timor-Leste (UNMIT).[50] Most of the missions facing the highest proportion of allegations held mandates which were more intrusive, such as the new Protection of Civilians (POC) mandates.[51] These missions also had large numbers of personnel. Missions established in the 20th century do not appear to have had as many allegations made against them as have recently established missions.

The author's data include only a few entries for missions established after 2005.[52] This may be because of the time-lag between when the misconduct occurred, and when these were publicly reported. Exceptionally, the UN Organization Stabilization Mission in the Democratic Republic of the Congo (MONUSCO) had some entries in the author's data.[53]

48 UNMIL had 7.0 allegations made per 10,000 UN police personnel per 12 months, UNOCI had 0, MINUSTAH had 2.6, ONUB had 0, UNMIS had 2.3, and UNMIT had 3.0. These rates are for the most part lower than earlier missions. (The rates for UNTAC, missions in Bosnia, UNMIK, UNTAET and MONUC were 11.5, 11.0, 3.7, 7.0 and 3.8 respectively. See the section above.)

49 Only those allegations concerning matters occurring in or after 2005 are counted.

50 For allegations against MONUSCO police personnel, see UNGA, 2011 OIOS PKO Report; UNGA, OIOS Report 2013. For allegations against UNMIS police personnel, see ibid. For allegations against UNMIT police personnel, see UNGA, 2014 OIOS PKO Report; UNMIT, UNMIT Human Rights and Transitional Justice Section Report: Report on Human Rights Developments in Timor Leste, August 2006–August 2007.

51 However, this does not include UNMIT and UNMIK. For the relationship between the mandates and the UN police's functions, see Chapter 2, Section 1. As regards crimes of a sexual nature, these can never fall within the mandate, and thus are not influenced by the nature of any mandate.

52 African Union-United Nations Hybrid Operation in Darfur (UNAMID), UN Mission in the Central African Republic and Chad (MINURCAT), UN Organization Stabilization Mission in the Democratic Republic of the Congo (MONUSCO), UN Organization Interim Security Force for Abyei (UNIFSA), United Nations Mission in the Republic of South Sudan (UNMISS), UN Supervision Mission in Syria (UNSMIS), United Nations Multidimensional Integrated Stabilization Mission in Mali (MINUSMA), and United Nations Multidimensional Integrated Stabilization Mission in the Central African Republic (MINUSCA).

53 2 allegations were made against UN police personnel, 2 against military contingent personnel, and 3 against civilian personnel. For allegations against MONUSCO military

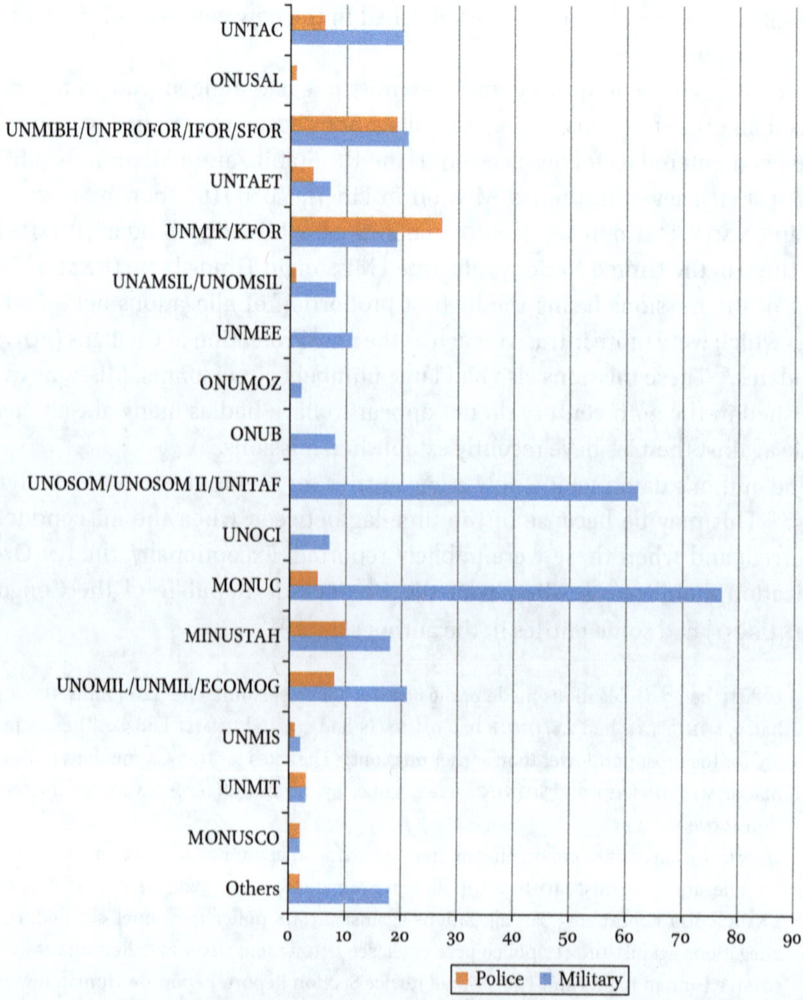

FIGURE 1 *Number of allegations against members of the UN police and military contingents in the author's data per mission*

Nature of Alleged Crimes

For reasons to be discussed later,[54] the nature of the alleged crimes affects the extent of any adverse impact on the UN. One aspect of this is whether

---

personnel, see UNGA, OIOS Report 2013; UNGA, 2011 OIOS PKO Report. For allegations against civilian personnel at MONUSCO, see ibid; UNGA, OIOS Report 2013.

54 See Section 2-2.

the alleged criminal conduct was committed during the exercise of UN police functions.[55]

In the author's data, 73 of the 89 criminal offences allegedly committed by UN police personnel were offences against the person, which might in certain circumstances fall within their official functions.[56] It is most unlikely that any sexual offences are linked to official functions, although being a member of the UN police may provide that person with more opportunities to carry out such offences. This may be the case if, for example, the alleged conduct occurred during police interrogation, arrest or detention. According to the author's data, there were 40 allegations of sexual offences by UN police officers, including four of rape. Others related to sexual slavery, sexual abuse (including involving minors), sexual exploitation and sexual harassment. There were also 21 allegations related to human trafficking.

In addition to allegations of sexual offences, three allegations related to the murder of local persons, and four assault or ill-treatment allegations were made which were unrelated to UN police functions. In addition, four allegations in the author's data pertained to torture or ill-treatment, which appeared to have occurred during the course of the suspects' work in detaining or interrogating people, or during patrols. There were also five allegations of excessive use of force, which injured or killed local persons. Out of nine allegations of criminal conduct that appeared to be linked to UN police duties, seven occurred in UNMIK, whilst the other two took place in UNTAC and MINUSTAH. In all three missions, the UN police were involved in actual policing duties.[57] In comparison, out of 240 allegations of offences against the person listed in the author's data as having been committed by military contingent personnel, 91 were of a non-sexual nature, including twelve allegations of murder, 22 instances of assault or ill-treatment, and 26 allegations resulted from either an excessive use of force or an indiscriminate attack. The disproportionately high rate of allegations against military personnel may reflect the different nature of the functions carried out by the UN police and military contingents.

There were only two allegations of motoring offences by UN police personnel in the author's data. They both concerned hitting and killing a local person while driving under the influence of alcohol. When searching for further information regarding traffic offences, records of some internal Boards of Inquiry convened in July and August 2010 were discovered, which were accessible to

55 This has implications for issues of immunity. See Chapter 6, Sections 1-4-1 and 1-4-2.

56 See n.28, n.30, n.31, n.32, n.34, n.37, n.38, n.43, n.44, n.47, n.53 for the sources for these allegations.

57 See Chapter 2, Sections 1-4, 1-5, 1-6 and 1-7.

certain non-UN personnel.[58] These records came from a completely separate source, and did not form part of the author's data. That Boards of Inquiry were held means that these were incidents in which UN Peace Operations personnel were killed, injured or died, or were incidents involving UN Peace Operations personnel which caused the death or injury of non-UN personnel, or cases in which UN property or equipment above a certain monetary value were lost or damaged.[59] Of these 35 incidents, nine concerned traffic accidents. All nine accidents were caused by UN Peace Operations personnel, seven of which involved fatalities, and two of which caused injuries to third persons. In only one case was there found to be no fault on the driver's part. Others involved speeding, falling asleep while driving, possible drunk-driving, and negligence. Those driving during these incidents included: one Military Observer, two military contingent members, three UN police personnel (including one FPU personnel), one international civilian staff and two local staff. The exact extent of UN traffic offences is unknown, but the BoI records, which appear to have been unintentionally made public, show that traffic offences are not uncommon. This information contrasts sharply with the complete lack of information officially released by the UN regarding traffic offences.

The author's data have 61 entries regarding alleged economic crimes, a significant majority of which were alleged to have been committed by civilian staff.[60] Some allegations were against military contingent members,[61] but only four were made against UN police personnel. While most economic crimes alleged to have been committed by military personnel concerned theft from local persons,[62] cases against UN police officers concerned fraud and the embezzlement of UN funds, as well as corruption involving local authorities.[63]

Across all categories of crimes, the majority of allegations against UN police officers did not directly relate to their official functions.[64] The exceptions

58 This document is on file with the author.

59 This is a list of the circumstances for which Boards of Inquiry are required to convene under the current UN internal rules. See Chapter 4, Section 2.

60 34 allegations were made against civilian staff, including four against UN Volunteers. Some allegations concerned both civilian staff and vendors.

61 18 allegations were made against military contingent members.

62 Ten out of 18 allegations concerned theft from a local person or property.

63 One related to entitlement fraud, and another to the embezzlement of training funds. Another case concerned corruption involving local authorities. All these three cases were substantiated by the OIOS. The other case related to the alleged involvement of several UN police personnel in weapons smuggling for economic gain.

64 According to the author's data, only 13 out of 89 allegations lodged against members of the UN police related to their official duties. However, in three cases, it is unclear whether or not they were related to the official functions.

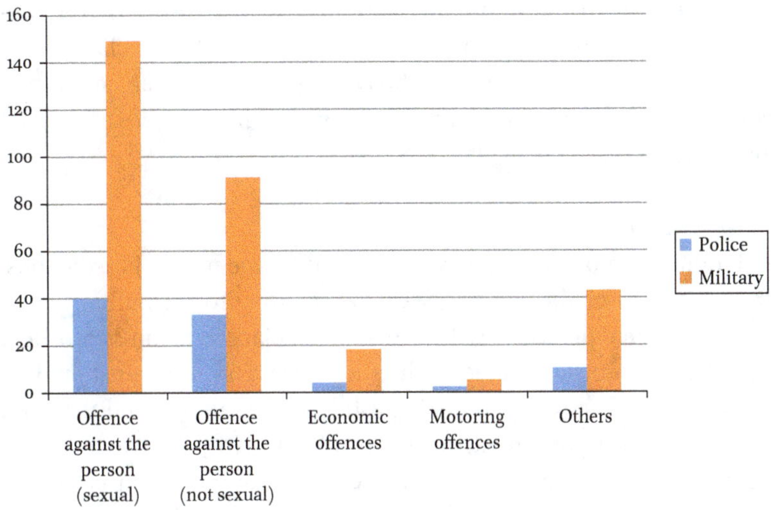

FIGURE 2 *Categories of alleged crimes by UN police and military personnel in the author's data*

included a few cases of ill-treatment of interviewees or detainees, and excessive use of force causing either injuries to, or the deaths of, demonstrators. It may not be a coincidence that most of these allegations concerned UNMIK.[65] It is conceivable that UNMIK personnel disproportionately committed crimes directly related to their official functions because of their executive policing functions. It is noteworthy that there is no indication that the more complex UN police functions have become, the more crimes these have triggered.

Nationality of Suspects

The author's data contain some information regarding the nationalities of suspects. The largest number of allegations against UN police officers concerned those from the US, Pakistan and Jordan,[66] and dealt with offences against the person, particularly sexual offences.[67] All but one had no link with their official

65 Ten out of 13 alleged crimes that appear directly related to the official functions were committed in UNMIK. The remaining allegations concerned MINUSTAH, UNMIT and UNTAC.

66 Eleven entries were against American police officers, nine against Pakistani officers, and five against Jordanian police officers. Romanians faced four allegations, whilst three allegations were made against Bulgarian police officers, two allegations each against Austrian, Nigerian, Zimbabwean and Filipino officers, and one allegation each against Finnish, British, Fijian, Argentinean, Egyptian, Indian, Russian, Nepalese, Mexican, Bulgarian, Canadian, Kenyan and Kosovar officers. As to the remaining allegations, the nationalities of the suspects are unknown.

67 Out of eleven allegations against UN police from the US, six were trafficking-related, one dealt with sexual slavery, one with the violation of confidentiality, one with weapons

functions.[68] Members of these military contingents were also relatively frequently complained about.[69] The kinds of alleged offences the military were accused of covered a wider range than those alleged to have been committed by UN police officers, but the majority of these were either offences of a sexual nature or excessive uses of force.[70]

Prosecution

In general, criminal proceedings may be brought in one of two jurisdictions: either the host State or the sending State.[71] According to the author's data, some form of criminal proceedings has been taken place in the mission's host State in 12 of the 89 entries related to the UN police. This number should be carefully examined. One needs to distinguish between UNMIK and UNTAET, where the UN was the government, and other missions. In these two missions, the authority to prosecute lay with the UN itself. Some of the concerns relating to the standards[72] of the host State did not apply in respect of these missions.

---

smuggling, one with corruption and one dealt with the sexual abuse of a minor. Out of nine crimes allegedly committed by Pakistani police officers, three concerned human trafficking-related offences, one dealt with sexual slavery, two with sexual abuse involving minors, one with rape and other sexual abuse, and one with weapons smuggling. Out of five allegations of criminal conduct by Jordanian police officers, three dealt with sexual crimes, and two with allegations of murder and abetting murder.

68 One case, concerning an American officer, dealt with a violation of confidentiality.

69 In the author's data, there were five entries against Jordanian military members, 29 allegations against American military members and twelve complaints against Pakistani military members. The nationalities of military contingents facing more than five allegations of misconduct were: Belgium (21), Morocco (20), Canada (19), Uruguay (18), Bulgaria (10), Italy (9), Nepal (8), the United Kingdom (7), France (5), Germany (5), India (5), South Africa (5) and Tunisia (5).

70 Four allegations against Jordanian military contingent members concerned sexual offences, whilst one dealt with excessive use of force. Eight alleged offences by American military members concerned sexual offences (three human trafficking allegations, two rapes and one sexual slavery allegation), eleven allegations of excessive use of force, two of murder, two of ill-treatment, whilst the remaining allegations concerned other types of crimes. Out of twelve allegations against Pakistani military personnel, four concerned sexual offences (including a rape allegation), four related to illegal trade and trafficking, one each of assault and egregious acts, and another allegation dealt with paying witnesses to falsify testimony related to criminal allegations. The remaining allegation concerned an indiscriminate attack against civilians.

71 For jurisdiction, see Chapter 5, Sections 3, 4.

72 These related mainly to human rights standards, in particular to due process guarantees for the accused. For more details, see Chapter 6, Section 2-2.

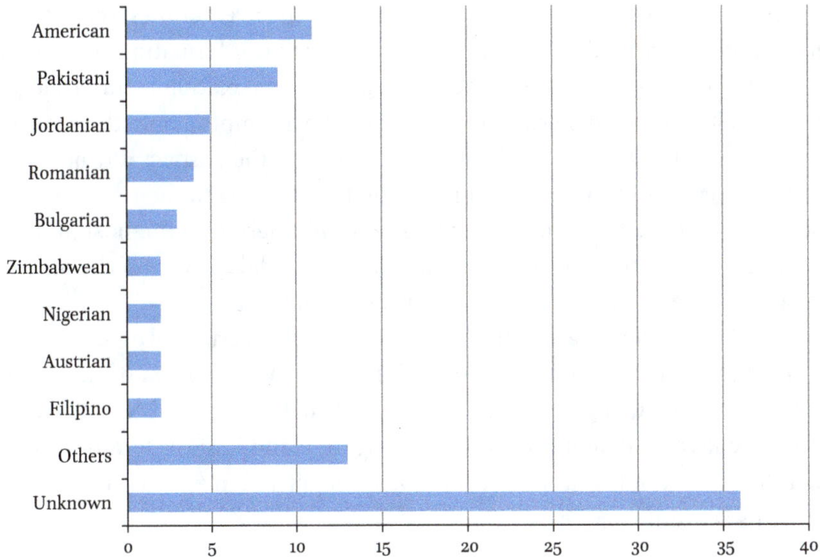

FIGURE 3 *Nationalities of UN police suspects in the author's data*

It is therefore natural that more prosecutions took place in Kosovo and East Timor.[73] All but one of the cases prosecuted concerned offences against the person.[74] Aside from UNMIK and UNTAET, the host State police only launched criminal investigations in two cases: one in MONUSCO, and one in MINUSTAH. Both concerned sexual offences and, in both cases, local police initiated the criminal investigations, even arresting the suspect in one case. However, no prosecutions eventuated in either case in the host State.

Out of 89 entries, there were only five cases in which information suggested that the suspect faced criminal proceedings back in their sending States. All of these took place after 2000, and all dealt with sexual crimes. Four concerned FPU officers, whilst the other concerned an individual police officer. In respect of these five cases, two of the suspects were from Pakistan, one was from Argentina, another was from Nepal, whilst the nationality of the suspects in the fifth case was not revealed. There are too few cases to make any concrete analysis of what types of crimes are more likely to be prosecuted, or which States are more likely to prosecute their nationals. Having said that, it appears

73 Three cases were prosecuted in UNTAET, and six cases in UNMIK. In addition, there was one case where the suspect was arrested, but was then released on the condition that he report daily to the authorities.

74 The remaining case related to a motoring offence.

that those cases which were prosecuted mostly involved crimes against the person and, in particular, sexual crimes. There is no information to suggest that UN police personnel were prosecuted anywhere in relation to fraud allegations.[75] As for traffic offences, one entry noted an attempt to hold the suspect criminally accountable in the host State. However, the suspect did not face court proceedings in the end.[76] None of the files relating to the UN's internal disciplinary proceedings on traffic offences were referred to the host State.[77] This may be because traffic offences may be seen as falling within the official functions of the UN police, and thus subject to immunity.

Overall, the author's data suggest that the majority of criminal offences have not been prosecuted. The UN responded internally to at least 41 of the 89 allegations contained in the author's data. However, the most the UN can do currently is to launch an administrative investigation and impose administrative sanctions, with the maximum penalty being repatriation.[78] As argued previously, this is insufficient.[79]

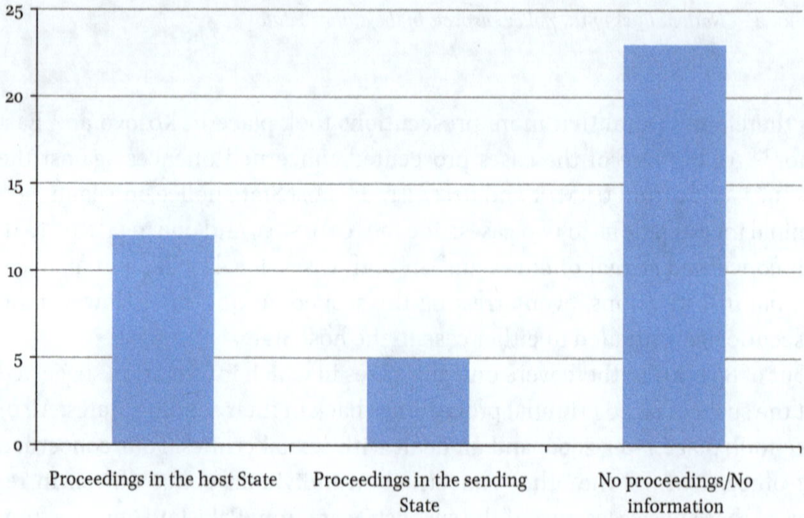

FIGURE 4 *Cases where criminal proceedings were brought against UN police*

75 There was, however, a case in which a high-ranking civilian staff member from UNMIK was prosecuted in Germany for fraud and embezzlement.

76 The case was investigated in East Timor, by the UN transitional government.

77 These are on file with the author.

78 The UN refers cases to the authorities of either the host or the national State for criminal prosecution; see Chapter 4, Sections 3-4 and 3-5.

79 See Chapter 1, Sections 1, 3 and 4.

2 Possible Patterns of Criminal Conduct

Because of the identified shortcomings in the author's data,[80] it is necessary to look elsewhere to obtain a better overall picture of the issue. Two sources over and above the author's data were consulted. The first source is that of UN reports. Two systematic sets of data have been collected by two different entities. The UN's Conduct and Discipline Unit (CDU) compiles data on the total number of allegations of misconduct, disaggregated according to the type of personnel, the type of misconduct and the mission concerned.[81] The UN's investigative body, the Office of Internal Oversight Services (OIOS), makes limited information public. It has published a list of its investigation reports annually since 2004.[82] The contents of these reports are sealed, but the Office indicates the number and kinds of reports this list contains.[83] The OIOS lists its investigation reports according to the type of personnel involved, gives a brief outline of the alleged misconduct, and states whether or not the allegation was substantiated. What is regrettable is that there is no means of knowing how many of the cases reported by the OIOS and the CDU overlap,[84] which prevents a better overall picture of the problems from emerging. In addition to these two sets of information, there are other UN reports dealing with specific offences, including sexual exploitation and abuse (SEA).[85] All these sets of data have only recently been compiled,[86] and the data cover not only criminal offences, but also disciplinary offences. None of these reports group together the kinds of offences in the same way as the author's data does. Nor do these

---

80 See Section 1.

81 UN CDU, 'Statistics' <https://cdu.unlb.org/Statistics/OverviewofStatistics.aspx> accessed 28 September 2016. For a discussion of the CDU's mandate and an analysis of it, see Chapter 4, Sections 3-2 and 3-5.

82 These reports are available at the OIOS website. UN OIOS, 'Office of Internal Oversight Services: Annual Reports' <http://www.un.org/Depts/oios/pages/annual_reports.html>.

83 Ibid.

84 Nonetheless, one report did indicate the proportion of the cases reported directly to the OIOS. If cases are reported directly to the OIOS, this means that the CDU would not have that data. Theoretically, therefore, 61% of OIOS data is also held by the CDU. The OIOS's final report on the pilot project reported that about 39% of the reports held by the OIOS were directly reported to the OIOS. UNGA, 'Comprehensive Report on the Pilot Project Designated by the General Assembly in Resolution 63/287' (21 February 2013) UN Doc. A/67/751, para. 15, (hereinafter 'Pilot Project Report').

85 Information on sexual exploitation and abuse is compiled annually by the Secretary-General pursuant to UNGA Res 57/306 (22 May 2003) UN Doc. A/RES/57/306.

86 The CDU has only collected and compiled data since 2007. Since 2004, the OIOS's annual reports have included some information on major investigations conducted by it.

reports reveal whether or not each complaint was substantiated.[87] These reports also make no distinction between criminal and other offences.[88] Therefore, the CDU and OIOS data, as well as any other UN reports, only provide a partial picture, and can only be used as supplementary sources.

The second source consisted of reports by non-governmental organizations (NGOs), academic writings, and insiders' writings about general problems or their own experiences. These reports can be used as supplementary materials, as they tend to report on a specific mission, a specific country, or a specific period of time. Because of the methodologies used for information collection for the author's data,[89] the information derived from these sources overlaps with that of the author's data. It is also subject to the same problems when attempting to grasp the scale and nature of the problems as with the other sources, that is, problems of under-reporting and an unsure evidence base for allegations.[90] Nevertheless, these reports may be helpful in providing a general picture of the problems.

Even taking into account all these different kinds of sources, it is impossible to draw conclusions as to the exact scale and seriousness of the issue. However, these sources may reveal the general scale of the problems and some patterns. A caveat should be attached to this statement: any patterns which may emerge will be based on the information available. Different patterns might emerge were there to be full disclosure of the relevant information. Nevertheless, the patterns sought are likely to be indicative of where the problems lie. Four patterns are sought in particular. The first is the balance between different crimes, according to the nature of violations. Given that what matters is the perception of the local police and the population, some crimes may have more of a negative impact on the local population than others, particularly if local people are directly harmed by the conduct, or if it is visible to them. The second pattern sought is the balance between criminal conduct which is directly linked to the discharge of the UN polices' official functions, and that

---

87 OIOS reports, by the way in which they are titled, indicate whether or not an allegation has been substantiated. 'Investigation report' is used for allegations that have been substantiated; 'contingent report' refers to substantiated reports regarding military members; and 'closure report' denotes unsubstantiated allegations. See for example the Activities of the Office of Internal Oversight Services on peace operations for the period 1 January to 31 December 2013, Report of the Office of Internal Oversight Services 2014. UN doc. A/68/337 (Part II), 25 February 2014, para. 11.

88 OIOS' 'Category I' misconduct includes criminal conduct. The CDU does not differentiate between categories on the basis of the seriousness of the misconduct.

89 See Section 1; see also Chapter 1, Section 3.

90 See Section 1.

which is not.[91] For instance, if a UN police officer uses excessive force to control a crowd and kills a person as a result, the conduct is directly related to his official functions.[92] On the other hand, if a UN police officer rapes a person after work in his private accommodation, there is no operational link. There may be some criminal conduct which falls between these two poles, such as conduct that may be indirectly related to the discharge of official functions, for example road traffic offences. If the data show a high proportion of criminal conduct directly related to their functions, this may either call into question what is asked of UN police officers, or their professional or personal qualifications, or both.[93] The third pattern sought is the rate of reported criminal conduct per mission. If certain missions are subject to a clearly disproportionate number of allegations, it may be because of the ease of reporting in that mission in comparison to other missions. It could also be linked to the local culture, or the population's perception of police accountability. It could even be related to the fact that the media have tended to focus their attention on a particular State involved in that mission. The final pattern sought is whether there is a disproportionately high number of allegations against officers from some sending States. It would be interesting to see, for example, if there is any pattern indicating that UN police officers from sending States with bad human rights records are also those against whom the most allegations are made, or if UN police officers from countries with a repressive public culture are more complained about than those from freer countries.

Each of the four patterns is sought not only as information in its own right, but also for how they relate to each other. Along the way, comparisons may be made between allegations against members of military and those against UN police, in order to see if there is any particular trend in this regard.

2-1 *Evidence of the Scale of Wrongdoing*

First, the general scale of wrongdoing, and any shift in that scale, will be assessed. This necessitates a consideration of how, over time, changes in the functions carried out by the UN police may have contributed to the number of crimes they are alleged to have committed.[94] The available information confirms the earlier finding that allegations did not surface in the public domain until the beginning of the 1990s.[95]

91 This has implications for immunity; see Chapter 6, Sections 1-4-1 and 1-4-2.

92 See Chapter 6, Sections 1-4-1 and 1-4-2.

93 On UN police's functions, see Chapter 2, Section 1.

94 See Chapter 2, Section 1.

95 See Section 1.

UNTAC was the first mission to catch the media's attention in relation to allegations of wrongdoing. Insiders' reports supported the media's reports.[96] Complaints were made by the local population about the general behaviour of international personnel, in particular about sexual misconduct.[97]

In the mid-1990s, during the Peace Enforcement missions in the Balkans, allegations increased dramatically, and were subsequently reported in the public domain.[98] The International Police Task Force (IPTF) in the UN Mission in Bosnia and Herzegovina (UNMIBH) became known not only for the allegedly widespread nature of UN police involvement in human trafficking, but also the subsequent dismissal of two whistleblowers.[99] Reports continued to emerge in

---

96 Some examples include: Holm and Eide, *Peacebuilding and Police Reform*, p. 51; Heininger, *Peacekeeping in Transition: The United Nations in Cambodia*; UNITAR and IPS, *UNTAC debriefing*; International Alert, *Gender Mainstreaming in Peace Support Operations: Moving beyond Rhetoric to Practice* (July 2002), p. 42; Mackay, 'Sex and the Peacekeeping Soldier: The New UN Resolution' (*Peace News*, June–August 2001) <http://peacenews.info/node/3602/sex-and-peacekeeping-soldier-new-un-resolution>; Kenneth Cain, Heidi Postlewait and Andrew Thomson, *Emergency Sex and Other Desperate Measures: A True Story from Hell on Earth* (Miramax 2004); Kien Serey Phal, 'The Lessons of the UNTAC Experience and the Ongoing Responsibilities of the International Community for Peacebuilding and Development in Cambodia' (1995) 7 *Global Change, Peace & Security* 129; Gabrielle Simm, *Sex in Peace Operations* (Cambridge University Press 2013), p. 24.

97 170 people signed an open letter to Yasushi Akashi, calling for measures to redress sexual harassment, an advisory committee on gender issues to be set up, and the dissemination of a code of conduct for UNTAC personnel. See 'An Open Letter to Yasushi Akashi'.

98 Human Rights Watch, *Hopes Betrayed*; McKenna, 'Sins of the Peacekeepers' (*Sunday Herald*, 30 June 2002) <http://www.sundayherald.com/25914>; Walsh and Byrne, 'UN Peacekeepers Criticized'; Kathryn Bolkovac, *The Whistleblower: Sex Trafficking, Military Contractors, and One Woman's Fight for Justice* (Palgrave Macmillan 2011); Lynch, 'Misconduct, Corruption by US Police Mar Bosnian Mission'. There were also a lot of reports on missions in Somalia, for example, 'Peacekeeper accused' (*Paksearch*, January 2002) <http://www.pakseach.com/br2002/jan/3/un%20peacekeeper%20accused%20of%20assaulting%20congo%20girl.htm>; Rakiya Omaar and Alexander De Waal, *Somalia – Human Rights Abuses by the United Nations Forces* (African Rights, July 1993). However, it is irrelevant to the UN police as UNOSOM I did not include a UN police contingent; and UNOSOM II had a minor UN police presence. The total figure included both military and police. UN DPKO, 'Somalia – UNOSOM I Facts and Figures' <http://www.un.org/en/peacekeeping/missions/past/unosom1facts.html> accessed 22 August 2014 UN DPKO, 'Somalia – UNOSOM II Facts and Figures' <http://www.un.org/en/peacekeeping/missions/past/unosom2facts.html> accessed 22 August 2014.

99 Bolkovac, *The Whistleblower: Sex Trafficking, Military Contractors, and One Woman's Fight for Justice* O'Meara, 'DynCorp Disgrace' (*Insight Magazine*, 14 January 2002) <http://www.corpwatch.org/article.php?id=11119>; Jamie Wilson and Kevin Maguire, 'American Firm

the early 2000s, particularly of allegations of widespread involvement of Peace Operations personnel in sexual offences.[100] Most notable were those which triggered a change in the UN's responses and mechanisms. These reports mostly concerned military personnel, but also UN police in the Democratic Republic of the Congo (DRC).[101]

A significant difference regarding reports of alleged crimes is the availability of additional information from the UN since 2000.[102] The list of reports of investigations by the OIOS indicates that 433 investigations were concluded between 2010 and 2013.[103] Out of 245 substantiated investigations, 22 involved UN police personnel. This amounted to 9 percent of the substantiated investigations, whereas the UN police comprised about 11.7 percent of all mission personnel. In comparison, substantiated reports against the military contingent amounted to 52.2 percent of the total number of reports, whereas the military contingent made up 70.7 percent of all Peace Operations personnel.[104]

However, this number represents the tip of the iceberg, as the OIOS did not investigate all allegations, not even instances of serious misconduct. Between 1 July 2009 and 30 June 2012, there were 1,026 case intakes, and 117 serious cases

in Bosnia Sex Trade Row Poised to Win MoD Contract' *The Guardian* (London, 29 November 2002) <http://www.theguardian.com/uk/2002/nov/29/military.politics> accessed 6 October 2014.

100 Holt and Hughes, 'Sex and the UN: When Peacemakers Become Predators'; Wallis, 'UN Staff in Congo Face Child Sex Claims'; Bowcott, 'Report Reveals Shame of UN Peacekeepers'; Neil MacFarquhar, 'Peacekeepers' Sex Scandals Linger, On Screen and Off' *New York Times* (New york, 7 September 2011); Martin, *Must Boys be Boys*; Corinna Csáky, *No One to Turn to – The Under-Reporting of Child Sexual Exploitation and Abuse by Aid Workers and Peacekeepers* (Save the Children – UK, 2008); Charlotte Rachael Proudman, 'Charitable Rape: Peacekeepers' Dirty Little Secrets' *The Independent Blogs* (22 May 2012) <http://blogs.independent.co.uk/2012/05/22/charitable-rape-peacekeepers-dirty-little-secrets/> accessed 24 May 2012.

101 UNGA, OIOS Bunia Report; UNGA, 'A Comprehensive Strategy to Eliminate Future Sexual Exploitation and Abuse in United Nations Peacekeeping Operations' (24 March 2005) UN Doc. A/59/710. On the subsequent changes in the UN system, see Chapter 4, Section 2.

102 See the introductory section in Section 2.

103 UN OIOS, 'Office of Internal Oversight Services: Annual Reports' <http://www.un.org/Depts/oios/pages/annual_reports.html>.

104 Numbers of personnel are calculated as an average over a 4 year period, when taking the December figures given by the DPKO in UN DPKO, 'Peacekeeping Fact Sheet Archive' <http://www.un.org/en/peacekeeping/resources/statistics/factsheet_archive.shtml> accessed 28 February 2015.

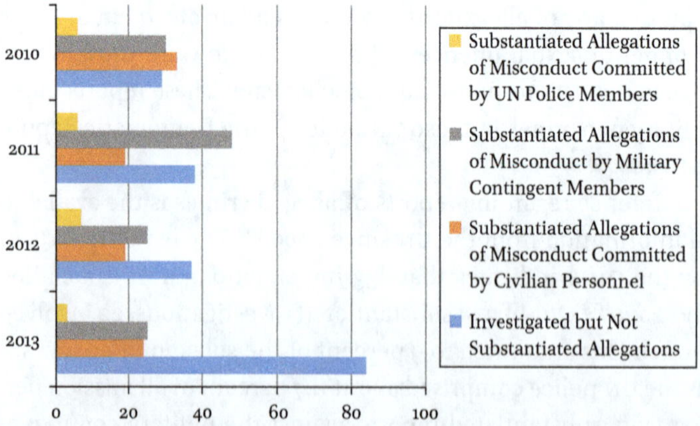

FIGURE 5 *The number of investigations undertaken by the OIOS in the years 2010–2013*

were referred to missions for investigation.[105] To put that into the context, data provided by the CDU is useful. The CDU provides the total number of allegations since 2007, disaggregated into categories, including types of personnel and allegations. According to its annual data, from 2007 until 2013, the number of allegations of serious misconduct[106] against UN police personnel ranged from 28 to 44, except for 2013 when this number dropped to 15.[107] Since 2007, the equivalent figures for military personnel[108] have ranged from 204 to 313 annually.[109] These figures indicate an average of 28 allegations per 10,000 personnel per year between 2007 and 2013 for UN police personnel, while the equivalent rate for the military is 30.5 allegations per 10,000 personnel per year.[110]

105 These were 'Category I' cases, which were referred to missions. 216 less serious cases ('Category II' cases) were also referred to missions. UNGA, Pilot Project Report designated by the General Assembly in UNGA Res 63/287 (21 February 2013) UN Doc. A/RES/63/287, Annex I.

106 For a consideration of the categorization of the type of allegations, see Chapter 4, Section 2. For the purposes of this thesis, it suffices to note that all allegations of criminal conduct are categorized as Category I cases.

107 The annual numbers were 44, 42, 31, 47, 28, 43, and 15 respectively (based on data as of 1 May 2014). These numbers included serious misconduct (Category I) allegations plus allegations of sexual exploitation and abuse. UN CDU, 'Statistics' <https://cdu.unlb.org/Statistics/OverviewofStatistics.aspx>.

108 Note that CDU data for military personnel includes data covering Military Observers.

109 The annual numbers were 246, 313, 237, 295, 236, 204 and 216.

110 The number of personnel is based on the number as it stands in December each year at UN DPKO, 'Fact Sheet archive' <http://www.un.org/en/peacekeeping/resources/statistics/factsheet_archive.shtml>.

The CDU figures do not include allegations made directly to the OIOS without the knowledge of CDU.[111] The scale of the allegations is thus larger than the CDU figures indicate.

These two figures are interesting for several reasons. First, they provide a more accurate picture of the sheer magnitude of misconduct. Because it is possible that people are making more complaints as they become more aware of the existence of complaint mechanisms,[112] the current figures cannot be extrapolated so as to attempt to gain an indication of the actual number of crimes committed before 2000. However, comparing all the data assists in obtaining a better picture of the problem. For example, if one takes UNTAC, the mission with the highest number of allegations in the 1990s, the rate of allegations is about 11.5 per 10,000 UN police personnel per year.[113] This is less than half of the total number of allegations listed by the CDU.

The rate of allegations against the England and Wales police forces, as cited above,[114] was much higher as compared to the rate of allegations against

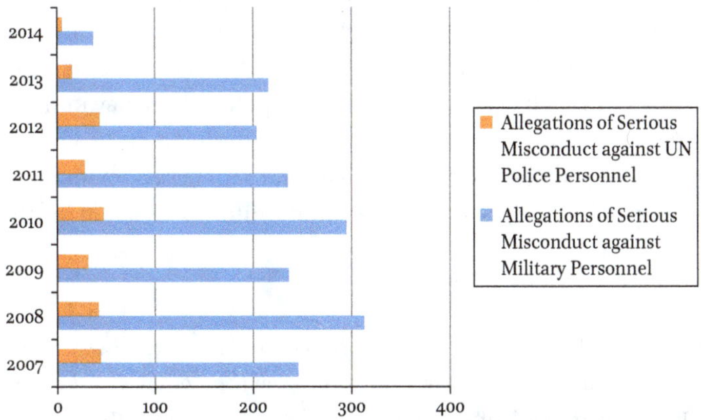

FIGURE 6 *Number of allegations made against UN police and military personnel between 2007 and 2014 according to the CDU**
*The number of allegations are calculated as the addition of alleged Category I misconduct and allegations of Sexual Exploitation and Abuse.

---

111 UN CDU, 'Statistics' <https://cdu.unlb.org/Statistics/OverviewofStatistics.aspx>.

112 This was suggested in the UNGA, Zeid Report, para. 8.

113 See Section 1 for the allegation rate per 10,000 personnel (17.3). This figure is the result of 17.3 divided by the duration of UNTAC (1.5 years). In the same way, for military personnel, the rate per 10,000 persons per year comes to 7.5.

114 The rate of allegations was 525.1 per 10,000 officers per year. See the introductory section to this chapter.

UN police personnel,[115] but the rate of substantiated allegations against the England and Wales police forces was similar to the rate of allegations against UN police personnel substantiated by the OIOS.[116] The rate of cases in which a conviction was obtained in respect of these allegations is much lower in the case of the UN police.[117] This could be because people are more confident about making complaints in England and Wales, or because these police forces respond to complaints; the two appear inter-related. It could also be due to the extent of disclosure about the rate of criminal and other misconduct by police officers. It is impossible to draw firm conclusions from the limited information available.

Second, both the OIOS and CDU figures indicate that more allegations are made against military personnel than UN police personnel.[118] However, the author's data consistently showed that there are broadly similar numbers of allegations made against these two groupings, with a slightly higher rate of allegations lodged against the UN police.[119]

Third, the OIOS and CDU figures indicate that even though military personnel are subject to more allegations than UN police personnel, those against the UN police are more likely to be substantiated.[120] This can mean many things. It may be that allegations are more difficult to substantiate against members of military contingents than against members of the UN police. This may indicate that, once the stage of an investigation is reached where the identification of a suspect is required, it is more difficult for a victim to identify a member of the military contingent, as they all wear the same uniforms and stay in the

115 See text accompanying n.13 and n.14.

116 OIOS substantiated 22 allegations against UN police personnel over 4 years, which gives an average of 5.5 substantiated allegations per year. In September 2013, there were 12,705 UN police officers across all missions. UN DPKO, 'Fact Sheet archive' <http://www.un.org/en/peacekeeping/resources/statistics/factsheet_archive.shtml>. This means there were 4.4 substantiated instances of criminal conduct per 10,000 UN police personnel per year.

117 It is impossible to present an accurate rate of prosecution. There are five entries in the author's data, in which suspects have been convicted. However, for one case, criminal proceedings took place *in absentia*.

118 See above within this section.

119 See Section 1.

120 The UN police make up 11.7 percent of the Peace Operations personnel. 9.0 percent of the substantiated allegations were made against them. The military contingent personnel constitute 70.7 percent of the personnel, and 52.2 percent of the substantiated allegations were lodged against them. This rate of substantiated allegations, when translated into the same number of personnel is about 172 (UN police): 165 (military contingent). This was calculated using figures cited above.

same compound.[121] It could also mean that military contingent members have a greater tendency to cover up their colleagues' misconduct.[122] It could also mean that military contingents tend to initiate their own investigations,[123] or that the UN trusts that that is the case. The lower rate of substantiated reports of allegations against the military may mean that the OIOS prioritizes investigating allegations against UN police members, either because it expects sending States to investigate their military members' misconduct, or for other reasons. For whatever reason, it appears that allegations concerning military misconduct are not less frequently made, as appears from the author's data.

The two supplementary datasets confirm that some missions have been subject to a much higher rate of allegations. Of the allegations listed by the OIOS in 2006 and 2007, about 85 percent were made against MONUC, UNMIL, MINUSTAH, UNMIS and UNOCI. These missions made up one third of the total operations running during that period.[124] Data from the CDU indicated that allegations of serious misconduct (Category I) against UN police personnel had been reported at disproportionately high rates in MINUSTAH,[125] UNMIL,[126] UNMIT,[127] UNMIS,[128] and UNOCI.[129] During this time, the six missions against whom the most allegations of serious misconduct by military personnel were reported were: MONUC, MINUSTAH, MONUSCO, UNMIL, UNOCI and UNAMID.[130]

121 UNGA, OIOS Bunia Report. There may be a similar problem for FPU personnel, as they are national units which are deployed together.

122 Ibid. Whether or not this applies to FPUs is unknown. However, it is possible that it does, given the nature of their deployment. It may be worth noting that, in one case in MONUSCO, when two FPU officers were arrested by the local police for alleged sexual abuse of a local woman, the FPU commander made an armed intervention and relieved the two arrested officers without negotiating or resorting to diplomatic channels. UNGA, OIOS Report 2013, para. 60.

123 Under the 2007 Memorandum of Understanding, States sending military contingents accept responsibility for conducting investigations into their members' misconduct. UNGA, 'Revised Draft Model Memorandum of Understanding, as annexed to UNGA, Report of the Special Committee on Peacekeeping Operations and its Working Group on the 2007 Resumed Session' (12 June 2007) UN Doc. A/61/19 (Part III) Article 7 quarter.

124 The data are taken from UNGA, OIOS 2008 Report, p. 7.

125 In total 95 allegations in the period between 2007 and 2014. CDU data are taken from UN CDU, 'Statistics' <https://cdu.unlb.org/Statistics/OverviewofStatistics.aspx>.

126 In total 40 allegations in the period between 2007 and 2014.

127 39 allegations in the period between 2007 and 2014.

128 26 allegations in the period between 2007 and 2014.

129 18 allegations in the period between 2007 and 2014.

130 213, 109, 88, 84, 82 and 42 allegations respectively in the period between 2007 and 2014.

2-2 *Nature of Alleged Criminal Offences*

The overall scale of criminal misconduct by UN police officers appears to be serious, but the problem may be intensified if the nature of some criminal offences is taken into account. This is because some offences are more visible to, and have a greater impact on, the local population. The categories of offences whose nature may have such an impact are: offences against the person, road traffic offences, and economic offences. Each of these categories is examined in turn.

2-2-1 Offences against the Person

Criminal offences against the person generally have a big impact. They are very visible to the local population, in particular if the victim is someone from the local community. A significant proportion of alleged crimes fall into this category. CDU data cannot be used, as they do not distinguish between alleged offences in such a way as to identify how many of these offences are offences against the person.[131]

Of a Sexual Nature

The first observable trend is that there have been numerous reports of misconduct of a sexual nature.[132] As stated, the majority of cases entered in the author's data fall into this category,[133] and quite a few media and NGO reports focus on sexual offences.[134] The Zeid Report stated that sexual exploitation and abuse appeared widespread in the DRC, involving both civilian and uniformed personnel.[135]

CDU statistics show that allegations of sexual exploitation and abuse by UN police personnel between 2007 and 2014 amounted to between 7 and 24 annually, averaging 12.4 per year.[136] Interestingly, the average rate of allegations of sexual exploitation and abuse was highest among civilian personnel, with the

131 The data are disaggregated into several different categories, but these categories do not reveal the information sought here. UN CDU, 'Statistics' <https://cdu.unlb.org/Statistics/OverviewofStatistics.aspx>.

132 See Section 1 above on UNTAC, missions in the Balkans, and sexual exploitation and abuse in West Africa, to name a few.

133 See Section 1.

134 See Section 2-1.

135 UNGA, Zeid Report, para. 8.

136 Since 2007, the annual number of allegations has been: 2007: 7; 2008: 16; 2009: 13; 2010: 10; 2011: 9; 2013: 7; and 2014: 13. UN CDU, 'Statistics' <https://cdu.unlb.org/Statistics/OverviewofStatistics.aspx>.

UN police having a higher rate than military personnel.[137] This is significant, because, overall, there have been more allegations against military contingent personnel than against UN police personnel,[138] but the position is switched when sexual exploitation and abuse allegations are examined.

Allegations of sexual exploitation and abuse by UN police officers were disproportionately reported in some missions. The majority of allegations against UN police personnel were made in respect of the following six missions: MINUSTAH,[139] UNMIL,[140] MONUC,[141] UNOCI,[142] UNMIT,[143] and UNMIS.[144] With respect to allegations of sexual exploitation and abuse by all categories of personnel in these missions, the numbers of allegations were largely similar.[145] These missions were also those which were subject to the highest number of allegations of criminal misconduct in general by all categories of personnel.[146]

---

137 Allegations of sexual exploitation and abuse committed by civilian personnel since 2007 amounted to 32, 26, 35, 30, 22, 23, 20 and 14 (an annual average of 25.3 allegations); whilst those involving military amounted to 56, 49, 55, 38, 40, 19, 37 and 24 (an annual average of 40.0 allegations). Ibid. Note that the CDU includes not only contingent members, but also Military Observers in the figure for military personnel (unlike the OIOS). The former shows an average of 12.4 allegations, while the latter lists 5.2 allegations for the years 2007–2013. Interestingly, the average rate of allegations against civilian personnel over the same seven years was the highest: 13.5 allegations per 10,000 personnel. The number of civilian personnel was calculated as the sum of the number of international civilian staff, the number of local civilian personnel and United Nations Volunteers, as of December each year. These numbers were obtained from the UN DPKO, 'Fact Sheet archive' <http://www.un.org/en/peacekeeping/resources/statistics/factsheet_archive.shtml>.

138 See Section 1 above.

139 37 allegations between 2007 and 2014.

140 16 allegations between 2007 and 2014.

141 10 allegations over the same 8-year period.

142 9 allegations.

143 9 allegations.

144 8 allegations.

145 As regards allegations against military personnel, the five missions with the highest rates of allegations were MONUC, MONUSCO, UNMIL, MINUSTAH and UNOCI. They had 123, 51, 44, 35, and 29 allegations against them respectively. All data were taken from CDT statistics. The Data were accessed on 30 August 2015, with the last update being made on 31 July 2015. UN CDU, 'Statistics' <https://cdu.unlb.org/Statistics/OverviewofStatistics.aspx>. This takes into consideration the fact that UNMIT did not have military contingents. UN DPKO, 'UNMIT Facts and Figures' <http://www.un.org/en/peacekeeping/missions/past/unmit/facts.shtml> accessed 16 August 2014.

146 See Section 1 above.

In 2012, a report noted an overall improvement for all personnel, but in particular for police personnel.[147] It commended the UN police for the decrease in the number of allegations against them in respect of sexual exploitation and abuse, which dropped to 4.1 per 10,000 deployed UN police personnel.[148]

Offences against the Person, Excluding Those of a Sexual Nature

Compared to offences of a sexual nature, other offences against the person have not been highlighted by the UN, the media or NGOs. The number of reported incidents falling into this sub-category has been relatively small.

UN sources disaggregate data in such a way that makes it impossible to distinguish which offences fall within the category of offences against the person. In other words, UN sources do not add anything to the information provided in the author's data.[149] Even if the number of intentional killings of persons outside the realm of work is small, it can nevertheless have an immense impact on the reputation of the mission.

2-2-2 Road Traffic Offences

All UN police personnel are required to have certain driving skills,[150] which is a reflection of their duties. This category of offences is difficult to analyze, as it is hard to determine whether a particular offence amounts to a crime, such as one involving dangerous driving. In addition, it is difficult to distinguish whether or not an offence was committed during the course of duty. This is more problematic than for other crimes. Road traffic offences are likely to involve local persons and, as such, are likely to be visible to the local population.

It is claimed that road traffic offences, including drunk and other forms of dangerous driving, are common in some missions.[151] It appears that the records

---

147 UNGA, 'Report of the Secretary-General on the Special Measures for Protection from Sexual Exploitation and Sexual Abuse' (17 February 2012) UN Doc. A/66/699.

148 The rates were 8.2 in 2010, 13.9 in 2009, and 6.1 in 2008.

149 On CDU's categorization, see the introductory sub-section in Section 2.

150 On the requirements, see Chapter 2, Section 3-1.

151 Catherine Lutz, Matthew Gutmann and Keith Brown, *Conduct and Discipline in UN Peacekeeping Operations:Culture, Political Economy and Gender – Report submitted to the Conduct and Discipline Unit, Department of Peacekeeping Operations United Nations* (Watson Institute for International Studies, Brown University, 19 October 2009), p. 5; Heininger, *Peacekeeping in Transition: The United Nations in Cambodia*; Klaas C Roos, 'Debriefing of Civilian Police Components: UN Transitional Authority in Cambodia (UNTAC)' in Nassrine Azimi (ed), *The Role and Functions of Civilian Police in United Nations Peace-Keeping Operations: Debriefing and Lessons* (Kluwer Law International 1996); Murdoch, 'UN Under Fire for Turning a Blind Eye to Peacekeepers Misconduct'.

of particularized offences confirm this.[152] However, road traffic offences are not well reported by the UN, the media and NGOs.

2-2-3 Theft, Fraud and Corruption

There are two possible scenarios regarding economic crimes. First, that the offence is visible to the local population, for example, theft from a local person. Second, that the theft, fraud or corruption is committed against the UN, or during UN business, and thus is not visible to the local populace (for example, if a UN police officer takes advantage of his position and illegally takes money from the UN, claims illegitimate entitlements, or makes use of the Organization's money for his own benefit). There is no case of the former type in the author's data.[153] However, money lost due to theft, fraud or corruption is money not spent on achieving the aim of the mission. Thus, indirectly, this type of offence has an immense impact on the mission beneficiaries.

It is claimed that theft and corruption are commonly committed by personnel in Peace Operations.[154] Like the author's data, the CDU's data also indicated that the largest number of allegations of both fraud and procurement-related offences were made against civilian staff,[155] while UN police personnel were allegedly involved in entitlement fraud, but not offences related to procurement.[156] The large number of allegations against civilian personnel may indicate that they are in positions which provide more opportunities to engage in fraud or procurement-related offences than are the UN police.

2-3 *Analysis in Relation to the Sending State*

It would be interesting to see if there are any sending States that have a disproportionately high rate of allegations against their police officers. However, such an analysis is very difficult because the UN does not reveal the nationality of the suspect in respect of allegations of misconduct. Whilst the UN has disclosed the nationality of suspects in news releases in the past,[157] it has

152 See Section 1.

153 See Section 1.

154 Lutz, Gutmann and Brown, *Report to CDU*, p. 5.

155 There were 83 entitlement fraud allegations and 52 allegations of procurement related offences between 2007 and 2014. UN CDU, 'Statistics' <https://cdu.unlb.org/Statistics/OverviewofStatistics.aspx>.

156 Altogether, there were all 23 entitlement fraud allegations against UN police personnel between 2007 and 2013. Procurement related offences were not reported in relation to UN police. Ibid.

157 UN DPKO, 'Jordanian Civilian Police Indicted on Rape Charges' (24 August 2001) <http://www.un.org/en/peacekeeping/missions/past/etimor/DB/db240801.htm> accessed 16

generally not done so in recent years. Exceptionally, it has published the nationality of suspects in relation to substantiated sexual exploitation and abuse cases in 2015.[158] In fact, it appears that opinions are divided within the UN as to whether or not information regarding the sending State should be made public. The Zeid Report recommended making the name of the sending State public if it failed to submit a case to its national authorities for prosecution.[159] While the OIOS may be eager to reveal this information, the Department of Peacekeeping Operations (DPKO) has been reluctant to do so.[160]

It is significant that the UN has been reluctant to disclose the nationalities of those against whom allegations are made. This could be legitimate if the UN is attempting to avoid discrediting sending States merely on the basis of allegations. However, the UN has also been hesitant to reveal the nationalities

---

December 2014; UN, 'Security Council Condemns "In the Strongest Terms" All Acts of Sexual Abuse, Exploitation by UN Peacekeeping Personnel' (31 May 2005) <http://www.un.org/press/en/2005/sc8400.doc.htm> accessed 16 December 2014.

158 In the data provided by OIOS and CDU, the nationalities of alleged perpetrators are not made public. See OIOS reports including UNGA, OIOS Congo Report; UNGA, 2014 OIOS PKO Report; UNGA, 'Report of the Office of Internal Oversight Services on Peacekeeping Operations' (13 March 2012) UN Doc. A/66/286 (Part II); UNGA, 2011 OIOS PKO Report; UNGA, 2010 OIOS PKO Report; UNGA, 2009 OIOS PKO Report and UNGA, OIOS Bunia Report. For CDU, see UN CDU, 'Statistics' <https://cdu.unlb.org/Statistics/OverviewofStatistics.aspx>. See also UN, 'Member of UN Mission in DR of Congo Accused of Sexual Abuse Sent Home for Trial' (26 May 2004) <http://www.un.org/apps/news/story.asp?NewsID=10882&Cr=congo>; 'UN Sex Abuse Sackings in Burundi'; Lynch, 'UN Says Its Workers Abuse Women in Congo' and UN News Center, 'Heeding Annan's Zero-Tolerance on Sex Abuse, UN Suspends Two Soldiers in Burundi' (17 December 2004) <http://www.un.org/apps/news/story.asp?NewsID=12853&Cr=sex&Cr1>, in which the UN did not disclose the nationality of the alleged perpetrators. However, the UN has occasionally revealed the nationality of suspects in its news pieces, amongst which are: UN News Center, 'Haiti – Three UN Peacekeepers Repatriated for Sexual Abuse' (13 March 2012) <http://www.un.org/apps/news/story.asp?NewsID=41538#.VUJL-mZzdWo>, and 'UN Says Scores Of Peacekeepers Ousted for Abuse'. UNGA, 2015 SEA Report.

159 Zeid Report, para. 82.

160 This reluctance may either be as a result of the UN's fear that if it reveals information, some States may be unwilling to send further personnel, or it might actually be the case that some States may be unwilling to send more officers. See above, introductory section. In this regard, note that an OIOS report stated that '[i]t should be noted that it was the intention of OIOS to name the troop contributing countries whose soldiers had been identified as having exploited and abused the local female population'. Instead, the DPKO decided to send the OIOS file to the sending States, but not to reveal the names of those States. UNGA, *Investigation by the Office of Internal Oversight Services into allegations of sexual exploitation and abuse in the United Nations Organization Mission in the Democratic Republic of the Congo* (5 January 2005), para. 29.

of those involved in substantiated allegations. It is difficult to comprehend the reason for this, other than that the UN does not want to reveal the extent to which the preponderance of violations is committed by police from certain States, particularly if these States are reliable sources of police officers for UN missions.[161] The UN may be desperate to secure sufficient UN police personnel, and thus may not wish to displease any sending States by naming them.[162]

Therefore, virtually the only information available is that provided in the author's data. Three States – the United States, Pakistan and Jordan – were identified as those whose UN police officers were frequently complained about. This is unsurprising, as these three States have been important contributors of both UN police and military contingents.[163] Even if a disproportionately large number of allegations were in fact made against officers from these three countries, it is impossible to draw any conclusions as to why these officers have received the most allegations, due to the limitations of the available information. More generally, it is wondered if UN police from States with poor human rights records have a higher rate of engaging in criminal conduct, or whether the professional pride that police officers from some States have may tend to assist in preventing criminal conduct. It is also possible that UN police officers from countries with repressive public cultures may be more likely to seize the opportunity to engage in criminal conduct of a sexual nature when abroad.[164] If police officers from certain sending States are subject to higher rates of al-

---

161 As mentioned above, some of the largest contributors of uniformed personnel have expressed concerns about being named as the result of misconduct by a few of their personnel. Fleshman, *Tough UN Line on Peacekeeper Abuses.*

162 '[T]he UN itself does not make it a practice to chastise the member countries which send abusive peacekeepers because of the fear that it will lose a source of volunteer peacekeepers if it offends the sending nation'. Alexandra R Harrington, 'Victims of Peace: Current Abuse Allegations Against UN Peacekeepers and the Role of Law in Preventing Them in the Future' (2005) 12 *ILSA Journal of International & Comparative Law* 125, p. 139. In addition, the Secretary-General admitted that the UN had no other choice but to use Fijian soldiers despite their involvement in the military coup in Fiji. Tracey Watkins, 'Ban Ki-Moon Backs UN Use of Fiji Soldiers' *Fairfax News NZ* (7 September 2011) <http://www.stuff.co.nz/national/politics/5577793/Ban-Ki-moon-backs-UN-use-of-Fiji-soldiers> accessed 24 August 2014. See also Chapter 2, Section 3-3; Chapter 4, Sections 3-4 and 3-5.

163 In April 2001, the US, Jordan and Pakistan were the first, second and fifth biggest police sending States. In April 2013, the US no longer sent large numbers of police, but Jordan and Pakistan remained the second and sixth biggest police sending States. UN DPKO, 'Fact Sheet archive' <http://www.un.org/en/peacekeeping/resources/statistics/factsheet_archive.shtml>.

164 In this regard, it is reported that a factor that increases misconduct is that Peace Operations personnel are removed from their cultural constraints back home. Fleshman, *Tough UN Line on Peacekeeper Abuses.*

legations of misconduct, and if some of these States are among the primary contributors of police officers, it may be possible that the major shift in sending States has resulted in an increase in the number of allegations made.[165]

2-4 *Possible Reasons for the Patterns*

The number of allegations of criminal conduct in early operations by the UN police was low. There may be a several reasons for this. First, it could have been lower because the number of UN Peace Operations and UN police personnel were also low. Second, it may have been because the actual rate of misconduct was low. If so, this may be due to the fact that the UN police were mostly limited to carrying out monitoring and advising functions.[166] Third, it is also possible that the real rate of misconduct was higher, but that these rates were not made public by the UN. In addition, the absence of media reports of misconduct may have added to the impression that the UN police were not committing many crimes. Fourth, it may be because the UN was not equipped to handle complaints in a systematic manner, and/or it had limited machinery for doing so. Fifth, it may be because general awareness amongst the local population of what to do in the case of misconduct was low, or that victims did not lodge complaints for some reason. Finally, it may be a combination of all of these possibilities.

Where increased numbers of reports of alleged criminal conduct surface, there may be a number of possible causes for this increase. One factor is the size of the mission. For example, in relation to the disproportionate reporting on UNTAC when compared to ONUSAL,[167] UNTAC had about ten times more UN police personnel and 43 times more military personnel compared to ONUSAL.[168] This, and the different durations of missions, could partially explain the difference in numbers of reported misconduct between UNPROFOR and missions in Angola.[169]

165 See Chapter 2, Section 3-3-1.

166 See Chapter 2, Section 1.

167 See Sections 1 and 2-1.

168 UN DPKO, 'El Salvador – ONUSAL Facts and Figures' <http://www.un.org/en/peacekeeping/missions/past/onusalfacts.html> accessed 22 August 2014; UN DPKO, 'UNTAC Facts' <http://www.un.org/en/peacekeeping/missions/past/untacfacts.html>.

169 UNPROFOR had 38,599 military personnel, including 684 Military Observers, 803 UN police officers and, separately, civilian personnel. UN DPKO, 'Former Yugoslavia – UNPROFOR' <http://www.un.org/en/peacekeeping/missions/past/unprof_p.htm>. On the other hand, at their peaks, UNAVEM I had only 70 Military Observers; UNAVEM II had a maximum of 350 military and 126 UN police personnel; UNAVEM III had 286 Military Observers, 3,649 troops, and 288 UN police personnel. UN DPKO, 'UNAVEM I Figures' <http://

Another factor may be the functions carried out by the UN police. For example, UNTAC police and, in fact, the mandate for the UNTAC mission in general, had much broader functions than ONUSAL.[170] It is also observed that relatively limited monitoring missions, such as the UN Mission for the Referendum in Western Sahara (MINURSO), were not subject to any public allegations of misconduct by Peace Operations personnel.[171] On the other hand, the UN Observer Mission in Sierra Leone (UNOMSIL) had many reports of misconduct laid against its personnel,[172] despite the fact that it was a very limited mission in terms of its size.[173] A military presence or general lawlessness could also contribute to a high rate of reported misbehaviour.

The rate of reporting may also be linked to the size of the military. UNTAC and ONUSAL had significantly different military presences.[174] This may or may not be linked to the general lawlessness in the host States. This may also have been triggered by the lack of preparedness and planning of the mission,[175] which in turn may have exacerbated a sense of lawlessness.

---

www.un.org/depts/DPKO/Missions/unavem1/UnavemIF.html>, UN DPKO, 'UNAVEM II Facts' <http://www.un.org/en/peacekeeping/missions/past/Unavem2/UnavemIIF.html>, UN DPKO, 'UNAVEM III' <http://www.un.org/Depts/DPKO/Missions/unavem_f.htm>.

170 See Chapter 2, Section 1-3. If any crimes are committed which do not fall within their official functions, then the mandate of the mission concerned is irrelevant.

171 There is no entry regarding allegations of misconduct in MINURSO in the author's data.

172 The author's data have fourteen entries for misconduct committed by personnel associated with UNOMSIL. The sources are: UNGA, OIOS West Africa Report; UN OCHA, Humanitarian Situation Report – Sierra Leone, February 01–28 2002; UN OHCHR, *Africa Quarterly Report*; 'Child Refugee Sex Scandal'; 'Sex-for-Aid Under UN Spotlight'; 'Aid-for-Sex Children Speak Out'; 'African Refugees Condemn Sex Abuses'; AFP, 'UN Says It Has Insufficient Evidence of Sexual Exploitation by Staff' (*Reliefweb*, 1 March 2002) <http://www.reliefweb.int/w/RWB.NSF/s/1D842B6723EC082BC1256B6F005D68CC> accessed 30 August 2015.

173 It had 210 Military Observers, 35 medical personnel, 107 international civilian staff, and 69 locally recruited staff. UN DPKO, 'Sierra Leone – UNOMSIL Facts and Figures' <http://www.un.org/en/peacekeeping/missions/past/unomsil/UnomsilF.html> accessed 22 August 2014.

174 UNTAC had 15,991 members of military at its peak. This appears to include both members of national contingents and Military Observers. UN DPKO, 'UNTAC Facts' <http://www.un.org/en/peacekeeping/missions/past/untacfacts.html>. ONUSAL had no national military contingents. It had 368 Military Observers at its peak. UN DPKO, 'El Salvador – ONUSAL Facts and Figures' <http://www.un.org/en/peacekeeping/missions/past/onusal facts.html>.

175 UNITAR and IPS, *UNTAC debriefing*, p. 17.

In some missions, it is possible that complaints about the behaviour of the UN police were better publicized than those against the military, possibly because complaints against military may have been handled within the contingent. It may also be the case that different complaint handling mechanisms in the case of the UN police and the military led to different levels of public reporting.

One convincing reason for the disproportionate reporting on allegations of criminal conduct appears to be the similarly disproportionate attention paid to certain missions or areas. Missions in the Balkans, Somalia and Sierra Leone attracted the most reports during the mid-1990s. In the Balkans, there were reports of human trafficking.[176] In Somalia, a few cases of severe ill-treatment of local persons by military members were widely reported.[177] UNOMSIL operated in an area where widespread sexual exploitation and abuse by humanitarian workers was reported.[178] It is probably partly due to the fact that data collection and information provided by the UN were not systematic in the 1990s. The UN typically responded to public scandals on an *ad hoc* basis.[179] In the missions mentioned above, it was alleged was that those cases were not isolated; rather, they were part of a widespread problem.

A comparatively high number of allegations against UNMIK and UNTAET personnel may be related to the very particular executive policing functions[180] the UN police carried out. It may also be proximity to the local population that resulted in a larger number of reports of criminal conduct. It is also possible that there were better complaint mechanisms in place for those missions. In other words, because the UN police were required to deliver all policing

---

176 See Section 2-1.

177 (*Social Council Research Council*) <http://www.ssrc.org/programs/gsc/gsc_quarterly/newsletter5/content/graybill.page/> accessed 15 August 2006; 'Somalia: Atrocities Committed by UN Troops' (*OZ*) <http://www.oz.net/~vvawai/sw/sw35/somalia.html> accessed 15 August 2005; 'UN Atrocities in Somalia' (*Shire*) <http://www.shire.net/big.brother/unatroc.htm> accessed 25 August 2006; Donald Charles Daniel and Bradd C Hayes, *Coercive Inducement and the Containment of International Crises* (US Institute of Peace Press 1999); Omaar and Waal, *Somalia – Human Rights Abuses by the United Nations Forces* Walsh and Byrne, 'UN Peacekeepers Criticized'; Zacarias, *The United Nations and International Peacekeeping*.

178 UNHCR and Save the Children-UK, *Note for Implementing and Operational Partners on Sexual Violence & Exploitation: The Experience of Refugee Children in Guinea, Liberia and Sierra Leone based on Initial Findings and Recommendations from Assessment Mission 22 October–30 November 2001* (February 2002), pp. 6–7; UNGA, OIOS West Africa Report.

179 See Chapter 4, Section 2 for the evolution of the system within the UN.

180 See Chapter 2, Section 1-5.

functions, they may have had more opportunities to commit crimes. Another possible explanation is that the record-keeping of allegations had improved. Alternatively, it could have been due to the fact that the UN was exercising governmental functions in these States. This meant that the pressure the UN was under to establish appropriate complaints intake and response machineries was greater than in other missions. If the establishment of these machineries is identified as the main reason for the high number of allegations, this may indicate that the scale of criminal misconduct in UNMIK and UNTAET reflect the actual scale of wrongdoing in other missions.

Since 2000, a few factors have emerged which may have a significant distorting effect on the numbers of complaints. One is that the UN's internal mechanisms for receiving, recording and responding to complaints have been rapidly developed,[181] which may have a big effect on the actual rate of complaints. If victims are more aware of, or more confident in, the internal mechanisms, it may be more likely that people would actually report misconduct. It could also mean that the characteristics of missions established after 2000 are such that Peace Operations personnel are likely to have more opportunities to engage in criminal conduct, or that people have gained more confidence in making complaints in the new missions. It is also possible that the cultural setting in States hosting these new missions is such that people are more likely to complain. Perhaps it is a combination of some of the potential reasons identified. However, it is impossible to identify reasons with any precision.

Care also needs to be taken in concluding that crimes of a sexual nature are the biggest problem for Peace Operations. As a result of public reports beginning to focus on sexual offences,[182] especially reports about sexual exploitation and abuse,[183] the UN started paying special attention to preventing sexual misconduct.[184] This may have distorted the information in many different ways. There may be more complaints about offences of this nature. The UN may respond to sexual offences more vigorously than other crimes if it considers sexual offences a priority. It may also be the case that the greater the attention paid to sexual offences, the greater the number of reports there would be of this category of offence.

The different rates of allegations of sexual crimes against different categories of personnel may be related to the extent of the contact they have with the

---

181 For the evolution of internal machineries, see Chapter 4, Section 2.

182 See Sections and 2-2-1.

183 UNGA, Zeid Report.

184 On the measures the UN has put in place to prevent sexual exploitation and abuse, see Chapter 4, Section 3-1-1.

local population. It is also a possibility that, where sexual misconduct is concerned, there is an increasing tendency amongst uniformed personnel to close ranks.[185] It is also possible that the new arrangements for investigating military contingent members have been working effectively, as there have been fewer reports made to the UN. All cases of sexual exploitation and abuse, no matter which category of personnel the suspect belongs to, are to be reported to the UN.[186] Thus the CDU should have a complete record of these, except for those reported directly to the OIOS.[187]

In relation to traffic offences, the low rate of reports may be an indication that the UN does not consider these to be sufficiently serious, or does not prioritize these. It may be because at least some of the cases may be subject to different internal proceedings.[188] It may be that the UN compensates the victim for any injury or damage to his property (or the victim's family in case of the victim's death),[189] and conducts no other proceedings, even where there was fault on the driver's part. It may also be that motoring offences are not well reported by the media and NGOs.

3 Evidence of Prosecution

If it is difficult to find information regarding misconduct, this difficulty is multiplied when attempting to find out what happened to the suspect.

During the mid-1990s in the Balkans, the problem was not only the type of crime committed, but also the ineffective action taken by the UN in response to these crimes. One prime example is the summary dismissal of whistleblowers, who suggested that human trafficking was not only widespread, but also that it took place with the acquiescence of some parts of the institution.[190] There were accounts of dismissals of UN police officers on disciplinary grounds, but

185 UN OIOS, 'Report of the Office of Internal Oversight Services on its Investigation into Allegations of Sexual Exploitation and Abuse in the Ituri Region (Bunia) in the United Nations Organization Mission in the Democratic Republic of the Congo' UN Doc. A/61/841, paras. 37–38; UNGA, 2011 OIOS PKO Report, para. 98. These reports dealt mainly with the military; however, the same tendency may exist within the UN police. See also n.122, above.

186 See Chapter 4, Section 3-1 (2) for the duty to report sexual exploitation and abuse.

187 On the relationship between the CDU and OIOS, see Chapter 4, Section 2.

188 See Chapter 4, Section 2 for different kinds of internal proceedings.

189 Claims for compensation are normally dealt with by the Civil Claims Unit. On available mechanisms, see Chapter 4, Section 2.

190 Bolkovac, *The Whistleblower: Sex Trafficking, Military Contractors, and One Woman's Fight for Justice*.

there was little recognition by the sending States that they should develop standard procedures for bringing criminal proceedings against UN police personnel who committed criminal offences.[191]

As demonstrated, attempts to bring criminal proceedings against mission personnel in the host State were made in those missions where the UN acted as the government.[192] Elsewhere, it appears that prosecutions were much less likely to occur. Prince Zeid suggested that the perception of impunity was widespread among the population, and that this perception was well-founded.[193] Where criminal proceedings were not brought in the host State, it could have been because the suspect was not present in that State: either he could have fled the host State, or finished his tour of duty, or has been sent back to his sending State as a disciplinary sanction, or been withdrawn by his sending State from the host State. It could also be because the host State could not gather the information necessary for prosecution. It could be because the capacity of the national legal system was weak or non-existent. In some cases, there may have been no legal system at all, or, if there was a legal system in place, it was not functional. Another possibility is that immunity worked as a barrier to bringing criminal proceedings. In some cases, immunity may have affected the host State's access to a witness, if the witness was one of the UN personnel. Even if immunity did not apply in a particular case, the national prosecutor may nevertheless have assumed that it was not possible to bring proceedings against a UN police officer on this basis.

In recent years, in particular since the new Memorandum of Understanding (MoU) was signed between the UN and the sending States of FPUs,[194] the

---

191 A report states that, by the end of 2002, 57 UNMIK Police were repatriated or dismissed. Amnesty International, 'Kosovo (Serbia and Montenegro): "So Does It Mean That We Have the Rights?" Protecting the Human Rights of Women and Girls Trafficked for Forced Prostitution in Kosovo', (2004). Those officers who were found to lack required skills were also repatriated. See, for example, for ONUMOZ, Ali Mahmoud, 'UN Operation in Mozambique (ONUMOZ)' in Nassrine Azimi (ed), *The Role and Functions of Civilian Police in United Nations Peace-Keeping Operations: Debriefing and Lessons* (Kluwer Law International 1996), p. 49; for UNAVEM, Muhammad Anwarul Iqbal, 'An Overview of the CIVPOL Operations in Angola (UNAVEM)' in Nassrin Azimi (ed), *The Role and Functions of Civilian Police in United Nations Peace-Keeping Operations: Debriefing and Lessons* (Kluwer Law International 1996), p. 98; Kjell Johansen, 'Civilian Police in Former Yugoslavia (UNPROFOR)' in Nassrine Azimi (ed), *The Role and Functions of Civilian Police in United Nations Peace-Keeping Operations: Debriefing and Lessons* (Kluwer International 1996), p. 119.

192 See Section 1.

193 UNGA, Zeid Report, para. 38.

194 UN, 'Model Memorandum of Understanding between the United Nations and the xxx Contributing Resources to the xxxx' UN Doc. (on file with author).

UN has increasingly aimed for UN police personnel to be held to account by their sending States. Currently, the UN refers a case to the sending State, and occasionally follows up with it as to what may have happened to the suspect. Information dealing with these follow-ups is very limited. The CDU publishes the number of follow-up communications that the UN has with sending States. The UN appears to have been more likely to follow up on allegations of crimes other than those dealing with sexual exploitation and abuse. With regard to sexual exploitation and abuse cases, the UN has sent between 47 and 82 items of correspondence to sending States every year between 2007 and 2014.[195] However, this information does not reveal what type of communication was sent or what the nature is of the information included in the correspondence. The UN has received widely differing numbers of responses to such inquiries.[196] Again, the type of communications sent to the UN, and the nature of the responses is not revealed.[197] The information shows only that 45.8 percent of follow-up correspondence relating to sexual exploitation and abuse cases precipitated some kind of response from States, whilst 41.6 percent of follow-ups in relation to other allegations were responded to by States. The fact that more than half of the inquiries were ignored is worrying. It may indicate that the UN is not sufficiently persistent in asking for information regarding measures taken against repatriated UN police personnel. If the UN requires sending States to prosecute their police officers upon repatriation, it needs to put more effort into checking whether this occurs. If the UN does not go further than sending a letter about substantiated offences, it cannot be said to be sufficiently serious about prosecution.

If it is the case that the UN only seeks to ensure prosecution in relation to crimes against the person, it may indicate that the UN does not consider other crimes to be equally serious, or that it may have decided not to prosecute other types of crime, given its priorities and resources. It may also be that some types of crimes are more appropriately responded to using other forms of proceedings. It may be that fraud or theft of property or money from the UN is seen by the UN as an internal matter. If the UN fires the personnel and recovers the property or money, it may consider this sufficient. Where the

195 Between 2007 and 2014, the UN sent 67, 69, 82, 74, 60, 47, 70 and 61 items of correspondence respectively.

196 Between 2007 and 2014, the UN received 23, 8, 14, 29, 26, 27, 64 and 52 responses respectively.

197 In these instances, between 2007 and 2014, the UN sent 72, 109, 74, 14, 84, 106, 78 and 102 items of correspondence, to which 16, 24, 24, 3, 28, 38, 71 and 62 responses were received. UN CDU, 'Statistics' <https://cdu.unlb.org/Statistics/OverviewofStatistics.aspx>.

local population is not aware of an offence, they do not stand to lose as much as where there is a lack of criminal proceedings. Nevertheless, the prosecution of such crimes may work as a deterrent for future offences of a similar kind.

Likewise, criminal proceedings do not appear to be instituted for traffic offences across the board. The UN normally convenes an internal administrative inquiry into the facts and, for UN police personnel, facts can be sent to the sending States.[198] At the same time, the Claims Unit – the internal body within each UN mission that deals with third-party claims of a civil nature – may deal with compensation matters.[199] This may be a sign that the UN does not consider traffic offences sufficiently serious, even where personnel were negligent or at fault. This is problematic. Traffic offences in which local persons are either injured or killed are very noticeable to the local population. If these offences become public knowledge, but no action is taken against the offenders, this may cause serious damage to the mission's reputation. Furthermore, it may set a bad example for the accountability of the police in the host State.

4 Conclusion

The scale and nature of allegations of criminal offences by UN police personnel have been shown to represent a threat to the legitimacy of missions. Where no action is taken, the damage is even greater, and there is a danger that irreparable harm may be caused not only to the mission, but also to the host State.

After the rapid increase in the number of allegations of misconduct in early 1990s, in particular in respect of UNTAC, allegations of misconduct continue to be made. The mid-1990s were particularly bad in this regard, mainly in relation to Transitional Administrations. It was also shown that allegations have been concentrated in certain missions. No determinative correlations between the functions and the scale of allegations could be found, but many of the missions subject to large numbers of allegations had ambitious mandates, as well as police functions related to carrying out or reforming the local police.

Offences against the person constitute a high proportion of criminal conduct. According to the author's data, about 82 percent of allegations fall into this category, with offences of a sexual nature being the most commonly

198 See Chapter 4, Sections 3-4 and 3-5.

199 See Kirsten Schmalenbach, 'Third Party Liability of International Organizations – A Study on Claim Settlement in the Course of Military Operations and International Administrations' (2006) 19 *Journal of International Peacekeeping* 33, p. 43.

reported.[200] This may indicate that the personal qualities of UN police officers may have the greatest impact on the rate and nature of the crimes committed.[201] According to the CDU's data, about half the allegations of serious misconduct relate to sexual exploitation and abuse. In addition, traffic offences affecting third persons appear to be frequent. Offences affecting the local population directly or indirectly include theft and fraud. These offences are problematic, as they impact on the effectiveness of the mission, but the rate of these offences by UN police personnel has been low.

The information located indicates that only a handful of cases have reached the stage of criminal prosecution in a legal forum. According to the author's data, criminal proceedings in a host State have taken place in only two cases, excluding those dealt with by Transitional Administrations. For the rest, information was either not readily available, or it may be that nothing happened to the suspect.

It was established that a majority of offences have nothing to do with the functions carried out by the UN police.[202] This finding necessitates research into what else could be done to reduce the likelihood of crimes occurring. In addition to operational measures, if individuals are effectively called to account, this might introduce a deterrent effect.

The uncertainty as to the existence of a standardized and proactive system for registering complaints, the lack of disaggregation of allegations into different categories of crimes (whether the acts were part of official functions, or by the suspect's nationality), all made it difficult to evaluate the scale and nature of the problem. Given the importance of the issue for the effectiveness and legitimacy of the missions and the reputation of the UN, greater transparency might have the beneficial effect of reducing the incidence of criminal behaviour. The sending State might be motivated by embarrassment to take more effective action, both before deployment and after repatriation. The same would be true in relation to follow-ups conducted by the UN. It is not clear whether the fear of the impact on recruitment is well-founded, or whether it is a pretext on the part of States, or the UN itself.

Thus, the next step is to consider what system the UN has in place for collecting, registering and centralizing information regarding allegations of misconduct committed in host States.

---

200 73 of 89 entries fell into this category.

201 On the personal qualities required, see Chapter 2, Section 3-2.

202 This has implications for the applicability of immunity for the UN police officers concerned. See Chapter 6, Sections 1-4-1 and 1-4-2.

CHAPTER 4

Current UN Machinery for Collecting Information Regarding Alleged Crimes for Domestic Criminal Proceedings

The previous chapter revealed evidence of crimes committed by UN police officers, and an apparent lack of criminal proceedings against the alleged offenders. Obviously, the UN does not simply ignore all these allegations. It has internal mechanisms for dealing with complaints of misconduct. It is thus essential to consider these mechanisms, even though their proceedings, as such, and the penalties they impose are not relevant because of their administrative and disciplinary nature. As a result, this Chapter does not provide a general description of the existing UN mechanisms. Rather, it will consider these mechanisms in light of the roles they play in assisting in the collection of evidence on the basis of which States may bring criminal proceedings. What matters is that they collect sufficient evidence of the right type so as to enable domestic courts to institute proceedings. It is also important for the UN to conduct proper follow up with States in order to secure criminal proceedings.

Since the crimes are committed in the host State, problems surrounding access to evidence, victims and witnesses do not normally arise for that State. If the host State is willing to investigate, and is capable of doing so,[1] it can investigate independently of the UN. It is more of a problem for sending States, as they are peculiarly dependent on the evidence collected during the UN's investigation process. For that reason, this Chapter will focus on sending States.

1 That is, in instances where the conduct is not carried out in the course of the official functions as, in that case, UN immunity does not prevent the host State from investigating. Where the host State is unsure about whether the conduct in question is covered by immunity, it may be reluctant to conduct an investigation. In addition, if, for example, it takes time to determine whether the conduct is related to the suspect's official functions, it may be problematic if the host State authorities have no access to the suspect during that period. This is primarily the case in relation to determining whether the suspect has immunity, or whether that immunity is to be waived. For details, see Chapter 6, Section 1-5. In addition, States hosting recent operations typically have no functioning legal system. In that case, the host State may not be able to investigate an allegation. See Chapter 2, Section 1. Moreover, if part of the role of UN police is to assist in the establishment of a functioning legal system, it may be in the UN's interest not to overburden the system with too many cases. See Chapter 6, Section 1-4.

 | DOI 10.1163/9789004328815_005

1 Benchmarks

The ultimate goal is to ensure that an individual UN police officer, who has allegedly engaged in criminal behaviour while on a UN operation, is subject to criminal proceedings and, if convicted, is given an appropriate criminal penalty. This work therefore examines whether the existing mechanism within the UN, and the arrangements between the UN and the States concerned, constitute an appropriate vehicle for facilitating that goal. In other words, if any step in the process – from the alleged commission of a crime to its potential prosecution and subsequent proceedings – is not designed and does not function in a manner that enables States to prosecute the personnel concerned, it will increase the risk of impunity. In order for the system that is currently in place to meet the desired goal, there appear to be four main benchmarks that should be met.[2]

Benchmark 1

First, the mechanism needs to investigate all matters that should be referred for domestic proceedings. In order for this to happen, the information needs to reach the Organization. For that to happen, persons both external and internal to the Organization need to know that certain conduct may amount to a crime, and that there are means for making a complaint. Those places where complaints may be made must be practically accessible to the public, without posing direct or indirect difficulties for any group of individuals, for example, illiterate and/or vulnerable people. The mechanism must be, and must be perceived as being, fair and effective, as people would be unlikely to lodge a complaint if they were not confident that their complaints would be taken seriously. When a complaint is lodged, the information must be centralized and properly registered. The information must be sent promptly to the appropriate bodies. Where criminal conduct is suspected, the relevant information must be sent promptly to an investigative body that deals with misconduct of a criminal nature. Determining whether or not an allegation contains criminal elements may require a preliminary investigation.

Benchmark 2

Second, alleged crimes must be properly investigated. Here, International Human Rights Law (IHRL) provides guidance as to what qualifies as an effective investigation. Where an allegation of criminal conduct is made, an

---

2 The benchmarks identified below do not derive from the UN's internal rules or policies, or any legal provisions of international law.

investigation needs to be commenced as soon as possible by professional investigators, so that all the potential evidence can be gathered effectively. The investigation should be conducted thoroughly, and by sufficiently independent investigators.[3] This means that the alleged offence cannot be investigated by a UN police officer working under or alongside the alleged offender. Given the way UN police personnel are deployed,[4] there may be a problem if the investigation is conducted by UN police personnel sharing the same nationality.[5] This would mean that allegations against FPU personnel should not be investigated by members of the same FPU. It would be desirable if investigators were appointed from outside the UN police, but where the UN police have only a small mission presence, this may be unrealistic. In such cases, those UN police officers tasked with investigating misconduct by the UN police should do just that. A thorough and effective investigation is required, leading to a determination of the facts and the identification of the perpetrator.[6] This can only be achieved with sufficient resources. For this reason, it would be desirable for the mission to have investigators who are assigned solely to investigate any alleged misconduct. An investigation must include the collection of physical evidence. This necessitates access to technical resources such as forensics, finger-print identification tools, autopsies, and crime scene investigation facilities.[7] In certain types of cases, information technology forensics may also be useful.

The second strand of this benchmark concerns the kind of information collected. In order for evidence to be used in criminal proceedings, it must be collected in such a way that it conforms with the rules of evidence in the jurisdiction where prosecution may take place. Where the overall procedure is not considered fair, there may be issues under IHRL.[8] There could be additional complex issues, as different States have different rules and standards

---

3 For more details on the requirements under IHRL, see Chapter 7, Section 3-1.

4 For the process of selection and deployment of UN police personnel, see Chapter 2, Section 3-3-1.

5 On the other hand, if the evidence is collected by investigators with the same nationality, this may help in the provision of appropriate evidence for use in their State's domestic criminal courts. For problems relating to the evidential standard, see Sections 3-3-1 and 3-3-2.

6 On the requirement under IHRL that an investigation be effective, see Chapter 7, Section 3-1.

7 Erling Grimstad, *Final Report, Review of the OIOS Investigations Division, United Nations* (Submitted to the Under-Secretary-General of Office of Internal Oversight Services, 2007), pp. 65–66, (hereinafter 'ID Review').

8 Issues relating to the due process rights of the personnel alleged to have committed a crime were raised in relation to the host State by the UN in its determination of the applicability of immunity, and the consideration of waiver. See Chapter 6, Section 1. Similar issues can also arise in relation to the sending State. See Chapter 6, Section 3-2.

of evidence. It is particularly problematic for proceedings in sending States, as their rules vary.[9] Evidence collected in a way which does not meet the prosecuting State's domestic legal requirements may not be useable. For example, some States only allow evidence gathered by specifically authorized persons to be presented in court.[10] Only some States allow hearsay to be used as evidence in court.[11] Some do not accept evidence that is collected in an unlawful manner.[12] There may also be issues in relation to the requirement that the chain of custody of evidence be properly recorded, in order for it to be usable in criminal proceedings.[13]

Benchmark 3

Benchmark 3 requires that the evidence gathered be made available to relevant States. This is because States, in particular sending States, are reliant on the information collected by the UN.[14] Thus, the procedure for referring or providing information about a case to the State concerned needs to be systematized. Many issues, such as those concerning the methods of investigation and evidential rules, may not arise in relation to the host State.[15] While it is legitimate to prioritize some criminal cases over others, decisions regarding referral must be subject to oversight at the point of referral to ensure that no serious criminal cases are neglected.

---

9 In this regard, it was observed that, '[c]omplying with the criminal investigative requirements of all UN staff contributing countries, particularly where criminal investigations are the prerogative of an investigating judge, could prove quite difficult for even the most professional of UN investigators'. William J Durch et al., *Improving Criminal Accountability in United Nations Peace Operations* (Stimson Center Report, 2009), p. 10, (hereinafter 'Improving Criminal Accountability').

10 UNGA, 'Report of the Ad Hoc Committee on Criminal Accountability of United Nations Officials and Experts on Mission' (15 April 2008) UN Doc. A/63/54, para. 17.

11 Hearsay evidence consists of statements made by witnesses outside a court setting. More States are excluding this evidence from being presented in court. David Alan Sklansky, 'Hearsay's Last Hurrah' (2009) 1 *Supreme Court Review* 1, p. 2.

12 For example, the 'fruit of the poisonous tree' doctrine is applied in the United States. This rejects the use of evidence gathered by unlawful means, including by unlawful search. *US v Rey* 663 F 2d 1086 DNM (2009); *Wong Sun et al. v US* 371 US 471 (1963), 83 S Ct 407; 9 L Ed 2d 441; 1963 US LEXIS 2431.

13 For example, under the US Federal Rules of Evidence, the establishment of the chain of custody is a requirement in order for evidence to be admissible. Jefferson L Ingram, *Criminal Evidence* (Elsevier 2011), pp. 582–584.

14 See introductory section above.

15 In relation to the host State, the investigative phases from information collection to investigation can, in principle, be independently conducted by the host State authorities parallel to the UN proceedings. See the text accompanying n. 1.

Benchmark 4

The last benchmark concerns issues arising after a case has been referred to the national authorities. The UN should conduct an effective follow-up with the relevant authorities to ensure that criminal misconduct is prosecuted, because there is a risk of impunity if it fails to do so. The risk would be higher if the State concerned were not willing to prosecute the accused personnel.[16] This means that the UN should check systematically with the State concerned regarding its decisions to prosecute or not to prosecute, its reasons for non-prosecution, the findings by any national inquiry into the alleged criminal conduct, and any sanctions imposed. It is foreseeable that sending States may need additional information, or evidence that is collected in a different way. The host State is able to do these things for itself, subject to any limits on its capacity to investigate an allegation, and issues of immunity.[17] The UN needs to create a mechanism to respond to requests for additional evidence or information.[18]

Central to these benchmarks is how effective each identified step is in ensuring that the individual UN police officers alleged to have committed crimes face criminal proceedings and, if convicted, face appropriate criminal penalties. The issue which arises is the degree to which virtually the only system[19] there is for investigating crimes committed by the UN police is capable of collecting evidence for criminal proceedings.

2 Evolution of the Approach to, and the Mechanisms for, Dealing with Criminal Misconduct

Prior to 1990, the means to process complaints against UN police personnel was not systemized.[20] An interesting field mechanism established in the 1970s

---

16 UNGA, 'Ensuring the Accountability of United Nations Staff and Experts on Mission with Respect to Criminal Acts Committed in Peacekeeping Operations' (16 August 2006) UN Doc. A/60/980, para. 84 (i).

17 See Section 3-3; Chapter 6, Section 1-4.

18 The need for a policy on how to deal with national authorities regarding criminal prosecution was identified earlier. In the early 2000s, such a policy did not exist. UN, 'Comprehensive Review of All Aspects of Boards of Inquiry Report' (2005) UN Doc. (on file with author), paras. 30–31, (hereinafter 'BoI Review').

19 This does not include cases where the host State investigates parallel to the UN's investigation. See the text accompanying n. 1.

20 The Field Administration Handbook of 1974 dealt with Military Observers, but not UN police officers. As an administrative category of personnel dealt with in the Handbook (Staff members, locally hired staff members, Representatives of States and Military Observers), Military Observers are the closest to the UN police. For Military Observers, the

was the Board of Inquiry, whose sole task was to collect facts regarding fatal or serious accidents involving UN staff members 'in the mission area'.[21] This mechanism was quite different from the later Boards of Inquiry, which were tasked to investigate misconduct. There was virtually no need for a complaint mechanism as very few allegations surfaced.[22] At that time, the only mode of recruitment of a UN police officer was through secondment by the sending State. This meant that sending States had relatively strong control over individual UN police personnel.[23] The limited number of both UN police personnel and sending States may also have contributed to the lack of alleged misbehaviour.[24]

In the 1990s, there began to be a more significant military and police presence,[25] and the UN began developing internal mechanisms.[26] This occurred around the time that Peace Operations changed their mandates from

---

Handbook described disciplinary procedures as coming under the authority of the Chief of Staff or Chief Military Observer. There was no set mechanism to conduct investigations of misconduct by UN police or Military Observers. UN, 'Field Administration Handbook' (January 1974) UN Doc. ST/OGS/L.2/Rev.3, p. F-5 (hereinafter 'FAH').

21 Ibid, p. D-59. This had nothing to do with criminal misconduct by UN police officers, but was a tool for investigating vehicular accidents. The Handbook did not specify that the Board was only established for that purpose, but that sub-section followed another sub-section which dealt with vehicular accidents ('Classification of Vehicle Accidents', p. D-58). Both sections came within the section dealing with General Services. Ibid, pp. D-58, D-59.

22 See Chapter 3, Sections 1 and 2-1.

23 Chapter 2, Section 3-3-1.

24 See Chapter 2, Section 1.

25 As described in Chapter 2, Section 1.

26 There is a record showing that the 'UN Field Administration Manual (FAM)' had relevant information on how to deal with complaints of misconduct. The FAM was reportedly transmitted to the Office of the Legal Affairs (OLA) for comments by the Director of Field Operations Division on 22 October 1992. However, apart from some excerpts in other materials, its content is not available. FAM was referred to in UN, 'Liability of the Organization for Claims Concerning Loss of or Damage to Personal Property of the Members of the Peacekeeping Contingents – Report of the Secretary-General Entitled 'Review of the Background and Development of Reimbursement to Member States Contributing Troops to Peacekeeping Operations' (A/44/605/Add.l) of 12 October 1989 – Financial Arrangements with States Contributing Troops for UNIFIL and UNFICYP – Reimbursability of Extra and Extraordinary Costs as They are Incurred by the States as a Result of their Soldiers' Participation in UNIFIL and UNFICYP – Loss and Damage to Personal Property Fall within the Category of Extra and Extraordinary Costs (15 July 1993)' (1993) 1993 UN Jurid YB 346, p. 346, (hereinafter 'Liability for UNIFIL and UNFICYP contingents').

monitoring to a more robust type of action.[27] The development of internal mechanisms may have come in response to reports of misconduct.[28] It may also have been due to the shift in the kind of allegations made, from those of a predominantly internal management type to individual misconduct complaints, which became more visible externally.[29] The UN needed to develop a field-based complaints system. In the mid-1990s, the UN started to use different *ad hoc* mechanisms to deal with the increasing number of complaints. The disciplinary measures for UN police personnel, although still *ad hoc*, were clarified to some extent, including confirmation that the Police Commissioner had the authority to discipline UN police officers. Around this time, it appears that the UN expanded its use of the Board of Inquiry (BoI).[30] At this stage, though, the rationale for BoI was the protection of the UN's financial interests.[31]

In the absence of standardized information collection procedures, complaints were lodged with different components. It appears that no personnel were assigned solely for the purpose of receiving or recording complaints,[32] or investigating misconduct allegations.[33] In general, little information is available on the details of the mechanism at that time. The issue of whether UN police personnel can and should be criminally prosecuted in the host State or

---

27 As analyzed in Chapter 2, Section 1.

28 In 2005, the OIOS found that the establishment of disciplinary mechanisms in the UN field missions had taken place in response to negative reports. UNGA, 'Report of the Office of Internal Oversight Services on the Global Review of Discipline in Field Missions led by the Department of Peacekeeping Operations' (8 March 2006) UN Doc. A/60/713, Summary, p. 2 (hereinafter 'OIOS Discipline Report'). See Chapter 3, Sections 1 and 2-1 for the details of these allegations.

29 As analyzed in Chapter 3, Sections 1, 2-1 and 2-2.

30 FAM, as cited above, has a chapter on the Board of Inquiry. Chapter 16, FAM, as cited in UN, Liability for UNIFIL and UNFICYP contingents, p. 346. The expanded model appears to be based on an earlier BoI. See the text accompanying n. 21.

31 The rationale for BoI in the FAM is found to be 'clearly financial'. UN, BoI Review.

32 The UN's internal directives are also silent on who should receive complaints. UN DPKO, 'Directives for Disciplinary Matters Involving Civilian Police Officers and Military Observers' (2003) UN Doc. DPKO/CPD/DDCPO/2003/001, DPKO/MD/03/00994, paras. 9–10, (hereinafter '2003 Directives'). It set out that any such allegation shall be reported to the Head of Mission directly or through a Personnel Conduct Officer. See also Françoise Hampson and Ai Kihara-Hunt, 'The Accountability of Personnel Associated with Peacekeeping Operations' in Chiyuki Aoi, Cedric De Coning and Ramesh Thakur (eds), *Unintended Consequences of Peacekeeping* (UNU 2007), p. 206, (hereinafter 'PKO Personnel Accountability').

33 See Section 5-3-3.

in their sending States did not really surface during this period. It was assumed that, if such a situation arose, prosecution would take place in the host State.[34]

Around the year 2000, those *ad hoc* measures began to be more systematized,[35] except for the complaints intake and registration, and the centralization of information. Instead, efforts were focused on clarifying disciplinary proceedings. The BoI was further developed as a primary vehicle for addressing misconduct in Peace Operations.[36] It was re-affirmed as an administrative body composed of three senior staff members. Its role was also clarified as being one which reviewed the findings of investigators and made recommendations regarding disciplinary action, if any, in individual cases of misconduct. Investigations were conducted by appointed investigators prior to Board proceedings, or by the Board members themselves,[37] which in reality

34 The UN's legal office (Office of Legal Affairs: OLA) concluded that the host State is able to prosecute UN police officers for criminal offences. UN, 'Letter to the Acting Chair of the Special Committee on Peacekeeping Operations, United Nations, Regarding Immunities of Civilian Police and Military Personnel' (2004) 2004 UN Jurid YB 323 (hereinafter 'OLA letter'.) OLA also held the opinion that the host State could prosecute UN police officers, thus repatriation is not provided for in the status-of-forces agreement (SOFA) or status-of-mission agreement (SOMA). UN, 'Legal Status of Certain Categories of United Nations Personnel Serving in Peacekeeping Operations – Civilian Police and Military Observers – Military Members of Military Components (3 May 2002)' (2002) 2002 UN Jurid YB 466, para. 6.

35 Parallel to the standardization of procedures, the UN also set up *ad hoc* codes and sections or offices within the mission. For example, UNMIK set up a Trafficking and Investigation Unit in 2001. Bruce Oswald and Sarah Jane Finnin, 'Combating the Trafficking of Persons on Peace Operations' (2006) 10 *International Peacekeeping: The Yearbook of International Peace Operations* 1, p. 22. This *ad hoc* response resulted in new mission appointments. In 2004, the first Personnel Conduct Officer was appointed to MONUC. Durch et al., *Improving Criminal Accountability*, p. 7.

36 UN DPKO, 'Directives for Disciplinary Matters Involving Civilian Police Officers and Military Observers' (2003) UN Doc. DPKO/CPD/DDCPO/2003/001; DPKO/MD/03/00994, in particular, paras. 15–22 (hereinafter '2003 Directives'). The *rationale* for BoI in the FAM was 'clearly financial'. UN, BoI Review, para. 15. However, over time, 'BOI reports have come to serve as the historical record of events and the rationale extends to assisting in determination of disciplinary measures that can be taken by the appropriate authorities, pursuance of criminal cases against individuals [...] among others'. Ibid, para. 16.

37 For Preliminary Investigations, see UN DPKO, 2003 Directives, para. 11 and Annex B, para. 2. The Board itself can seek expert advice. Ibid, Annex A, para. 2. In addition, '[i]n some instances, the BOI is asked to serve as the investigation that establishes the facts'. UN, BoI Review, para. 28.

often meant UN police personnel.[38] It is unknown how often UN police personnel who shared the suspect's nationality were involved in such investigations.

While the BoI system had advantages,[39] its major problem was resources. Investigators and Board members were selected and appointed by the Head of the Mission to carry out tasks for BoIs *in addition to* their normal functions. A BoI dealing with a UN police misconduct case was convened by the Head of Mission, and was composed of at least three senior staff members, including someone from the UN police.[40] The appointment of senior managers to the Board, in particular when allegations were frequently made, stretched their capacity.[41] These senior managers did not welcome having to perform the additional tasks sitting on BoIs required, and missions often had difficulties finding people to sit on the Boards.[42] This, along with confusion regarding the rules, may have contributed to BoI procedures being lengthy.[43] Neither the investigators conducting the preliminary investigation nor the Board members were professional investigators, which raised issues about the quality of their investigations.[44] As a result, the effectiveness of BoIs was questioned. In addition, the composition of some BoIs raised questions where their members

---

38 A UN report stated that many missions took advantage of police expertise in dealing with investigations, even though it was not referred to in the FAM. UN, BoI Review, para. 27. An independent report stated that excessive use of force cases are normally investigated by the internal affairs unit of the UN police. Annika S Hansen, *From Congo to Kosovo: Civilian Police in Peace Operations* (Oxford University Press for the International Institute for Strategic Studies 2002), p. 30. Another UN report in 2008 confirmed that the Internal Affairs Unit conducts investigations into disciplinary matters. UNGA, 'Report of the Secretary-General on the Comprehensive Report of Conduct and Discipline Including Full Justification of All Posts' (20 March 2008) UN Doc. A/62/758, paras. 23–28 (hereinafter '2008 Discipline Report'). Another independent study mentioned that the OIOS provides feedback on investigations to the relevant mission components. For UN police, the relevant component is its internal affairs unit. Durch et al., *Improving Criminal Accountability*, p. 13.

39 See Section 3-3-1 for details.

40 UN DPKO, 2003 Directives, paras. 17, 19–20.

41 It was documented that some members of BoIs were unwilling to serve on another Board. UN, BoI Review, para. 7.

42 Ibid, para. 7.

43 Ibid, para. 34. In 2011, with the new standing operating procedure (SOP) on Boards of Inquiry, a two-week time limit was set for the initiation of a BoI. UN DPKO/DFS, 'Standing Operating Procedure "Board of Inquiry"' (1 March 2011) UN Doc. Ref. 2011.15, (hereinafter '2011 BoI SOP').

44 The phrase 'enthusiastic amateurs' was used to describe those investigators in: UNGA, 'A Comprehensive Strategy to Eliminate Future Sexual Exploitation and Abuse in United

were drawn solely from one mission component.[45] Independent, prompt and thorough investigations, especially when faced with an increasing number of allegations, were not achieved with the BoI mechanism.

Parallel to the BoI system, the Office of the Internal Oversight Services (OIOS) was established in 1994. This Office was created as an oversight mechanism to assist the Secretary-General in delivering his internal oversight responsibilities, in order to increase the accountability of the UN as an organization.[46] The OIOS's initial remit was reviewing managerial responsibilities, auditing operations and evaluating the implementation of policies. The Investigation Division existed from the time the OIOS was created, but its focus was on managerial misconduct, misconduct involving personal disputes, and misconduct related to the management of funds, assets and procurement.[47] At the time the OIOS was established, BoIs constituted the main mechanism dealing with misconduct in Peace Operations.[48] With the publicity attracted by sexual exploitation and abuse (SEA) allegedly carried out by members of UN field presences in the early 2000s,[49] the UN's practice was severely criticized, most notably in

Nations Peacekeeping Operations' (24 March 2005) UN Doc. A/59/710 (hereinafter 'Zeid Report').

45 The lack of transparency was also raised. UN, BoI Review, para. 32.

46 UN OIOS, 'About Us' <http://www.un.org/Depts/oios/pages/about_us.html> accessed 8 October 2014. See also: UN, 'Secretary-General's Bulletin on the Establishment of the Office of the Oversight Services' (7 September 1994) UN Doc. ST/SGB/273, para. 10.

47 UNGA Res 48/218 B (12 August 1994) UN Doc. A/RES/48/218 B, op. para. 5 (c); and UN, 'Reporting of Inappropriate Use of United Nations Resources and Proposals for Improvement of Programme Delivery' (7 September 1994) UN Doc. ST/AI/397.

48 Internal Directives on disciplinary proceedings clearly stated that, within the mission, the BoI was the sole mechanism for dealing with serious misconduct, including criminal offences, by UN police officers. UN DPKO, 2003 Directives, para. 15. The Zeid Report noted that, where the OIOS was requested to investigate alleged misconduct, its investigations were to be considered as preliminary investigations for disciplinary purposes. UNGA, Zeid Report, para. 35.

49 UNGA, 'Investigation into Sexual Exploitation of Refugees by Aid Workers in West Africa' (11 October 2002) UN Doc. A/57/465 (hereinafter 'OIOS West Africa Report'); UNGA, 'Investigation by the Office of Internal Oversight Services into Allegations of Sexual Exploitation and Abuse in the United Nations Organization Mission in the Democratic Republic of the Congo' (5 January 2005) UN Doc. A/59/661 (hereinafter 'OIOS Congo Report'); UNGA, 'Report of the Office of Internal Oversight Services on its Investigation into Allegations of Sexual Exploitation and Abuse in the Ituri Region (Bunia) in the United Nations Organization Mission in the Democratic Republic of the Congo' (5 April 2007) UN Doc. A/61/841 (hereinafter 'OIOS Bunia Report').

the Zeid Report.[50] The Zeid Report highlighted the shortcomings of the UN's response at different stages of its investigations. One shortcoming which was addressed was the way investigations were conducted in the BoI system, which did not provide sufficient bases for criminal prosecutions in States willing to undertake these.[51] The Report further noted that the criticism that the Organization and its managers were unaccountable even when they failed to tackle the SEA problem was well-founded,[52] as UN efforts were *ad hoc* and inadequate.[53] It suggested a number of recommendations, including a change in the BoI system so as to entrust investigations to a more professional and independent body.[54] This worked as a major trigger for change.[55] The disadvantages of the BoI system became increasingly apparent: BoIs were time-consuming and resource-heavy,[56] and their procedures were assessed as unnecessary, and as duplicating other efforts.[57]

The UN took multiple steps in response to these criticisms. With the GA's endorsement,[58] the OIOS's investigative capacity was re-visited in 2005. Under the new arrangement, all serious misconduct, including criminal conduct

---

50 UNGA, Zeid Report.

51 Ibid, para. 28.

52 Ibid, para. 37.

53 Ibid, para. 11.

54 Ibid, para. 32.

55 Elizabeth F Defeis, 'UN Peacekeepers and Sexual Abuse and Exploitation: An End to Impunity' (2008) 7 *Washington University Global Study Law Review* 185, p. 186. Most of the Zeid Report's recommendations were accepted by the Secretary-General, and were followed up, including the standardization and clarification of rules, the use of professional investigation capacity, and the creation of oversight mechanisms for alleged misconduct and disciplinary issues.

56 Long delays in completing cases were identified as one of the problems related to BoIs. The average number of days needed to complete BoI proceedings for misconduct cases was 86.25 days. UN, BoI Review, paras. 2, 11.

57 Ibid, paras. 18–19. The Zeid Report also pointed out that the BoI procedures, which involved preliminary investigations, duplicated the work down in the BoI investigations. UNGA, Zeid Report, para. 29.

58 UNGA Res 59/287 (13 April 2005) UN Doc. A/RES/59/287; UNGA Res 59/300 (30 June 2005) UN Doc. A/RES/59/300; together with recommendations by the Special Committee on Peacekeeping Operations, as contained in the Official Record (UNGA, 'Report of the Special Committee on Peacekeeping Operations and its Working Group' [GAOR 59th Session Supp no 19, 31 January-25 February 2005; 4–8 April 2005] UN Doc. A/59/19/Rev.1). It was decided that cases of serious misconduct and/or criminal behaviour should be investigated by independent, professional investigators, and that the OIOS should be 'the internal body entrusted with investigations in the UN'. UNGA Res 59/287, op. para. 3.

and all SEA cases, were to be investigated by the OIOS Investigation Division.[59] Along with that change, the BoI system was streamlined. The use of BoIs was brought closer to their original administrative role, in that the Board did not itself conduct investigations.[60] As of 2011, BoIs are only mandatory in specific circumstances, that is, an incident or accident resulting in the death or serious injury of a mission member or a third party when a member of a mission personnel is involved; major loss or damage of UN property or third-party owned property when a mission member is involved; and major loss or damage of military/FPU contingent-owned equipment.[61] It is significant that all the circumstances in which BoIs are currently mandatory could involve criminal behaviour. Other cases were to be investigated by the OIOS, and followed up by the Department of Peacekeeping Operations (DPKO).[62] The authority of the BoI to recommend any action related to discipline, legal liability or compensation was removed.[63] It still retained fact-finding power (including making findings on the presence of personal fault), and to determine whether the act was committed as part of the official functions.[64] Parallel to that, a significant step was taken in 2005 with regard to the centralization of allegations, and the registration thereof: the creation of the Conduct and Discipline Team (CDT)/ Unit (CDU).[65] The CDU is located at the UN Headquarters, and provides 'overall

59 UN, 'Code Cable on the Guidance on Cooperation with OIOS on Investigation' (22 November 2005) UN Doc. (on file with author) (hereinafter 'Nov 2005 Code Cable'), para. 2; and '[a]uthority and responsibility for investigating all allegations of misconduct on the part of all UN personnel for high risk and complex cases has, in effect, been given to OIOS by General Assembly resolution 59/287'. Ibid, attached 'Interim procedures to implement General Assembly resolution 59/287 on investigations into misconduct in peacekeeping missions', para. 6.

60 The UN's internal directive stated in 2008 that BoIs are not 'an investigative nor judicial process', and they do not 'consider questions of compensation, legal liability or disciplinary action'. UN DPKO/DFS, 'Policy Directiveon the Boards of Inquiry' (27 May 2008) UN Doc. Ref. 2008.23, para. 3 (hereinafter '2008 BoI Directive').

61 A new Standard Operating Procedure for BoIs entered into force in March 2011. UN DPKO/DFS, 2011 BoI SOP, para. 6.

62 Even where a situation is one which demands a mandatory BoI, that is, where serious misconduct is involved, it is generally the OIOS that investigates. If this is the case, no other investigation is conducted. E-mail communication with senior UN official, 16 September 2014.

63 UN DPKO/DFS, 2011 BoI SOP, para. 35.

64 Negligence/gross negligence, wilful misconduct or wilful intent of any individual. Ibid, paras. 61, 63.E.(b).

65 'The Conduct and Discipline Unit (CDU) was formally established in the Department of Field Support in 2007, following the initial formation of a Conduct and Discipline Team

direction for conduct and discipline issues' in Peace Operations, including policies, training, outreach activities and dealing with allegations. CDTs operate in the field as principal advisers to Heads of Mission on conduct and discipline issues for all mission personnel.[66] Most importantly, for the purposes of this chapter, they constitute the central point for receiving complaints, registering all complaints received in a web-based database, and referring them to the appropriate bodies for investigation and action.[67]

The new arrangement had advantages, but also disadvantages.[68] It soon became apparent that the biggest problem was resources, given the volume of cases it had to deal with. The OIOS suffered from a large backlog of pending cases.[69] As the OIOS was not primarily based in the field, it experienced difficulties in conducting investigations promptly, and gaining access to victims, witnesses and crime scenes.[70] This was a new problem, which arose with the shift from BoIs to the OIOS. On the whole, the new arrangements solved some, but not all the problems.

---

in the Department of Peacekeeping Operations in 2005'. UN CDU, 'Conduct and Discipline Unit' <https://cdu.unlb.org/> accessed 6 October 2014, (hereinafter 'CDU web').

66 Ibid.

67 The tasks include: advising personnel and mission leadership on all matters of conduct and discipline; ensuring coherence of administrative and disciplinary procedures; leading a process of reviewing existing policies and developing strategies for addressing problems; acting as a central repository of information; undertaking awareness-raising activities for mission personnel and the host population; ensuring remedial actions are taken; and liaising with complainants and victims. Ibid; Durch et al., *Improving Criminal Accountability*, pp. 13–14. See also UNGA, 'Comprehensive Report Prepared Pursuant to General Assembly Resolution 59/296 on Sexual Exploitation and Sexual Abuse, Including Policy Development, Implementation and Full Justification of Proposed Capacity on Personnel Conduct Issues' (24 May 2006) UN Doc. A/60/862, (hereinafter '2006 SEA Report').

68 A detailed analysis of these advantages and disadvantages is included in Section 3-3.

69 For example, see UNGA, 'Report of the Office of Internal Oversight Services' (19 September 2001) UN Doc. A/56/381. It shows the shift in the number of pending cases. In 1994, there was one open case at the end of the reporting period, and the number increased every year. At the end of June 2001, there were 274 open cases.

70 UNGA, 'Comprehensive Report on the Pilot Project Designated by the General Assembly in Resolution 63/287' (21 February 2013) UN Doc. A/67/751, paras. 17, 43, (hereinafter 'Pilot Project Report'). See also Durch et al., *Improving Criminal Accountability*, p. 11, discussing the fact that the OIOS investigators' presence in missions increased, following an increased demand for OIOS investigations, but that the innovation of concentrating the OIOS in regional hubs would not meet the needs of prompt investigations into serious crimes. For more details, see Section 3-3.

Eventually, the UN modified these arrangements. The OIOS started to send some of the less complicated cases back to the mission for investigation. These cases were given to mission personnel, such as police investigators and Security Officers, to investigate. Security Officers are civilian mission personnel primarily tasked to ensure the safety and security of the mission and its personnel.[71] It is more likely that the response will be prompt where the OIOS sends cases back to the mission immediately,[72] but the earlier issue of an independent and professional investigation would emerge again with this arrangement. Once more there is a risk that misconduct will be investigated by police in the same unit as the suspect.[73]

One significant shift occurred in the early 2000s. As already noted, prior to that, it was assumed that criminal proceedings would be brought in the host State.[74] The UN has been consistent in stating that UN police personnel could face criminal proceedings in the host State if the conduct in question did not occur while they were carrying out their official functions.[75] For example, in UNMIK and UNTAET, the SRSGs repeatedly clarified that Peace Operations personnel with functional immunity, such as the UN police,[76] could be subject to criminal proceedings in the host State should they commit criminal acts, and that the SRSGs indeed agreed to such proceedings in the host State.[77] While the UN has maintained this theoretical approach, it has faced dramatically

---

71 The OIOS provides training to those involved in investigations in the mission. See the account of investigation training for Security Officers in UNGA, 'Report of the Office of Internal Oversight Services' (11 September 2003) UN Doc. A/58/364, para. 138.

72 For example, OIOS' reports show the reduction of long-pending cases between 2010 and 2013. At the end of each year, there were 71, 58, 67 and 52 such reports respectively. UNGA, 'Report of the Office of Internal Oversight Services on Peacekeeping Operations' (13 March 2012) UN Doc. A/66/286 (Part II), para. 9 (hereinafter '2012 OIOS PKO Report'); UNGA, 'Report of the Office of the Internal Oversight Services on the Activities of the Office of Internal Oversight Services on Peace Operations for the Period 1 January to 31 December 2013' (25 February 2014) UN Doc. A/68/337 (Part II), para. 14, (hereinafter '2014 OIOS PKO Report'). The main increase in the number of OIOS investigators took place before 2010. Durch et al., *Improving Criminal Accountability*, p. 11.

73 See Section 3-3-1.

74 See n. 34.

75 For example, see UN, OLA letter, p. 324; UN DPKO, 2003 Directives, para. 8.

76 The majority of personnel working for UN Peace Operations, including the UN police with the exception of the Police Commissioner, enjoy immunity only in relation to their official acts. See Chapter 6, Section 1-4.

77 See the cases cited in Chapter 3, section 3. On immunity, see Chapter 6, Sections 1-4 and 2-2-2.

different and unexpected conditions in host States in the newer Operations,[78] namely either the complete lack of a legal system, or the lack of a system meeting IHRL.[79] In such situations, the UN's interests are not protected if it has to subject its personnel to criminal proceedings that fail to meet required standards.[80] Where no functional legal system existed, it was impossible to expect any proceedings to occur. As a result, the UN has started to look into the possibility of criminal prosecution in sending States.[81] Two studies were undertaken by two different groups of legal experts. Of the two, the first considered the host State as the primary forum for criminal prosecution, while the second focused on the possibility of criminal prosecution in sending States.[82] It is understandable that the UN is not ready to submit its personnel to a host State's judicial system where that system has collapsed or is dysfunctional, or suffers from long delays.[83] In relation to FPU personnel, their sending States

78 See Chapter 2, Section 1.

79 UNGA, Zeid Report, paras. 67(b), 83.

80 Ibid, para. 83. It was acknowledged that it was simply not 'feasible' to subject UN personnel to the host State's criminal justice system where it was dysfunctional. Ibid, para. 29.

81 Some claimed that the UN police are now subject to the exclusive criminal jurisdiction of the sending State. William J Durch, *United Nations Police Evolution, Present Capacity and Future Tasks* (The Henry L Stimson Center, Discussion Paper, 2010), p. 18, (hereinafter 'UNPOL Evolution'). This is inaccurate.

82 The first group, appointed in October 2005, looked into 'the best way to [...] ensure that [...] United Nations staff and experts on mission would never be effectively exempt from the consequences of criminal acts committed at their duty station, nor unduly penalized, in accordance with due process'. The report was made public in August 2006, after a long review of the language used in it. UNGA, 2006 Legal Experts Report, (hereinafter '2006 Legal Experts Report'). The second group was appointed in September 2006, and reported on 'ways of standardizing the norms of conduct applicable to all categories of peacekeeping personnel' with particular attention paid to SEA, which is relevant to this research. UNGA, 2008 Ad Hoc Committee Report. The second group also examined (b)'[...] whether, and if so how, the standards in the Secretary-General's Bulletin [...] could bind [military] contingent members [...] prior to the conclusion of a memorandum of understanding' with a troop contributing State, according to the mandate. While this is intended for military contingents, the MoU was also concluded between the UN and the sending States of FPUs. UN, 'Model Memorandum of Understanding between the United Nations and the xxx Contributing Resources to the xxxx' UN Doc. (on file with author), (hereinafter 'FPU MoU').

83 Somalia, the Democratic Republic of Congo, Cote d'Ivoire, and Sudan could be prime examples. It was observed in a study that 'rule of law institutions have ceased to operate' in the DRC, Liberia and Cote d'Ivoire, and 'are largely dysfunctional' in Haiti. Scott N Carlson, *Legal and Judicial Rule of Law Work in Multi-Dimensional Peacekeeping Operations: Lessons-Learned Study* (UN DPKO, 2006), Section 2. An independent study suggest-

have formally agreed in recent years to take the action necessary for bringing criminal proceedings.[84]

These arrangements, and their evolution, are highly complicated. In order to assess the effectiveness of these mechanisms in facilitating criminal proceedings, each vehicle will be assessed from the point of the collection of information, to the UN's facilitation on criminal proceedings, to any follow up it conducts.

3 Analysis of the Mechanisms' Performance

Benchmark 1

3-1 Information Collection

The first step in facilitating any potential criminal proceedings is ensuring that all available information is gathered about the alleged criminal conduct. The most common way an allegation is made is through a report or complaint by someone either outside or inside the mission. It is also possible that the UN receives some general information or reported suspicions from different sources. These sources of information are analysed separately to assess how effectively information is collected.

3-1-1 *Reporting*

This chapter will deal first with reports by persons external to the mission.

(1) External Reporting

Complaints may be brought to the attention of the mission by victims, witnesses or third parties who have information about alleged misconduct. Third party reporters can be the victim's family members, representatives of civil society organizations (including those representing women or youth), representatives of religious institutions, staff of international or national NGOs,[85]

---

ed using the World Bank's Governance Indicators, and the Freedom House's measurement of civil and political rights, to assess the situation. Durch et al., *Improving Criminal Accountability*. pp. 49–50 and Table A-3, pp. 78–82.

84 UN, FPU MoU, Article 7.19. Since then, a similar general agreement has been reached between the UN and sending States of IPOs. UNGA, 'Report of the Secretary-General on the Special Measures for Protection from Sexual Exploitation and Sexual Abuse' (13 February 2015) UN Doc. A/69/779, para. 53, (hereinafter '2015 SEA Report').

85 The OIOS recommendations on the application of wider protection and detection measures included the 'designation of local officials or nongovernmental organizations to receive reports of sexual exploitation and abuse'. UNGA, OIOS Bunia Report, para. 56.

personnel of inter-governmental organizations such as the UN High Commission for Refugees, representatives of the local administration, chiefs of clans, or traditional local leaders.

a Awareness

In order for anyone to report criminal misconduct, he or she must be aware that a particular act contravenes a criminal code, or at least some code,[86] that it can be reported, and how and where to report it. In addition, it should be assumed that for someone to make a report, they need some awareness of what to expect when lodging a complaint. Until the end of the 20th century, there was not much information regarding the extent to which the local population and persons external to the Organization were aware of either the criminal code or complaint mechanisms.

The early 2000s heralded many changes in the system. During this period, the SEA reports focussed attention on the lack of awareness, as well as the insufficient outreach done by the UN to raise awareness. For example, in 2005, there were no public information programmes designated specifically to inform local women about their rights, and how to report a crime in Haiti and Liberia,[87] two of the missions where serious misconduct was most frequently reported. An NGO report criticized the fact that, too often, information on how to report abuse, and on what would happen to the perpetrator, was unclear to the local community.[88] The reporting mechanism was apparently also unclear to some international third parties.[89]

Awareness of where to report misconduct has become less important for external persons since the early 2000s, because internal reform has clarified that misconduct can be reported to any mission member.[90] In relation to SEA, additional outreach activities have been conducted, using alternative methods. Mission websites also often have posts on codes of conduct and how to

---

86 It may be that the reporter does not know whether the alleged conduct constitutes a crime, but knows that the conduct is wrong in light of some other code, rule or custom.

87 Sarah Martin, *Must Boys be Boys? Ending Sexual Exploitation and Abuse in UN Peacekeeping Missions* (Refugees International, October 2005), p. 21.

88 Ibid, p. iii.

89 The report quoted a UN government representative: '[i]f we get credible information, we'll get complaints into the proper channels. But it's not always clear to us how to do that'. Ibid, p. 21.

90 See Section 3-1-1 (1). However, in that case, they need to be under an obligation to pass the information on to the appropriate investigative body, through an appropriate channel. On the obligation to pass on information, see Section 3-2.

report misconduct, in particular SEA incidents.[91] Reporting of SEA by personnel working for other organizations has also been made easier through the coordinated approach of UN agencies and a network of NGOs.[92]

There are two issues with this approach. One is that the focus has been almost entirely on SEA, and not on other criminal conduct.[93] The other is that a large proportion of awareness raising methods has been dependent on literacy, as a result of which important messages may fail to reach a vulnerable population.[94] Some reported activities involving local actors, such as holding meetings with local government officials, liaising with educational institutions, or carrying out information sessions with the local population,[95] may

91 These activities were conducted by missions, using methods such as radio broadcasting, distribution of printed materials, targeted campaigns, exhibitions, and symposiums. Information sheets have been distributed to target populations. Recent information sheets are based on the model information sheet developed by the Sexual Exploitation and Abuse Task-Force. Some new ideas, such as an orange wrist band, T-shirts and bumper stickers with a simple message against SEA, have been used along with more traditional public information tools, like posters. UN, 'Protection from Sexual Exploitation and Abuse by UN and Related Personnel' <http://www.un.org/en/pseataskforce/tools_engage.shtml> accessed 12 December 2012.

92 UNGA, 2006 SEA Report, para. 9. In this regard, there is also an inter-agency task force working on prevention of sexual exploitation and abuse. PSEA Task Force, 'Protection from Sexual Exploitation and Abuse by Our Own Staff' <http://www.pseataskforce.org/> accessed 28 September 2016.

93 See Section 3-1-1 for more details.

94 The Zeid report observed that victims were often poorly educated frightened young women and children. UNGA, Zeid Report, para. 12. See also UNGA, OIOS Bunia Report, which reported the poor education levels and vulnerability of the victims, as well as the difficulties encountered in reaching them, para. 11. In another context, surveys in refugee camps in Kenya revealed that about twenty to forty percent of the population was illiterate, and messages related to SEA were not understood. Kirsti Lattu, *To Complain or Not to Complain: Still the Question, Consultations with Humanitarian Aid Beneficiaries on Their Perceptions of Efforts to Prevent and Respond to Sexual Exploitation and Abuse* (Humanitarian Accountability Partnership, 2007), p. 49, (hereinafter 'Complain or Not Complain').

95 In response to a survey conducted in 2010, nine Peace Operations claimed to have conducted external communications activities. United Nations Operation in Cote d'Ivoire (UNOCI), United Nations Organization Stabilization Mission in the Democratic Republic of the Congo (MONUSCO), United Nations Mission in Liberia (UNMIL), United Nations Stabilization Mission in Haiti (MINUSTAH), United Nations Mission in Sudan (UNMIS) and three other missions reported carrying out outreach activities on the prevention of SEA. UNGA, 'Report of the Secretary-General on the Special Measures for Protection from Sexual Exploitation and Sexual Abuse' (18 February 2011) UN Doc. A/65/742, para. 31 (hereinafter '2011 SEA Report'). Those activities included holding meetings with local

have mitigated the barrier of illiteracy to some extent. The UN observed that such activities had raised awareness amongst the local population, and that this improved awareness had resulted in more complaints being made.[96] It is not clear how effective this has been, as there are too many variables in determining the number of complaints. It is probable that the increased awareness of the local population has been responsible for some of the increase in the number of allegations, but it could also be argued that the newly developed complaint system failed to deter criminal behaviour in the first place.

The problem of poor awareness, however, is deeper than simply informing the population that they can make a complaint. Surveys in refugee camps in Kenya showed that the majority of the population believed that there were cases of SEA, yet about half of those interviewed said that SEA incidents were the victims' own fault.[97] Staff turnover further confused the population, as this made it unclear with whom to lodge a complaint.[98] In another survey, conducted in Kenya, Thailand and Namibia, the respondents indicated that they were not able to lodge a complaint because they were not invited to participate in designing the complaint mechanism, and there was no feedback mechanism available for suggesting improvements to the system. The vast majority of the interviewees also indicated that they would not complain.[99] Although the interviewees were not part of the host population of Peace Operations, but rather were beneficiaries of humanitarian aid, these surveys showed that awareness-raising activities must be carefully planned in order to be effective. Compared to humanitarian aid agencies, Peace Operations generally operate

---

government officials, liaising with educational centres and schools, as well as carrying out information sessions with the local population. The five named missions were the missions against which the highest number of SEA allegations was made. UNGA, 'Report of the Secretary-General on the Special Measures for Protection from Sexual Exploitation and Sexual Abuse' (17 February 2012) UN Doc. A/66/699, para. 32 (c) (hereinafter '2012 SEA Report'). Some of those activities were held in collaboration with civil society and local authorities. UNGA, 2008 Discipline Report, para. 40.

96 The UN observed in 2006 that the increase in the number of SEA allegations involving personnel associated with UN Peace Operations can in part be explained by the heightened awareness of the host population about the UN standards of conduct. UNGA, 2006 SEA Report, para. 57.

97 Xefina Consulting, *Preventing Sexual Exploitation and Abuse (PSEA) Project: KAPB Survey Results* (Report to International Rescue Committee, September 2007), p. 8 (hereinafter 'KAPB Survey').

98 Lattu, *Complain or Not Complain*, p. 49.

99 They also claimed that too little information was provided about the complaint mechanism. Ibid, p. 49.

within a shorter time-span with more categories of staff,[100] who operate on rotation.[101] This further complicates matters for the host population of Peace Operations. The issue is also related to empowerment. People might be aware of the code of conduct and where to report misconduct, but may not believe that they are entitled to make complaints or that the complaint process is effective. This may be a larger problem for vulnerable people.[102]

Current mechanisms appear to fall short of meeting the desired benchmark. The UN has made significant efforts to raise awareness since the early 2000s, but the methods used have insufficiently targeted vulnerable groups. It is difficult to know the extent to which awareness-raising activities have reached the targeted population, apart from an indication that the number of complaints rose after 2003–4, when two major SEA reports were released.[103] Furthermore, it is unknown at this stage whether or not awareness amongst the local population has increased due to having a realistic picture of what to expect after lodging a complaint.

b *Practicality*

Even where awareness is not an issue, if it is not easy for a victim or witness to come forward, a complaint may not be lodged.

100 In addition to different categories of civilian personnel, Peace Operations have military contingents, military observers and UN Police. Chapter 2, Section 1.

101 For the military contingent, Military Observers and UN police, the average tour of duty is one year, but depending on the length of the mandate, sending States and other variables, it can be shorter. Chapter 2, Section 1.

102 Despite 68% of the people having participated in an awareness raising programme, many participants believed that they do not have rights. Moreover, some people were not aware that some sexual acts constitute crimes. A study observed that problems may arise due to the nature of the society concerned, for example, a gender unequal society where people assume sexual conduct involves violence to a certain extent. Corinna Csáky, *No One to Turn to – The Under-Reporting of Child Sexual Exploitation and Abuse by Aid Workers and Peacekeepers* (Save the Children – UK, 2008), p. 13, (hereinafter 'No One to Turn to').

103 UNGA, OIOS Bunia Report; UNGA, OIOS West Africa Report. However, a survey in 2008 by Save the Children revealed that none of the 341 local people in 38 focus groups, consulted in Haiti, South Sudan and Cote d'Ivoire, could name the focal points in Peace Operations. Csáky, *No One to Turn to*, p. 13. The number of allegations of sexual exploitation and abuse by Peace Operations personnel has generally decreased since 2007. UN CDU, 'Statistics' <https://cdu.unlb.org/Statistics/OverviewofStatistics.aspx> accessed 28 September 2016.

In earlier missions, the means and methods for receiving allegations of misconduct were *ad hoc*.[104] The weakness of complaint mechanisms underlined in the Zeid Report[105] also applied to other forms of misconduct.[106]

In recent missions, reports can be made in writing (including by dropping a written complaint in a locked drop-box, or sending electronic mail), verbally in person, or by telephoning a hotline.[107] This has widened the means of lodging a complaint, although most of these require access to electronic equipment, and still require that the complainant be able to write. A complainant is not required to identify him/herself.[108] Furthermore, a pattern of behaviour, without specifying a particular incident, or a genuine suspicion, can also be reported.[109] In terms of a contact point, anyone can directly lodge a complaint at the OIOS, not necessarily in written form.[110] In addition, Peace Operations commonly use multiple contact points, including the CDT, focal points on SEA and Gender,[111] managers and commanders, and human resource personnel.[112]

---

104 For more details, see Hampson and Kihara-Hunt, 'PKO Personnel Accountability', pp. 305–306. UNGA, OIOS Discipline Report, para. 7.

105 UNGA, Zeid Report, paras. 7, 40. UNGA, 2006 SEA Report, para. 4. It was also reflected in the Statement of Commitment adopted by the SEA Task Force, which consisted of the UN, UN agencies and NGOs working mostly in the area of humanitarian aid. It declares the commitment to making the complaint mechanisms accessible. UN, 'SEA Task Force "Statement of Commitment on Eliminating Sexual Exploitation and Abuse by UN and Non-UN Personnel"' <http://www.un.org/en/pseataskforce/docs/statement_of_commitment_on_eliminating_sexual%20_exploitation.doc> accessed 6 October 2014, point no. 4.

106 UNGA, 2006 SEA Report, para. 4. This is because the means available to lodge a complaint have been common to all misconduct. In fact, allegations of SEA had better complaint mechanisms. While missions have designated a focal point for receiving complaints on sexual exploitation and abuse cases, all other misconduct complaints are filed with multiple entities within a mission. UNGA, OIOS Discipline Report, 2006, para. 7.

107 UNGA, 2006 SEA Report, para. 19. There is also discussion regarding future development of a community-based reporting system. UNGA, 2015 SEA Report, para. 43.

108 UN OIOS, 'Frequently Asked Questions' <https://oios.un.org/page?slug=frequently-asked-questions> accessed 3 June 2015.

109 Ibid.

110 UN OIOS, 'Overview of Investigations; How to Report Misconduct' (November 2008) <http://www.un.org/Depts/oios/pages/id_brochure.pdf> accessed 8 October 2014 (hereinafter 'OIOS Brochure').

111 Gender Advisors and Child Protection Advisors are also involved in providing advice according to their respective expertise. UNGA, 2006 SEA Report, paras. 47–48.

112 This includes the 'Serve with Pride' video. UN, 'Serve with Pride' <http://www.un.org/en/pseataskforce/video_english.shtml> accessed 6 October 2014.

Reports may also be made to any mission personnel, who then report these to relevant focal points.[113] Corresponding to this, it is now an obligation for all mission personnel to pass on any allegations which are made to them, using the relevant channels.[114] The internal rule clarifies that the failure to do so will result in disciplinary action against the personnel concerned.[115] The SEA Task Force has also provided guidance on the complaint mechanisms accessible to the host population.[116] By 2011, all missions had established complaint mechanisms for accusations against UN mission personnel.[117]

Therefore, it appears that complaint mechanisms are now more physically accessible to the population than ever before. The new system requires only that the potential complainant have access to any mission personnel. By virtue of being a victim or witness to a case of criminal behaviour by UN police, they are likely to have access to at least some personnel. The OIOS reported that its presence in mission areas appeared to have facilitated the better receipt of complaints.[118]

---

113 UNGA, 2011 SEA Report, para. 30 (c).

114 UN DPKO, 2003 Directives, para. 9; UN, 'Secretary-General's Bulletin on the Protection against Retaliation for Reporting Misconduct and for Cooperating with Duly Authorized Audits or Investigations' (19 December 2005) UN Doc. ST/SGB/2005/21, para. 1.1. See also UN, 'Secretary-General's Bulletin 'Special measures for protection from sexual exploitation and sexual abuse' (9 October 2003) UN Doc. ST/SGB/2003/13, para. 3-2 (e), in relation to sexual exploitation and abuse.

115 UN, 'Information Circularon the Reporting of Suspected Misconduct' (24 March 2005) UN Doc. ST/IC/2005/19, para. 5, (hereinafter 'IC on Reporting'), applies to staff members of the UN. UN DPKO, 'Undertaking and Declaration by Experts on Mission: UN Police Officer/Corrections Officer/Military Observers/Military Liaison Officer' UN Doc. (on file with author), para. 6 and the last un-numbered paragraph.

116 In 2009, Guidelines on Community-Based Complaining Mechanisms were drafted by the SEA Task-Force. This provides guidance and principles for making the complaint mechanisms more accessible to the host population. It also states that cultural considerations should be taken into account when designing complaint mechanisms. UN, 'Task-Force on Sexual Exploitation and Abuse, Draft Guidelines on the Community-Based Complaints Mechanisms Regarding Sexual Exploitation and Abuse by UN and non-UN Personnel' (15 September 2009) accessed 1 January 2015.

117 In addition, there are focal points in the regional presence which receive complaints in the field.

118 UNGA, 2011 SEA Report. In 2012, there were investigators in Nairobi, Vienna, and in seven Peace Operations. UNGA, Pilot Project Report, para. 1. It is possible that the presence of resident OIOS investigators may result in an increase in the number of reports, possibly as these investigators are more visible, thus helping to build trust in the investigations process. Ibid, para. 34, summary p. 1.

Nonetheless, some barriers remain due not to inaccessibility, but rather the cultural acceptability or appropriateness of the means available for complaining. These barriers may be particularly difficult for the rural population, illiterate people and girls or women. Child victims of SEA stated that they had particular difficulties using the reporting mechanisms.[119] Even though the UN acknowledged that having regular contact with civil society groups is useful,[120] two of the three missions (in Kosovo, Lebanon and Haiti) studied for a research project in 2009 had no regular or extensive contact with women's groups in those countries.[121] In cases of a sexual nature in particular, it may be difficult for a victim to come forward without the support of such a local organization. Generally, problems continue to be experienced by victims and witnesses in remote places, and these are exacerbated where language poses additional barriers.[122]

c *Insufficient Victim and Witness Protection*

Another factor that may hinder complaints from being lodged is the fear of retaliation, often accompanied by a lack of confidence in the protection scheme.[123] In societies in which Peace Operations typically operate, in

119 Some children said that they would have difficulty accessing officials without the involvement of their parents or guardians and, even if they gained access, the authorities would not believe their stories. In such cases, access to a reliable third party is essential for children making reports, but it may be challenging, in particular for orphans and children in especially vulnerable situations. Csáky, *No One to Turn to*, p. 13.

120 UNGA, 2012 SEA Report, para. 32 (c); UNGA, 2008 Discipline Report, para. 40. Indeed, it was the head of a local organization who brought complaints of sexual abuses of minors by foreign forces working alongside the UN mission in the Central African Republic to the UN's attention. Marie Deschamps, Hassan B Jallow and Yasmin Sooka, *Taking Action against Sexual Exploitation and Abuse by Peacekeepers – Report of an Independent Review on Sexual Exploitation and Abuse by International Peacekeeping Forces in the Central African Republic* (17 December 2015), Appendix A, para. 2, (hereinafter '2015 CAR Report').

121 Catherine Lutz, Matthew Gutmann and Keith Brown, *Conduct and Discipline in UN Peacekeeping Operations:Culture, Political Economy and Gender – Report submitted to the Conduct and Discipline Unit, Department of Peacekeeping Operations United Nations* (Watson Institute for International Studies, Brown University, 19 October 2009), p. 7. The UN is currently developing a mechanism for community-based reporting. UNGA, 2015 SEA Report, para. 43.

122 Even if complaints may be made in the victim's national language, some victims or witnesses may only speak a local dialect.

123 On the link between the fear of retaliation and a lack of confidence, see the text accompanying n. 125. This Chapter will not address the issue of incentives for victims to report misconduct. For example, some victims ceased being interested in testifying against

particular where they are deployed to build or rebuild the judicial infrastructure, the real and perceived danger of retaliation may be more acute.

The OIOS found that victims of SEA in Bunia (DRC) and West Africa were often frightened.[124] A survey in a humanitarian setting indicated the extent to which the fear of retaliation and lack of safety deters reporting. A primary reason given for not reporting SEA incidents was fear of revenge by the perpetrator.[125] Beneficiaries of humanitarian aid worried about their security were they to complain.[126] Some child victims were concerned about being punished by their parents or other family members for falling victim to SEA, or for reporting on behalf of others.[127] Fear of retaliation is closely linked to the actual or perceived lack of confidentiality.[128] The UN attempts to secure confidentiality by having private rooms for hearing complaints, and using telephone hotlines and secure e-mail addresses to receive complaints.[129]

However, victim protection goes further than securing confidentiality. The stigma attached to being a victim of a crime, particularly those of a sexual nature, is so great in some societies[130] that victims will not come forward without better protection. The lack of such measures cannot be overlooked if the UN is serious about facilitating criminal accountability. Retaliation can occur not only in respect of victims and witnesses, but also third parties who may be in a position to report misconduct or support victims.[131] The UN is aware of the need to ensure that alleged victims are provided with support, including psycho-social assistance through coordination with humanitarian

alleged SEA offenders upon learning that they would not gain any economic benefit from testifying. UNGA, OIOS Bunia Report, para. 13 (b).

124 Some were frightened because of their prior negative experiences with the Congolese authorities, and some were frightened reportedly because they had been intimidated or bribed by peacekeeping personnel. Ibid, paras. 13 (d), 13 (e).

125 Xefina Consulting, *KAPB Survey*, p. 10. About one third of the population consulted in a survey in Haiti thought that the fear of retaliation by perpetrators was deterring child victims from reporting SEA incidents. Csáky, *No One to Turn to*, p. 13.

126 Lattu, *Complain or Not Complain*, p. 49.

127 Csáky, *No One to Turn to*, p. 13.

128 In Dadaab, Kenya, research revealed that 15.5 percent of refugees and 43.7 percent of incentive workers expressed a 'fear of lack of confidentiality' in reporting a case of sexual exploitation and abuse. Xefina Consulting, *KAPB Survey*, p. 50. Another survey showed that beneficiaries of humanitarian aid worry particularly about the lack of confidentiality, were they to complain. Lattu, *Complain or Not Complain*, p. 49.

129 UNGA, 2006 SEA Report, para. 19.

130 For example, see Csáky, *No One to Turn to*, p. 13.

131 See ibid, p. 16, where it was reported that local authorities sometimes fear physical retaliation by perpetrators, especially if they are armed.

organizations.[132] In 2011, however, a survey indicated that the strategy was yet to be fully operationalized. Only two of the thirteen missions which responded to the survey have referred a victim for medical assistance, counselling or legal services, and only one mission referred a victim to a safe shelter. Ten missions did not even have a safe house, secure shelter or community centre to which to refer victims.[133]

Again, efforts made to protect victims and witnesses have almost exclusively focussed on SEA. This focus is justified to some extent by the particularly sensitive nature of sexual crimes, and the burden these place on the victims.[134] Nevertheless, the protection of victims, witnesses, and the third parties who assist them, should not be forgotten no matter what type of crime is alleged to have occurred.

d *Lack of Expectation/Perception of Ineffectiveness*

The decision not to report a crime may be related to the lack of expectation that anything will happen following such a report. In some cases, this may be influenced by one or more of the factors discussed above.[135] This lack of expectation is rooted in a lack of trust that the UN will address the misconduct appropriately. The vast majority of the beneficiaries of humanitarian assistance in the above-mentioned surveys said they would not complain, partly due to the lack of a relationship of trust.[136] In 2005, many Haitians were apparently not convinced that the UN took the issue of SEA seriously,[137] and victims refused to give evidence.[138] Following a series of SEA cases in Bunia, the OIOS

132 UNGA, Zeid Report, para. 54. In the case of SEAs, the UN provides basic assistance to victims and to children born as a result of SEA, according to their individual needs, even before the allegations have been substantiated. UNGA Res 62/214 (7 March 2008) UN Doc. A/RES/62/214, Annex, paras. 4, 6–7.

133 UNGA, 2012 SEA Report, para. 29. However, there are missions that have taken measures to improve assistance to victims. UNGA, 'Report of the Secretary-General on Special Measures for Protection from Sexual Exploitation and Sexual Abuse' (14 February 2014) UN Doc. A/68/756, para. 56, (hereinafter '2014 SEA Report'). However, in 2015, it was reported that the situation still has not been appropriately addressed. UNGA, 2015 SEA Report, para. 65.

134 See the text accompanying n. 127.

135 For example, this may be related to the lack of awareness, as discussed above in Section 3-1-1 (1) a.

136 Lattu, *Complain or Not Complain.*

137 They perceived the civilian police patrolling the neighbourhood as not doing anything but talking to women. Martin, *Must Boys be Boys*, p. 5.

138 Ibid, p. 21.

investigation also faced a serious problem, in that victims and witnesses were unwilling to come forward. In that investigation, only one case out of 217 SEA allegations was fully substantiated, largely due to a lack of cooperation by the victims.[139] As these reports indicate, the lack of trust can be a real deterrent to making complaints. It is possible that this is more of a problem with SEA allegations than with other crimes. It may also be that part of this distrust results from a perception of authorities in general or during a time of conflict.[140] Part of it, however, is driven by the observation that nothing had happened in respect of previously reported cases.[141] In such communities, the UN has additional work to do to nurture a culture of accountability. Providing information to the victims on the progress and outcomes of investigations is one way to ensure some trust in the system.[142]

(2) Internal Reporting

In order for the UN to ensure full disclosure, another source of information needs to be secured, that of a member of a UN Peace Operation, military, police or civilian making a report about another member of the mission. Reporting can be done by a victim of or witness to a particular criminal conduct, or by a third party who becomes aware that a colleague is involved in criminal misconduct.[143]

a *Awareness*

The first requirement is that the personnel working for Peace Operations be aware of the codes that they and other mission personnel are bound by,[144] and

139 UNGA, OIOS Bunia Report.

140 Csáky, *No One to Turn to*, p. 14. See also UNGA, OIOS Bunia Report, para. 13 (e).

141 Csáky, *No One to Turn to*, p. 13.

142 It is also crucial to provide some feedback to alleged victims on their complaints to the mission. At the end of the mission's investigation, the alleged victim should be informed of the outcome of the investigation and, in general terms, of any action taken as a result of a complaint. UNGA, Zeid Report, para. 55.

143 Where mission personnel receive information (as a third party), the procedure is similar to where an external person lodges a complaint with anyone in the mission. For that reason, there is no separate consideration of this category.

144 Different categories of personnel may be subject to different codes of conduct. Therefore, it is possible that a certain conduct that is prohibited for one category of personnel is not prohibited for another category of personnel. However, what constitutes a crime in the host State is the same for all categories of personnel. See also the GA's request to the SG to ensure that all staff are aware of what constitutes misconduct and criminal conduct, as well as the consequences of committing such acts. UNGA Res 59/287.

that they know where and how to report an allegation. In addition, there presumably needs to be awareness of what to expect when reporting alleged misconduct. Evidence cited in an OIOS report issued in the early 2000s indicates that a significant number of those working for a Peace Operation were unaware of how to lodge a complaint.[145] A large number of survey respondents indicated that they had not received a briefing or had not otherwise received information on the UN Standard of Conduct.[146] The report found varying degrees of a lack of discipline in all missions, partly due to the inadequate guidance provided by the UN Headquarters. That is, the UN Headquarters had not informed mission personnel of the terms of policies, procedures and guidelines, and had not properly enforced these policies and procedures at Headquarters or in the field.[147] Around the same time, an NGO observed that UNMIL employees were confused as to who to report to, and that UNMIL lacked a clear and transparent process for reporting SEA incidents. Apparently, no two people interviewed in 2004 could identify the correct focal person.[148]

Since the reforms made following the SEA reports, awareness amongst mission personnel has become critically important, as the new system permits external persons to report misconduct to any mission personnel.[149] This requires all mission personnel to be aware not only of where they must go to report a complaint, but also what to do if they receive a complaint from non-UN personnel. Since the new system became operational, the UN's awareness-raising efforts have been conducted by CDTs. This includes messages regarding the prevention of misconduct and SEA, as well as the behaviour expected of

145 UNGA, OIOS Discipline Report, paras. 30, 43. The Zeid Report also observed a low level of awareness of the code in MONUC. UNGA, Zeid Report, para. 13. It identified the lack of awareness of the UN standard of conduct as one of the main problems relating to sexual exploitation and abuse. See also UNGA, 2006 Legal Experts Report, para. 84 (h), where it observed that there was considerable uncertainty amongst UN officials about the role of the OIOS, and how it interacts with other administrative proceedings.

146 UNGA, OIOS Discipline Report, para. 43. This is despite the fact that the information is contained in the 'Undertaking and Declaration by Experts on Mission: UN Police Officer/Corrections Officer/Military Observers/Military Liaison Officer', which is signed by all UN police personnel. The current form of Undertaking is contained in UN DPKO, 'Guidelines for United Nations Police Officers on Assignment with Peacekeeping Operations' UN Doc. DPKO/PD/2006/00135.

147 UNGA, OIOS Discipline Report; UNGA, 2006 SEA Report, para. 5.

148 Martin, *Must Boys be Boys*, p. 15.

149 UNGA, 2011 SEA Report, para. 30 (c); UN DPKO, 2003 Directives, para. 9; UN, SGB Whisltblower Protection, para. 1.1. Also see UN, SGB on SEA, para. 3-2 (e), in relation to sexual exploitation and abuse. See Section 3-1-1 (1) b.

UN personnel. It is delivered through e-mail messages, broadcast messaging, posters and administrative instructions.[150] A number of missions use Standard Operating Procedures (SOPs) for reporting suspicions of misconduct, including those regarding acts of a sexual nature.[151] Mandatory induction training for newly-recruited personnel includes a session on the prevention of SEA, and these training materials have been made available on-line.[152] Additional training modules have been developed, targeting senior and middle managers.[153] The UN's efforts in disseminating information on reporting mechanisms are significant.[154] However, whether or not the level of awareness has reached the desired level as a result of these improvements is difficult to measure. The OIOS reported that there is no clear cause and effect relationship between the number of personnel in mission areas and the number of complaints, but that it is probable that the visibility of the OIOS presence may increase awareness of, and accessibility to, the OIOS for mission personnel.[155] On the one hand, reports of SEA incidents have decreased in recent years, but on the other, they persist albeit at a lower frequency.

In fact, the issue of awareness needs to be further addressed. In Peace Operations, especially in uniformed components, the majority of personnel are men. As of December 2015, only around ten percent of UN police officers were female,[156] and this was after the UN prioritized the deployment of women police officers.[157] Combined with the actual or perceived lack of functioning

---

150 UNGA, 2012 SEA Report, para. 28.

151 The internal guidance is applicable across missions: UN, IC on Reporting.

152 Training materials are available at UN DPKO, 'Peacekeeping Resource Hub' <http://peacekeepingresourcehub.unlb.org/PBPS/Pages/Public/Home.aspx> accessed 6 October 2014.

153 UN DFS, 'Standard Training Module 2: Combating Sexual Exploitation and Abuse, Role of Mid-Level Managers and Commanders' <www.un.org/en/pseataskforce/docs/dpko_dfs_standard_training_module_2_role_of_mid_level_manager_ppt> accessed 6 October 2014.

154 UNGA, OIOS Discipline Report. A UN report claimed that the new training programme instituted since 2006 covers awareness-raising of the code of conduct and personnel accountability. UNGA, 'Report of the Secretary-General on the Progress of Training in Peacekeeping' (21 December 2010) UN Doc. A/65/644, para. 38, (hereinafter 'SG Report on Training'.).

155 UNGA, Pilot Project Report, para. 34.

156 Data from December 2015. All together there were 1,411 female UN police officers out of a total of 13,858 UN police. UN DPKO, 'Troop and Police Contributors' <http://www.un.org/en/peacekeeping/resources/statistics/contributors.shtml> accessed 18 February 2016.

157 For example, States sending military and police officers have not only been encouraged to send female personnel, but also to send women-only troops and FPUs as part of the policy to increase the representation of women in missions. UN DPKO, 'Women in

legal systems, the acceptance of sexual misconduct by previous national authorities in some areas,[158] and issues relating to the national culture and expectations of a group of uniformed personnel deployed from the same sending States, misconduct of a sexual nature is to some extent condoned.[159] Where this is the case, a tradition of silence has evolved alongside this attitude.[160] It is difficult to make a complaint or to report a colleague for misconduct against this backdrop. Even in the US, where making a complaint is much more common in everyday life, female military officers at military academies reported only one-third of the incidents that they experienced.[161] Members of the CDT reported problems regarding the culture of masculine privilege.[162] An OIOS survey in 2005 found that many uniformed personnel were deterred by a 'code of silence' in reporting misconduct. Some of the respondents noted that the work environment was not always conducive to reporting misconduct.[163] This attitude was described by a member of a Peace Operation as 'a culture of boys protecting boys',[164] both in military and civilian groups.[165] While this attitude

Peacekeeping' <http://www.un.org/en/peacekeeping/issues/women/womeninpk.shtml> accessed 23 September 2014.

158 Csáky, *No One to Turn to*, pp. 8–9, 15–17.

159 It is sometimes condoned even by the SRSG. It is reported that a former SRSG responded '[b]oys will be boys', when faced with sex scandals. Judy Ledgerwood, *UN Peacekeeping Missions: The Lessons from Cambodia* (PN 1994), p. 7. Another report went further in stating that the hyper-masculine culture encourages SEA. Martin, *Must Boys be Boys*, p. ii.

160 Martin, *Must Boys be Boys*, p. ii.

161 Ibid, p. 3.

162 Lutz, Gutmann and Brown, *Report to CDU*, p. 7.

163 UNGA, OIOS Discipline Report, para. 21. When the OIOS investigators contacted military contingent members and commanders, their attitude was one of trying to protect their national honour from any accusation. See also the UNGA, OIOS Bunia Report.

164 Martin, *Must Boys be Boys*, p. 7. An independent study also found that, '[r]eports from the Congo and elsewhere, for example, showed that commanders sometimes participate in SEA, cover up for friends and colleagues, and ignore the fact that such acts are occurring or that whistleblowers are being harassed [...] the small group loyalty common to military organizations is also a significant factor in erecting a wall of silence around misconduct, something made even worse when sub-cultural differences and divisions emerge within national militaries, leading to attempts to cover up within contingents as well as between them'. Lutz, Gutmann and Brown, *Report to CDU*, p. 9.

165 A former Personnel Conduct Officer reported that many of the mission personnel were complicit in this problem, either by participating in the misconduct, covering up for colleagues, or by averting their eyes from the problem. Jane Rasmussen, 'MONUC: Sexual Exploitation and Abuse, End of Assignment Report' (25 February 2005) UN Doc. (on file with author), (hereinafter 'Rasmussen Report').

may slowly be changing,[166] encouraging reporting in this environment requires extra effort on the part of the UN.

b *Duty to Report*

One measure taken by the UN was to make it a duty for all personnel in Peace Operations to report any information regarding misconduct, or any suspicion of misconduct.[167] Managers have an additional duty to respond to such information.[168]

All Personnel

In the 1990s, it was not clear if there was a legal obligation for all categories of mission personnel to report misconduct. Since 2003, the UN has made it a duty for all personnel, including UN police personnel, to report suspected misconduct.[169] Reports may be made to officials further up the chain of command, or to the OIOS.[170] Since the establishment of the CDU/T, all misconduct information, if not directly reported to the OIOS, must be referred to the CDU/T.[171] Currently, the obligation to report is contained in multiple internal regulations and documents, but confusion may result from the fact that there are many reporting channels, and it may be difficult to know which one to use.[172] In addition, in relation to SEA, all personnel associated with Peace Operations have a duty to report concerns about, and suspicions of, a fellow worker through the

166 Martin, *Must Boys be Boys*, p. iii.

167 See Section 3-1-1 (2) b 'All personnel'.

168 See Section 3-1-1 (2) b 'Managers'.

169 'Any member of the field mission who becomes aware of such acts shall report them to the Head of Mission', UN DPKO, 2003 Directives, para. 9. With regard to UN Secretariat staff members, the duty is also stipulated in the UN, IC on Reporting, para. 5.

170 UN, IC on Reporting, para. 5. Allegations can be reported to the OIOS, CDTs or to other authorized mission personnel, including the Head of the Mission, Military Provost Marshall, or the Security Investigation Unit. UN, 'Code Cable on the Clarification of Conduct and Discipline Issues' (1 February 2006) UN Doc. (on file with author), para. 7, (hereinafter 'Feb 2006 Code Cable').

171 The Mission CDT works as 'the focal point for conduct and discipline matters within missions', and 'shall receive' allegations of misconduct. UN, Feb 2006 Code Cable, para. 3.

172 In 2003, the Directives stated that misconduct should be reported to the Head of Mission. UN DPKO, 2003 Directives, para. 9. However, at the time the Directives were issued, the reporting mechanisms were still unclear. For details regarding the centralization of information, see Section 3-2.

established reporting channels.[173] As with all factors behind under-reporting, it is difficult to know the exact extent to which this duty is carried out.

Managers

The requirement that all personnel must report misconduct will be meaningful only if managers are aware of what they are supposed to do. The UN has made it clear in recent years that, when an allegation of misconduct is reported, the head of department or office has the responsibility and the obligation to review the information. If there is reason to believe that a staff member has engaged in misconduct, the head must undertake a preliminary investigation, including fact-finding.[174] In recent years, it has also been made clear that the performance of managers is assessed partly through taking their responses to reports of suspected misconduct into account. Managers appear to understand their duties well in this respect.[175]

However, in reality their enforcement of the rules appears inconsistant. Taking into account the reports of managers' acquiescence in the face of SEA misconduct,[176] in order for the rules to have some effect, there needs to be action taken against those managers who fail to enforce these rules. In this respect, in 2015, the Department of Field Support (DFS) led an initiative to create an accountability framework for conduct and discipline, in order to hold both

173 UN, SGB on SEA, para. 3.2.(e) (hereinafter 'SGB on SEA'). This Bulletin applies to all personnel via their Individual Undertakings. For details of codes that apply to UNPOL officers, see Chapter 5, Section 2.

174 UN, 'Revised Disciplinary Measures and Procedures' (2 August 1991) UN Doc. ST/AI/371, (hereinafter '1991 AI'). The same obligation is contained in the UN, SGB on SEA, Section 4, and also in UN DPKO, 'Directives for Heads of Police Components in Peacekeeping Operations' (21 November 2006) UN Doc. DPKO/PD/2006/00122, para. 42, (hereinafter 'Directives for Heads'); UN DPA/DPKO/DFS, 'Policy on Accountability for Conduct and Discipline in Field Missions' (1 August 2015) UN Doc. Ref. 2015.10, paras. 14.2, 14.3, 17.5, (hereinafter '2015 Policy on Accountability').

175 The review found that managers of UN Peace Operations were aware that they would be held accountable through their performance management systems should they fail to implement measures to prevent SEA. UNGA, 2011 SEA Report, para. 27; UN DPA/DPKO/DFS, 2015 Policy on Accountability, para. 14.3.

176 A former Personnel Conduct Officer observed that '[m]anagement culture in the mission, both civilian and military, appears to have encouraged sexual exploitation and abuse by not taking the phenomenon seriously, ignoring and suppressing reports, standing passively by as the staff members who reported sexual exploitation and abuse were harassed and ridiculed'. Rasmussen, Rasmussen Report, p. 4. See also the reported culture of 'boys protecting boys'. Section 3-1-1, (2).

individuals and leaders personally accountable for failing to carry out their duties.[177] The UN confirmed that where managers encouraged or condoned SEA, this would be reflected in their performance appraisals.[178] However, current SOPs do not make specific mention of this aspect of these appraisals.[179] How many such instances are missed at this stage is unknown, but, taking into account earlier reports of the totally arbitrary manner in which allegations were handled,[180] and the apparent tendency to return UN police personnel to their sending States,[181] it is difficult to imagine that this trend has been reversed. Given that there is so little evidence in the public domain on this issue, it is impossible to determine whether or not that policy requiring that managers who fail to act on a report be disciplined is being implemented.

c *Inadequate Protection of Whistle-Blowers*

Mission personnel in possession of relevant information may fail to come forward if there is, or is perceived to be, inadequate protection of whistle-blowers. In fact, a major deterrent to internal personnel reporting suspected misconduct is the fear of retaliation.[182] The fear of retaliation can exist in a normal work environment, but certain aspects of the environment within Peace Operations function may exacerbate these fears. Furthermore, arguably, uniformed personnel need better protection than civilian personnel, given that uniformed personnel may work in a more closed environment.[183] For security and operational reasons, as well as cultural and linguistic ones, UN police personnel are likely to congregate together both during and after work. In the case of FPUs,

---

177 UN DPA/DPKO/DFS, 2015 Policy on Accountability.

178 UNGA, 'Report of the Secretary-General Special on Measures for Protection from Sexual Exploitation and Sexual Abuse' (28 February 2013) UN Doc. A/67/766, para. 36, (hereinafter '2013 SEA Report'); UN DPA/DPKO/DFS, 2015 Policy on Accountability, paras. 14.2, 14.3, 17.5.

179 UN DPKO, 'Standard Operating Procedures on the Performance Appraisal of United Nations Police Officers' (19 December 2006) UN Doc. Ref. 2006.29, DPKO/PD/2006/00132, (hereinafter 'SOP Appraisal').

180 See Section 2 for more details.

181 See text accompanying n. 321.

182 Grimstad, *ID Review*, p. 35; UN, 'Accountability Frameworks in the United Nations System' (2011) UN Doc. JIU/REP/2011/5, paras. 69–70, (hereinafter '2011 Accountability Report').

183 In relation to the closed environment of uniformed personnel, it was also observed that 'the small group loyalty common to military organizations is also a significant factor in erecting a wall of silence around misconduct, something made even worse when subcultural differences and divisions emerge within national militaries, leading to attempts to cover up within contingents as well as between them'. Lutz, Gutmann and Brown, *Report to CDU*, p. 9.

this likelihood is even greater. FPU personnel come from the same State, bring their national command structure with them, and work and live together. That particular behaviour is condoned in some parts of Peace Operations[184] would further isolate any potential whistle-blower. In such an environment, especially if a superior is implicated,[185] or if more than one person in the Unit is implicated, the chances of the whistle-blower becoming isolated are high. One factor that may provide some encouragement is their ability to report misconduct directly to the OIOS. Nonetheless, to overcome the reluctance to report misconduct, there must be further protection provided to whistle-blowers. The mere prohibition of retaliation against whistle-blowers is not likely to have the desired effect.

The UN has, thus far, not managed to protect whistle-blowers effectively. A survey conducted in 2004 confirmed that UN personnel fear retribution for reporting misconduct.[186] Another OIOS survey also indicated that, across all missions, a lack of protection against reprisals for reporting misconduct was the main reason that many personnel are unwilling to report misconduct.[187] The Zeid Report also highlighted that there is a perception amongst mission personnel that whistle-blowers are not protected, and that little is done to address this problem.[188] In fact, the fear is not only about retribution by the alleged wrongdoers, but discrimination by their managers for reporting misconduct.[189] International civilian staff in Bunia were unwilling to report misconduct by colleagues because of the fear of being stigmatized and punished as 'whistle blowers'.[190] The ineffectiveness of whistle-blower protection was again marked as a worrying issue throughout the UN system in 2011.[191] In December 2006, the European Parliament expressed 'serious concern over

184 As discussed above, Section 3-1-1 (2).

185 This was apparently the case in the Congo. Rasmussen, Rasmussen Report, p. 4.

186 UN Wire, 'Survey Finds UN Staff Fear Retribution for Reporting Misconduct' (10 June 2004) <http://www.unwire.org/UNWire/20040610/449_24749.asp> accessed 5 June 2006. This survey concerned only UN personnel. Given the particular circumstances prevalent in the field, it is likely that there is a similar, if not worse, problem for whistle-blowers in missions.

187 UNGA, OIOS Discipline Report, para. 21. Also see Martin, *Must Boys be Boys*, p. 6.

188 UNGA, Zeid Report, para. 13.

189 UNGA, OIOS Discipline Report, para. 21. See also Kathryn Bolkovac, *The Whistleblower: Sex Trafficking, Military Contractors, and One Woman's Fight for Justice* (Palgrave Macmillan 2011).

190 Martin, *Must Boys be Boys*, p. 6.

191 UN, 2011 Accountability Report, paras. 69–70.

reports of a "culture of silence" in some U.N. missions, stemming from the fear of punishment and retaliation'.[192]

There is some evidence to suggest that these fears are grounded in reality. More significantly, the main problem appears to be that whistle-blowers are discriminated against for reporting misconduct by their managers.[193] For example, two contractors working as UN police in a mission in the Balkans were fired for reporting serious misconduct by their colleagues. One of their claims for compensation for summary dismissal was upheld by the tribunal.[194] Other accounts of retaliation have also been reported.[195] In another UN office at OIOS, when an investigator repeatedly asked about the way her supervisor dealt with an important piece of evidence for an investigation, the supervisor threatened to give her a negative performance appraisal.[196] Considering that

---

192 European Parliament, 'Resolution on the Involvement of UN Forces in Sexual Abuse in Liberia and Haiti' (14 December 2006) <http://www.europarl.europa.eu/sides/getDoc.do?Type=TA&Reference=P6-TA-2006-0606&language=RO> accessed 8 October 2014. This 'code of silence', through which reporting misconduct is strongly discouraged, was also observed by the OIOS. UNGA, OIOS Discipline Report, para. 21.

193 UNGA, OIOS Discipline Report, para. 21. See also Bolkovac, *The Whistleblower: Sex Trafficking, Military Contractors, and One Woman's Fight for Justice*.

194 Kathryn Bolkovac was a UN police officer employed through the private company DynCorp. In 2002, she won her case against DynCorp for summary dismissal, which was heard by a British employment tribunal. She had been summarily dismissed for reporting serious misconduct by their colleagues in a mission in Bosnia. Ben Johnston was an air mechanic, and was fired for reporting 'sexual slavery' and arms trafficking. His case was concluded through an out-of-court financial settlement. Jamie Wilson and Kevin Maguire, 'American Firm in Bosnia Sex Trade Row Poised to Win MoD Contract' *The Guardian* (London, 29 November 2002) <http://www.theguardian.com/uk/2002/nov/29/military.politics> accessed 6 October 2014. A separate case, heard by the UN Dispute Tribunal, upheld the claim lodged by a former senior civilian official at UNMIK that he had been fired following his report of corruption by his supervisors, and that the UN had failed to protect him. This ruling was later overturned in the Appeals Court. Kristen Saloomey, 'Panel Says UN Failed to Protect Whistleblower' *Al Jazeera* (23 June 2012) <http://www.aljazeera.com/video/americas/2012/06/201262322950126228.html> accessed 6 October 2014; Julian Borger, 'UN Tribunal Finds Ethics Office Failed to Protect Whistleblower' *The Guardian* (London, 27 June 2012) <http://www.theguardian.com/world/2012/jun/27/un-tribunal-whistleblower-james-wasserstrom> accessed 6 October 2014; 'UN Tribunal Overturns Ruling Backing Whistleblower' *The New Zealand Herald* (4 September 2014) <http://www.nzherald.co.nz/world/news/article.cfm?c_id=2&objectid=11320116> accessed 6 October 2014.

195 Human Rights Watch, *Hopes Betrayed – Trafficking of Women and Girls To Post-Conflict Bosnia and Herzegovina for Forced Prostitution* (November 2002, vol 14, no 9 (D), 2002), pp. 55–56, (hereinafter 'Hopes Betrayed'); Rasmussen, Rasmussen Report, p. 4.

196 *Nguyen-Kropp Postica v Secretary-General of the United Nations* Cases no UNDT/NY/2010/107; UNDT/NY/2011/004 Judgment no UNDT/2013/176 (UNDT, 20 December 2013).

this incident took place in the very office that investigates misconduct, it is logical to presume that retaliation against whistle-blowers is a very real problem.

What the UN did in response was merely to set out a clear policy to protect staff who report misconduct in UN Peace Operations.[197] It prohibits any 'direct or indirect detrimental action recommended, threatened or taken'[198] as a result either of staff reporting misconduct, or co-operating with an investigation/inquiry. The Secretary-General's Bulletin on Whistleblower Protection protects UN staff members, but the UN has undertaken to apply the same protection to Experts on Mission who are serving in a Peace Operation.[199] While there are many written policies dealing with the matter, there is little evidence to support the argument that the UN is making a serious attempt to protect whistle-blowers. The UN may be concerned about how its reputation might be adversely affected by reports of misconduct.[200] There is no evidence that any UN Peace Operations personnel were subject to disciplinary action as a result of his or her actions against a whistle-blower. The OIOS is responsible for investigating cases of retaliation against whistle-blowers, with a possible reference from the Ethics Office, but OIOS has no data on how frequently the whistle-blower scheme is used.[201] Separate reports indicated in September 2014 that the Ethics Office had managed to protect less than one percent of the 343 staff who came to it for help since its establishment in 2006.[202] The UN's own tribunal held that the Organization's protection mechanisms for whistle-blowers

197 This policy concerned protection against retaliation for reporting misconduct and for co-operating with duly authorized audits or investigations, UN, SGB Whistleblower Protection, (hereinafter 'SGB Whistleblower Protection').

198 Ibid, para. 4.

199 For example, Secretary-General's Bulletin on the mandate of OIOS contains the following clause: '(n)o action may be taken against staff or others as a reprisal for making a report or disclosing information to, or otherwise cooperating with, the Office'. UN, SGB OIOS Establishment, para. 18 (f).

200 Analogously, it is reported that a similar concern led the UN to conceal the cholera outbreak in Haiti that resulted from a national military contingent's poor sewage system. 'In 2010, the U.N. didn't want anyone to talk about this', Katz said, in a phone interview with CNN. 'They were directly castigating anyone who would bring up the topic'. Ivan Watson and Joe Vaccarello, 'UN Sued for "Bringing Cholera to Haiti", Causing Outbreak that Killed Thousands' *CNN* (New York, 10 October 2013) <http://edition.cnn.com/2013/10/09/world/americas/haiti-un-cholera-lawsuit/> accessed 6 October 2014.

201 When an independent body reviewed the performance of the OIOS Investigation Division, the OIOS was unable to report how many cases were referred to it by the Ethics Office. If the Ethics Office considers it appropriate, the case may be investigated by the OIOS. However, the OIOS did not have sufficient numbers of investigators available to do this. See Grimstad, *ID Review*, pp. 35–36.

202 'UN Tribunal Overturns Ruling Backing Whistleblower'.

were 'fundamentally flawed'.[203] Given the extent of the fear of retaliation, the effectiveness of whistle-blower protection policy reveals a significant shortfall in its capacity to ensure reporting.

d Perception of Ineffectiveness

The mistrust of a disciplinary mechanism can significantly discourage the reporting of misconduct, either in its own right, or combined with other concerns. This does indeed appear to be behind the under-reporting of misconduct by mission personnel. For example, a lack of confidence in the disciplinary process, accompanied by the actual or perceived lack of support from managers who are meant to enforce the disciplinary process and take corrective action, were commonly indicated as reasons for not reporting misconduct.[204] Women, in particular, were apparently dissatisfied with the UN's ability to deal with conduct and discipline issues.[205] The concerns that no action will be taken against a suspect, and the fears that reporters may suffer retribution for reporting misconduct, appear to discourage mission personnel from reporting misconduct.

3-1-2 *Initiation of an Investigation/Inquiry Where no Complaint is Lodged*

Another way a mission may gain information about alleged misconduct is for it to proactively search for information. It is encouraging that, in theory, there is nothing that prohibits the initiation of an investigation/inquiry by the relevant authorities without having received a specific allegation of misconduct. In fact, such authority is explicitly conferred on the following actors in UN internal documents: the Heads of Police Components in Peace Operations are authorized to conduct investigations[206] with or without an allegation being made; the OIOS is explicitly authorized to initiate investigations without

---

203 The Dispute Tribunal found that 'the organisation's ethics office failed to protect Wasserstrom against such reprisals from his bosses, and that the UN's mechanisms for dealing with whistle-blowers were 'fundamentally flawed', to the extent the organisation had failed to protect the basic rights of its own employees'. There were allegedly 297 cases where whistle-blowers complained of retaliation for their attempts to expose wrongdoing inside the UN at the time of reporting. Borger, 'UN Tribunal Finds Ethics Office Failed to Protect Whistleblower' However, this ruling was overturned at the Appeals Court. 'UN Tribunal Overturns Ruling Backing Whistleblower'.

204 UNGA, OIOS Discipline Report, para. 21. See also Martin, *Must Boys be Boys*, p. 6; Rasmussen, Rasmussen Report, p. 4; UN, 2011 Accountability Report, para. 70.

205 UNGA, OIOS Discipline Report, para. 49.

206 They are authorized to 'conduct investigations, make inquiries and request information, reports and consultations' in order to discharge their responsibilities in respect of

hindrance;[207] and CDU/Ts can take the initiative to look into matters of conduct and discipline without having received a specific complaint, and can recommend areas for investigation by the appropriate authorities.[208]

However, all of the above entities are facing resource shortages. The investigative capacity of missions is frequently reported as being inadequate.[209] The OIOS has been struggling with a heavy investigative load, and has tried out different ways of dealing with the backlog of investigations.[210] Given that the number of allegations is well over 800 per year,[211] and given that the CDT has extensive involvement in a wide range of tasks,[212] it is difficult to imagine that CDT members have much time to proactively seek information regarding misconduct. It is probably appropriate to view the power of these entities to initiate investigations *proprio motu* as one that is rarely used in reality.

3-2 Centralization of Information

An effective system is necessary to centralize the information following a report of misconduct. This is even more essential where various focal points of complaints exist. An effective system would provide clear guidance for all those involved in implementing it, as well as what type of information should be sent where, and within what time-frame.

Prior to the establishment of the CDU, the information flow was not systematized. There was no repository of information,[213] nor were there any set tools

---

maintaining good order and discipline within the UN police. UN DPKO, Directives for Heads, para. 41.

207 UN, SGB OIOS Establishment, paras. 3–4. See also UN OIOS, 'OIOS Brochure' (November 2008) <http://www.un.org/Depts/oios/pages/id_brochure.pdf>, p. 2, which highlights that the OIOS may undertake proactive investigations.

208 E-mail communication with a senior UN official, 20 February 2013; communication with two senior UN officials, June 2016.

209 UN, BoI Review, paras. 6–8. Rasmussen, Rasmussen Report, pp. 3–4. UNGA, Pilot Project Report, paras. 25–28.

210 Among other OIOS reports, see UNGA, Pilot Project Report, para. 18.

211 UN CDU, 'Statistics' <https://cdu.unlb.org/Statistics/OverviewofStatistics.aspx>.

212 As set out above, in Section 2.

213 UNGA, OIOS Discipline Report, para. 7. There was no entity in MONUC that kept comprehensive data relating to misconduct. Rasmussen, Rasmussen Report, p. 2. This was also the case at the UN Headquarters. At the Headquarters, 'there is no single office responsible for tracking cases of indiscipline referred by the missions. Depending on the nature of the case and the alleged offender, cases may be referred to the Office of Human Resources Management, the Personnel Management and Support Service, the Military Division or the Civilian Police Division in the Department of Peacekeeping Operations, or the Investigations Division in the OIOS. As such, monitoring the state of discipline cases under the

or procedures.[214] Gender Advisers and Child Protection Advisers were involved in providing advice within their respective area of expertise.[215] Administrative personnel, such as the Director of Administration, the Chief Administrative Officer and the Head of Police Component, typically supported this work by collating and forwarding documentation on serious misconduct cases involving UN police officers to the Department of Peacekeeping Operations.[216] Some cases were dealt with within the UN police structure,[217] and some were taken up by different focal points or units,[218] including by the SEA focal points.[219] Because there were many avenues for making complaints, but no system to centralize them, there were various points at which complaints could potentially be dropped.[220] There was also a possibility of duplication, if complaints were made simultaneously at different contact points. Where data existed, some of it was either incomplete, or significantly flawed.[221]

Since the establishment of the CDU and its teams (CDT), it has functioned as the central repository for this information. The CDT has a presence in a dozen missions.[222] Acting as a repository, it keeps misconduct records on a

current structure at Headquarters and in the missions is difficult. Moreover, OIOS found that there are no tools and procedures for recording and tracking cases. In addition, no mechanisms have been established at Headquarters or in the field to ensure consistent application of policies, procedures and guidelines on discipline'. UNGA, OIOS Discipline Report, para. 7.

214 UNGA, OIOS Discipline Report, para. 7.

215 UNGA, 2006 SEA Report, paras. 47–48.

216 Ibid, para. 49.

217 This raises questions regarding a possible lack of independence on the part of UN police investigators. See Section 3-3-1.

218 For example, some cases that fell within the mandate of Human Rights component of the mission were assisted by the unit. Chuck Call and Michael Barnett, 'Looking for a Few Good Cops: Peacekeeping, Peacebuilding and CIVPOL' (1999) 6 *International Peacekeeping* 43, p. 51.

219 UNGA, 2006 SEA Report, para. 19.

220 For an internal account of the failure to conduct investigations into very serious allegations in MONUC, see Rasmussen, Rasmussen Report, p. 1.

221 UNGA, OIOS Discipline Report, paras. 25–29. Where data were kept in the mission and at the headquarters, they sometimes did not match up. For example, MONUC recorded eight SEA cases in 2004, while DPKO headquarters reported 76 SEA cases involving MONUC personnel during the same period. Ibid, para. 27.

222 Conduct and Discipline Teams (CDTs) are based in peacekeeping missions in Côte d'Ivoire (UNOCI), Democratic Republic of the Congo (MONUC), Chad and Central African Republic (MINURCAT), Western Sahara (MINURSO), Haiti (MINUSTAH), Darfur (UNAMID), Kosovo (UNMIK), Lebanon (UNIFIL), Liberia (UNMIL), Sudan (UNMIS), Timor-Leste

central database.[223] This works well with one exception. The CDU does not have access to complaints that were made directly to the OIOS.[224] Separately, the OIOS records and assesses all allegations reported to it, including those referred to it from the CDU.[225] It is positive that, for the first time, the UN has gained some idea of the scale and nature of misconduct through the data provided by the CDU. However, because the extent of duplication of recording between the two agencies is unknown, it is difficult to ascertain the exact number of cases of misconduct.[226] In order to reduce this duplication, it would be better if the 'central repository' role was shifted to the OIOS. The OIOS is better able to maintain its independence, and to provide a better overall picture of misconduct.

The CDU does not itself perform any investigative functions. Rather, it collects misconduct allegations, allocates them to Categories I or II according to their seriousness, makes recommendations for onward investigation by the OIOS, and hands over all allegations and information on potential serious misconduct to the OIOS.[227] At this stage, allegations of a less serious nature are forwarded to the relevant mission components, such the police's Internal Affairs

---

(UNMIT), and in special political missions in Afghanistan (UNAMA), Burundi (BINUB) and Iraq (UNAMI). This information was correct as of 3 June 2014, although at that point, UNMIT and MONUC no longer existed, and MONUC was replaced by MONUSCO in July 2010. Note also that BINUB and UNAMI fall outside the scope of this thesis. During 2011, there were 12 teams based in missions, covering 19 missions, as well as the UN Logistics Base in Italy. UNGA, 'Report of the Secretary-General on the Criminal Accountability of United Nations Officials and Experts on Mission' (31 July 2012) UN Doc. A/67/213, para. 415, (hereinafter 'SG Report on Criminal Accountability').

223 UN CDU, 'Conduct and Discipline Teams' <http://cdu.unlb.org/AboutCDU/ConductandDisciplineTeams.aspx> accessed 3 June 2014; UN DPA/DPKO/DFS, 2015 Policy on Accountability, paras. 17.7, 17.8, 18.6, 18.18.

224 UNGA, 2008 Discipline Report, para. 20.

225 UNGA, 'Secretary-General's Report on Special Measures for Protection from Sexual Exploitation and Sexual Abuse' (17 February 2009) UN Doc. A/63/720, para. 9, (hereinafter '2009 SEA Report').

226 The OIOS stated that 39 percent of the 1026 matters in total that were brought in front of it were also directly reported it. UNGA, Pilot Project Report, paras. 14–16. In addition, the Police Division also maintains a database of allegations of misconduct committed by UN police personnel. Communication with senior UN officials, July 2016.

227 The OIOS divides misconduct into two categories. Serious misconduct or criminal conduct is called Category I misconduct. For minor misconduct or Category II misconduct, heads of mission retain the responsibility to investigate. UN, Nov 2005 Code Cable; UN DPA/DPKO/DFS, 2015 Policy on Accountability, paras. 17.7, 17.8, 18.3, 18.6, 18.18.

Unit.[228] The CDU thus plays a vital role in receiving, assessing and referring allegations of all kinds of misconduct for appropriate action.[229]

The involvement of the CDUs provides some safeguards for ensuring that complaints are responded to, as compared to earlier procedures. As the information on misconduct by UN police personnel is now assessed by CDUs as to where it should be referred, this is an improvement when compared to the earlier practice whereby the UN police itself assessed whether alleged conduct was serious.[230] CDTs report directly to the Head of the Mission,[231] which increases the likelihood that misconduct allegations against UN police personnel will be dealt with more independently and with greater impartiality.

Benchmark 2

3-3 Investigation

Effective investigation is critical if the results of these investigations are to be used to institute criminal proceedings. Early investigative practice does not permit a proper assessment to be made of the effectiveness of these investigations. Investigations by the UN police were not always carried out.[232] Where

---

228 The Special Investigation Unit for civilian staff, the Internal Affairs Unit for police, or the Provost Marshall for military personnel. UN, Feb 2006 Code Cable, para. 3. In the 2015 policy document, the police component's internal investigation unit is called the Internal Investigation Unit. UN DPA/DPKO/DFS, 2015 Policy on Accountability, para. 18.16.

229 UNGA, 2006 SEA Report, para. 39; UN DPA/DPKO/DFS, 2015 Policy on Accountability, paras. 17.7, 17.8, 18.6, 18.18.

230 Under the Directives, it is not clear who makes the decision on the categorization of misconduct. As reports are to be made to the Head of Mission if the information relates to 'an act of serious misconduct or an act that has the potential to damage the image, credibility or integrity of the United Nations', it appears that categorization was carried out by individuals who had reported the information. UN DPKO, 2003 Directives, para. 9.

231 The Head of Mission may then delegate the daily management of the CDT to the Chief of Staff. UNGA, 2006 SEA Report, para. 53; UN DPA/DPKO/DFS, 2015 Policy on Accountability, paras. 18.7, 18.10, 20.2.

232 Human Rights Watch, *Hopes Betrayed*; 'A police officer and divorced mother of three, Kathryn Bolkovac was looking for a fresh start when she signed up as a UN peacekeeper in Bosnia' *The Guardian Weekend* (London, 22 January 2011) 19; Colum Lynch, 'Misconduct, Corruption by US Police Mar Bosnian Mission' *Washington Post* (Washington, 29 May 2001) <http://www.balkanpeace.org/index.php?index=article&articleid=11668> accessed 12 August 2014; Amnesty International, *Kosovo (Serbia and Montenegro): So Does It Mean That We Have the Rights? – Protecting the Human Rights of Women and Girls Trafficked for Forced Prostitution in Kosovo* (EUR 70/010/2004, 2004); UNMIK, 'UNMIK Online' (13 August 2001) <http://www.unmikonline.org/press/2001/trans/tr130801.html> accessed 24 August 2005. One actual instance of conflict of interest was reported. For example, in a case

allegations were responded to, some investigations were halted before they were completed.[233] Records indicate that some instances of misconduct were responded to without any formal procedures having taken place,[234] some with a large degree of arbitrariness.[235] Some were dealt with within the UN police, whilst some were dealt with through different focal points or units.[236] Given this situation, it would have been impossible for each unit involved to see patterns emerging, or to gain a picture of the broad context within which alleged misconduct was committed. After the clarification of the role of the BoI,[237] it was the BoI which conducted or facilitated investigations in relation to serious misconduct.[238]

3-3-1 *The BoI System*

The BoI system had some flaws. One problem was finding qualified investigators to staff it. Preliminary investigations were conducted by persons appointed by the Head of Mission, which could include any civilian personnel.[239] This

in UNMIK, police officers from the same duty station investigated allegations of sexual misconduct by their colleagues. OSCE Mission in Kosovo, *Kosovo Review of the Criminal Justice System – Themes: Legal Representation, Detention, Trafficking & Sexually Related Crimes, Municipal & Minor Offence Courts* (Department of Human Rights and Rule of Law, October 2001). For an internal account of the failure to conduct investigations into very serious allegations in MONUC, see Rasmussen, Rasmussen Report, p. 1.

233 Human Rights Watch, *Hopes Betrayed*, pp. 56–60. At best, the suspects were sent back home. Commissioner Klaas Roos, the commander of the CIVPOL component of the UN Transitional Authority in Cambodia (UNTAC). See UNTAC Evaluation Report UN CIVPOL UNTAC Cambodia, Phnom Penh, Cambodia. Unpublished Document, August 1993, p. 5, as cited in Duncan Chappell and John Evans, *The Role, Preparation and Performance of Civilian Police in United Nations Peacekeeping Operations* (1997), p. 74. Mission commanders have been initiating the repatriation of 'problematic' UN police officers, including those with significantly inadequate skills. Chuck Call and Michael Barnett, 'Looking for a Few Good Cops: Peacekeeping, Peacebuilding and CIVPOL' in Tor Tanke Holm and Espen Barth Eide (eds), *Peacebuilding and Police Reform* (Frank Cass 2000), p. 52.

234 UNICEF, *Trafficking in Human Beings in Southeastern Europe* (June 2002).

235 For example, see cases where the alleged officers were talked into voluntary repatriation. Human Rights Watch, *Hopes Betrayed*.

236 For example, the human rights division of the mission sometimes assisted in dealing with some allegations. Call and Barnett, 'Few Good Cops', p. 51.

237 UN DPKO, 2003 Directives.

238 The definition of 'serious misconduct' is provided in the Directives. The UN police determine whether particular conduct falls within the category of 'serious misconduct' or 'minor misconduct' and, if it constitutes 'serious misconduct', it is obligatory for UN police to refer it to the Board. Ibid, para. 14.

239 Ibid, para. 11.

meant that preliminary investigations were often conducted by 'enthusiastic amateurs', even sensitive cases.[240] When presented with the findings of a preliminary investigation, a BoI would examine the case, and might conduct an additional investigation.[241] For matters involving the UN police, investigations were often referred to the police's internal unit for investigation.[242] There was no requirement that the investigators be appointed from outside the pool of normal UN police personnel. This raised questions regarding the independence and impartiality of investigators.[243] Another problem was the thoroughness of investigations, as investigators were tasked with conducting investigations for the Board on top of their normal jobs.[244] On the other hand, where UN police investigators were assigned, provided they had investigatory skills and experience,[245] the quality of their investigations was likely to have been better. Some investigations were conducted by Security Officers, Human Rights monitors or Child Protection advisors.[246] Overall, this mixed practice meant that the quality of investigations varied tremendously, and was often unsatisfactory, meaning that the Board was unable to use it.[247] For example, MONUC struggled to conduct investigations for the BoI to use in relation to numerous SEA allegations.[248] The lack of qualified investigators also caused delays in BoI

---

240 UNGA, Zeid Report, para. 32. This is despite the acknowledgement that 'trained managers should only investigate less serious misconduct and non-crime investigation'. UNGA Res 62/247 (24 April 2008) UN Doc. A/RES/62/247, paras. 12, 15.

241 UN DPKO, 2003 Directives, Annex, in particular paras. 5, 9, 10.

242 Several mission components have been involved in investigations. These include: the Special Investigation Unit for civilian staff, the Internal Affairs Unit for the UN police, and the Provost Marshall for military personnel. UNGA, 2008 Discipline Report, paras. 23–28.

243 Durch et al., *Improving Criminal Accountability*, p. 28. See also UN, BoI Review, para. 8.

244 As discussed above, in Section 2.

245 The required skills were not always met by all UN police personnel. See Chapter 2, Section 3-3.

246 UN DPKO, 2003 Directives, para. 11.

247 UN, BoI Review, para. 2. The Chief Legal Adviser and the Senior Police Adviser in UNAMA also noted that the investigative capacity of the Mission's investigation team needed to be enhanced. They revealed that investigation reports were often not complete, and that members of Boards of Inquiry had to seek additional information. Investigation units in Peace missions lacked the required number of investigators or the skill sets to conduct preliminary investigations of allegations of misconduct, resulting in some reports being of a poor quality. UNGA, OIOS Discipline Report, paras. 34–35; UN, BoI Review, paras. 6, 8, 27; UNGA, Zeid Report, para. 28.

248 UN, BoI Review, para. 8.

proceedings,[249] so that the 'prompt' test failed to be met in providing an effective response.[250] This lack of promptness posed a serious problem in relation to misconduct committed by UN police, as UN police personnel rotate. They often only perform one year of service, sometimes the period is even shorter.[251] Once the suspect leaves the mission, it is virtually impossible for the UN to gain access to him or her without the close cooperation of the sending State.[252]

There was also insufficient means to conduct a thorough investigation. Investigative tools, such as forensics, autopsies, DNA sample checks and other crime scene investigation facilities, were not available to investigators under the BoI system.[253] For example, the lack of a mechanism for securing evidence at the same time as providing medical care for victims was problematic.[254]

Another problem was the standard used for evidence collection. BoIs use a different evidential standard from that of criminal investigations.[255] Under the most recent rule, 'reasonable inference' is the standard used for establishing facts, although assumptions are prohibited.[256] Moreover, this standard was only clarified in 2011 amidst the comprehensive review and reform. Prior to that, the standard was unclear.[257] Where information was gathered for the use

249 Long delays were assessed as being one of the flaws of Boards of Inquiry. Ibid. paras. 5, 34. Some investigations were halted while waiting for particular personnel to arrive in the mission. Ibid, para. 6.

250 Later in 2011, with a new Standard Operating Procedure (SOP) in place for Boards of Inquiry, the time limit for the initiation of an investigation was set at 48 hours. Preliminary reports must be completed within 72 hours according to the new requirements. Note, however, that the BoI's functions have changed dramatically. See UN DPKO/DFS, 2011 BoI SOP, para. 19.

251 Durch et al., *Improving Criminal Accountability*, p. 33. The tour of duty for UN police in United Nations Verification Mission in Guatemala (MINUGUA) lasted six months. Carlos Abad Ruiz, 'Role and Functions of the Civilian Police in Human Rights Verification Missions' in Nassrine Azimi (ed), *The Role and Functions of Civilian Police in United Nations Peace-Keeping Operations* (Kluwer Law International 1996), p. 90.

252 Grimstad, *ID Review*, p. 69.

253 UNGA, Zeid Report, para. 32.

254 Ibid, para. 53.

255 '[I]nternal inquiries by the United Nations do not follow the prescriptions of criminal laws'. UNGA, 'Comprehensive Report on All Processes Involved in the Investigation and Prosecution of Crimes Committed against Deployed United Nations Peacekeepers' (9 December 2011) UN Doc. A/66/598, para. 11, (hereinafter 'Report on Investigation').

256 UN DPKO/DFS, 2011 BoI SOP, Annex III, Guidelines for BOI members on the Conduct of Inquiries, Section 4.

257 For example, see 2003 Directives UN DPKO, 2003 Directives, which contain information on the procedures and forms to be used by BoI members. However, the Directives do not make any reference to an evidential standard.

of BoIs, the standard of this information would have meant that a large portion of it did not meet the evidential standards for criminal prosecution.[258]

There is an additional difficulty relating to the standard of evidence. Rules of evidence differ to a great extent from one State to another, and thus it is inherently difficult to provide the right type of evidence collected in the right way, in particular to sending States' authorities.[259] These evidential requirements cannot be met even if the UN investigative bodies make the utmost effort to do so.[260]

3-3-2 *The OIOS System*

The OIOS system must be analysed in two stages. The first stage concerns situations in which the OIOS conducts the investigations, and the second stage concerns the OIOS' referral of certain cases back to the mission concerned.

(1) Investigation by OIOS Investigators

The starting point is that after the review of the system, the OIOS Investigation Division has become the main investigative authority for serious misconduct, including criminal conduct.[261] All serious misconduct must be referred to the OIOS.[262] After their initial assessment of the information, allegations that are prioritized for investigation will then undergo a preliminary fact-finding inquiry to decide whether the available evidence warrants further investigation.[263]

258 The DPKO's reliance on the BoI for providing the basis for criminal proceedings against UN police by their sending States 'allows national authorities to query and even reject the BOI findings on the basis of evidentiary standards, insufficiency of evidence, due process provisions or other aspects'. BoI Review UN, BoI Review, para. 30.

259 For details of possible requirements under domestic laws, see Section 2, *Benchmark* 2.

260 In addition, if the procedures during which the evidence is collected are unfair, this may give rise to problems under IHRL. However, an analysis of whether or not the proceedings are fair falls out of the scope of this work. See also n. 11.

261 The OIOS is mandated by UNGA Res 48/218 B, to investigate possible violations of rules or regulations, mismanagement, misconduct, the waste of resources or the abuse of authority. UN OIOS, 'Investigation Division' <http://www.un.org/Depts/oios/pages/id.html> accessed 13 December 2012. For more details regarding this mandate, see UN, SGB OIOS Establishment.

262 The OIOS divides misconduct into two categories. Category I includes all criminal conduct. All category I matters must be referred to the OIOS, without exception. UN, Feb 2006 Code Cable, para. 8.

263 UNGA, 2009 SEA Report, para. 5. The OIOS records and assesses all allegations, including those they receive directly, prioritizes allegations for investigation, refers allegations back to the mission for operational or practical reasons, suspends allegations pending further investigation, or dismisses allegations if there is insufficient evidence, as it deems

Some problems have been solved through the introduction of the OIOS investigations. Falling outside the mission structure, the OIOS reports directly to the Secretary-General.[264] This means it is free to investigate any cases it sees fit, even those involving institutional problems within a mission, or those implicating senior mission personnel. Although the OIOS is not completely independent in terms of its budget and human resources,[265] it has not been deterred from publishing reports which are highly critical of the UN's internal organs.[266]

It appears fair to state that the OIOS is capable of conducting a better quality of investigation than other entities. This is firstly due to the quality of its investigators. Unlike managers and Security Officers, OIOS investigators are specifically required to have investigative skills, including evidence collection skills, as well as knowledge of criminal investigations.[267] A second reason relates to the OIOS's division of labour. The OIOS employs professional investigators, who are assigned solely to investigating misconduct.[268] There is thus a better chance of thorough investigations. Third, the OIOS has established a formal quality control mechanism for draft investigation reports. Each report is assigned to a reviewer who reviews it to ensure that facts described are logical and make sense, that the allegations concern acts which indeed come within

---

appropriate. Ibid, para. 9; UN OIOS, *Investigations Manual* (available at <http://wwwunorg/Depts/oios/pages/id_manual_mar2009pdf> accessed 6 October 2014).

264 UNGA Res 48/218 B, op. para. 5 (a).

265 UNGA, 'Note by the Secretary-General on the Investigations Function in the United Nations System' (13 July 2012) UN Doc. A/67/140, paras. 25, 28, (hereinafter 'JIU Report').

266 For example, in its report on the status of discipline in the Peace Operations, it was highly critical of that status and the attendant machinery. UNGA, OIOS Discipline Report. Another example is UNGA, 'Report of the Office of Internal Oversight Services on the Investigation Conducted by the Investigations Task Force into Fraud and Corruption Allegations at Pristina Airport' (14 March 2006) UN Doc. A/60/720.

267 OIOS investigators are required to have knowledge and an understanding of administrative investigation, knowledge of criminal investigation management and administration, must be capable of collecting evidence, interviewing witnesses and suspects, and writing reports, amongst other things. A Master's degree or the equivalent in law or a related area, or a university first degree, with qualifying experience, is required. They are also required to have professional experience of investigative work, and practical experience of investigation management and administration. The vacancy announcements for OIOS investigators have the same or very similar requirements. For example, see the following professional investigator vacancy announcement: UN Jobs, 'Investigator, Vienna' (18 January 2012) <http://unjobs.org/vacancies/1326958725958> accessed 6 October 2014.

268 At the Investigation Division, UN OIOS, 'Investigation Division' <http://www.un.org/Depts/oios/pages/id.html>.

the category of either crimes or misconduct, and are well-written.[269] If reports are reviewed in terms of their quality, it may be more likely that they will be used as a basis for prosecution. Fourth, the OIOS is better equipped with investigative tools. It has access to technical investigative tools in the field, such as facilities to take and check finger prints, information technology forensics, and equipment to take and test DNA samples.[270] Assistance is also available from the Digital Forensics Unit based in the UN Headquarters, Nairobi and Vienna. This Unit provides services for forensic recovery, the analysis of digital information, and related training.[271]

However, some problems remain. Above all, OIOS investigations are also an administrative process 'irrespective of the type of conduct being investigated'.[272] OIOS Investigation Reports only establish the facts, and are conducted in order to support a decision on whether or not to initiate disciplinary proceedings.[273] This means that, notwithstanding these improvements, the methodology and standards of investigation required for criminal prosecution are not met.[274] One cannot expect the evidence collection to be conducted so as to meet the higher standards imposed for the purposes of criminal prosecution simply by requiring that investigations must be conducted in a manner that can 'withstand the rigour of criminal prosecution'.[275] The OIOS, for example, cannot and does not secure crime scenes for the purposes of criminal investigation.[276] The OIOS is authorized to conduct criminal investigation in cooperation with national authorities and,[277] if it does so, may address some of the shortcomings

---

269 The Professional Practices Section (PPS) was the section that guaranteed the quality of investigations. It was located within the OIOS. UNGA, JIU Report, para. 40. Since January 2014, the section has been expanded and renamed as the Operational Standards and Support Section (OSSS). The OSSS conducts 'ad-hoc and sample quality reviews'. UNGA, 'Report on the Activities of the Office of Internal Oversight Services on Peace Operations for the Period from 1 January to 31 December 2014' (23 February 2015) UN Doc. A/69/308 (Part II), para. 11, (hereinafter '2015 OIOS PKO Report').

270 The OIOS frequently uses its equipment to take and test DNA samples. The OIOS also has the resources to take fingerprints in the field, but these are virtually never used. The OIOS has an internal forensic unit. UN OIOS, *Investigations Manual*, p. 48. Communications with two UN officials, January 2015.

271 UNGA, 2012 OIOS PKO Report, para. 7.

272 UN OIOS, *Investigations Manual*, p. 33.

273 Ibid, p. 77.

274 Ibid, p. 33. This is on top of the additional difficulty of meeting different evidential requirements for different sending States, as discussed earlier. See Sections 1 and 3-3.

275 Ibid, p. 33.

276 Ibid, p. 96.

277 Ibid, para. 6.6.4.

for collecting evidence. However, where the OIOS collects evidence, the standard of proof it uses for evidence is that of reasonable inference, which is lower than that required for criminal prosecution.[278] OIOS investigators themselves are not required to be criminal investigators, and apparently the quality of their investigations reflects this.[279] The OIOS investigation processes, including procedures for the collection of evidence and the unreliable electronic case management system, have also been subject to criticism.[280]

The problems experienced in meeting the varying evidential requirements set by national laws are the same as those for BoIs.[281] For example, where the domestic laws of some States place restrictions on who can gather evidence, evidence collected by the OIOS cannot be used as it stands.[282]

New problems have also arisen. The biggest problem relates to access to victims, witnesses and physical evidence. The OIOS has investigation offices sited in only five operations. Other missions are covered by headquarters or regional centres.[283] In some cases between 2008 and 2009, one investigator was shared by four missions, while the maximum was four investigators in one mission.[284] The frequent turnover of investigators, and the failure to deploy investigators in a timely manner, accelerates the resource problems.[285] On top of that,

278 Ibid, p. 26.

279 William J Durch, *UN Peacekeeping, American Politics,and the Uncivil Wars of the 1990s* (Macmillan 1997), p. 32.

280 For example, the unreliable, unsecured and time-consuming nature of the electronic case management system has been pointed out in the review. These flaws in the case management system also prevent an effective comparison being made between OIOS and CDU cases. Grimstad, *ID Review*, pp. 42–43, 68. Certain State delegations were of the view that the procedures for the collection of evidence by the OIOS were too irregular to be admissible in criminal proceedings. UNGA, 2008 Ad Hoc Committee Report, para. 17.

281 See Section 3-3-1.

282 UNGA, 2008 Ad Hoc Committee Report, para. 17.

283 At the end of 2014, only MONUSCO, UNMIL, MINUSTAH, UNOCI, and UNMISS had resident investigators. UNGA, 2015 OIOS PKO Report, para. 7.

284 There were 43 Professional positions, of which 31 were based in the three regional centres, and 12 were located in seven missions. Supporting these 43 Professional posts and positions were 13 General Service posts and positions, and 1 Field Service post. For a more detailed account of the developments since then, see UNGA, Pilot Project Report, paras. 7–9.

285 Moreover, the majority of OIOS resident investigators based in mission areas voiced a strong wish to leave the mission environment. Ibid, para. 43. In 2015, OIOS again reported on the difficulties it encounters in filling vacancies. UNGA, 'Report on the Activities of the Office of Internal Oversight Services for the period from 1 July 2014 to 30 June 2015' (13 August 2015) UN Doc. A/70/318 (Part I), p. 2.

investigations into misconduct in those operations without an OIOS presence pose a serious difficulty.[286] If immediate access to victims, complainants and witnesses cannot be secured, it will make it very difficult to secure evidence. Even where OIOS investigators are stationed in the mission, they are normally based in the mission headquarters in capital cities, which may also hinder prompt access to the scene of incidents. In such circumstances, the OIOS must rely on other investigators on the ground.

Two separate trends can be seen when considering the issue of the promptness of investigations. One is that, in the new system, there is a clear time limit for taking the initial steps, such as the seven day limit within which the OIOS must decide whether to investigate the matter itself, or refer the case to the mission.[287] The second is that, in addition to complaints made directly to the OIOS, it was also given a new load of alleged serious misconduct cases. Thus, it suffered a severe backlog of investigations.[288] Furthermore, the OIOS's procedures for initiating investigations, and its decisions regarding which investigations

286 The OIOS conducted a three-year pilot project to assess the desirability of concentrating investigators in regional centres, instead of deploying them in missions. The project found that having resident teams of investigators provided clear advantages for achieving effective investigations. UNGA, Pilot Project Report, para. 17.

287 UN, Feb 2006 Code Cable, para. 9.

288 The OIOS reported that the average open caseload carried by the Investigation Division in 2007 was 285, including 206 cases (73%) from Peace Operations. The last quarter of the same year was a little better, with 254 open cases, including 174 cases from Peace Operations. UNGA, 'Report on the Activities of the Office of Internal Oversight Services for the Period from 1 January to 31 December 2007' (25 February 2008) UN Doc. A/62/281 (Part II), para. 10. In relation to sexual exploitation and abuse, by the end of 2010, 74% of cases reported in 2008, 60 percent of cases reported in 2009, and 38% of cases reported in 2010, had been completed. UNGA, 2011 SEA Report, para. 12. The situation for the following year showed some improvement: investigations into 77% of the instances reported in 2008, 71% of cases reported in 2009, 60% of the instances reported in 2010, and 26% of the cases reported in 2011 had been completed. UNGA, 2012 SEA Report, para. 14. In 2011 and 2012, the OIOS Investigation Division managed to prevent the backlog of investigations from increasing further. There were 87 intake matters for investigation, and 101 completed Investigation Reports during this period. UNGA, 'Report of the Office of Internal Oversight Services on Peacekeeping Operations' (1 March 2011) UN Doc. A/65/271 (Part II), para. 13. In 2012, there were 114 new reports requiring investigation, and 119 completed investigation reports. UNGA, 2012 OIOS PKO Report, para. 9. As for the length of time investigations were pending, in 2010, 71 cases (51.08%) were pending for more than 12 months and, in 2011, 58 cases (39.19%) were pending for more than 12 months. In that period, 11.51% and 4.73% of cases were pending for more than 36 months. Ibid, p. 8.

to prioritize, were criticized as complicated and time-consuming.[289] For these reasons, the OIOS exercised its right,[290] which appeared to have initially been set out as an exception,[291] to refer cases back to the mission.

(2) Investigations by Mission Personnel

When the OIOS refers cases back to missions, investigations are conducted by mission personnel. Who investigates a case varies.[292] Some confusion remains as to who can investigate, who is no longer authorized to investigate, and who investigates in practice. Internal guidelines for the investigation of misconduct appear to contradict each other. The 2003 Directives stated that preliminary investigations shall be conducted by persons appointed by the Head of Mission, including civilian personnel.[293] However, the UN's internal *Codes Cable*[294] instructed that the components that were previously responsible for conduct and discipline issues (including the heads of administration and human resource sections within the police components) could no longer play any role in receiving, handling or tracking misconduct issues.[295] According to one *Code*

289 Grimstad, *ID Review*, pp. 67–71.

290 The OIOS has the right to 'entrust trained programme managers to conduct investigations on its behalf'. This is stipulated in UNGA Res 59/287, op. para. 8.

291 GA Res 59/287 also decided that serious misconduct and/or criminal behaviours must be investigated by professional investigators. Ibid, op. para. 9. Immediately after the adoption of GA resolutions 59/287 and 59/300, all missions were requested to hand over all Category I investigations in relation to all categories of mission personnel to the OIOS. UN, Nov 2005 Code Cable, para. 2.

292 See the section above, which deals with investigators in the mission. Sections 3-3-1 and 3-3-2 (2).

293 UN DPKO, 2003 Directives, para. 11.

294 A *Code Cable* is a mode of internal communication within the UN, and may include internal policies, guidelines or codes that can be binding on the recipient. It is suggested that this mode of communication is the most important internal communication tool between the UN headquarters and the missions. It is not only an administrative communication tool, but is 'a means of diplomacy to issue politically motivated notices'. *Codes Cables* must be signed by the official at the highest level of the DPKO or the Head of Mission (HoM), and must be addressed to the highest level officials. Joel Gwyn Winckler, 'Protectionism within the Organization of United Nations Peacekeeping: Assessing the Disconnection between Headquarters and Mission Perspectives' (2014) 5 *Journal of International Organizations Studies* 71, p. 73.

295 UN, Nov 2005 *Code Cable*; UN, 'Clarification of Roles within Mission Administration with Regard to Conduct and Discipline Issues' (4 June 2007) UN Doc. (on file with author), (hereinafter 'June 2007 *Code Cable*').

Cable, they are required to cooperate with CDT as appropriate.[296] A separate Directive states clearly that the Head of Police is authorized to carry out investigations and inquiries, and to request information, reports and consultations with regard to all disciplinary matters.[297] In order to deliver that obligation, the Police Component is required to establish an 'internal investigation unit' to assist in preliminary investigations as anticipated in the Directives dealing with disciplinary matters.[298] Investigations can be initiated by the Head of the Police, but the Head of the Mission needs to be involved to some extent – either to appoint the persons to such an investigation team, or to coordinate with the OIOS and CDU/T.[299] Mission investigators have two roles: the first consists of making preliminary findings on the facts; the second consists of conducting a full investigation with regard to cases of criminal misconduct that have been referred back to the mission by the OIOS.[300] All completed investigation reports dealing with misconduct belonging to both categories, substantiated or not, are transmitted to the OIOS.[301] The current practice seems to be a practical compromise based on the various requirements for effective investigation. In fact, in 2007 and 2008, the OIOS investigated less than 30 percent of allegations itself, referring most investigations back to the missions.[302] The very fact that there is some confusion regarding the investigative responsibility for criminal

296 UN, June 2007 *Code Cable*, paras. 8–9.

297 UN DPKO, Directives for Heads, para. 41.

298 Ibid, para. 51. This is consistent with the 2015 policy. UN DPA/DPKO/DFS, 2015 Policy on Accountability, para. 18.16. In practice, normally the Chief of Staff within the mission police component deals with police personnels' conduct and discipline issues, in support of the Police Commissioner. Communication with senior UN officials, July 2016.

299 See Section 3-3-2. According to a policy adopted in 2015, the Head of Mission is responsible for mandating investigation, and commanders and managers have an obligation to advise the CDT of any allegations of misconduct. The Head of Police Component must ensure that relevant information and recommendations are conveyed to the Head of Mission and, in turn, the Head of Mission has an obligation to report on these to the Secretary-General. UN DPA/DPKO/DFS, 2015 Policy on Accountability, paras. 14.2, 14.3, 17.5, 18.7, 18.10, 20.2, 20.3, 20.4. In practice, UN police officers sometimes are assigned to the CDT to support its work. Communication with senior UN officials, June and July 2016.

300 UN, Feb 2006 *Code Cable*, para. 11.

301 Ibid, para. 13.

302 In 2007, the OIOS investigated 29% (134 reports) of allegations, referring 23% (108 reports) to mission components. 2008 OIOS PKO Report, para. 9. In 2008, OIOS investigated 24% (81 reports) itself, referring 33% (112 reports) to mission components. UNGA, 'Report of the Office of Internal Oversight Services on Peacekeeping Operations' (23 February 2009) UN Doc. A/63/302 (Part II), para. 6. The equivalent number or percentage of referrals was not given in reports released since 2010. Even where an investigation is carried out

matters is a cause for concern. Additionally, where allegations of serious misconduct are sent back to the missions for investigation, earlier problems with investigations within those missions would persist.[303]

In fact, Security Officers in the field are still asked to conduct full formal investigations into serious misconduct cases in parallel to OIOS investigations.[304] This confusion, and the conducting of investigations by non-professional investigators, remains an obstacle to achieving the goal of all investigations of alleged crimes being conducted by competent investigators. An independent report concluded that investigations conducted by non-professional investigators and/or entities, which are part of the management structure, can result in conflicts of interests, improper handling of information, inconsistent application of standards, and problems with due process, as well as cases being dropped or taking undue time to complete.[305]

It is difficult to justify the OIOS's practice of continuing to refer the majority of cases to entities within the missions, in particular because it was the very concern about investigations conducted by non-professionals that triggered the shift from investigations within the mission to those by the OIOS.[306] Indeed, senior mission personnel have voiced concerns that the OIOS is referring too many cases back to the missions for investigation, for which the missions have inadequate resources.[307] The OIOS nonetheless intends to continue this practice. In 2009, it introduced investigation training programmes to raise the awareness and improve the technical know-how of UN personnel involved in investigations, and to transfer the skills of Investigation Division personnel to non-professional UN personnel.[308] It also published an Investigation Manual for managers and mission components with investigative roles.[309] Practically speaking, while amateur investigators with some training are better than those

by mission personnel, the OIOS retains overall responsibility for any referred cases. UN DPA/DPKO/DFS, 2015 Policy on Accountability, para. 18.3.

303 See Section 3-3-1.

304 UNGA, JIU Report, para. 20.

305 Ibid, para. 21.

306 See Section 2.

307 UNGA, Pilot Project Report, para. 26. Several other senior mission personnel expressed the desire that personnel at the Special Investigation Unit under the Department of Safety and Security (DSS) be given adequate training in conducting investigations. Ibid, paras. 25–28.

308 UNGA, 'Report of the Office of Internal Oversight Services on Peacekeeping Operations' (23 February 2010) UN Doc. A/64/326 (Part II), para. 16, (hereinafter '2010 OIOS PKO Report').

309 UN OIOS, *Investigations Manual*.

without training, the standards of investigation cannot be improved through a 'quick fix' involving brief training or being given a manual to read. The Manual has also been criticized as lacking sufficient instructions on conducting an investigation.[310] Considering that criminal investigation requires highly specialized skills, it is submitted that investigations conducted by non-professional investigators may pose a serious problem.[311]

The OIOS maintains that the cases referred back to the missions remain OIOS cases, and that the OIOS stands by as an available resource.[312] However, considering that the reasons behind referring cases back were largely linked to a lack of resources, this may not be practically achievable in reality.

3-3-3 *Question of Access to the Suspect*

The UN's ability and willingness to facilitate proper criminal accountability is tested during investigations if the suspect leaves the host State before an investigation is completed.[313] This could happen if the suspect either flees or completes his or her tour of duty, or where the sending State withdraws its personnel before the UN investigation is completed. The absence of a suspect may prevent the investigations from being thorough. If the host State had initiated criminal proceedings, this would make prosecution virtually impossible.[314] If the suspect becomes unavailable before the UN's investigation is complete, or at least during the period in which the suspect is required to answer to the investigatory authorities, this will result in the UN having no grounds to press for that suspect's prosecution by the sending State.[315] This may result in impunity if the sending State is therefore not willing to prosecute its returned personnel.[316] The UN requires that the UN police officer under investigation remain

310 Grimstad, *ID Review*, p. 97.

311 UNGA, JIU Report, para. 23. In this respect, it was stated that '[i]nternationally there are not as yet any effective training courses to equip someone without prior experience for the role of investigator'. Ibid, para. 62.

312 UN OIOS, *Investigations Manual*, p. 90; UN DPA/DPKO/DFS, 2015 Policy on Accountability, para. 18.3.

313 UNGA, 2006 Legal Experts Report, para. 84 (i).

314 That is, without extradition or other means of transferring the suspect back to the host State. For a consideration of the human rights obligations of States in relation to the request for the transfer of a suspect, see Chapter 7, Section 4.

315 In such a situation, the repatriation would be voluntary, rather than repatriation on disciplinary grounds. This gives the UN no grounds on which to request information regarding any disciplinary or criminal action taken against the suspect.

316 UNGA, 2006 Legal Experts Report, para. 84 (i).

in the host State until the investigation against him is complete,[317] but it is not very successful in ensuring this happens. Some UN police suspects have fled the country during investigation,[318] or have been given the option of 'voluntary' resignation even after evidence emerged to support the claim of serious wrongdoing, instead of being subject to disciplinary sanctions.[319] Sometimes sending States appear to be involved in the repatriation of personnel before an investigation is complete.[320] It was suggested that this practice may be *de*

317 UN DPKO, 2003 Directives, para. 13. It also states '[l]eaving the mission area without authorization from UN Headquarters to avoid disciplinary procedures or criminal charges shall not be allowed and shall require the Member State concerned to return the individual(s) to the mission area to facilitate the disciplinary process', para. 26. For FPUs, UN, FPU MoU, Article 7 quarter, 7.14.

318 See Judicial System Monitoring Programme, 'JSMP' (6 November 2002) <http://66.102.9.104/search?q=cache:oVvw99PcDQIJ:www.jsmp.minihub.org/News/Summary%25201-8%2520November.pdf+rape+Police+Jordan&hl=ja> accessed 28 July 2005; UNTAET, 'Media Release: Jordanian Civilian Police Indicted on Rape Charges' (24 August 2001) <http://www.un.org/en/peacekeeping/missions/past/etimor/DB/db240801.htm> accessed 28 August 2015; East Timor Action Network (ETAN), 'UN Policeman Charged with Rape in East Timor' (19–25 August 2001) <http://www.etan.org/et2001c/august/19-25/24unpolc.htm> accessed 3 September 2005; UN, 'Police Officers Suspected of Rape Will Enjoy No Immunity UN Official Says' (6 July 2001) <http://www.un.org/peace/etimor/news/01jul06.htm> accessed 22 August 2005; UN, 'Police Officer Serving with UN Mission in East Timor Charged with Rape' (24 August 2001) <http://www.un.org/peace/etimor/news/01aug24.htm> accessed 22 August 2005; UNTAET, 'Media Release' (6 July 2001) <http://www.un.org/peace/etimor/DB/db060701.htm> accessed 22 August 2005; 'UN Peacekeeper Charged with Rape' *BBC* (London, 24 August 2001) <http://news.bbc.co.uk/2/hi/asia-pacific/1508473.stm> accessed 25 August 2006; Frederick Rawski, 'To Waive or Not to Waive: Immunity and Accountability in UN Peacekeeping Operations' (2002) 18 *Connecticut journal of international law* 103; Amnesty International, *Serbia and Montenegro (Kosovo): The Legacy of Past Human Rights Abuses* (EUR 70/009/2004, 31 March 2004, 2004); US Office, 'US Office Pristina' <http://www.usofficepristina.rpo.at/hrkos2.htm> accessed 22 August 2005. In another case, an entire Formed Police unit was repatriated before the completion of investigation. Human Rights Watch, 'EU Should Ensure International Mission is Accountable' (10 March 2008) <https://www.hrw.org/news/2008/03/09/kosovo-eu-should-ensure-international-mission-accountable> accessed 29 August 2015.

319 Duncan Chappell and John Evans, 'The Role, Preparation and Performance of Civilian Police in United Nations Peacekeeping Operations' (1998) 24 *Commonwealth Law Bulletin* 1248, p. 154. See also Human Rights Watch, *Hopes Betrayed*.

320 Amnesty International, 'News' <http://news.amnesty.org/library/index/engeur700052002?open&of=eng-2eu> accessed 23 August 2005. Another account given was that members of Romanian FPU who shot and killed allegedly peaceful demonstrators in UNMIK were repatriated by the sending State before completion of the UN investigation against the UN's wishes. See Durch et al., *Improving Criminal Accountability*, p. 28.

facto encouraged by the time and energy-consuming process that the UN and the related personnel must go through, which may make them consider that it would be much easier to send the suspect back without proper proceedings.[321]

Benchmark 3

3-4 Decision Making Process on Referral of Cases

After an internal investigation has been completed, the UN must decide whether or not to refer a case to a State for possible criminal prosecution. In most cases, a referral would entail the UN sending information to the State concerned so that the latter can seek prosecution based on that information. However, in some cases, in particular where the UN is the victim of the crime (such as where that crime concerns fraud or theft), the UN may refer that case to the relevant State's national court for prosecution.[322] In the case of the host State, criminal proceedings may start before the completion of the internal investigation.[323] In the case of the sending States, the UN decides what to do with the result upon the completion of the investigation.[324]

For the purposes of this work, how the UN decides on disciplinary or administrative sanctions is irrelevant. The pertinent decision is how the UN decides whether to refer a case to a State for potential criminal prosecution, and what it does to ensure that proceedings are brought in that State. That said, normally only those cases in which an allegation has been substantiated will be referred to the national authorities for possible criminal proceedings.[325]

(1) *The BoI System*

In the case of the BoI system, where the host State sought criminal prosecution, the SRSG was vested with the authority to agree whether such proceedings could take place.[326] The decision as to whether proceedings could continue

---

321 E-mail communication with a former UN Legal Advisor, 13 October 2014.

322 This may take place parallel to civil proceedings, but a consideration of civil proceedings is outside the scope of this work.

323 This depends on the determination of issues of immunity. See Chapter 6, Section 1-5.

324 As will be seen later, in Section 3-5.

325 In exceptional cases, it is possible that the UN may refer information relating to unsubstantiated allegations to the national authorities, for example, if the failure to substantiate an allegation is due to a lack of access to the repatriated suspect.

326 UNGA, 'Report of the Secretary-General on the Model Status-of-Forces Agreement for Peace-Keeping Operations' (9 October 1990) UN Doc. A/45/594, para. 47(a), (hereinafter 'Model SOFA'). Decisions were made as to the facts of the case, as well as who bore personal responsibility for the misconduct. Board members also made recommendations as to disciplinary action. UN DPKO, 2003 Directives, para. 16. The Board's findings were

had two phases: the first was whether the act concerned was covered by immunity; the second was whether, where an act was covered by immunity, it should be waived.[327] The SRSG's decision, together with the BoI file, was then sent to Headquarters along the departmental reporting line. The decision to refer a case to the sending State presumably rested with the SG,[328] although this was not normal UN practice.[329] Legal advisors were involved at different stages, from the review of BoI proceedings,[330] to the decision to refer a case to national authorities.[331]

After the Board had completed the process and had made recommendations, there appeared to be a lack of management support and follow-up within the UN.[332] Confusion persisted as to who was responsible for the review and monitoring of the implementation of BoI recommendations at UN Headquarters, with many recommendations being forgotten about.[333] There was no clear policy on how the BoI process was to interface with either the host or sending State's national authorities regarding the criminal investigation.[334]

---

then forwarded to the Head of Mission, often the SRSG, who would make a decision on whether disciplinary action should be taken. Ibid, para. 23.

327 See Chapter 6, Section 1-5.

328 UNGA, 'Report of the Office of Internal Oversight Services on the Activities of the Procurement Task Force for the Period from 1 July 2007 to 31 July 2008' (15 September 2008) UN Doc. A/63/329/Add.1, para. 18, (hereinafter '2008 Procurement TF Report').

329 See Section 2.

330 UN DPKO, 2003 Directives, para. 19.

331 If a referral was made to the host State, this involved legal advisor in the mission. If a referral was made to a sending State, this involved a legal advisor at the Headquarters (the Police Division has a Legal Advisor), and the Office of Legal Affairs. Administrative personnel who carried out administrative and personnel processes relating to administrative or disciplinary action taken by the UN were supported by it. UNGA, 2006 SEA Report, para. 49. Decisions regarding the facts and disciplinary action were final, and there was no internal court for UN police to challenge these. *El Moctar v Secretary-General of the United Nations* Case no UNDT/NBI/2011/011, Judgment no UNDT/2012/113, (UNDT, 24 July 2012); *Prisacariu v Secretary-General of the United Nations* Case no UNDT/NY/2012/023, Judgment No UNDT/2014/045 (UNDT, 23 April 2014).

332 UN, BoI Review, para. 2. UNGA, OIOS Discipline Report, para. 41.

333 UN, BoI Review, para. 5.

334 'If DPKO holds national authorities responsible and accountable for taking disciplinary and criminal action against their nationals, then there must be a clear policy on how the BOI process interfaces with national investigations of serious misconduct. This clarity does not exist at present. There is almost no guidance to field missions on how they can facilitate national investigations of disciplinary incidents'. In addition, guidance on when and how to cooperate with host State criminal proceedings needs to be clarified. 'Cooperation with the investigations of host country authorities should also be clarified.

The situation has been improved to a large extent by the reforms, and by streamlining the BoI system. Some requirements are more clearly set out in the new BoI rules.[335] In the new and limited BoI system, while BoI findings do not provide advice on the action needed, procedures to be followed after the BoI has completed its work have largely remained unchanged.[336] One role played by the BoI remains significant. It determines whether or not the misconduct took place in the course of the performance of official duties, or whether a death or injury was connected to the performance of official duties in any way.[337] This determination has a significant influence on the ability of a State to prosecute UN police personnel using information collected by BoI.[338] One advantage of the new system is that the CDU tracks all misconduct, except for cases that are only known to the OIOS. For those cases, there is additional oversight to ensure that they are not forgotten.

A potential problem regarding the system of referral of BoI cases to national authorities is that the UN maintained that BoI reports were confidential documents. Even where reports were shared with a sending State, it was stipulated that the report could not be used as a basis for criminal proceedings.[339] This is not a problem for the purposes of bringing criminal proceedings if evidence is shared and is available to the State concerned to use. Where the 'raw'

When an act of misconduct amounting to a criminal act occurs and involves military observers, civilian police or UN civilian staff, all of whom do not enjoy immunity from local criminal process, the SG has an obligation to ensure the proper administration of justice. Yet, there is no guidance on how and when the field mission should cooperate and coordinate with local authorities. This may give rise to the perception among the host population of impunity of mission members'. ibid, paras. 30–31.

335 For example, UNMIL requires Board members to be of different nationalities. UNMIL, 'CIVPOL: International Police Service – Standard Operating Procedures' (June 2004) UN Doc. (on file with author).

336 UN DPKO/DFS, 2011 BoI SOP.

337 Ibid, Annex III Guidelines for BOI Members on the Conduct of Inquiries, Section 4. This presumably refers to the initial determination, as the final determination as to whether conduct falls within the official functions is made by the Secretary-General. See the texts accompanying n. 346 and n. 347.

338 See Chapter 6, Section 1-4 for the implications of this determination.

339 The UN document makes this a stipulation with regard to sending States. When a BoI report is shared with a sending State, it remains a UN internal document, and is for official use only. It is 'not to be made public in any way, including for judicial or legislative proceedings'. UN DPKO/DFS, 2008 BoI Directive, para. 16. See also UN DPKO, 2003 Directives, para. 22. See also UNGA, Zeid Report, para. 28 on complaints made by troop contributing countries (TCCs) that they do not receive all the BoI files because of the UN's policy not to release any document that may be used to make a complaint against it.

information was also to be used, the evidence provided by the UN could only act as a trigger for the State concerned to conduct its own investigation. This means that that State would have to collect the same evidence all over again.

(2) *The OIOS System*

OIOS investigation reports contain recommendations for the relevant managers.[340] All investigation reports are transmitted to the DPKO and the respective managers or commanders for follow-up action.[341] Cases are tracked by the CDU except for those exclusively reported to the OIOS.[342] The Permanent Mission of the sending State of the UN police officer concerned is informed of the outcome of the investigation through the CDU at Headquarters, after consultation with the Police Division and the Office of Legal Affairs, as appropriate.[343]

---

340 This includes appropriate administrative or disciplinary action to be taken against the implicated person. UN OIOS, *Investigations Manual*, p. 78.

341 UNGA, 2006 SEA Report, para. 51. UN, Nov 2005 *Code Cable*, Annexed Interim Procedures, para. 4. The findings are then used for disciplinary and administrative purposes by the manager. No appeal process is available to UN police personnel. *El Moctar v Secretary-General of the United Nations*; *Prisacariu v Secretary-General of the United Nations*. Where disciplinary sanctions were decided in a summary manner without BoI being involved, some missions allowed appeals after a preliminary decision. UNMIL, UNMIL SOP, para. 7.9.

342 See Section 3-2.

343 UNGA, 2008 Discipline Report, para. 29. The following account reveals the lengthy procedure in place. The OIOS provides its completed investigation reports to the SG or his designee, which include information and recommendations regarding matters of jurisdiction, or disciplinary actions to be taken. 'Concerned programme managers' are also informed through reporting mechanisms. UN OIOS, *Investigations Manual*, p. 75. In the case of UNPOL officers in Peace Missions, the OIOS report is provided to the Under Secretary-General of the Department of Peacekeeping Operations and the Head of Mission of the concerned Peace Operation for their comment and action. UN, Nov 2005 *Code Cable*, para. 12. Subsequently, the CDU at the Headquarters review the report to assess the propriety of the procedures followed, the investigation findings, and the resulting recommendations. UNGA, 2008 Discipline Report, para. 29. In cases of less serious misconduct, police supervisors in the mission assess the findings in consultation with mission CDUs. Each case is formally transmitted to the Assistant Secretary-General of the Office of Human Resources by the USG of DPKO, following which the headquarters of CDT interfaces with Field Personnel Division in the Department of Field Services (DFS). (The *Code Cable* states that the 'Personnel and Management Support Services (PMSS)' in DPKO must be involved, but since 2005, there has been a reform of the offices and units supporting Peace Operations. The equivalent to PMSS in the current organogram is the Field Personnel Division in DFS. See the organizational chart: UN DPKO, 'Department of Peacekeeping Operations' <http://www.un.org/en/peacekeeping/about/dpko/>

The OLA will be consulted in cases in which UN police officers have been identified as having been involved in a criminal activity,[344] primarily to give advice on providing information on the case to the appropriate national system for prosecution. As with the BoI system, the decision to refer a case to a national jurisdiction is made by the USG of DPKO,[345] but the final decision in all referrals is taken by the Secretary-General.[346] Where the host State initiates criminal proceedings by requesting that a suspect's immunity either be clarified or waived, the SRSG will make the decision in the SG's name.[347]

It is ultimately the SG who takes a decision on: (i) whether or not a particular action constitutes misconduct; and (ii) the action to be taken against the personnel concerned.[348] The result of the investigation, or recommendations of actions based thereon, are not final. Legal advice on the propriety of any action falls within the mandate of the Legal Counsel and the Office of the Legal Affairs.[349]

---

accessed 14 February 2013). They will then coordinate with the Office of Human Resources Management (OHRM), OLA, if necessary, and the Police Division for cases involving UN police personnel. UN, Nov 2005 *Code Cable*, para. 28. The Permanent Mission of the UN police officer concerned is informed of the outcome of the investigation through CDU. UNGA, 2008 Discipline Report, para. 29. When it involves repatriation of individual UN police personnel or members of an FPU, the Police Advisor/Police Division in the Department of Peacekeeping Operations will consult with the Under Secretary-General of the Department and, after his/her clearance, provide advice to the Police Commissioner/Senior Police Advisor in the mission. UN, Nov 2005 *Code Cable*, Annex (Interim procedures to implement General Assembly resolution 59/287 on investigations into misconduct in peacekeeping missions), para. 4. If it is the Head of Police who considers it necessary to repatriate UN police personnel, he or she must recommend this to the USG of DPKO and, in the process, the DPKO Police Advisor should be informed so that he or she can take up the matter with the PCC concerned UN DPKO, Directives for Heads, para. 41. The advice from the DPKO to the Police Commander is communicated through the CDU at Headquarters. At this point, CDU at Headquarters enters the individual's name in the conduct and discipline database, so that the person concerned will not be considered for further service in a Peace Operation. UNGA, 2008 Discipline Report, para. 30.

344 UN, Nov 2005 Code Cable, Annex, Interim procedures, para. 4.

345 Ibid, para. 12.

346 UNGA, 2008 Procurement TF Report, para. 18.

347 UNGA, Model SOFA, para. 47(a).

348 The Secretary-General's note states that, '[T]he final determination of whether any rules have in fact been breached is made by the Secretary-General and his programme managers [...]' (emphasis added). UNGA, 2008 Procurement TF Report, para. 3. Generally speaking, the Secretary-General and his programme managers make such decisions jointly. However, if there is any disagreement, the Secretary-General has the ultimate authority.

349 Ibid, para. 3.

It is problematic if the SRSG's decision (taken in the name of the SG) to refer a case to the national authorities of the sending State for criminal prosecution is made not purely on legal grounds, but also takes account of political considerations. It is reported that the SG considers both the political implications and the UN's interests before he makes that decision.[350] In relation to cases in which the UN has been the victim of financial loss caused by its personnel or contractors, the SG himself has reported that referral to national authorities for legal action must be made after 'a careful evaluation process which encompasses an analysis of policy considerations'.[351] Examples of factors to be considered in such cases include:

> [...] the impact on privileges and immunities; the likelihood of the success of the claim if pursued; the impact upon the reputation of the Organization caused by becoming party to a lawsuit; an evaluation of the expected cost and benefit of entering into such action in view of the high costs and uncertainties of litigation; the exposure of the Organization to financial and other risks; and the potential impact on the internal justice system of the Organization.[352]

While this statement was made in relation to cases in which criminal and civil legal actions are both in view, where a crime is involved, political considerations should not prevent the criminal prosecution of an alleged wrongdoer. In an independent report, the inspectors concluded that executive heads of UN Secretariat offices were given an excessive degree of discretion when dealing with the findings of, and recommendations made in, investigation reports, and that this could include 'concealing evidence and/or burying the findings'.[353] This is a weighty observation about actions that could block individual criminal accountability, and appears to be contrary to the UN's obligations. These obligations are set out in the new MoU, and include notifying the sending State about any well-founded allegations of misconduct by FPU personnel, accompanied by the findings of the UN's internal investigation.[354]

350 Durch et al., *Improving Criminal Accountability*, p. 43, in which it was stated that a determination that there has been criminal conduct, and decisions to refer a case to national authorities, are made by the Secretary-General upon advice from the OLA, taking both the political considerations and the interests of the Organization into account.

351 UNGA, 2008 Procurement TF Report, para. 18.

352 Ibid, para. 19.

353 UNGA, JIU Report, para. 35.

354 UN, FPU MoU, Article 7.21. Currently, there is a general agreement between the UN and sending States of IPOs that this also applies to IPOs. UNGA, 2015 SEA Report, para. 53.

The other issue is time. The aforementioned procedures for determining both sanctions and referral to national authorities mean that decisions are made after a considerable amount of time has passed. These lengthy procedures mean that it would be difficult to respond to the requirements of a time-sensitive criminal prosecution.[355] Considering the short tours of duty undertaken by UN police,[356] the requirement of promptness is more pressing than in normal domestic circumstances.

Benchmark 4

3-5 Follow-Up of Cases Referred to the Sending State

Following the referral of a case to the State concerned, there needs to be systematic follow-up. As it poses particular problems for the sending State, and as the current practice is to make more referrals to sending States,[357] the following analysis focuses on sending States.

One of the most obvious issues is the lack of transparency regarding follow-ups. While it is acknowledged that there has been some improvement on this front, the improvement is from revealing no information to little information. Unlike before 2007, the UN now publishes the numbers of cases referred to national authorities, and the number of cases in which it received some kind of response from those authorities.[358] While the UN is clearly facing challenges in receiving responses from sending States,[359] information on follow-up action stops there. The data are not disaggregated according to the category of personnel. Therefore, it is not known whether the UN follows up more frequently on misconduct committed by military personnel, or that committed by UN police personnel. There is also no means of knowing whether States are more likely to respond to the UN's queries in relation to misconduct by military personnel or UN police personnel. There is no information as to which States cases were referred to, how long these States took to respond after they received these referrals, or what type of responses the UN received. Partial information is available on what in fact happened to the alleged offenders.[360]

---

355 Durch et al., *Improving Criminal Accountability*, p. 33.

356 For the military contingent, Military Observers and UN police, the average tour of duty is one year, but depending on the length of the mandate, sending States and other variables, it can be shorter. See Chapter 2, Section 3-3-1.

357 See Section 3-4.

358 UN CDU, 'Statistics' <https://cdu.unlb.org/Statistics/OverviewofStatistics.aspx>.

359 UNGA, 2013 SEA Report, para. 21, UNGA, 2014 SEA Report, para. 17 (b), (hereinafter '2014 SEA Report'). UNGA, 2011 SEA Report, para. 21.

360 UNGA, 2013 SEA Report, para. 15. In the near future, the UN plans to publish the nationality of those involved in substantiated allegations of sexual exploitation and abuse. UNGA, 2015 SEA Report, para. 55.

The lack of information about what kinds of responses particular States have sent prompts one to wonder, for example, if the UN includes in its figures letters that simply state that the State concerned has decided that there is no foundation to the allegations, and that the alleged UN police offender has been cleared of all charges.[361] If the UN is satisfied with such a response and makes no further inquiry, it would show a lack of political will on the UN's part. In fact, there is an account regarding cases of sexual abuse and exploitation in which some States' responses were not satisfactory.[362]

The rates of response indicate that States' bureaucratic competence or political will is generally weak. The overall rate of response was about 30 percent between the years 2007 and 2012.[363] In 2013, there was a sudden increase in the rate of response to around 91 percent. It is almost impossible to provide an explanation for this sudden rise,[364] although it may partly be due to new ways of seeking responses,[365] or it may be influenced by the new MoU regarding military contingents, which requires sending States to act as primary investigative authorities. However, the MoU also stipulated that the UN would conduct

---

361 One senior UN official confirmed that only those responses that contain information about alleged cases are counted. However, the same official also informed the author that a letter is counted as one response even if that refers to multiple allegations, and that two letters referring to a single case are counted as two responses. Communication with a senior UN official, June 2016.

362 UNGA, 2014 SEA Report, para. 28.

363 Each year between 2007 and 2012, there were between 47 and 82 cases related to sexual exploitation and abuse, and between 14 and 109 cases of other types of misconduct. The response rate is between 11.6% and 57.5% for SEA cases, and between 22.0% and 35.9% for other cases. On average, the response rate regarding case follow ups is 30.3%. The statistics are available at UN CDU, 'Statistics' <https://cdu.unlb.org/Statistics/OverviewofStatistics.aspx>.

364 In 2013, 70 letters were sent to States in relation to cases of sexual exploitation and abuse. The UN received 64 responses. 78 letters were sent to States in relation to cases which did not concern sexual exploitation and abuse. 71 responses were received. This amounts to a 91.4 and 91% response rate respectively. It should be noted that responses are not necessarily received in relation to cases which were referred in the same year. In 2014 and 2015, 61 and 107 letters were issued in relation to cases of sexual exploitation and abuse. The UN received 52 and 115 responses respectively. The UN sent 102 and 109 letters to States in relation to other cases. In response, the affected States responded with 62 and 80 letters. This amounts to a 99.4% and 67.3% response rate respectively. Ibid.

365 UNGA, 2014 SEA Report, para. 46. A senior UN official indicated that this sudden rise in the response rate may be related to the CDU's new method for counting letters. Communication with a senior UN official, June 2016.

an investigation where the States concerned chose not to investigate.[366] One piece of progress is that the new MoU, regarding FPU personnel, sets out the sending State's obligation to pursue the prosecution of its FPU personnel where the host State fails to do so.[367] It is submitted that there should also be a legally binding agreement between the UN and sending States that the latter would take the action necessary for bringing criminal proceedings against those IPOs who are alleged to have committed criminal conduct while on mission.

There is in fact one perplexing tendency in relation to information made public by the UN. In the early years, for example in the 1990s, the UN seemed to have had no problem in revealing the nationality of those accused of misconduct.[368] Recent cases, however, show that the UN appears not to reveal the nationality of alleged perpetrators. This applies to criminal, disciplinary and civil cases across the board. The nationality of suspects is not revealed in the OIOS's annual reports, annual reports on sexual exploitation and abuse, or

---

366 UNGA, 'Revised Draft Model Memorandum of Understanding, as annexed to UNGA, Report of the Special Committee on Peacekeeping Operations and its Working Group on the 2007 Resumed Session' (12 June 2007) UN Doc. A/61/19 (Part III), (hereinafter '2007 MoU').

367 UN, FPU MoU, Article 7 quinquiens, Section 7.18.

368 The information was made public through media releases and daily briefings by the mission and UN headquarters. Amongst them, see UN Press Release, 'Special Committee on Peacekeeping Operations Begins (New York)' (4 April 2005) <www.un.org/News/Press/docs/2005/gapk186.doc.htm> accessed 8 October 2014; UN, 'Jordanian Civilian Police Indicted on Rape Charges' (24 August 2001) <http://www.un.org/en/peacekeeping/missions/past/etimor/DB/db240801.htm> accessed 8 October 2014. Reports of some cases were also found through UN sources, and contained the nationalities of UN police suspects. UNTAET, 'Media Release: Jordanian Civilian Police Indicted on Rape Charges' (24 August 2001) <http://www.un.org/en/peacekeeping/missions/past/etimor/DB/db240801.htm>; UN, 'Police Officers Suspected of Rape Will Enjoy No Immunity UN Official Says' (6 July 2001) <http://www.un.org/peace/etimor/news/01jul06.htm>; UN, 'Police Officer Serving with UN Mission in East Timor Charged with Rape' (24 August 2001) <http://www.un.org/peace/etimor/news/01aug24.htm>; UNTAET, 'Media Release' (6 July 2001) <http://www.un.org/peace/etimor/DB/db060701.htm>; UNTAET, 'Media Release' (3 August 2001) <http://www.un.org/peace/etimor/DB/db030801.htm> accessed 25 July 2005; UNMEE, 'SG Annan Responds to Eritrean Allegations against UNMEE' (May 2004) <http://www.unmeeonline.org/index.php?option=com_content&task=view&id=935&Itemid=53> accessed 15 July 2008; UN, 'Probe Closed of Police Officers Connected to Deadly Shootings in Kosovo' (19 May 2004) <http://www.un.org/apps/news/story.asp?NewsID=10794&Cr=kosovo&Cr1=&Kw1=unmik&Kw2=misconduct&Kw3=> accessed 26 August 2006; UN Wire, (20 April 2004) <http://unwire.org/UNWire/20040420/Current_Print.asp> accessed 26 August 2005.

statements by the UN in response to particular incidents.[369] There was some indication that opinion within the UN is divided on whether to reveal the nationality of suspects against whom an allegation has been substantiated. The UN is also thought to be divided on the issue of whether or not to reveal the nationality of suspects where the States concerned fail to cooperate in holding suspects to account for the crimes they have committed.[370] It made analyzing the following issues virtually impossible: the relationship between the nationality of the suspect and the rate of criminal conduct; identifying which States continuously failed to respond to follow-up inquiries from the UN; and which States had undertaken proper proceedings and applied appropriate sanctions against individual UN police personnel. It is regrettable that, even if suspects came from States with very poor records of tackling misconduct, the UN did not reveal their nationalities. There may have been political considerations for keeping the information internal,[371] in particular if it were considered that this information might have had a negative impact on sending States' willingness to send more personnel for future missions. In this regard, an observation was made that the UN has an internal culture of reluctance, close to being a taboo, about speaking out about differences between national contingents, and that this results in the 'fear of offending particular member states by comparing their behavior with others, particularly, in this case, by suggesting differing degrees of criminality'.[372] Currently, this trend is being partially reversed. The SG intends to start publishing the nationality of the wrongdoers in cases of sexual

369 UNGA, 2014 SEA Report; UNGA, 2013 SEA Report; UNGA, 2012 SEA Report; UNGA, 2011 SEA Report; UNGA, Report of the Secretary-General, 'Special measures for Protection from Sexual Exploitation and Sexual Abuse' (18 February 2010), UN Doc. A/64/669;UNGA, 2009 SEA Report; annual reports by the OIOS on peacekeeping operations, including UNGA, 2014 OIOS PKO Report; UNGA, 2012 OIOS PKO Report; UNGA, 2011 OIOS PKO Report; UNGA, 2010 OIOS PKO Report; UNGA, 2009 OIOS PKO Report.

370 An OIOS report in 2013 recorded that the OIOS continues to investigate and to provide assistance to investigations of military contingent members, despite the new MoU. Five such cases were referred back to the missions concerned by the sending States due to the low level of misconduct. UNGA, Pilot Project Report, para. 19. The Zeid Report suggested that States which fail to cooperate should be named, para. 82.

371 Marco Odello, 'Tackling Criminal Acts in Peacekeeping Operations: The Accountability of Peacekeepers' (2010) 15 *Journal of Conflict and Security Law*, p. 351. This can be coupled with the sending State's reluctance to admit wrongdoing: the Zeid report stated that sending States were reluctant 'to admit publicly to acts of wrong doing'. UNGA, Zeid Report 67(a). This may apply to the police as well. Durch et al., *Improving Criminal Accountability*, p. 28.

372 Lutz, Gutmann and Brown, *Report to CDU*, p. 5.

exploitation and abuse, where these have been substantiated in the UN's internal proceedings.[373]

In addition, where an allegation of a crime is substantiated, it is necessary for the UN to agree with the sending State that the suspect must go back to the sending State. If the suspect is free to leave the host State to go to a third State, this will lessen the chance that he will be prosecuted. This agreement could be included in MoUs in relation to FPU personnel, and in *Notes Verbales* in relation to IPOs. In order to ensure that this can be achieved, the UN requires the authority to hold the suspect until he is sent back to the sending State, and the mechanisms for doing so. This can be done through detaining the suspect, or in other ways, but these will all involve the modification of the agreement between the sending and host States. When the suspect is sent back to the sending State, his return should be accompanied by any information generated by the UN's investigation into the alleged crime. This transfer of information is required in relation to FPUs,[374] and should be replicated in relation to IPOs. In order to maximize the prospect of prosecution, information should be sent to a particular contact point, preferably a prosecutor in the sending State. In fact, when a State sends its police officers to join a UN mission, there should be an agreement between the UN and the sending State as to who should act as the particular contact point on the issue of individual accountability, so that the follow up on each case is made smoother.

It is not known whether or not there is a routine procedure the UN and States follow for cooperating on additional investigations and other judicial procedures. In the early 2000s, there was no such system.[375] Judicial cooperation between States and the UN has been encouraged,[376] but there are few

373 UNGA, 2015 SEA Report, para. 55. An independent report, which analyzed how effectively the UN dealt with allegations of sexual exploitation and abuse by members of non-UN and UN forces, has also revealed the nationality of alleged wrongdoers. Deschamps, Jallow and Sooka, *2015 CAR Report*.

374 UN, FPU MoU, Article 7, Section 7.21.

375 UN, BoI Review, paras. 30–31.

376 UNGA Res 62/63 (8 January 2008) UN Doc. A/RES/62/63, para. 4; UNGA Res 63/119 (15 January 2009) UN Doc. A/RES/63/119, op. para. 3; UNGA Sixth Committee, 'Draft Resolution on the Criminal Accountability of United Nations Officials and Experts on Mission' (27 October 2011) UN Doc. A/C.6/66/L.16 op. para. 3; UNGA Res 64/110 (15 January 2010) UN Doc. A/RES/64/110, op. para. 3;UNGA Res 65/20 (10 January 2011) UN Doc. A/RES/65/20, op. para. 3; UNGA Res 66/93 (13 January 2012) UN Doc. A/RES/66/93, op. para. 3; UNGA Res 67/88 (14 January 2013) UN Doc. A/RES/67/88, op. para. 3.

details available as to either side's legal obligations.[377] One exception is that States sending FPU personnel are obliged to cooperate with the host State's criminal proceedings where these take place.[378] Where an agreement results in a legally binding obligation,[379] there is no prescribed procedure for what should happen if the obligation is breached by either party. Where mechanisms are subject to *ad hoc* responses, they may not exert sufficient pressure to ensure that criminal accountability is enforced. There is an urgent need for the UN to consider a more established mechanism for follow-up and post-investigation cooperation.

3-6 Conclusion

The UN's internal proceedings have not been effective in facilitating individual criminal accountability. The UN is in a difficult position: it has neither the authority nor the mechanisms necessary to address individual criminal accountability itself. This is not likely to change.[380] The best the UN can do is to attempt to facilitate criminal proceedings in one State or another.

In order for the UN to effectively facilitate the criminal accountability of individual UN police personnel, its administrative and disciplinary proceedings need to be carefully designed. The system needs to effectively receive information on potential criminal misconduct, and each subsequent stage – from

377 For FPUs, the Model FPU MoU sets out the UN's obligation to provide 'a complete report of the findings of the investigation' to the sending State, but there is no obligation following this transfer of information. UN, FPU MoU, Article 7 sexiens, 7.21. No equivalent exists for Individual Police Officers (IPOs). On cooperation between the UN and the host State, where either or both have an interest in alleged offences, they nevertheless have an obligation to assist each other in carrying out 'all necessary investigations'. This includes assistance after the initial referral. UNGA, Model SOFA, para. 44.

378 UN, FPU MoU, para. 7.18. This is presumably only where the host State has a functioning legal system that can deliver trials in accordance with requirements of IHRL, and where the conduct in question either does not attract immunity or where immunity is waived. See Chapter 2, Section 1 on the varying legal environments of host States. See Chapter 6, Section 1-4 on the applicability of immunity. See Chapter 6, Section 1-5 on the waiver of immunity.

379 Under the General Convention, the UN is bound to cooperate with appropriate local authorities to facilitate the proper administration of justice. Convention on the Privileges and Immunities of the United Nations (adopted 13 February 1946, entered into force 17 September 1946) 1 UNTS 15, Section 21. This is stipulated in relation to Officials, but the OLA considers that the UN is under a legal obligation to cooperate with the appropriate local authorities to facilitate the proper administration of justice in all States. UN, OLA letter. This applies in relation to State parties.

380 For a discussion of criminal jurisdiction, see Chapter 5, Section 3-4.

the centralization and registration of such information, to investigation, to decision-making on what to do with the investigation results, to following up substantiated cases with States – must be tailored to maximize the chances of criminal accountability taking place. In addition, an independent oversight of the UN's dealings on misconduct would result in greater effectiveness.

The UN has made a significant effort since the mid-1990s, and it continues to do so. Disciplinary codes, as well as the rules and procedures to be followed in administrative and disciplinary proceedings have been clarified. Awareness-raising activities have been conducted to raise both internal and external awareness about what constitutes criminal misconduct, and how and where to lodge a complaint. The time-consuming BoI system has been reviewed, streamlined and largely replaced with a new system involving the OIOS and CDU. This has addressed the quality of investigation to some extent.[381] Most notably, a significant improvement is the introduction by the UN of a centralized record and tracking system.[382]

One general observation is that the overall effort regarding personal accountability is heavily focused on SEA. For example, in response to the OIOS's recommendation that there should be a formal coordination mechanism for all relevant components on conduct and discipline, the DPKO stated that it would make these mechanisms clear through SEA directives.[383] In terms of awareness-raising, the UN's efforts have almost exclusively centred round SEA.[384] Data on the status of investigations is only available for SEA cases.[385] While it is an important issue, the UN also urgently needs to address other types of misconduct. According to the data collected by the CDU between 2007 and 2015, SEA allegations included in Category I misconduct allegations ranged between 23 and 40 percent for all categories of personnel, and between 15 and 53 percent for UN police personnel.[386] Other misconduct, such as theft, corruption, and drunk and other dangerous ways of driving, is also common in some missions.[387] Reports of SEA allegations against UN police officers have slowly decreased since 2007, from 24 allegations in 2007 to 16 in 2015. Category

381 See Sections 2 and 3-3.

382 See Section 3-2.

383 UNGA, OIOS Discipline Report, recommendation 21.

384 See Section 3-1-1 (1).

385 UN CDU, 'Statistics' <https://cdu.unlb.org/Statistics/OverviewofStatistics.aspx>.

386 Ibid.

387 Lutz, Gutmann and Brown, *Report to CDU*, p. 5; Communications with senior UN officials, June and July 2016.

I allegations[388] involving UN police officers, but which exclude SEA cases, do not show a similar decrease.[389] The proportion of all reported misconduct cases which is SEA cases does not justify leaving aside other types of serious misconduct.[390]

There remain multiple flaws in the system. One part of the solution is to ensure that all allegations are properly recorded, and result in investigations. While awareness and access to complaint mechanisms have been improved, lodging a complaint is still heavily reliant on the complainant being literate.[391] The protection of victims, witnesses and internal whistle-blower appears in the code, but all available information indicates that implementation is problematic.[392] The code must be properly implemented, including taking disciplinary action against personnel and managers who fail to report misconduct or to pass relevant information to the appropriate internal unit, or to respond promptly and appropriately. The central repository of allegations should be better designed. The UN has created a centralized case database, but due to considerations regarding independence and confidentiality, the central repository does not have access to OIOS cases.[393] It would be better if OIOS were to function as the central repository in that case.

A second part of the solution lies with the quality of investigations. Efforts to ensure independent and professional investigations into allegations led the UN to refer all allegations of serious misconduct to the OIOS. However, the OIOS's struggle to carry out prompt investigations resulted in it returning many cases to the mission.[394] The UN needs to find a way to ensure that allegations are investigated by qualified investigators.

Efforts were also made to improve the quality of investigations, but the standard of proof, the ways in which investigations are conducted, and the results of investigations remain administrative in nature, and do not meet the standard to be used for criminal prosecution in States. The evidence collected is not likely to be useful in criminal prosecutions. Some barriers in respect of evidential rules are not unique to UN investigations. For example, different requirements imposed by domestic rules of evidence cannot realistically be

388 This is a distinction made by the Office of the Internal Oversight Services (OIOS). All allegations relating to criminal acts and serious misconduct are included in Category I.

389 The data shows that 21, 40, 15, 38, 21, 13, 18, 14 and 27 allegations were made between 2007 and 2015 respectively.

390 Such as murder, theft and motoring offences. See Chapter 3, Section 2-2.

391 See Section 3-1-1.

392 See Sections 3-1-1 (1) c and 3-1-1 (2) c.

393 See Section 3-2.

394 See Section 3-3.

expected to be overcome by increasing the professionalism of UN investigations. Therefore, States are likely to require information over and above that which the UN provides. Currently, there is no set mechanism within the UN for obtaining additional evidence or evidence of the type that can be used in criminal proceedings. This mechanism needs to be agreed with States as otherwise it will be very difficult for willing States to prosecute the UN police personnel. This also raises the question of whether States need to harmonize their rules, for example by agreeing on the minimum standard for admissible scientific evidence.

The third part of the solution lies with the decision to refer a case to a national authority for prosecution. There is an apparent lack of policies dealing with when and how to cooperate with national investigatory authorities. It is now mandatory for the UN to notify the sending State where an allegation of misconduct by a member of FPU has been established as being well-founded, and to send any findings reached by the UN investigation to the sending State. Similar formal agreements need to be reached between the UN and sending States of IPOs.[395] In general, the decision to actively refer a case for criminal prosecution appears to remain within the discretion of the Secretary-General. This is problematic.[396]

Most significantly, the fourth part of the solution lies in addressing the UN's failure to provide an effective response once it completes an investigation. Where its investigation substantiates an alleged crime, virtually all the UN does is to send this information to the suspect's sending State. States are then requested to respond to the UN, disclosing information regarding any investigation or proceedings they have undertaken, the results of any such investigation and the sanctions imposed and, if not pursued further, the reasons for this. States only respond to one third of such requests, and the UN appears to accept this rate of response. The UN does not take any further action to ensure that States actually do what they claim to do.[397] For example, the UN could make public the names of States that do not respond to the UN's inquiries. In such circumstances, the efforts exerted in conducting investigations are not also exerted to ensure criminal accountability. The inevitable conclusion is that, for whatever reasons, the UN does not put much effort into reaching its aim of 'Zero Tolerance',[398] in particular in relation to what happens after allegations

---

395 See Section 3-4.

396 See Section 3-4.

397 See Section 3-5.

398 'Zero Tolerance' has been used as a policy to tackle the SEA issues throughout the UN. In 2002, the then-SG stated that 'Sexual exploitation and abuse by humanitarian staff cannot

have been substantiated. There is a mismatch between the promises made, and their delivery.

One clear trend has emerged from this analysis, and that is the varying extent to which arrangements in relation to IPOs and FPUs are systematized. In relation to FPUs, there is an obligation on the UN to send all information regarding substantiated cases of misconduct to the sending State.[399] The obligation of the sending State to bring the case to the prosecuting authorities is also clear only in relation to FPUs.[400] The obligation of the sending State to cooperate with the host State where the latter seeks prosecution is also set out in relation to FPUs.[401] It is probable that the difference in arrangements regarding IPOs and FPUs has arisen because those regarding FPUs are much more recent. The UN may consider the FPU arrangements to constitute good practice. In that case, it is necessary to replicate this arrangement in relation to IPOs insofar as the difference in the mode of deployment does not affect the content of the agreement between the UN and the sending State.

This Chapter has analyzed the ways in which the UN assists in the gathering of evidence in order for host or sending States to prosecute a UN police suspect. Following the initial collection of evidence, the States concerned are required to take action. In order for these States to bring criminal proceedings against UN police officers for crimes they have committed, they must first have criminal jurisdiction over the matter. Thus, the next Chapter will consider the issue of jurisdiction.

be tolerated'. UNGA, OIOS West Africa Report, para. 3. The UN SG reiterated: 'Let me be clear: the United Nations, and I personally, are profoundly committed to a zero-tolerance policy against sexual exploitation or abuse by our own personnel. This means zero complacency. When we receive credible allegations, we ensure that they are looked into fully. It means zero impunity'. UN CDU, 'CDU web' <https://cdu.unlb.org/>.

399 UN, FPU MoU, Article 7 sexiens, Section 7.21.

400 Ibid, Article 7 sexiens, Section 7.22.

401 Ibid, Article 7 quinquiens, Section 7.18.

CHAPTER 5

Criminal Jurisdiction under International and National Law

1 Introduction

Previous chapters have shown that, across all missions, UN police do not appear to have been prosecuted when they have committed serious crimes.[1] It has also been shown that the absence of prosecutions is not because there is no mechanism to address serious misconduct.[2] Rather, there are mechanisms in place within the UN for this purpose. Relying, in part, on the outcome of the investigations carried out by those mechanisms, both host and sending States are in a position to bring prosecutions against UN police personnel who have been alleged to have engaged in criminal behaviour. There is, however, a mismatch between the existence of such mechanisms, and the apparent lack of criminal proceedings.[3] This necessitates inquiring whether there are legal barriers which create difficulties for States, which would otherwise be willing to bring criminal proceedings.

The first potential legal barrier is criminal jurisdiction. In discussing this matter, a distinction must be made between prescriptive and enforcement jurisdiction. Prescriptive jurisdiction refers to the legally binding criminal law norms themselves, whilst enforcement jurisdiction refers to the enforcement of those norms, which involves the exercise of jurisdiction.[4] As this work

---

1 See Chapter 3, Section 3.

2 See Chapter 4, Sections 2 and 3.

3 See Chapter 3, Section 3.

4 This theory divides jurisdiction into two categories: legislative or prescriptive jurisdiction, and enforcement jurisdiction. The *Lotus* case distinguished prescriptive from enforcement jurisdiction, holding that the former was considered as the jurisdiction required to prescribe rules, whilst the latter was the jurisdiction required to enforce these rules. SS *Lotus* (*France v. Turkey*) PCIJ Rep Series A No10, pp. 18–19. Mann describes enforcement jurisdiction as one which concerns the lawfulness of those acts of a State which give effect to its national regulation. The existence of legislative jurisdiction is not considered sufficient basis on which to exercise enforcement jurisdiction in another State's territory. F A Mann, 'The Doctrine of International Jurisdiction Revised after Twenty Years' in W Michael Reisman (ed), *Jurisdiction in International Law* (Aldershot 1999), pp. 139–236. Brownlie, however, claims that there is no essential distinction between the limits on legislative jurisdiction and enforcement

 | DOI 10.1163/9789004328815_006

analyses what may hinder criminal prosecution, and seeks ways to encourage prosecution, this chapter mostly focuses on enforcement jurisdiction.

First, in order for criminal proceedings to be brought against members of the UN police, the police must be legally bound by criminal law. All of those who are to be involved in potential criminal proceedings, namely the individual members of the UN police, States and the UN, need to have the same understanding of the legal regimes to which the UN police are subject. This work thus seeks to clarify whether UN police personnel are bound by the criminal law of the host State and/or their sending States and, if they are, how this is given effect. In addition, whether the UN ensures (a) that the relevant criminal codes apply to UN police officers; and (b) that States, as well as individual members of UN police, are aware of the binding nature of these criminal codes, and how this is done, will also be examined.

Second, whether States can exercise criminal jurisdiction over misconduct by UN police officers will be considered. The first issue arising in this regard is whether States are free to exercise criminal jurisdiction under international law. Determining this requires an analysis of the notion of permissive jurisdiction,[5] which grants the authority to prosecute an alleged author of criminal conduct.

---

jurisdiction. He sees them as being two sides of the same coin. Ian Brownlie, *Principles of Public International Law* (3rd edn, Oxford University Press 1979), p. 309. According to another theory, jurisdiction is divided into three categories: legislative, judicial and executive jurisdiction. See, for example, Michael Akehurst, 'Jurisdiction in International Law' in Michael Reisman (ed), *Jurisdiction in International Law* (pp. 25–138, Ashgate 1999), pp. 25–138. The Council of Europe has also taken this position. See Council of Europe, *Extraterritorial Criminal Jurisdiction* (1990). Legislative jurisdiction is the jurisdiction to 'establish in general the contents and scope of application of certain national norms and prescriptive rules'. Judicial jurisdiction refers to the application of the 'established jurisdiction in a particular litigation or proceedings'. Executive jurisdiction means the jurisdiction to actually enforce orders or prescriptive rules deriving from the judiciary or legislature. Ibid, p. 18. Akehurst defines legislative jurisdiction as constituting the power of a State to apply its laws to cases involving a foreign element; judicial jurisdiction as the power of a State's courts to try cases involving a foreign element; and executive jurisdiction as a State's power to perform acts in the territory of another State. Akehurst, 'Jurisdiction in IL', p. 59. Thus, the discussion appears to focus on extra-territorial jurisdiction, or jurisdiction in relation to cases involving 'foreign' elements.

5 The obligation on States under international law to investigate and prosecute a suspect when s/he is present in their territory only applies in relation to limited international crimes under the Geneva Conventions and other specific treaties. Even in instances such as these, the obligation on States is that of *aut dedere aut judicare* (the obligation to extradite or to prosecute). This is a qualified obligation. The State's obligation to prosecute will be discussed in Chapter 7, Section 1.

Thus, the type of jurisdiction considered here is enforcement jurisdiction.[6] The question is whether international law places any restrictions on States' exercise of criminal jurisdiction and, if so, what is prohibited in relation to the host, sending and other States.

Even where States are able to exercise criminal jurisdiction under international law, their domestic law may place limitations on their ability to bring proceedings against suspects. Therefore, national criminal laws need to be examined to see if States are able to bring such proceedings under their domestic laws. Where feasible, and where these are found to exist, practical barriers to exercising jurisdiction will also be identified.

There is currently no standard criminal code that applies to all UN police personnel, nor is there a UN criminal tribunal where the UN can itself bring criminal proceedings against its own personnel.[7] Whilst a recent argument posits that the UN should establish its own model criminal code,[8] create a hybrid criminal tribunal, and exercise criminal jurisdiction,[9] the evaluation

---

6 Or judicial jurisdiction, according to the theory that divides jurisdiction into three categories: legislative, judicial and executive jurisdiction. See n. 4. above.

7 UNGA, 'Note by the Secretariat: Criminal Accountability of United Nations Officials and Experts on mission' (11 September 2007) UN Doc A/62/329, para. 16.

8 William J Durch et al., *Improving Criminal Accountability in United Nations Peace Operations* (Stimson Center Report, 2009), pp. 59–60.

9 UNGA, 'Ensuring the Accountability of United Nations Staff and Experts on Mission with Respect to Criminal Acts Committed in Peacekeeping Operations' (16 August 2006) UN Doc. A/60/980, paras. 33–37. This argument, which challenges the generally accepted position that the UN cannot exercise criminal jurisdiction, is made on the basis that international tribunals may be created either through treaties, or through the powers invested in the Security Council. Another suggestion was that a high-ranking Civil Provost should be appointed in major missions. The Civil Provost would be the principal contact point with the host State's criminal justice system, and would 'marshal resources on the UN side of the collaborative criminal justice effort and also work with OIOS forensic field investigators'. The Civil Provost would not solve problems relating to criminal jurisdiction, but would provide support on behalf of the UN for the host State's exercise of criminal jurisdiction. Durch et al., *Improving Criminal Accountability*, pp. 60–65. Ibid, pp. 21–22, citing UNGA, 'Final Act of the United Nations Diplomatic Conference of Plenipotentiaries on the Establishment of an International Criminal Court' (17 July 1998) UN Doc. A/CONF.183/10; UNSC Res 827 (25 May 1993) UN Doc. S/RES/827, establishing the UN International Criminal Tribunal for the Former Yugoslavia (ICTY); UNSC Res 955 (8 November 1994) UN Doc. S/RES/955, establishing the UN International Criminal Tribunal for Rwanda; UNSC Res 1244 (10 June 1999) UN Doc. S/RES/1244, establishing the UN Interim Administration Mission in Kosovo (UNMIK); UNSC Res 1272 (25 October 1999) UN Doc. S/RES/1272, establishing the UN Transitional Administration in East Timor (UNTAET); and UNSC Res 1315 (14 August 2000) UN Doc. S/RES/1315, establishing the Special Court for Sierra Leone.

of such a prospect is outside the scope of this work. However, if such a tribunal were to be formed, its task would be to consider breaches of national criminal law.

The applicability of International Criminal Law (ICL) is not considered in this chapter for two reasons. One reason is that it is very unlikely that the UN police would engage in international crimes.[10] There have not been any allegations thus far that the UN police have, in fact, engaged in international crimes.[11] The other is that there is no question of the applicability of ICL, as the very notion underlying ICL is that the crimes set out in it are so grave that it applies to all persons irrespective of borders.[12] Therefore, the analysis herein is focused on the domestic criminal laws of States, primarily those of the host and sending States.

2 Criminal Laws to Which the UN Police are Subject

2-1 *The Host State's Criminal Law*

One possibility is that members of the UN police are subject to the criminal law of the host State. As the host State is the territorial State in which the alleged

10 Piracy, war crimes and slavery are international crimes under customary international law. Antonio Cassese, *International Criminal Law* (Oxford University Press 2003), pp. 284–285. However, note that Cassese observes that piracy has a different nature from war crimes and slavery, and that there is thus doubt as to whether piracy is an international crime. However, it is subject to universal jurisdiction. Convention on the High Seas (adopted 29 April 1958, entered into force 30 September 1962) 450 UNTS 11, Preamble; Geneva Academy of International Humanitarian Law and Human Rights, *Counterpiracy under International Law* (Academy Briefing No 1, August 2012), pp. 14–15. With the exception of these crimes, international crimes are defined by a treaty, which requires States to prosecute a person if there is reason to believe that he has committed an international crime. In addition, crimes under the Rome Statute are international crimes. On the sources of international crimes, see Cassese, *International Criminal Law*, pp. 25–37. Given how international crimes are defined, it is unlikely that non-military members of UN missions would commit such crimes, although they could be viewed as an accomplice where a third party commits an international crime.

11 See Chapter 3, Sections 1 and 2.

12 Cassese, *International Criminal Law*, pp. 23–25. Problems may arise in incorporating international crimes in domestic criminal law, in defining international crimes in domestic criminal law, and in applying domestic law (where it criminalizes international law) extra-territorially. In addition, there may be an issue regarding immunity. Ibid, pp. 301–311, 321–326.

offence took place, it is almost universally accepted that its criminal laws are applicable.[13]

2-1-1 The Obligation to 'respect'

It is not clearly stated anywhere that UN police personnel are bound by the host State's criminal code. The main documents dealing with Peace Operations simply state that UN police officers have an obligation 'to respect' local laws and regulations. The first legal instrument that evidences this is the Status-of-Forces Agreement (SOFA). A SOFA is a legally binding agreement governing the relationship between the UN Peace Operation and the host State.[14] It sets out the rights, obligations and duties between the two,[15] as well as the applicable laws, and the status of the Operation and its personnel.[16] SOFAS can take two different forms: either they are treaties signed by the Secretary-General and a representative of the host State, or they consist of letters of exchange between the two parties. Both constitute a valid and legally binding SOFA.[17] Where an Operation does not have a military component, the agreement between the UN and the host State is called a Status-of-Mission Agreement (SOMA).[18] In most Peace Operations, the UN and the host State have agreed on a SOFA/SOMA, but some missions have either been established without these,[19] or have begun

---

13 The *Lotus* Court stated in 1927 that, 'in all systems of law the principle of territorial character of criminal law is fundamental'. *Lotus* (*France v Turkey*) (Judgment) PCIJ Rep Series A No 10, para. 20.

14 Bruce Oswald, *Documents on the Law of UN Peace Operations* (Oxford University Press 2010), p. 12.

15 United Nations Law Reform Project, 'UN Peacekeeping and The Model Status of Forces Agreement' (Experts' Workshop), p. 1.

16 Oswald, *Documents*, p. 12.

17 United Nations Law Reform Project, 'UN Peacekeeping and The Model Status of Forces Agreement', para. 64.

18 Ralph Zacklin, 'United Nations Management of Legal Issues' in Jessica Howard and Bruce Oswald CSC (eds), *The Rule of Law on Peace Operations, 'Challenges of Peace Operations' Project Conference* (Law School, University of Melbourne, 11–13 November 2002, Kluwer Law International 2002), p. 118.

19 For example, no SOFA was concluded between the UN and the host State for UN Transitional Administration in East Timor (UNTAET). However,, military contingents were governed by SOFAS entered into by the sending States and the host State. United Nations Law Reform Project, 'UN Peacekeeping and The Model Status of Forces Agreement', para. 84. No SOFA was agreed between Eritrea and the UN despite a Security Council resolution requesting that the parties conclude a SOFA. Ibid, para. 87. UNSC Res 1320 (15 September 2000) UN Doc. S/RES/1320, op. para. 6. No SOFA was concluded for the UN Disengagement Observer Force (UNDOF), because there were disputes as to who held the authority to

before any such agreements were entered into.[20] Eventually, the UN began to rely on a model agreement it had drawn up, partly as a response to such situations.[21]

The Model SOFA was drafted in 1990,[22] and serves as a basis for negotiating and drafting specific SOFA agreements.[23] In recent Peace Operations, the UN considers the Model SOFA provisionally binding on both it and the host State, until such time as a mission-specific SOFA has been concluded.[24] When a Security Council resolution, made under Chapter VII, has been passed which stipulates that it applies on a provisional basis, it becomes fully legally binding.[25] Inasmuch as the Model SOFA was based on SOFAs from previous UN Peace Operations, it reflected the practice of earlier operations.[26] Whether this

---

sign such an agreement. Bruno Simma and others, *The Charter of the United Nations: A Commentary*, vol 2 (Oxford University Press Oxford 2002), case of UNDOF.

20 The African Union-United Nations Mission in Darfur (UNAMID) was deployed before the mission-specific SOFA was concluded. That SOFA was finally concluded more than six months after the deployment of the mission. United Nations Law Reform Project, 'UN Peacekeeping and The Model Status of Forces Agreement', paras. 62, 85. MONUC took more than five months to conclude a SOFA. Ibid, para. 86.

21 However, the provisional use of the model SOFA was not included in the UN's initial plans. Ibid, para. 61.

22 It was drafted in response to a request from the General Assembly, and was included in Report of the Secretary-General, 'The Model status-of-forces agreement for peace-keeping operations' (1990) UN Doc A/45/594.

23 In the case of SOMA, it only applies *mutatis mutandis*. Ibid, para. 2. Zacklin, 'Legal Issues', p. 119.

24 Oswald, *Documents*, p. 34.

25 See for example, the Security Council resolutions establishing the following missions: UNAMID, UNSC Res 1769 (31 July 2007) UN Doc S/RES/1769, op. para. 15 (b); UN Mission in the Central African Republic and Chad (MINURCAT) UNSC Res 1778 (25 September 2007) UN Doc S/RES/1778, op. para. 4; UN Mission in Sudan (UNMIS) UNSC Res 1590 (24 March 2005), UN Doc. S/RES/1590, op. para. 16 (ii); UN Mission in the Central African Republic (MINURCA) op. para. 19, UNSC Res 1159 (27 March 1998) UN Doc S/RES/1159; UN Mission in Ethiopia and Eritrea (UNMEE), UNSC Res 1320 (15 September 2000) UN Doc S/RES/1320, op. para. 6; UN Mission in Sierra Leone (UNAMSIL), UNSC Res 1270 (22 October 1999), UN Doc S/RES/1270), op. para. 16; UN Stabilization Mission in Haiti (MINUSTAH), UNSC Res 1542 (30 April 2004), UN Doc S/RES/1542, op. para. 11; UN Operation in Burundi (ONUB), UNSC Res 1545 (21 May 2004), UN Doc S/RES/1545. op. para. 10; UN Operation in Côte d'Ivoire (UNOCI), UNSC Res 1528 (27 February 2004), UN Doc S/RES/1528, op. para. 9; and UNSC Res 1291 (24 Feb 2000), UN Doc S/RES/1291 expanding MONUC's mandate, op. para. 10.

26 United Nations Law Reform Project, 'UN Peacekeeping and The Model Status of Forces Agreement', para. 9. However, at least some parts of the Model SOFA are not reflective of

practice can be considered as evidence of customary law is a difficult question. In part, this is because not much of the content appears to reflect customary international law in relation to the status of foreign visiting forces belonging to the UN.[27]

SOFAs often include the obligation of the UN Peace Operation, and its members, to '*respect* all local laws and regulations'.[28] This obligation contains two sets of rules: one is that all personnel 'shall *respect* all local laws and regulations', and the other is a corresponding obligation on the Special Representative requiring him or her to 'take all appropriate measures to ensure the observance of these obligations'.[29] The obligation of UN personnel to respect local laws and regulations has also been written into the Convention governing the scope of States' obligations in respect of the safety of personnel working for the UN.[30]

This obligation is also set out in the rules that apply directly to the conduct of UN police officers. All UN police officers are required to sign an Individual Undertaking and Declaration.[31] It appears that this requirement is being met;

---

earlier practice, for example, those rules governing the status of the Police Commissioner. See Chapter 6, Section 1-3.

27 Dieter Fleck (ed) *The Handbook of the Law of Visiting Forces* (Oxford University Press 2001), pp. 493–494.

28 (Emphasis added). UNGA, 'Report of the Secretary-General on the Model Status-of-Forces Agreement for Peace-Keeping Operations' (9 October 1990) UN Doc. A/45/594, Annex, para. 6, (hereinafter 'model SOFA'). See also the SOFAs for UNAMID, MINUSTAH, UNMIS and the UN Mission in South Sudan (UNMISS): UNSC Res 1769 (31 July 2007) UN Doc. S/RES/1769, op. para. 5; UNSC Res 1542 (30 April 2004) UN Doc. S/RES/1542, op. para. 5; UNSC Res 1590 (24 March 2005) UN Doc. S/RES/1590, op. para. 5; UNSC Res 1996 (8 July 2011) UN Doc. S/RES/1996, op. para. 5. However, it should be noted that some SOFAs excluded this provision, for example, SOFAs for the UN Transitional Authority in Eastern Slavonia, Baranja and Western Sirmium (UNTAES), the UN Mission of Observers in Tajikistan (UNMOT), the UN Observer Mission in Georgia (UNOMIG), and the UN Observer Mission in Rwanda-Uganda (UNOMUR). See United Nations Law Reform Project, 'UN Peacekeeping and The Model Status of Forces Agreement', para. 187.

29 (Emphasis added). The model SOFA refers to 'those' obligations'. UNGA, Model SOFA, para. 6. This formula appears to suggest that the obligation that the Secretary-General is required to ensure is the 'obligation to respect'.

30 Convention on the Safety of United Nations and Associated Personnel (adopted on 9 December 1994, entered into force on 15 January 1999) 2051 UNTS 363, Article 61, (hereinafter the 'Safety Convention').

31 Undertaking and Declaration by Experts on Mission: UN Police Officer/Corrections Officer/Military Observers/Military Liaison Officer, (hereinafter 'Undertaking'); Annex 3 to UN DPKO, 'Guidelines for United Nations Police Officers on Assignment with Peacekeeping

at least, this has been the case in recent years.[32] By signing it, each officer agrees to be *bound* by all the laws and regulations contained therein.[33] These include: the Regulations Governing the Status, Basic Rights and Duties of Officials other than Secretariat Officials, and Experts on Mission;[34] the Directives for Disciplinary Matters involving Civilian Police Officers and Military Observers;[35] the Directive on Sexual Harassment in UN Peacekeeping and Other Field Missions, *aides-memoirs* entitled 'Ten Rules: Code of Personal Conduct for Blue Helmets' (blue cards); and 'We are UN Peacekeepers'.[36]

Operations' UN Doc. DPKO/PD/2006/00135, (hereinafter '2007 Guidelines'). All UN police officers are required to sign it upon deployment, in presence of an authorized witness.

32 In 2011, the Police Adviser at the Department of Peacekeeping Operations confirmed that, in the five years prior to this, every single UN police officer had signed an Undertaking upon deployment to a mission. Ann-Marie Orler, 'Professionalism: UN Policing 2012' (2011) 8 *UN Police Magazine* 3, p. 4.

33 All Mission Directives, Standard Operating Procedures (SOPs), Mission policies and other applicable issuances. UN DPKO, Undertaking, para. 10.

34 Historically speaking, first, the Secretary-General announced that a UN 'Code of Conduct' for staff members was to be adopted as part of the development of a transparent and effective system of accountability. The Secretary-General released a report in 1997 on the proposed Code of Conduct. UNGA, 'Report of the Secretary-General on the Proposed United Nations Code of Conduct' (17 October 1997) UN Doc. A/52/488. In the report, he referred to the status of officials other than Secretariat officials, experts on mission, and the Secretary-General himself. The report recommended that the General Assembly consider whether these personnel should be subject to a similar code. Ibid, para. 2. Subsequently, in 1998, the Bulletin on the 'Code of Conduct' for staff members was published. UN, 'Secretary-General's Bulletin on the Status, Basic Rights and Duties of United Nations Staff Members (entered into force 1 January 1999)' (10 December 1998) UN Doc. ST/SGB/1998/19, (hereinafter '1998 Bulletin'). This Bulletin was revised in 2002. UN, 'Secretary-General's Bulletin on the Status, Basic Rights and Duties of United Nations Staff Members (entered into force on 1 December 2002)' (1 November 2002) UN Doc. ST/SGB/2002/13, (hereinafter '2002 Bulletin'). It is a compilation of the complex rules and regulations applicable to UN staff members. The parallel Bulletin on the Status, Basic Rights and Duties of Officials other than Secretariat Officials, and Experts on Mission, entered into force on 1 July 2002. UN, 'Secretary-General's Bulletin on the Regulations Governing the Status, Basic Rights and Duties of Officials other than Secretariat Officials, and Experts on Mission (entered into force 1 July 2002)' (18 June 2002) UN Doc. ST/SGB/2002/9, (hereinafter 'Regulations'). Oswald, *Documents*, p. 366. For a brief history of the development of the Secretary-General's Bulletins, and details of the rules and regulations, see ibid, pp. 341–345, 366–369.

35 UN DPKO Undertaking, para. 2.

36 Oswald, *Documents*, p. 368.

Amongst these, the only code that sets out the obligation to '*comply* with local laws' is the Regulation governing Experts on Mission.[37] This language indicates a stronger obligation than merely to *respect* local laws. It appears, though, that this obligation applies specifically with regard the Experts' private legal obligations.[38] The remainder of the codes all express this obligation as the requirement to 'respect' local laws and regulations.[39] This wording is taken from the Vienna Convention of the Laws of Diplomatic Relations.[40]

37 (Emphasis added). UN, Regulations, Regulation 2 (j).

38 See the commentary to Regulation 2 (j). See also Regulation 1 (e) on privileges and immunities, which stipulates that there is an obligation 'to observe the laws and police regulations' of the host State in relation to private conduct: '[…] privileges and immunities furnish no excuse to those who are covered by them to fail to observe the laws and police regulations of the State in which they are located; nor do they furnish an excuse for non-performance of their private obligations'.

39 Directives binding on the UN police state that they 'shall respect all local laws and regulations'. UN DPKO, 'Directives for Disciplinary Matters Involving Civilian Police Officers and Military Observers' (2003) UN Doc. DPKO/CPD/DDCPO/2003/001; DPKO/MD/03/00994, para. 6, (hereinafter 'Directives'). Rule 2 of another set of binding rules stipulates the obligation on the part of the UN police to 'respect the law of the land of the host country'. Rule 4 also prohibits 'immoral acts of sexual physical or psychological abuse or exploitation', and Rule 6 requires them to account properly for UN money and property. UN DPKO, 'Ten Rules: Code of Personal Conduct for Blue Helmets' UN Doc. (on file with author), (hereinafter 'Ten Rules'). Another code requires that UN police officers 'will always […] respect local laws, customs and practices […]'. It also requires that they 'will never […u]se unnecessary violence or threaten anyone in the custody; commit any act that could result in physical, sexual or psychological harm or suffering to members of the local population, especially women and children'. It further states that they will not 'commit any act involving sexual exploitation and abuse, sexual activity with children under 18, or exchange of money, employment, goods or services for sex; […] be abusive or uncivil to any member of the public; wilfully damage or misuse any United Nations property or equipment […], participate in any illegal activities, corrupt or improper practices, attempt to use our positions for personal advantage, to make false claims or accept benefits to which we are not entitled'. UN DPKO, 'We are United Nations Peacekeeping Personnel' UN Doc. (on file with author), hereinafter 'We are Peacekeeping Personnel').

40 Article 41 sets out the obligations of those who enjoy privileges and immunities 'to respect the laws and regulations of the receiving State'. Vienna Convention on Diplomatic Relations (adopted 18 April 1961, entered into force on 24 April 1964) 500 UNTS 95, (hereinafter 'Vienna Convention'). It is submitted that using the convention governing diplomatic relations in this particular UN context may cause problems. This is because the two contexts are not identical. Diplomatic missions are not operational within the domestic sphere of the host State. If diplomats commit crimes, they can be declared *persona non grata* by the host State, which works to safeguard the system from abuse. See Chapter 6, Section 1-1.

The obligation to *respect* local laws and regulations is doubly stressed in the Memorandum of Understanding (MoU). An MoU is a formal agreement between the UN and each sending State, which contains the legally binding rights and obligations of both parties during a mission.[41] Part of the agreement deals with matters of discipline, investigations and UN standards of conduct for the relevant personnel. An MoU also includes the administrative, financial, and logistical terms and conditions that govern the contribution of personnel by sending States.[42] The model for such agreements has existed since 1991. It covers a wide range of issues, such as command and control, the applicable law, and the accountability of contributed personnel.[43] It was drafted primarily with military contingents in mind, but its provisions clearly stated that the agreement applies *mutatis mutandis* to civilian personnel, including UN police.[44] Most importantly, it serves as a basis for the negotiation and drafting of a specific MoU in relation to other seconded personnel. Formed Police Units (FPUs) are deployed under an MoU within the contingent-owned-equipment system (CoE).[45] For IPOs, the arrangement varies. Some MoUs cover IPOs *mutatis mutandis*, as suggested by the 1991 Model.[46] For the rest, IPOs are not covered by MoUs, but are covered by the content of *Codes Cables*, which is not made public. Revisions of the Model MoU have gradually strengthened it in respect of disciplinary issues, investigations, accountability, and applicable Codes of Conduct.[47] What is significant is that the Codes of Conduct

41 Oswald, *Documents*, pp. 12, 51.

42 Ibid, p. 12.

43 Ibid, pp. 51–52.

44 UNGA, 'Report of the Secretary-General on the Model Agreement between the United Nations and Member States Contributing Personnel and Equipment to United Nations Peace-Keeping Operations' (23 May 1991) UN Doc. A/46/185, para. 18, (hereinafter '1991 MoU'); Carsten Stahn, *The Law and Practice of International Territorial Administration: Versailles to Iraq and Beyond*, vol 57 (Cambridge University Press 2008), para. 2.

45 UN DPKO/DFS, 'Policy (Revised) on Formed Police Units in United Nations Peacekeeping Operations' (1 March 2013) UN Doc. Ref.2009/32, para. 9, (hereinafter '2013 FPU policy').

46 UNGA, 1991 MoU, para. 18.

47 Following the reform of the UN's reimbursement scheme, the 1991 model was revised, and was renamed 'the Contribution Agreement'. Later, in 1997, the document was reproduced as 'the Model Memorandum of Understanding'. Most recently, in 2007, the Model MOU was amended following issues and concerns about applicable laws, jurisdiction and accountability, including issues surrounding sexual exploitation and abuse by Peace Operations personnel. UNGA, 'Revised Draft Model Memorandum of Understanding, as annexed to UNGA, Report of the Special Committee on Peacekeeping Operations and its Working Group on the 2007 Resumed Session' (12 June 2007) UN Doc. A/61/19 (Part III) Annex, (hereinafter '2007 Model MoU'). The 2007 Model MoU thus incorporated additional

applicable to contributed personnel have been incorporated as an annex to the Model MoU (entitled 'We are Peacekeeping Personnel'),[48] which is essentially a combination of the two 1997 *aides memoires*: 'Ten Rules: Code of Personal Conduct for Blue Helmets' and 'We are UN Peacekeepers', and the Secretary-General's Bulletin on Sexual Exploitation and Abuse.[49] It is apparent that the UN is using the MoU as a further means of ensuring that the obligation to 'respect' local laws and regulations is fulfilled.[50]

It is necessary to consider what is meant by 'respect'. Is this an obligation to *obey*, or merely an obligation to *take account of* local law? In considering this issue, it is necessary to distinguish between the normative content of local criminal law, and the accountability of suspects through the local criminal law enforcement system. The obligation to respect local laws does not automatically mean that UN police are subject to the jurisdiction of the local courts for breaches of the law, even where immunity is not at issue. In fact, the provisions are carefully worded, and avoid specific reference to the UN polices' legal obligation to comply with local laws and regulations. Research found that these provisions are a reflection both of a complex reality and the delicate balance between the desire that all UN personnel should make their utmost effort to observe the local laws and regulations, and the perceived difficulties in doing so.[51] On some occasions, the UN appears to take a conservative approach. For example, the Capstone Doctrine,[52] the renewed set of principles and guidelines for Peace Operations issued in 2008, considers that a UN operation should show respect 'to local customs, institutions and laws', and explains that it has

---

articles on discipline, investigations, accountability, the exercise of jurisdiction by the sending State, and applicable Codes of Conduct, in the form of Annexes. Oswald, *Documents*, pp. 51–52. In the 1996 revised version, there was no particular mention of the UN police. UNGA, 'Note by the Secretary-General on the Reform of the Procedures for Determining Reimbursement to Member States for Contingent-Owned Equipment' (9 July 1996) UN Doc. A/50/995, (hereinafter '1996 Model MoU'). However, the 2007 version refers to FPUS. UNGA, 2007 MoU, Annex A, para. 1.

48 Annex H to the 2007 Model MoU. UNGA, 2007 MoU.

49 Durch et al., *Improving Criminal Accountability*, pp. 22–23.

50 However, it should be noted that the main motivation for the UN to incorporate the Code of Conduct through a MoU was the need to clarify the prohibitions on sexual exploitation and abuse. See ibid, pp. 22–23 for the background to incorporating the Codes into the MoU.

51 United Nations Law Reform Project, 'UN Peacekeeping and The Model Status of Forces Agreement', paras. 187–188.

52 UN DPKO/DFS, 'United Nations Peacekeeping Operations: Principles and Guidelines' (January 2008) UN Doc. –, (hereinafter 'Capstone Doctrine').

a 'direct effect upon the perception of its legitimacy'.[53] The tone of this Doctrine is not very strong, and certainly does not indicate that local criminal law legally binds the UN police or any other mission personnel. On the other hand, a General Assembly document emphasized that the UN's efforts in raising the awareness of its personnel should continue to focus on 'the obligation of all United Nations personnel to *observe* the laws of the host State'.[54] The obligation to *observe* the law is stronger than that of *respect* for the law.

There are some legitimate reasons for leaving the obligation vague. Some conduct, which is in accordance with the functions and roles that the UN police are required to carry out, may nevertheless breach local criminal law, for example, carrying arms and detaining people.[55] In this regard, it is necessary to identify those laws that would hinder the UN police from delivering their functions. The UN should then enter into an agreement with the host State to ensure that the UN police are exempt from those laws from the outset. Separately, some local laws may be contrary to human rights laws, norms and standards.[56] In such circumstances, the UN needs to negotiate an agreement with the host State which would exclude these laws from applying to its personnel.[57] In fact, the UN has taken this approach in some of its documents.[58]

However, the UN appears to accept that its police are bound by the host State's criminal law, at least in principle. It has repeatedly emphasized that

---

53 Ibid, p. 36.

54 (Emphasis added). UNGA, 'Report of the Secretary-General on the Criminal Accountability of United Nations Officials and Experts on Mission' (22 July 2013) UN Doc. A/68/173, para. 27, (hereinafter '2013 SG Report on Criminal Accountability').

55 See Chapter 2, Section 1, for the functions and roles of the UN police.

56 United Nations Law Reform Project, 'UN Peacekeeping and The Model Status of Forces Agreement', p. 38, para. 188; Durch *et al.* observed this as 'the de facto requirement that UN personnel only be subject to judicial processes that satisfy basic international human rights standards'. Durch et al., *Improving Criminal Accountability*, p. 27. See also UNGA, 'A Comprehensive Strategy to Eliminate Future Sexual Exploitation and Abuse in United Nations Peacekeeping Operations' (24 March 2005) UN Doc. A/59/710, paras. 67 (b), 87. The latter paragraph (para. 87) deals with the fact that the UN did not anticipate that its personnel would be working in places where the legal system is so devastated.

57 An example would be a criminal law in the host State that prohibits a consensual same-sex relationship. If UN police were to be exempt from this law, immunity would not be applicable should UN police officers engage in such acts. Chapter 6, Section 1-4.

58 UN police officers 'shall respect the legislation applicable in the mission area insofar as it is not in conflict with internationally recognized human rights standards or United Nations Rules, Regulations and other issuances'. UN DPKO, 2007 Guidelines, para. 36. It is possible that, in relation to operational conduct, immunity may be invoked to protect UN police personnel. See Chapter 6, Sections 1-4-1, 1-4-2.

UN police officers can be prosecuted in the host State, save for the issue of immunity.[59] The fact that the UN accepts that criminal proceedings can be brought at all must be an indication that it accepts that UN police officers are obliged to comply with the criminal laws of the host State.

2-1-2 What Can the UN Do to Ensure that Its Police Personnel are Aware of the Content of Local Laws and Their Obligation to Respect These?

Certain documents have been provided to UN police personnel individually, in order to make them aware of the possibility that they might be subject to criminal proceedings in the host State.[60] The most important of these documents is the 'Undertaking', which requires that the UN police accept that substantiated cases of sexual exploitation and abuse may 'be referred to the competent national authorities for the purposes of criminal prosecution'.[61] The Undertaking does not specify which national authorities would receive referred cases, thus maintaining the possibility that criminal proceedings will take place in the host State. In relation to other conduct, the reference in the Undertaking is limited to potential disciplinary action in cases where UN police officers are found to have breached their codes of conduct.[62] It is not clear why potential criminal prosecution is mentioned only in relation to sexual exploitation and abuse. It may merely be a reflection of the fact that the UN is focusing on

59 UN DPKO, 2003 Directives, para. 8; 2007 Guidelines, para. 30; UNGA, UN, 'Secretary-General's Bulletin "Special measures for protection from sexual exploitation and sexual abuse"' (9 October 2003) UN Doc. ST/SGB/2003/13, (hereinafter 'SEA Bulletin'). The SEA Bulletin's Section 5 does not distinguish between the host State and the sending State. It simply states that cases may be referred to the national authorities for criminal prosecution. 'Where there is a functional legal system in the host State, a crime will be investigated and prosecuted in accordance with the laws, practices and procedures of that State'. UNGA, 2006 Legal Experts Report, para. 14.

60 The documents consist of an 'Undertaking', 'We Are Peacekeepers', Secretary-General's Bulletin on Sexual Exploitation and Abuse, Regulations Governing the Status, Basic Rights and Duties of Officials other than Secretariat Officials, and Experts on Mission, among other mission directives and Standard Operating Procedures. UN DPKO, 'Undertaking and Declaration by Experts on Mission: UN Police Officer/Corrections Officer/ Military Observers/Military Liaison Officer' UN Doc. (on file with author), (hereinafter 'Undertaking'). UN, SGB on SEA; UN, Regulations.

61 UN DPKO, Undertaking, para. 9.

62 This is contained in the final paragraph of the Undertaking, the paragraphs of which are not numbered.

these crimes,[63] but it would be more appropriate to cover all serious crimes.[64] 'We are United Nations Peacekeeping Personnel' states that, 'We realize that the consequences of failure to act within these guidelines may [...] result in administrative, disciplinary or criminal action', thereby making it clear that criminal action may result from any crime committed.[65]

The question arises as to what the UN is doing to ensure that the UN police are aware of the content of local criminal law. The possibility that UN personnel may be unaware of this content has been raised before.[66] Such information would be mission-specific, and therefore could be expected to be given in the pre-deployment or in-theatre training.[67] However, there is no evidence that the UN in fact provides this information during training.[68] It may cause a problem, for example, where the UN emphasizes that its police officers are

---

63 See Chapter 4, Sections 2, 3-6. For a discussion of how sexual exploitation and abuse became the focus of the revision of the Codes of Conduct for Peace Operations personnel, see Durch et al., *Improving Criminal Accountability*, pp. 22–23.

64 The reasons for making this argument are given in Chapter 3, Sections 1, 2. A similar view was expressed in UNGA, 'Criminal Accountability of United Nations Officials and Experts on Mission' (11 September 2007) UN Doc. A/62/329, in relation to the suggested convention. See para. 70(d), (hereinafter 'Secretariat Note').

65 See the final point made in UN DPKO, We are Peacekeeping Personnel.

66 United Nations Law Reform Project, 'UN Peacekeeping and The Model Status of Forces Agreement', para. 188.

67 On the different types of training, see Chapter 2, Section 3-3-2.

68 The content of the pre-deployment training, as stated in the 1997 guidelines, only touches upon the local 'penal system' as part of the session on the 'UNCIVPOL Monitoring in-theatre'. This focuses on their monitoring tasks, and not on the content of the local criminal code to which the UN police are subject. UN DPKO, *Selection Standard and Training Guidelines for UNCIVPOL* (UN 1997), pp. 20–26, (hereinafter '1997 Selection Guidelines'). Likewise, the content of 'in-theatre training' includes Standing Operating Procedures, but not criminal codes. *Ibid*, pp. 28–29. There is no information on local criminal law in the pre-deployment training kits that are handed out to UN police. To view the content contained in the standardized Core Pre-Deployment Training (CPTM) document, which was developed by the UN in 2009, see: <http://www.peacekeepingbestpractices.unlb.org/PBPS/Library/SG%20Report%20A%2065%20644.pdf>. The UN Pre-deployment Training Standard for Police Officers is available at: <http://pbpu.unlb.org/PBPS/Library/Training%20Standards%20for%20police%20-%20Experts%20on%20Mission.pdf>, last accessed 30 September 2014. To view the content of the Specialized Training Materials for Formed Police Units, see UN DPKO, 'Specialized Traihing Materials for Formed Police Units' <http://research.un.org/FPUPackage> accessed 29 September 2016. The content of in-theatre training is not accessible to the public. It is tailored to each mission. However, it does not involve training which deals with the criminal law or criminal procedural law of the host State. Telephone interview with a senior legal officer, 17 September 2014.

prohibited under its disciplinary rules from engaging in sexual acts with persons below eighteen years old, but where it does not inform officers of the age of consent according to local criminal law.

2-2 *The Sending State's Criminal Law*

Whether or not the sending States' criminal laws bind UN police personnel is dependent on those States' criminal codes.[69] For the purposes of this work, what is important is whether or not sending States can in fact bring criminal proceedings against their national police officers who are engaged in UN missions.[70] Therefore, whether or not the sending States' criminal laws apply to UN police deployed in UN Peace Operations will be discussed together with whether sending States' domestic laws provide for the exercise of criminal jurisdiction.[71]

This section has found that the issue which obstructs the prosecution of the UN police is not whether or not there is a code to which they are subject; rather, it concludes that there may be difficulties in determining which States can exercise criminal jurisdiction over the UN police.

3 International Law Governing Jurisdiction

In order for States to exercise criminal jurisdiction, this must be provided for in international law. International law imposes certain limits on a State's freedom to decide on the contents of its criminal law.[72] It is therefore necessary to consider whether States are free to exercise jurisdiction where this is not prohibited by international law, or whether jurisdiction may only be exercised where this is explicitly permitted by international law.[73]

The *Lotus* decision determined which State can exercise criminal jurisdiction in a particular matter. It divided the issue into four categories: prescriptive jurisdiction within a territory; prescriptive jurisdiction outside a territory;

---

69 That is, the issue of prescriptive jurisdiction. See n. 4. above.

70 That is, the issue of enforcement jurisdiction. See n. 4. above.

71 Section 4-2.

72 The Council of Europe observed that any limitations are dependent on the grounds for each extra-territorial criminal jurisdictional claim. Council of Europe, *Extraterritorial Criminal Jurisdiction*, pp. 16, 26–27. For details, see Cedric Ryngaert, *Jurisdiction in International Law* (Oxford University Press 2008), pp. 102–104.

73 See, for example, States' various arguments on this point in *The Legality of the Threat or Use of Nuclear Weapons* (Advisory Opinion) [1996] ICJ Rep 238, para. 21.

enforcement jurisdiction inside a territory; and enforcement jurisdiction outside a territory. It found that States can apply their laws both within and outside their territories, unless there is an international law rule which prohibits them from doing so.[74] In relation to enforcement jurisdiction, States are free to exercise jurisdiction within their territories in the absence of a prohibition under international law.[75] However, they cannot exercise jurisdiction outside their own territories, unless there is a permissive rule under international law.[76]

This decision was subject to the criticism that it was too liberal an approach. Many have supported a more restrictive approach.[77] The *Lotus* Court deemed it a customary rule,[78] but the current scope of customary law dealing with this issue may be different.[79] The *Nuclear Weapons* case emphasized that the *Lotus* decision needs to be considered in light of the particular context at the time.[80] Some argue that the content of this customary rule is quite different from the way in which it was formulated in the *Lotus* case.[81] Others argue that there is another position, which falls somewhere between the absence both of prohibition and permission, such as tolerance.[82] However, the original two approaches do not pose any difficulties for the more established bases for exercising jurisdiction.[83]

---

74 *Lotus*, pp. 18–19.

75 *Ibid*, pp. 18–19.

76 It ruled that States cannot exercise enforcement jurisdiction outside their territories 'except by virtue of a permissive rule derived from international custom or from a convention'. Ibid, pp. 18–19.

77 American Law Institute, *Restatement (Third) Foreign Relations Law of the United States* (1987), pp. 235–236; Iain Cameron, *The Protective Principle of International Criminal Jurisdiction* (Dartmouth 1994), p. 319; F A Mann, 'The Doctrine of International Jurisdiction Revisited after Twenty Years' (1964) 111 *Recueil des Cours de l'Académie de Droit International de La Haye*, p. 35; Rosalyn Higgins, *Problems and Process: International Law and How We Use It* (Oxford University Press 1994), p. 77; Ryngaert, *Jurisdiction*, p. 22; *Case concerning Barcelona Traction, Light and Power Co Ltd (Belgium v Spain) (New Application: 1962)* (Second phase) [1970] ICJ Rep 3, para. 70.

78 *Lotus*, pp. 18–19.

79 Mann, 'Jurisdiction after Twenty Years', p. 35; Ryngaert, *Jurisdiction*, p. 21.

80 *The Legality of the Threat or Use of Nuclear Weapons* (Declaration of Bedjaoui P) [1996] ICJ Rep 268, para. 21.

81 Ryngaert, *Jurisdiction*, pp. 27–31.

82 *Accordance with International Law of the Unilateral Declaration of Independence in Respect of Kosovo* (Declaration of Simma J) [2010] ICJ Rep 478, paras. 8–10.

83 The difference may only become relevant when considering a less well-established basis. See Section 3-3 below.

Under international law, there are four main bases on which States may exercise criminal jurisdiction. These are: territoriality, active personality, passive nationality and protective jurisdiction. Territoriality consists of the jurisdiction of the State on whose territory the crime was committed. Active nationality is the exercise of jurisdiction by the State of nationality of the suspect, whilst passive nationality is exercised by the State of nationality of the victim. Protective jurisdiction amounts to an exercise of jurisdiction in order to protect the national interests of the State claiming jurisdiction. The first two bases are not contested. However, passive nationality is more controversial. Protective jurisdiction is much more controversial still.[84]

3-1 *Host State Jurisdiction*

The host State is the territorial State in which the criminal conduct was committed. At the time of the commission of the crime, the suspect, the victim and witnesses are usually all located in the territorial State.[85] Territorial jurisdiction is the least contested and most firmly established basis of criminal jurisdiction.[86] That is because jurisdiction is one of the most tangible forms of the exercise of sovereign power by States.[87] Sovereignty is territorial and, accordingly, jurisdiction is also essentially territorial,[88] although the territoriality of criminal law 'by no means coincides with territorial sovereignty'.[89] It is the

84 Harvard Law School's Reseach on International Law, 'Draft Convention on Jurisdiction with Respect to Crime' (1935) 29 *American Journal of International Law* 435, Article 3 (Territorial Jurisdiction); Article 5 (Jurisdiction over Nationals); Articles 7, 8 (Protection); Articles 9, 11 (Universality). Akehurst, 'Jurisdiction in IL', p. 32; Cassese, *International Criminal Law*, pp. 282–283; REDRESS/FIDH, *Extraterritorial Jurisdiction in the European Union – A Study of the Laws and Practice in the 27 Member States of the European Union* (December 2010), pp. 16–21. One of the few cases in which jurisdiction was exercised based on the effect doctrine was that of the *Attorney-General v Eichmann* (Israel Sup Ct 1962), 36 Int'l L Rep 277, 1968 (English translation).

85 This is generally the case. However, there are some exceptions. For example, there could be an incident in which an act in one territory causes an effect in another territory. See the facts in *Solomou and Others v Turkey* App no 36832/97 (ECtHR, 24 June 2008).

86 Harvard Law School's Reseach on International Law, 'Draft Convention on Jurisdiction with Respect to Crime', p. 495. The *Lotus* Court stated in 1927 that, 'in all systems of law the principle of territorial character of criminal law is fundamental'. *Lotus*, p. 20.

87 *Legal Status of Eastern Greenland Case* (*Denmark v Norway*) (Judgment) PCIJ Rep Series A/B, No 53, 48.

88 Mann, 'The Doctrine of International Jurisdiction Revised after Twenty Years', p. 140.

89 *Lotus*, p. 20.

State's power to exercise criminal jurisdiction within its territory over a person who has committed a criminal offence according to its criminal law which is at issue.[90] Nothing in international law prohibits the host State from exercising criminal jurisdiction.[91]

There are advantages in relation to the host State's assertion of criminal jurisdiction. Cassese argues that the advantage of the territorial principle is fourfold: the ease of evidence collection; the better protection of the rights of the accused; broader accountability to the community; and the assertion of the authority of the territorial State on its territory.[92] The Legal Experts at the Sixth Committee of the General Assembly cited the availability of evidence and witnesses, as well as the achievement of a greater sense of justice for local communities, as favouring the exercise of jurisdiction by the host State.[93] In the context of criminal conduct committed by the UN police during Peace Operations, all these advantages are present, save the protection of the rights of the accused. The argument that the territorial State may provide better protection for the accused only works in respect of cases where the accused is accustomed to the State in question, either through nationality or long-term residence. UN police personnel are, by definition, foreigners, who are not accustomed to the law, custom or language of the host State. In addition, in recent missions, host States have typically suffered from a lack of an effective legal system.[94] As such, in order to protect the accused, it has recently become less and less appropriate for them to be tried in the host State. However, procedurally, it is still the most convenient place to hold criminal proceedings. More importantly, considering the *raison-d'être* of the mission in the first place, it serves the purpose of the Operation better if victims, as well as the whole of the local community, can see justice being done.[95]

In brief, international law allows the host State to exercise criminal jurisdiction over criminal conduct committed by UN police officers during their service in the host State. From the point of view of the *rationale* behind prosecution, as well as practically speaking, it is the best forum in which to bring

---

90 Akehurst, 'Jurisdiction in IL', p. 32.

91 This is the case except where immunities apply. For a discussion of immunity, see Chapter 6, Section 1-4.

92 Cassese, *International Criminal Law*, pp. 278–279.

93 UNGA, 2006 Legal Experts Report, p. 10, para. 27.

94 See Chapter 2, Section 1.

95 Recent missions generally aim to build or rebuild the rule of law, and to improve the accountability of national institutions. See Chapter 2, Section 1-7.

criminal proceedings. However, two issues impede the bringing of criminal proceedings in the host State: first, concerns regarding the accused UN police personnel's due process rights;[96] and, second, issues relating to immunity.[97]

3-2 *The Sending State's Jurisdiction*

It is also possible that the UN police officer's sending State may exercise jurisdiction. The sending State is also normally the State of nationality of UN police personnel. Depending on the rules which govern who can become a police officer in a State, there may be UN police personnel who are sent to a mission by State A, but who are nationals of State B. This may happen, for example, if the person concerned is a permanent resident of State A.[98] Those with dual nationalities would encounter no additional issues.[99] The percentage of UN police personnel who are residents, but not nationals of the sending State, is unknown. The following analysis will focus on nationals of sending States.

It is possible that sending States can exercise criminal jurisdiction based on the principle of 'active nationality'. As with most bases of criminal jurisdiction, the active nationality principle is based on a link between the conduct and the State claiming jurisdiction.[100] In the case of the active nationality principle, the link is the nationality of the accused. This basis is firmly established in international law, as can be seen from discussions at the General Assembly's Sixth Committee. No State sitting on this Committee has challenged the authority of sending States to exercise criminal jurisdiction.[101]

96 This is the main reason for the UN's shift from general support for host State proceedings to supporting proceedings in sending States. See Chapter 4, Section 2.

97 See Chapter 6, Sections 1-4 and 2.

98 For certain crimes, States have a tendency to broaden the grounds for active nationality to include those who are resident in their territory. For example, UK legislation allows the criminal prosecution of its residents with regard to war crimes committed during the Second World War. Brazil has the same approach in relation to genocide. Cassese, *International Criminal Law*, p. 282.

99 On the selection and deployment of UN police personnel, see Chapter 2, Section 3-3-1.

100 Harvard Law School's Reseach on International Law, 'Draft Convention on Jurisdiction with Respect to Crime', p. 519, Article 5 (a). Akehurst, 'Jurisdiction in IL', p. 32.

101 Replies from States at the Sixth Committee during discussions on the Criminal Accountability of UN Officials and Experts on Mission. UNGA, 'Report of the Sixth Committee on the Criminal Accountability of United Nations Officials and Experts on Mission' (23 November 2015) UN Doc. A/70/506; UNGA, 'Report of the Secretary-General on the Criminal Accountability of United Nations Officials and Experts on Mission' (31 July 2014) UN Doc. A/69/210, (hereinafter '2014 SG Report on Criminal Accountability'); UNGA, 2013 SG Report on Criminal Accountability; UNGA, 'Report of the Secretary-General on the Criminal Accountability of United Nations Officials and Experts on Mission' (31 July 2012) UN Doc.

Scholars have also generally found this principle to be firmly established in international law.[102]

The variation in State practice, it seems, revolves around the requirement of double criminality. Some States see the active nationality principle as being applicable only where the conduct in question is also a crime under the law of the State where the crime was committed.[103] The double criminality requirement does not require an act to fall into the same category of crime in both States. Rather, it requires the act to be punishable under both their laws. The acts addressed by this work are by definition criminal in every jurisdiction.[104] Therefore, the issue of double criminality is unlikely to arise.

If jurisdiction is exercised according to the active nationality principle, the UN police personnel accused of committing crimes are most likely to be

---

A/67/213, (hereinafter '2012 SG Report on Criminal Accountability'); UNGA, 'Report of the Secretary-General on the Criminal Accountability of United Nations Officials and Experts on Mission' (23 September 2011) UN Doc. A/66/174/Add.1, (hereinafter '2011 SG Report on Criminal Accountability'); UNGA, 'Report of the Secretary-General on the Criminal Accountability of United Nations Officials and Experts on Mission' (29 July 2010) UN Doc. A/65/185, (hereinafter '2010 SG Report on Criminal Accountability'); UNGA, 'Report of the Secretary-General on the Criminal Accountability of United Nations Officials and Experts on Mission' (28 July 2009) UN Doc. A/64/183, (hereinafter '2009 SG Report on Criminal Accountability'); UNGA, 'Report of the Secretary-General on the Criminal Accountability of United Nations Officials and Experts on Mission – Addendum' (28 July 2009) UN Doc. A/64/183/Add.1; UNGA, 'Report of the Secretary-General on the Criminal Accountability of United Nations Officials and Experts on Mission – Addendum' (26 September 2008) UN Doc. A/63/260/Add.1; UNGA, 'Report of the Secretary-General on the Criminal Accountability of United Nations Officials and Experts on Mission' (11 August 2008) UN Doc. A/63/260, (hereinafter '2008 SG Report on Criminal Accountability'); UNGA, Report of the Secretary-General on the Criminal Accountability of United Nations Officials and Experts on Mission – Addendum (28 July 2009), UN Doc. A/63/260/Add.1.

102 Akehurst, 'Jurisdiction in IL', p. 36. Higgins stated that, in principle, international law accepts the nationality principle, provided that the exercise of it is not excessive, and that there is no attempt to enforce it within the territory of another State. Rosalyn Higgins, 'Allocating Competence: Jurisdiction' in W Michael Reisman (ed), *Jurisdiction in International Law* (Aldershot 1999), p. 283. This means that the nationality principle is an acceptable basis for the exercise of judicial jurisdiction, but not for executive jurisdiction, if one considers the theory that there are three different categories of jurisdiction. For the categorization of jurisdiction, see n. 4. Cassese observed that, 'It is striking that countries such as the UK, which have no constitutional or other prohibition on the extradition of their nationals, normally do not provide for active nationality as a basis for jurisdiction'. Cassese, *International Criminal Law*, p. 281.

103 Cassese, *International Criminal Law*, p. 281.

104 See Chapter 1, Section 6. However, the scope of offences may vary.

accustomed to the law, language and customs of their own States.[105] On the other hand, practical difficulties with regard to evidence collection would constitute an obstacle to successful prosecution. The Sending States' access to the victims, witnesses, crime scenes, and other pieces of evidence, is likely to be severely limited.[106] Even in cases where States are in principle willing to prosecute, if they are unable to obtain the necessary evidence, there is little chance of a successful prosecution. In these circumstances, national authorities are unlikely to proceed with such cases.

3-3 *Exercise of Criminal Jurisdiction by Other States*

Other bases of criminal jurisdiction are less well-established. Traditionally under international law, a genuine connection was required between the conduct and the State claiming jurisdiction for that jurisdiction to be exercised.[107] It remains to be seen what States consider as being sufficient for establishing the required link, and thus permitting the exercise of criminal jurisdiction.

3-3-1 Exercise of Criminal Jurisdiction by the State of Nationality of the Victim

Where the victim is neither a national of the host State nor the sending State, there is a third potential basis for criminal jurisdiction: the passive nationality principle. This principle aims to protect nationals living or residing abroad.[108] It has been invoked by several States[109] in relation to a limited number of crimes.[110] Taking the *Lotus* approach, there is no general prohibition on States 'extend[ing] the application of their laws and the jurisdiction of their courts

---

105 Cassese cites this as a reason for supporting the territorial principle. Cassese, *International Criminal Law*, pp. 278–279. See also Section 3-1.

106 On the difficulties faced by sending States in obtaining the right kind of evidence, collected in the correct manner during UN investigations, see Chapter 4, introductory section, Section 1.

107 ICJ, *Nottebohm case on diplomatic protection, Lichtenstein v. Guatemala*, ICJ Report 4 (1995). *Nottebohm case* (*Lichtenstein v Guatemala*) (*Second phase*) (Judgment of 6 April 1955) [1955] ICJ Rep 4.

108 Cassese, *International Criminal Law*, p. 282.

109 For information regarding States which support this principle, see Section 4-3.

110 Cassese, *International Criminal Law*, p. 283. However, note that universal jurisdiction is, and should be, invoked more often in relation to these crimes under international law. Ibid, p. 284. REDRESS/FIDH, *EU jurisdiction study*, p. 17. Sometimes passive nationality is invoked as a 'fall back' option for invoking jurisdiction. See cases in France and Spain, for example. Ibid, p. 19.

to persons, property and acts outside their territory'.[111] When challenging this principle, the *nulla poena sine lege* principle is sometimes raised.[112] Presumably the accused must be able to predict that, where he commits a certain act in the host State, this would be a criminal offence.[113] Non-retroactivity may also be an issue if a new form of extra-territorial jurisdiction were to be applied.[114] However, the crimes dealt with here are, by definition, serious crimes that constitute criminal offences in virtually all States, so it may be presumed that suspects know that their acts are criminal, even though they may not anticipate that the victim's State of nationality might exercise criminal jurisdiction over them, for example, if suspects are unaware of the victim's nationality.

This basis for claiming the exercise of criminal jurisdiction remains controversial, as the link between the situation and the State concerned may be considered insufficient. This is particularly the case in relation to ordinary crimes.[115] It may not add much in practice in any case. Upon repatriation or completion of service, the alleged offender is likely to be present in another State, either the host or sending State. Thus, bringing a prosecution may require extradition.[116] Witnesses, if any, are likely to be present in the host State or in another State, depending on their place of normal residence. Just as evidence collection may be very difficult for sending States, so too might victims' States encounter difficulties. Exercise of criminal jurisdiction by the State of nationality of the victim would mean that it would be difficult for the community served by the UN mission to see justice being served, although the victim would in all likelihood experience this. From the point of view of the rights of

111 *Lotus*, pp. 18–19. Note, however, the position taken by Higgins, who argued that this decision applied due to the particular circumstance of the case. In *Lotus*, the collision of two ships occurred on the high seas, which do not fall under the jurisdiction of any States. She argued that the *Lotus* decision does not support the use of the passive nationality principle for a crime committed in the territory of another State. Higgins, *Problems and Process: International Law and How We Use It*, p. 66.

112 Council of Europe, *Extraterritorial Criminal Jurisdiction*, p. 23.

113 Ibid, pp. 22–23.

114 Ibid, p. 23.

115 Ryngaert, *Jurisdiction*, pp. 92ff; Jurgen Meyer, 'Vicarious Administration of Justice: An Overlooked Basis of Jurisdiction' (1990) 31 *Harvard International Law Journal* 108, p. 113. Regula Echle, 'Passive Personality Principle and the General Principle of Ne Bis In Idem' (2013) 9 *Utrecht Law Review* 56, pp. 57, 60. See also Akehurst, 'Jurisdiction in IL', pp. 92–96, who claims that the passive nationality principle is not established in international law except for specific crimes, such as terrorism-related offences.

116 Before a suspect may be extradited, it is normally required that the offence in question satisfies the double criminality test. Cassese, *International Criminal Law*, p. 282.

the accused, this jurisdictional basis does not provide an advantage. However, one possible area where the exercise of criminal jurisdiction has some prospect of success is where the victim is also a UN staff member. If neither the host nor sending State has a functioning legal system, or if both have a system with significant problems regarding fair trial standards, but the victim's State has a functioning legal system that adheres to human rights standards, that State may have the best prospect in bringing fair criminal proceedings.

3-3-2 Universal Jurisdiction

A possibility open to all States is that of universal jurisdiction. Unlike other bases of jurisdiction, there is no connection between the State claiming jurisdiction and the conduct itself. It is based solely on the nature of the crime, that is, where the violation is so grave that it shocks the human conscience.[117] Universal jurisdiction has been exercised in respect of piracy since the 17th century, albeit in order to protect the interests of States.[118] War crimes have been recognized as attracting universal jurisdiction and, after World War II, torture and certain acts of terrorism were added to the list of crimes that attract universal jurisdiction, in order to safeguard universal values.[119] The arguments against universal jurisdiction, which are based on the *nulla poena sine lege* principle and non-retroactivity, can be refuted in the same way as in the case of passive nationality.[120]

There are two versions of this principle. The narrower and more widely-accepted version is that the State in whose territory the suspect is found may exercise jurisdiction.[121] The broader version of universal jurisdiction includes

---

117 Harvard Law School's Reseach on International Law, 'Draft Convention on Jurisdiction with Respect to Crime', p. 573, Article 10; Ryngaert, *Jurisdiction*, pp. 100–101; Cassese, *International Criminal Law*, pp. 284–285.

118 Cassese, *International Criminal Law*, p. 284.

119 Akehurst, 'Jurisdiction in IL', p. 40; Cassese, *International Criminal Law*, pp. 284–285. Some States have claimed universal jurisdiction over other crimes which are contained in their criminal codes, such as sexual offences, corruption, immigration offences, pornography distribution, narcotics distribution, and human trafficking. Ryngaert, *Jurisdiction*, pp. 104–106. For details of this national legislation, see Section 4-3.

120 See Section 3-3-1.

121 The narrower version of universal jurisdiction is criticised for not being truly 'universal', as it is only permitted if a suspect is within a State's territory. '[B]y the loose use of language, [this] has come to be referred to "universal jurisdiction", though it is an obligatory territorial jurisdiction over persons, albeit in relation to acts committed elsewhere'. *Arrest Warrant of 11 April 2000* (*DRC v Belgium*) (Sep Op Higgins, Koojimans and Buergenthal) [2002] ICJ Rep 63, para. 41.

situations in which a State claims jurisdiction over a foreigner for an act committed outside its territory, while he or she is outside its territory. This is termed absolute universal jurisdiction. Except for more recent treaties and draft treaties, universal jurisdiction exists only in the narrower sense in international law.[122] Exercising universal jurisdiction in the narrower sense is obligatory for grave breaches of the Geneva Conventions and their Additional Protocols, and torture under the Torture Convention.[123]

Even if it is accepted that States may exercise universal jurisdiction where it is not prohibited, this may only be done in respect of international crimes.[124] The criminal offences committed by UN police are not likely to amount to international crimes, according to the data collected.[125] Moreover, there are difficulties in exercising jurisdiction on this basis. First, it must be resorted to with care in order to ensure there is no possibility that it could be used to prosecute UN personnel for political purposes.[126] Second, as the link between the State seeking to exercise jurisdiction and the crime in question is either non-existent, or involves the mere presence of the suspect in the territory, the practical difficulties are considerable.[127] Third, it does not immediately contribute to a sense of accountability in the local community, nor is a third State best placed to protect a suspect's rights.[128] At best, it may work indirectly, through encouraging States with firmer links to the situation concerned to bring criminal proceedings.[129] If universal jurisdiction were to result in States with links to the conduct bringing prosecutions, it would assist in combating impunity, and ensuring that justice is served in respect of serious crimes.

---

122 Akehurst, 'Jurisdiction in IL', pp. 40–41; *Arrest Warrant of 11 April 2000* (*DRC v Belgium*) (Sep Op Guillaume P) [2002] ICJ Rep 35. See also the *Arrest Warrant of 11 April 2000* (*DRC v Belgium*) (Diss Op Van den Wyngaert) [2002] ICJ Rep 137, para. 54–55, in which he stated that 'there is no rule of conventional nor customary international law to the effect that universal jurisdiction in absentia is prohibited'.

123 This arises where a State has reason to believe that a suspect has committed a crime under the Geneva Conventions. Here, it has an obligation to search for him and, having found him, it is required to prosecute him, or extradite him. The obligation is the same in relation to torture under the Convention against Torture. Ryngaert, *Jurisdiction*, pp. 110–111.

124 Cassese, *International Criminal Law*, pp. 284–285.

125 There is no such case in the author's data. On the author's data, see Chapter 3, Section 1.

126 This also relates to the *rationale* for which immunity is accorded. See Chapter 6, Section 1-1.

127 See Section 3-2.

128 See Sections 3-1 and 3-2.

129 Such as the sending State.

3-3-3 The Protective Principle and the Effect Doctrine

There is another principle upon which States may exercise jurisdiction: the protective principle. However, this principle is based on the idea that States should be protected from offences perpetrated abroad which jeopardize their sovereignty or their right to political independence.[130] As criminal acts committed by UN police personnel do not fall into this category of conduct, this principle is not relevant to this work.

Some States invoke the effect doctrine. In terms of this doctrine, a person can be convicted of a crime in the State where the effects of his or her act are felt, even without the requirement that the act is a criminal offence in the State where it occurred. The big difference between the effect doctrine and the protective principle is that, in the case of the former, the effect must be felt in the State concerned. However, the effect doctrine is controversial.[131] One view is that the effect doctrine extends the concept of territoriality.[132] However, the kinds of crimes committed by UN police personnel are unlikely to attract a claim of jurisdiction based on this principle.[133]

4 National Laws Dealing with Jurisdiction

Another possibility is that the exercise of criminal jurisdiction by the State concerned may be limited by its national laws. Whether or not a State has criminal jurisdiction over a person is different from whether or not that person

130 Akehurst, 'Jurisdiction in IL', pp. 96–100.

131 Ibid, pp. 34–35.

132 Council of Europe, *Extraterritorial Criminal Jurisdiction*, p. 27.

133 For the nature of crimes committed by the UN police, see Chapter 3, Section 2-2. However, note that there were two cases where the alleged conduct involved 'spying'. In both cases, the host States requested the UN to expel the personnel concerned, which was subsequently done. 'Eritrea Expels Five UN Staff Over Espionage' *AFP* (5 September 2006) <http://www.reliefweb.int/node/434798> accessed 26 August 2008; IRIN, 'Eritrea: UN Protests at Staff Expulsions' (*Reliefweb*, 7 September 2006) <http://www.reliefweb.int/rw/rwb.nsf/db900sid/LSGZ-6TED8W?OpenDocument&query=unmee> accessed 29 August 2015; UN, 'UN News: As Eritrea Decides to Expel 5 UN Personnel, Annan Decries "Pattern of Hostility"' (6 September 2006) <http://www.un.org/apps/news/story.asp?NewsID=19735&Cr=eritrea&Cr1=#> accessed 20 August 2015; 'Eritrea Expels Five UN Staff over Episonage' *AFP* (5 September 2006) <http://www.reliefweb.int/rw/rwb.nsf/db900sid/HMYT-6TCR4P?OpenDocument&query=unmee> accessed 20 August 2015; 'UN Says 10 Withdrawn from Iraq' *BBC* (7 September 2001) <http://news.bbc.co.uk/1/hi/world/americas/1531854.stm> accessed 18 September 2015; 'Iraq Expels Five UN Staff' *CNN* (5 September 2001) <http://archives.cnn.com/2001/WORLD/meast/09/05/iraq.un/index.html>.

is subject to a particular criminal law. In the case of criminal law, the two are claimed to coincide,[134] but, in fact, there are situations in which there is a breach of a State's legal regime, but where that State's court does not have the authority to hear that case. For example, where the criminal court of State A can only prosecute conduct if an act constitutes a crime under its criminal law, as well as under that of the place where the conduct was committed (this is the double criminality requirement), there may be conduct that is a crime in State A, but not State B. This means that State A cannot bring proceedings in relation to that conduct. Thus, although the two differ from each other, there is nevertheless a significant overlap between them.

4-1 *The Host State*

Under national law, there is no question that the host State possesses the power to prosecute suspects. Virtually all national legal systems assert territorial jurisdiction.[135]

4-2 *Sending States*

For the State of nationality of the UN police personnel concerned to be able to prosecute them, it is necessary that its national criminal law either generally asserts jurisdiction on the basis of nationality, or makes specific provision for such proceedings in the case of these personnel.[136] Criminal prosecution would presumably occur after the suspects have returned to their home States, and thus these States would exercise enforcement jurisdiction in their own territories.

4-2-1 Extra-territorial Jurisdiction Over Nationals for All Crimes

Many States retain criminal jurisdiction over their nationals who are abroad.[137] In this respect, there is a difference between common-law countries and civil-law countries. Traditionally, common-law countries have been reluctant to extend criminal jurisdiction to conduct committed abroad. This position has now softened, and many of them have established jurisdiction for nationals

---

134 Council of Europe, *Extraterritorial Criminal Jurisdiction*, p. 20.

135 See Section 4-1.

136 In some exceptional cases, permanent residents could also be prosecuted.

137 The UN requires that UN police officers are either police officers or retired police officers in their sending States. Sending States generally only send police officers to the UN who are their nationals, or who are permanent residents in their territories. Thus there is a link between the sending States and those personnel they send to the UN. For further details of this national link, see Chapter 2, Section 3-1.

abroad, at least for certain offences.[138] On the other hand, the criminal laws of civil-law countries continue to apply to their nationals, even when they are abroad.[139]

In countries observing Islamic law, this is usually combined with another legal tradition.[140] The four major sending States with this type of legal system are Bangladesh, Jordan, Pakistan and Yemen.[141] The criminal laws in these mixed legal systems assert that their courts can hear cases in which crimes have been committed by their nationals whilst abroad.[142]

---

138 Ryngaert, *Jurisdiction*, pp. 85–88. For example, India is a common-law country, but its penal code is also applicable to extra-territorial offences. Penal Code (India, 1860 Act no 45 of 1860 of 6 October 1860), Introduction, Preamble, para. 8. See also India's response to the UN General Assembly's Sixth Committee. UNGA Sixth Committee, '68th Session: 10th & 11th Meetings (AM & PM) – Criminal Acts by United Nations Officials, Experts on Mission Must Not Go Unpunished, Sixth Committee Told as Debate Begins' (16 October 2013) UN Doc. GA/L/3460.

139 Akehurst, 'Jurisdiction in IL', p. 37.

140 JuriGlobe, 'Muslim Law Systems and Mixed Systems with a Muslim Law Tradition' <http://www.juriglobe.ca/eng/sys-juri/class-poli/droit-muslman.php> accessed 26 June 2015.

141 Afghanistan and Saudi Arabia have more 'pure' Islamic legal systems, but neither of them has contributed police personnel for Peace Operations as of April 2013. For data, see UN DPKO, 'Troop and Police Contributors' <http://www.un.org/en/peacekeeping/resources/statistics/contributors.shtml> accessed 18 February 2016.

142 For example, Bangladesh stipulates that: 'Any person liable, by any Bangladesh Law, to be tried for an offence committed beyond Bangladesh shall be dealt with according to the provisions of this Code for any act committed beyond Bangladesh in the same manner as if such act had been committed within Bangladesh'. Penal Code (Bangladesh, Act no XLV of 1860 of 6 October 1980), Preamble, para. 3. Jordan stipulates that: 'Article 10 of the Penal Code (No. 16 of 1960), as amended, provides for exercise of jurisdiction: over any Jordanian who, as perpetrator, instigator or accomplice, commits, outside the Kingdom, a felony or misdemeanour punishable by Jordanian law; [...] over any alien resident in the Kingdom who, as perpetrator, instigator or accomplice, commits, outside the Kingdom, a felony or misdemeanour punishable by Jordanian law, if his extradition has not been requested or accepted'. This information was obtained from UNGA, 2008 SG Report on Criminal Accountability, para. 22. Pakistan stipulates in Article 3: 'Any person liable, by any Pakistani Law, to be tried for an offence committed beyond Pakistan shall be dealt with according to the provision of this Code for any act committed beyond Pakistan in the same manner as if such act had been committed within Pakistan', Penal Code, (Pakistan, Act XLV of 6 October 1860). Yemen stipulates that: 'The laws of Criminal Proceedings are applicable on all Yemeni citizens, as well as the citizens of other countries and those without any citizenship whatsoever'. Republican Decree for Law no 13 for the Year 1994, Concerning the Criminal Procedures (Yemen), Article 17–2 and the Penal Code states the penal code is applicable to cases where Yemeni court exercises jurisdiction according to

In order to analyze the reach of sending States' criminal laws, a sample of sending States from two different time periods was selected. That is, States providing more than 100 police personnel to UN missions in either April 2001 or April 2013 were chosen. There were 22 such States in 2001,[143] and 24 in 2013.[144] These States provided 82.0 percent[145] and 86.1 percent[146] of all UN police personnel respectively, during those times. In total, excluding duplications, 37 States form part of this sample. A large majority, 29 countries, have jurisdiction for crimes committed by their nationals who are abroad.[147] 17 of the 29 countries require the offence in question to constitute a crime in the State where

criminal procedural law. Republican Decree for Law no 12 for the Year 1994, Concerning Crimes and Penalties (Yemen), Article (3).

143 US, Jordan, India, Germany, Pakistan, Ghana, Portugal, UK, Ukraine, France, Poland, Bangladesh, the Philippines, Turkey, Argentina, Spain, Malaysia, Russia, Australia, Austria, Egypt and Nepal. UN DPKO, 'Troop and Police Contributors' <http://www.un.org/en/peacekeeping/resources/statistics/contributors.shtml>.

144 Bangladesh, Jordan, India, Nepal, Senegal, Pakistan, Nigeria, Rwanda, Egypt, Burkina Faso, Yemen, Tanzania, Ghana, Sierra Leone, Niger, Cote d'Ivoire, Indonesia, Zambia, Togo, Turkey, Benin, Burundi, the Philippines and Tunisia. UN DPKO 'Monthly Summary of Contributions (Police, UN Military Experts on Mission and Troops), as of 30 April 2013', ibid.

145 This amounts to 6,332 out of a total of 7,724 UN police officers (April 2001).

146 This amounts to 10,812 officers out of a total of 12,562 UN police officers (April 2013).

147 Bangladesh, Benin, Jordan, India, Niger, Senegal, Pakistan, Rwanda, Egypt, Burkina Faso, Yemen, Tanzania, Cote d'Ivoire, Indonesia, Togo, Zambia, Turkey, Burundi, Germany, Portugal, Ukraine, France, Poland, Argentina, Spain, Malaysia, Russia, Tunisia and Austria. This information was provided by these States at the General Assembly's Sixth Committee, and was cross checked against criminal law and criminal procedural laws. UNGA, Report of the Sixth Committee on the Criminal Accountability of United Nations Officials and Experts on Mission; UNGA, 2014 SG Report on Criminal Accountability; UNGA, 2013 SG Report on Criminal Accountability; UNGA, 2012 SG Report on Criminal Accountability; UNGA, 2011 SG Report on Criminal Accountability; UNGA, 2010 SG Report on Criminal Accountability; UNGA, 2011 SG Report on Criminal Accountability; UNGA, 2009 SG Report on Criminal Accountability; UNGA, Report of the Secretary-General on the Criminal Accountability of United Nations Officials and Experts on Mission – Addendum; UNGA, Report of the Secretary-General on the Criminal Accountability of United Nations Officials and Experts on Mission – Addendum; UNGA, 2008 SG Report on Criminal Accountability. In addition, some have extended the active personality principle, so that it covers permanent residents or habitual residents. For example, Malaysia and Russia have extended their criminal law to cover their residents or *domiciliaries* in respect of criminal offences committed abroad. IBA, *Report of the Task Force on Extraterritorial Jurisdiction* (IBA 2009), p. 145. Ukraine has gone further, extending its coverage to stateless persons. Criminal Code of Ukraine (entered into force on September 1, 2001), Article 7.

the offence was committed (double criminality).[148] There are eight States where criminal law, as a whole, does not automatically apply to their nationals abroad.[149]

Where double criminality is required, there are some acts which a sending State's authorities cannot prosecute even though its criminal law applies. However, this is generally not an issue for crimes within the scope of this work because they are crimes in virtually every jurisdiction.[150]

4-2-2 Extra-territorial Jurisdiction Over Nationals for Particular Acts

Where States lack the power to prosecute their nationals for all acts constituting a criminal offence under their criminal laws, they can adopt criminal laws that allow for prosecution of certain crimes based on the active personality principle. For example, Sierra Leone[151] and the US[152] have established jurisdiction over human-trafficking offences committed abroad by their nationals.[153]

A range of extra-territorial sexual offences are criminalized both in the US and the UK.[154] In addition, murder, manslaughter, bigamy and perjury can be prosecuted in the UK, even if committed abroad by UK nationals.[155] Some other types of conduct are also subject to extra-territorial jurisdiction in some

148 Rwanda, Egypt, Burkina Faso, Yemen, Cote d'Ivoire, Indonesia, Togo, Burundi, Germany, Portugal, France, Spain Russia, Tunisia, Benin, Niger and Austria. IBA, *ETJ Report. Code Pénal* (*Niger, tel qu'Amendé par la Loi* no 2008–18) 2003.

149 Nepal, Nigeria, Ghana, Sierra Leone, the Philippines, the United States, the United Kingdom and Australia. Ibid. An Act Revising the Penal Code and Other Penal Laws, Act No. 3815, 8 December 1930, The Revised Penal Code of the Philippines. Nepal: *Muluki Ain* (General Code), 2020 (1963).

150 See Chapter 1, Section 6.

151 'A court in Sierra Leone shall have jurisdiction to try an offence under this Act where the act constituting the offence has been carried out – (a) wholly or partly in Sierra Leone; (b) by a citizen of Sierra Leone anywhere [...]', The Anti-Human Trafficking Act (Sierra Leone, Act Supplement to the Sierra Leone Gazette vol CXXXVI, no 44 of 18 August 2005) 2005, s.14.

152 UNGA, 2009 SG Report on Criminal Accountability, para. 25.

153 Nepal has criminalized human trafficking against its citizens both in and outside Nepal. Human Trafficking and Transportation (Control) Act (Nepal, 2064 [2007], shrawan 8, 2064 [24 July 2007, Act no 5 of the Year 2064 [2007]), s.1(3).

154 In the case of the US, it has criminalized sex with minors. Substantial sexual offences can be prosecuted under the UK's laws, which cover UK nationals and residents. UNGA, 2009 SG Report on Criminal Accountability, para. 25; UK: The Sex Offenders Act (c 51) (UK) 1997, s.7(1); Sexual Offences Act (c 43) (UK) 2003, s.72 (1).

155 Those resident in the UK may also be prosecuted. See The Offences Against the Person Act (UK) 1861 c 100, ss. 9 & 57(1) (UK); Perjury Act (UK) 1911, c.6, s.8 (UK).

States, such as fraudulent activities and other federal crimes in the US,[156] terrorism-related offences in the UK,[157] and treason in Ghana.[158]

These act-specific clauses or pieces of legislation have served to remove further obstacles to the prosecution of UN police personnel by his or her State of nationality for these acts.

4-2-3 Extra-territorial Jurisdiction Over Particular Categories of Persons

Some States also claim jurisdiction over all acts prohibited by their criminal law where these are committed by certain categories of their nationals. Often these are offences committed either by members of a State's armed forces serving abroad, or by public officials in the course of their duties abroad.[159] In relation to the sample of States listed above, of the eight States which do not have extra-territorial jurisdiction over their nationals for all crimes committed outside their borders, two States (Sierra Leone[160] and the Philippines[161]) have jurisdiction over their public officials for acts they commit in the course of their duties. While the former category does not include UN police personnel,[162] the latter 'public official' category may include them.[163] Australia has made a

156 In addition, the US can exercise criminal jurisdiction over the following conduct if some part of the crime is committed in its territory: distributing the proceeds of unlawful activity, the crime of violence in furtherance of unlawful activity, and corruption related offences. UNGA, 2009 SG Report on Criminal Accountability, paras. 26–28; UNGA, 2008 SG Report on Criminal Accountability, para. 35.

157 See Michael Hirst, *Jurisdiction and the Ambit of the Criminal Law* (Oxford University Press 2003), pp. 50–73.

158 These are included in Ghana. Criminal Code (Ghana, Act 29) 1960 (Consolidated up to 1999); The Criminal Code (Amendment) Act (Ghana, Act 646) 2003, s.180(3). Also included is false reporting, where it injures the reputation of the State. Ibid, s.185(4).

159 Akehurst, 'Jurisdiction in IL', p. 37. Issues surrounding immunity may arise in such a case.

160 Sierra Leone, The Criminal Procedure Acts (Sierra Leone, Act No 32) 1965, s.42 (1).

161 Penal Code (The Philippines, as Revised by an Act Revising the Penal Code and Other Penal Laws, Act no 3815, 8 December 1930), Article 2(4).

162 Except for any cases in which members of FPU are fulfilling military police functions and serve in the armed forces in their home State. The question arises as to whether the law applies to them, if they are part of the armed forces back home and are subject to the law applicable to armed forces, even if they are not functioning as armed forces in Peace Operations.

163 National police personnel are not considered to be carrying out national duties whilst they are serving in UN peace operations. A question arises as to whether or not the 'public official' category under the domestic criminal laws may be applied to UN police members, even if they are considered to be performing the functions of the UN mission, and not their national policing duties.

specific amendment to its criminal law to ensure that it has jurisdiction over crimes committed by its Federal Police officers who take part in UN Peace Operations.[164] The question arises as to whether jurisdiction can be exercised with regard to those retired police officers who serve as UN police. That is, whether the law covers only those who are serving police officers, or whether it also covers those who only act as police officers abroad. A separate issue is that of UN police officers who are recruited through a private company, as they may not fall into the category of 'public officials'. A further question concerns whether FPU personnel who fall under Ministries of Defence, may be subject to a separate body that can bring criminal proceedings against them for acts committed during the mission.[165]

Therefore, at least three sample countries have specific clauses which appear to apply their criminal law to certain categories of persons, including their police personnel working abroad.[166] In total, 32 out of the 37 sample countries (which make up about 86.5 percent of the States, covering 84 percent of the police personnel from the sample countries)[167] have criminal jurisdiction in relation to all criminal conduct committed by their police personnel abroad.[168]

164 2003 Amendment to the Crimes (Overseas) Act (Australia) 1964. While not a sample State, New Zealand ensures that their police personnel, who serve as UN police abroad, are subject to its jurisdiction through two additional pieces of legislation. The United Nations (Police) Act (NZ) 1964, which governs police who form part of a UN force; Crimes and Misconduct (Overseas Operations) Act (NZ, Public Act 2004 no 17) 2004, which governs anyone serving as part of an 'overseas operations force'. In addition, for example, the Swedish Penal Code provides that 'crimes committed outside the Realm shall be adjudged according to Swedish law and by a Swedish court: [...] if the crime was committed in the course of duty outside the Realm by a policeman [...], who performs boundless assignments according to an international agreement that Sweden has ratified'. Criminal Code (Sweden, 'Brottsbalken') 1965. See also Chapter 2, Section 3-3.

165 On the different kinds of FPU personnel, see Chapter 2, Section 1-6.

166 Australia, Sierra Leone and the Philippines.

167 On 30 April 2013, the total number of personnel coming from those 37 sample States was 11,164 officers. April 2013 Contributions. Of these, 9,387 officers came from the 32 States where all criminal conduct by UN police personnel is subject to their criminal codes.

168 Bangladesh, Jordan, India, Senegal, Pakistan, Rwanda, Egypt, Burkina Faso, Yemen, Tanzania, Niger, Cote d'Ivoire, Indonesia, Togo, Zambia, Turkey, Benin, Burundi, Germany, Portugal, Ukraine, France, Poland, Spain, Malaysia, Russia, Australia, Sierra Leone, and the Philippines. As mentioned above, some require the conduct to be committed by the UN police in the course of their duties, which, depending on the interpretation of the law, may exclude their private conduct. The Philippines and Sierra Leone are examples of States in which this is the case.

In addition, some States have asserted criminal jurisdiction over specific offences committed abroad. Overall, a majority of sending States can exercise criminal jurisdiction over UN police personnel for the kinds of criminal conduct in question.[169] There are only five States out of the sample countries that may have a problem exercising criminal jurisdiction over their national police personnel. This means the problem relating to the lack of criminal jurisdiction on the part of the sending State may arise only in relation to 16 percent of personnel amongst sample countries.[170] This was reflected in the responses by Member States to the UN General Assembly's Sixth Committee.[171]

In addition, the rules and regulations which apply specifically to the police in their sending States may remain applicable when they are serving in missions. For the most part, this is of minor relevance for the present study, but where a national police force has its own court which can deal with criminal cases, this issue may become more important.[172] This may be more relevant for FPU personnel, as some FPU officers are members of the military police or of police forces that are institutionally situated within Ministries of Defence.[173]

---

169 For more details on the applicability of the national laws of sending States, see Ai Kihara-Hunt, 'Mechanisms of Individual Criminal Accountability of Civilian Police in Peace Support Operations' (LLM thesis, University of Essex 2004) pp. 68–74.

170 UN police personnel from these countries represent 14.5 percent of the total UN police personnel. In April 2013, there was a total of 12,562 UN police personnel. The number of police personnel coming from those five States was 1,842 in total.

171 UNGA, Report of the Sixth Committee on the Criminal Accountability of United Nations Officials and Experts on Mission; UNGA, 2014 SG Report on Criminal Accountability; UNGA, 2013 SG Report on Criminal Accountability; UNGA, 2012 SG Report on Criminal Accountability; UNGA, 2011 SG Report on Criminal Accountability; UNGA, 2010 SG Report on Criminal Accountability; UNGA, 2009 SG Report on Criminal Accountability; UNGA, 2008 SG Report on Criminal Accountability; UNGA, Report of the Secretary-General on the Criminal Accountability of United Nations Officials and Experts on Mission – Addendum.

172 For example, the Armed Police Force in Nepal has its own internal court that deals with criminal cases committed by its personnel. This Court is similar to the Court established for these purposes for the Nepalese Army. UN OHCHR, *Nepal Conflict Report* (Available at <http://wwwohchrorg/EN/Countries/AsiaRegion/Pages/NepalConflictReportaspx> accessed 10 January 2015) 2012, pp. 190–191, 199–200.

173 For example, the Italian *Carabinieri* belongs to Italy's Armed Forces, and its personnel are subject to courts-martial. See US Department of State, 'Italy Human Rights Practices, 1995' (March 1996) <http://dosfan.lib.uic.edu/ERC/democracy/1995_hrp_report/95hrp_report_eur/Italy.html> accessed 3 September 2014, section entitled 'Respect for Human Rights', section a. Other units that deliver law enforcement functions within military establishments include: the US Military Police and Special Forces, the French Gendarmerie, the Spanish Guardia Civil, the Chilean *Carabineros*, and the Argentine Gendarmes. Michael

4-2-4 What Actions Does the UN Take to Ensure that Sending States' Criminal Laws Apply to the UN Police?

An MoU is the obvious vehicle for legal agreements between the UN and the sending States regarding FPU personnel. Until 2007, Model MoUs did not stipulate any requirements for sending States with regard to the reach of their criminal law.[174] The 2007 Model MoU refers extensively to the sending States' obligation to apply national laws to any members subject to national military law.[175] It includes explicit assurances by the sending States that they will exercise the required criminal and disciplinary jurisdiction over such personnel.[176] It has been recommended that each specific MoU between the UN and a State sending an FPU should have the same obligation inserted in it.[177]

Where a specific agreement exists between the UN and States regarding IPOs, it depends on what is written in it. Where an MoU is considered to apply *mutatis mutandis* between the UN and sending States to both IPOs and FPUs,[178] it is unclear what legal obligations it gives rise to in relation to IPOs. Where no agreement exists, there is no vehicle for the UN to oblige the sending State to ensure that any act that would constitute a crime if committed within that State's territory is treated as a crime by that State.

Following reports of sexual exploitation and abuse in the DRC, the UN has been concerned about the lack of a vehicle for ensuring criminal

---

J Dziedzic, 'Policing the New World Disorder: Addressing Gaps in Public Security during Peace Operations' in Max G Manwaring and John T Fishel (eds), *Toward Responsibility in the New World Disorder – Challenges and Lessons of Peace Operations* (Frank Cass 1998), p. 144.

174 The 1991 Model MoU required sending States to exercise criminal jurisdiction over military contingent personnel, and thus required sending States to subject military personnel to their applicable criminal laws. UNGA, 1991 MoU, para. 25. However, it was silent on how the UN police were to be dealt with in this regard. Neither the 1996 Contribution Agreement nor the 1997 Model MoU refers to criminal law or criminal jurisdiction. Contribution Agreement, UN, 'Model Memorandum of Understanding between the United Nations and [participating State] contributing resources to [the United Nations Peacekeeping Operation]' UN Doc. (on file with author).

175 UNGA, 2007 MoU, Article 7, 7.22 in particular. This was done following a recommendation by the first experts' group. UNGA, 2006 Legal Experts Report, para. 64 (c).

176 UNGA, 2007 MoU, Article 7, 7.22 and 7.23.

177 This was recommended to the General Assembly by the UN Secretariat. UNGA, 2007 Secretariat Note, para. 69 (c).

178 As stated in UNGA, 1991 MoU, para. 18.

accountability,[179] and the issue has been taken up at the General Assembly.[180] In the main, two approaches have been taken: first, there has been a long-standing attempt to draft a convention dealing with establishing criminal jurisdiction over nationals;[181] and, second, sending States have been urged to extend the applicability of their criminal laws to nationals serving in UN Peace Operations, and to establish criminal jurisdiction to enforce these laws.[182] A Convention has been drafted, but has yet to be adopted,[183] and the General Assembly resolution simply 'strongly urges all States to consider establishing' jurisdiction over serious crimes in particular, or at least where double

---

179 UNGA Res 59/300 (30 June 2005) UN Doc. A/RES/59/300 endorsed the recommendations in UNGA, 'Report of the Special Committee on Peacekeeping Operations and its Working Group' (GAOR 59th Session Supp no 19, 31 January-25 February 2005; 4–8 April 2005) UN Doc. A/59/19/Rev.1, that the SG appoint a group of legal experts 'to advise on the best way' to ensure the criminal accountability of UN staff and experts on mission. Ibid, para. 40 (a). A significant part of the discussion in the Special Committee centered on the measures required to eliminate SEA.

180 See, in general, the discussions held at UNGA Sixth Committee, '68th Session and Previous Sessions: Criminal Accountability of United Nations Officials and Experts on Mission' <http://www.un.org/en/ga/sixth/68/CrimAcc.shtml> accessed 1 October 2014.

181 It also addresses jurisdiction over habitual residents and those who are found in that State's territory. This is contained mainly in two resolutions: UNGA Res 62/63 (8 January 2008) UN Doc. A/RES/62/63; UNGA Res 63/119 (15 January 2009) UN Doc. A/RES/63/119.

182 Sending States are '*Strongly urge*[*d* ...] to consider establishing to the extent that they have not yet done so jurisdiction, particularly over crimes of a serious nature, as known in their existing domestic criminal laws, committed by their nationals while serving as United Nations officials or experts on mission, at least where the conduct as defined in the law of the State establishing jurisdiction also constitutes a crime under the laws of the host State' in UNGA Res 62/63, op. para. 3; UNGA Res 63/119, op. para. 3; UNGA Sixth Committee, 'Draft Resolution on the Criminal Accountability of United Nations Officials and Experts on Mission' (27 October 2011) UN Doc. A/C.6/66/L.16, op. para. 3; UNGA Res 64/110 (15 January 2010) UN Doc. A/RES/64/110, op. para. 3; UNGA Res 65/20 (10 January 2011) UN Doc. A/RES/65/20, op. para. 3; UNGA Res 66/93 (13 January 2012) UN Doc. A/RES/66/93, op. para. 3; UNGA Res 67/88 (14 January 2013) UN Doc. A/RES/67/88, op. para. 3; UNGA Res 105 (18 December 2013) UN Doc. A/RES/68/105, op. para. 3; UNGA Res 69/114 (18 December 2014) UN Doc. A/RES/69/114, op. para. 3; UNGA Res 114 (18 December 2015) UN Doc. A/RES/70/114, op. para. 6.

183 As of November 2014, neither the Sixth Committee, nor the Working Group it established, has been able to agree to begin negotiations based on the draft convention. See the Working Group's report UNGA Sixth Committee, '67th Session: Summary Record of the 24th Meeting' (28 December 2012) UN Doc. A/C.6/67/SR24, pp. 3, 6–7. Also see UNGA Sixth Committee, 'Report of the Sixth Committee on the Criminal Accountability of United Nations Officials and Experts on Mission' (19 November 2013) UN Doc. A/68/461.

criminality is satisfied.[184] In other words, the UN lacks any means to oblige sending States to apply their criminal laws.

Even where the MoU obliges sending States to exercise their criminal law over their nationals, or where States claim that their criminal laws apply to UN police personnel who are their nationals, it is not known whether the UN monitors their legislation in order to confirm their claims. Given that it takes the UN several years to collect the relevant information, which is in any case by no means complete, it arguably would take the UN several more years to confirm all this information.[185] Thus, it is difficult to imagine that the UN actually checks the information.

The fact that the UN's efforts to ensure the criminal accountability of its personnel stemmed from reports of sexual exploitation and abuse appears to have resulted in the UN disproportionately prioritizing these types of crimes.[186] There are two issues raised by this approach. The first is that the UN treats crimes of sexual exploitation and abuse as a single category and, as a result, does not make it clear that very different forms of conduct may thus fall within this category. This leads to a risk that personnel may fail to understand that some forms of conduct of sexual exploitation and abuse amount to crimes.[187] The second is that criminal conduct not falling in the SEA category may be left unaddressed or ignored.[188]

As noted above, depending on the domestic laws and practice of their sending States, UN police officers may be subject to the criminal law and police

---

184 UNGA Res 62/63, op. para. 3.

185 See the SG Reports, n. 171.

186 For example, the first experts' report to the GA Sixth Committee recommended that the sending States' jurisdiction should be asserted in relation to 'serious crimes against the person, in particular those involving sexual exploitation and abuse'. UNGA, 2006 Legal Experts Report, para. 47. This was also recognized in UNGA, 2007 Secretariat Note, para. 70 (d). The High Panel on Peace Operations, which submitted its report in June 2015, also focused on sexual exploitation and abuse. UNGA/SC, 'Uniting Our Strength for Peace – Politics, Partnerships and People – Report of the High-Level Independent Panel on United Nations Peace Operations' (16 June 2015) UN Doc. A/70/95-S/2015/446, paras. 258–269. Also see Somini Sengupta and Rick Gladsone, 'Panel Urges Changes in Using UN Soldiers' *The New York Times* (New York, 16 June 2015) <www.nytimes.com/2015/06/17/world/html?smid> accessed 26 June 2015.

187 This was raised in the UNGA, 2006 Legal Experts Report, para. 18.

188 In this regard, the Legal Experts Report recommended the adoption of a convention requiring States to assert criminal jurisdiction over their nationals abroad for serious crimes against the person. Ibid, para. 47. However, the UN Secretariat emphasized that such jurisdiction should be asserted in respect of all crimes. UNGA, 2007 Secretariat Note, para. 70 (d).

code in force in these territories. In relation to FPUs, the UN accepts offers for the secondment of their personnel from sending States regardless of the type of police forces these FPU personnel work for back home, or whether they are part of the armed forces or the civilian police forces, armed or unarmed. In light of the severe difficulties experienced by the UN in securing the required number of UN police personnel,[189] it is difficult to imagine the UN basing decisions regarding which police personnel to accept for missions on whether or not they are subject to the same laws which are applicable to their armed forces.

4-3 *The National Laws Governing the Jurisdiction of Other States*

States other than that of the State of nationality or the host State may have jurisdiction based on the other principles identified above.[190]

Many States' laws provide for criminal jurisdiction based on the passive nationality principle. For example, Spain,[191] Italy,[192] France,[193] Romania[194] and Panama,[195] claim jurisdiction on this basis. Burkina Faso,[196] Greece[197] and Germany[198] provide for criminal jurisdiction based on the passive nationality principle, subject to there being double criminality; and Portugal provides for criminal jurisdiction based on the passive nationality principle, but only for certain domestic crimes.[199] Poland allows criminal jurisdiction based on

189 See Chapter 2, Section 3-3.

190 See Section 2-3.

191 Organic Act 1/2009 (Spain, 3 November 2009), which introduced amendments to Sections 4 and 5 of Article 23 of The Organic Law of the Judiciary 6/1985 (Spain, LOPJ – *Ley Organica del Poder Judicial*) 1985.

192 Criminal Code (Italy, Codice Penale) 1930, Article 10, as cited in REDRESS/FIDH, *EU jurisdiction study*, p. 165.

193 Penal Code (France) 2005, Articles 113–7.

194 Criminal Code (Romania) 1969, Article 5.

195 Criminal Code (Panama) 2007, Article 20. As Panama claimed in UNGA, 2012 SG Report on Criminal Accountability, para. 7 (b).

196 *Loi no 043/96/ADP du 13 Novembre 1996 Portant Code Pénal* (Burkina Faso) 13 December 1996, Article 4.

197 UNGA, 2008 SG Report on Criminal Accountability, para. 19; Penal Code (Greece) 1950, Article 7(1).

198 Criminal Code (Germany, Version promulgated on 13 November 1998, Federal Law Gazette [*Bundesgesetzblatt*] I p. 3322, last amended by Article 3 of the Law of 2 October 2009, Federal Law Gazette I p 3214), s.7(1) and (2).

199 Criminal Code (Portugal) 1982, Article 5(1) (b) and (e). As cited in REDRESS/FIDH, *EU jurisdiction study*, p. 215.

the passive personality principle only if the suspect is in its territory.[200] The majority of European States use the passive nationality principle as a basis for exercising jurisdiction over acts committed abroad, but only in relation to specific crimes.[201]

Extra-territorial jurisdiction based on the protective principle and/or effect doctrine is provided for in a number of States' criminal laws. Ukraine,[202] the Philippines,[203] Panama,[204] Togo,[205] Indonesia[206] and Yemen[207] are examples of States which do this. However, there have not been any cases involving a UN police officer that have threatened the security of a third State, or otherwise triggered the protective principle and/or effect doctrine. These bases, therefore, add little.

Finally, universal jurisdiction is provided for under most States' national laws for certain crimes.[208] Normally, acts covered by this type of jurisdiction are international crimes,[209] but some States provide universal jurisdiction for specific and serious domestic crimes, such as murder, manslaughter, human

200 Criminal Code (Poland) 1997, Article 110(1), as cited in REDRESS/FIDH, *EU jurisdiction study*, p. 210.

201 23 States out of 29 EU member States have jurisdiction based on the passive nationality principle in relation to at least one crime. REDRESS/FIDH, *EU jurisdiction study*, p. 17. Note that the investigation into Augusto Pinochet in Chile in 1998 was undertaken on the basis of the passive personality principle. It led to a request from the UK for his extradition to the UK and, in 1990, the Argentine officer Alfredo Astiz was convicted of the torture and disappearance in Argentina of two French nuns, and was sentenced to life imprisonment. The trial was conducted *in absentia*. Cassese, *International Criminal Law*, p. 283.

202 The Criminal Code (Ukraine, entered into force 1 September 2001). See paragraph 1 of Chapter I 'FINAL AND TRANSITIONAL PROVISIONS'), Article 8 as amended by Law No 3316-IV (3316–15) of 12.01.2006.

203 Penal Code (The Philippines, as Revised by an Act Revising the Penal Code and Other Penal Laws, Act no 3815, 8 December 1930), Article 2–2.

204 Criminal Code (Panama) 2007, Article 20. As claimed in UNGA, 2012 SG Report on Criminal Accountability, para. 7 (a).

205 Penal Code (Togo, *Code Pénal*) 1980, Article 7.

206 Penal Code (Indonesia, *Undang-undang RI no 27 Tahun 1999, Tanggal 19 Mei 1999*) 1982, Article 4.

207 Penal Code (Yemen, Republican Decree for Law no 12 for the Year 1994 Concerning Crimes and Penalties) 1994, Article (3).

208 All 29 EU member States exert universal jurisdiction for at least one international crime. REDRESS/FIDH, *EU jurisdiction study*, p. 21.

209 '[T]he crimes over which such jurisdiction may be exercised are of such a gravity and magnitude that they warrant their universal prosecution and repression'. Cassese, *International Criminal Law*, p. 285.

trafficking, assault, rape, and the distribution of pornography.[210] Some of them have additional requirements, such as double criminality,[211] or the presence of the suspect in their national territory.[212] Other States will only invoke universal jurisdiction in order to prosecute a suspect if an official request is received from the victim or his or her State of nationality.[213] Some States invoke universal jurisdiction for crimes that attract a particular types of punishment,[214] whilst others invoke it for any and all ordinary crimes if they meet double

210 Germany, Sweden and Norway. Germany: Criminal Code (Germany, Version promulgated on 13 November 1998, Federal Law Gazette [Bundesgesetzblatt] I, p. 3322, last amended by Article 3 of the Law of 2 October 2009, Federal Law Gazette I, p. 3214), s.6. 15 out of 29 EU member States claim criminal jurisdiction based on universal jurisdiction for particular ordinary crimes. REDRESS/FIDH, *EU jurisdiction study*, p. 21. Sweden: Criminal Code (Sweden, '*Brottsbalken*') 1965, Chapt. 2, as cited in REDRESS/FIDH, *EU jurisdiction study*, p. 245. Norway: Criminal Code (Norway, The General Civil Penal Code, Act of 22 May 1902 no 10, with subsequent amendments, the latest made by Act of 21 December 2005 no 131) 1902, Section 12 (4), as cited in REDRESS/FIDH, *EU jurisdiction study*, p. 202.

211 Germany, Poland and Sweden. Germany: Criminal Code (Germany, Version promulgated on 13 November 1998, Federal Law Gazette [*Bundesgesetzblatt*] I p. 3322, last amended by Article 3 of the Law of 2 October 2009, Federal Law Gazette I p. 3214), s.7 (2). Poland: Criminal Code (Poland) 1997, under Articles 113–126, as cited in REDRESS/FIDH, *EU jurisdiction study*, p. 210. Sweden: UNGA, 2009 SG Report on Criminal Accountability, para. 24. However, where international crimes are concerned, the double criminality requirement is considered unnecessary because the offence is an international crime under international law regardless of the contents of the territorial State's legal regulations. Cassese, *International Criminal Law*, p. 283.

212 Canada, The Netherlands, Italy, Germany, Norway, Poland, Sweden. Canada with regard to war crimes and crimes against humanity. UNGA, 2008 SG Report on Criminal Accountability, para. 12; Criminal Code and the Crimes against Humanity and War Crimes Act, s.7. The Netherlands in relation to crimes under Section 2 Paragraph 1 (a) of International Crimes Act (The Netherlands) 2003. Italy: UNGA, 2010 SG Report on Criminal Accountability, para. 25. Germany: German Criminal Code, s.7-2. Norway: New General Civil Penal Code (Norway) 2005, s.5. Poland: Criminal Code (Poland) 1997, under Articles 113–126, as cited in REDRESS/FIDH, *EU jurisdiction study*, p. 210. Sweden: statement by Ms. Karolina Wieslander, Legal Advisor, Ministry of Justice, cited in ibid, p. 246.

213 Poland: Criminal Code (Poland) 1997, under Articles 113–126, as cited in REDRESS/FIDH, *EU jurisdiction study*, p. 210.

214 Italy for crimes requiring more than three years of imprisonment, Poland for crimes with entailing more than two years imprisonment, Sweden for crimes carrying more than four years imprisonment. Italy: Criminal Code (Italy, Codice Penale) 1930, Article 10, as cited in REDRESS/FIDH, *EU jurisdiction study*, p. 165. Poland: Criminal Code (Poland) 1997, under Articles 113–126, as cited in REDRESS/FIDH, *EU jurisdiction study*, p. 210.

criminality requirements.[215] Some States will reject a request for the extradition of a suspect if the requesting State has made the request on the basis of universal jurisdiction.[216]

In short, a number of third States' national laws would permit the prosecution of UN police personnel who are suspected of having committed particularly serious crimes, and who then pass through their territories.[217] In practice, this is most unlikely to arise unless the UN was to seek prosecution. In addition, there may be circumstances in which the victim's State wished to exercise criminal jurisdiction, particularly where the legal systems of both the host and sending States may not function in accordance with human rights standards.

4-4 *Competing Bases of National Jurisdiction*

The analysis above leads one to conclude that exercising jurisdiction mostly falls either to the host State or the sending State. The issue of which of the two States should exercise criminal jurisdiction should be addressed in the agreement between the UN and the sending States and, in the case of FPU personnel, this should be stipulated in the MoU.[218] The arrangement in respect of IPOs is less clear, but the practice appears to be the same as for FPU personnel, in that the host State has the primary claim to exercising jurisdiction, failing which sending States are required to do their best to exercise criminal jurisdiction over their IPOs.[219]

Under international law, the system relating to jurisdiction is concurrent jurisdiction.[220] Traditionally, jurisdiction requires a State to have a close connection with the situation concerned, but this connection does not have to be 'the

215 Criminal Code (Hungary) 2012, s.4 (a) and (b), as cited in REDRESS/FIDH, *EU jurisdiction study*, p. 152. Romania and Czech Republic can claim universal jurisdiction over all criminal conduct provided the double criminality requirement is satisfied and the suspect is in the territory. Romania: Criminal Code (Romania) 1969, Article 6 (1). Czech: Criminal Code (Chech) 2009, s.8.

216 Germany: Criminal Code (Germany, Version promulgated on 13 November 1998, Federal Law Gazette [Bundesgesetzblatt] I p. 3322, last amended by Article 3 of the Law of 2 October 2009, Federal Law Gazette I p. 3214), p. 3322, last amended by Article 3 of the Law of 2 October 2009, Federal Law Gazette I p. 3214, s.7, 2.

217 'Passing through' includes visits for a conference, meeting or holiday.

218 UN, 'Model Memorandum of Understanding between the United Nations and the xxx Contributing Resources to the xxxx' UN Doc. (on file with author).

219 On the increase in moves to ensure that the sending State has also established criminal jurisdiction, see Chapter 4, Section 3-5.

220 Ryngaert, *Jurisdiction*, p. 127; *Lotus*, pp. 30–31.

closest' connection.[221] It is argued that there is no obligation to exercise their jurisdiction reasonably.[222] On this point, it is submitted that the obligation on a State to act in 'good faith' under general principles of international law[223] may mean that jurisdiction needs to be claimed and exercised reasonably. Given that these two bases – territoriality and active nationality – for criminal jurisdiction are the most established, there may be circumstances in which both the host and sending States claim criminal jurisdiction. In such a case, the territory in which the suspect is located may have a stronger claim. Thus, the sending State, having found a suspect in its territory who is a UN police officer holding its nationality, may want to bring criminal proceedings against him. If the host State seeks to adjudicate on the same crime, it may be legitimate for the sending State to reject the claim for the suspect to be extradited to the host State.

In short, it is theoretically possible that a problem may arise in deciding which State has the stronger claim to jurisdiction, if more than one State claims jurisdiction. However, in reality, the major problem lies in the lack of criminal proceedings, and not with competing claims of criminal jurisdiction.[224]

5 Conclusion

Both international and domestic law have been examined to determine whether they constitute a legal barrier to a State's exercise of criminal jurisdiction. Under international law, the host State has an unchallenged claim of criminal jurisdiction, based on the territoriality principle. In addition, the concurrent nature of jurisdiction under international law does not prevent other States from exercising criminal jurisdiction.[225]

Depending on where the suspect is found, the territorial State and the sending State have the strongest claim to jurisdiction under international law. Other bases for jurisdiction are less well-established, but theoretically, third States have multiple bases for claiming criminal jurisdiction. Foremost amongst these are passive personality and universal jurisdiction, where relevant.[226]

221 Ryngaert, *Jurisdiction*, p. 129.

222 Ibid, p. 129.

223 *Nuclear Tests Case (Australia v France) (Merits)* [1974] *ICJ Rep 253*; Malcolm N Shaw, *International Law* (6th edn, CUP 2008), p. 103; Michel Virally, 'Review Essay: Good Faith in Public International Law' (1983) 77 *American Journal of International Law* 130.

224 See Chapter 3, Section 3.

225 See Section 3.

226 See Section 3.

At the level of national law, the host State automatically has jurisdiction because the crime is committed there. Whether sending States can exercise criminal jurisdiction over UN police personnel varies, according to their national laws. For most States, their criminal laws apply to all criminal conduct committed by UN police personnel deployed in UN Peace Operations, by virtue either of their penal codes or special laws applicable to police deployed abroad.[227] Some States have adopted laws dealing with specific crimes committed by their nationals abroad.[228] Increasingly, the UN's approach is that sending States are responsible for prosecuting crimes committed by their nationals serving as UN police.[229] In relation to FPUs, the MoU between the UN and sending States makes it clear that these States are obliged to apply their criminal laws to their personnel and, in fact, must exercise jurisdiction over them.[230] For IPOs, depending on the content of a specific MoU or *Note Verbale*, the exercise of jurisdiction based on the relevant criminal law may differ significantly.

The UN has inserted the formula 'the obligation to respect' in several documents relating to the application of the criminal law of the host State. According to the individual undertaking that all UN police personnel sign at the time they are appointed, together with internal codes applicable to them, they have a legal obligation to 'respect' local laws, including criminal law. While the exact content of the obligation to 'respect' local law is unclear, the fact that the UN accepts that its police personnel can be prosecuted in the host State[231] indicates that it considers that they are bound by that State's criminal law. This is the same for members of UN police personnel deployed in FPUs.[232] UN police

227 See Section 4-2.

228 See Section 4-2-2.

229 See Chapter 4, Section 3-5.

230 UN, FPU MoU.

231 See Section 2.

232 For clarification by the UN on the status of FPUs, and the exercise of host State criminal jurisdiction over these units, see UNGA, 'Comprehensive Report on All Processes Involved in the Investigation and Prosecution of Crimes Committed against Deployed United Nations Peacekeepers' (9 December 2011) UN Doc. A/66/598, para. 26 and footnote 2. In 2006, an OIOS report stated that, '[t]he Department of Peacekeeping Operations accepted this recommendation commenting that the Office of Legal Affairs had been requested to clarify the legal status and therefore disciplinary regime that applied to formed police units. In the interim, all peacekeeping missions had been informed to apply the disciplinary regime of "experts on mission" to formed police units'. UNGA, 'Report of the Office of Internal Oversight Services on the Global Review of Discipline in Field Missions led by the Department of Peacekeeping Operations' (8 March 2006) UN Doc. A/60/713, para. 76.

officers are provided with information through various codes and documents as to the possibility of prosecution in the host State.[233] However, there is no evidence that the UN in fact makes them aware of the *content* of the host State's criminal law. It is particularly important that this should be done, especially where criminal codes vary, such as on the age of consent for engaging in sexual acts.[234]

This leads to the conclusion that there is little evidence that jurisdiction, either at the international or national level, constitutes a major legal obstacle to the prosecution of crimes committed by UN police officers. Instead, the problem may lie either in the failure of States to assert criminal jurisdiction, or in the issues that arise after jurisdiction has been asserted. Thus, the next chapter will discuss immunity as a potential legal barrier to prosecution.

233 See Section 2-1.

234 See Section 2-1-2.

CHAPTER 6

Immunity as a Potential Legal Barrier

The previous chapter revealed that jurisdiction poses no major legal barriers to States bringing criminal proceedings against UN police officers.[1] However, there is another possible legal barrier which has often been cited in this regard: the issue of immunity.[2] This chapter examines the extent to which the law of immunity actually acts as a barrier to prosecuting UN police personnel. Questions regarding immunity mainly arise in relation to: (i) the type of conduct by UN police personnel for which immunity is granted; (ii) the period of time for which immunity from criminal prosecution is granted; and (iii) the criminal jurisdiction(s) in relation to which immunity is granted.

Other contexts in which immunity may have an adverse impact on the individual criminal accountability of UN police personnel are: immunity from its property being searched by any State, the inviolability of UN documents and archives;[3] and the immunity of the UN police or other personnel from being summoned by a court to give testimony as a witness.[4] However, these are auxiliary issues, and thus will not form the focus of this chapter.

A further question relates to the procedure by which immunity is asserted. Even where the law does not in principle hinder prosecution and where the

1 This deals with the issue of whether those States are prohibited from bringing criminal proceedings against UN police officers for criminal acts committed by them during their missions. It is a separate question from whether or not sending States in fact bring criminal proceedings. There may be many other reasons for which States may decide not to bring criminal proceedings. For details, see Chapter 5, Section 3.

2 William J Durch et al, *Improving Criminal Accountability in United Nations Peace Operations* (Stimson Center Report, 2009) p. 33; Marco Odello, 'Tackling Criminal Acts in Peacekeeping Operations: The Accountability of Peacekeepers' (2010) 15 *Journal of Conflict and Security Law*; Andrew Ladley, 'Peacekeeper Abuse, Immunity and Impunity: The Need for Effective Criminal and Civil Accountability on International Peace Operations' (2005) 1 *Politics and Ethics Review* 81; Elizabeth F Defeis, 'UN Peacekeepers and Sexual Abuse and Exploitation: An End to Impunity' (2008) 7 *Washington University Global Study Law Review* 185, p. 192; Anthony J Miller, 'Legal Aspects of Stopping Sexual Exploitation and Abuse in UN Peacekeeping Operations' (2006) 39 *Cornell International Law Journal* 71, p. 90.

3 Article 2, Section 4. This is also explicitly stated in relation to the personnel category 'Experts on Mission'. Convention on the Privileges and Immunities of the United Nations (adopted 13 February 1946, entered into force 17 September 1946) 1 UNTS 15, Section 22 (c).

4 This is included in the immunity from all legal proceedings. Ibid, Article IV, Section 12; Article V, Section 18 (a); Article VI, Section 22 (b).

 | DOI 10.1163/9789004328815_007

scope of immunity is clear, if the procedure to assert or deny it is either unclear or open to abuse, it may nonetheless prevent prosecution.

In the first instance, law itself will be analyzed with respect to both the scope of immunity and the procedure in relation to its application or waiver. Subsequently, insofar as the practice differs from the law, this practice will be examined in light of that law.

1 The Law of Immunity

1-1 *The* Rationale *for Immunity*

In order to analyse the exact scope of immunity for UN police personnel, it is first necessary to set out the *rationale* for this immunity, as the scope is closely connected to the *rationale*. Immunity derives from the needs of the UN. It is aimed at protecting the UN from any undue influence or control by a member State,[5] to the extent necessary for it to fulfil its purposes.[6] A strong link exists between the immunity accorded to the UN, and those provided for its

5 August Reinisch, 'Privileges and immunities' in Jan Klabbers and Asa Wallendahl (eds), *Research Handbook on the Law of International Organizations* (Edward Elgar Publishing 2011), p. 134.

6 The Charter of the United Nations (adopted 26 June 1945, entered into force 24 October 1945) 1 UNTS XVI, Article 105. Seidl-Hohenveldern describes the fundamental nature of the Organization's immunity protection as follows: 'The main goal behind all rules concerning international organizations is the aim to enable the organization to fulfil its functions. A very important sub-goal thereof is to ensure the independence of the organization from any interference by any individual member state. This sub-goal thus implies granting the organization immunity from domestic jurisdiction of any member state and from corresponding enforcement measures'. Ignaz Seidl-Hohenveldern, 'Failure of Controls in the Sixth International Tin Agreement' in Niels Blokker and Sam Muller (eds), *Towards More Effective Supervision by International Organizations, Essays in Honour of Henry G Schermers*, vol I (Multinus Nijhoff 1994), p. 270. Immunities 'are strictly designed to protect the interests of the organization in preventing any coercion or threat thereof in respect of the performance by the experts of their missions'. See UN, 'Legal Status of Experts Employed by Specialized Agencies – Question whether Salaries and Emoluments of Experts on Mission Should be Accorded Exception from National Taxation in Pursuance of the 1947 Convention on the Privileges and Immunities of the Specialized Agencies – Scope of the Privileges and Immunities Enjoyed by UNIDO Experts and UNDP Volunteers' (1992) 1992 UN Jurid YB, p. 486, (hereinafter 'Experts' Immunity Opinion'). See also Written Statement Submitted on behalf of the Secretary-General, *Mazilu* Pleadings, para. 63. Anthony J Miller, 'United Nations Experts on Mission and their Privileges and Immunities' (2007) 4 *International Organizations Law Review* 11, p. 40, (hereinafter 'EoM Immunity').

personnel; or, rather, the latter derives from the former. As such, immunity for UN personnel does not derive from who they are, but from the fact that they form a part of the machinery that enables the UN to fulfil its purposes.[7] In other words, in order for the UN to deliver its functions, not only the Organization but also the personnel through which it operates, must be protected from any coercion or threats by any State in respect of their performances. Therefore, the *rationale* for granting immunity is not that UN personnel need to be protected, but that they need it to be able to do their jobs. This *rationale* is different from that underlying sovereign or diplomatic immunity. Sovereign immunity derives from the agreement amongst States to mutually respect each other's sovereign dignity.[8] Diplomatic immunity has two aspects. One is the need to protect diplomatic envoys from other States' courts, in the sense or to the extent that they are the personification of their State. The other is that diplomatic envoys need to be protected from any undue influence exerted by the receiving State in order to perform their functions.[9] The latter point overlaps with the *rationale* for immunity for the UN and its personnel. There are thus some similarities between the immunity provided to diplomats and that provided to UN personnel, in particular with regard to the immunity applicable in the host State.[10] Nevertheless, in the UN's case, this need to protect its functions is the only *rationale* for granting immunity. This *rationale* is significant in that it provides a test for the geographic scope, duration and subject matter of any specific immunity protection.[11] This means that immunity should be limited to covering the needs of the Organization. Thus, immunity is, generally

7 Bruce Oswald, *Documents on the Law of UN Peace Operations* (Oxford University Press 2010), p. 315, (hereinafter 'Documents').

8 *Jurisdictional Immunities of the State (Germany v Italy: Greece intervening)* (Judgement) [2012] ICJ Rep 99, para. 57; *Jones and Others v UK* ECHR 2014, para. 188; Thomas R Van Dervort, *International Law and Organization: An Introduction* (Sage Thousand Oaks 1998), pp. 304–305; Antonio Cassese, *International Criminal Law* (Oxford University Press 2003), pp. 265–267; Charles J Lewis, *State and Diplomatic Immunity* (3rd edition edn, Lloyd's of London Press 1990), p. 2.

9 Cassese, *International Criminal Law*, pp. 265–267; Ian Brownlie, *Principles of Public International Law* (3rd edn, Oxford University Press 1979), pp. 346–347; Van Dervort, *International Law and Organization: An Introduction*, pp. 289–290; Grant V McClanahan, *Diplomatic Immunity* (Hurst & Company 1989), p. 82; Lewis, *State and Diplomatic Immunity*, p. 2.

10 See Section 1-4.

11 Derek William Bowett and George Paterson Barton, *United Nations Forces: A Legal Study* (The Lawbook Exchange 2008), p. 432.

speaking, not absolute.[12] This limitation means that if something is not necessary to the effective functioning of the organization, immunity should not be given or, alternatively, that it should last only for such time as is necessary.

The International Court of Justice (ICJ) illustrated the principal idea behind the need for immunity for personnel working for the UN in the *Reparations* case:[13]

> In order that the agent may perform his duties satisfactorily, he must feel that this protection is assured to him by the Organization, and that he may count on it. To ensure the independence of the agent, and, consequently, the independent *action* of the Organization itself, it is essential that in performing his duties he need not have to rely on any other protection than that of the Organization.[14]

The issue of immunity is so fundamental that the UN Charter itself specifies the immunity protection granted to the Organization and its personnel.[15] Article 105 states that organizational immunities are provided 'as are necessary for the fulfilment of its purposes'.[16] Individual immunities are similarly provided 'as are necessary for the independent exercise of the functions of its personnel in connextion [*sic*] with the Organization'.[17]

The *rationale* for immunity – the need to protect the exercise of their functions, or 'necessity' –[18] is evidenced in another legal instrument: the Convention on the Privileges and Immunity of the United Nations (hereinafter the

12 There are some people who are granted absolute immunity, as will be explained in Section 1-4-2 (1).

13 *Reparation for Injuries Suffered in the Service of the United Nations* (Advisory Opinion) [1949] ICJ Rep 174, (hereinafter 'Reparations').

14 (Emphasis added.) Ibid, para. 183.

15 The idea of immunity for international organizations pre-dates the existence of the UN. Regarding the development of the idea of immunity for the UN, see Anthony J Miller, 'Privileges and Immunities of United Nations Officials' [2007] *International Organizations Law Review* 169, (hereinafter 'UN Official's Immunity').

16 UN Charter, Article 105-1.

17 Ibid, Article 105-2.

18 The immunity of international organizations is based on the notion of functional necessity. Seidl-Hohenveldern, 'Failure of Controls in the Sixth International Tin Agreement', p. 151. In this work, in order to distinguish 'functional necessity' as the *rationale* for immunity, and 'functional immunity' as a type of immunity, the term 'functional necessity' is avoided.

'General Convention').[19] As articulated later,[20] it is an instrument that mirrors the UN Charter. It is therefore not surprising that it echoes the *rationale* provided in the Charter. Individual immunities shall be accorded 'as are necessary for the independent exercise of their functions',[21] and 'in the interests of the United Nations and not for the personal benefit [*sic*]'.[22]

1-2 *Sources*

For reasons discussed later,[23] the source of a particular immunity may have implications for the scope of immunity. The UN Charter provides only the underlying purpose of immunity, without giving any further details.[24] Subsequently, the General Convention was drafted to give effect to Article 105-3 of the UN Charter, 'with a view to determining the details of the application of the privileges and immunity of the Organization and its personnel'.[25] As such, the General Convention is a legal instrument that interprets or 'operationalizes' the Charter.[26] The UN and States are both parties to it. However,

---

19 General Convention.

20 For details of the relationship between the UN Charter and the General Convention, see Section 1-2.

21 General Convention, Article VI, Section 22 for Experts on Mission.

22 Ibid, Article IV, Section 14 for Representatives of Members; Article V, Section 20 for Officials; Article VI, Section 23 for Experts on Mission. There is a separate legal agreement between the UN and the host State, normally called the 'Status-of-Forces Agreement' (SOFA). While SOFAs do not provide any details on the *rationale* for individual immunity, it relies on the UN Charter and the General Convention to provide the bases of the immunity provisions. This would mean that SOFAs do not separately confirm or provide a *rationale* for immunity. On SOFAs, see Section 1-2. On the provisions in the SOFA, see UNGA, 'Report of the Secretary-General on the Model Status-of-Forces Agreement for Peace-Keeping Operations' (9 October 1990) UN Doc. A/45/594, Articles 3-5, (hereinafter 'model SOFA').

23 See Sections 1-3 and 1-4.

24 See Section 1-1.

25 Article 105-3 of the UN Charter sets out the General Assembly's authority either to make recommendations or to propose conventions to the member States. UN, 'Question of Privileges and Immunities of the United Nations, of Representatives of Member States and of Officials of the Organization – Statement Made by the Legal Counsel at the 1016th Meeting of the Sixth Committee of the General Assembly on 6 December 1967' (1967) 1967 UN Jurid YB 311, p. 313, para. 9.

26 Scott P Sheeran, 'A Constitutional Moment?: United Nations Peacekeeping in the Democratic Republic of Congo' (2011) 8 *International Organizations Law Review* 55, p. 31. The interpretative nature of the General Convention is also provided in the preamble, General Convention.

whereas the States in question all have the same obligations, the UN's obligations are different.[27] Issues may arise where relevant States, either the host or sending States, are not party to the General Convention. In such cases, the General Convention does not apply to those States.[28]

Since neither the UN Charter nor the General Convention refer to the UN police, where it is considered that a particular immunity derives from these documents, it is deemed to do so by virtue of the nature of their assignment falling either into the category of 'Experts on Mission', or that of high-ranking 'Officials' in the case of the Police Commissioner.[29]

Quite apart from the general provision on immunity, there is a bilateral agreement between the UN and the host State of a Peace Operation, the Status-of-Forces Agreement (SOFA).[30] SOFAs provide immunity to the mission and its personnel in respect of the host State.[31] Where a mission specific SOFA does

---

27 The UN is not normally a party to any treaties. However, in respect of the General Convention, which has the effect of a bilateral treaty, the UN is always considered to be one of the parties to this treaty. (The other party is always a State.) When the Sub-Committee on Privileges and Immunities within the Sixth Committee described the Convention as a unique treaty that has the UN on one side and each individual State on the other, it appears possible to interpret it in such a way that each State party is only concerned with the UN's functioning in that particular State. UNGA Sixth Committee 'First Report of the Sub-Committee on Privileges and Immunities' (26 January 1946) UN Doc. A/C.6/17, pp. 2–3.

28 Unless either the whole or part of the General Convention is considered customary. See sub-section below on the status of the General Convention.

29 See Section 1-3.

30 See Chapter 5, Section 2-1-1.

31 Oswald, *Documents*, p. 34. 'SOFAs are framed within the paradigm of international law but their effect is primarily on the application of the domestic law of the host State in relation to both the peace operation and members serving in the operation'. Bruce Oswald and Adrian Bates, 'Privileges and Immunities of United Nations Police' in Bryn W. Hughes, Charles T. Hunt and Boris Kondoch (eds), *Making Sense of Peace and Capacity-Building Operations: Rethinking Policing and Beyond* (Martinus Nijhoff Publishers 2010), p. 164; United Nations Peacekeeping Law Reform Project, 'UN Peacekeeping and The Model Status of Forces Agreement – Background Paper' (Experts' Workshop, London, 26 August 2010), paras. 38, 48, 60. It is separate from and independent of any SOFAs that may be agreed upon between the host State and all or some of the States sending military contingents. Françoise Hampson and Ai Kihara-Hunt, 'The Accountability of Personnel Associated with Peacekeeping Operations' in Chiyuki Aoi, Cedric De Coning and Ramesh Thakur (eds), *Unintended Consequences of Peacekeeping* (UNU 2007), p. 199. See also United Nations Peacekeeping Law Reform Project, 'SOFA Workshop Paper', para. 84. The relationship between the immunity provided for in the SOFA and those provided for in other legal instruments will be discussed in Section 1-4 (below). In a Peace Operation

not exist, the UN claims that the model SOFA applies on a provisional basis.[32] This has been asserted in recent Security Council resolutions establishing missions.[33] Were the applicability of the SOFA to be successfully contested, this may have implications for the scope of immunity.[34]

The relationship between the General Convention and the SOFA may be significant because the scope of immunity may be different depending upon the interpretation of their inter-relationship. There are two possible views on this relationship. The first argues that SOFA *makes* the immunity provisions of the General Convention applicable to Peace Operations and, more precisely, in relation to the host State, whether or not it has ratified the General Convention.[35] This appears to imply that it is the SOFA that works as a bridge between UN police personnel and their immunity. In other words, without a SOFA, it is not clear whether the UN police personnel and the Police Commissioner can claim immunity.

If it is indeed the case that immunity for UN police personnel is reliant on there being a SOFA, this means that whatever immunity is granted to these personnel is only applicable in relation to the host State. The view that immunity

that does not include a military component, a Status of Mission Agreement (SOMA) is normally agreed in place of a SOFA. UN DPKO, *Handbook on United Nations Multidimensional Peacekeeping Operations* (UN 2003), p. 13; United Nations Peacekeeping Law Reform Project, 'SOFA Workshop Paper', paras. 7–8. The author will use the term 'SOFA' to include SOMA in such missions.

32 See Chapter 5, Section 2-1-1. However, the provisional use of the model SOFA was not included in the UN's initial plans. United Nations Law Reform Project, 'UN Peacekeeping and The Model Status of Forces Agreement' (Experts' Workshop), para. 61.

33 See, for example, the Security Council resolutions establishing the following missions: African Union-United Nations Hybrid Operation in Darfur (UNAMID), UNSC Res 1769 UNSC Res 1769 (31 July 2007) UN Doc. S/RES/1769, op. para. 15 (b); UN Mission in the Central African Republic and Chad (MINURCAT), UNSC Res 1778 (25 September 2007) UN Doc. S/RES/1778, op. para. 4; UN Mission in Sudan (UNMIS), UNSC Res 1590 (24 March 2005) UN Doc. S/RES/1590, op. para. 16 (ii); UN Mission in the Central African Republic (MINURCA) op. para. 19; UNSC Res 1159 (27 March 1998) UN Doc. S/RES/1159; UN Mission in Ethiopia and Eritrea (UNMEE), UNSC Res 1320 (15 September 2000) UN Doc. S/RES/1320, op. para. 6; UN Mission in Sierra Leone (UNAMSIL), UNSC Res 1270 (22 October 1999) UN Doc. S/RES/1270, op. para. 16; UN Stabilization Mission in Haiti (MINUSTAH), UNSC Res 1542 (30 April 2004) UN Doc. S/RES/1542, op. para. 11; UN Operation in Burundi (ONUB), UNSC Res 1545 (21 May 2004) UN Doc. S/RES/1545, op. para. 10; UN Operation in Côte d'Ivoire (UNOCI), UNSC Res 1528 (27 February 2994) UN Doc. S/RES/1528, op. para. 9; and UNSC Res (24 February 2000) UN Doc. S/RES/1291 expanding MONUC's mandate, op. para. 10.

34 See Section 1-4.

35 Oswald, *Documents*, p. 35.

is reliant on there being a SOFA would also have a significant impact on immunity for UN police personnel serving in missions which do not have a SOFA, or where a mission begins before a SOFA is agreed. In these circumstances, it could be argued that these personnel are not covered by immunity, as questions remain with regard to the provisional applicability of the model SOFA in such situations.[36]

The second view holds that immunity exists independently of a SOFA. According to this view, it is not the SOFA that gives UN police immunity. Rather, it is the practice of the States and the UN that causes UN police personnel to come within the immunity category of 'Experts on Mission'. Thus, the model SOFA simply reflects this practice.[37] The same applies to the Police Commissioner, as he is considered a high-ranking Official, which is reflected in the SOFA.[38] In this case, the SOFA acts only as a complementary instrument for immunity in respect of the host State.[39] This seems to be the position taken by the UN.[40] Given the fundamental nature and vital necessity of immunity,[41]

36 See Chapter 5, Section 2-1-1.

37 UNGA, Model SOFA, para. 26. It is claimed that the Model SOFA reflects practice at the point at which it was drafted. Ibid, accompanying letter from the Secretary-General, para. 1. See also the United Nations Peacekeeping Law Reform Project, 'SOFA Workshop Paper', para. 9. However, note that practice related to the UN police was not established at the time the report was published.

38 UNGA, Model SOFA, para. 24.

39 Where the host State is a party to the General Convention, the mission and its personnel 'shall enjoy the privileges and immunity specified in the [SOFA] as well as those provided for' in the General Convention. Ibid, para. 3, in particular footnote d.

40 'As a general rule, the basic privileges and immunity of a United Nations peace-keeping operation consist of provisions that flow from the Convention on the Privileges and Immunity of the United Nations adopted by the General Assembly on 13 February 1946'. Ibid, footnote to para. 3. UN, 'Letter to the Acting Chair of the Special Committee on Peacekeeping Operations, United Nations, Regarding Immunities of Civilian Police and Military Personnel' (2004) 2004 *UN Jurid YB* 323, p. 324. This supports the view that the SOFA classifies certain personnel (in this case, the Military Observers and staff members of the Force Commander) as Experts on Mission, as an example of UN practice. Miller, 'EoM Immunity', p. 29. See also Oswald, *Documents*, p. 34. 'If the model SOFA does not apply and no operation-specific SOFA has been concluded between the UN and the host country then the status of the operation and most of the members of that operation, except for the military contingent and locally recruited personnel [...], will be governed by the Convention on the Privileges and Immunity of the United Nations'.

41 See Section 1-1 above.

it would be most appropriate to consider that immunity exists under the UN Charter, as interpreted in the General Convention.[42]

This would mean that where both the host and sending States and, for that matter, any other States that may seek to exercise criminal jurisdiction, have ratified the General Convention, there are two separate sources of immunity granted to the UN police personnel (including the Police Commissioner). These two kinds of immunity may vary in their scope. Where a State is not party to the General Convention, it is important to establish whether the whole of the General Convention, or only some of its provisions, are deemed to have acquired customary status.

The Status of the General Convention

There are some who consider the entire General Convention to have become customary. The UN Office of Legal Affairs (OLA) has suggested that the provisions of the Convention became a 'part of the general international law governing the relations of States and the United Nations' in 1967.[43] It has near-universal ratification, as it has been ratified by 160 States.[44] However, this issue is still open to debate.[45] Nevertheless, the UN Charter itself requires all member States to give effect to Article 105-2 of the Charter. The UN has taken

42 On the application of the General Convention, see Section 2.

43 UN, Question of Privileges and Immunities of the United Nations, of Representatives of Member States and of Officials of the Organization – Statement Made by the Legal Counsel at the 1016th Meeting of the Sixth Committee of the General Assembly on 6 December 1967, pp. 311–314. See also Ralph Zacklin, 'United Nations Management of Legal Issues' in Jessica Howard and Bruce Oswald CSC (eds), *The Rule of Law on Peace Operations, 'Challenges of Peace Operations' Project Conference* (Law School, University of Melbourne, 11–13 November 2002, Kluwer Law International 2002), p. 119.

44 This was the situation as of 7 November 2014. The ratification status is available at UN, 'United Nations Treaty Collection' <https://treaties.un.org/> accessed 7 November 2014. On the relationship between the large number of ratifications and customary status of this Convention, see Raphaël Van Steenberghe, 'The Obligation to Extradite or Prosecute Clarifying its Nature' (2011) 9 *Journal of International Criminal Justice* 1089, p. 4. In *North Sea Continental Shelf* case, the ICJ explicitly endorsed the idea that ratification of a treaty by a large number of States may lead to the transformation into customary law of its provisions through its influence on the practice of non-State parties. *North Sea Continental Shelf case* (*Federal Republic of Germany v Denmark/The Netherlands*) [1969] ICJ Rep 3, pp. 43–44.

45 For example, in a case heard by the International Tin Council (ITC), a judge stated that, 'International organizations such as the ITC have never, so far as I know, been recognized at common law as entitled to sovereign status. They are accordingly entitled to no sovereign or diplomatic immunity in this country save where such immunity is granted by

the stance that the Charter itself obligates all member States to give effect to the privileges and immunities set out therein, 'whether or not they have acceded to the Convention'.[46] However, because the obligations enshrined in the UN Charter are very vague, it is unclear where the details of these obligations should be sought.

1-3 *Status of UN Police Personnel in Terms of Immunity*

The type and scope of immunity are determined according to the status of the UN personnel concerned. Thus, it is essential to clarify their status.

UN Police Personnel in General

The UN Charter refers only to 'Representatives of Members', and 'officials of the Organization'.[47] However, people who are not 'officials of the Organization', but nonetheless deliver the Organization's functions, were recognized and included in the discussion of who constitutes 'officials'.[48] Subsequently, at the time the General Convention was drafted, the view was taken that the UN needed to assure the privileges and immunity for those experts who were not UN staff members.[49] For this reason, where early instruments and documents,

---

legislative instrument, and then only to the extent of such grant'. *Standard Chartered Bank v ITC and Others* [1987] 1 WLR 641, 648 (Bingham J), pp. 647–648.

46 UN, Question of Privileges and Immunities of the United Nations, of Representatives of Member States and of Officials of the Organization – Statement Made by the Legal Counsel at the 1016th Meeting of the Sixth Committee of the General Assembly on 6 December 1967, para. 9. See also the International Law Commission (ILC), which considers that the obligation to give effect to the privileges and immunity to officials derives directly from the UN Charter. Ibid, p. 313, para. 9; ILC, 'The Practice of the United Nations, the Specialized Agencies and the International Atomic Energy Agency concerning their Status, Privileges and Immunities: Study Prepared by the Secretariat' (1967) *ILC YB* vol 2 154, p. 265. para. 246.

47 UN Charter, Article 105-2.

48 The Sub-Committee to the Sixth Committee on Privileges and Immunity in submitting a draft of the future Article 105 noted that 'officials' include 'the agents (functionaries, etc.) of the Organization and of its organs, authorities or agencies'. UN, 'Report Submitted by Subcommittee to Committee IV, UN Conference on International Organization, vol 13' (18 May 1945) UN Doc. 412 IV/2/A/2 (2), p. 779. Also note that, during the Preparatory Commission of the United Nations, experts travelling for the Organization were mentioned. See also UN, 'Summary Report of the Second Meeting of Committee IV/2, UN Conference on International Organizations, vol 13' (11 May 1945) UN Doc. 228, IV/2/10, p. 74, which refers to 'Representatives and members and officials of the United Nations organization and their staffs'.

49 Miller, 'EoM Immunity', pp. 17–19.

including the UN Charter, refer to 'officials', it is clear that the term was intended to include experts who are not officials, but who are nevertheless entrusted by the UN to deliver some of its functions.

This category of persons is referred to as 'Experts on Mission' in the General Convention, as distinguished from 'Officials'.[50] Officials are those personnel appointed as staff members who are bound by Staff Rules and Regulations,[51] while 'Experts on Mission' are defined as those who are not 'Officials', but who are, nonetheless, 'performing missions for the UN'.[52] This definition of Experts on Mission is ambiguous, and has left member States confused concerning the difference between the two categories.[53] The UN has provided its interpretation of this definition on multiple occasions.[54] According to the UN, an expert

---

50 General Convention, Article VI.

51 UN, Question of Privileges and Immunities of the United Nations, of Representatives of Member States and of Officials of the Organization – Statement Made by the Legal Counsel at the 1016th Meeting of the Sixth Committee of the General Assembly on 6 December 1967, p. 284, para. 340.

52 General Convention, Article VI, Section 22. The categories of 'Official' and 'Expert on Mission' are therefore mutually exclusive. This is not the case for 'Representative of a Member State' and 'Expert on Mission'. For example, there were individuals representing member States who simultaneously served as members on the UN Pension Board. They were considered Experts on Mission while performing functions for the Pension Fund. This meant that they enjoyed diplomatic immunity in relation to the host State, as well as immunity for official acts in other States. Miller, 'EoM Immunity', p. 30.

53 Miller, 'EoM Immunity', pp. 20–21. When this category of personnel emerged for the first time in the draft convention recommended by the Sub-Committee on Privileges and Immunities within the General Assembly's Sixth Committee, there was virtually no discussion of it. This may have caused confusion as to the nature of this category, as well as the immunity afforded to this group. UNGA Sixth Committee Sub-Committee Report; Ai Kihara-Hunt, 'Why Does the Immunity Afforded to UN Personnel Not Appropriately Reflect the Needs of the Organization?: The Case of the UN Police' (2016) 17 *United Nations Studies* 205, pp. 211–212, (hereinafter 'Inappropriate Immunity').

54 ILC, 1967 ILC Immunities Study, p. 284. See also UN, 'Question of Whether Contractors' Personnel Could be Considered as 'Experts on Mission' – Article VI, Section 22, of the 1946 Convention on the Privileges and Immunities of the United Nations – Status of Consultants' (1998) 1998 *UN Jurid YB* 481; *Applicability of Article VI, Section 22, of the Convention on the Privileges and Immunities of the United Nations* (Written Statement Submitted on behalf of the Secretary-General of the United Nations) [1989] ICJ Rep 173, pp. 185–188; UN, 'Memorandum dated 17 April 1981 from the Assistant Administrator, Bureau for Finance and Administration, to the Field Offices of UNDP and UNDP Headquarters Staff' (17 April 1981) UN Doc. UNDP/ADM/FIELD/762; UNDP/ADM/HQRTS/503, available in *Applicability of Article VI, Section 22, of the Convention on the Privileges and Immunities of the United Nations*, p. 127.

is assigned a specific task, often based on a contract.[55] A person's status as an Expert on Mission is determined at the time of his appointment according to different contractual conditions, chiefly the nature of his contractual relations and his terms of service with the UN. These matters are decisive in categorizing someone.[56] The Secretary-General (SG) has authority over an expert only in relation to a particular assignment, unlike the case of Officials. Furthermore, Experts on Mission cannot be assigned to any other activity.[57]

The ICJ examined the elements of 'Experts on Mission' in two cases. In the *Mazilu* case, the Court was asked to rule on whether the applicability of privileges and immunity granted to Experts on Mission should be granted to a person who was appointed as a Special Rapporteur of the UN's Sub-Commission on Prevention of Discrimination and Protection of Minorities in respect of his own State of nationality.[58] The ICJ held that Experts on Mission are those assigned to a mission by the Organization. The experts:

> [...] may or may not be remunerated, may or may not have a contract, may be given a task requiring work over a lengthy period or a short time. The essence of the matter lies not in their administrative position but in the nature of their mission.[59]

The 'mission' often includes travel, but 'embrace[s] in general the tasks entrusted to a person, whether or not those tasks involve travel'.[60] In the *Cumaraswamy* case, the ICJ considered whether a Special Rapporteur at the UN Commission on Human Rights was immune from legal proceedings in his State of nationality, in relation to what he had said during interviews he had given.[61] The Court followed its finding in the *Mazilu* case, stating that, 'what is decisive is that [the Experts on Mission] have been entrusted with a mission by the [UN]'.[62] The word 'experts' suggests that there are professional skills they can

55 Miller, 'EoM Immunity', p. 21; ILC, 1967 ILC Immunities Study, para. 340.

56 ILC, 1967 ILC Immunities Study, paras. 340–341.

57 Miller, 'EoM Immunity', p. 21. ILC, 1967 ILC Immunities Study, para. 340.

58 *Applicability of Article VI, Section 22, of the Convention on the Privileges and Immunities of the United Nations* (Advisory Opinion) [1989] ICJ Rep 177.

59 Ibid, para. 48.

60 Ibid, para. 49.

61 *Difference Relating to Immunity from Legal Process of a Special Rapporteur of the Commission on Human Rights* (Advisory Opinion) [1999] ICJ Rep 62, [hereinafter 'Cumaraswamy (Advisory Opinion)'].

62 Ibid, para. 42.

offer.[63] While the Court noted that some Experts on Mission have participated in peacekeeping forces,[64] it did not include UN Police in the list of examples of Experts on Mission.[65]

That notwithstanding, UN police personnel are considered to be 'Experts on Mission' by the UN, whose practice it is to classify as such a person who is entrusted to perform a specific and important task for it, even if that person is neither a staff member nor a representative of a member State.[66] Based on their professional skills, UN police officers are specifically called on to provide their services to the UN for a certain period of time. They are assigned a mission by the SG. IPOs hold individual contracts with the SG, while members of FPUs are deployed as units. The description of IPOs fits neatly into the 'Experts on Mission' category of personnel, as expanded upon by the ICJ in the cases cited above. As FPU personnel are also employed to perform duties based on specific professional skills, they also appear to match the requirements for being 'Experts on Mission'. However, their mode of employment does not reflect the typical character of Experts on Mission.[67]

---

63 Miller, 'EoM Immunity', p. 28. *Cumaraswamy* (*Advisory Opinion*), p. 83, para. 43, emphasizing that the mission is 'entrusted' by the UN, which appears to indicate that the protection of the General Convention is granted to those persons who are given a specific task requiring professional expertise.

64 *Mazilu* (*Advisory Opinion*), para. 48. An observation was made in the Secretariat study for the ILC that, '[i]n adopting Article VI of the United Nations Convention, the General Assembly had in mind peace missions in particular'. ILC, 1967 ILC Immunities Study, p. 284.

65 It included Military Observers and members of the Force Commander's staff. *Applicability of Article VI, Section 22, of the Convention on the Privileges and Immunities of the United Nations*, at 133 (Document No. 144). This is understandable due to the limited existence of UN Police in Peace Operations.

66 Immunities accorded to persons on the basis of their link with the UN are divided into different categories. Personnel falling within the scope of the General Convention are placed into three categories: Representatives of Members, Officials, and Experts on Mission. Officials are then sub-divided into Officials and high-ranking Officials. General Convention, Article V, Sections 18, 19 and Article VI, Section 22. See UN, Question of Whether Contractors' Personnel Could be Considered as 'Experts on Mission' – Article VI, Section 22, of the 1946 Convention on the Privileges and Immunities of the United Nations – Status of Consultants, pp. 481–482; Oswald, *Documents*, pp. 315, 366. Locally recruited personnel who are paid hourly are excluded from the Officials category. UNGA, 'Recommendations Presented by the Secretary-General, Categories of Officials to which the Provisions of Article V and Article VII Shall Apply' (16 October 1946) UN Doc. A/116; UNGA, 'Recommendations Presented by the Secretary-General, Categories of Officials to which the Provisions of Article V and Article VII shall apply – Addendum' (9 Novermber 1946) UN Doc. A/116/Add.1.

67 See Chapter 2, Sections 1-6 and 3-3-1 for FPU's mode of employment.

Separately, SOFAs explicitly categorize UN police personnel as Experts on Mission in relation to the host State. For example, the model SOFA provides that UN police personnel 'shall be considered as experts on mission within the meaning of Article VI of the Convention'.[68] Mission-specific SOFAs do not modify this provision.

The OLA has observed that both mission-specific SOFAs and the model SOFA consistently place UN police officers in the same category and, even where an individual SOFA has not been agreed or where a model SOFA is not made applicable to a specific mission, the UN police's status remains governed by the General Convention as being Experts on Mission.[69] There has not been any challenge to the categorization of UN police officers as Experts on Mission, at least since the mid-1990s. Therefore, it is submitted that UN police personnel are Experts on Mission because the nature of their assignment with the UN corresponds to the nature of the work conducted by Experts on Mission, as defined in the General Convention.[70]

Since the recruitment and deployment process of FPU personnel,[71] as well as their command structure,[72] are similar to those of military contingents, there were suggestions that FPUs should be subject to the exclusive criminal jurisdiction of their sending States, as are the military contingents.[73] If that

---

68 UNGA, Model SOFA, para. 24.

69 The UN has consistently claimed that the immunity provided for in the General Convention applies independently of the SOFA. See Section 1-2. UN, Letter to the Acting Chair of the Special Committee on Peacekeeping Operations, United Nations, Regarding Immunities of Civilian Police and Military Personnel, p. 324. This is the view that SOFA classifies certain personnel (in this case it was Military Observers and staff members of the Force Commander) as Experts on Mission, as an example of UN practice. Miller, 'EoM Immunity', p. 29.

70 See Section 1-2. It is also of note that the model SOFA was drafted to set out the practice that had been in place before then. In other words, the UN claims that it had already been UN practice to consider UN police personnel as Experts on Mission at the time the model SOFA was drafted. UNGA, Model SOFA, attached letter by the Secretary-General, para. 1. For an analysis of the UN's practice, see Section 2.

71 See Chapter 2, Section 3-3 on their recruitment and deployment.

72 Members of an FPU report to their national commander, who reports to the Police Commissioner. In some large missions, commanders of FPUs report to the Deputy Chief Operations, who is in charge of FPU operations. UN DPKO/DFS, 'Formed Police Units in United Nations Peacekeeping Operations' (1 March 2010) UN Doc. Ref. 2009. 32, paras. 46, 51–54.

73 It has been suggested that FPUs and those police who may have to take up enforcement tasks be given the same immunity as armed forces. 'The Special Committee continues to believe that the tasks of such personnel require adaptation of the current rules governing their legal status, by assigning them immunity equivalent to those of armed military

were the case, FPU personnel would be immune from all host State criminal proceedings, but not immune to criminal proceedings instigated by their sending States. Since the UN is increasingly reliant on FPUs, discussions on the criminal accountability of Experts on Mission in peace operations have been held at the Sixth Committee of the General Assembly. It was clarified that both IPOs and members of FPUs are considered to be Experts on Mission.[74]

UN Police Commissioner

The status of a UN Police Commissioner differs from that of other members of the UN police. For reasons which are discussed below, the Police Commissioner is considered to be a high-ranking Official in the Organization.

The Police Commissioner is selected and appointed by the SG, with the consent of the Security Council, and reports directly to the SRSG, unlike the other members of the UN police.[75] While some ambiguity remains regarding the difference between Officials and Experts on Mission, this selection and appointment process, as well as the direct employment relationship between the UN and the Police Commissioner, indicate that the position of Police Commissioner shares more characteristics with those of an Official.[76] Thus, the Police Commissioner position differs from those of Experts on Mission, who lack a direct employment relationship with the UN.[77]

---

personnel, bearing in mind the need for accountability'. UNGA, 'Report of the Special Committee on Peacekeeping Operations and its Working Group' (GAOR 59th Session Supp no 19, 31 January-25 February 2005; 4–8 April 2005) UN Doc. A/59/19/Rev.1, para. 81.

74 See, for example, UNGA, 'Ensuring the Accountability of United Nations Staff and Experts on Mission with Respect to Criminal Acts Committed in Peacekeeping Operations' (16 August 2006) UN Doc. A/60/980.

75 United States Institute for Peace, 'Guide for Participants in Peace, Stability, and Relief Operations' <http://www.usip.org/node/5545> accessed 9 November 2014. See above, section entitled '*UN Police Personnel in General*', for the status of other members of the UN police.

76 See above, section entitled '*UN Police Personnel in General*'. ILC, 1967 ILC Immunities Study, p. 284. See also UN, Question of Whether Contractors' Personnel Could be Considered as 'Experts on Mission' – Article VI, Section 22, of the 1946 Convention on the Privileges and Immunities of the United Nations – Status of Consultants; *Applicability of Article VI, Section 22, of the Convention on the Privileges and Immunities of the United Nations*, pp. 185–188; UN, Memorandum dated 17 April 1981 from the Assistant Administrator, Bureau for Finance and Administration, to the Field Offices of UNDP and UNDP Headquarters Staff, available in *Applicability of Article VI, Section 22, of the Convention on the Privileges and Immunities of the United Nations*, p. 127.

77 They are selected by their sending States and are appointed by the SG for a specific task. However, as noted earlier, those Experts on Mission who are assigned to UN Peace

Within the category of Officials, there is a sub-category containing a limited number of high-ranking Officials, whose duties and responsibilities are so vital that they require a different type of immunity.[78] The General Convention provides that this category is limited to the SG and Assistant Secretaries-General (ASGs),[79] but since it was drafted, there have been new developments in the Organization. For example, during the reorganisation of the UN structure, a new category of Under Secretaries-General (USGs) were created. They are deemed to be in the same immunity category as the SG, because:

> [...] the magnitude and importance of their functions and operations are such that the privileges and immunity envisaged in Section 19 of the General Convention are as necessary for their independent exercise of their functions as they were to the Assistant Secretaries-General.[80]

Whether the Police Commissioner's functions can be considered to have the same magnitude and importance so as to require protection under Section 19 of the General Convention is questionable. Just like the USG, at the time the Convention was drafted, Police Commissioners did not exist in any mission, so it is the reasoning that matters in such a consideration. Guidance provided by the UN states that the protection offered by Section 19 of the General Convention is based on the principle that 'the officials ranking immediately below the executive' should enjoy the same level of protection as the SG.[81] While the Police Commissioner certainly leads one of the core functional groups of the Peace Operation,[82] he reports to the SRSG, which means that the internal ranking of the Police Commissioner is at least twice removed from the SG. In some missions, the Police Commissioner reports to the Deputy SRSG.[83] In

---

Operations (i.e. UN police and Military Observers), are not typical of the Experts on Mission that the UN had in mind when drafting the General Convention. Ibid.

78 UN, 'Report of the Preparatory Commission of the United Nations' (23 December 1945) UN Doc. PC/20, p. 62; Yu-Long Ling, 'A Comparative Study of the Privileges and Immunities of United Nations Member Representatives and Officials with the Traditional Privileges and Immunities of Diplomatic Agents' (1976) 33 *Washington & Lee Law Review* 91, p. 131.

79 General Convention, Article V, Section 19.

80 Ling, 'Comparative Study', pp. 132–133.

81 ILC, 1967 ILC Immunities Study, para. 332: Section 19 applies to all USGs instead of ASGs. '[...] the principle that the officials ranking immediately below the executive [...]', para. 3 of the memorandum.

82 See Chapter 2, Sections 1 and 2.

83 UNGA, 'Report of the Secretary General on the United Nations Police' (15 December 2011) UN Doc. A/66/615, para. 21.

smaller missions, some heads of police are appointed at a lower professional rank. Those lower-ranking heads are called Senior Police Advisors,[84] and they may not enjoy the same immunity as the Police Commissioner. A question remains as to whether all heads of UN police components can be considered to be equally high-ranking Officials by virtue of the nature of their appointments.

The model SOFA places the 'head of the United Nations civilian police', normally the Police Commissioner, in this category of high-ranking Officials.[85] Mission-specific SOFAs have followed this method of categorization since at least the 1990s.[86]

If it can be established that, under customary law, the UN Police Commissioner is a high-ranking Official within the meaning of Section 19 of the General Convention, he would be assumed to have the same immunities which are accorded to that category of personnel independently of the SOFA. The UN has taken the position that the model SOFA reflects its practice.[87] This would mean that the Police Commissioner is categorized as a high-ranking Official by virtue of the nature of his appointment. It is difficult to find any authority for this interpretation of the UN Police Commissioner's immunity coverage, as the issue has never been pursued in the courts.[88] Where a SOFA is non-existent or, more precisely, is considered to be non-existent, it is possible that the Police Commissioner's status is less than that of a high-ranking Official, and is possibly that of an ordinary Official or an Expert on Mission.[89]

The immunity categories to which ordinary UN police personnel and the Police Commissioner belong determine the scope of their immunity.

1-4 *Scope of Immunities for UN Police Personnel*

There are two issues which need to be distinguished. The first relates to the acts which are covered and, depending on this, immunity can be absolute

84 Ibid, para. 20.

85 He 'shall have the status specified in Section 19 and 27 of the Convention'. UNGA, Model SOFA, Section 24. Section 24 puts the Special Representative, the Commander of the military component, and 'such high-ranking members of the Special Representative/Commander's staff' in the same category, and thus there is a theoretical possibility that other senior UNPOL officers can be added to the same category.

86 UN, Letter to the Acting Chair of the Special Committee on Peacekeeping Operations, United Nations, Regarding Immunities of Civilian Police and Military Personnel.

87 UNGA, Model SOFA, attached letter of the SG, para. 1.

88 The debate as to whether there is a customary international law on privileges and immunity of international organizations and, if so, the precise content of such law, has remained controversial. Different national courts have dealt with this issue differently. Reinisch, 'Privileges and immunities', p. 135.

89 For the implications of this difference, see Section 1-4.

or functional. Absolute immunity applies in respect of all acts, regardless of whether or not the act was carried out in an official capacity or in the performance of an official mission.[90] Functional immunity, on the other hand, only applies to official acts.[91] Private acts having nothing to do with official functions, such as committing rape in private accomodation after working hours, would be covered by absolute immunity, but not by functional immunity.

The second distinction relates to what the relevant immunity shields the person from. The main immunity provided to Peace Operations personnel concerns their arrest and detention[92] and, separately, any legal proceedings against them.[93] For UN police personnel, immunity from legal proceedings can arise where they are considered to be either a suspect or a witness to a crime. Where a UN police officer commits a crime, and another UN police officer is a witness to that crime, two separate immunity claims can arise in relation to any resultant legal proceedings.

1-4-1 UN Police Personnel in General

Conduct Covered

As some types of immunity only cover certain acts, it is necessary to consider what types of conduct are covered by immunity. Article VI of the General Convention provides two different types of immunity to Experts on Mission, as far as criminal proceedings are concerned: immunity from personal arrest or detention,[94] and immunity from criminal proceedings, if these arise in respect of their official statements and functions.[95]

Section 22 of the General Convention states that:

---

90 General Convention, Article IV, Section 11 a; Article V, Section 19; Article VI, Section 22 a.

91 Ibid, Article IV, Section 11 a; Article V, Section 18 a and Article VI, Section 22 b. UNGA, Model SOFA, Article 46.

92 General Convention, Article VI, Section 22 a; Article V, Section 19 together with Vienna Convention on Diplomatic Relations (adopted 18 April 1961, entered into force on 24 April 1964) 500 UNTS 95, Article 29, (hereinafter 'Vienna Convention'). See Section 1-4.

93 General Convention, Article V, Sections 18 a and Section 10 together with Vienna Convention Article 31–1, General Convention, Article VI, Section 22 b. There are other immunities, such as immunity from search, and the inviolability of documents, but these have little relevance for this work. For example, see ibid, Article VI, Section 22 c, f.

94 General Convention, Section 22 a.

95 Ibid, Section 22 b. See also Section 46, which assures immunity from 'legal process in respect of words spoken or written and all acts performed by them in their official capacity' for all members of a UN Peace Operation. This issue could be relevant in respect of potential immunity for UN personnel who give statements to courts as witnesses.

> Experts [...] performing missions for the United Nations shall be accorded such privileges and immunities as are necessary for the independent exercise of their functions [...] In particular, they shall be accorded:
> a. immunity from personal arrest or detention and from seizure of their personal baggage;
> b. in respect of words spoken or written and acts done by them in the course of the performance of their mission, immunity from legal process of every kind.

The first form of immunity is not accorded to Officials,[96] and reflects the circumstances in which Experts on Mission are likely to operate, which requires an additional safeguard.[97] In relation to the second form of immunity, UN police officers are immune from proceedings only in respect of acts committed as part of their official functions,[98] and not in respect of acts performed in their private capacities. This means that there is a possibility that, with regard to some private acts, a UN police officer can be prosecuted, but cannot be arrested or detained during his mission. If criminal proceedings are to be brought against a person, arrest is a necessary step. If he can be prosecuted, but cannot be arrested or detained, immunity from arrest may, in practice, also prevent criminal proceedings from taking place.

This immunity from arrest and detention may have been adapted from diplomatic immunity, as diplomatic immunity enshrines personal inviolability.[99] Because part of the *rationale* for immunity is similar, i.e. the need to secure the smooth functioning of personnel in the receiving/host State,[100] the scope of immunity is arguably also comparable. As such, the immunity of UN personnel was initially developed in an analogous fashion to that of diplomatic

96 Within the meaning of the General Convention, Article V. See also UN, 'Immunity from Legal Process of United Nations Officials – Memorandum to the Deputy *Chef de Cabinet*' (1963) 1963 *UN Jurid YB* 188, para. 1, for confirmation that Officials do not enjoy immunity from arrest and detention. See further UN, Memorandum dated 17 April 1981 from the Assistant Administrator, Bureau for Finance and Administration, to the Field Offices of UNDP and UNDP Headquarters Staff, para. 4, where it confirms that Experts on Mission enjoy 'complete immunity from arrest and detention', while Officials do not.

97 Miller, 'EoM Immunity', pp. 40–42; *ILC YB* 1967 ILC, 1967 ILC Immunities Study, para. 343. Both acknowledge that Experts on Mission have immunity from arrest and detention which is separate from their immunity from legal proceedings.

98 See also UNGA, Model SOFA, Section 46.

99 Vienna Convention, Article 29; Vienna Convention on Consular Relations (adopted 24 April 1963, entered into force 19 March 1967), 1 UNTS 596, Article 41.

100 See Section 1-1.

immunity.[101] However, there is an important difference between the two, in that the immunity which protects UN personnel is not attached to the personnel themselves, but rather to the functions they carry out.[102] In addition, diplomatic immunity is only applicable in relation to the receiving State,[103] while the immunity of UN personnel also applies elsewhere, as will be examined later.[104] If a diplomat commits a crime and his immunity is not waived, the receiving State can declare him *persona non grata* and expel him. Moreover, he does not enjoy immunity in his own State. This system works to safeguard against the abuse of immunity.[105] An equivalent system does not exist in respect of immunity granted by the UN. In absence of safeguards, it may be argued that immunity from arrest and detention is problematic. The fact that there is no safeguard may strengthen the argument that UN personnel should only have immunity for official functions, and not from arrest or detention.[106] This chapter will deal later with how the UN applies this immunity in fact.[107]

In relation to immunity from criminal proceedings, the essence of UN immunity is functional, in that it only covers official acts. However, diplomatic immunity is different, as it also covers criminal proceedings in the receiving State, regardless of the character of the conduct in question.[108] The limitation

101 This may have caused uncertainty in relation to the geographical scope of immunity afforded to UN personnel. Kihara-Hunt, 'Inappropriate Immunity', pp. 213–214; Martin Hill, *Immunities and Privileges of International Officials: The Experience of the League of Nations* (The Lawbook Exchange 2003), pp. 11–13; Miller, 'EoM Immunity', p. 18; Ling, 'Comparative Study', pp. 131–133; McCLanahan, *Diplomatic Immunity*, p. 76.

102 See Section 1-1. Also see General Convention, Article V, Section 20; Article VI, Section 23. For high-ranking Officials, see Section 1-4-2.

103 There is also a limited immunity for diplomats in transit States. Vienna Convention, Article 40.

104 See later section called *Geographic scope* and Section 1-4-2, *Geographic scope of absolute immunity*.

105 Stipulating that someone has been termed *persona non grata* has been used in cases where the receiving State's request for a waiver of immunity is not accepted by the sending State. McCLanahan, *Diplomatic Immunity*, pp. 127–128, 139. Whether or not the designation of *persona non grata* works to safeguard against the abuse of immunity depends on the likelihood that the sending State will bring criminal proceedings.

106 On the geographic scope of immunity, see Section 1-4.

107 See Section 2.

108 Vienna Convention, Article 31-1. In relation to consular officers and employees, their immunity only shields them from prosecution in relation to 'acts performed in the exercise of consular functions'. Vienna Convention on Consular Relations, Article 43-1.

of immunity to 'official acts' is also reflected in the SOFA.[109] The key, then, is identifying what comes within 'official acts'. Substantively, there are no detailed guidelines as to what constitutes an 'official' act, and determining what constitutes an official act is based on the facts of a particular case.[110] The closest the UN has come to clarifying the scope of an 'official' act was its opinion regarding the difference between 'on-duty' and 'off-duty' acts. It stated that:

> The primary factor of determining an 'off-duty' situation [... is] whether the member of a peacekeeping mission was acting in a non-official/non-operational capacity when the incident occurred, and not whether he/she was in military or civilian attire at the time of the incident or whether the incident occurred inside or outside the area of operations.[111]

In addition, both the Security Council resolution establishing the mission and the SG's report, which provides a detailed mission design, may be taken into account in determining what is 'official',[112] as they define the roles and functions of UN police personnel.[113] The determining factor is whether the UN police member concerned was acting in an official capacity, or not. This is ambiguous at best, and leaves a large space for different interpretations. This guidance

109 UNGA, Model SOFA, Article 46. '[A]ll members of PO to be immune from legal proceedings in relation to words spoken or written and all acts performed by them in their official capacity'.

110 *Cumaraswamy* (*Advisory Opinion*), para. 52.

111 UN, 'Liability of the United Nations for Claims Involving Off-Duty Acts by Members of Peace-Keeping Forces – Determination of "Off-Duty" and "On-Duty" Status' (1986) 1986 UN Jurid YB 300, p. 300. See also Oswald and Bates, 'Privileges and Immunities of United Nations Police', p. 181.

112 For example, 'Mandate language has important implications for the application and waiver of functional immunity', Durch et al, *Improving Criminal Accountability*, p. 42. Also see Oswald and Bates, 'Privileges and Immunities of United Nations Police', p. 181.

113 For details of the roles and functions of UN police, see Chapter 2, Section 1. Information may also be sought on whether the orders given to the UN police were lawful and authorized in accordance with UN internal law. Oswald and Bates go further and state that '[i]f the UNPOL member's act is not expressly or impliedly mandated then the relevant host State authorities should be informed that no immunity exists'. Oswald and Bates, 'Privileges and Immunities of United Nations Police', pp. 181–182. The article cites the Zeid Report, but that is not what that Report states. It merely states that if the SG determines that a particular act or omission was not within the official duty of the person concerned, the SG will inform the host State of this. UNGA, 'A Comprehensive Strategy to Eliminate Future Sexual Exploitation and Abuse in United Nations Peacekeeping Operations' (24 March 2005) UN Doc. A/59/710, para. 86.

makes it easier to assert that an allegation of rape after working hours in a private residence falls outside the 'official functions' demarcation, but it may be more difficult to determine whether an allegation of rape, which is claimed to have occurred during an investigation at a detention centre by a UN police officer, falls within the category of official functions. Difficulties such as this have arisen more frequently in recent and complex Peace Operations, as UN police officers become more involved in actual policing tasks.[114]

However, one important element can be gleaned from this guidance: the determination of whether the conduct concerned is official is made at the time of the incident. The mere fact that a UN police officer is present in the area of operations does not mean that he is on duty by virtue of being there. Rather, the official character of his conduct is determined by whether he is actually on duty at the time he committed the offence. This appears to reject the argument that UN police officers are on duty '24/7' while they are on a mission.[115] However, whenever UN police officers are required to be on stand-by by virtue of their roles in the mission, this determination may be more ambiguous.

Two cases warrant discussion in this context. The first was a civil case, in which redress was sought in relation to allegations of sexual harassment and battery by Officials. The sexual misbehaviour was alleged to have been committed in a UN office while the alleged offenders were performing their official functions. The US courts upheld the defendants' claim that those acts were covered by functional immunity. In particular, the Appeals Court found that whether or not the alleged acts of sexual harassment or battery were of an official nature was irrelevant. It found that what matters is whether the act was performed whilst delivering official functions, regardless of how improper the behaviour may have been.[116] This finding contrasts with the decision in the second case, that of *Ranollo*. Mr. Ranollo was a driver for the SG, and was caught speeding whilst driving the SG back from a meeting. The UN's claim that

114 See Chapter 2, Section 1.

115 UN, *United Nations Civilian Police Handbook* (UN 1995), pp. 28–29. Also note that the OLA has suggested that the link between the act in question and the official duty should not be interpreted narrowly in the host State, as the person concerned is present in the host State in the performance of his duties. ILC, 1967 ILC Immunities Study, pp. 266–267, para. 251, citing a letter by the OLA.

116 See *Cynthia Brzak and Nasr Ishak v The United Nations, Kofi Annan, Wendy Chambering, Ruud Lubbers, et al* 551 F Supp 2d 313 (SDNY 2008); Docket No. 08-2799-cv *Cynthia Brzak and Nasr Ishak v The United Nations, Kofi Annan, Wendy Chambering, Ruud Lubbers, et al* 597 F 3d 107 (2010); *Cynthia Brzak and Nasr Ishak v The United Nations, Kofi Annan, Wendy Chambering, Ruud Lubbers, et al* (Certiorari – Summary Dispositions) Order list 562 US 09–1481.

Mr. Ranollo was performing his official functions was rejected by the court.[117] These two cases show that the determination of what comes within the term 'official act' is not well established.

SOFAs merely confirm the UN police personnel's immunity category in respect of the host State,[118] and do not provide any further guidance on the scope of immunity. Some argue that a criminal act is *per se* excluded from being considered part of the UN police's official functions.[119] There is no text in any legal instrument which clarifies this point. However, it seems strange to suggest that a criminal act is automatically excluded from constituting an official function. If this were the case, the issue of immunity from criminal proceedings would not have arisen in the first place.

There are a number of elements that must be taken into account in determining what constitutes an official act. The Guidelines for UN Police officers deal with all criminal offences, and state that UN Police officers are subject to the jurisdiction of the host State in respect of any criminal offences committed by them in that State.[120] Some mission-specific guidelines contain a similar statement.[121] However, the guidelines are misleading, as official conduct, even if criminal in nature, may be covered by immunity.[122] Even where potential

117 *Westchester County v William Ranollo* New Rochelle City Ct, 8 November 1946, 187 Misc 777; 67 NYS 2d 31 (City Ct of New York, New Rochelle 1946); (1946) 13 ILR 168–171.

118 See Section 1-3, above.

119 For example, De Brabandere claims, '[i]n general, offences falling under the exercise of normal criminal jurisdiction will not be considered "official acts"; immunity will thus not be applicable in these cases'. Eric De Brabandere, 'Immunity as a Guarantee for Institutional Autonomy' in Richard Collins and Nigel D White (eds), *International Organizations and the Idea of Autonomy: Institutional Independence in the International Legal Order* (Routledge 2011), p. 286.

120 UN DPKO, 'Guidelines for United Nations Police Officers on Assignment with Peacekeeping Operations' UN Doc. DPKO/PD/2006/00135, para. 30. UN DPKO, 'Functions and Organization of United Nations Formed Police Units' (9 November 2006) UN Doc. DPKO/PD/2006/00060, para. 4.6 also contained a similar sentence. The revised 2010 policy on FPUs does not contain an equivalent clause. UN DPKO/DFS, 'Formed Police Units in United Nations Peacekeeping Operations' (1 March 2010) UN Doc. Ref.2009.32.

121 For example, see UN DPKO, 'Guidelines for Civilian Police Officers on Assignment with the United Nations Assistance Mission in Afghanistan (UNAMA)' (January 2005) UN Doc. –, para. 32.

122 In the context of the immunity of State officials from foreign criminal jurisdiction, Special Rapporteur Kolodkin of the International Law Commission stated in his report that the immunity as a whole would be meaningless if one were to view immunity *rationae materiae* as not extending to illegal acts. UNGA, 'Second Report on Immunity of State Officials from Foreign Criminal Jurisdiction' (10 June 2010) UN Doc. A/CN.4/631, para. 31. See also

criminal liability arises in relation to an *ultra vires* act, for example, the excessive use of force by UN police officers while legitimately controlling a crowd, the act cannot immediately be considered as falling outside their official functions. However, there is nothing stopping the UN from waiving immunity in circumstances such as these.[123]

When the crime under consideration is an international crime, the case for annulling the effect of immunity is stronger.[124] It then becomes a question of which law is more firmly established: the law of immunity, or the law prohibiting international crimes. As yet, no case has been heard regarding the applicability of the immunity of UN personnel in relation to an international crime. For this reason, cases dealing with other types of immunity in relation to international crimes are examined briefly. In *Jones* and *Al-Adsani* cases, the European Court of Human Rights (ECtHR) ruled that immunity shielded both the respondent States and State officials from the applicants' civil claims in relation to alleged acts of torture.[125] In *Italy v Germany*, the ICJ upheld the immunity of the State from civil proceedings in relation to war crimes.[126] Another case that dealt with this issue was the *Arrest Warrant* case.[127] Here, the Court upheld the immunity of an incumbent Minister of Foreign Affairs in respect of a third State's attempt to exercise judicial jurisdiction for alleged war crimes and crimes against humanity.[128] A contrasting case is that of *Pinochet*, in which the UK House of Lords denied immunity to a former Head of State for a series

UNGA, 'Fourth Report on the Immunity of State Officials from Foreign Criminal Jurisdiction' (29 May 2015) UN Doc. A/CN.4/686, para. 31.

123 See Section 1-5-2.

124 In this regard, Rawski argued that, while there has been no comprehensive statement from the SG's office about when waiver is *obligatory*, recent rhetoric in the SG's reports, in the General Assembly and in recent practice in the field suggests that, in cases of 'serious breaches' of international law, refusal to waive immunity would violate Sections 20 and 23 of the General Convention. Frederick Rawski, 'To Waive or Not to Waive: Immunity and Accountability in UN Peacekeeping Operations' (2002) 18 *Connecticut Journal of International Law* 103, p. 114, (hereinafter 'To Waive or Not to Waive').

125 *Jones v UK*; *Al-Adsani v UK* ECHR 2001-XI. See also *Kalogeropoulou and Others v Greece and Germany* (Admissibility) EHCR 2002-X. See further Lorna McGregor, 'Torture and State Immunity: Deflecting Impunity, Distorting Sovereignty' (2007) 18 *European Journal of International Law* 903.

126 *Germany v Italy*. However, this finding was not without controversy. See *Jurisdictional Immunities of the State (Germany v Italy: Greece intervening)* (Diss Op Trindade) [2012] ICJ Rep 179.

127 *Arrest Warrant of 11 April 2000 (DRC v Belgium)* (Judgment) [2002] ICJ Rep 3.

128 Or 'enforcement jurisdiction'. See Chapter 5, Section 1.

of criminal proceedings relating to alleged acts of torture.[129] In addition, domestic courts have begun finding the immunity of State officials inapplicable in relation to specific international crimes.[130] This different approach by different courts appears to have been justified by distinguishing immunity for criminal proceedings from that of immunity from civil claims.[131] However, the ICJ and ECtHR's approach, which is that immunity is procedural in character and does not conflict with the unlawful nature of the conduct,[132] appears to support the claim that immunity is applicable in criminal proceedings in domestic courts. However, this may be handled differently by international tribunals.[133] In any case, it is extremely unlikely that a situation such as this will come before a court in the near future, as this situation requires: (i) that a UN police officer commits a war crime, a crime against humanity, the crime of genocide or another international crime (e.g. torture) during his service with the UN; and (ii) that the SG either finds that the act falls within the official functions of UN police personnel *and* refuses to waive immunity, or, in the case of a Police Commissioner, he refuses to waive immunity.

In summary, UN police personnel are given functional immunity. It is generally accepted that this means that they are immune both from arrest and detention, and from criminal proceedings in relation to acts carried out in the performance of their official functions. In relation to other acts, the law provides that they are immune from arrest and detention while on mission. However, questions remain as to whether this is appropriate. It is important that where UN Police personnel have immunity in one State, that should not mean that they can act with impunity. This will largely depend on whether or not

---

129 *Regina v Bow Street Metropolitan Stipendary Magistrate, ex parte Pinochet* [1999] UKHL 17, [2000] 1 AC 147, (hereinafter 'Pinochet').

130 *Boery v Ghaddafi* Cour de Cassation [2001] 125 ILR 490; *Bouterse v Public Prosecutor* Court of Appeal of Amsterdam (Gerechtshof Amsterdam) 20 November 2000, para. 4.2. See also *Arrest Warrant of 11 April 2000* (*DRC v Belgium*) (Sep Op Higgins, Koojimans and Buergenthal) [2002] ICJ Rep 63, para. 85; *Prosecutor v Furundzija* (Trial Judgement) ICTY-95-17/1-T (10 December 1998), para. 155.

131 *Germany v Italy*, paras. 87, 91; *Jones v Ministry of Interior Al-Mamlaka Al-Arabiya AS Saudiya* (*the Kingdom of Saudi Arabia*) [2006] UKHL 26, paras. 31–32; *Yousuf v Samantar* 699 F 3rd 763 (4th Circuit). See also the opinion of Lord Millet, *Pinochet*, para. 179ff. However, see *Ferrini v Germany* [2004] Italian Court of Cassation, Decision No 5044/2004, 128 ILR 658. The Court distinguished the *Ferrini* case from the *Al-Adsani* case on the basis that the alleged crimes were committed in Italian territory.

132 *Germany v Italy*, paras. 81–91; *Jones v UK*, para. 198; *Kalogeropoulou and Others v Greece and Germany.*

133 *Arrest Warrant* (*Judgement*), paras. 58, 61.

they can be prosecuted in another State. Thus, the next section analyses the geographical scope of immunity.

Geographic Scope

The need for immunity is based on ensuring that States do not prevent the UN from carrying out its functions.[134] The most likely place the UN can be prevented from doing so is in the territory of the host State. For this reason, it is apparent that UN police personnel need immunity for official acts in relation to the host State's courts. A separate question is whether they need immunity from the courts of other States. In other words, immunity is dependent on a consideration of whether the possibility of prosecution in any other State, including the sending State, would pose a barrier to the UN delivering its functions. It is also a question of whether the possibility of arrest and detention of UN police officers may adversely affect the UN's smooth functioning, even in States other than the host State.

The geographical scope of UN police officers' immunity must be analysed separately: first, the immunity accorded through the General Convention must be examined and, second, immunity bestowed via SOFAs must be scrutinized. In considering the scope of the former, the status of the General Convention is significant. The General Convention applies to all State parties. There appear to be two different views in respect of a State party's obligation to give effect to immunity under the Convention. One is that the effect is limited to the bilateral relationship between the UN and each State party, which means that every State is obliged to give effect to immunity in relation to acts committed in its territory.[135] This view does not necessarily contradict the ICJ's findings in cases dealing with Special Rapporteurs belonging to UN human rights bodies. In these cases, the Court ruled that immunity was also applicable to the States of nationality of the two Rapporteurs, as they were considered partly to be delivering official functions in their States of nationality.[136] If this view is taken, immunity for the conduct of the UN police will not be an issue in their sending States.

---

134 See Section 1-1.

135 When the Sub-Committee on Privileges and Immunity within the Sixth Committee described the Convention as a unique treaty, with the UN on one side and each individual State on the other, this can arguably be interpreted to mean that each State party is only concerned with the UN's functioning within its territory. UNGA Sixth Committee Sub-Committee Report, pp. 2–3.

136 *Mazilu* (*Advisory Opinion*), (hereinafter '*Mazilu* (*Advisory Opinion*)'); *Cumaraswamy* (*Advisory Opinion*).

The second view holds that all States are bound to give effect to immunity in relation to acts regardless of where they were committed. It appears that a number of States consider that immunity applies globally to acts of the UN police. For example, in their submissions to the Sixth Committee of the General Assembly, Portugal, Switzerland, Australia, Bulgaria, Cyprus and Paraguay expressed their understanding that, under the General Convention, immunity also applies in sending States.[137] Occasionally, the UN also appears to have indicated that immunity applies globally. In relation to Military Observers, who belong to the 'Experts on Mission' category for immunity purposes and who serve in Peace Operations, the UN made it clear that they should not face criminal

137 Portugal acknowledged the application of the General Convention to their Officials or Experts on Mission, in respect of Portugal's exercise of criminal jurisdiction over them. UNGA, 'Report of the Secretary-General on the Criminal Accountability of United Nations Officials and Experts on Mission' (28 July 2009) UN Doc. A/64/183, para. 22; UNGA, 'Report of the Secretary-General on the Criminal accountability of United Nations Officials and Experts on Mission' (29 July 2010) UN Doc. A/65/185, para. 34. Switzerland made it clear that immunity applies in such cases. UNGA, 'Report of the Secretary-General on the Criminal Accountability of United Nations Officials and Experts on Mission' (23 September 2011) UN Doc. A/66/174/Add.1, para. 19. See also in UNGA, 'Report of the Secretary-General on the Criminal Accountability of United Nations Officials and Experts on Mission' (11 August 2008) UN Doc. A/63/260, para. 33, Australia stated that 'the Crimes (Overseas) Act 1964 would apply, for example, extraterritorially to Australian Federal Police deployed as United Nations police who *were* covered by the immunity provided for' in the General Convention (emphasis added). Bulgaria stated very clearly that it considers that the General Convention would bar prosecution in relation to official acts in the host State and in the State of nationality and that, in such a case, prosecution can only happen after the waiver of immunity. UNGA, Report of the Secretary-General on the Criminal accountability of United Nations Officials and Experts on Mission, paras. 12–13. Cyprus, when talking about the prosecution of its nationals, stated that it should be 'without prejudice to any privileges and immunity such persons may enjoy under international law binding Cyprus'. Ibid, para. 16. Panama said representatives of the UN enjoyed immunity from legal process under its Penal Code, and that they cannot be prosecuted after their return to Panama. Ibid, para. 30. Paraguay recognized immunity in the context of both territorial and extraterritorial jurisdiction. Ibid, para. 32. Note, however, that some States may be of the opinion that the immunity accorded to Officials and Experts on Mission only take effect in relation to the host State. Iraq's position is described in UNGA, Report of the Secretary-General on the Criminal Accountability of United Nations Officials and Experts on Mission, paras. 8–10. Iraq stated that, if the prosecution of crimes committed by an Official or Expert on Mission is not brought in the host State, both States and the General Assembly should make sure that there are mechanisms in place to address such crimes.

proceedings when they return home.[138] A report on criminal accountability written by a panel of legal experts, which was established by the Secretary-General, also took the position that immunity is relevant to States other than the host State.[139] The logic underlying this position is that the UN's global functions must be protected in all States. If the geographical scope of immunity is interpreted in this way, immunity for UN police officers would apply equally in their sending States.[140]

It is submitted that the immunity from criminal proceedings accorded to the UN police should be interpreted as applying in all States which have ratified the General Convention. This is because the fact that the UN has declared immunity applicable to an act committed by a UN police officer in relation to the host State necessarily means that that act came within his official functions. Because the rationale for immunity is to protect the UN so that it can deliver its functions smoothly without any hindrance by States, this protection must be accorded by all States. In a State which is not party to the General Convention, the obligation does not arise, unless the Convention, or some of its provisions, are considered to be customary.[141]

A SOFA only provides immunity in relation to the host State.[142] If one holds the view that the SOFA provides the basis for the status of UN police officers, then the existence and scope of their immunity is dependent on that SOFA.

138 The UN made it clear that Military Observers on Peacekeeping Missions must not be subjected to criminal proceedings upon their return to their State of nationality, as this would be incompatible with the obligations of Member States under the UN Charter. UN, Immunity from Legal Process of United Nations Officials – Memorandum to the Deputy *Chef de Cabinet*, paras. 4–6. In relation to Officials of the UN, the OLA made it clear that they enjoy immunity both in the host State and their States of nationality. ILC, 1967 ILC Immunities Study, para. 335.

139 UNGA, A/60/980 paras. 20–22. Discussions at the Ad Hoc Committee on Criminal Accountability of Officials and Experts on Mission at the General Assembly were also mindful of the fact that they may enjoy immunity in their home States. When the transfer of a criminal prosecution from one jurisdiction to another was discussed, it was asserted that any measures taken should not remove the immunity enjoyed by the Officials or Experts on Mission. A/63/54, Annex II, para. (i). The same caveat can be seen in the following draft Resolutions: A/C.6/64/L.8, op para. 2; A/C.6/66/L.16, (27 October 2011) op. para. 2. See also GA Res. 62/63 of 6 December 2007, which states that the resolution is without prejudice to immunity.

140 See also Miller, pp. 38, 43. He takes the position that if the designation as an Expert on Mission is valid, it would operate in all States party to the General Convention.

141 Or in relation to acts committed in that State only, depending on the view taken on the effect of the General Convention. See the discussion above, as well as Section 1-2, above.

142 As discussed in Section 1-2, above.

This means either that there is no immunity for UN police personnel outside the host State, or that there may be immunity for personnel outside the host State which derives from the UN Charter. However, the Charter's scope is ambiguous, and must be determined on a case-by-case basis. It would be detrimental to the smooth functioning of the UN if its personnel could not rely solely on the protection provided by the Organization.[143]

Neither the General Convention nor SOFAs distinguish between the two different kinds of immunity – immunity from legal proceedings, and immunity from arrest and detention – in terms of their geographical scope. This leads one to draw the provisional conclusion that UN police personnel are granted immunity both from legal proceedings and from arrest and detention in all States party to the Convention.[144]

This global applicability of immunity has significant implications for the consideration of the appropriate application of immunity to UN police personnel and, more generally, to UN personnel. It is this aspect which distinguishes the immunity of UN personnel from the immunity of State officials or diplomats. As regards the latter, immunity before the courts of foreign States does not mean global immunity and therefore impunity. At least theoretically, these officials can be tried in their States of nationality.[145] The UN and its personnel do, however, have global immunity. When the UN invokes immunity or considers the use of waiver, this should be taken into account. What the UN actually does in practice will be discussed later.[146]

Temporal Scope

It is necessary to consider the temporal scope of immunity because this determines whether or not some crimes can be prosecuted after the UN police officer in question has completed his work. Immunity shields UN police officers from legal proceedings in relation to official acts carried out during the time they hold office, but does that protection cease when they leave office? In light of the *rationale* for immunity, two arguments arise: one is that, although their actual performance cannot be interfered with, UN police personnel can be subjected to proceedings after they have completed their tours of duty. Another

143 *Reparations*, p. 183.

144 Or in all States, if the General Convention is considered customary. See Section 1-2.

145 See Section 1-1. See also *Arrest Warrant* (*Judgement*), paras. 60–61; *Jones v UK*, para. 174; McCLanahan, *Diplomatic Immunity*, pp. 127–128, 139.

146 See Section 2. For a discussion of the implications of the way that immunity of UN personnel has been developed, see Kihara-Hunt, 'Inappropriate Immunity'.

argument is that if they know that they may be subject to legal proceedings, it may cause them to act in a more restrained fashion at the time.

The General Convention provides different temporal scopes for different types of immunity. The immunity from arrest and detention is accorded 'during the period of their missions, including the time spent on journeys in connection with their missions'.[147] The immunity from legal proceedings in relation to official acts is accorded not only during the mission, but it 'shall continue to be accorded notwithstanding that the persons concerned are no longer employed on missions for the United Nations'.[148] The SOFA merely repeats that immunity for the official acts of all Peace Operations personnel continues after the mission has ended.[149] Since UN police personnel are deployed from their sending States to the host State for their missions, this has implications for the geographical scope of immunity, in that immunity from arrest and detention would not apply once they are back in their sending States after the missions, but would apply to acts performed as part of official functions, even after the missions have ended.

1-4-2 UN Police Commissioner

A UN Police Commissioner enjoys a different type of immunity. Because there is only one Police Commissioner in each mission, it is arguable that it is not critical to clarify the scope of his immunity. However, it is important to do so because he is granted a particularly wide scope of immunity, as will be demonstrated, and it is possible that this type of immunity is more open to abuse.

As shown above, some uncertainties remain as to how the provisions of the General Convention apply to the Police Commissioner if there is no applicable SOFA.[150] However, if the provisions of the General Convention apply either by virtue of the importance of his position, or via a SOFA, the determining provision states that:

> In addition to the immunities and privileges specified in Section 18, the Secretary-General and all Assistant Secretaries-General shall be accorded [...] the privileges and immunities [...] accorded to diplomatic envoys, in accordance with international law.[151]

147 General Convention, Article VI, Section 22 a.

148 Ibid, Article VI, Section 22 b.

149 UNGA, Model SOFA, Section 46.

150 See Section 1-2.

151 General Convention, Article V, Section 19.

First, the Police Commissioner is accorded functional immunity under Section 18 of the General Convention. The scope of that immunity is that of 'Officials', which means the same scope of immunity accorded to UN police officers (as analyzed above), without immunity from arrest and detention.[152] On this basis, the Police Commissioner enjoys global immunity in relation to acts he committed in the performance of his official functions, which endures even after he leaves office.[153] However, the Police Commissioner also has the 'privileges and immunities [...] accorded to diplomatic envoys'.[154]

Conduct Covered

The scope of immunity accorded to diplomatic envoys is provided for in the Vienna Convention on Diplomatic Relations, and states that, 'A diplomatic agent shall enjoy immunity from the criminal jurisdiction of the receiving State'.[155] This article has codified theory and practice of States over more than two centuries.[156] There is no exception to this rule. It is therefore an absolute immunity attached to a person, which covers all their conduct. In addition, this diplomatic immunity also shields the Police Commissioner from giving evidence in court, as well as from any execution measures in relation to any potential criminal acts.[157] A diplomatic agent is inviolable, and thus shall also not be liable to any form of arrest or detention.[158] However, it is important to note that the immunity of diplomats is limited to the receiving State.[159] A diplomat can be declared *persona non grata*, which works as a safeguard against the abuse of diplomatic immunity.[160] This is not the case for high-ranking UN

152 See Section 1-4-1.

153 See Section 1-4-1. In relation to the Police Commissioner, under SOFAs, functional immunity is provided for in two places. One is by reference to the General Convention, and the other is in relation to all mission personnel. Article 46 of the model SOFA confirms that immunity, which is attached to words (either spoken or written) as well as acts performed in their official functions by members of UN peace operations, shall continue to apply even after their employment by the UN ceases. The Police Commissioner's inviolability ceases once his functions have concluded. One then needs to take Article 40 into account, and acknowledge his immunity in the transit State, both on his way to taking up his assignment, and on his return to his home State. UNGA, Model SOFA, Article 46.

154 General Convention, Article V, Section 19.

155 Vienna Convention, Article 31-1.

156 McCLanahan, *Diplomatic Immunity*, p. 128.

157 Vienna Convention, Articles 31-2 and 31-3.

158 Ibid, Article 29.

159 There is also limited immunity for diplomats in transit States. Ibid, Article 40.

160 See Section 1-4-1.

Officials. This may have implications for the consideration of what is an appropriate application of immunity to the Police Commissioner.

SOFAs do not provide any additional guidance on the scope of immunity granted to the Police Commissioner.[161] By virtue of this, the Police Commissioner's immunity shields him from arrest, detention, and all other forms of legal proceedings in relation to his entire conduct.

Geographical Scope of Absolute Immunity

The geographical scope of the absolute immunity provided to the Police Commissioner must be examined in order to clarify which States may be able to prosecute him.

The Vienna Convention clearly states that immunity applies in relation to the receiving State.[162] In particular, it makes it clear that diplomatic agents are not exempt from the jurisdiction of the State of nationality.[163] In the context of Peace Operations, this means that immunity applies only in the host State. However, '[I]nviolability and such other immunity as may be required to ensure his transit or return' is additionally granted to him.[164]

Accordingly, it may be possible to argue that the absolute immunity enjoyed by the Police Commissioner via the General Convention applies in respect of the host State and the transit State, and that the scope of immunity in the latter may be narrower than that in the host State. As the courts have not yet heard a case dealing with the issue of the scope of absolute immunity of a Police Commissioner, or a diplomatic agent in a transit State, its exact scope is unclear.

However, considering that there is a fundamental difference between the functions of the UN Police Commissioner and those of diplomats, it is necessary to take a step back to examine what the appropriate geographical scope would be. Diplomatic immunity applies as between two States. The *rationale* for UN immunity is the need to protect the global functioning of the UN, particularly from interference by *any* State.[165] Therefore, the UN Police Commissioner is a high-ranking Official of an international organization that discharges its functions globally, whilst diplomats represent their State in its relationship with the receiving State. Diplomats enjoy immunity in the places they travel to, and in the places where they exercise diplomatic functions. The equivalent of this for senior members of the UN – those who qualify for absolute immunity – is

161 On the category of the Police Commissioner in terms of his immunity, see Section 1-3.

162 Vienna Convention, Article 31-1.

163 Ibid, Article 31-4.

164 Ibid, Article 40.

165 See Section 1-1.

immunity in any UN member State. It follows that, in order for the Police Commissioner to receive protection which is equivalent to that held by diplomats, he also needs global immunity.

As discussed, there are two ways of including the Police Commissioner in the category of high-ranking Officials for the purposes of the application of absolute immunity.[166] If absolute immunity is provided to the Police Commissioner by virtue of the General Convention, this means that immunity should apply in all States which have ratified the General Convention. If the General Convention is considered customary, immunity should apply in all States.

If, on the other hand, one considers that the status of the Police Commissioner as a high-ranking Official is dependent on SOFA, the geographical scope of immunity is limited to the host State. As indicated above, this is problematic. Given the nature of the protection required for the UN to carry out its functions,[167] the Police Commissioner is likely to require absolute immunity in all UN member States. Alternatively, if one takes a more restrictive view, it is possible to argue that his absolute immunity is limited to the host State, and that a narrower scope of immunity should be granted in the transit State.[168]

Temporal Scope

The Police Commissioner's absolute immunity may cease either at the time he leaves office, or it may continue afterwards. The temporal scope of his immunity depends on what is necessary to guarantee the smooth functioning of the UN, and has implications for the way in which the Police Commissioner may deliver his functions. If there is a possibility that the Police Commissioner may later be subjected to legal proceedings in relation to his *private* conduct during his mission, this may lead him to deliver his *official* functions in a more restricted way. Preventing this may require that absolute immunity should continue even after his mission. If this is not the case, his absolute immunity will cease at the end of his mission.

As the General Convention links the scope of immunity for the Police Commissioner to the immunity accorded to diplomats, it is necessary to consider the Vienna Convention, which sets out a clear temporal boundary. Absolute immunity applies 'from the moment he enters the territory of the receiving State on proceeding to take up his post', or 'from the moment when his appointment is notified' to the relevant ministry of the receiving State.[169] It shall cease when he leaves the country, or after a 'reasonable period' following the

166 See Section 1-3.

167 See Section 1-1.

168 However, note that, even then, he has global functional immunity.

169 Vienna Convention, Article 39-1.

end of his official functions. After that, his immunity subsists only with regard to acts performed in the exercise of his official functions.[170] In other words, he cannot be arrested and detained, or criminally prosecuted, for acts performed as part of his official functions even after he ceases to hold office. However, he can be prosecuted after he leaves office for acts performed in his private capacity during his official term of office.[171] The underlying reasoning must therefore be that the possibility of prosecution after he leaves office in relation to private acts committed during his tenure is not likely to restrict the way in which he performs his official functions whilst in office.

The Police Commissioner is therefore likely to have absolute immunity in respect of all conduct committed during his mission, from the moment of his appointment to the end of his appointment, in relation to all UN member States. His immunity for acts committed in his private capacity ceases when his term in office ends.[172]

1-5 *Determining the Scope of Immunity, and When it May be Waived*

1-5-1 Who Determines What Comes within the Scope of Immunity

As the scope of immunity is dependent on whether or not the act was committed 'in the course of the performance of the mission',[173] or 'performed by them in their official capacity' in the Police Commissioner's case,[174] the procedure to determine what comes within the 'official' category is a key issue. This determination does not affect the immunity from arrest and detention granted to both UN police personnel in general, and the Police Commissioner in particular.[175]

The SG has the authority to deliver this determination:

---

170 Ibid, Article 39-2.

171 However, this issue is unlikely to arise in practice, because the diplomat will normally leave the receiving (host) State at the same time as he leaves office.

172 There was a case in which the immunity attached to the former UN High Commissioner for Refugees, Ruud Lubbers, and others, came into question. The allegation was that the defendants committed sexual assault and battery during a meeting in Geneva, and subsequently took actions that adversely affected the claimants' career. By the time the case was brought before a court, the former High Commissioner had left office. The UN's plea that their immunity should shield them from legal proceedings against them was upheld by US courts. As noted, the court considered the acts concerned as being acts performed in the performance of their functions, and that those acts attracted functional immunity. This confirms that the functional immunity attached to high-ranking Officials is global, and continues after they cease to hold office. *Brzak and Ishak v UN et al (F. Supp. 2d)*, *Brzak and Ishak v UN et al (F. 3d 107) Brzak and Ishak v UN et al (Order list 562 US 09–1481)*.

173 General Convention, Article VI, Section 22 b.

174 Ibid, Article V, Section 18 a.

175 See Sections 1-4-1 and 1-4-2 above.

> The Secretary-General, as the chief administrative officer of the Organization, has the primary responsibility to safeguard the interests of the Organization; to that end, it is up to him to address whether its agents acted within the scope of their functions and, where he so concludes, to protect these agents, including experts on mission, by asserting their immunity.[176]

The UN claims that the SG has the exclusive power to make this determination, and has taken the position that this power is conferred on the SG by the General Convention.[177] The Regulations governing Experts on Mission provide that, 'the Secretary-General should inform and may take into account the views of the legislative bodies that appointed the officials or experts on mission',[178] but they do not actually require the SG to follow these views. The only body which may review the SG's decisions is the ICJ, which provides a dispute settlement mechanism in this respect.[179] Where differences arise in the interpretation or

---

176 *Cumaraswamy* (*Advisory Opinion*), p. 87. Although the immunity at issue in the case related to civil proceedings against an Expert on Mission, the rationale and process for determining whether an act was 'official' are the same for criminal immunity.

177 UN, 'Exclusive Authority of the Secretary-General as Regards Permission to Execute the Waivers of Privileges and Immunities Required by a Member State from Staff Members Maintaining or Seeking Permanent Resident Status in that State – Policy of the United Nations in that Respect' (1969) 1969 *UN Jurid YB* 224, p. 225. See also the statement of the Legal Counsel to the Fifth Committee in 1981 which noted that the SG had a right under the international instruments conferring privileges and immunity 'to independently determine whether or not an official act had been involved'. UN, 'Privileges and Immunities of Officials of the United Nations and the Specialized Agencies – Concept of Functional Immunity – Right of the Secretary-General under the International Instruments in Force to Independently Determine, in Case a Staff Member is Being Subjected to Legal Process, Whether an Official Act is Involved – Meaning of the Term "Officer" in the Conventions on the Privileges and Immunities of the United Nations and of the Specialized Agencies' (1981) 1981 *UN Jurid YB* 161, p. 161. See also UN, 'Question of Who Can Determine Whether the Acts of United Nations Officials are Performed in their Official Capacity – Section 20 of the Convention on the Privileges and Immunities of the United Nations (24 January 1995)' (1995) 1995 *UN Jurid YB* 403, p. 404. See also Miller, 'EoM Immunity', p. 45.

178 UN, 'Secretary-General's Bulletin, Regulations Governing the Status, Basic Rights and Duties of Officials other than Secretariat Officials, and Experts on Mission' (18 June 2002) UN Doc. ST/SGB/2002/9 Regulation 1 (e).

179 General Convention, Article VIII. See also *Difference Relating to Immunity from Legal Process of a Special Rapporteur of the Commission on Human Rights* (Written Statement submitted on behalf of the Secretary-General of the United Nations) (ICJ 2 October 1999), <http://wwwicj-cijorg/docket/files/100/8658pdf>, accessed 30 November 2011.

application of the General Convention, the matter shall be referred to the ICJ, whose opinion shall be accepted as decisive by the parties.[180]

If the chief administrator of the UN has the sole authority to determine what comes within the scope of the supposedly 'functional' immunity, this raises the question as to whether, in practice, there are some situations in which the SG, or someone to whom he has delegated this power, claims immunity where it is clear that immunity should not be applied to him.[181] If there is no mechanism to challenge this decision, the determination is not rebuttable. If there are circumstances in which immunity is inappropriately invoked, machinery for safeguarding it from abuse becomes important.

The question, then, is whether the SG's authority is exclusive in deciding whether immunity applies.[182] The UN itself considers his authority to be exclusive. The OLA confirmed that, 'the competence to determine what constitutes an "official" or "unofficial" act performed by a staff member is vested solely in the Secretary-General'. The OLA further stated that the UN had neither recognised nor accepted that national courts, or any other authorities of member States, have jurisdiction for making this determination.[183] UN Staff Regulations confirm this position:

---

180 General Convention, Article VIII, Section 30.

181 On the practice in this regard, see Section 2-1.

182 It is not certain whether the SG is solely vested with the authority to determine whether the immunity initially applies. Oswald and Bates, 'Privileges and Immunities of United Nations Police', p. 180. Rawski argued that the SG's delegate, the Security Council or the Court can make such a determination. Rawski, 'To Waive or Not to Waive', pp. 112–113.

183 UN, Question of Who Can Determine Whether the Acts of United Nations Officials are Performed in their Official Capacity – Section 20 of the Convention on the Privileges and Immunities of the United Nations (24 January 1995), pp. 403–404. The OLA has answered the question of who can determine whether the acts of UN officials are performed in their official capacity. In the case in question, the *rationale* and process are the same as for Experts on Mission. However, there have been a few cases in which national courts have questioned the scope of immunity granted to UN officials. For example, in 1949, in *Coplon*, a court decided that an act of espionage fell outside the defendant's functions. *US v Coplon et al* US Dist Ct SDNY 10 May 1949, 84 F Supp 472 (SDNY 1949). The same court interpreted the functional immunity of a UN official as meaning that the act in question fell outside the defendant's official functions. *US v Melekh* US Dist Ct SDNY, 28 November 1960, 190 F Supp 67 (SDNY 1960). In 1979, the District Court of Haifa in Israel tried a Senegalese UN military member for trafficking arms, stating that he could not claim immunity because 'the defendant was not in the framework of his job during the time he allegedly perpetrated the transfer of explosives for the PKO'. UN, 'District Court of Haifa, The Government of Israel against Papa Coli Ben Dista Saar: Judgement of 10 May 1979: Question of the Jurisdiction of an Israeli Court Regarding a Member of a National Contingent within

> In any case where an issue arises regarding the application of these privileges and immunity, the staff member shall immediately report the matter to the Secretary-General, *who alone* may decide whether such privileges and immunity exist [...].[184]

The ICJ, however, does not consider that the SG has *exclusive* power in this regard. Rather, the court issued a caveat:

> When national courts are seized with a case in which the immunity of a United Nations agent is at issue, they should immediately be notified of any finding by the Secretary-General concerning this immunity. That finding, and its documentary expression, creates a presumption *which*

UNIFIL, Accused of Smuggling Explosives into Israeli Territory – Claim of Immunity from Territorial Jurisdiction – Question Whether the Accused Could be Considered as a Member of a Foreign Military Force Present in Israel with the Consent and Permission of the State – Extent of the Immunity of Jurisdiction of Members of Such Forces in the Absence of a Specific Agreement on the Matter between the Host State and the Country of the Military Forces Origin – Question Whether the Accused Could be Considered as Enjoying Immunity from Jurisdiction as a Member of a United Nations Force' (1979) 1979 UN Jurid YB 205, p. 207, in the case of 'The Government of Israel against Papa Coli Ben Dista Saar', District Court of Haifa, Judgment of 10 May 1979. For further cases, see Miller, 'UN Officials Immunity', pp. 197–198. See also Miller, 'EoM Immunity', p. 43; UN, Exclusive Authority of the Secretary-General as Regards Permission to Execute the Waivers of Privileges and Immunities Required by a Member State from Staff Members Maintaining or Seeking Permanent Resident Status in that State – Policy of the United Nations in that Respect, p. 225; UN, Privileges and Immunities of Officials of the United Nations and the Specialized Agencies – Concept of Functional Immunity – Right of the Secretary-General under the International Instruments in Force to Independently Determine, in Case a Staff Member is Being Subjected to Legal Process, Whether an Official Act is Involved – Meaning of the Term 'Officer' in the Conventions on the Privileges and Immunities of the United Nations and of the Specialized Agencies, p. 161; UN, Question of Who Can Determine Whether the Acts of United Nations Officials are Performed in their Official Capacity – Section 20 of the Convention on the Privileges and Immunities of the United Nations (24 January 1995) p. 404. This appears to be consistent with the *Reparations* judgment, p. 183.

184 (Emphasis added.) UN, 'Secretary-General's Bulletin, Staff Rules, Staff Regulations of the United Nations and Staff Rules 100.1 to 112.8' (1 January 2002) UN Doc. ST/SGB/2002/1; as amended by the following: UN, 'Amendments to the 100 Series of the Staff Rules (ST/SGB/2002/1)' (1 January 2003) UN Doc. ST/SGB/2003/1; UN, 'Amendments to the 100 Series of the Staff Rules (ST/SGB/2002/1)' (1 January 2004) UN Doc. ST/SGB/2004/1; UN, 'Amendments to the 100 Series of the Staff Rules (ST/SGB/2002/1)' (1 January 2005) UN Doc. ST/SGB/2005/1 and UN, 'Amendments to the 100 Series of the Staff Rules (ST/SGB/2002/1)' (1 January 2006) UN Doc. ST/SGB/2006/1, Section i i (f).

> *can only be set aside for the most compelling reasons* and is thus given the greatest weight by national courts.[185]

There is no explanation as to what such 'compelling reasons' are, and opinion regarding the interpretation of this paragraph is divided. In the same case, Judge Koroma found that the SG's findings on the applicability of the General Convention should be 'given due weight and respect',[186] but that the Convention 'does not stipulate that it is conclusive, let alone binding'.[187] He cited the various views of different States participating in the proceedings, none of which confirmed that the SG's views are exclusive and final.[188]

In the context of Peace Operations, the SG's power to define whether the act in question is related to that person's official functions has been delegated to the SRSG.[189] SOFAs contain a provision to the effect that either the SRSG or the Commander of a military contingent shall agree with the host government as

185 (Emphasis added.) *Cumaraswamy* (*Advisory Opinion*), para. 61.

186 The same applies to his decision on the maintenance or waiver of immunity.

187 *Difference Relating to Immunity from Legal Process of a Special Rapporteur of the Commission on Human Rights* (Diss Op Koroma) [1999] ICJ Rpt 111, para. 13.

188 'According to the United States, "the views of the Secretary-General in a given case are highly relevant"; the United Kingdom takes the position that it is "essential that all due weight is given to [the views of the Secretary-General] by the national courts". Italy had expressed the following viewpoint on the issue: "once [...] a decision has been adopted, both the government and the judicial authorities of the State where the issue of immunity has been raised are nonetheless obliged to give immediate and careful consideration to the delicate problems of immunity, and they must take due account of the weight to be accorded to the determination made in this regard by the Secretary-General of the United Nations. *It would be going too far to say that this imposes a legal duty on the courts of the State where the issue of immunity has been raised to stay all proceedings until the issue of immunity has been settled at the international level.* But, at the very least, it is to be expected that those courts would display caution by avoiding hasty decisions which might entail responsibility on the part of that State". (Emphasis added.) Ibid, para. 19. On the other hand, this information needs to be balanced against the fact that the US and Italy are the two of the few countries whose courts have ignored the UN's claim for immunity in relation to UN premises and personnel. See August Reinisch, *International Organizations Before National Courts* (Cambridge University Press 2000). See also Reinisch, "Privileges and immunities", pp. 143–146. See also Bekker, who observes that the "most compelling reasons" approach in the *Cumaraswamy* case is inconsistent with the idea expressed in the *Reparations* case that the UN must be able to protect its staff'. Peter H E Bekker, 'Difference Relating to Immunity from Legal Process of a Special Rapporteur of the Commission on Human Rights' (1999) 93 *American Journal of International Law* 921, p. 921.

189 Oswald, *Documents* pp. 35, 316.

to whether or not criminal proceedings should be instigated.[190] This appears to include the process of determining whether the act in question was carried out in the performance of the functions of the said personnel.[191] Furthermore, the SG's report containing the model SOFA sets out that, where agreement cannot be reached between the SRSG and the host government on this point, a panel of three arbitrators is to be established, whose finding is then final and binding.[192] The position in the Convention, wherein the SG has sole authority to decide what comes within a grant of immunity, and the position in the SOFA, wherein immunity issues must be agreed between the UN and the host State, appear contradictory. The arbitration panel provided for in the SOFA can be considered 'another mode of settlement', which has been agreed to by the parties concerned, and is provided for in the General Convention.[193] There is a tension between the claim that the SG has the exclusive authority to determine the scope of immunity, and the existence of these dispute resolution mechanisms, but in order to safeguard against abuse, such mechanisms are desirable.

1-5-2 Waiver

Where a person *prima facie* qualifies for immunity, there is nevertheless a possibility that immunity can be waived. It does not apply where there is no immunity in the first place. As provided for in the General Convention,[194] the process of waiver is theoretically identical for the Police Commissioner and other UN police officers.[195] The relevant section states that:

> The Secretary-General shall have the right and the duty to waive the immunity of any official in any case where, in his opinion, the immunity would impede the course of justice and can be waived without prejudice to the interests of the United Nations.[196]

190 UNGA, Model SOFA, para. 47 a.

191 However, this does not apply in the case of military contingents.

192 UNGA, Model SOFA, attached letter by the Secretary-General, para. 2. There is no evidence that such a panel has ever been formed. See Oswald and Bates, 'Privileges and Immunities of United Nations Police', p. 184. This is presumably the case except for issues regarding differences 'arising out of the interpretation or application of the present arrangements, which involve a question of principle concerning the [General] Convention', which shall be dealt with according to the Convention's dispute settlement mechanisms. This means referral to the ICJ. UNGA, Model SOFA, para. 54.

193 General Convention, Article VIII, Section 30.

194 Ibid, Article V, Section 20 and Article VI, Section 23 respectively.

195 UN, 'Extent of the Immunity from Local Prosecution Enjoyed by United Nations Officials under Existing International Agreements' (1974) 1974 *UN Jurid YB* 188, p. 188.

196 General Convention, Article V, Section 20. 'Official' reads 'expert' in ibid, Article VI, Section 23.

Immunity does not have to be waived all together. Where both civil and criminal proceedings are sought against a UN police member in relation to one act, immunity could be waived only in relation to the civil claim. For example, this can happen in relation to a traffic offence.[197] Immunity from arrest and detention, and immunity from judicial proceedings, must be waived separately.[198]

Who Waives?

The Convention is clear that it is the SG's opinion that matters. The UN has also consistently stated that the waiver decision falls within the SG's exclusive authority.[199] The agent whose immunity is in question is not permitted to waive his or her own immunity.[200] The only body which can review the SG's waiver decision is the ICJ, which acts as a dispute settlement mechanism.[201] The consideration of the appropriateness of the SG's exclusive authority to decide the scope of immunity also applies in respect of a decision to waive immunity.[202]

While there is no formal delegation of the authority to waive immunity,[203] in the Peace Operations context, the SRSG takes up this role in the name of the SG.[204] The requirement in the model SOFA that the SRSG must reach an agreement with the host Government on 'whether or not criminal proceedings

---

197 UN, 'Status of Military Observers Serving with a United Nations Mission' (1964) 1964 *UN Jurid YB* 261.

198 Miller, 'EoM Immunity', p. 47.

199 The right and duty to waive immunity, and the authority to do so, is 'vested exclusively (except for his own privileges and immunity, which the Security Council may waive) in the Secretary-General'. UN, Exclusive Authority of the Secretary-General as Regards Permission to Execute the Waivers of Privileges and Immunities Required by a Member State from Staff Members Maintaining or Seeking Permanent Resident Status in that State – Policy of the United Nations in that Respect, pp. 224–225. UN, Secretary-General's Bulletin, Staff Rules, Staff Regulations of the United Nations and Staff Rules I00.1 to 112.8, as amended by UN, Amendments to the 100 Series of the Staff Rules (ST/SGB/2002/1); UN, Amendments to the 100 Series of the Staff Rules (ST/SGB/2002/1); UN, Amendments to the 100 Series of the Staff Rules (ST/SGB/2002/1) and UN, Amendments to the 100 Series of the Staff Rules (ST/SGB/2002/1), Section i I (f).

200 Miller, 'UN Officials Immunity', p. 238. See also Oswald, *Documents*, p. 315.

201 General Convention, Article VIII. See also *Applicability of Article VI, Section 22, of the Convention on the Privileges and Immunities of the United Nations.*

202 See above, Section 1-5-1.

203 Miller, 'UN Officials Immunity' pp. 239–240.

204 Oswald states that the waiver decision is made by the SG. 'Pursuant to the model SOFA and UN practice, the SRSG determines whether the acts of the member of the peace operation are related to "official duties". If the SRSG so determines, the Secretary-General can still waive immunity in regards to that act'. Oswald, *Documents*, p. 35. See also Oswald and Bates, 'Privileges and Immunities of United Nations Police', p. 184, where they state that '[r]egardless of the approach taken as a matter of law, the practice of the UN appears

should be instituted',[205] would involve a waiver decision. There thus remain some uncertainties with regard to the claimed exclusivity of the SG's authority to waive immunity. It remains to be seen how these additional mechanisms may work to safeguard the system from the potential abuse of immunity.

Circumstances in Which Immunity Must or May be Waived

The General Convention stipulates that the SG can and must waive immunity, 'where [...] the immunity would impede the course of justice and can be waived without prejudice to the interests of the United Nations'.[206] This formula suggests that the decision to waive or not to waive immunity is not entirely within the discretion of the SG, but rather, where certain circumstances arise, it must be waived. It was the intention of the Preparatory Commission that, not only can the SG waive immunity in the specified circumstances, but that the SG will indeed do so in each case that satisfies this two-fold test.[207]

The first strand of this test concerns where the maintenance of immunity may impede the course of justice. A related obligation on the UN to cooperate with member States in facilitating the proper administration of justice is provided for in the General Convention.[208] There is little further guidance on when this threshold has been met.[209] Rawski suggested that affirming immunity for

---

to be that the Secretary-General is always *consulted* in relation to decisions concerning waivers'. (Emphasis added.).

205 UNGA, Model SOFA, Article 47 a.

206 General Convention, Article V, Section 20; Article VI, Section 23, for 'officials' and 'experts on mission' respectively.

207 UN, Prep Commission Report, para. 7. The UN also took the position that it is the UN's legal obligation 'to cooperate with the appropriate local authorities to facilitate the proper administration of justice'. It was emphasized, therefore, that the immunity of a UN police officer may be waived even if the act concerned was committed in the course of performing his functions, where 'immunity for that act would impede the course of justice and that immunity can properly be waived'. UN, Letter to the Acting Chair of the Special Committee on Peacekeeping Operations, United Nations, Regarding Immunities of Civilian Police and Military Personnel, p. 324.

208 General Convention, Article V, Section 21. While an equivalent to Section 21 does not exist for Experts on Mission, it is obvious that it applies to all those listed in the General Convention. The equivalent was the same during the existence of the League of Nations. Miller, 'EoM Immunity', p. 43. On the test for waivers, see: UN, Status of Military Observers Serving with a United Nations Mission, p. 262; UN, 'Request by the Government of a Member State that United Nations Technical Assistance Experts Sign a Declaration under an Act on State Security' (1973) 1973 *UN Jurid YB* 166, pp. 166–167.

209 The *travaux preparatoires* of the General Convention does not provide guidance on this issue. *Mazilu* (*Advisory Opinion*), para. 46.

crimes that amount to serious breaches of international law would be an example of a circumstance where immunity not only *can* be waived, but *must* be waived.[210] Even in relation to serious crimes that do not amount to international crimes, it is possible that the same argument can be made, in particular because of the UN police's important role in building respect for the rule of law.[211] A further potential consideration is the rights of the victims, and whether maintaining immunity may lead to impunity, or be perceived as leading to impunity.[212]

The second strand is whether immunity can be waived without prejudice to the UN's interests, which are multifaceted. On the one hand, presumably the UN wants to continue operating, so it may not be in its interest for its personnel to be subject to proceedings, fair or otherwise. At the same time, it is in its interests to be seen to be adhering to the rule of law. If UN personnel are alleged to have engaged in criminal behaviour, the UN may be prejudiced if these personnel are seen as having 'got away with it'. There may be circumstances, however, in which cooperating with a national court entails the disclosure of confidential materials. In such circumstances, it is possible that the UN would wish to maintain immunity from proceedings.[213] However, it may be more appropriate to maintain immunity only in relation to those materials.

There may be circumstances where proceedings in the host State would be fundamentally flawed.[214] Examples of these include the host State's failure to comply with human rights standards, in particular those related to a fair trial.[215] Where the local judicial system is not functioning properly,[216] or is overburdened with cases, or has severely under-staffed courts, there may be a

---

210 Rawski, 'To Waive or Not to Waive', p. 114.

211 See Chapter 1, Section 2; Chapter 2, Section 1.

212 UNGA, 2006 Legal Experts Report, para. 22.

213 Wolfgang Munch, 'Wrongdoing of International Civil Servants – Referral of Cases to National Authorities for Criminal Prosecution' (2006) 10 *Max Planck Yearbook of United Nations Law* pp. 84–85.

214 On the conditions in the host State, see Chapter 2, Section 1.

215 Miller, 'UN Officials Immunity', p. 247; Oswald and Bates, 'Privileges and Immunities of United Nations Police', p. 183; United Nations Law Reform Project, 'UN Peacekeeping and The Model Status of Forces Agreement' p. 24, para. 117; Miller, 'EoM Immunity', p. 47. Miller argues that, if the host State's legal system does not satisfy human rights standards, it would not be in the interests of the UN to waive immunity because the UN Charter requires the UN to uphold, promote and respect human rights. See also UNGA, Zeid Report, para. 187; Miller, 'Legal Aspects of Stopping Sexual Exploitation and Abuse in UN Peacekeeping Operations', pp. 89–95.

216 UNGA, 2006 Legal Experts Report, para. 22.

practical issue of whether or not justice would be delivered. These factors can be considered as forming part of the UN's interests, and may justify the UN not waiving immunity.

2 Application of Immunity in Practice

It has become clear that, theoretically, immunity should not be a major barrier to the prosecution of UN police personnel by a willing State, at least for the majority of incidences of criminal conduct.[217] Where the alleged crime was committed outside someone's official functions, there is no immunity. Where *prima facie* immunity is applicable, it should usually be in the interests of the UN to ensure that proceedings take place in relation to serious crimes. Immunity should therefore be waived in relation to many of the offences that the UN police are committing. However, evidence shows that there are barriers to criminal prosecution.[218] It is possible that immunity is applied differently in practice. Thus, it is necessary to ask whether either an inappropriate assertion of immunity, or an inappropriate refusal of waiver of immunity, is blocking the criminal prosecution of UN police personnel by those States who are willing to prosecute them.

Before examining these two questions, it is necessary to consider the unique formula identified in the previous section in relation to immunity from arrest and detention, in order to determine whether or not immunity is invoked in practice.[219] Because immunity from arrest and detention theoretically applies to a broader category of acts than acts performed solely within the exercise of the UN police personnel's functions, granting immunity in these circumstances runs the risk of leading to impunity.[220]

The UN mostly appears to have applied immunity from arrest and detention in respect of UN police personnel only in relation to acts committed within the performance of their functions.[221] The UN's OLA seemed to have taken this position in 2004, when it stated that:

---

217 If the conduct is unrelated to their official functions; or if the conduct in question was carried out in the exercise of their official functions, but was done so in a way manifestly different from the way that was desired, immunity must be waived by the SG. See Section 1.

218 See Chapter 3, Section 3.

219 Section 1-4-1.

220 Section 1-4-1.

221 However, the UN's practice is not very consistent, as is demonstrated later in this section, and in Section 2-2-2.

> As experts performing missions for the United Nations, civilian police officers enjoy "functional immunity", that is, immunity *for purposes of the official acts done by them in the course of the performance of their official functions*. Their privileges and immunity, *which include immunity from personal arrest and detention*, are granted solely to enable them to perform their official functions [...] United Nations civilian police officers may therefore be made subject to local civil and criminal jurisdiction for acts committed by them in the host country that are done by them *otherwise* than in the performance of their official functions.[222]

This statement is carefully worded, but it appears to indicate that the OLA considers that all privileges and immunities held by UN police officers, including immunity from arrest and detention, to be limited to official acts.[223] This reinforces the OLA's earlier position with regard to UN police personnel and, more precisely, with regard to those in UNMIK and UNTAET.[224] Some writers also support this position.[225] The UN has, in some cases, indicated that it will follow this limited interpretation with regard to immunity from arrest and detention. For example, in a case in which two UN police officers were alleged to have committed rape in a hotel room after working hours, their immunity was declared inapplicable, because rape was considered to be outside the scope of their official functions.[226]

The UN is certainly free not to invoke immunity from arrest and detention in respect of UN police officers. It is unfortunate, however, that its practice in this

222 (Emphasis added.) UN, Letter to the Acting Chair of the Special Committee on Peacekeeping Operations, United Nations, Regarding Immunities of Civilian Police and Military Personnel, p. 324.

223 See also UN, 'Legal Status of Certain Categories of United Nations Personnel Serving in Peacekeeping Operations – Civilian Police and Military Observers – Military Members of Military Components (3 May 2002)' (2002) 2002 *UN Jurid YB* 466.

224 Ibid, pp. 467–468, paras. 5, 7.

225 UNGA, Zeid Report, para. 86. Oswald and Bates, 'Privileges and Immunities of United Nations Police', p. 182.

226 However, note that this conclusion was reached after a heated internal debate on the coverage of immunity and the lawfulness of their arrests. See Rawski, 'To Waive or Not to Waive', p. 120. The Secretary-General's report on Peace Operations, published in 2015, missed the opportunity to clarify the scope of immunity afforded to various categories of Peace Operations personnel. UNGA/SC, 'Uniting Our Strength for Peace – Politics, Partnerships and People – Report of the High-Level Independent Panel on United Nations Peace Operations' (16 June 2015) UN Doc. A/70/95-S/2015/446, para. 284.

regard varies greatly,[227] which makes it difficult to determine the UN's position on this issue. At the very least, it would be helpful if it was easily foreseeable what the coverage of immunity is likely to be, in particular if immunity from arrest and detention for UN police officers is considered to apply with regard to acts other than those performed in the exercise of their official functions. This is important because this uncertainty may cause national authorities to avoid seeking prosecution and, as a result, may contribute to impunity.[228] In some cases in which UN police officers were allegedly involved in serious crimes which were completely unrelated to their official functions, immunity was considered to apply *prima facie*. These examples will be discussed later.[229] However, this work will assume that the UN's interpretation of the immunity from arrest and detention granted to UN police personnel is that it applies only with regard to acts performed within the exercise of their functions.

It is unclear what the practice of the application of immunity from arrest and detention is in reality with regard to the Police Commissioner, who is covered by absolute immunity. No case has arisen in any national court which has questioned this immunity, nor has the issue been raised at the UN, at least in the public domain. It could be argued that the Police Commissioner has a stronger case for the global protection of his personal inviolability due to the vital nature of his position for the UN's delivery of its functions.[230]

Another issue that warrants a brief mention is immunity from legal proceedings, as it applies to UN personnel who are required to appear in front of a national court to give testimony. In such circumstances, for example, in the case of international tribunals, the UN provides a waiver of immunity for the personnel concerned to provide witness statements.[231] However, it is not

---

227 Rawski, 'To Waive or Not to Waive', pp. 119–120, 123; Durch et al, *Improving Criminal Accountability*, p. 35.

228 This is claimed to be the case in Bosnia in relation to alleged sexual and trafficking offences involving American UN police personnel. Robert Capps, 'Sex-Slave Whistle-Blowers Vindicated' (*Salon*, 7 August 2002) <http://www.salon.com/2002/08/06/dyncorp/> accessed 16 October 2012.

229 Section 2-2-2.

230 See Sections 1-3, 1-4-2.

231 In *Prosecutor v Blaškić*, the ICTY Trial Chamber issued a subpoena against a former UN official in order to call the official to testify. This was possible only because the UN SG waived immunity in this instance. The subpoena was upheld by the Appeals Chamber. *Prosecutor v Blaškić* (Decision of Trial Chamber I on Protective Measures for General Philippe Morillon, Witness of the Trial Chamber) ICTY-95-14-T (12 May 1999); *Prosecutor v Blaškić* (Judgment on the Request of the Republic of Croatia for Review of the Decision of the Trial Chamber II of 18 July1997) ICTY-95-14-A (29 October 1997). *Prosecutor v Akeyasu*

known to what extent this has been done in practice in relation to crimes committed by the UN police in Peace Operations.

2-1 *Inappropriate Assertions of Immunity*

2-1-1 Does the UN Claim Immunity Where it Should Not?

On the assumption that the UN considers the immunity accorded to the UN police officers, including their immunity from arrest and detention, to apply only in relation to acts performed during the course of their official functions,[232] any claim of immunity for an act which is unrelated to these functions would be inappropriate.

There are examples in which the UN has invoked immunity in relation to acts committed by UN police officers in their private capacities. For example, in a case in which a UN police officer allegedly engaged in the sexual abuse of a trafficked minor in a private house, the suspect's immunity was invoked and maintained.[233] There were apparently ten cases in UNMIK, involving UN police officers, for which immunity was asserted for serious crimes in potentially inappropriate circumstances.[234] In such cases, the issue is not that UN police

---

(Decision on the Motion to Subpoena a Witness) ICTR-96-4-T (19 November 1997). The UN often imposes some conditions before it will waive immunity, such as the proceedings must be held in a closed session; the personnel must be accompanied by a legal advisor; and/or the questions asked of the personnel must fall within a limited scope. Karim A.A. Khan, Caroline Buisman and Christopher Cosnel, *Principles of Evidence in International Criminal Justice* (1st edn, Oxford University Press 2010), p. 571. However, Honourable Justice Robertson doubted whether it was justifiable to impose such conditions in order for UN Officials to testify before an international tribunal. *Prosecutor v Brima et al* (Decision on Prosecution Appeal Against Decision on Oral Application for Witness TF1-150 to Testify Without Being Compelled to Answer Questions on Grounds of Confidentiality) SCSL-2004-16-AR73 (26 May 2006); *Prosecutor v Brima et al* (Sep and Conc Op Robertson, Decision on Prosecution Appeal against Decision on Oral Application for Witness TF1-150 to Testify Without Being Compelled to Answer Questions on Groudns of Confidentiality) SCSL-04-16, AC (26 May 2006); *Prosecutor v Brima et al* (Diss Op Donerty on the Prosecution's Oral Application for Leave to Be Granted to Witness TF1-150 to Testify Without Being Compelled to Answer Any Questions on Grounds of Confidentiality) SCSL-04-16-T, TC II (22 September 2005).

232 See above, Section 2.

233 OSCE Mission in Kosovo, *Kosovo Review of the Criminal Justice System – Themes: Legal Representation, Detention, Trafficking & Sexually Related Crimes, Municipal & Minor Offence Courts* (Department of Human Rights and Rule of Law, October 2001), p. 52.

234 Rawski, 'To Waive or Not to Waive', p. 119.

officers are accorded functional immunity, but, rather, that their immunity is inappropriately invoked.

No case has been brought against a UN Police Commissioner to date. It is therefore not known what the UN would do in these circumstances. The Police Commissioner enjoys absolute immunity during the period of his mission.[235] Therefore, the issue will only arise where immunity is invoked in respect of any acts committed by him in his private capacity after his assignment as Police Commissioner has ended.

2-1-2 Availability of the Means with Which to Challenge an Inappropriate Claim of Immunity

Where immunity is claimed in apparently inappropriate cases, it raises a secondary issue as to whether that claim can be challenged. If not, there is a real risk that it will lead to impunity. Bearing in mind that the consequence of asserting immunity is that immunity should be given effect globally,[236] this would be the case where the coverage of immunity was determined essentially by what falls within the official functions.[237]

There are two dispute resolution mechanisms, as identified above.[238] The first is the use of the ICJ to challenge the SG's decision, as provided for in the General Convention.[239] In practice, the SG's determination of the applicability of immunity in relation to UN police personnel has never been placed before the ICJ. The ICJ has only been requested to provide advice on whether two UN Special Rapporteurs fell within the 'Experts on Mission' category.[240] Taking into consideration the situation of the host State, it may be difficult for this State to challenge the UN's decision at the ICJ.[241] In relation to the sending State, immunity does not appear to pose a major barrier to prosecution. However, States may hesitate to start proceedings if they think that the UN will invoke immunity. Rather, the practical issues identified previously may pose problems for sending States.[242] In recent years, the problems faced by sending

235 Section 1-4-1.

236 Section 1-4.

237 Section 1-4.

238 Section 1-5.

239 General Convention, Article VIII, Section 30.

240 *Mazilu* (*Advisory Opinion*); *Cumaraswamy* (*Advisory Opinion*).

241 On the situation of the host State, see Chapter 2, Section 1. It may, however, be noteworthy that the Democratic Republic of Congo brought a case to the ICJ, that of the *Arrest Warrant* (*Judgement*) case, and that its claim was supported by the ICJ.

242 Chapter 5, Section 3-2.

States have been discussed in the context of the UN's attempt to ensure that they are able to criminally prosecute suspects under their domestic law.[243]

The second mechanism in relation to the host State is a three-person arbitration tribunal.[244] Information suggests that an arbitration tribunal has never been utilized in Peace Operations.[245] Thus, in the host State, even in cases where that State's authorities have demanded prosecution, no resort has been made to this tribunal for formally challenging immunity. The demand for prosecution has sometimes been made through political contacts.[246]

As a result, the SG's power in relation to the determination of immunity for Peace Operations personnel has never been challenged. This poses a serious problem in practice. Because the SG's powers have not been challenged, he is able to use his power in any way he sees fit.

2-2 *Inappropriate Use of Waiver*

2-2-1 The Decision Not to Waive Immunity

When an act committed by a UN police officer is *prima facie* covered by immunity, it should still be waived by the SG if the two-pronged test ('in his opinion, the immunity would impede the course of justice and can be waived without prejudice to the interests of the United Nations')[247] is satisfied.[248] It would, for example, be obligatory for immunity to be waived if there is an allegation of serious ill-treatment by a UN police officer during an interrogation, or of indiscriminate shooting during a peaceful demonstration, with a fatal outcome. The author's data contain illustrations of both examples, in relation to which criminal proceedings were not brought, and where it appears that waiver was not sought by any national authorities.[249] Although some traffic offences

---

243 UNGA, Zeid Report, paras. 88–89;UNGA Res 62/63 (8 January 2008) UN Doc. A/RES/62/63, op. para. 3; UNGA Res 63/119 (15 January 2009) UN Doc. A/RES/63/119, op. para. 3; UNGA Res 64/110 (15 January 2010) UN Doc. A/RES/64/110, op. para. 3; UNGA Res 65/20 (10 January 2011) UN Doc. A/RES/65/20, op. para. 3; UNGA Res 66/93 (13 January 2012) UN Doc. A/RES/66/93, op. para. 3; UNGA Res 67/88 (14 January 2013) UN Doc. A/RES/67/88, op. para. 3; UNGA Sixth Committee, 'Draft Resolution on Criminal Accountability of United Nations Officials and Experts on Mission' (3 November 2014) UN Doc. A/C.6/69/L.11, op. para. 3; and discussions in the GA Sixth Committee. See Chapter 5, Section 4-2.

244 UNGA, Model SOFA, para. 53.

245 Oswald and Bates, 'Privileges and Immunities of United Nations Police', p. 184.

246 For example, see the cases cited in Rawski, 'To Waive or Not to Waive', pp. 119–120.

247 General Convention, Article V, Section 20 and Article VI, Section 23.

248 Section 1-5-2.

249 See Chapter 3, Sections 1 and 3. It is not known whether the UN has ever waived immunity before receiving a request from a national authority.

appear to be criminal in character, it appears that national authorities often do not seek prosecution for these.[250] It remains a theoretical possibility that waiver could be inappropriately refused for official acts that are performed in a markedly unacceptable manner. However, the evidence indicates that this is not a problem in practice.

2-2-2 Inappropriate Use of Waiver

One issue that appears to lie in between these two positions (an inappropriate assertion of immunity which is not waived, and the inappropriate refusal of waiver of appropriate immunity), is the inappropriate use of waiver where immunity does not apply. It appears that the UN frequently assumes that immunity exists, when, in fact, it does not.

In 2002, in Kosovo, a UN police officer was alleged to have murdered his language assistant. His immunity was waived, rather than being found to be inapplicable,[251] although apparently this only took place after a serious discussion among the senior mission leadership regarding the necessity of the waiver.[252] In relation to two separate allegations (one of rape and one of murder) in Kosovo, immunity was waived instead of being considered inapplicable.[253] Since the suspects were eventually prosecuted, this is only a theoretical problem. However, it would be better if the scope of immunity, as well as the procedure for applying it, were to be appropriately implemented. This is important because this practice could give national authorities the impression that the decision whether or not to bring criminal proceedings in relation to conduct not falling within the official functions remains solely in the hands of the SRSG. That may prevent national authorities from prosecuting this criminal conduct. However, it would also be helpful for the sake of clarity if the law were to be appropriately applied.

The UN's practice in relation to the host State is that it assumes immunity exists in relation to all acts. This means that the UN considers whether it should waive immunity without first determining whether immunity applies at all. It also fails to specify what type of immunity, immunity from legal proceedings, or immunity from arrest and detention, it is waiving. In other words, the two separate steps which examine whether or not immunity *prima facie* exists, and

250 See Chapter 3, Sections 2-2-2 and 3.

251 OSCE Mission in Kosovo, *Kosovo Review of the Criminal Justice System, September 2001 – February 2002 – Themes: Independence of the Judiciary, Detention, Mental Health Issues* (Department of Human Rights and Rule of Law, 2002), pp. 41–42.

252 Rawski, 'To Waive or Not to Waive', p. 120.

253 Ibid, pp. 119–120.

whether or not to waive immunity if it does exist, are mixed together. As a result, the term 'waiver' is used, both by the UN itself and national courts, in two ways: to indicate a finding of the non-existence of immunity, and to indicate a decision to waive immunity.[254]

In relation to sending States, unlike the practice with regard to host States, the question of waiver of immunity has not arisen. The issue, then, is whether the UN has clarified whether immunity applies to the act in question and, if it waives immunity in cases where it is found to exist, in what circumstances the UN will refer a case to a sending State for possible prosecution. Information regarding these matters is extremely limited, in particular considering that the active referral of allegations of criminal conduct to sending States by the UN is only a recent phenomenon.[255]

3 Conclusion

3-1 *Theory*

The starting point for determining the scope of immunity accorded to UN police personnel and the Police Commissioner is the unique *rationale* for granting immunity to the UN and its personnel. Unlike sovereign or diplomatic immunity, it exists solely to enable the UN to pursue the aims entrusted to it by its member States, and in order to do that, it must enable its personnel to deliver their functions without undue hindrance by any States. This means immunity for the UN police and the Police Commissioner is limited to what is necessary for them to perform their duties.

3-1-1 UN Police Personnel

There are two main sources of immunity for UN Police personnel: the General Convention and the SOFA. The former grants immunity in the territory of all States which are party to the Convention and, depending on the status of the Convention, it can be considered to apply globally.[256]

254 Miller, 'EoM Immunity', p. 297; UN, Letter to the Acting Chair of the Special Committee on Peacekeeping Operations, United Nations, Regarding Immunities of Civilian Police and Military Personnel, p. 324. In July 2013, a former senior legal officer at the OLA confirmed this in an e-mail communication with the author.

255 Prior to that, it was left to the sending States to voluntarily prosecute their nationals who serve as Experts on Mission upon their return. On the increased move by the UN to encourage sending States to prosecute their nationals who serve as Experts on Mission, see Chapter 4, Section 2.

256 Section 1-2.

UN police personnel enjoy functional immunity. The General Convention shields UN police personnel from arrest and detention in relation to all acts committed during the mission, and from all kinds of legal proceedings, but only in relation to official acts. The former protection ends when their mission ends, whilst the latter protection continues even after the completion of the mission. Theoretically, therefore, immunity does not work as a barrier to prosecuting a UN police officer for crimes such as a rape committed after working hours in private accommodation. However, no State can arrest or detain a suspect during his mission without a waiver of immunity. In other words, UN police personnel can be prosecuted anywhere, but the courts cannot exercise their enforcement jurisdiction. Immunity does not bar a suspect from being prosecuted for acts not related to his official functions after he ceases to serve as a UN police officer.[257]

SOFAs confirm the immunity provided for in the General Convention in relation to the host State. This means that while a UN police officer is on a mission in the host State, he cannot be arrested or detained, but he can be prosecuted for acts he commits outside his official functions.[258]

Where immunity exists, it is still possible for it to be waived. The waiver can and must be granted if the course of justice would otherwise be impeded, and where waiving immunity does not prejudice the interests of the Organization. Therefore, where maintaining immunity would lead to impunity for a serious crime, theoretically, it is expected that immunity would be waived.[259]

The decision as to what comes within the official functions of the UN police officer in question, and whether to waive his immunity, if it is found to exist, is for the SG alone to make.[260] His decision cannot be set aside by national courts, unless 'most compelling reasons' exist to do so.[261] There is an *ad hoc* dispute resolution mechanism – the arbitration panel. Where disagreement arises with regard to the interpretation of the General Convention, the matter can be referred to the ICJ.[262]

3-1-2 UN Police Commissioner

The same sources provide the Police Commissioner with absolute immunity. The Police Commissioner is shielded from both legal proceedings, and from

257 Section 1-4-1.
258 Section 1-4-1.
259 Section 1-5-2.
260 Section 1-5-1.
261 *Cumaraswamy* (*Advisory Opinion*), para. 61.
262 Section 1-5-2.

arrest or detention in relation to all acts committed by him during his assignment in the territory of all States party to the Convention. Depending on the status of the General Convention, the geographical scope of his immunity may be global. After the Police Commissioner leaves office, his immunity only protects him in relation to his official acts. SOFAs confirm the same scope of immunity in respect of host State authorities. The option of a waiver also exists in relation to Police Commissioners, and the decision-maker and the procedure is the same as those for ordinary members of the UN police.

This conclusion shows that the law works as a barrier to criminal prosecution by States to some extent, but mostly only in respect of official acts. There is an additional protection from arrest and detention in relation to all acts carried out by a UN police officer during the mission, but his immunity for unofficial acts ceases at the end of his tour of duty. If this is the legal position, and if this is properly applied in practice, questions are unlikely to arise regarding the lack of prosecution for criminal acts that do not have the required link with the official functions of the person in question.

The scope of immunity can be presented as follows:

TABLE 1 *UN police officers*

	Legal basis	During the mission	After the mission
Host State	SOFA immunity GC immunity	Functional immunity and personal inviolability	Functional immunity
State of Nationality	SOFA immunity	–	–
	GC immunity	Functional immunity (and personal inviolability, but this is unlikely to be useful)	Functional immunity
Transit State	SOFA immunity	–	–
	GC immunity	Functional immunity and absolute personal inviolability	Functional immunity
Other States	SOFA immunity	–	–
	GC immunity	Functional immunity (and personal inviolability, but this is unlikely to be useful)	Functional immunity

TABLE 2 *UN Police Commissioners* (*UN PCs*)

	Legal basis	During the mission	After the mission
Host State	SOFA immunity	Absolute immunity, including personal inviolability	Functional immunity
	GC immunity	Absolute immunity including personal inviolability (if he qualifies as a high-ranking official)	
State of Nationality	SOFA immunity	–	–
	GC immunity	Absolute immunity. including personal inviolability	Functional immunity
Transit State	SOFA immunity	–	–
	GC immunity	Absolute immunity, including personal inviolability	Functional immunity
Other States	SOFA immunity	–	–
	GC immunity	Absolute immunity, including personal inviolability	Functional immunity

3-2 *Practice*

However, in practice, there are situations in which immunity acts as a barrier to criminal prosecution, in particular with regard to host States. The UN applies immunity from legal proceedings for UN police personnel and the Police Commissioner in almost the same way as absolute immunity. That is, it applies it regardless of whether or not the act was performed within the exercise of their functions, while appropriately disregarding the separate immunity from arrest and detention for acts committed outside their official functions. An independent study recognized that one of the barriers to prosecution is:

> [...] the broad-spectrum nature of functional immunity as applied to experts on mission "during the period of their missions", without distinction between behaviour on and off duty.[263]

This practice raises the question as to what causes the UN to apply immunity law in the way that it does. It may be that the explanation lies in the state of the legal system in the host State.[264] The UN may be trying to protect its own

263 Durch et al, *Improving Criminal Accountability*, p. xii.

264 See Chapter 2, Section 1; Chapter 6, Section 1-5-2.

personnel from legal proceedings in places without a functioning legal system, or where the legal system fails to meet human rights standards.[265] It is of legitimate concern that the UN does not and should not hand over its personnel to be subject to such criminal proceedings, in particular in light of the UN's obligation to 'uphold, promote and respect human rights'.[266] It becomes an even more serious matter because sending States are concerned about subjecting their personnel to the host State's criminal proceedings and, in turn, the UN is concerned about receiving fewer personnel if it allows the host State to prosecute UN police officers.[267] This must be seen within the bigger picture of the UN's constant struggle to secure personnel to serve in UN Peace Operations.[268]

---

265 Miller, 'EoM Immunity', p. 47; Oswald, *Documents*, p. 36. 'Whilst the general position is that civilian members are subject to the jurisdiction of the host country in respect of any criminal offences that may be committed by them in the host country, the SRSG may not give permission for criminal proceedings to be commenced if there are concerns with the human rights standards of the local justice system or if the host country does not have a well-functioning court system'. The UN has also been attempting to secure fair trial standards in the host State by inserting new clauses in individual SOFAs in recent missions. For example, the SOFA for the UN Mission in Sudan (UNMIS) contains a clause that states that 'the courts and authorities of Sudan shall ensure that the member of UNMIS [...] is brought to trial and tried in accordance with international standards of justice, fairness and due process of law, as set out in the International Covenant on Civil and Political Rights, to which Sudan is a party'. Agreement between the Government of Sudan and the United Nations concerning the Status of the United Nations Mission in Sudan, (adopted and entered into force 28 December 2005), 2005 *UN Jurid YB* 44, para. 51 (a). See also Oswald and Bates, 'Privileges and Immunities of United Nations Police', p. 183.

266 UNGA, Zeid Report, para. 87.

267 A senior UN police officer summarized the perception of the waiver of immunity well when he said, '[w]aiving immunity is a very difficult thing to do. We are hard pressed to get police to serve here'. Human Rights Watch, *Hopes Betrayed – Trafficking of Women and Girls To Post-Conflict Bosnia and Herzegovina for Forced Prostitution* (November 2002, vol 14, no 9 (D), 2002), p. 60. See also Oswald and Bates, 'Privileges and Immunities of United Nations Police', p. 183, where they argue that, '[a]t the very least it must be in the interest of successfully recruiting UNPOL to serve in UN peace operations to ensure that any UNPOL member receives a fair trial and, if convicted, the member is not imprisoned in facilities that do not meet minimum international standards. From the time of UNEF I, it was already acknowledged that shielding the host State from criminally prosecuting UN personnel was an essential principle to ensuring that the UN is able to successfully recruit personnel to serve in its operations'. Note, though, that this was in relation to national military contingents. UNGA, 'Summary Study of the Experience Derived from the Establishment and Operation of the Force: Report of the Secretary-General' (9 October 1958) UN Doc. A/3943, para. 163.

268 Chapter 2, Section 3-3.

However, for reasons of clarity, it would be helpful to address that concern separately, because it is clear that the SG's power does not extend to creating a new form of immunity.[269] Leaving the scope of immunity unclear, or its application inconsistent, seriously increases the risk of impunity, unless the UN *ensures* that the sending State brings proceedings. It also makes it difficult to predict how it will be applied.

The complexities of the immunity scheme also mean that there are additional practical barriers that victims of UN police misconduct must negotiate in order to lodge complaints. These complexities may also prevent States from proceeding with criminal cases.

If the UN is trying to balance the need to protect its functions with its own actual or perceived accountability, it needs a separate mechanism to deal with these matters. Misuse or abuse of immunity is not only problematic under international law, but also detrimental to the interests of the UN.[270]

The UN must also consider another factor in relation to immunity. The assumption that UN police officers who have been repatriated for alleged misconduct will face fair legal proceedings back home is false. Most of the sending States have, in recent years, been subject to criticism by human rights bodies in relation to fair trial standards, including due process guarantees. For example, out of the top ten sending States in 2013, nine have been subject to clear criticism for failing to meet fair trial standards in the most recent review by the HRC, and in the Universal Periodic Review process.[271] If the UN's commitment

---

269 See Sections 2-1-1 and 2-2-2.

270 UN, Prep Commission Report, para. 7.

271 See UN Human Rights Council, 'Report of the Working Group on the Universal Periodic Review: Bangladesh' (8 July 2013) UN Doc. A/HRC/24/12, paras. 129.73, 129.74, where the right of defence, the impartiality of judges, and access to fair trial for all detainees are questioned; UN Human Rights Committee, 'Concluding Observations of the Human Rights Committee: Jordan' (18 November 2010) UN Doc. CCPR/C/JOR/CO/4, paras. 9, 11 where the Human Rights Committee criticized the denial of access to lawyers for detainees, resort to detention without charges, and absence of effective access to guarantees of trial; India, UN Human Rights Committee, 'Concluding Observations of the Human Rights Committee: India' (4 August 1997) UN Doc. CCPR/C/79/Add.81, para. 27, where the Human Rights Committee recommended making court reforms necessary for conducting speedy trials; UN Human Rights Committee, 'Concluding Observations of the Human Rights Committee: Nepal' (10 November 1994) UN Doc. CCPR/C/79/Add.42, para. 18, where it calls on Nepal to take appropriate measures to give effect to the independence of judiciary; UN Human Rights Committee, 'Concluding Observations of the Human Rights Committee: Senegal' (28 December 1992) UN Doc. CCPR/C/79/Add.10, paras. 5, 14 where *incommunicado* detention, and a lack of access to lawyer for detainees, as well as some forms of pre-trial detention outside the scope provided by law and lack of access to counsel by detainees are questioned; UN Human Rights Committee, 'Concluding Observations of the

to promoting 'human rights and fundamental freedoms' is to make sense, the UN must have a mechanism which elicits a formal assurance from sending States that repatriated personnel would face a fair trial.[272] Otherwise, this would not only infringe the fundamental principles of the Charter, but would allow UN personnel to be subject to differing standards of justice, depending on their nationality.

In fact, the other side of the coin is that there is no guarantee that UN police personnel who are repatriated will face any criminal proceedings, fair or otherwise, even if the alleged criminal conduct is referred to the sending States. In addition, if they do, there is no assurance that the proceedings or sentences would be appropriate. It should be noted that major sending States have recently been subject to the criticism that they do not hold their national police officers to account for the crimes they commit within their domestic contexts. In 2013, out of the same top ten sending States, nine have been clearly criticized in this regard by the most recent review by the HRC, or in the Universal Periodic Review session.[273] In such circumstances, a question arises as to who

---

Human Rights Committee: Nigeria' (24 July 1996) UN Doc. CCPR/C/79/Add.65 paras. 12, 13, 15, 16, 17, 20, where Nigeria's revocation of normal constitutional guarantees of fundamental rights, including fair trial rights in particular, and the power of special tribunals was questioned; UN Human Rights Committee, 'Concluding Observations of the Human Rights Committee: Rwanda' (7 May 2009) UN Doc. CCPR/C/RWA/CO/3, para. 17, where a local justice system was observed to be failing to operate in accordance with the basic rules pertaining the right to a fair trial; UN Human Rights Committee, 'Concluding Observations of the Human Rights Committee: Egypt' (28 November 2002) UN Doc. CCPR/CO/76/EGY, para. 16 (b), where it was criticized that terrorism-related offences by civilians are tried in military and security courts without any guarantee of the courts' independence, and the right to appeal; and UN Human Rights Council, 'Report of the Working Group on the Universal Periodic Review: Burkina Faso' (8 July 2013) UN Doc. A/HRC/24/4, paras. 135.68, 135.69, 135.111, 136.3, where the denial of prisoners' legal rights including due process rights, as well as independence of judiciary, was questioned. In relation to Pakistan, observations were made as to the improvement of fair trial guarantees, but not with respect to the initial lack of such guarantees. UN Human Rights Council, 'Report of the Working Group on the Universal Periodic Review: Pakistan' (26 December 2012) UN Doc. A/HRC/22/12.

272 Durch et al, *Improving Criminal Accountability*, p. 46.

273 See UN Human Rights Council, UPR Bangladesh report, paras. 129.33, 129.68, 129.75, 129.76, 129.78, 129.79, 129.80, 129.81, 129.82, 129.83, 129.84, 129.85, 129.86, where multiple comments were made with respect to the reported impunity in relation to extrajudicial executions, torture and brutality, as well more generally with regard to human rights violations by law enforcement agencies; UN Human Rights Committee, HRC Jordan Concluding Observations, para. 9, where practice of torture by public officials and the lack of a genuine complaint mechanism was noted; UN Human Rights Committee, HRC India Concluding Observations, paras. 18, 21, 23, 24, where it was stated that special powers afforded to

might have an obligation to ensure that: (i) criminal proceedings are brought against UN police officers; (ii) proceedings are appropriate; (iii) sanctions are appropriate; and (iv) proceedings are conducted in accordance with human rights standards.

It is clear that the legal barriers hindering the criminal prosecution of the UN police are minor. Jurisdiction is not a major barrier, nor is immunity, if appropriately invoked and appropriately waived. Practical issues do exist, but they do not explain all the problems encountered. In other words, it has been established that, in most cases, States are free to bring criminal proceedings against UN police members. If it is the case that States are in fact not willing to bring criminal proceedings, it is necessary to consider how this unwillingness can be addressed.

---

security forces and armed forces in some areas, coupled with the alleged failure of police and other security forces to respect the rule of law, including their resorting to torture or ill-treatment and arbitrary detention, are resulting in a climate of impunity, and the denial of victims' right to remedies in relation to those members; UN Human Rights Committee, HRC Concluding Observations Nepal, para. 10, where it was stated that members of security forces have not been brought to justice, or punished for arbitrary executions, enforced or involuntary disappearance, torture, and arbitrary or unlawful detention; UN Human Rights Committee, Concluding Observations of the Human Rights Committee: Senegal, paras. 5, 11, where the Human Rights Committee criticized the government's passivity in conducting timely investigations into the ill-treatment and torture of detainees, and extrajudicial executions in light of the allegations of indiscriminate killing of civilians by army and police, disappearance, torture and ill-treatment; UN Human Rights Council, Report of the Working Group on the Universal Periodic Review: Pakistan, paras. 122.111, 122.114, 122.115, 122.116, where the working group recommended that the current impunity for enforced disappearances, abduction and human rights violations should be dealt with; UN Human Rights Committee, Concluding Observations of the Human Rights Committee: Nigeria, paras. 17, 18, where the lack of investigation, prosecution and punishment of those responsible for extrajudicial and summary executions, disappearances, torture and ill-treatment and other human rights violations was criticized, and where it was observed that this was resulting in a state of impunity; UN Human Rights Committee, Concluding Observations of the Human Rights Committee: Rwanda, paras. 12, 13, where the apparent impunity enjoyed by the police forces in particular in relation to enforced disappearances, summary or arbitrary executions was criticized; UN Human Rights Committee, Concluding Observations of the Human Rights Committee: Egypt, para. 13, where Egypt was criticized for the systematic pattern of torture, cruel, inhumane or degrading treatment by law-enforcement personnel, and the general lack of investigations and punishment of those responsible, as well as reparations for victims; UN Human Rights Council, UPR Burkina Faso report, paras. 42, 135.67, where it was recommended that investigations be conducted into allegations of torture and ill-treatment. The recommendation with regard to Burkina Faso appears to fall short of including a criticism of the lack of such investigations.

CHAPTER 7

Is There an Obligation to Investigate and Prosecute?

Previous chapters established that the legal and practical obstacles which potentially impede the prosecution of UN police personnel do not explain the extent to which they are not prosecuted for crimes they have committed. It is often difficult to distinguish between the genuine difficulties a State may face in bringing criminal proceedings, and its unwillingness to do so. Where States are unwilling, it may be useful to identify the ways in which they can be pressured into bringing prosecutions. If a State's failure to prosecute were to constitute a breach of international law, would this motivate it to bring a prosecution? This chapter seeks to clarify whether the failure by States to prosecute an alleged UN police suspect amounts to a violation of international law.

This chapter does not deal with the *responsibility* for the original criminal conduct. This is because imputing conduct to a State does not normally arise in relation to the UN police, as they are not 'State agents' belonging to the sending State.[1] It is clear that States are *free to* bring criminal proceedings against members of the UN police, subject to considerations of immunity. However, this chapter considers whether there is a potential *obligation* on States to bring criminal proceedings for such conduct.[2] This is primarily a question under

1 This is reflected in the agreements between the UN and the individual UN police personnel, and between the UN and sending States of Formed Police Units (FPUs). See the Undertaking and Declaration by Experts on Mission: UN Police Officer/Corrections Officer/Military Observers/Military Liaison Officer, Annex 3 to UN DPKO, 'Guidelines for United Nations Police Officers on Assignment with Peacekeeping Operations' UN Doc. DPKO/PD/2006/00135, (hereinafter 'Undertaking'). There is an earlier and simpler Undertaking: the DPKO, Text of Undertaking to be signed by Civilian Police Officers. (On file with author.) Even where the individual who carried out the conduct in question does not come within the category of a State organ, it is possible that that conduct may be attributed to the State in certain limited circumstances. This may be relevant in exceptional cases in relation to FPUs. This is discussed in Section 5 below. UN, 'Model Memorandum of Understanding between the United Nations and the xxx Contributing Resources to the xxxx' UN Doc. (on file with author), (hereinafter 'FPU MoU').

2 In any case, UN police conduct is unlikely to be attributable to the sending State. The conduct of FPUs may be attributable to their sending States in exceptional circumstances. See Section 5 of this chapter.

 | DOI 10.1163/9789004328815_008

international human rights law (IHRL). This chapter examines first, whether States are under an obligation to investigate and prosecute a serious crime committed by a UN police officer and, if so, what the scope of that obligation is. This is followed by a similar consideration of the UN's obligations in this regard.

In seeking to establish, first, that an *obligation* exists and, second, what its scope might be, it is important to note that there may be exceptional rules for international crimes. International crimes are those crimes that are subject to international jurisdiction under a treaty, or are subject to universal jurisdiction, or are listed in the Rome Statute.[3] However, it is highly unlikely that UN police officers would engage in such grave crimes.[4] Therefore, this chapter does not discuss whether international crimes affect either the existence or scope of the obligation to investigate or prosecute.

Before dealing with whether States have such an obligation, a brief mention of the major human rights monitoring mechanisms will be made. This machinery is important because it is able to enforce human rights norms. This may make it more likely that States can be persuaded to re-evaluate their conduct and adhere to these norms.

1 IHRL Monitoring Mechanisms

The advantage of IHRL is that it contains mechanisms that can deal with individual cases of human rights violations.[5] There are two types of mechanisms: first, there are treaty-based mechanisms, which have both monitoring and enforcement functions. They can investigate how States give effect to the obligation to prosecute and, more precisely, how they give effect to that obligation in

3 These include war crimes, crimes against humanity, genocide, torture, and crimes listed in the Rome Statute of the ICC. Some acts of terrorism can also constitute international crimes. Antonio Cassese and Paola Gaeta, *Cassese's International Criminal Law* (Oxford University Press 2013), p. 63ff. Rome Statute of the International Criminal Court (17 July 1998, entered in force 1 June 2002) 2187 UNTS 90, (hereinafter 'Rome Statute').

4 No such case was recorded in the author's data.

5 Six of the treaty monitoring bodies (Human Rights Committee [HRC], Committee on the Elimination of Racial Discrimination [CERD], Committee against Torture [CAT], Committee on the Elimination of Discrimination against Women [CEDAW], Committee on the Rights of Persons with Disabilities [CRPD], and Committee on Enforced Disappearances [CED]) can hear individual petitions. UN OHCHR, 'Monitoring the Core International Human Rights Treaties' <http://www.ohchr.org/EN/HRBodies/Pages/TreatyBodies.aspx> accessed 27 December 2014.

relation to Peace Operations personnel outside their national territory.[6] Some treaty bodies can also hear individual petitions regarding potential breaches of treaty obligations.[7] The issue of non-prosecution could be challenged through these petitions. Second, there are Charter-based mechanisms, which include Special Procedures. Their key role is elaborating the scope of a norm in relation to a particular thematic issue or a particular State, depending on their mandate.[8] Special Rapporteurs are independent experts, who have some discretion regarding the issues they consider. Special Rapporteurs could therefore focus on the issue of non-prosecution specifically in relation to their thematic mandates. For example, the Special Rapporteur on torture,[9] and the Special Rapporteur on violence against women,[10] could adopt the issue of non-prosecution in respect of the impact it has on their particular theme.[11] There is, however, no mandate specifically dealing with either the issue of accountability in general, or the specific issue of the accountability of UN Peace Operations personnel.[12]

6 There are nine core human rights treaties and bodies which monitor States' compliance: HRC, Committee on Economic, Social and Cultural Rights (CESCR), CERD, CEDAW, CAT, Committee on the Rights of the Child (CRC), Committee on Migrant Workers (CMW), CRPD and CED. See ibid. For the purposes of this work, the most relevant treaty is the International Covenant on Civil and Political Rights (adopted 16 December 1966, entered into force 23 March 1977), 999 UNTS 171, (hereinafter 'ICCPR'). Its monitoring body is the Human Rights Committee (HRC).

7 As already noted, six of the treaty monitoring bodies (HRC, CERD, CAT, CEDAW, CRPD, and CED) can hear individual petitions. UN OHCHR, 'Treaty bodies' <http://www.ohchr.org/EN/HRBodies/Pages/TreatyBodies.aspx>.

8 UN OHCHR, 'Special Procedures of the Human Rights Council' <http://www.ohchr.org/EN/HRBodies/SP/Pages/Welcomepage.aspx> accessed 27 December 2014.

9 Special Rapporteur on torture and other cruel, inhuman or degrading treatment or punishment, as created by UN CHR Res 1985/33 (13 March 1985) UN Doc. E/CN.4/RES/1985/33, extended every three years since, most recently by UN Human Rights Council Res 25/13 (15 April 2014) UN Doc. A/HRC/RES/25/13.

10 Special Rapporteur on violence against women, its causes and consequences, as created by UN CHR Res 1994/45 (4 March 1994) UN Doc. E/CN.4/1994/132, extended every three years since, most recently by UN Human Rights Council Res 23/25 (14 June 2013) UN Doc. A/HRC/RES/23/25.

11 For example, the Special Rapporteur on the promotion of truth, justice, reparation and guarantees of non-recurrence, created by UN Human Rights Council Res 18/7 (13 October 2011) UN Doc. A/HRC/RES/18/7, extended by UN Human Rights Council Res 27/3 (03 October 2014) UN Doc. A/HRC/RES/27/3.

12 If such a mandate were to be established, it would be useful in addressing the difficulties inherent in the unique context of UN Peace Operations. These difficulties include issues of jurisdiction and immunities, which do not normally arise in the domestic context. However, a consideration of the possible creation of a new Special Procedures

There are also regional mechanisms. These are the European Court of Human Rights (ECtHR);[13] the Inter-American Commission on Human Rights (IACHR);[14] the Inter-American Court of Human Rights (IACtHR);[15] and the African Commission, and the African Court on Human and People's Rights.[16] As these institutions can hear individual petitions, it is possible that, in certain circumstances, the issue of non-prosecution of a UN police member may be considered by them.[17]

Resorting to human rights machinery may also have the advantage of generating publicity and raising awareness of the issue of accountability. The pressure engendered through this process may enable the UN and States to elicit more information on general or particularized misconduct in UN Peace Operations.

The question then arises as to whether IHRL requires the investigation and, where appropriate, the prosecution of serious crimes.

2 A State's Obligation to Investigate and Prosecute UN Police Officers, in Relation to Serious Crimes

Under IHRL, there are three dimensions of obligation in respect of rights: (1) the obligation to respect the right; (2) the obligation to protect the right;

---

mandate falls outside the scope of this work. The issues of jurisdiction and immunities are addressed in Chapters 5 and 6. There are two mechanisms established by the General Assembly and the Security Council, which partially address issues related to this work. These are the Special Representative of the Secretary-General for Children and Armed Conflict, and the Special Representative of the Secretary-General on Sexual Violence in Conflict. Neither of them are human rights mechanisms, but they serve as spokespersons on these issues, and advise the Secretary-General on the issues covered by their mandates. The former mechanism was established by UNGA Res 51/77 (20 February 1997) UN Doc. A/RES/51/77, and has been extended every three years, most recently by UNGA Res 69/157 (3 February 2015) UN Doc. A/RES/69/157. The latter mechanism was established by UNSC Res 1888 (30 September 2009) UN Doc. S/RES/1888.

13 The ECtHR falls under the Council of Europe. Council of Europe, 'European Court of Human Rights,' <http://www.echr.coe.int/Pages/home.aspx?p=court&c=#n1354801701084_pointer> accessed 27 December 2014.

14 The IACHR falls under the Organization of American States. OAS, 'Inter-American Commission on Human Rights' <http://www.oas.org/en/iachr/> accessed 27 December 2014.

15 OAS, 'Inter-American Court of Human Rights' <http://www.corteidh.or.cr/index.php/en> accessed 27 December 2014.

16 AU, 'African Commission on Human and People's Rights' <http://www.achpr.org> accessed 27 December 2014.

17 There may be an issue of the machinery's competence in terms of *ratione personae* and *ratione loci*.

and, (3) the obligation to fulfil the right. The first obligation is also called the 'negative obligation', whilst the other two obligations are known as 'positive obligations'.[18] Negative obligations require a State to refrain from infringing a right, whilst positive obligations require a State to do something to guarantee a right.[19] States are required to protect individuals who are within their territory and subject to their jurisdiction[20] from acts which would be human rights violations were they to be carried out by State agents.[21] This obligation also requires that States investigate and prosecute any such acts.[22] The first question is whether such obligations exist in general. If they are found to exist, their source and scope will be discussed.

2-1 *Existence of the Obligation in General*

This section focuses on a State's duty to conduct an effective investigation into allegations that certain crimes have been committed by UN police officers,[23] and its duty to prosecute private wrongdoers where these allegations are

18 UN Human Rights Committee, 'General Comment 31 on the Nature of the General Legal Obligation Imposed on States Parties to the Covenant' (29 March 2004) UN Doc. CCPR/C/21/Rev.1/Add.13, (hereinafter 'General Comment 31').

19 Ibid, paras. 6–7.

20 This formula is contained in the ICCPR, Article 2. Under the ECHR and American Convention on Human Rights, each State party has human rights obligations only in relation to persons subject to its 'jurisdiction'. There is no requirement that they be 'within the territory'. Convention for the Protection of Human Rights and Fundamental Freedoms (European Convention on Human Rights, as amended) (ECHR) 213 UNTS 222, Article 1; American Convention on Human Rights (adopted 22 November 1969, entered into force 18 July 1978) 1144 UNTS 123, Article 1.

21 UN Human Rights Committee, General Comment 31, para. 18. *Joaquín David Herrera Rubio v Colombia* 2 Selected Decisions of the Human Rights Committee 192; *José Vicente and Amado Villafañe Chaparro, Dioselina Torres Crespo, Hermes Enrique Torres Solis and Vicencio Chaparro Izquierdo v Colombia* 6 Selected Decisions of the Human Rights Committee 135, para. 8.8 (this case is also known as *Arhuacos v. Colombia*); *Osman and Osman v UK* ECHR 1998-VIII, para. 115; *L C B v UK* ECHR 1998-III 1403, para. 36. See also Jean-François Akandji-Kombe, *Positive Obligations under the European Convention on Human Rights* (Council of Europe, Human Rights Handbooks No 7, 2007), p. 16, (hereinafter 'Positive Obligations'), where it explains that such obligations are those that 'call for the organisation of domestic procedures to ensure better protection of persons, those that ultimately require the provision of sufficient remedies for violations of rights'.

22 It is claimed that this aspect of the obligation is more onerous if the violation is committed by State agents. See Section 5 below for further details. The obligation to investigate and prosecute is sometimes called the 'procedural obligation'. For example, Akandji-Kombe, *Positive Obligations*, p. 16.

23 This is because a member of the UN police is not a State agent at the time he is working for a UN Peace Operation. See the introductory section of this chapter.

substantiated.[24] IHRL is primarily concerned with the conduct of States, but it also covers a State's conduct in relation to the acts of private individuals. A State's responsibility in respect of a private actor's criminal act that infringes on another's rights can be engaged, 'not because of the act itself, but because of the lack of due diligence to prevent the violation or to respond to it'.[25] General Comment 31 of the Human Rights Committee (HRC) states:

> There may be circumstances in which a failure to ensure Covenant rights [...] would give rise to violations by States Parties of those rights, as a result of States Parties permitting or failing to take appropriate measures or to exercise due diligence to prevent, punish, investigate or redress the harm caused by such acts by private persons or entities.[26]

This was confirmed in a case where a victim's Convention right was infringed by a private person.[27]

Regional human rights mechanisms have also found that States have an obligation to respond appropriately to breaches of human rights by private actors. *Velasquez Rodriquez* is the leading IACtHR case in this regard. It establishes the procedural obligation to prevent or respond to an IHRL violation that is not initially directly attributable to the State, either because it is the act of a private person or the person(s) responsible have not been identified.[28] The rationale for this obligation is:

---

24 For ease of reference, this obligation is referred to throughout this chapter as the 'obligation to investigate and prosecute'.

25 *Velásquez Rodríguez v Honduras* Inter-Am Ct HR Series C No 4 (29 July 1988), para. 172.

26 UN Human Rights Committee, General Comment 31, para. 8. The HRC also affirmed that an effective remedy must be available to victims of torture, and that the perpetrators must be held responsible whether they are public officials or other persons acting on behalf of the State, or private persons. UN Human Rights Committee, 'General Comment 20 on the Prohibition of Torture, or Other Cruel, Inhuman or Degrading Treatment or Punishment, Article 7' (30 September 1992) UN Doc. HRI/GEN/1/Rev.1, paras. 2, 13.

27 *Khilal Avadanov v Azerbaijan* Communication no 1633/2007 (Human Rights Committee, 25 October 2010), para. 9.5, in relation to ill-treatment by a private person. Also note that in the *Herrera Rubio* case, although it was not established that the victim was murdered by a State agent, the Committee affirmed the State's obligation to establish effective facilities and procedures to ensure a thorough investigation. *Herrera Rubio v Colombia*.

28 *Velásquez Rodríguez*, para. 172.

> Where the acts of private parties that violate the Convention are not seriously investigated, those parties are aided in a sense by the government, thereby making the State responsible on the international plane.[29]

Similarly, the Inter-American Commission found that if a State does not properly enforce those rules which prohibit violations, this could be a factor in the commission of subsequent violations.[30] The IACtHR has confirmed this approach.[31]

The ECtHR has also heard cases probing the appropriateness of the State's response to private criminal acts, for example, *M. C. v. Bulgaria*, which involved rape and sexual assault. The lack of a thorough investigation into allegations of rape was, in itself, found to be a violation of Article 3 of the Convention.[32] Cases dealing with the appropriateness of the State's response to the deprivation of life by private individuals addressed the State's duty to investigate and prosecute after the deaths.[33] One of the cases in *Al-Skeini* dealt with the duty to investigate a killing where the person who fired the fatal shot was not identified.[34] In another case which concerned a local authority's failure to prevent

---

29 Ibid, para. 177.

30 For example, in relation to domestic violence in the private sphere, the IACHR emphasized that, '[t]he failure to prosecute and convict the perpetrator under these circumstances is an indication that the State condones the violence suffered by Maria da Penha, and this failure by the Brazilian courts to take action is exacerbating the direct consequences of the aggression by her ex-husband'. *Maria da Penha Maia Fernandes v Brazil* Inter-Am Com HR Series L No 54/01, paras. 55–56.

31 *Godinez-Cruz v Honduras* (Merits) Inter-Am Ct HR Series C No 5 (20 January 1989) paras. 181–182, citing *Velásquez Rodríguez*, para. 172; *Caballero Delgado and Santana v Colombia* Inter-Am Ct HR Series C No 22 (8 December 1995), para. 56.

32 In this case it was held that, '[…] the effectiveness of the investigation of the applicant's case and, in particular, the approach taken by the investigator and the prosecutors in the case fell short of the requirements inherent in the States' positive obligations – viewed in the light of the relevant modern standards in comparative and international law – to establish and apply effectively a criminal-law system punishing all forms of rape and sexual abuse'. *M C v Bulgaria* ECHR 2003-XII, para. 185.

33 *Menson and Others v UK* ECHR 2003-V; *Angelova and Iliev v Bulgaria* ECHR 2007-IX; *Gongadze v Ukraine* App no 34056/02 (ECtHR, 8 November 2005); *Dink v Turkey* App no 2668/07 (ECtHR, 14 September 2010).

34 *Al-Skeini and Others v UK* [2011] ECHR 1093. This case is significant in that the killing took place outside the respondent State's territory, although the situation was said to be under its control for the purpose of application of the Convention.

an explosion at a rubbish dump, resulting in the deaths of slum-dwellers, the State's obligation to investigate these deaths adequately was examined.[35]

It appears that, in general, the obligation to investigate and prosecute exists under IHRL treaties in relation to criminal conduct which would be a violation of a right protected in one of these treaties, had it been committed by a State agent.[36] In order to determine the scope of this obligation, it is necessary to establish how it arises.

2-2 *Two Ways in which the Obligation to Investigate and Prosecute Arises*

There are two ways in which this obligation arises. One is reading it into each treaty right, and the other is to interpret the content of each right in light of the right to a remedy.

Reading the Obligation into Each Right

Some of the HRC's responses appear to read this obligation into each right. General Comment 31 of the ICCPR states that:

> [...] the Covenant itself envisages in some articles certain areas where there are positive obligations on States Parties to address the activities of private persons or entities.[37]

General Comment 6 on the right to life concludes that the deprivation of life through criminal acts should be punished.[38] In the *Herrera Rubio* case, which dealt with the disappearance of the applicant's parents, the HRC held that an effective investigation was a requirement under the right to life.[39]

---

35 *Öneryildiz v Turkey* ECHR 2004-XII. The obligation to investigate was also found to be violated in suicide cases. In *Mammadov*, the authority's failure to interview the person who committed suicide before death, despite the availability of information about her life-threatening injuries, was found to be in violation of the obligation to investigate. *Mikayil Mammadov v Azerbaijan* App no 4762/05 (ECtHR, 17 December 2009), para. 130.

36 In general, there are positive obligations on State parties to guarantee the rights contained in the Covenant, by protecting individuals against 'acts committed by private persons or entities that would impair the enjoyment of Covenant rights in so far as they are amenable to application between private persons or entities'. UN Human Rights Committee, General Comment 31, para. 8.

37 Ibid, para. 8.

38 UN Human Rights Committee, 'General Comment 6 on Article 6 (The Right to Life)' (30 April 1982) UN Doc. HRI/GEN/1/Rev.1, para. 3.

39 *Herrera Rubio v Colombia*. Note, however, that in the earlier examination of the case, the Committee referred to the State's obligation under Article 2, which requires that the State

In *M. C. v. Bulgaria*, the ECtHR found a violation due to the lack of an effective investigation into a crime.[40] The Court also found violations of the right to be free from torture and ill-treatment, and the right to a private and family life.[41] However, the Court found that no separate issue arose under the right to a remedy.[42] The first leading ECtHR case on the obligation to investigate, the *McCann* case, dealt with this obligation under the right to life.[43] This was followed by a number of cases before the European Court on right to life issues, including those dealing with fatal shootings, crimes by a private individual taking or threatening life, suspicious deaths and medical malpractice.[44]

---

give effect to the victim's right to a remedy. Ibid, para. 10.3. The HRC's examination of Article 16 (the right to recognition before the law) in *Kimouche* may be worth noting. It was found that under the circumstances (the victim's arrest by the authorities followed by a lack of provision of information), the lack of investigation placed the victim outside the protection of the law. *Messaouda Kimouche v Algeria* Communication no 1328/2004 (Human Rights Committee, 10 July 2007), para. 7.9.

40 It was held that, '[…] the effectiveness of the investigation of the applicant's case and, in particular, the approach taken by the investigator and the prosecutors in the case fell short of the requirements inherent in the States' positive obligations – viewed in the light of the relevant modern standards in comparative and international law – to establish and apply effectively a criminal-law system punishing all forms of rape and sexual abuse'. *M C v Bulgaria*, para. 185.

41 Articles 3 and 8.

42 *M C v Bulgaria*, para. 187.

43 *McCann and Others v UK* Series A No 324.

44 *Hugh Jordan v UK* ECHR 2001-III; *McKerr v UK* ECHR 2001-III; *Kelly and Others v UK* App no 30054/96 (ECtHR, 4 May 2001); *Shanaghan v UK* App no 37715/97 (ECtHR, 4 August 2001); *McShane v UK* App no 43290/98 (ECtHR 28 May 2002); *Finucane v UK* ECHR 2003-VIII; *Öğur v Turkey* ECHR 1999-III; *Tanis and Others v Turkey* ECHR 2005-VIII. In *Tanis and Others*, the Court also found a violation under the right to a remedy. In one of the *Al-Skeini* incidents, Article 2 was found to be breached because a full and independent investigation into the deaths did not take place, even though the applicant's relative received a substantial sum in the settlement of his civil claim, together with the admission of liability on the part of the British Army. *Al-Skeini and Others v UK*. In *Menson and Others*, the Court stated that all life-threatening injuries in suspicious circumstances should lead to an effective official investigation, even where there is no indication that the authority concerned knew or should have known. *Menson and Others v UK*. See also *Yaşa v Turkey* ECHR 1998-VI; *Angelova and Iliev v Bulgaria*. In *Silih*, the official inquiry into the death of a man due to medical malpractice by a doctor at a public hospital was found to be too slow and had other deficiencies, resulting in a violation of the right to life. In its judgment, the Court ruled that this obligation applies in cases related to medical care both in public and private sector. '[T]he procedural obligation of Article 2 requires the States to set up an effective independent judicial system so that the cause of death

The IACtHR also took this approach. In the *Velasquez-Rodriguez* case, the Court found a violation of the right to life, as a result of the State's general obligation under the Convention to 'ensure' this right, but did not raise the question of the right to a remedy.[45] This approach has been followed in subsequent cases.[46]

Reading the Scope of Each Right in Conjunction with the Right to a Remedy

It is also possible to identify a procedural obligation in relation to various rights by reading the scope of each right in conjunction with the right to a remedy. Part of the HRC's General Comment 31 appears to take this approach, by referring to the potential circumstances in which a violation of these rights would arise due to a State's failure to guarantee them, as required by Article 2.[47] ICCPR Article 2, paragraph 3 concerns the State Parties' obligation to provide an effective remedy for victims in the event of a breach. This appears to suggest that the obligation to investigate and prosecute may arise from reading a substantive right in conjunction with the right to a remedy. General Comment 20 on the right to be free from torture and ill-treatment also takes this approach.[48] Cases involving alleged torture or ill-treatment, arbitrary detention and issues

---

of patients in the care of the medical profession, whether in the public or the private sector, can be determined, and those responsible made accountable'. *Silih v Slovenia* ECHR 2009, para. 192. See also *Calvelli and Ciglio v Italy* ECHR 2002-I; *Powell v UK* ECHR 2000-V; *Dodov v Bulgaria* ECHR 2008; *Eugenia Lazăr v Romania* App no 32146/05 (ECtHR, 16 February 2010); *Mehmet Şentürk and Bekir Şentürk v Turkey* App no 13423/09 (ECtHR, 9 April 2013). In a number of cases involving a violation of Article 3, the Court also found the requirement of effective investigation was not satisfied. In those cases, the acts of torture/ill-treatment were carried out by State agents. *Menesheva v Russia* App no 59261/00 (ECtHR, 9 March 2006); *Bekos v Greece* App no 15250/02 (ECtHR, 13 December 2005); *Tanli v Turkey* ECHR 2001-III; *Kurt v Turkey* ECHR 1998-III.

45 *Velásquez Rodríguez*, paras. 166, 172–182. The Court ruled that there was no issue under the right to judicial protection (Article 25).

46 *Godinez-Cruz v Honduras*, paras. 170–171, 197–198, 203; *Caballero Delgado and Santana v Colombia*, paras. 55–59, 72; *Paniagua-Morales v Guatemala* Inter-Am Ct HR Series C No 37 (8 March 1998), paras. 173–174.

47 UN Human Rights Committee, General Comment 31, para. 8. Article 2 deals with the States Parties' obligation to give effect to the rights enshrined in the Covenant, and paragraph 3 ensures that there are effective remedies for any violation of Covenant rights. Those two are inter-related, as set out in ibid, para. 8.

48 UN Human Rights Committee, General Comment 20, para. 14.

regarding recognition before the law have followed this path.[49] In several cases dealing with acts by private persons, the HRC has taken this route to recognizing this obligation.[50]

The ECtHR has observed that whether issues are raised under the right to a remedy is dependent on the existence of a 'close procedural and practical relationship between the criminal investigation and the remedies available to those applicants in the legal system as a whole'.[51] The scope of Article 13 (the right to a remedy) varies depending on the nature of the complaint.[52] In *Kurt*,

49 *Ali Medjnoune v Algeria* 9 Selected Decisions of the Human Rights Committee 182, para. 10; *Zheikov v Russia* Communication No 889/1999 (Human Rights Committee, 17 March 2006), para. 7; *Sundara Arachchige Lalith Rajapakse v Sri Lanka* Communication no 1250/2004 (Human Rights Committee, 14 July 2006), para. 9.5, where the Committee found a violation of Article 2.3 in conjunction with Article 7, and subsequently held it unnecessary to consider possible violation under Article 7 alone. In a recent disappearance case, the Committee also examined the issue of effective investigation under Article 2.3 in conjunction with Article 7. *El Hassy v Lybia* Communication no 1422/2005 (Human Rights Committee, 24 October 2007), para. 6.9. See also *Hassan Abbousedra v Lybia* Communication no 1751/2008 (Human Rights Committee, 25 October 2010), para. 7.10. In this case, the HRC found a violation of Articles 6.1 and 7, read in conjunction with Article 2.3. In the *Kimouche* case, the HRC examined substantive articles on their own, then examined Article 2.3 in conjunction with those substantive rights. It found a violation of Article 2.3 in conjunction with Articles 7, 9, and 16, as well as a separate violation of Article 2.3 read in conjunction with Article 7. *Kimouche v Algeria*, paras. 7.9, 7.10.

50 *Marija and Dragana Novakovic, on behalf of their son, Zoran Novakovic (deceased) v Serbia* Communication no 1556/2007 (Human Rights Committee, 21 October 2010), para. 7.3. The Committee used an argument under Article 5 in conjunction with Article 2.3 to reach this conclusion. In this regard, it is noteworthy that the HRC found that Article 2 cannot be invoked in isolation, but can only be invoked in conjunction with another Covenant right. *R A V N v Argentina* 3 Selected Decisions of the Human Rights Committee 20, para. 5.3. In *Avadanov*, the Committee found a violation of Article 7 read in conjunction with Article 2.3 in respect of the authority's failure to conduct an adequate investigation into the allegations of ill-treatment by a private person. *Avadanov v Azerbaijan*, para. 9.5. See also *M G B and S P v Trinidad and Tobago* 3 Selected Decisions of the Human Rights Committee 36, para. 6.2.

51 *Öneryildiz v Turkey*, para. 148; *Salman v Turkey* ECHR 2000-VII, para. 109. In *Öneryildiz*, a violation was found under the right to a remedy on account of the lack of a prompt administrative procedure for compensation, but not on account of the lack of an effective investigation into the deaths of the applicant's relatives. *Öneryildiz v Turkey*, paras. 91–96, 150–155.

52 *Menesheva v Russia*; Fernando Felipe Basch, 'The Doctrine of the Inter-American Court of Human Rights Regarding States' Duty to Punish Human Rights Violations and Its Dangers' 23 *American University International Law Review* 195, p. 222.

the Court compared the procedural requirements under Article 5 (the right to liberty and security) with those in Article 13, and ruled that the latter includes a:

> [...] thorough and effective investigation capable of leading to the identification and punishment of those responsible and including effective access for the relatives to the investigatory procedure.[53]

Thus, Article 13 is broader than Article 5.[54] In relation to the right to life, an observation was made that the investigation requirement under Article 2 is more focused on official investigations leading to the establishment of criminal liability, whilst that under Article 13 is more focused on civil remedies to enable the victims or their relatives to seek compensation.[55] The ECtHR's requirements relating to effective investigation and subsequent prosecution are increasingly demanding, which transforms the requirements into substantive rights.[56]

The IACtHR has also considered the duty to investigate and prosecute under the right to a remedy.[57] It has further considered the issue from the perspective of the right of a victim to a fair trial. It has taken a view that fair trial guarantees serve to protect the defendants as well as victims in criminal proceedings.[58]

---

53 *Kurt v Turkey*, para. 140. The Court refers to *Aksoy v Turkey* ECHR 1996-VI, para. 98; *Aydin v Turkey ECHR 1997-VI*, para. 103; *Kaya v Turkey* ECHR 1998-I, paras. 106–107.

54 *Kurt v Turkey*, para. 140.

55 Bernadette Rainey, Elizabeth Wicks and Clare Ovey, *Jacobs, White and Ovey: The European Convention on Human Rights* (Oxford University Press 2014), p. 160, (hereinafter 'European Convention'). This judgment was based *inter alia* on the Court's judgment in *Öneryildiz v Turkey*.

56 Akandji-Kombe, *Positive Obligations*, pp. 16–17. In *Tanis and Others*, the ECtHR found violations related to the duty to investigate under Article 2, Article 3 and subsequently under Article 13. *Tanis and Others v Turkey*.

57 'Article 25 in relation to Article 1 (1) [...] obliges the State to guarantee to every individual access to the administration of justice and, in particular, to simple and prompt recourse, so that inter-alia, those responsible for human rights violations may be prosecuted and reparations obtained for the damages suffered'. *Loayza-Tamayo v Peru* Inter-Am Ct HR Series C No42 (27 November 1998) para. 168.

58 *Bulacio v Argentina* Inter-Am Ct HR Series C No 100 (18 September 2003), para. 162; *Genie-Lacayo v Nicaragua* Inter-Am Ct HR Series C No 30 (29 January 1997), para. 75; *Blake v Guatemala* Inter-Am Ct HR Series C No 36 (24 January 1998), paras. 96–97; *Tradesman v Colombia* Inter-Am Ct HR Series C No 109 (5 July 2004), para. 219; *La Palmeras v Colombia* Inter-Am Ct HR Series C No 90 (6 December 2001), paras. 59–67; *Durand v Peru* Inter-Am Ct HR Series C No 68 (16 August 2000), paras. 111, 131, 146.

2-3 *Does it Matter Which Substantive Right is at Issue?*

The cases cited above relate to specific rights. It is thus necessary to clarify if the obligation to investigate exists only in relation to certain rights, and not others.

General Comment 31 provides that:

> The [ICCPR] itself envisages *in some articles* certain areas where there are positive obligations on States Parties to address the activities of private persons or entities.[59]

It suggests that the obligation to bring those responsible to justice arises in relation to:

> [...] those violations recognized as criminal under either domestic or international law, such as torture and similar cruel, inhuman and degrading treatment (article 7), summary and arbitrary killing (article 6) and enforced disappearance (articles 7 and 9 and, frequently, 6).[60]

In the *El Hassy* and *Kimouche* cases, the HRC emphasized that the obligation to investigate is particularly important in relation to enforced disappearances, acts of torture and the right to life.[61] In the latter case, the HRC also highlighted the relationship between the requirement to investigate and a violation of Article 16 (the right to recognition before the law).[62]

It is possible that this obligation may arise only in relation to limited rights, although clearly the list provided is not exhaustive. It is also clear that it is not limited to international crimes, but it may be that it arises only in relation to serious crimes. The HRC has found that this obligation exists in relation to disappearance cases, as well as alleged criminal conduct in relation to the right to life, the right not to be tortured or subjected to ill-treatment and arbitrary detention.[63]

---

59 (Emphasis added.) UN Human Rights Committee, General Comment 31, para. 8.

60 Ibid, para. 18.

61 *El Hassy v Lybia*, para. 8; *Kimouche v Algeria*, para. 2.8.

62 *Kimouche v Algeria*, para. 7.9.

63 This obligation arises even in cases in which either the conduct concerned was committed by private individuals, or where the State's involvement was suspected, but not established. *Novakovic v. Serbia*, para. 7.3; *Chaparro v Colombia*, para. 8.8. (This case is also known as *Arhuacos v Colombia*); *Herrera Rubio v Colombia*, para. 10.3. In addition, in relation to the deprivation of life by State agents, see *Marcellana and Gumanoy v The Philippines* Communication no 1560/2007 (Human Rights Committee, 30 October 2008),

Different regional bodies have applied this obligation to different rights. Under the ECHR, this approach was taken to the right to life,[64] and cases of rape and sexual assault (which raise the potential infringement of the right to be free from torture and ill-treatment, as well as the right to a private and family life).[65] While there is a suggestion that the obligation to investigate and prosecute only arises in relation to core rights[66] or in relation to 'grave facts',[67] the ECtHR has held that this obligation is dependent on the circumstances of each case.[68] It observed that not all infringements of the right to a private and family life necessarily require criminal remedies.[69] Since then the Court has found that an obligation to investigate exists in relation to rape,[70] and

para. 7.3. For other disappearance cases, see *Yasoda Sharma v Nepal* Communication no 1469/2006 (Human Rights Committee, 6 November 2008), para. 3.2; *Rafael Mojica v Dominican Republic* 5 Selected Decisions of the Human Rights Committee 70, para. 5.5; *Rosario Celis Laureano v Peru* 6 Selected Decisions of the Human Rights Committee 63, para. 8.3; *El Hassy v Lybia*, para. 8. The requirement that a full and thorough investigation be held was found to exist in relation to ill-treatment and incommunicado detention in *Medjnoune* case. *Medjnoune v Algeria*, para. 10.

64 *Öneryildiz v Turkey*. In addition, there are a number of cases in which the lack of effective investigation or prosecution and punishment was raised in relation to the deprivation of life by a State agent. *Kaya v Turkey*, para. 86; *Tanrikulu v Turkey* ECHR 1999-IV; *Kemal Kiliç v Turkey* ECHR 2000-III; *McCann v UK*; *Paul and Audrey Edwards v UK* ECHR 2002-II, para. 69; *Ergi v Turkey* ECHR 1998-IV; *Güleç v Turkey* ECHR 1998-IV. See also the cases listed above in n.44.

65 *M C v Bulgaria*; *X and Y v The Netherlands* Series A No 91. In addition, where a State agent is alleged to have tortured or ill-treated a victim, there is a clear case-law that the obligation to investigate and prosecute exists. See generally, *supra*, n.44.

66 That is chiefly in relation to Articles 2 and 3. Basch, 'The Doctrine of the Inter-American Court of Human Rights Regarding States' Duty to Punish Human Rights Violations and Its Dangers', pp. 222–223. This view is based on the language used by the European Court. For example, the Court emphasized 'the fundamental importance of the rights protected by Articles 2 and 3' in *Menesheva v Russia*.

67 The examples given are suspicious death and ill-treatment. Basch, 'The Doctrine of the Inter-American Court of Human Rights Regarding States' Duty to Punish Human Rights Violations and Its Dangers', pp. 222, 226.

68 In one case, the Court also attached a caveat to the obligation to investigate and prosecute under Article 13 (the right to a remedy). It stated that the cases arising from the conflict in south-east Turkey in the 1990s must be considered in that context, which was characterized 'by the absence of any such investigations into the applicants' complaints'. *Öneryildiz v Turkey*, para. 134.

69 *X and Y v The Netherlands*, para. 24; *Jankauskas v Lithuania* App no 59304/00 (ECtHR, 16 December 2003).

70 *M C v Bulgaria*.

life-threatening or fatal assaults.[71] It has also held that the response to a loss of life does not itself have to be criminal. In the case of a death through medical negligence at a private clinic, it was found that a civil remedy sufficed.[72]

The Inter-American system has held that the obligation applies to cases involving disappearance, arbitrary detentions, kidnapping, ill-treatment and the deprivation of life. These cases involved the infringement of multiple rights, and the obligation to investigate and prosecute, where appropriate, was found in relation to the rights to liberty, humane treatment, and life.[73] This indicates that most of the crimes committed by UN police officers would trigger an obligation to investigate.[74] Furthermore, the Court's language suggested that the obligation to investigate and prosecute arises in relation to every breach of the Convention, regardless of whether the infringement is due to State or private acts,[75] although the scope of this obligation may depend on which right is at stake, as well as the severity of the breach.[76]

3 Scope of the Obligation

3-1 *Obligation to Investigate*

The first part of the obligation entails a requirement to investigate the allegation. The HRC observed that States must exercise due diligence by investigating

---

71 *Kemal Kiliç v Turkey*; *Menson and Others v UK*; *Angelova and Iliev v Bulgaria*. The Court also dealt with the requirement that there be official investigations into suicides. *Mammadov v Azerbaijan*. In addition, there are numerous cases in relation to instances in which States were alleged to have been involved in killings or torture/ill-treatment under Articles 2 and 3. See in general, *supra*, n.44.

72 *Ciglio v Italy*. It examined the necessity of criminal proceedings in relation to cases dealing with the right to life. In the case at hand, no violation was found in relation to the absence of any criminal sanctions imposed on a doctor who was negligent. This was due to the fact that Italian law stipulates a particular time limit for bringing criminal proceedings in certain types of cases.

73 *Velásquez Rodríguez*; *Godinez-Cruz v Honduras*, paras. 170–171, 197–198, 203; *Caballero Delgado and Santana v Colombia*, paras. 55–59, 72; *Paniagua-Morales v Guatemala*.

74 For a discussion of the nature of crimes committed by UN police, see Chapter 3, Section 2-2.

75 'The State is obliged to investigate every situation involving a violation of the rights protected by the Convention'. *Velásquez Rodríguez*, para. 176; *Godinez-Cruz v Honduras*, para. 175. *Paniagua-Morales v Guatemala*, para. 174. See in general Basch, 'The Doctrine of the Inter-American Court of Human Rights Regarding States' Duty to Punish Human Rights Violations and Its Dangers', pp. 196–200.

76 Diane F Orentlicher, 'Settling Accounts: The Duty to Prosecute Human Rights Violations of a Prior Regime' (1991) 100 *Yale Law Journal* 2537, p. 2578.

allegations of violations promptly, thoroughly and effectively, through independent and impartial bodies.[77] In *Herrera Rubio*, although it was not established that the victim was murdered by a State agent, the Committee found that States Parties are obliged to establish effective facilities and procedures to ensure a thorough investigation by an appropriate impartial body. It is interesting to note that the Committee observed that an investigative 'facility and process' must be 'established', which may indicate that investigative bodies must, to a certain extent, be institutionalized, rather than investigations being carried out on an *ad hoc* basis. Furthermore, the investigation itself must be conducted in good faith.[78]

In other cases involving the actual or potential deprivation of life by State agents, it was found that there must be a criminal investigation.[79] It was reasoned that procedural requirements can only be ensured through a complete and exhaustive investigation into the cause of death, and the events leading to it. Such an investigation is guaranteed through criminal, not civil proceedings.[80] Proceedings must be brought promptly. The State's failure to provide legitimate reasons for a delay in initiating criminal proceedings in relation to the

---

77 UN Human Rights Committee, General Comment 31, para. 15. In *Rajapakse*, the Committee found that the fact that an investigation was not opened by the Attorney General until over three months after the incident at hand, despite the fact that the victim was hospitalized and unconscious for 15 days, was found to fail the 'prompt' test. It observed that the expeditious and effectiveness requirements are particularly important in cases involving torture. *Rajapakse v Sri Lanka*, paras. 9.4, 9.5.

78 This obligation was found in relation to cases of missing and disappeared persons in circumstances which might involve a violation of the right to life. In this case, the complainant's parents were picked up by State agents. The next day, State agents came to the complainant's house, and informed him that they had found his parents' bodies. However it could not be proved that the State agents murdered them. The Committee found that the burden of proof was not on the complainant, as the State may have exclusive access to some of the relevant information. In such circumstances, the State has an obligation to give due weight to the complainant's allegations. *Herrera Rubio v Colombia*, para. 10-5. See also *Eduardo Bleier v Uruguay* 1 Selected Decisions of the Human Rights Committee 109, para. 13.3; *Almeida de Quinteros v Uruguay* 2 Selected Decisions of the Human Rights Committee 138, para. 11; *El Hassy v Lybia*; para. 6.9.

79 *Nydia Erika Bautista de Arellana v Colombia* 6 Selected Decisions of the Human Rights Commitee 103, para. 8.2. This finding was reiterated in *Jose Vicente, Chaparro v Colombia*, paras. 5.2, 8.8.

80 See also the case concerning the killing of a 'suspected terrorist' by a State agent: *Marcellana and Gumanoy v The Philippines*, para. 7.3. Another case concerned a killing by police. See *Vadivel Sathasivam and Parathesi Saraswathi v Sri Lanka* Communication no 1436/2005 (Human Rights Committee, 8 July 2008), para. 3.6.

death, which was allegedly due to improper medical treatment, was, in itself, a breach of the State's obligation to properly investigate the case.[81]

Similarly, under the European system, requirements are those of means, and not of result.[82] Where there is an actual or potential loss of life, there must be 'some form of effective official investigation', whether or not the offender is established as being a State agent.[83] Whatever form such an investigation takes, the authorities are required to act once the matter has come to their attention, regardless of whether the next-of-kin has lodged a complaint.[84] Such an investigation must be carried out promptly,[85] in order to maintain public confidence in the authority's adherence to the rule of law, and to prevent the perception of their collusion in or tolerance of unlawful acts.[86] For an investigation to be effective, there are two requirements. The first is that it must be adequate; and the second is that it must be independent.[87] Under the first requirement, the investigation must be thorough,[88] and must be capable of leading to the identification and punishment of those responsible.[89]

81 *Novakovic v. Serbia*, para. 7.3.

82 *Jaloud v the Netherlands* [2014] ECHR 1292, para. 166; *Ramsahai and Others v the Netherlands* [2007] ECHR 393, para. 324; *Silih v Slovenia*, para. 193; *Edwards v UK*.

83 *McCann v UK*, para. 161. The Courts in *Kaya* and *Ergi* also stated that procedural requirements under the right to life require that the loss of human life must be subject to an effective official investigation. *Kaya v Turkey*, para. 87; *Ergi v Turkey*, para. 82. See also *Hugh Jordan v UK* ; *McKerr v UK*; *Kelly and Others v UK*; *Shanaghan v UK*; *McShane v UK*; *Finucane v UK*.

84 *Kelly and Others v UK*, para. 94; *Ilhan v Turkey* ECHR 2000-VII, para. 63; *Ahmet Özkan and Others v UK* App no 21689/93, (ECtHR, 6 April 2004), para. 310; *Isayeva v Russia* App no 57950/00 (ECtHR, 6 July 2005) , para. 210;*Jaloud v the Netherlands*, para. 186.

85 In the *Ramsahai* case, the fact that the police officers involved in the shooting were not questioned until three days later was questioned by the Court. *Ramsahai and Others v the Netherlands*, paras. 399–431. In *Angelova and Iliev*, four years of a stalled investigation into an allegedly racially motivated killing was found to be ineffective. The Court stated that the requirement of 'promptness and reasonable expedition' applies especially where death is alleged to follow a racially motivated attack. *Angelova and Iliev v Bulgaria*, paras. 97–98.

86 *Yaşa v Turkey*; *Çakıcı v Turkey* [1999] ECHR 43; *Tanrikulu v Turkey*; *Mahmut Kaya v Turkey* ECHR 2000-III.

87 *Ramsahai and Others v the Netherlands*, paras. 324–325; *Hugh Jordan v UK* , para. 105ff; *Akpinar and Altun v Turkey* ECHR 2007-III; *Osmanoglu v Turkey* App no 48804/99 (ECtHR, 24 January 2008); *Beker v Turkey* App no 27866/03 (ECtHR, 24 March 2009).

88 In the *Finucane* case, the official investigation was found inadequate because it only identified the man who shot the victim, and failed to examine the evidence that suggested the involvement of members of Royal Ulster Constabulary. *Finucane v UK*.

89 *Ramsahai and Others v the Netherlands*, paras. 324–325; *Menesheva v Russia*, para. 67.

Therefore, an investigation must take reasonable steps to secure the evidence, including testimonies of witnesses, forensic evidence and, where appropriate, autopsy.[90] The domestic law must enable the authority to conduct an effective investigation.[91] The investigation must be carried out on the basis of 'objective evidence'.[92] Where the deprivation of life was caused by lethal force, it must be capable of determining whether the force used was justified in the prevailing circumstances.[93] It also means attempting to identify those responsible.[94] Under the second requirement, the investigation must be headed by, and carried out by, persons who are institutionally and practically independent from those implicated in events.[95] An investigation, and its results, must be subject

---

90 *Jaloud v the Netherlands*, para. 186; *Ahmet Özkan and Others v UK*, paras. 310, 312; *Isayeva v Russia*, paras. 200, 212. See also *Salman v Turkey*; *Tanrikulu v Turkey* and *Gül v Turkey* App no 22676/93 (ECtHR, 14 December 2000). It was required that non-military witnesses must be questioned promptly in order to satisfy the procedural requirement under the right to life. *Al-Skeini and Others v UK*, para. 171. In addition, '[t]he mere fact that an appropriate measure was not taken to prevent collusion (of suspect with other witnesses) amounts to a shortcoming in the adequacy of investigation'. *Jaloud v the Netherlands*, paras. 206–208. In *Ramsahai*, the authority's failure to test the hands of police officers for gunshot residue, the lack of photographs of the injuries, its failure to reconstruct what happened in the incident, and the lack of examination of the weapons and ammunitions of the two police officers who may have been involved in the incident, was found to be inadequate. *Ramsahai and Others v the Netherlands*. See also *Guiliani and Gaggio v Italy* ECHR-2011.

91 For example, in the *Hugh Jordan* case, the authorities lacked the power to compel a police officer to testify as a witness, and he refused to give evidence or to be cross-examined. The jury also lacked the power to give a verdict as to the lawfulness of the killing. This was found to be ineffective. *Hugh Jordan v UK*.

92 *Ergi v Turkey*.

93 *Kaya v Turkey*, para. 87; *Güleç v Turkey*, para. 78; *Ahmet Özkan and Others v UK*, para. 312; *Isayeva v Russia*, para. 212.

94 *Ahmet Özkan and Others v UK*, para. 312; *Isayeva v Russia*, para. 212; *Hugh Jordan v UK*, para. 107; *McKerr v UK*, para. 113. The Court also stated that 'an investigation sufficient to inform a judicial finding as to whether the force used was or was not justified in the circumstances is crucial to the exercise, by any State agent prosecuted in ensuing criminal proceedings, of the rights of the defence'. *Jaloud v the Netherlands*, para. 200; *Edwards v UK* Series A No 247 B, para. 36.

95 *Kelly and Others v UK*, para. 95; *Güleç v Turkey*, paras. 81–82; *Oğur v Turkey*, paras. 91–92; *Ergi v Turkey*, paras. 83–84. 'For an investigation into alleged unlawful killing by State agents to be effective, it is necessary for the persons responsible for and carrying out the investigation to be independent from those implicated in the events. This means not only a lack of hierarchical or institutional connection but also a practical independence'. *Al-Skeini and Others v UK*, para. 167; *Shanaghan v UK*, para. 104; *Jaloud v the Netherlands*, para. 186.

to sufficient public scrutiny.[96] This includes the adequate involvement of the victim's next-of-kin in the investigation, including sufficient access to the investigation, and to related information.[97] A violation can be found even where the investigation was not conducted in 'bad faith'.[98] Furthermore, the obligation to investigate remains applicable in difficult situations. This is the case both where the security situation is fragile, including in the context of armed conflict, as well as military occupation.[99] In one of the cases under *Al-Skeini*,

---

'[T]he independence, and hence the effectiveness, of an investigation into an allegedly unlawful killing may be called into question if the investigators and the investigated maintain close relations with one another'. *Ramsahai and Others v the Netherlands*, para. 337; *Jaloud v the Netherlands*, para. 188. In *Ramsahai*, the two police officers who were believed to be involved in the incident were held together with other police officers after the incident. This raised the question of whether the investigation was independent. *Ramsahai and Others v the Netherlands*, para. 337. *In Al-Skeini*, after finding that the report of the 'Special Investigation Branch investigation was sent to the Commanding Officer, who was responsible for deciding whether or not the case should be referred to the Army Prosecuting Authority', the Court considered that the fact that investigation branch did not have the discretion 'to decide for itself when to start and cease an investigation', and did 'not report 'in the first instance to the [Army Prosecuting Authority]' rather than to the military chain of command', meant that it was not sufficiently independent from the suspects to satisfy the requirements of Article 2. *Al-Skeini and Others v UK*, para. 172. See also *Reavey v UK* App no 34640/04 (ECtHR, 27 November 2007).

96 *Kelly and Others v UK*, para. 98. For the same reasons, it was found that 'there must be a sufficient element of public scrutiny of the investigation or its results to secure accountability in practice as well as in theory. The degree of public scrutiny required may well vary from case to case. In all cases, however, the victim's next-of-kin must be involved in the procedure to the extent necessary to safeguard his or her legitimate interests'. *Al-Skeini and Others v UK*, para. 167; *Jaloud v the Netherlands*, para. 186; *Ahmet Özkan and Others v UK*, paras. 311–314; *Isayeva v Russia*, paras. 211–214.

97 *Güleç v Turkey*, para. 82. This obligation arose as part of the right to a remedy. See also *Mojsiewiew v Poland* App no 11818/02 (ECtHR, 24 March 2009); *Gül v Turkey*, para. 93; *Öğur v Turkey*, para. 92.

98 *Ramsahai and Others v the Netherlands*. See also Rainey, Wicks and Ovey, *European Convention*, p. 162.

99 The ECtHR reached this conclusion in a number of cases that took place in Southern Turkey. In the *Kaya* case, the Turkish authorities claimed that they were not in sufficient control of the territory in which the crime had been committed, and so were unable to travel there to investigate. *Kelly and Others v UK*, para. 97; *Yaşa v Turkey*, paras. 102–104; *Çakıcı v Turkey*, paras. 80, 87, 106; *Tanrikulu v Turkey*, para. 109; *Mahmut Kaya v Turkey*, paras. 106–107. In *Al-Skeini*, it was ruled that this was also the case in the area under control of the State, but which fell outside its borders. *Al-Skeini and Others v UK*, para. 164. 'It is clear that where the death to be investigated under Article 2 occurs in circumstances of generalised violence, armed conflict or insurgency, obstacles may be placed in the way

it was found that the obligation to investigate also arises even where it was unclear who fired the fatal shot, killing the victim.[100]

Under the Inter-American system, the Court, in *Velasquez Rodriquez,* ruled that the State is obliged to 'carry out a serious investigation', and 'to identify those responsible'.[101] The Court held that the State's obligation to investigate covers every situation involving a violation of a right which is protected by the Convention,[102] even in difficult circumstances. The investigation must 'have an objective', and must be treated by the State as a legal duty, which is not dependent on the victim, or his/her next-of-kin, bringing a complaint or proving the facts.[103] If it did not take 'reasonable measures', the State would be responsible for failing to meet its obligation to protect an individual's rights through the exercise of due diligence. The Court observed, as did the HRC, that this obligation has a systemic nature. Thus, it involves the organization of:

> [...] governmental apparatus and, in general, all the structures through which public power is exercised, so that they are capable of juridically ensuring the free and full enjoyment of human rights.[104]

The absence of a pertinent explanation by the State was taken as indicating the absence of an investigation to establish responsibility. That was viewed in one case as amounting to a denial of justice, and to a breach of its obligation 'to properly investigate the death of the victims and take appropriate action against those found guilty'.[105] The requirements under this obligation should

---

of investigators and, as the United Nations Special Rapporteur has also observed [...], concrete constraints may compel the use of less effective measures of investigation or may cause an investigation to be delayed'. See also *Jaloud v the Netherlands,* para. 186; *Bazorkina v Russia* ECHR 2006-I, para. 121; *Georgia v Russia (II)* (Admissibility) App no 38263/08 (ECtHR, 19 December 2011). Even in such circumstances, the requirements to safeguard life under Article 2 entail that 'all reasonable steps must be taken to ensure that an effective, independent investigation is conducted into alleged breaches of the right to life'. *Kaya v Turkey,* paras. 86–92; *Ergi v Turkey,* paras. 82–85.

100 *Al-Skeini and Others v UK,* para. 164. It may also be worth noting that, in disappearance cases, the obligation to investigate continues until the whereabouts and fate of the missing person is accounted for. *Varnava and Others v Turkey* ECHR 2009, para. 185.

101 *Velásquez Rodríguez,* para. 174.

102 Ibid, para. 176.

103 Ibid, para. 177.

104 Ibid, para. 166.

105 *Marcellana and Gumanoy v The Philippines,* para. 7.4.

be considered in light of the relevant modern standards in comparative and international law to 'establish and apply effectively a criminal-law system'.[106]

3-2 *Obligation to Prosecute and Punish*

The second part of the obligation entails the prosecution and punishment of the suspect.

The HRC stated that, where an investigation reveals a violation of certain Covenant rights, State Parties are obliged to ensure that those responsible are brought to justice.[107] This duty arises *a fortiori* in cases where the perpetrators have been identified.[108] Courts in the European and Inter-American systems also largely support this position.[109] Recent cases before the IACtHR go further and suggest that, in cases of serious human rights violations, the victim or victim's relatives have the right to secure prosecution.[110] Where those responsible are identified through investigations, criminal proceedings should be brought against them, and appropriate criminal sanctions imposed.[111]

However, the obligation to prosecute is not absolute. Private individuals do not possess the right to demand that the State prosecute or, for that matter, convict a suspect.[112] Even the Convention against Torture does not stipulate that the obligation entails more than 'submit[ting] the case to its competent authorities for the purpose of prosecution'.[113] Thereafter, prosecutorial

106 *M C v Bulgaria*, para. 185.

107 UN Human Rights Committee, General Comment 31, para. 18; *Rajapakse v Sri Lanka*, para. 9.3; *El Hassy v Lybia*, para. 8; *Kimouche v Algeria*, para. 2.8.

108 *Kimouche v Algeria*, para. 3.5; *Chaparro v Colombia*, para. 8.8.

109 *Ramsahai and Others v the Netherlands*, para. 325; *Menson and Others v UK*; *Menesheva v Russia*; *Tanli v Turkey*, paras. 213, 217, 220, 238–239; *Ognyanova v Bulgaria* App no 46317/99 (ECtHR, 23 February 2006), paras. 169. 196, 199.

110 'Article 8 (1) [...] also includes the rights of the victim's relatives to judicial guarantees [...and] recognizes the right [...] to have [the crimes] effectively investigated, [...] those responsible prosecuted for committing said unlawful acts; [and] to have the relevant punishment, where appropriate, meted out'. *Blake v Guatemala*, paras. 96–97.

111 *Kaya v Turkey*, para. 87; *Velásquez Rodríguez*, para. 174.

112 *H C M A v The Netherlands* 3 Selected Decisions of the Human Rights Committee 19, para. 11.6; *S E v Argentina* 3 Selected Decisions of the Human Rights Committee 41, para. 5.5; *R A V N v Argentina*, para. 5.5; *Chaparro v Colombia*, para. 8.8; *Rajapakse v Sri Lanka*, para. 9.3. Under the European system, see, for example, *Öneryildiz v Turkey*, which clarifies that this right does not exist for the victim either under the right to a remedy or other provisions of the Convention.

113 *Questions relating to the Obligation to Prosecute or Extradite* (*Belgium v Senegal*) [2012] ICJ Rpt 422, para. 94. Under Article 7, para. 1. Even with the strongest form of the obligation to prosecute, as provided in the Geneva Conventions, it does not mean that prosecutors are

discretion may be exercised. This necessitates a consideration of whether the obligation to prosecute is reconcilable with prosecutorial discretion.

3-2-1 Prosecutorial Discretion

In many national legal systems, prosecutors have a discretionary power to decide whether or not to initiate criminal proceedings, and which specific charges(s) to lay against the suspected perpetrator(s).[114] The basis for prosecutorial discretion differs, including the extent of public interest in pursuing prosecution.[115] Public interest, in turn, is determined by various factors, including the strength of evidence, the prospect of conviction, the seriousness of the offence, the degree of harm or damage caused, the need to deter reoccurrence, the existence of an alternative mode of disposition, and its influence on the State's relations with other States.[116]

The extent of the limitations on prosecutorial discretion is not clearly set out. The obligation to prosecute is formulated in treaties as the obligation to submit a case to the relevant authority for the purpose of prosecution.[117] This formulation is intended to accommodate prosecutorial discretion.[118]

One limitation on prosecutorial discretion relates to the reasons for not prosecuting a suspect. Human rights bodies have found a violation in relation to the obligation to prosecute, when the reason for prosecutor's decision to not pursue prosecution of an alleged criminal conduct is not sufficiently set out.[119] In the *Herrera Rubio* case, the HRC found a violation on these grounds.[120] Where a prosecutor fails to consider all the relevant information in deciding to drop the prosecution of an alleged crime, this may be considered a violation of the obligation to prosecute. For example, the ECtHR found that a prosecutor's

deprived of their discretionary powers. The Geneva Conventions are silent on the extent to which prosecutorial discretion is permitted. Raphaël Van Steenberghe, 'The Obligation to Extradite or Prosecute Clarifying its Nature' (2011) 9 *Journal of International Criminal Justice* 1089, pp. 1108–1109.

114 Daniel D Ntanda Nsereko, 'Prosecutorial Discretion before National Courts and International Tribunals' (2005) 3 *Journal of International Criminal Justice* 124, p. 2.

115 Ibid, p. 5.

116 Ibid, pp. 5–6.

117 For example, the Convention against Torture and Other Cruel, Inhuman or Degrading Treatment or Punishment (adopted 10 December 1984, entered into force 26 June 1987) 1465 UNTS 85, Article 7–1.

118 Van Steenberghe, 'The Obligation to Extradite or Prosecute Clarifying its Nature', pp. 1108–1109.

119 *Herrera Rubio v Colombia*, paras. 6.1–6.4, 10.2–11.

120 *Herrera Rubio v Colombia*, para. 10.5.

decision to close an investigation was in violation of this obligation, because he failed to give consideration to the relevant factors.[121]

One ground that is frequently questioned by human rights bodies is where the prosecutor claims that his decision was based on a lack of evidence. This will be discussed below.

Lack of Evidence

Prosecutors often decide not to prosecute a case where there is a lack of sufficient evidence[122] and, correspondingly, little prospect of a conviction.[123] It is important to distinguish two potential reasons for there being a lack of evidence: first, following a thorough investigation, there may be insufficient evidence to prosecute; second, the lack of evidence may be the result of an inadequate investigation. The first constitutes a legitimate reason for not bringing a prosecution, as the duty to prosecute applies '*a fortiori* in cases in which the perpetrators of such violations have been identified'.[124] However, the second reason may constitute a violation of the obligation to investigate.[125] Where a thorough investigation was not conducted and, as a result, a prosecutor is left with insufficient evidence, the prosecutor appears to be required to order a further investigation.[126]

In addition, the State cannot base its decision not to prosecute on a lack of evidence, without demonstrating that it has tried to gather evidence. For example, in relation to a case of kidnapping and killing of individuals by armed group members, the Committee held that the State's submission that the

121 The authorities claimed that evidence of physical resistance was not found, leading to the closure of investigation. However, the Court found that the State was required to take other elements into consideration. *M C v Bulgaria*, paras. 61–65, 180, 185.

122 Van Steenberghe, 'The Obligation to Extradite or Prosecute Clarifying its Nature', p. 1109.

123 Nsereko, 'Prosecutorial Discretion before National Courts and International Tribunals', pp. 5–6.

124 *Chaparro v Colombia*, HRC, para. 8.8.

125 Separately, where there is sufficient evidence which has been uncovered by the investigation, but there is no subsequent prosecution, this may call into question the obligation to prosecute. *Questions relating to the Obligation to Prosecute or Extradite* (*Belgium v Senegal*), para. 94.

126 For example, in *Zheikov*, the Human Rights Committee concluded that the complainant's allegation of ill-treatment was not adequately investigated. This was because the Prosecutor's office closed the case due to insufficient evidence, despite the fact that the names of the duty officers who may have been involved in the alleged ill-treatment were given to the Prosecutor's office. *Zheikov v Russia*, paras. 2.2–2.3, 7. See also M.C. *v Bulgaria*; *Herrera Rubio*, para. 10.5.

prosecutorial authorities had decided not to initiate criminal proceedings due to a lack of sufficient evidence, without providing any specific information as to whether investigations were carried out in order to determine the responsibility of individuals identified by witnesses, was not accepted as a legitimate reason for relieving the State of its obligation.[127] This means that the burden of proof for demonstrating that the decision to not prosecute a case is based on the results of a thorough investigation rests with the State.

This leads to the conclusion that, where national legal systems permit, prosecutors have some discretion in deciding whether to prosecute a crime. However, if no prosecution is pursued, this could be incompatible with the obligation, depending on the reasons for this. Lack of evidence constitutes a legitimate reason for non-prosecution, provided that certain investigative standards have been met. That is an obligation of best effort. The submission by the Secretary-General, in respect of the *Reparations* case, argued that the breach of the duty to protect was based partly on the failure to take all the measures required by international law to bring the culprits to justice.[128] Therefore, it is possible to argue that there may be circumstances in which the duty to investigate alleged violations in good faith may bring about a *duty* to prosecute a certain person.[129]

However, where prosecutorial discretion is misused, there is often no means of challenging the prosecutor's decision within the domestic legal system.[130] The only recourse in these circumstances may be to lodge a complaint with a relevant human rights mechanism.

---

127 *Marcellana and Gumanoy v The Philippines*, para. 7.3.

128 The Secretary-General stated that another element that needs to be taken into account is the liability of the government for actions committed by irregular forces in the territory under Israeli control. Marjorie M Whiteman, *Digest of International Law*, vol 8 (US Government Printing Office 1967), p. 743.

129 Deirdre Fottrell, 'How much Due Diligence is Due? The Concept of 'Due Diligence' in the context of Human Rights Violations' (LLM thesis, University of Essex 2002), p. 21. It is, however, clear that there is no right on the part of the victim to demand that a certain suspect to be prosecuted. *H C M A v The Netherlands*, para. 11.6; *S E v Argentina*, para. 5.5; *R A V N v Argentina*, para. 5.5. See also *Chaparro v Colombia*, para. 8.8. As indicated, the IACtHR appears to take the position that this is the case in relation to serious human rights violations. See text accompanying n.110.

130 It was observed that common-law States permit a wide range of prosecutorial discretion. Gary Chan Kok Yew, 'Prosecutorial Discretion and the legal limits in Singapore' (2013) 25 *Singapore Academy of Law Journal* 15, p. 20.

3-2-2 *Obligation to Criminalize Certain Behaviour*

In some circumstances, the State with the obligation to prosecute may claim that it cannot bring criminal proceedings because the behaviour in question is not criminal under its domestic law. In *X and Y*, heard by the ECtHR, the issue was the impossibility of instituting criminal proceedings because of the gap in criminal law provisions dealing with having sexual intercourse with a mentally disabled person of a particular age, against his or her will. The Court ruled that this act must be criminalized, and the State's failure to do so was itself a violation of the victim's right to a private life.[131] Under the ICCPR, States are similarly obliged to criminalize torture and ill-treatment within the meaning of Article 7. States should indicate which provisions of their criminal law penalize breaches of this prohibition, and specify the penalties for such acts, regardless of the offender's status.[132] The obligation to criminalize certain behaviour forms part of the State's obligation to give effect to the rights enshrined in each treaty.[133]

4 The Obligation of the Host State to Investigate and Prosecute

The host State, being the State in which the act in question was committed, is the first State which has an obligation to investigate and prosecute. IHRL unquestionably binds a State in respect of the people who are within its territory, and subject to its jurisdiction.[134] The host State's obligations are only briefly

131 *X and Y v The Netherlands*, in particular, paras. 21–30. See also Akandji-Kombe, *Positive Obligations*, p. 16, where it is explained that the State's duty to provide individuals with sufficient protection to prevent their rights from being infringed entails the right to effective investigation and, more widely, the State's duty 'to enact criminal legislation which is both dissuasive and effective'.

132 UN Human Rights Committee, General Comment 20, para. 13.

133 As can be seen in General Comment 31, para. 4.

134 The ECtHR held that, 'jurisdiction' in respect of IHRL is different from that of criminal jurisdiction. It does not concern the allocation of competences among States. Kjetil Mujezinović Larsen, *The Human Rights Treaty Obligations of Peacekeepers* (Cambridge University Press 2012), pp. 180–181. The HRC stated that 'anyone within the power or effective control' of a State is within the State's 'jurisdiction'. UN Human Rights Committee, General Comment 31, para. 10. '[A]s a general rule, the notion of "jurisdiction" within the meaning of Article 1 of the Convention must be considered as reflecting the position under public international law'. *Affaire Gentilhomme, Schaff-Benhadji and Zerouki v France App nos 48205/99, 48207/99 and 48209/99* (ECtHR, 14 May 2002). That notion is "primarily" or "essentially" territorial'. *Banković and Others v Belgium and Others (Admissibility)* ECHR 2001-XII, paras. 59–61. *Assanidze v Georgia* ECHR 2004-II, para. 137. As the State in which

discussed, because it is unlikely to be able to investigate and prosecute, rather than unwilling to do so.

The biggest problem is that States and territories where UN Peace Operations are deployed are, by their very nature, struggling to build or rebuild State institutions.[135] It is also possible that the host State is unable to protect human rights adequately, including by conducting an appropriate investigation and prosecution,[136] due to its lack of effective control over its territory and/or the persons within it.[137] The question arises as to whether the host State has an obligation in such a situation to prosecute UN police officers' crimes. That is, is the host State's *de jure* sovereignty sufficient to engage its responsibility?[138]

There is no question regarding any negative obligations on the part of the host State, as UN police officers are by definition foreign police personnel deployed to the host State under UN command. The question is limited to what the host State is obliged to do in response to a crime committed by one person against another person in its jurisdiction.

It has been held that treaty obligations must not be interpreted in such a way as to 'impose an impossible or disproportionate burden' on States.[139] For example, recognizing the particular circumstances of Kosovo, that whilst it was theoretically part of Serbia, its territory was under the control of a UN interim administration (UNMIK), the HRC suggested that UNMIK to report to it instead.[140] However, this arrangement did not mean that the territorial State (Serbia) lacked any jurisdiction whatsoever within the meaning of ICCPR.[141] At a minimum, it constituted the realization that it would be impractical to

---

the act in question was committed, it is not disputed that the host State *can* prosecute a UN police officer for criminal acts committed during his service with a Peace Operation in the host State. This is a separate issue from that of immunity.

135 See Chapter 2, Section 1.

136 *Velásquez Rodríguez*, para. 177.

137 UN Human Rights Council, 'Report of the Special Representative of the Secretary-General on the issue of human rights and transnational corporations and other business enterprises, John Ruggie -Guiding Principles on Business and Human Rights: Implementing the United Nations "Protect, Respect and Remedy" Framework' (21 March 2011) UN Doc. A/HRC/17/31, Commentary to Principle 7.

138 John Cerone, 'Reasonable Measures in Unreasonable Circumstances: A Legal Responsibility Framework for Human Rights Violations in Post-Conflict Territories under UN Administration' in Nigel D White and Dirk Klaasen (eds), *The UN, Human Rights and Post-Conflict Situations* (Manchester University Press 2005), p. 67.

139 See amongst others, *Özgür Gündem v Turkey* ECHR 2000-III, para. 43.

140 UN Human Rights Committee, 'Concluding Observations of the Human Rights Committee: Serbia and Montenegro' (12 August 2004) UN Doc. CCPR/CO/81/SEMO, para. 3.

141 Larsen, *Treaty Obligations of Peacekeepers*, pp. 87–89.

require Serbia to make efforts to protect the human rights of people present in the territory of Kosovo, and to allow complaints to be brought against Serbia for its failure to protect their rights.[142]

The ECtHR has also addressed this issue. In *Ilaşcu*, it ruled that, 'where a Contracting State is prevented from exercising its authority over the whole of its territory by a constraining *de facto* situation', the territorial State's jurisdiction continues. Therefore, the territorial State is still required to do everything it can, within the limits of its authority, to guarantee the rights of the people in its territory. However, the Court also acknowledged that the scope of a State's jurisdiction may be reduced by the factual situation, and that it must be considered 'only in the light of the Contracting State's positive obligations towards persons within its territory'.[143] The Court emphasized that the State must endeavour to continue to guarantee the enjoyment of these rights, taking into account 'all the legal and diplomatic means available to it vis-à-vis foreign States and international organizations'.[144] In the *Assanidze* case, the Court explained the steps taken in defining what comes within the 'jurisdiction' of a Contracting State. Once the territory in question is determined to be an integral part of a State's territory, that State is presumed to be competent. The Court must then determine whether 'there is valid evidence to rebut that presumption'.[145]

The Constitutional Court of Bosnia and Herzegovina also affirmed that, 'the state in whose territory the violation of the rights occurred retains the responsibility to take appropriate steps to protect the victims', even if 'the violation is a result of the actions of representatives over whom the [...] state has 'no *de facto* control', and even if 'the threat against human rights came from an international organization'.[146] In the *Bilbija* case, the same Court ruled that the

142 Ibid, p. 234.

143 In another case, the ECtHR held that States must not make reservations in order to exclude the territorial applicability of the Convention, except in respect of dependent territories. *Matthews v UK* [1999] ECHR 12, para. 29. ECtHR, *Ilaşcu and Others v Moldova and Russia* ECHR 2004-VII, para. 333.

144 *Ilaşcu and Others v Moldova and Russia* , para. 333. The '*Ilaşcu* principle', as it is called in Larsen, *Treaty Obligations of Peacekeepers*, p. 202, is also referred to in *Assanidze v Georgia*, para. 146. The Court held that each Contracting State remains responsible for events occurring anywhere within its national territory. 'Even though it is not inconceivable that States will encounter difficulties in securing compliance with the rights guaranteed by the Convention in all parts of their territory, each State Party to the Convention nonetheless remains responsible for events occurring anywhere within its national territory'.

145 *Assanidze v Georgia*, para. 139.

146 *Bogdan Subotić* (2005) AP-696/04 (The Constitutional Court of Bosnia and Herzegovina, 23 September 2005) , paras. 51–52.

State had breached its obligations to ensure an effective legal remedy under Article 13 of ECHR, as no such remedy was available against individual decisions of the High Representative.[147]

Applying this reasoning to the Peace Operations context, it appears that, at least to some extent, the host State remains obliged to protect the rights of persons within its territory and subject to its jurisdiction, to the maximum extent possible. This might suggest that the host State has an obligation to demand a thorough investigation on the part of the UN and, if it cannot itself prosecute, to insist that the UN ensure that the sending State should do so.[148]

There may be exceptional cases, such as those host States in which there has long been a UN mission, and where State institutions function normally.[149] In such a case, the host State itself will be expected to investigate and, where appropriate, prosecute. The obligation to investigate may therefore vary according to the situation in, and capacity of, the host State at that time. Thus, the same host State may be found to have a different extent of obligation at different times.

This raises a number of questions. Where the UN functions as the transitional government in a host State, this State may be relieved of its IHRL obligations, at least to some extent. Another issue arises where a UN police officer, who has allegedly committed a crime, has returned to his sending State, because his tour of duty has ended, or he has been withdrawn from the host State by his sending State, or as a result of the UN's disciplinary proceedings.[150] Where the host State wishes to prosecute the UN police officer in these circumstances, it must request the suspect's transfer. Is the host State required to request such a transfer and, if so, under what circumstances? Moreover, if such a request is made, is there an obligation on the part of the sending State to comply? It is unclear whether transfer can only be done under an extradition treaty, or also under some other arrangement. Under the new MOU concerning FPU personnel, the sending State is required to cooperate with the host State, if the latter seeks to bring proceedings.[151] However, it is unclear what the obligation to

---

147 *Bilbija et al* (2006) AP-953/05 (Constitutional Court of Bosnia and Herzegovina, in the Appeal of Milorad Bilbija et al, 8 July 2006).

148 *Özgür Gündem v Turkey*, para. 43.

149 For example, Cyprus, or those States in which the UN aimed to secure the proper functioning of the State institutions, such as Kosovo, and Bosnia and Herzegovina.

150 On the possibility of a suspect being withdrawn from a mission by his sending State, and the possibility that his tour of duty ends before the investigation is complete, see Chapter 4, Sections 3-3-3 and 3–4. On the UN's disciplinary proceedings, see Chapter 4, Sections 2 and 3.

151 UN, FPU MoU, Article 7 quinquiens 7.18.

cooperate entails. It may be possible for an MoU to include arrangements for the transfer of a suspect.

5 The Sending State's Obligation

Due to the environment in which Peace Operations operate, the best possible forum for prosecution, in many cases, may be the sending State. The sending State is in a peculiar situation, as it is not the State in whose territory the crime has been committed, but it may be the State in whose territory the suspect is present. That is, the sending State does not control the territory in which the act was committed, nor does it 'control' victim of the crime, but it does have control over the suspect. By virtue of this, it also has at least partial control of any investigation into the crime. This requires a consideration of whether the scope and extent of the obligation to investigate and prosecute is different for the sending State than it would be if the crime was committed in its territory.

Where the territory in which the crime was committed is located outside the State's borders, but is under its *de facto* 'control' or 'authority',[152] all of the State's obligations under both treaty and customary law apply.[153] This means the obligation to investigate and prosecute applies to the extent of its control.[154]

152 This means that a certain degree of control over a territorial space is asserted by the State concerned.

153 In two cases, the ICJ held that the occupying State is bound by the entirety of human rights' treaties and customary obligations. The Court further made it clear that the occupying power is responsible both for not violating international obligations, and for preventing violations by other actors. *Legal Consequences of the Construction of a Wall in the Occupied Palestinian Territory* (Advisory Opinion) [2004] ICJ Rep 316; *Armed Activities on the Territory of the Congo* (*DRC v Uganda*) [2005] ICJ Rep 168. The ECtHR has also heard cases in which a Contracting State was in control of the territory of another State. In the *Loizidou* ruling, it held that Turkey was in 'effective control over the territory', and that, in such a situation, it was not necessary to establish the existence of effective control over the specific conduct by the State's authorities. *Loizidou v Turkey* Series A No 310. The *Cyprus v Turkey* and the *Ilaşcu* cases followed the *Louzidou* decision, and elaborated on the requirement that the troops contributed decisively to the survival and existence of the local authorities. *Cyprus v Turkey* ECHR 2001-IV; *Ilaşcu and Others v Moldova and Russia*. The *Bankovic* case essentially re-iterated the *Louzidou* case, limiting the basis of jurisdiction to the fact of control over the relevant territory. In *Bankovic*, the Court held that the Convention only applies within the territories of Contracting States, even in an extraterritorial context. That interpretation was rebutted in later cases. The *Issa* case clarified that the Convention is applicable beyond the regional limits of Europe, if a Contracting State is exercising *de facto* control over the territory in question.

154 *Al-Skeini and Others v UK*.

There is clear case-law obliging States to investigate the killing of an individual abroad, in cases where the crime concerned was committed by a State agent. However, it is unclear whether the obligation to conduct an investigation in these particular circumstances only arises in the place where the killing took place, or also arises as an obligation to continue the investigation when the suspect is back in its territory.[155] It is possible that the scope of this obligation differs depending on the right affected.

To date, no human rights body has examined a case that deals with the State's obligation to bring criminal proceedings against its national for a criminal act committed abroad, where that national is not a State agent.[156] This does not mean that the obligation does not exist. The HRC's General Comment does not exclude the possibility that the same obligation exists in such situations. In particular, where a crime is of a cross-border nature, such as drugs-trafficking, human-trafficking, sex-tourism involving a minor, or transnational terrorism-related crimes, the protection would be meaningless if the obligation to respond to a crime did not exist for crimes committed abroad.

In fact, the global fight against impunity for serious crimes arguably supports the idea that the sending State has an obligation in this respect. With regard to crimes committed by the UN police in Peace Operations, the argument that supports the fight against impunity works in favour of finding that there is an obligation on the part of the sending State. This argument is based on the nature of these crimes, which are of international concern.[157] Because of the nature of the roles played by the UN police in UN Peace Operations, and the potential impact that serious crimes can have on UN missions, these crimes should arguably be of international concern, although certainly not to the same extent as international crimes. In addition, UN police officers are not

155 Two cases that dealt with the obligation to investigate, in relation to killings by State agents in Iraq, only concerned the obligation to conduct an effective investigation in Iraq. The Court did not discuss whether or not the obligation requires the investigation to continue after the suspects were back in their States of nationality (UK and the Netherlands respectively). *Jaloud v the Netherlands*; *Al-Skeini and Others v UK*.

156 One of the cases within *Al-Skeini* involved a situation where the person who fired the fatal shot was not identified. This means that the shot could have been fired by a private individual. Care needs to be taken in considering this case, as the situation was said to be under the respondent State's control, albeit it outside that State's territory. *Al-Skeini and Others v UK*.

157 UNGA Res 2840 (XXVI) (18 December 1971) UN Doc. A/RES/2840 (XXVI); UNGA Res 3074 (XXVIII) (3 December 1973) UN Doc. A/RES/3074 (XXVIII); UN ECOSOC Res 1989/65 (24 May 1989) UN Doc. ECS/RES/1989/65, principle 18.

only nationals of their sending State,[158] but are also qualified to serve as UN police by virtue of their previous status as State agents.[159] The sending State retains disciplinary authority and responsibility for serving police officers.[160] Most of them are selected to join a UN mission by their sending States.[161] This, along with the fact that the environment in the host State means that they are unlikely to be prosecuted there, may make it arguable that the sending State has an additional obligation to respond to crimes committed by its police officers. This is especially the case if, due to completing his service, or as a result of UN disciplinary proceedings, the suspect has returned to the sending State. If the suspect is back in the sending State, virtually no other State can prosecute the crime. Avoiding impunity in these circumstances would require the sending State to act.

Therefore, it is arguable that sending States have certain obligations to respond to crimes committed by their UN police, based on their obligation to fight against impunity.

6 Special Circumstances Pertaining to Formed Police Units (FPUs)

As already stated, the question as to the attribution of the conduct of a UN police officer to the sending State does not normally arise.[162] There may, however, be some exceptional cases in which certain conduct by FPU members can be attributed to their sending States.[163] This is relevant only insofar as it affects the obligation to respond to that act. The determination of the attribution of UN police conduct to the UN and/or the State is governed by Article 7 of the Draft Articles on the Responsibility of International Organizations (DARIO).[164]

158 See Chapter 2, Section 3-1.

159 However, UN police officers do not perform their UN duties as State agents. See Section 1. On the criteria for the selection of UN police, see Chapter 2, Section 3-3-1.

160 Chapter 2, Section 3-3; Chapter 4, Section 2; Chapter 5, Section 2.

161 This is with the exception of a few individual UN police officers, who applied directly to the UN, and were selected by it. See Chapter 2, Section 3-3-1.

162 See Section 1.

163 The distinction between direct and indirect responsibility is one of terminologies in the Law of Responsibility. It corresponds better with the common human rights terminologies of negative and positive obligations, or the obligation to respect, protect and fulfil. See Larsen, *Treaty Obligations of Peacekeepers*, p. 121.

164 Article 7 states that '[t]he conduct of an organ of a State [...] that is placed at the disposal of another international organization shall be considered under international law an act of the latter organization if the organization exercises effective control over that conduct'.

The decisive question is who has effective control over particular conduct.[165] The 'effective control' test is not applied to the overall conduct of the organ or the personnel, but rather to each specific act, in order to determine to whom the conduct is attributable.[166] The 'effective control' test is a factual question, dealing with the circumstances surrounding the conduct in question, and not the legal status of UN police personnel.

As national military contingents are governed by the same Article, some ideas can be borrowed from how cases concerning military contingents have

---

UNGA, 'Draft Articles on the Responsibility of International Organizations, as appears in International Law Commission Report on the Work of its Sixty-Third Session (26 April to 3 June and 4 July to 12 August 2011), para. 87' (26 April to 3 June and 4 July to 12 August 2011) UN Doc. A/66/10, Article 7, (hereinafter 'DARIO'). The conduct of UN police personnel may be governed by two DARIO articles depending on the factual link between the personnel and the sending State. If the personnel are fully seconded, the rule dealing with the attribution of the conduct of such personnel is governed by Article 6, and their conduct is attributed only to the UN. (Commentaries, Comment (1) to Article 7.) Article 6 deals with the 'organ' of the organization, and this includes 'agents', who are 'charged by an organ of the organization with carrying out, or helping to carry out, one of its functions – in short, any person through whom it acts', regardless of his/her official status. (*Reparation for Injuries Suffered in the Service of the United Nations* (Advisory Opinion) [1949] ICJ Rep 174.) However, if seconded personnel retain a link with their seconding State, Article 7 applies. It is claimed that a State's security organs are unlikely to completely surrender this link with their home State (see Aurel Sari, 'UN Peacekeeping Operations and Article 7 ARIO: The Missing Link' (2012) 9 *International Organizations Law Review* 77, pp. 79–80). This is despite the UN's guidelines which state that UN police officers are not supposed to receive instructions from any other source than the Organization itself. UN DPKO, 2007 Guidelines, p. 6. See also the DPKO/DFS policy on FPU suggesting three command models. In all cases, FULLCOM (full command) is with PCCs. See para. 47. Taking all these into consideration, it appears more appropriate to apply Article 7. UN DPKO/DFS, 'Policy (Revised) on Formed Police Units in United Nations Peacekeeping Operations' (1 March 2013) UN Doc. Ref.2009/32. This is the case for the FPUs, as their members hold the same nationality under the national command. See Chapter 2, Section 1-6.

165 UNGA, 'Draft Articles on the Responsibility of International Organizations with Commentaries, as appears in International Law Commission Report on the Work of its Sixty-Third Session (26 April to 3 June and 4 July to 12 August 2011), para. 88' (26 April to 3 June and 4 July to 12 August 2011) UN Doc. A/66/10, Commentary (8) to Article 7, (hereinafter 'DARIO with Commentaries').

166 The ILC, in its Commentaries, also cite scholarly interpretation of this 'effective control' test. See Commentary (8) to Article 7. In addition to the scholarship referred to in the Commentaries, see Christopher Leck, 'International Responsibility in United Nations Peacekeeping Operations: Command and Control Arrangements and the Attribution of Conduct', 10 *Melbourne Journal of International Law* 346 (2009), p. 348.

dealt with attribution. In principle, the UN assumes 'exclusive control' over military contingents in UN operations, and thus assumes responsibility for their acts.[167] However, this assumption is rebuttable where military contingents are found to have persisted in seeking, or acting on, orders received from their sending States.[168] The cases before the Dutch courts, relating to the Srebrenica massacre, indicate the unsettled approaches in the determination of attribution of conduct.[169]

---

167 UNGA, DARIO with Commentaries, Comments to (5) – (6) to Article 7.

168 For example, several national contingents making up the UNOSOM II force were found to be 'totally outside the command and control of the United Nations'. UNSC, 'Report of the Commission of Inquiry Established Pursuant to Security Council Resolution 885 (1993) to Investigate Armed Attacks on UNOSOM II Personnel Which Led to Casualties Among Them' (1 June 1994) UN Doc. S/1994/653, paras. 243–244.

169 This case concerned the responsibility of the Dutch contingent (Dutchbat) in UNPROFOR. On one hand, the District Court considered that their acts and omissions 'should be attributed strictly, as a matter of principle, to the United Nations' (*Nuhanovic v The State of the Netherlands* Case no 265615/HA ZA 06–1671 (DC Hague, 10 September 2008), English translation available at <http://zoekenrechtspraaknl> Accessed 29 December 2014), and that the assumption could only be overturned if 'Dutchbat was instructed by the Dutch authorities to ignore UN orders or to go against them, and Dutchbat behaved in accordance with this instruction' (ibid, para. 4.14.1). The Court found no such evidence. On the other hand, the Court of Appeal focused on the criterion of 'effective control' in relation to the particular circumstances of the case, and held that the State was responsible for turning Bosnian Muslim men away from its compound, effectively handing them over to Bosnian Serb forces. They were then massacred. The Court looked into whether the State would have been able to prevent that conduct after finding that the Dutch authorities did not give a specific instruction which was contrary to UN orders. In the course of examination, the Court also set out the possibility that there could be the dual attribution of conduct to the Netherlands and the UN. It thus considered the existence of 'effective control' by the former, but without considering the same by the latter. *Nuhanovic v The State of the Netherlands* Case no 265618 HA ZA 06–1672 (Court of Appeal in the Hague, 5 July 2011), English translation available at <http://zoekenrechtspraaknl> Accessed 29 December 2014, para. 5.9. 'The question whether the State had "effective control" over the conduct of Dutchbat which Mustafic et al. consider to be the basis for their claim, must be answered in view of the circumstances of the case. This does not only imply that significance should be given to the question whether that conduct constituted the execution of a specific instruction, issued by the UN or the State, but also to the question whether, if there was no such specific instruction, the UN or the State had the power to prevent the conduct concerned. Moreover, the Court adopts as a starting point that the possibility that more than one party has "effective control" is generally accepted, which means that it cannot be ruled out that the application of this criterion results in the possibility of attribution to more than one party. For this reason the Court will only examine if the State exercised "effective control" over the alleged conduct and will not answer the question whether the

UN also had "effective control"'. Consequently, the State was held responsible. The Supreme Court upheld the Court of Appeal's ruling. *The State of the Netherlands (Ministry of Defence and Ministry of Foreign Affairs) v Hasan Nuhanovic* (Judgement of 6 September 2013) Supreme Court of the Netherlands. Note also that, in response to the State's argument that the mission had already failed at the time, and that the State thus was not in 'effective control' over the conduct, the Court responded that the fact that Dutchbat could not exert any influence outside the compound did not 'detract from the fact that the State had effective control over Dutchbat's conduct in the compound'. *The State of the Netherlands (Ministry of Defence and Ministry of Foreign Affairs) v Hasan Nuhanovic* Case no 12/03324 LZ/TT (Judgement of 6 September 2013) Supreme Court of the Netherlands, English translation available at: <http://wwwrechtspraaknl/Organisatie/Hoge-Raad/OverDeHogeRaad/publicaties/Documents/12%2003324pdf> Accessed 10 March 2015. Note that the Commentaries state that it is also possible that States are co-responsible for the conduct of the UN, in a subsidiary manner. (UNGA, DARIO with Commentaries, Comment (6) to Article 3 of DARIO states, for example, 'an international organization may have cooperated with a State in the breach of an obligation imposed on both'.) This part refers to parallel responsibility: if it directs and controls the UN in the commission of the act in question (Draft Article 59), aids or assists (Draft Article 58), coerces (Draft Article 60), or avoids its own obligation by causing the Organization to commit the act (Draft Article 61), or if it has accepted responsibility for that act (Draft Article 62). To hold States accountable for their voting decisions or similar acts in the administration of international organisations may be one possible method for increasing the available remedies. [Council of Europe, *Accountability of International Organisations for Human Rights Violations* (Committee on Legal Affairs and Human Rights, Doc 13370, 2013), para. 74, (hereinafter 'COE Accountability Report')]. This form of accountability would seem to be most legitimate in cases where a State voted for a programme that involves what could be seen as amounting to a *prima facie* human rights violation in and of itself, such as the SC sanctions regime (ibid, para. 74). It is also noted that, if one considers the lack of criminal prosecution for a serious crime, such as the conduct in question, and not the serious crime itself, this would be a matter in which the relevant State would be responsible for its own conduct (non-prosecution), rather than incurring subsidiary responsibility. The next level or aspect of State responsibility occurs when States allow the International Organization to commit the conduct in question as a result of their lack of vigilance over the Organization's conduct. This approach was taken in several cases at the ECtHR. This obligation requires States to ensure that the transfer of competences does not result in the infringement of the rights and freedoms set out in the Convention. For example, in *Matthews*, the Court observed that, '[t]he Convention does not exclude the transfer of competences to international organisations provided that Convention rights continue to be "secured". Member States' responsibility therefore continues even after such a transfer'. (*Matthews v UK*, para. 32. See also *Etienne Tête v France* Series A No 54; *M & Co v Germany* Series A No 64.) This type of responsibility is not so much about the direct responsibility of the State over the conduct as such, but more about the State's conduct, that is, its lack of vigilance over the International Organization's conduct, and is thus of greater relevance when considering the responsibility of States in their roles as member States of the

UN. However, if, for example, a State sends a large number of police personnel to a UN mission whilst knowing that it engages in the systematic infringement of human rights law, such as arbitrary arrest and detention, or the denial of fair trial rights to those accused of committing crimes, there may be the space to argue that the State can be held responsible for 'allowing' the UN to commit the conduct in question. However, note the 'Mothers of Srebrenica' case, in which the conduct was found to be attributed to the UN, but that the UN was protected by immunity. *Mothers of Srebrenica Association v State of the Netherlands* Case no 10/04437 EV/AS (Supreme Court of the Netherlands, 13 April 2012), English translation available at: <http://wwwrechtspraaknl/Organisatie/Hoge-Raad/Supreme-court/Summaries-of-some-important-rulings-of-the-Supreme-Court/Pages/Ruling-Dutch-Supreme-Court-Mothers-of-Srebrenicaaspx> Accessed 1 January 2015. Several cases have raised the issue of the attribution of conduct of a national military contingent operating under the UN flag, at both human rights and domestic courts. *Behrami and Behrami v France and Sarmati v France, Germany and Norway* (Admissibility) App nos 71412/01, 78166/01 (ECtHR, 2 May 2007) were the first cases to be heard by the ECtHR in this regard. The Court did not discuss the possibility of the dual attribution of conduct to the UN and the sending States, even though dual attribution is acknowledged by the ILC. (Note that the ILC's Articles appear to assume that conduct is normally attributed to one entity. UNGA, DARIO with Commentaries, Commentaries to ARIO Article 7. For example, in (4), it states, 'The criterion for attribution of conduct *either to* the contributing State *or* organization or to the receiving organization is based according to article 7 on the factual control that is exercised over the specific conduct taken by the organ or agent placed at the receiving organization's disposal' [emphasis added]. See also: Sari, 'UN Peacekeeping Operations and Article 7 ARIO: The Missing Link'). However, it is also acknowledged that the same conduct can be simultaneously attributed to the Organization and State(s). UNGA, DARIO with Commentaries, Comment (7) to Article 3, ARIO Commentaries, states, 'Another example may be that of conduct which is simultaneously attributed to an international organization and a State and which entails the international responsibility of both the organization and the State'. Instead, it only considered that the decisive test for attribution is 'ultimate authority and control', and found that the Security Council retained such ultimate authority and control, while 'operational command only was delegated' to the contingents of the respondent States. (*Behrami and Behrami v France and Sarmati v France, Germany and Norway*, para. 133.) It thus found that the conduct in question was attributable to the UN alone. This approach was followed in subsequent cases at the same Court, which dealt with the attribution of conduct by national contingents at UNMIK. For example, *Kasumaj v Greece* (Admissibility) App no 6974/05 (ECtHR, 5 July 2007); *Gajić v Germany* (Admissibility) App no 31446/02 (ECtHR, 28 August 2007). This approach has been open to criticism. Kjetil Mujezinović Larsen, 'Attribution of Conduct in Peace Operations: The 'Ultimate Authority and Control' Test' (2008) 19 *European Journal of International Law* 509, pp. 521–522; Marko Milanović and Tatjana Papić, 'As Bad as it Gets: The European Court of Human Rights's Behrami and Saramati Decision and General International Law' (2009) 58 *International and Comparative Law Quarterly* 267, pp. 283–286; Aurel Sari, 'Jurisdiction and International Responsibility in Peace Support Operations: The Behrami and Saramati Cases' (2008) 8 *Human Rights Law Review* 151,

Following the same logic, there remains a limited possibility that certain conduct could be attributed to the sending State, depending on its level of involvement.[170] This could occur if the conduct is carried out in response to an explicit order by the sending State. In addition, some sending States have explicitly acknowledged that their police personnel carry their human rights

---

p. 164; Francesco Messineo, 'The House of Lords in Al-Jedda and Public International Law: Attribution of Conduct to Un-Authorized Forces and the Power of the Security Council to Displace Human Rights' (2009) 56 *Netherlands International Law Review* 35, pp. 39–43. The ECtHR appears to have failed to apply the factual 'effective control' test as visualized by the ILC. Compared to the approach the same Court has taken to other cases dealing with the attribution of conduct of non-state actors to the State, as discussed above, in which it emphasized the factual link between the actor and the State, this seems peculiar. This may be better explained in terms of the Court's attempt to refrain from ruling on matters involving the UN (Larsen, *Treaty Obligations of Peacekeepers*, p. 435). The *Al-Jedda* complaints concerned the detention of a person by British troops, which were operating in Iraq following authorization by Security Council resolution 1546 (2004). The UK's House of Lords found that the detention was attributable to the UK rather than to the UN, because the conduct of the British troops was not carried out under the 'effective command and control' of the UN. *R (on the application of Al-Jedda) (FC) v Secretary of State for Defence* (Sep Op Bingham LJ) [2007] UKHL 58, paras. 22–24; Opinion of Baroness Hale of Richmond, para. 124; Opinion of Lord Carswell, para. 131. Note, however, that the Opinions compare the situations surrounding *Behrami* and *Saramati* in Kosovo to the case in question in Iraq, reasoning that the situations differ. The issue of internment was then heard by the ECtHR, which found the conduct attributable to the UK, not the UN, because the Security Council had 'neither effective control nor ultimate authority and control over the acts and omission of troops', and that the internment 'took place within a detention facility [...] controlled exclusively by British forces'. On this basis, it found that the applicant was 'within the authority and control of the United Kingdom throughout his detention'. (*Al-Jedda v UK* [2011] ECHR 1092, paras. 84–85.)

170 Although in a majority of cases, the conduct of UN police personnel is attributed to the UN. This is because UN police personnel technically only work with the UN's interests in view, and are not supposed to receive instructions from their own governments. UN DPKO, 'Undertaking and Declaration by Experts on Mission: UN Police Officer/Corrections Officer/Military Observers/Military Liaison Officer' UN Doc. (on file with author); UN DPKO, 2007 Guidelines, Annex 3. See also UNGA, 'Draft Articles on Responsibility of States for Internationally Wrongful Acts, with Commentaries, in the Report of the International Law Commission, 53rd Session (23 April – 1 June and 2 July – 10 August 2001), para. 77' (23 April – 1 June and 2 July – 10 August 2001) UN Doc. A/56/10. The commentary to Article 6 explains that, for conduct to be attributed to the receiving State, it must be 'under its exclusive direction and control, rather than on instructions from the sending State'. If applied analogously to the UN police, this would mean that the UN police conduct in question must have been carried out under the exclusive direction and control of the UN, without the UN police receiving any related instructions from their sending State.

obligations with them when they are assigned to international operations, including UN Peace Operations.[171] This conduct would amount to a violation of the State's negative human rights obligations. Where a negative obligation is infringed, the extent of the obligation to investigate and prosecute the responsible individual(s) may be more onerous.[172]

It should be noted that the agreements entered into between the UN and sending States in relation to FPUs provide that sending States agree to impose criminal sanctions on individual FPU officers who commit criminal acts in cases where the host State does not do so, for whatever reason.[173] The wording of these agreements may be influenced by the potential IHRL obligations of the sending States, even though these agreements do not cite IHRL.

7 Does Immunity have any Impact on a State's Obligation to Prosecute?

To the extent that circumstances oblige either or both the host and sending States to investigate and, where appropriate, prosecute, immunity may prevent this from happening.

Three separate issues could arise in relation to the impact of immunity on the scope of the obligation to prosecute. The first is where the State prosecutor rightly or wrongly thinks that the suspect has been granted immunity by the UN, and decides not to prosecute the suspect on this basis. The second issue concerns where the UN inappropriately grants immunity to a suspect. In this situation, may/must a State ignore this immunity and prosecute the

171 Italy has confirmed that the ICCPR applies to the acts of Italian military and police officers stationed abroad, whether committed in the context of peace or armed conflict. UN Human Rights Committee, 'Concluding Observations to Italy's Fifth Periodic Report' (24 April 2006) UN Doc. CCPR/C/ITA/CO/5. Germany has affirmed that the ICCPR applies to persons subject to its jurisdiction in situations where its troops or police forces operate abroad, especially in the context of peace operations. Larsen, *Treaty Obligations of Peacekeepers*, pp. 205–206. Note, however, that this does not mean that the sending State will be held responsible for the conduct in question, as the issue of attribution must first be considered.

172 For example, in relation to the right to life, having the 'duty to prevent, investigate and punish violations of the right to life by private actors' is arguably 'more onerous when evidence indicates that government officials are involved', Sarah Joseph, Jenny Schultz and Melissa Castan, *The International Covenant on Civil and Political Rights*, vol 386 (Oxford University Press 2000), pp. 128–130.

173 Model MOU, Article 7 quinquiens, 7.22. UN, FPU MoU, Article 7 quinquiens, 7.19.

suspect? The third issue arises where the UN has waived a suspect's immunity, but where the suspect is challenging the State's proceedings against him, on the basis that immunity should not have been waived.

In relation to the first issue, one of the factors a prosecutor must take into account when deciding whether to prosecute a crime is immunity. However, does immunity provide a legitimate basis on which to exercise prosecutorial discretion? No case has yet been heard concerning a situation where there has been a lack of criminal proceedings on the basis of a grant of immunity. The *Al-Adsani* case has come closest to considering this issue. In this case, there was a *civil* claim for compensation for torture, which was blocked by sovereign immunity.[174] In *Germany v. Italy,* the ICJ held that, because Germany had immunity, the Italian courts had breached the jurisdictional immunity of the State by hearing civil cases in which victims sought compensation from Germany in relation to war crimes.[175] Thus, there appears to be strong evidence that States would be not be in breach of their IHRL obligations if they did not bring criminal proceedings against a suspect who had been granted immunity.

A second issue concerns the situation in which the UN inappropriately grants immunity to a suspect, and does not waive it even though it was inappropriate to have given it in the first place.[176] In these circumstances, it is not clear whether States must give effect to this immunity, and thus refrain from bringing criminal proceedings, or whether they can or must ignore it, and bring a prosecution against the suspect. In this regard, the ICJ's decision, that the Secretary-General's finding in relation to immunity 'can only be set aside for the most compelling reasons' by national courts,[177] appears to indicate that, in most circumstances, national courts are obliged to give effect to immunity asserted by the UN. However, if the UN invokes immunity for a serious crime committed outside official functions, or possibly in relation to an international crime, this may satisfy the 'most compelling reasons' test.[178]

The third issue could arise where the UN decides to waive a defendant's immunity. It should be remembered that waiver assumes that the act would

174 *Al-Adsani v UK* ECHR 2001-XI.

175 *Jurisdictional Immunities of the State* (*Germany v Italy: Greece intervening*) (Judgement) [2012] ICJ Rep 99.

176 The UN may grant immunity inappropriately either through overstepping the bounds of a source of immunity through incorrectly interpreting this source, or because it has wrongly determined that the conduct fell within the suspect's official functions. See Chapter 6, Section 2.

177 *Difference Relating to Immunity from Legal Process of a Special Rapporteur of the Commission on Human Rights* (Advisory Opinion) [1999] ICJ Rep 62, para. 61.

178 See Chapter 6, Section 1-5-1.

otherwise be covered by immunity. If UN personnel have a right to immunity in order to permit them to deliver their functions, and given that UN personnel must be able to rely solely on the UN's protection,[179] this raises the question as to whether a defendant is permitted to challenge the decision to remove his or her immunity.

Having analysed this obligation in relation to States, this chapter will now examine if the UN has any obligation to investigate and prosecute crimes committed by the UN police and, if so, what the scope of this obligation would be.

8 Does the UN have an Obligation to Investigate and Prosecute Crimes Committed by UN Police Officers?

In order for the UN to have a specific procedural obligation, first it is necessary to establish whether or not the UN has such an obligation under IHRL.

Even if the UN is found to have obligations under IHRL, the UN clearly cannot be expected to deliver the same obligations as States, because it does not have the same relationship with the individuals whose rights it is supposed to protect.[180] However, in some Peace Operations, the UN has some control over the local population. In particular, in the case of transitional administrations, the relationship between the UN and the local population is the same as between a State and its nationals. Because of this, the UN has virtually the same obligations as States in this particular circumstance.[181]

179 *Reparations*, para. 183.

180 A key element of IHRL is the relationship between State power and that State's responsibility to those under its jurisdiction. Scott P Sheeran, 'A Constitutional Moment?: United Nations Peacekeeping in the Democratic Republic of Congo' (2011) 8 *International Organizations Law Review* 55, p. 79, (hereinafter 'Constitutional Moment').

181 There were two transitional administrations where the UN assumed all governmental functions: UNMIK and UNTAET. See Chapter 2, Section 1-5. In 2002, the position of Kosovo Ombudsperson was established to receive complaints concerning any abuse of authority by 'the Interim Civil Administration and any emerging local institutions and any non-state actors claiming or exercising authority', UNGA, 'Report of the Secretary-General on the United Nations Interim Administration Mission in Kosovo' (12 July 1999) UN Doc. S/1999/779, para. 89; UNMIK Regulation no 2000/38 of 30 June 2000 on the Establishment of the Ombudsperson Institution in Kosovo. The Ombudsperson looked into UNMIK's response to allegations of ill-treatment by UN police personnel. Recalling that an investigation into ill-treatment allegations must be capable of leading to the identification and punishment of those responsible, and considering that UNMIK's response merely amounted to 'steps to discipline' the publically unidentified personnel without any criminal proceedings taking place, the Ombudsperson found that this response fell

8-1 *Applicability of IHRL to the UN*

The UN is not party to any human rights treaties. Thus, for the UN to have any human rights obligations, these must derive from other sources. There are two main arguments that support the contention that the UN is bound by IHRL. The first relies on the UN Charter, whilst the second is based on customary law.[182] These will be discussed in turn.[183]

---

short of meeting the required human rights standards. *Shefqet Maliqi, against the United Nations Mission in Kosovo* (UNMIK) Registration no 361/01, (the Kosovo Ombudsperson, 13 March 2002). The Human Rights Advisory Panel (HRAP) in Kosovo (established by UNMIK Regulation no 2006/12 of 23 March 2006 on the Establishment of the Human Rights Advisory Panel) also heard many complaints alleging violations of ECHR in relation to the right to property. In *Shaip Canhasi,* the Panel found that UNMIK had violated the right to life due to lack of an effective investigation into the killing of the complainant's wife. *Shaip Canhasi v UNMIK* Case no 004/08 (The Human Rights Advisory Panel, 15 July 2008). In *Jočić,* the HRAP found that UNMIK had violated Article 2 and 3 of the ECHR by failing to adequately investigate the disappearance and subsequent death of a Kosovo Serb civilian. *Svetlana Jočić v UNMIK* Case no 34/09 (Human Rights Advisory Panel, 23 April 2013). See Amnesty International, *Serbia (Kosovo): UNMIK Legacy – The Failure to Deliver Justice and Reparations to the Relatives of the Abducted* (EUR 70/009/2013, 2013), Kosovo: UNMIK's Legacy, where the failure to deliver justice and reparation to the relatives of the abducted is discussed. Another argument specifically developed in relation to transitional administrations is that the UN 'steps into' fulfil the human rights obligations of the host State. Karen Kenny, *UN Accountability for its Human Rights Impact: Implementation through Participation* (Manchester University Press 2005), p. 441. The UN itself acknowledges the need to comply with the host State's human rights obligations. The HOM [Head of Mission] shall ensure that the peace operation's performance and impact in integrating human rights is monitored, taking into consideration country-specific human rights indicators, including compliance with international human rights obligations by the host country. UN OHCHR/DPKO/DPA/DFS, 'Policy on Human Rights in United Nations Peace Operations and Political Missions ' (1 September 2011) UN Doc. Ref. 2011.20, para. 39.

182 There are other arguments regarding the basis on which the UN is bound by IHRL. These arguments are: obligations deriving from the nature of human rights (Andrew Clapham, *Human Rights Obligations of Non-State Actors* (Oxford University Press 2006), p. 87; Frédéric Mégret and Florian Hoffman, 'UN as a Human Rights Violator – Some Reflections on the United Nations Changing Human Rights Responsibilities' (2003) 25 *Human Rights Quarterly* 314, p. 317, (hereinafter 'UN as Human Rights Violator'); obligations deriving from States own membership of the UN; and being bound by virtue of the IHRL obligations of the host State.

183 The strongest case for making the argument that the UN has IHRL obligations is where the UN functions as the transitional administration. In these circumstances, it is generally uncontested that the UN would be fully bound by IHRL. Cerone, 'Reasonable Measures', p. 60; Sheeran, 'Constitutional Moment', p. 79. The ECtHR has taken the position that where

8-1-1 The UN is Bound by IHRL on the Basis of the UN Charter

The *Reparations* case establishes that the UN's rights and duties are dependent on its purposes and functions, as specified or implied in its constitutive instrument, and are then developed through its practice.[184] It was held that the UN:

> [...] must be deemed to have those powers which, though not expressly provided in the Charter, are conferred upon it by necessary implication as being essential to the performance of its duties [...]

Although this finding is related to the UN's rights, it is reasoned that it must also apply in relation to its obligations.[185] The first argument follows this approach, reasoning that the UN Charter implicitly requires the UN to act in accordance with IHRL. A similar view is that the UN's purposes and principles are at the core of the Charter and, as such, the Charter is considered to be legally binding on the UN as a whole.[186] According to Article 1 of the Charter, one of the UN's purposes is to achieve international cooperation in encouraging respect for human rights.[187] What precisely this Article requires of the UN

---

a State is in effective control of territory outside its borders, the State has full human rights obligations. *Cyprus v Turkey*. Note, however, that the possibility of the existence of a state of emergency and derogation from human rights obligations, as well as the possibility of national actors sharing human rights obligations, was raised. See Mégret and Hoffman, 'UN as Human Rights Violator', pp. 334–5. The Kosovo Ombudsperson clarified that, to the extent that the Security Council resolution created UNMIK 'as a surrogate state', 'all ensuing obligations, including affirmative obligations to secure human rights to everyone within UNMIK jurisdiction' were imposed on the international administration. Ombudsperson Institution of Kosovo, *On Certain Aspects of UNMIK Regulation No 2000/59 Amending UNMIK Regulation 1999/24 on the Law Applicable in Kosovo* (27 Oct 2000) (Special Report no 2 2000). These obligations could arise as a result of the host State's treaty obligations, according to agreements made prior to the UN governing the territory.

184 *Reparations*, p. 178.

185 The content of the UN's legal capacity, and its rights and duties, 'must depend upon its purposes and functions as specified or implied in its constituent documents and developed in practice', ibid, para. 180. The Secretary-General commented in relation to Peace Operations, 'the international responsibility of the UN for the activities of UN forces is an attribute of its international personality and its capacity to bear international rights and obligations'.

186 Zenon Stavrinides, 'Human Rights Obligations under the United Nations Charter' (1999) 3 *The International Journal of Human Rights* 38, p. 40; Mégret and Hoffman, 'UN as Human Rights Violator', p. 317.

187 The Charter of the United Nations (adopted 26 June 1945, entered into force 24 October 1945) 1 UNTS XVI, Article 1.

is unclear. However, under Article 55, the UN is obliged to promote 'universal respect for, and observance of, human rights and fundamental freedoms for all'.[188] This does not mean that the UN has a duty to protect, promote or fulfil human rights.[189] Rather, it places an obligation on the UN to assist other entities to do so.[190] However, promoting universal respect for human rights can only be achieved if the UN itself respects human rights.[191] This argument reinforces that IHRL is 'characteristically embedded' in the UN's operations in general.[192] The UN's OLA has confirmed that the UN takes the position that the UN Charter provides an obligation for the UN to 'uphold, promote and encourage respect for human rights'.[193]

The human rights principles in the Charter are embodied by,[194] and interpreted in, in a number of documents,[195] such as the Universal Declaration of Human Rights (UDHR), and the twin Covenants.[196] According to this approach, the UDHR and the two Covenants can be used to elaborate on the meaning of the Charter. Some claim that the UN Charter, the Universal Declaration and the

---

188 This obligation is set out in Article 55, and should be read together with Article 56. Kenny, *UN Accountability for its Human Rights Impact: Implementation through Participation*, p. 442. Notice the wording of Article 55, which requires that the UN 'shall' promote human rights and fundamental freedoms.

189 'Protecting, promoting or fulfilling' are the three different dimensions of human rights obligations. See Section 2.

190 Mégret and Hoffman, 'UN as Human Rights Violator', p. 319.

191 Kenny, *UN Accountability for its Human Rights Impact: Implementation through Participation*, p. 442. The UN is bound by international human rights standards because it is tasked with promoting such standards. [Amnesty International, *Peace-keeping and Human Rights 13* (IOR 40/001/1994, 1994)].

192 Mégret and Hoffman, 'UN as Human Rights Violator', p. 318.

193 UN, 'Letter dated 1 April 2009 from UN Office of Legal Affairs to the UN Department of Peacekeeping Operations, available in "UN Army Told Not to Join Congo Army in Operation"' *New York Times* (New York, 9 December 2009) <http://www.nytimes.com/2009/12/10/world/africa/10congo.html> accessed 3 January 2015.

194 It is argued that the Charter imposes binding norms on the UN, including the Secretariat. The Universal Declaration of Human Rights (UDHR) must also be respected by the Secretariat. For another approach, see n.197 and the text accompanying it.

195 Erika De Wet, *The Chapter VII Powers of the United Nations Security Council* (Hart 2004), pp. 199–200; White and Klaasen, *The UN, HR and Post-Conflict Situations*, p. 6, who state that these instruments provide the legal principles which govern UN practice.

196 ICCPR; International Covenant on Economic, Social and Cultural Rights (adopted 16 December 1966, entered into force 3 January 1976), 993 UNTS 3, (hereinafter 'ICESCR').

two Covenants are regarded as forming the UN's constitution.[197] Thus, another, possibly tenuous, argument which has been made, is that the UN is bound by these treaties.

8-1-2 The UN is Bound by IHRL on the Basis of Custom

Another argument is that the UN is bound by customary human rights law. The ICJ has affirmed that international organizations, including the UN, are bound by the 'obligations incumbent upon them under general rules of international law, under their constitutions or under international agreements to which they are parties'.[198] 'General rules of international law' can be divided into customary law and general legal principles.[199] Thus, the second argument posits that the UN is bound by IHRL to the extent it has customary law status. Many scholars take this position.[200]

---

197 For example, P.M. Pierre-Marie Dupuy, 'The Constitutional Dimension of the Charter of the United Nations Revisited' (1997) 1 *Max Planck Yearbook of United Nations Law* 1, p. 1. It is argued that the Charter imports many of these norms as binding on the Organization, including the Secretariat, and that the Universal Declaration of Human Rights (UDHR) must also be respected by the Secretariat. Nigel D White and Dirk Klaasen (eds), *The un, hr and Post-Conflict Situations* (Manchester University Press 2005), p. 7.

198 *Interpretation of the Agreement of 25 March 1951 between the WHO and Egypt* (Advisory Opinion) [1980] ICJ Rep 73, para. 37. In relation to WHO, the Court found that there is an obligation to give a reasonable period of notice to the host State when terminating an existing arrangement, and to consult the host State in good faith on the transfer of the Organization's regional office. At a general level, Rosalyn Higgins has stated that all UN activities must comply with both the Charter and general international law. Rosalyn Higgins, *Problems and Process: International Law and How We Use It* (Oxford University Press 1994), p. 181. Its obligations are not restricted to those which are explicitly accepted by the UN. C Tomuschat, *International Law: Ensuring the Survival of Mankind on the Eve of a New Century: General Course on Public International Law*, vol 281 (Martinus Nijhoff 2001), pp. 24–25.

199 Council of Europe, *COE Accountability Report*, para. 15. In this regard, Hannum observed that 'neither national courts nor lawyers always distinguish clearly between custom and general principles'. Hurst Hannum, 'The Status of the Universal Declaration of Human Rights in National and International Law' (1995) 25 *Georgia Journal of International and Comparative Law* 287, p. 352. '[O]n certain general and well-recognized principles, namely: elementary considerations of humanity, even more exacting in peace than in war; the principle of the freedom of maritime communication; and every State's obligation not to allow knowingly its territory to be used for acts contrary to the rights of other States'. *Corfu Channels case (UK v Albania)* (Merits) [1949] ICJ Rep 4, para. 22.

200 Mégret and Hoffman, 'UN as Human Rights Violator', p. 317. Clapham took the position that international organizations have a duty to protect the customary human rights of everyone falling under their control regardless of their nationality, to the extent that their

Finally, the UN itself has affirmed that it is bound by customary international law. The UN's OLA affirmed the position that customary international law obliges the UN to 'uphold, promote and encourage respect for human rights, international humanitarian law and refugee law'.[201] Also of note is that an 'applicable portion' of the UDHR is incorporated into the rules that bind the military and the UN police in Peace Operations.[202] Another convention 'universally recognized [that] standards of human rights as contained in international instruments' apply to UN personnel.[203]

---

functions permit. This obligation is both the duty to respect human rights and the duty to protect human rights. Clapham, *Human Rights Obligations of Non-State Actors* pp. 19, 68. Kondoch considers that the UN is bound by customary international law *mutatis mutandis*, as this automatically results from the finding that the UN has a legal personality. 'The UN possesses legal personality which means that it can be bound by customary international law *mutatis mutandis*'. Boris Kondoch, 'Human Rights Law and UN Peace Operations in Post-Conflict Situations' in Nigel D White and Dirk K Laasen (eds), *The UN, Human Rights and Post-Conflict Situations* (Manchester University Press 2005), p. 36. See also Rosalyn Higgins, *The Development of International Law through the Political Organs of the United Nations* (Oxford University Press 1963); Tomuschat, *International Law: Ensuring the Survival of Mankind on the Eve of a New Century: General Course on Public International Law*; August Reinisch, 'Securing the Accountability of International Organizations' (2001) 7 *Global Governance* 131, p. 136. However, see the discussion in José E Alvarez, *International Organizations as Law-Makers* (Oxford University Press Oxford 2005), p. 171.

201 UN, 'Letter dated 1 April 2009 from UN Office of Legal Affairs to the UN Department of Peacekeeping Operations, available in "UN Army Told Not to Join Congo Army in Operation"'.

202 Under 'We Are Peacekeeping Personnel' in MOU. UN, 'Model Memorandum of Understanding between the United Nations and [participating State] contributing resources to [the United Nations Peacekeeping Operation] ' UN Doc. A/C.5/60/26, annex A; UN, FPU MoU.

203 '[N]othing in this Convention shall affect: (a) the applicability of international humanitarian law and universally recognized standards of human rights as contained in international instruments in relation to the protection of United Nations operations and United Nations and associated personnel or the responsibility of such personnel to respect such law and standards'. UNGA Res 49/59 (9 December 1994) UN Doc. GA Res 49/59. Convention on the Safety of United Nations and Associated Personnel (adopted on 9 December 1994, entered into force on 15 January 1999) 2051 UNTS 363, Article 20 (a). The UN's policy on the integration of human rights into Peace Operations requires all personnel to act 'in accordance with [IHRL] and International Humanitarian Law', and to 'understand how their tasks intersect with human rights'. They shall refrain from committing human rights abuses or being associated with human rights violations and, if they do, they will be 'held accountable'. The Head of Mission is tasked with ensuring their compliance with their obligations, and he or she must issue all necessary instructions in this regard. UN

Thus, it appears likely that the UN is bound by fundamental IHRL obligations arising from the Charter or customary law.[204] This work proceeds on the assumption that customary IHRL is applicable to the UN.

8-2 *Content of the UN's Obligations*

This section examines what these customary obligations might be. Human rights obligations are usually defined only in general terms.[205] Discussion regarding the detailed contents of the UN's IHRL obligations is scarce and, where it exists, it often focuses on the UN's obligations in the context of transitional administrations.[206] Even the observation that some norms, such as the right to life, personal security, basic due process guarantees, freedom from arbitrary detention, torture or cruel treatment, slavery and *apartheid*-like racial discrimination,[207] have crystallized into customary international law, does

OHCHR/DPKO/DPA/DFS, Policy on Human Rights in United Nations Peace Operations and Political Missions , paras. 36, 38. Clapham claims that the UN is bound by IHRL because it has declared itself bound by it. Clapham, *Human Rights Obligations of Non-State Actors*, p. 127.

204 White and Klaasen, *The UN, HR and Post-Conflict Situations*. They go further and state that 'the UN is bound to respect, and ensure respect for, human rights', p. 7.

205 Kondoch, 'Human Rights Law and UN Peace Operations in Post-Conflict Situations', p. 41.

206 On the human rights obligations of the UN as a transitional administrator, see Section 7.

207 Cerone, 'Reasonable Measures', p. 62. Clapham claims that 'the rules prohibiting arbitrary killing, slavery, torture, detention, and systematic racial discrimination' are now recognized as rules of customary international law. In addition, he claims that other rights, including 'the right to self-determination, the right to basic sustenance, freedom of opinion, equality rights, and the right to fair trial' have entered in the area of customary international law. (Clapham, *Human Rights Obligations of Non-State Actors*, p. 86). The scope of the rights to life, liberty and security of person under the UDHR is too general to be a useful international norm, although protection of the right to life has been cited frequently as falling within customary international law. Hannum stated that the prohibition against slavery under the UDHR is also 'universally held to form part of customary law'. According to Hannum, the prohibition against 'torture or [...] cruel, inhuman or degrading treatment or punishment' under Article 5 of the UDHR has been confirmed as customary. The prohibition provided under Article 9 of the UDHR against arbitrary arrest, detention or exile is customary only if it is 'prolonged'. Those who urge acceptance of the UDHR in *toto* as customary law are clearly in a minority. UDHR Article 8's guarantee of an effective remedy before domestic courts for violations of human rights is not generally included in the list of customary law rules. Hannum claims that the right to a fair trial is often considered among those now guaranteed under customary law. Hannum, 'The Status of the Universal Declaration of Human Rights in National and International Law', pp. 340–346. Sheeran states that certain basic human rights norms have crystallised into customary international law, and thus bind all States. Human rights obligations considered non-derogable

not mean that the UN is required to meet all the obligations related to these rights at all times. The same consideration applies to duties arising from non-derogable IHRL.[208]

One of the difficulties the UN encounters in meeting the obligation to respond to a crime is that it does not generally have the same kind of relationship that a State has with those under its authority. The UN also lacks a number of powers and functions that States have,[209] most notably, the authority and capacity to bring criminal proceedings against suspects. However, the UN has the authority and ability to conduct investigations into disciplinary offences by the UN police and, indeed, it claims that authority to do so.

A challenge remains in determining the exact content of the obligations, and in what situations such obligations apply.[210] A further complexity is the possibility that the UN's IHRL obligations differ depending on the functions, responsibilities, roles and activities of each mission.[211] It is possible to take a

---

are: the right to life; the prohibition of torture or cruel and degrading treatment; the prohibition of slavery and servitude or civil imprisonment; the impermissibility of retroactive punishment; the right to recognition before the law; and freedom of thought, religion and conscience. He argues that these rights are possibly in the realm of customary human rights law. Sheeran, 'Constitutional Moment', p. 29. Non-derogable rights under the ICCPR are listed under ICCPR, Article 4(2). The HRC stated that proclaiming these rights as non-derogable in nature was a recognition, in part, of their peremptory nature. The Committee also noted that, in its view, 'elements' of other norms would be non-derogable, and that those norms included humane treatment, the right to liberty (in connection with forced displacement), and the right to an effective remedy. UN Human Rights Committee, 'General Comment 29, States of Emergency (Article 4)' (31 August 2001) UN Doc. CCPR/C/21/Rev.1/Add.11, para. 11.

208 Sheeran observes that non-derogable human rights 'represent the clearest application of the "human rights and fundamental freedoms" referred to in Article 1(3) of the Charter'. Sheeran, 'Constitutional Moment', p. 81.

209 Mégret and Hoffman, 'UN as Human Rights Violator', p. 321.

210 Still, difficult issues remain, including the possibility of derogation in times of emergency, and whether the principle of proportionality applies to the UN. Sheeran, 'Constitutional Moment', pp. 81–82. For a further consideration of derogation and other forms of limitations of human rights obligations in UN operations, see Guglielmo Verdirame, *The UN and Human Rights: Who Guards the Guardians?* (Cambridge University Press 2011), pp. 243–366.

211 The UN has different capacities in different Peace Operations, in terms of the 'control' it exercises over the local population. The UN's human rights obligations are minimal in respect of most 'traditional' Peace Operations – those which are intended purely to monitor ceasefires or buffer zones. On the other extreme is where the UN acts as the transitional administration, that is, where the UN functions as the government. Other operations generally fall somewhere within these two points. This requires careful analysis, as

'sliding-scale' approach, or to argue that the UN's obligations should be proportionate, relative to its functions, mandates,[212] and activities.[213] This may differ not only from one operation to the next, but also within the same operation. However, a more detailed analysis of the exact content of the UN's human rights obligations falls outside the scope of this work. For these reasons, it is assumed that the content of customary human rights law is similar to the content the human rights treaties.[214] Specifically, it is assumed that the

---

some operations played a bigger role than was provided for in their written mandates. For example, the mandate of UNOSOM II did not explicitly provide such extensive powers as to reach the threshold of effective control over a territory, but, in the absence of a functioning domestic government, it found itself in *de facto* control over a part of the territory, providing a wide range of governmental functions. Guglielmo Verdirame, 'UN Accountability for Human Rights Violations in Post-Conflict Situations' in Nigel D White and Dirk Klaasen (eds), *The UN, Human Rights and Post-Conflict Situations* (Manchester University Press 2005) p. 234; Carsten Stahn, *The Law and Practice of International Territorial Administration: Versailles to Iraq and Beyond*, vol 57 (Cambridge University Press 2008) pp. 6–7. UNTAC, UNTAG and UNAMSIL also found themselves providing some governmental functions at certain times. J G Merrills, *International Dispute Settlement* (4th edn, Cambridge University Press 2005) pp. 243–244, 260. As stated, a key element of IHRL is the relationship between a State's power and its responsibility to those under its jurisdiction. Where the United Nations acts in a quasi-sovereign role or exercises public power, it surely must give rise to human rights obligations. The UN has never claimed that its activities are free from human rights obligations. Sheeran, 'Constitutional Moment', p. 79. Alvarez, *International Organizations as Law-Makers*, p. 179. In both UNMIK and UNTAET, regulations were adopted to require all persons undertaking public duties or holding public office to observe the standards of the major human rights treaties. UNMIK Regulation no 1999/24 on the Law Applicable in Kosovo (12 December 1999); UNTAET Regulation no 1999/1 on the Authority of the Transitional Administration in East Timor. There is then the question of the extent to which obligations arise for the UN, in light of its competence, functions and practice. *Reparations*, p. 179.

212 There is also the issue of the mandates which are set down in the Security Council resolutions, which could be incompatible with the human rights obligations of the UN. For example, where the UN is allowed to take 'all necessary means to maintain law and order', this may infringe on the right to liberty. For a consideration of derogation and other forms of limitations of human rights obligations in UN operations, see Verdirame, *Who Guards the Guardians*, pp. 243–366.

213 Cerone, 'Reasonable Measures', p. 49. Note, however, the *Bankovic* decision, in which the Court rejected this sliding-scale approach in relation to participating NATO States' human rights obligations in respect of damages caused by NATO bombing in Belgrade. *Banković and Others v Belgium and Others*.

214 On the State's obligation to investigate, prosecute and punish a crime that infringes on a right enshrined in treaties, see Sections 3 to 5. It may also be relevant to note that the International Law Association's Committee on Accountability of International Organizations

UN has an obligation to investigate serious crimes which are alleged to have been committed by those over whom it exercises control, in the same way that a State would have, were the crime to be committed by a State agent within its national territory.

8-2-1 Two Kinds of Potential Obligations

The first question is whether the UN has an obligation to investigate and prosecute a crime committed by a UN police officer. The second is whether the UN is required to assist States in meeting their obligations to investigate and prosecute. These will be discussed in turn.

(1) *The UN's Obligation to Investigate and Prosecute*

Obligation to Investigate

Where IHRL requires that an investigation be conducted, this should be prompt, thorough and effective.[215] It is necessary to translate this into terms appropriate for a UN mission. The requirement is to initiate and conduct prompt, through and effective investigations by a sufficiently independent investigative body into crimes that infringe on a right, when committed by UN police officers. In light of the requirement of due diligence, the UN arguably has an obligation to begin an investigation on its own initiative, and to ensure that this investigation is conducted by professional investigators, who are sufficiently independent institutionally-speaking, and in reality. This is likely to mean that investigation by the UN police is not necessarily problematic, but that there is likely to be a problem if the suspect and the investigator have the same nationality.[216] The investigative body must not be *ad hoc*. The investigation must

---

recognizes that, as a general principle of law and as a basic international human rights standard, the right to a remedy applies in relation to international organizations. International Law Association, *Report of the Seventy-First Conference, Accountability of International Organizations: First Report* (2004), p. 207. Some argue that customary international law includes an individual's right to a remedy against international organizations. Karel C Wellens, *Remedies against International Organisations* (Cambridge University Press 2002), p. 10. Wellens takes this position in spite of the acknowledgement that, if one looks at these obligations purely in terms of customary international law, they may be more limited than those enshrined in treaties. For example, whether customary law requires States to 'ensure' rights, as has been required by treaties, appears unsettled. See Cerone, 'Reasonable Measures', p. 59.

215 As presented in Section 3-1.

216 See Section 3-1. In *Jaloud*, the nature and extent of the independence of the investigatory body was examined. The Court found that, although the investigation was heavily reliant on police information and support, it was not necessarily problematic. *Jaloud v*

be thorough, including interviewing relevant witnesses and securing evidence. Once a suspect is identified, the UN should take measures to avoid any collusion with potential witnesses. For the investigation to be effective, all available means must be resorted to, and the response must be prompt. This appears to exclude the possibility that all investigators be located at the UN headquarters.

Obligation to Prosecute

The UN does not have the authority or capacity to prosecute those UN police officers who are alleged to have committed crimes. As a result, the UN's obligation to prosecute must be interpreted in another way, such as imposing on the UN the requirement to use its best endeavours to ensure that a suspect is prosecuted by a State. There are two possible manifestations of this obligation. One is the obligation not to obstruct a State which is conducting a prosecution, and the other is the obligation to equip States in bringing criminal proceedings. The obligation not to obstruct a prosecution would entail limiting the use of immunity to appropriate cases, and waiving it promptly where required.[217] The obligation may also require the UN to clarify those aspects of immunity granted to UN police which are unclear, in particular its geographic coverage, the scope of official acts, and the circumstances in which the UN would waive immunity. If any aspect of immunity is unclear, this could hinder the prompt initiation of criminal proceedings by States. Furthermore, vital evidence may be lost whilst the UN is in the process of determining whether the act in question is covered by immunity.

The obligation to use its best endeavours to enable States to prosecute would mean that the UN is required to give the evidence that it has collected to the appropriate State authority, in a form which would permit the receiving State to bring criminal proceedings as promptly as possible. This is vital, as the UN has something (evidence) without which States and, in particular, sending States, may not be able to deliver their obligations.

When a UN investigation establishes that a disciplinary offence has been committed that is also criminal in nature, leading it to fire the suspect, the UN should be able to detain that person until he is repatriated to his sending State, in order to ensure that he does not flee to another country. At the same time, the UN should transfer all the information from its own investigation to a specific,

---

the Netherlands, paras. 191–194. However, in *Ergi*, the prosecutor's heavy reliance on an incident report, written by *gendarmerie*, in deciding on the facts of the case, was found to be in breach of the right to life. *Ergi v Turkey*, para. 83.

217 On the appropriate circumstances in which to claim immunity, see Chapter 6, Section 1-4. On the circumstances in which immunity should be waived, see Chapter 6, Section 1-5-2.

previously designated person in the sending State, who has responsibility for ensuring that prosecutions are brought where appropriate. This might mean altering the MoU to require each sending State to identify the correct person to receive the information, and to give an undertaking to act on it. In fact, the obligation of the sending States to prosecute is clearly set out in the MoU between the UN and sending States in relation to FPUs. However, it should also be included in *Note Verbales* in relation to IPOs. The details of cooperation in potential criminal proceedings against UN police personnel need to be decided between the two parties and clearly set out.

The obligation would also require the UN to initiate and continue follow-up with the sending State until either criminal proceedings are finalized (i.e. criminal sanctions are imposed, or the person is acquitted), or the UN is convinced that there is a good reason not to initiate criminal proceedings, taking into account the sending State's IHRL obligations. Where the UN attempts to follow up, but where the sending States' responses only contain general remarks, such as 'it is taken seriously', 'an investigation is underway', or 'the person in question has been properly disciplined', the UN must demand further details regarding the measures taken, the results of any investigation, the reason for any delay, or the reason the case has been closed, if this has occurred.[218]

In essence, the UN needs to be prepared to respond when a crime has been committed by UN police personnel. This requires having permanent systems in place to deliver its due diligence obligations in this regard. Given the nature and expected effect of criminal sanctions, the condemnation of the wrongdoing needs to be public. This may require the UN to assist, or at least not obstruct, any public criminal proceedings.[219]

(2) *The UN's Obligation to Assist States in Delivering their Obligations*

In addition to obligations based on their primary responsibilities, States also have, in some contexts, an obligation to assist others in the delivery of their obligations. Does the UN have such an obligation and, if so, does it apply in this context, so as to require that the UN assist States in delivering effective investigations and prosecutions? This argument is based on two sources. The first is the UN Charter. The UN is required to 'achieve international co-operation [...]

---

218 See Chapter 4, Section 3-5.

219 'Responsibility [...] could be ascribed to the international organization, as in the case of state responsibility, if there had been some element of negligence on the part of the international organization in allowing the offence to occur'. C F Amerasinghe, *Principles of the Institutional Law of International Organizations* (2nd edn, Cambridge University Press 2005), p. 406.

in promoting and encouraging respect for human rights and for fundamental freedoms',[220] and to 'be a centre for harmonizing the actions of nations in the attainment of these common ends'.[221] Based on these articles, there is a view that the UN must assist other entities in protecting, promoting and fulfilling human rights.[222]

The second possible source is IHRL. An analogy may be made with the obligation imposed on States by the International Covenant on Economic, Social and Cultural Rights (ICESCR) to cooperate with, and assist States in, achieving human rights goals. Drawing on several articles, in particular Article 2 of the ICESCR,[223] it can be argued that all State Parties have an obligation to cooperate and assist others in the realization of Covenant rights.[224]

Even if such a legal obligation could in theory exist, it would be necessary to show that it forms part of customary human rights law, and that it applies outside the context of economic, social and cultural rights. More specifically, it would need to apply to the obligation to investigate and, where appropriate, prosecute. It appears difficult to find evidence to support such a contention.

However, if this obligation were found to exist, it would entail the UN assisting a sending State to make an arrangement between itself and the host State to conduct its own investigation, if that is what is required for the sending State to prosecute its UN police officer. It may also entail responding to requests for additional evidence, or evidence in a different form, from the sending State for the purposes of prosecution. It may require technical cooperation, such as providing specific expertise or equipment in order for that State to conduct an effective investigation.

It is submitted that the stronger argument regarding whether the UN has an obligation to investigate and prosecute is that based on the UN's own obligation to investigate and, where appropriate, use its best endeavours to secure criminal prosecution, as discussed in the previous sub-section.

---

220 UN Charter, Article 1-3.

221 Ibid, Article 1-4.

222 Mégret and Hoffman, 'UN as Human Rights Violator', p. 319.

223 Articles 2, 11, 15, 22 and 23.

224 International organizations and States have 'a strong and continuous responsibility to take whatever measures they can to assist governments to act in ways which are compatible with their human rights obligations'. UN Committee on Economic Social Cultural Rights, *Globalization and Economic, Social and Cultural Rights, Statement by the Committee on Economic, Social and Cultural Rights at the 18th Session* (*27 April – 15 May 1998*) Available at <http://www2ohchrorg/english/bodies/cescr/docs/statements/Globalisation-1998doc> accessed 10 January 2015, 1998.

9 Conclusion

The obligation to investigate, prosecute and punish certain criminal conduct is firmly enshrined in IHRL. It requires States to conduct a prompt, thorough and effective investigation, carried out by a sufficiently independent body, into allegations of crimes. The investigation must be of such a nature as to be capable of identifying the perpetrator. Where the evidence warrants it, there is an obligation to prosecute the wrongdoer. This obligation is not absolute. The standard is that of due diligence and of best effort, taking into account all available means. Prosecutorial discretion is acknowledged, but this discretion is not without limits. Where a case is closed without charges being brought against a suspect, and where a State has not made its 'best effort' to bring charges, it may be found to have violated its obligation to prosecute.

Cases decided by human rights bodies indicate that this obligation forms part of substantive human rights, including the right to life, physical integrity, liberty and security, and a private life.[225] In some cases, the State's obligation under these substantive rights must be read in conjunction with the victim's right to a remedy, or that of their next-of-kin. Certain kinds of behaviour must be criminalized and, where this behaviour occurs, civil redress will not suffice.

In the context of UN Peace Operations, the host State has an obligation to investigate and prosecute. However, the problem in respect of the host State is rarely that it is unwilling to prosecute; rather, it is often that it lacks the capacity to do so. As IHRL does not require States to deliver impossible tasks, the content of the host State's obligation will depend on its capacity. Where, exceptionally, a host State has the capacity to investigate and prosecute,[226] it must meet this obligation in full.

The circumstances regarding sending States are more complicated, because the criminal conduct is committed outside their borders. However, the obligation to investigate and prosecute does not explicitly distinguish between crimes committed within a State's territory, and those committed outside its territory. Where the suspect is present in the sending State, it may have an obligation to investigate and, in particular, to prosecute him. The fact that the individual has usually been seconded by the State itself, and is usually one of its own police officers, may add weight to this argument. An additional factor is

225 These cases have dealt with: killings by State agents or by private persons; death due to medical malpractice or incident; torture or ill-treatment; disappearance; rape; and sexual assault.

226 Examples of host States which have had the capacity to investigate and prosecute include Cyprus, Kosovo and Bosnia and Herzegovina.

the need to combat impunity, at least in circumstances in which the host State is not itself in a position to investigate and prosecute.

Generally, the conduct of a member of UN police is not attributable to the sending State. Where, exceptionally, it is attributable to that State, its obligation to investigate and, where appropriate, prosecute, may be more onerous.[227]

The obligation of a State to respond to a crime may conflict with the immunity afforded to the UN police officer who committed that crime. Legitimate claims to immunity are likely to be accepted by human rights bodies, either as part of prosecutorial discretion or as a requirement that forms part of general international law. It is not clear whether, where immunity has been inappropriately claimed, a State has an obligation to disregard that immunity. Another issue which is unclear is whether a defendant can challenge a decision to waive his immunity.

The UN may also have an obligation to respond to crimes committed by UN police officers. If one takes the position that the UN is bound by customary human rights law, and that the content of customary obligations is similar to those enshrined in human rights treaties, it can be argued that the UN has an obligation to investigate and, where appropriate, prosecute, particularly since the UN police are UN agents.

However, the UN's obligations to investigate and prosecute are different to those of States because of the different relationship between it and those under its control. Since the UN has control over the initial investigation, the obligation to investigate can be delivered through the UN conducting its own investigation. The requirement that an investigation take place promptly would require that some investigators be present in missions. The UN's responses must not be of an *ad hoc* nature. Investigations must be conducted by professional investigators, who are sufficiently independent of the suspect. This, in turn, means that UN police officers who share the same nationality as the suspect should not investigate allegations against him. Once a suspect is identified, the UN must take measures to prevent the suspect colluding with other potential witnesses. An effective investigation requires the UN to resort to all available means. Thorough investigation requires that the UN interview witnesses outside the UN.

The obligation of best endeavours to ensure that criminal proceedings are brought, where appropriate, means not making inappropriate immunity claims, or refusing to waive immunity when it should be waived. It may also require the UN to clarify the scope and procedure of immunity. This obligation also entails the investigation being conducted in such a way that its findings

227 See Section 6.

can be used in criminal proceedings brought by a State. This means that the standard of investigation needs to be that of a criminal investigation and, where it is known which State may prosecute, that the UN do its best to collect evidence according to that State's legal requirements. In order to ensure that the investigation is thorough, the UN may be required to hold the suspect during the investigation, either by detaining him, or otherwise ensuring he does not flee. Where criminal conduct is substantiated in the UN's investigation, the suspect must be handed over to a State which is willing to prosecute him. At the same time, information collected by the UN needs to be sent to the relevant State and, subsequently, a systematic follow-up with that State is required.

Finally, although tenuous, it is also possible to argue that the UN has an obligation to assist States in delivering their procedural obligations. If this obligation is found to exist, it may mean that the UN must assist a State, which is seeking to prosecute, to obtain additional evidence. It may also require the UN to assist the State in making an arrangement to send its own investigators.

In short, it is submitted that the States' obligation to investigate a crime, which would have been a human rights violation were it to be committed by a State agent, exists in relation to serious crimes committed by the UN police. The obligation exists both for host and sending States, although the extent of the host State's obligation is dependent on the nature of its legal system. The UN may also have an obligation to conduct an effective investigation, and to do its best to ensure that the suspect is prosecuted. Where such an obligation is a possibility, it may be in the UN's interests to deliver that potential obligation, even before it is clearly found to exist by a human rights body.

CHAPTER 8

Conclusion

This work has focused on the individual criminal accountability of UN police officers, who work in UN Peace Operations. It has analyzed various ways to ensure that, where it is alleged that an individual UN police officer has engaged in criminal conduct, the matter is investigated and, where appropriate, the officer prosecuted. This issue has become vitally important because of the nature of the work the UN police undertake, and the impact that a lack of response to these crimes may have both on the UN, and on the effectiveness and perceived legitimacy of its Peace Operations.

This issue has increased in importance as a result of the evolution of UN Peace Operations. The environments into which UN police are deployed increasingly suffer from fragile security, and lack basic national institutions. Thus, Peace Operations have become more intrusive. The evolution of the UN police is also reflected in its increased size. Beginning as a small police contingent serving in a single mission, there are now more than 12,000 UN police officers in the field.[1] The issue of the criminal accountability of the UN police has also become more important due to the dramatic transformation of the functions they carry out. Since the 1990s, these functions have been clearly distinguished from those of military contingents. The nature of the functions that the UN police are entrusted with have shifted from monitoring the behaviour of the local police, to building or rebuilding the police force and other national institutions. More importantly, their functions involve inculcating the values of the rule of law, including the notion of accountability. In doing so, the UN police are required to act as role models.[2] Thus, the effective delivery of individual criminal accountability of UN police officers is of increasing importance to the effectiveness and legitimacy of UN Peace Operations across the world.

UN police officers are selected and trained primarily by their sending States, save for a limited number who are selected directly by the UN. This applies to both Individual Police Officers (IPOs) and Formed Police Unit (FPU) personnel. Two types of qualities are sought in respect of UN police officers: first, the expertise to deliver the requisite functions, with a focus on policing experience, language and driving skills; and, second, personal integrity. The analysis in this work makes it clear that there is a major problem in securing

1 See Chapter 2, Section 2.

2 See Chapter 2, Section 1.

 | DOI 10.1163/9789004328815_009

a sufficient number of qualified personnel in a timely manner. It appears that the increasing reliance on FPUs is partly due to the difficulties in securing police personnel.[3]

In connection to the selection of personnel, there has been a major shift in the States which send UN police to missions. In the 1990s, it was mainly western States which sent police to UN missions. Currently, sending States are concentrated in South Asia and Africa. The majority of UN police personnel come from only a handful of States.[4] It is recommended that specialized training, which targets policing in the Peace Operations context, be given to police officers in these States or regions. Those who complete the course should be awarded a certificate, and should be given priority over those who have not successfully completed this training when recruitment is carried out for a Peace Operation.

It is clear that crimes have been, and continue to be, committed by UN police personnel. However, due in part to the fact that there is little publicly available data that properly indicates the scale of this problem,[5] it is difficult to assess its true extent.[6] In an attempt to address this issue, the author constructed a database using what little information there is regarding the incidence of alleged crimes.[7] It became clear from this (limited) data that serious crimes have been committed by UN police personnel, and that a large proportion of these are crimes against the person. The author's data showed that a majority of these offences are unrelated to their official functions.[8] This indicates that the element that has the greatest impact on the commission of crimes may be not the mandate, the functions, or the environment they are deployed in; instead, it appears to be the personal qualities of UN police personnel. Thus, the issue of the proper selection of personnel appears vital. In most cases for which data are available, criminal proceedings did not appear to have been brought against the suspects, either in the host or sending States.[9]

3 See Chapter 2, Section 3.
4 See Chapter 2, Section 3-3-1.
5 See Chapter 3, introductory part, Section 4.
6 See Chapter 3, Sections 2 and 3.
7 The contents of the database form the basis of the analysis in Chapter 3. This set of data is called 'the author's data' to distinguish this from other data.
8 Chapter 3, Section 2-2. It is possible that crimes that are related to the UN police's official functions are dealt with internally within the UN, and that information about such crimes is not made publicly available. If that is the case, it may be that information in the public domain concentrates more on crimes that are not related to the UN police's official functions.
9 See Chapter 3, Section 3.

This apparent absence of criminal proceedings is not the result of there being no mechanism to deal with allegations of criminal conduct. The current UN machinery is triggered by complaints.[10] This indicates that a certain proportion of allegations do not reach the UN, in particular because victims and witnesses face greater obstacles in lodging complaints in societies in which Peace Operations are deployed.[11] Since the mid-1990s and, in particular, since the Zeid Report was issued, the UN has taken measures to address the issue of the individual criminal accountability of UN personnel.[12] The *ad hoc* mechanism was reformed and, initially, all misconduct investigations were entrusted to the Board of Inquiry (BoI) system. However, BoI investigators lacked the requisite investigative skills.[13] Since then, a number of measures have been taken: mechanisms have been created for raising awareness of what constitutes misconduct; how to lodge a complaint and how to handle a complaint, both within the UN and outside it, have been publicized; codes of conduct and complaint mechanisms have been established; procedures have been introduced to ensure the smoother receipt of complaints, as well as the centralization of these complaints; and agreements have been entered into with States regarding arrangements for investigation and prosecution.[14]

Currently, the two main offices entrusted with disciplinary issues are the Office of the Oversight Services (OIOS), and the Conduct and Discipline Unit (CDU) and its field teams (CDTs). The OIOS has investigators who are assigned solely to conduct investigations, and the office is responsible for investigating all allegations of serious misconduct. The CDU is tasked with serving as a focal point for all misconduct allegations, including the centralization of information, and data management. The selection standards for UN police personnel have been clarified, an internal policy has been developed to protect whistleblowers, and the UN has begun to refer some allegations of criminal misconduct to sending States.[15] The problem of UN police misconduct has also been acknowledged by the General Assembly, which has discussed the criminal accountability of civilian personnel, including the UN police.[16]

---

10 Under IHRL, States are not only required to investigate upon receiving complaints, but must also use their own initiative to determine if violations have occurred. See Chapter 7, Section 3-1.

11 Chapter 4, introductory section, Section 3-1.

12 UNGA, 'A Comprehensive Strategy to Eliminate Future Sexual Exploitation and Abuse in United Nations Peacekeeping Operations' (24 March 2005) UN Doc. A/59/710.

13 Chapter 4, Sections 2 and 3-3-1.

14 Chapter 4, Sections 2, 3-2 and 3-3.

15 Chapter 4, Section 2.

16 Chapter 1, Section 1.

Nevertheless, the analysis in this work has revealed persistent shortcomings. There is no evidence that the policy on the protection of whistle-blowers is being effectively implemented.[17] Even though the need for professional and independent investigations has resulted in the UN referring all serious misconduct to the OIOS, due to the OIOS being overloaded with cases, about half of the investigations referred to it are now sent back to the originating mission to investigate.[18] Furthermore, OIOS investigations do not serve the needs of criminal investigations, as the evidence gathered by the OIOS cannot be used in criminal proceedings.[19]

In fact, the OIOS was originally established for a specific purpose, and its investigators may be qualified to fulfil that purpose,[20] but they appear to lack the ability to investigate 'ordinary' crimes. One possibility would be to create a special unit within OIOS to investigate criminal conduct by UN personnel, but a putative unit would be likely to be based in New York, which would be problematic. Another possibility would be to designate UN police to investigate allegations against mission personnel. To ensure impartiality, UN police would not be permitted to investigate allegations against other UN police with the same nationality. These investigators could come under the control of an OIOS investigator.[21]

Regarding data, the CDU does not collect all data dealing with misconduct, as the data concerned are independently collected and managed by both the OIOS and the CDU.[22] Without accurate and comprehensive data, it is difficult for the UN to respond to, or prevent, criminal misconduct. It is recommended that a single office should be responsible for collecting comprehensive data on misconduct and, given that the OIOS's data are confidential, for it to be the office responsible for collecting and managing the entire database.[23] The UN should also seek to ensure that the system for collecting information on criminal misconduct does so regardless of whether a complaint has been lodged or not.

The UN should also seek information about misbehaviour proactively. At the very least, it should respond to all allegations that reach any mission members,

---

17 Chapter 4, Section 3-1 (2) c.

18 Chapter 4, Section 2.

19 Chapter 4, Section 3-3-2.

20 Chapter 4, Section 3-3-2.

21 In certain recent missions, *ad hoc* arrangements are made to allocate UN police personnel within the CDT. Communication with senior UN officials, June 2016.

22 Chapter 4, Section 3-2.

23 Chapter 4, Section 3-2.

even if no formal complaint is made. Every member of a mission should be under an obligation to forward such information to a designated person. A failure to do so should result in a serious sanction.[24] The data collected by the UN regarding criminal misconduct should be disaggregated according to the mission during which the misconduct occurred, the type of alleged misconduct, the personnel category into which the suspect falls, the type of victim, and the nationality of the suspect.[25]

A separate issue is the extent to which this information should be made public. It is submitted that the majority should be made public.[26] Transparency is, in and of itself, necessary for the UN because it is trying to inculcate good governance, which involves being transparent. In addition, by making the information public, civil society will join the UN in bringing pressure to bear on States to resolve the issue of the individual criminal accountability of UN Peace Operations personnel.[27]

In relation to making public the nationality of the suspect, there are two possible approaches. One is to make public the nationality of all suspects in respect of whom substantiated allegations of criminal conduct have been made which warrant prosecution. The other is to publish the names of States that fail to act on receipt of a report of substantiated criminal misconduct. The latter may work as a sanction against non-cooperation.[28]

The UN's responses have also disproportionately focused on sexual crimes.[29] Other equally serious crimes also need to be addressed effectively.[30]

Once information is made available, criminal prosecution can take place in either the host or the sending State. It is noteworthy that, in recent years, the UN has shifted its focus from the host State to sending States in terms of providing potential legal fora for prosecution.[31] The shift appears to have taken place as a result of mission environments, as well as the state of the host State's legal

24 Chapter 4, Section 3-2.

25 Chapter 4, Sections 3-1 and 3-2.

26 The information that should be made public is as follows: the date on which the criminal misconduct was committed, the mission during which the crime was committed, the nature of the criminal conduct, a brief summary of the alleged crime, the personnel category to which the suspect belongs, the suspect's nationality, the type of the victim(s) if any, the nationality(ies) of the victim(s), and a brief explanation of what action has been taken.

27 Chapter 4, Sections 3-1 and 3-2.

28 Chapter 4, Sections 3-5 and 3-6.

29 Chapter 4, Section 3-1-1.

30 Chapter 4, Section 3-6.

31 Chapter 4, Section 2.

system.[32] The recent Memorandum of Understanding (MoU) between the UN and States sending FPUs to missions establishes that the sending State is required to prosecute the suspect if the host State does not do so itself.[33] This should be written into the *Note Verbale* between the UN and States sending IPOs.

However, the idea that sending States should be required to prosecute their own police officers for misconduct should be complemented with practical measures to enable them to do so. The practical difficulties inherent in bringing criminal proceedings based on evidence gathered by another entity for disciplinary purposes cannot be underestimated. It is very difficult for the sending State to respond promptly to an allegation of serious criminal conduct against its national UN police officer, and to investigate an act that occurred outside its borders. Thus, where an allegation is made that there has been criminal misconduct, the UN should put in place arrangements for ensuring that evidence is collected promptly, and in a form which is able to serve the needs of a criminal prosecution. In some cases, this may entail an agreement between the host State, the sending State and the UN, which would enable the sending State to send its own investigators to the host State. In other cases, it may mean that UN investigators conduct an investigation under the guidance of the sending State, in order to ensure that the right kind of evidence is collected in the right form. In either case, it would be useful to have a contact person in each sending State with whom to negotiate practical arrangements.[34] By systematizing the entire procedure, reliance on the individual Special Representative of the Secretary-General (SRSG)'s willingness to pursue the issue of criminal accountability could be minimized.

There are other practical steps that need to be taken after the initial collection of evidence. Where sending States require additional information, the UN would need to assist in gathering it. It also needs to follow up systematically in order to ensure that the sending State does all it can to investigate and, where facts warrant it, to prosecute a suspect. Where the UN has substantiated an allegation of criminal misconduct, the UN should also be equipped with the power to detain or otherwise hold the suspect until it hands him over to the State which will prosecute him. This would ensure that the suspect does not flee to another jurisdiction to avoid facing criminal proceedings. At the same time, the UN should transfer all the information from its own investigation to

---

32 Chapter 2, Section 1; Chapter 4, Section 2.

33 UN, 'Model Memorandum of Understanding between the United Nations and the xxx Contributing Resources to the xxxx' UN Doc. (on file with author), (hereinafter 'FPU MoU').

34 Chapter 4, Section 3-5.

a person in the prosecuting State, who has been previously designated for this purpose. This person would have the responsibility for ensuring that the State concerned makes its best efforts to prosecute the suspect. This may involve a modification of the MoU, and the same modification should be written into *Notes Verbales* between the UN and the State sending IPOs.

It is often claimed that one of the main legal obstacles to the prosecution of a suspect is the limits imposed on the exercise of criminal jurisdiction by States. However, international law poses no difficulties for either the host or sending State in relation to bringing criminal proceedings. The former can rely on the territorial principle, whilst the latter may rely on the active nationality principle.[35] Under its domestic laws, the host State will not encounter any problem in exercising jurisdiction.[36] There may, however, be a problem under domestic law for the sending State. There is generally no problem in this regard in relation to sending States which have a civil-law system, as their criminal laws provide criminal jurisdiction over their nationals for acts committed abroad. This work has shown that a significant proportion of common-law countries also claim to be able to exercise criminal jurisdiction in these circumstances. The majority of sending States, from whom the bulk of UN police come, can exercise jurisdiction either by ensuring that they can prosecute nationals for all relevant crimes even when committed abroad, or by making criminal law applicable to public officials or security personnel when they are abroad.[37] On this basis, it is recommended that the UN only accept police officers from those States that are able to show that they can exercise jurisdiction. Quite apart from States exercising criminal jurisdiction, recent argument posits that the UN should establish its own model criminal code,[38] create a hybrid criminal tribunal similar to the Special Court for Sierra Leone or the Extraordinary Chambers in Cambodia, and exercise criminal jurisdiction over crimes committed by personnel serving in Peace Operations.[39] This option

35 Chapter 5, Sections 4-1 and 4-2.

36 Chapter 5, Section 3-1.

37 Chapter 5, Section 4-2.

38 William J Durch et al., *Improving Criminal Accountability in United Nations Peace Operations* (Stimson Center Report, 2009), pp. 59–60.

39 UNGA, 'Ensuring the Accountability of United Nations Staff and Experts on Mission with Respect to Criminal Acts Committed in Peacekeeping Operations' (16 August 2006) UN Doc. A/60/980, paras. 33–37. Another suggestion was that a high-ranking Civil Provost should be appointed in major missions. The Civil Provost would be the principal contact point with the host State's criminal justice system, and would 'marshal resources on the UN side of the collaborative criminal justice effort and also work with OIOS forensic field investigators'. The latter role would not solve the problems relating to criminal

may warrant further consideration, but rather in the form of a special chamber of the already-existing ICC, in order to mitigate resource problems.

This research also showed that, in theory, immunity can only shield UN police officers from prosecution in relation to acts committed in the performance of their official duties. Since most of the criminal acts in question have nothing do to with their official performance, immunity should not apply to these. The law provides additional immunity to UN police from arrest and detention, but, in reality, this does not appear to be invoked on its own unless the offence itself is also protected by immunity. The UN Police Commissioner, whilst in office, has immunity for all his conduct.

Some uncertainty remains about the geographic coverage of immunity. If the entire scope of immunity derives from the General Convention,[40] the scope of cover in relation to official acts will be global, both for UN police officers and the UN Police Commissioner.[41] However, if the immunity concerned is dependent on a Status-of-Forces Agreement (SOFA),[42] it is limited in relation to the host State.[43] It is submitted that the UN should make its understanding of the demarcation of immunity clear, so that both States who seek prosecution of the UN police, and the UN police themselves, know what conduct is protected by immunity and where.[44]

The waiving of immunity is a complex issue. Immunity can and must be waived by the Secretary-General (SG) when, 'in his opinion, the immunity would impede the course of justice and can be waived without prejudice to the interests of the [UN]'.[45] It is unclear whether this two-fold test should be understood as requiring waiver *unless* it harms the UN's interests, or whether its application is much more discretionary. There is no mechanism to challenge the SG's decision, except for taking the issue to the ICJ.[46] It could be problematic if immunity is not waived when it should be waived.[47]

---

jurisdiction, but would provide support on behalf of the UN for the host State's exercise of criminal jurisdiction. Durch et al., *Improving Criminal Accountability*, pp. 60–65.

40 Convention on the Privileges and Immunities of the United Nations (adopted 13 February 1946, entered into force 17 September 1946) 1 UNTS 15.

41 Chapter 6, Section 1-4.

42 UNGA, 'Report of the Secretary-General on the Model Status-of-Forces Agreement for Peace-Keeping Operations' (9 October 1990) UN Doc. A/45/594. There are also mission-specific SOFAs. See Chapter 6, Section 1-2.

43 Chapter 6, Section 1-4.

44 Chapter 6, Section 3.

45 General Convention, Article V, Section 20. 'Official' reads 'expert' in ibid, Article VI, Section 23.

46 Chapter 6, Section 1-5-2.

47 Chapter 6, Section 2-2.

In Peace Operations, the determination both of what comes within the UN polices' official functions for the purposes of deciding the issue of the applicability of immunity, and whether or not to waive it where it is found to exist, is made by the SRSG in the name of the SG.[48] Two main problems arise in this regard: the first is that the UN sometimes invokes immunity where no such immunity exists, and then 'waives' this non-existent immunity. It would be better if the UN were to simply and clearly state that there was no such immunity in the first place.[49] Second, the UN sometimes invokes immunity, and does not waive it even where it does not in fact exist. In some cases, it appears that the real reason for this is the UN's concern about handing over its personnel to a legal system that either may not be able to conduct a trial at all, or that is unable to protect a suspect's right to a fair trial. While that is a legitimate concern, it is recommended that this issue be dealt with separately via another mechanism.[50] It is possible that inappropriate claims of immunity amount to a breach of human rights obligations by the UN. To the extent that this is the case, States may be required not to give effect to such immunity.[51]

Given that States are *free* to exercise jurisdiction in relation to criminal conduct committed by the UN police in a majority of cases, an obstacle to prosecution may either be practical, or it may indicate that States are reluctant to exercise jurisdiction. Where reluctance is the problem, it may be possible to argue that the State has an *obligation* to investigate and prosecute (where appropriate) under international human rights law (IHRL). This is the case in relation to allegations of crimes which would be human rights violations had they been committed by State officials. As the territorial State, the host State is subject to this obligation, although the extent of that obligation depends on its

48 Chapter 6, Sections 1-5 and 2.

49 Chapter 6, Section 2-1.

50 Chapter 6, Sections 2-2-1 and 3-1-2.

51 An important development in this regard is that the courts, both national supreme courts and international human rights courts, are exploring the question of the effect of inappropriate immunity by international organizations. They have questioned whether asserting the claimed immunity would deprive individuals of equivalent protection to the protection they enjoy under the law. Guglielmo Verdirame, *The UN and Human Rights: Who Guards the Guardians?* (Cambridge University Press 2011), p. 396. Quite independently of IHRL, the ICJ has called into question the exclusive power of the SG to determine the applicability of immunity. The Court found that the SG's decision 'creates a presumption *which can only be set aside for the most compelling* and is thus given the greatest weight by national courts'. (Emphasis added.) *Difference Relating to Immunity from Legal Process of a Special Rapporteur of the Commission on Human Rights* (Advisory Opinion) [1999] ICJ Rep 62, para. 61.

ability to meet it.[52] It is submitted that the obligation also arises in respect of sending States. While the offence is committed outside its territory, the suspect is nevertheless its national and, moreover, he or she is selected and sent as its representative to a Peace Operation. Once a suspect is back in its territory, the sending State has an obligation to investigate the misconduct, and to do its best to prosecute serious crimes committed by its UN police officer, depending on its circumstances.[53]

The UN may also have certain obligations in this respect. If it is taken as given that the UN has customary human rights obligations, and that the content of its customary obligations is similar to its treaty obligations,[54] it is arguable that the UN has an obligation to: (1) conduct a prompt, effective and impartial investigation; and, (2) to use its best endeavours to ensure that suspects are prosecuted.[55] Where it is clear that the misconduct constitutes a crime, the obligation to investigate may require the UN to conduct its disciplinary investigation according to criminal law standards. The obligation to use its best endeavours may require the UN to hold the suspect, and then to hand him or her over to the prosecuting authority of the State concerned. When the UN hands over the suspect, it should also hand over all the results of its investigations to enable the State to prosecute him or her. This obligation may also require that the UN conduct a systematic follow-up with that State to establish whether it has carried out the prosecution and, if not, why not.[56] It also means that the UN is required *not to shield* a suspect from prosecution, and *to do its best to ensure* prosecution.[57] This further means that the UN must refrain from resorting to inappropriate claims of immunity, or refusing to waive immunity where it is inappropriate to do so.

The research conducted for this work indicates that the problems encountered in ensuring the criminal accountability of the UN police are much more fundamental. One key aspect of the problem is that the UN[58] may be getting offers of police personnel that they have difficulty accepting.[59] The UN receives police personnel from States where the police are not routinely

52 Chapter 7, Sections 2 and 3.

53 Chapter 7, Sections 3 and 5.

54 Chapter 7, Section 8-1.

55 Chapter 7, Section 8-2-1.

56 Chapter 7, Section 8-2-2.

57 Chapter 7, Section 8-2-2.

58 Chapter 2, Section 3.

59 The SG admitted this in relation to military contingents. The SG stated that the UN had no choice but to accept Fijian military contingents, even though some States had imposed sanctions against Fiji after the *coup d'etat*. Tracey Watkins, 'Ban Ki-Moon Backs UN Use of

called to account.[60] If that is the case, there is little prospect of sending States bringing criminal proceedings against their police officers who are accused of committing crimes. If a sending State does not recognize the importance of accountability, it is not likely that pressure exerted on it by the UN to do so will have any real impact. However, there could be an impact if the pressure exerted on a State brought shame on it, leading it to change its behaviour.[61]

This appears mostly not to be the fault of the UN. Nevertheless, the UN should improve its transparency in relation to accountability issues[62] and, more broadly, in relation to its operations in general. There should be no hesitation on its part to make publicly available data regarding the nationality of those police personnel against whom allegations of serious misconduct have been established. Nor should the UN hesitate to publicize the names of States that are not willing to bring criminal proceedings against suspects, following the UN's referral of such cases to them. It is possible that the UN is concerned that disclosing such information would reveal the extent to which UN police officers accused of serious misconduct disproportionately come from a limited number of States, which also happen to be the largest and most constant source of UN police officers. However, if information reveals that the majority of wrongdoers come from certain States, this should not be of major concern to the UN. Instead, the UN should consider imposing conditions on those sending

---

Fiji Soldiers' *Fairfax News NZ* (7 September 2011) <http://www.stuff.co.nz/national/politics/5577793/Ban-Ki-moon-backs-UN-use-of-Fiji-soldiers> accessed 24 August 2014.

60 Chapter 2, Section 3.

61 In one case, members of a Moroccan military contingent were alleged to have been involved in sexual assault and they have been prosecuted subsequent to media reports. 'UN Soldiers Arrested in DR Congo' *BBC* (London, 13 February 2005) <http://news.bbc.co.uk/2/hi/africa/4262743.stm> accessed 24 August 2005; 'UN Troops Held Over Sex Crimes' *CNN* 15 February 2005) <http://www.cnn.com/2005/WORLD/africa/02/15/un.congo.peacekeepers/> accessed 25 August 2006; 'Morroco Soldiers Face Sexual Abuse Charge' *CNN* (13 February 2005) <http://www.cnn.com/2005/WORLD/africa/02/13/morroco.abuse.reut/> accessed 26 August 2006; Scoop, 'UN-Arrest of 6 Peacekeepers for Sexual Abuse' (16 February 2005) <http://www.scoop.co.nz/stories/WO0502/S00429.htm> accessed 23 August 2006; 'Peacekeepers Held for Sex Crimes' *CBS News* (15 February 2005) <http://www.cbsnews.com/stories/2005/02/15/world/main674173.shtml> accessed 15 August 2006; 'UN Soldiers Arrested for Alleged Sexual Abuse' *China Daily* (16 February 2005) <http://china.org.cn/english/international/120416.htm> accessed 16 May 2007; Michael Fleshman, *Tough UN Line on Peacekeeper Abuses* (Africa Survival, April 2005, 2005).

62 See Chapter 4, 3-1-1 (2) c on the lack of information regarding how the whistle-blower protection policy is implemented; Chapter 4, Section 3-5 on the lack of transparency regarding follow-up by the UN regarding actions taken against suspects; and Chapter 4, 3-5 on the issue of concealing the nationality of a perpetrator.

States with accountability problems. For example, where there is an indication that certain States have major issues regarding accountability, it could require those States to make changes, and to provide evidence of this, before accepting further police personnel from them.

By concealing the nationality of suspected wrongdoers, and by concealing the names of States which fail to make efforts to investigate and prosecute crimes committed by their nationals, the UN is, in fact, colluding with those States. If the real problem is the quality of police personnel that the UN attracts, this problem needs to be acknowledged by the UN and its member States. In some situations, the UN may have to choose between having police personnel who are of poor quality, and having no police personnel. This is an issue that the political organs of the UN should resolve. All actors are tacitly aware of these problems, which need to be explicitly discussed with States.

Another action which is not currently being undertaken by the UN, but which could be taken, is the monitoring of the requirements States must meet. Where, for example, the UN establishes selection criteria for UN police personnel, but does not monitor whether the personnel who are sent meet these criteria,[63] the perception will be that these criteria do not really matter. It may be that the UN is not willing to reveal the extent to which UN police officers are not qualified for the job. If that is the case, the UN Secretariat would be missing an opportunity to advise the Security Council about this problem. If problems in this regard lie with the sending States, and not the UN Secretariat, if the UN Secretariat nevertheless covers these up, it is also at fault. With regard to many of these points, the UN has shown that it has identified the issues correctly, but the measures it has adopted, and its attitude toward non-compliance, suggest that the UN does not think these things actually matter.

The issues identified in this assessment of the UN's approach to UN police personnel's criminal accountability are closely connected to how the UN operates. Without an accurate assessment of where the key problems lie, as well as adopting the means for addressing these problems effectively with greater transparency, this predicament cannot be resolved. Instead, what is a very real problem will continue to simply be concealed.

63 Chapter 2, Section 3-3.

Bibliography

International Treaties and Instruments

Agreement between the Government of Bosnia and Herzegovina and the United Nations on the Status of the United Nations Protection Force in Bosnia and Herzegovina (UNPROFOR), 15 May 1993, 1772 UNTS 77.

Agreement between the Government of Sudan and the United Nations concerning the Status of the United Nations Mission in Sudan, (adopted and entered into force 28 December 2005), 2005 UN Jurid YB 44.

Agreement between the Supreme National Council of Cambodia and the United Nations on the Status of the United Nations Transitional Authority in Cambodia, 7, May 1992, 1673 UNTS 364.

Agreement between the United Nations and the Republic of the Congo (Leopoldville) Relating to the Legal Status, Facilities, Privileges and Immunities of the United Nations Organizations in the Congo, 27 November 1961, 414 UNTS 229.

American Convention on Human Rights (adopted 22 November 1969, entered into force 18 July 1978) 1144 UNTS 123.

Convention against Torture and Other Cruel, Inhuman or Degrading Treatment or Punishment (adopted 10 December 1984, entered into force 26 June 1987) 1465 UNTS 85.

Convention for the Protection of Human Rights and Fundamental Freedoms (European Convention on Human Rights, as amended) (ECHR) 213 UNTS 222.

Convention on the High Seas (adopted 29 April 1958, entered into force 30 September 1962) 450 UNTS 11.

Convention on the Privileges and Immunities of the United Nations (adopted 13 February 1946, entered into force 17 September 1946) 1 UNTS 15.

Convention on the Safety of United Nations and Associated Personnel (adopted on 9 December 1994, entered into force on 15 January 1999) 2051 UNTS 363.

Covenant of the League of Nations, adopted 28 April 1919, entered into force 10 January 1920 [1919] UKTS 4 (Cmd 153).

Exchange of Letters concerning an Agreement between the United Nations and the Government of Egypt concerning the Status of the Untied Nations Emergency Force in Egypt, 8 February 1957, 260 UNTS 61.

Exchange of Notes Constituting an Agreement Concerning the Establishment of a United Nations Observer Mission in El Salvador (ONUSAL), 16 and July 1991, 9 August 1991, 644 UNTS 177.

Exchange of Letters Constituting an Agreement Concerning the Privileges and Immunities of the United Nations Observer Mission for the Referendum in Western Sahara (MINURSO), 13 December 1991 and 15 January 1992, 1662 UNTS 169.

Geneva Convention for the Amelioration of the Condition of the Wounded and Sick in Armed Forces in the Field of August 12, 1949 (adopted 8 December 1949, entered into force 21 October 1950) 75 UNTS 30.

Geneva Convention for the Amelioration of the Condition of the Wounded, Sick and Shipwrecked Members of the Armed Forces at Sea of August 12, 1949 (adopted 8 December 1949, entered into force 21 October 1950) 75 UNTS 84.

Geneva Convention Relative to the Protection of Civilian Population in Time of War of August 12, 1949 (adopted 8 December 1949, entered into force 21 October 1950) 75 UNTS 286.

Geneva Convention Relative to the Treatment of Prisoners of War of August 12, 1949 (adopted 8 December 1949, entered into force 21 October 1950) 75 UNTS 134.

Convention for the Protection of Human Rights and Fundamental Freedoms (European Convention on Human Rights, as amended) (ECHR) 213 UNTS 222.

International Covenant on Economic, Social and Cultural Rights (adopted 16 December 1966, entered into force 3 January 1976), 993 UNTS 3.

International Covenant on Civil and Political Rights (adopted 16 December 1966, entered into force 23 March 1977), 999 UNTS 171.

Protocol Additional to the Geneva Conventions of 12 August 1949, and Relating to the Protection of Victims of International Armed Conflicts (Protocol I) 1979 UNTS 4.

Protocol on the Tasks to Be Fulfilled in Angolan Territory (with Additional Protocol), 9 June 1989, 1537 UNTS 13.

Rome Statute of the International Criminal Court (17 July 1998, entered in force 1 June 2002) 2187 UNTS 90.

The Charter of the United Nations (adopted 26 June 1945, entered into force 24 October 1945) 1 UNTS XVI.

Vienna Convention on Consular Relations (adopted 24 April 1963, entered into force 19 March 1967), 1 UNTS 596.

Vienna Convention on Diplomatic Relations (adopted 18 April 1961, entered into force on 24 April 1964) 500 UNTS 95.

National Laws

Code Penal (Niger, Loi N° 2003-025 du 13 Juin 2003 Modifiant la Loi N° 61-27 du 15 Juillet 1961, portant Institution du Code Pénal, Journal Officiel Spécial N° 4 du 7 Avril 2004).

Code de Procedure Penale (Niger, Loi N° 61-33 du 14 Août 1961 portant Institution du Code de Procédure Pénale, Modifiée par la Loi N° 2003-026 du 13 Juin 2003, la Loi N° 2004-21 du 16 Mai 2004 et la Loi N° 2007-04 du 22 Février 2007).

Code Pénal (Niger, tel qu'Amendé par la Loi no 2008–18) 2003.

Crimes and Misconduct (Overseas Operations) Act (NZ, Public Act 2004 no 17) 2004.

Criminal Code (Chech) 2009.

Criminal Code (Germany, Version promulgated on 13 November 1998, Federal Law Gazette [Bundesgesetzblatt] I p. 3322, last amended by Article 3 of the Law of 2 October 2009, Federal Law Gazette I p. 3214).

Criminal Code (Ghana, Act 29) 1960.

Criminal Code (Hungary) 2012.

Criminal Code (Italy, Codice Penale) 1930.

Criminal Code (Norway, The General Civil Penal Code, Act of 22 May 1902 no 10, with subsequent amendments, the latest made by Act of 21 December 2005 no 131) 1902.

Criminal Code (Panama) 2007.

Criminal Code (Poland) 1997.

Criminal Code (Portugal) 1982.

Criminal Code (Romania) 1969.

Criminal Code (Sweden, 'Brottsbalken') 1965.

Human Trafficking and Transportation (Control) Act (Nepal, 2064 [2007], shrawan 8, 2064 [24 July 2007], Act no 5 of the Year 2064 [2007]).

International Crimes Act (The Netherlands) 2003.

Loi no 043/96/ADP du 13 Novembre 1996 Portant Code Pénal (Burkina Faso) 13 December 1996.

New General Civil Penal Code (Norway) 2005.

Organic Act 1/2009 (Spain, 3 November 2009).

Penal Code (Bangladesh, Act no XLV of 1860 of 6 October 1980).

Penal Code (France) 2005.

Penal Code (Greece) 1950.

Penal Code (India, 1860 Act no 45 of 1860 of 6 October 1860).

Penal Code (Indonesia, Undang-undang RI no 27 Tahun 1999, Tanggal 19 Mei 1999) 1982.

Penal Code, (Pakistan, Act XLV of 6 October 1860).

Penal Code (The Philippines, as Revised by an Act Revising the Penal Code and Other Penal Laws, Act no 3815, 8 December 1930).

Penal Code (Togo, Code Pénal) 1980.

Penal Code (Yemen, Republican Decree for Law no 12 for the Year 1994 Concerning Crimes and Penalties) 1994.

Perjury Act (UK) 1911.

Republican Decree for Law no 12 for the Year 1994, Concerning Crimes and Penalties (Yemen).

Republican Decree for Law no 13 for the Year 1994, Concerning the Criminal Procedures (Yemen).

Sexual Offences Act (c 43) (UK) 2003.
The Anti-Human Trafficking Act (Sierra Leone, Act Supplement to the Sierra Leone Gazette vol CXXXVI, no 44 of 18 August 2005) 2005.
The Criminal Code (Amendment) Act (Ghana, Act 646) 2003.
The Criminal Code (Ukraine, entered into force 1 September 2001).
The Criminal Procedure Acts (Sierra Leone, Act No 32) 1965.
The Offences Against the Person Act (UK) 1861.
The Organic Law of the Judiciary 6/1985 (Spain, LOPJ – Ley Organica del Poder Judicial) 1985.
The Sex Offenders Act (c 51) (UK) 1997.
The United Nations (Police) Act (NZ) 1964.
UNMIK Regulation no 1999/24 on the Law Applicable in Kosovo (12 December 1999).
UNMIK Regulation no 2000/38 of 30 June 2000 on the Establishment of the Ombudsperson Institution in Kosovo.
UNMIK Regulation no 2006/12 of 23 March 2006 on the Establishment of the Human Rights Advisory Panel.
UNTAET Regulation no 1999/1 on the Authority of the Transitional Administration in East Timor.
2003 Amendment to the Crimes (Overseas) Act (Australia) 1964.

Cases and Decisions

Accordance with International Law of the Unilateral Declaration of Independence in Respect of Kosovo (Declaration of Simma J) [2010] ICJ Rep 478.
Affaire Gentilhomme, Schaff-Benhadji and Zerouki v France App nos 48205/99, 48207/99 and 48209/99 (ECtHR, 14 May 2002).
Ahmet Özkan and Others v UK App no 21689/93, (ECtHR, 6 April 2004).
Akpinar and Altun v Turkey ECHR 2007-III.
Aksoy v Turkey ECHR 1996-VI.
Al-Adsani v UK ECHR 2001-XI.
Al-Jedda v UK [2011] ECHR 1092.
Al-Skeini and Others v UK [2011] ECHR 1093.
Ali Medjnoune v Algeria 9 Selected Decisions of the Human Rights Committee 182.
Angelova and Iliev v Bulgaria ECHR 2007-IX.
Applicability of Article VI, Section 22, of the Convention on the Privileges and Immunities of the United Nations (Advisory Opinion) [1989] ICJ Rep 177.
Applicability of Article VI, Section 22, of the Convention on the Privileges and Immunities of the United Nations (Written Statement Submitted on behalf of the Secretary-General of the United Nations) [1989] ICJ Rep 173.

Armed Activities on the Territory of the Congo (DRC v Uganda) [2005] ICJ Rep 168.
Arrest Warrant of 11 April 2000 (DRC v Belgium) (Diss Op Van den Wyngaert) [2002] ICJ Rep 137.
Arrest Warrant of 11 April 2000 (DRC v Belgium) (Judgment) [2002] ICJ Rep 3.
Arrest Warrant of 11 April 2000 (DRC v Belgium) (Sep Op Guillaume P) [2002] ICJ Rep 35.
Arrest Warrant of 11 April 2000 (DRC v Belgium) (Sep Op Higgins, Koojimans and Buergenthal) [2002] ICJ Rep 63.
Assanidze v Georgia ECHR 2004-II.
Aydin v Turkey ECHR 1997-VI.
Banković and Others v Belgium and Others (Admissibility) ECHR 2001-XII.
Bazorkina v Russia ECHR 2006-I.
Behrami and Behrami v France and Sarmati v France, Germany and Norway (Admissibility) App nos 71412/01, 78166/01 (ECtHR, 2 May 2007).
Beker v Turkey App no 27866/03 (ECtHR, 24 March 2009).
Bekos v Greece App no 15250/02 (ECtHR, 13 December 2005).
Bilbija et al. (2006) AP-953/05 (Constitutional Court of Bosnia and Herzegovina, in the Appeal of Milorad Bilbija et al., 8 July 2006).
Blake v Guatemala Inter-Am Ct HR Series C No 36 (24 January 1998).
Boery v Ghaddafi Cour de Cassation [2001] 125 ILR 490.
Bogdan Subotić (2005) AP-696/04 (The Constitutional Court of Bosnia and Herzegovina, 23 September 2005).
Bouterse v Public Prosecutor Court of Appeal of Amsterdam (Gerechtshof Amsterdam) 20 November 2000.
Bulacio v Argentina Inter-Am Ct HR Series C No 100 (18 September 2003).
Caballero Delgado and Santana v Colombia Inter-Am Ct HR Series C No 22 (8 December 1995).
Çakıcı v Turkey [1999] ECHR 43.
Calvelli and Ciglio v Italy ECHR 2002-I.
Case concerning Application of the Convention on the Prevention and Punishment of the Crime of Genocide (Bosnia and Herzegovina v Serbia and Montenegro) (Judgment of 26 February 2007) [2007] ICJ Rep 43 (ICJ).
Case concerning Barcelona Traction, Light and Power Co Ltd (Belgium v Spain) (New Application: 1962) (Second phase) [1970] ICJ Rep 3.
Case concerning Military and Paramilitary Activities in and against Nicaragua (Nicaragua v US) (Merits) [1986] ICJ Rep 12.
Certain Questions of Mutual Assistance in Criminal Matters (Djibouti v France) (Judgment) [2008] ICJ Rep 172.
Corfu Channels case (UK v Albania) (Merits) [1949] ICJ Rep 4.
Cynthia Brzak and Nasr Ishak v The United Nations, Kofi Annan, Wendy Chambering, Ruud Lubbers, et al. (Certiorari – Summary Dispositions) Order list 562 US 09-1481.

Cynthia Brzak and Nasr Ishak v The United Nations, Kofi Annan, Wendy Chambering, Ruud Lubbers, et al. Docket No. 08-2799-cv 597 F 3d 107 (2010).

Cynthia Brzak and Nasr Ishak v The United Nations, Kofi Annan, Wendy Chambering, Ruud Lubbers, et al. 551 F Supp 2d 313 (SDNY 2008).

Cyprus v Turkey ECHR 2001-IV.

Difference Relating to Immunity from Legal Process of a Special Rapporteur of the Commission on Human Rights (Advisory Opinion) [1999] ICJ Rep 62.

Difference Relating to Immunity from Legal Process of a Special Rapporteur of the Commission on Human Rights (Diss Op Koroma) [1999] ICJ Rpt 111.

Difference Relating to Immunity from Legal Process of a Special Rapporteur of the Commission on Human Rights (Written Statement submitted on behalf of the Secretary-General of the United Nations) (ICJ 2 October 1999), <http://wwwicj-cijorg/docket/files/100/8658pdf>, accessed 30 November 2011.

Dink v Turkey App no 2668/07 (ECtHR, 14 September 2010).

Dodov v Bulgaria ECHR 2008.

Durand v Peru Inter-Am Ct HR Series C No 68 (16 August 2000).

Eduardo Bleier v Uruguay 1 Selected Decisions of the Human Rights Committee 109.

Almeida de Quinteros v Uruguay 2 Selected Decisions of the Human Rights Committee 138.

Edwards v UK Series A No 247 B.

El Hassy v Lybia Communication no 1422/2005 (Human Rights Committee, 24 October 2007).

El Moctar v Secretary-General of the United Nations Case no UNDT/NBI/2011/011, Judgment no UNDT/2012/113, (UNDT, 24 July 2012).

Ergi v Turkey ECHR 1998-IV.

Etienne Tête v France Series A No 54.

Eugenia Lazăr v Romania App no 32146/05 (ECtHR, 16 February 2010).

Ferrini v Germany [2004] Italian Court of Cassation, Decision No 5044/2004, 128 ILR 658.

Finucane v UK ECHR 2003-VIII.

Food and Agriculture Organization v Istituto Nazionale di Previdenze per i Dirigenti di Aziende Industriali (INPDAI) [1992] Italian Court of Cassation 87 ILR 1–10.

Gajić v Germany (Admissibility) App no 31446/02 (ECtHR, 28 August 2007).

Genie-Lacayo v Nicaragua Inter-Am Ct HR Series C No 30 (29 January 1997).

Georgia v Russia (II) (Admissibility) App no 38263/08 (ECtHR, 19 December 2011).

Godinez-Cruz v Honduras (Merits) Inter-Am Ct HR Series C No 5 (20 January 1989).

H C M A v The Netherlands 3 Selected Decisions of the Human Rights Committee 19.

Gongadze v Ukraine App no 34056/02 (ECtHR, 8 November 2005).

Guiliani and Gaggio v Italy ECHR-2011.

Gül v Turkey App no 22676/93 (ECtHR, 14 December 2000).

Güleç v Turkey ECHR 1998-IV.

Hassan Abbousedra v Lybia Communication no 1751/2008 (Human Rights Committee, 25 October 2010).

HRH Prince Abdul Aziz Bin Fahd Bin Abdul Aziz v Mrs Janan George Harb [2015] EWCA Civ 481.

Hugh Jordan v UK ECHR 2001-III.

Ilaşcu and Others v Moldova and Russia ECHR 2004-VII.

Ilhan v Turkey ECHR 2000-VII.

Imakayeva v Russia ECHR 2006-XIII.

Interpretation of the Agreement of 25 March 1951 between the WHO and Egypt (Advisory Opinion) [1980] ICJ Rep 73.

Isayeva v Russia App no 57950/00 (ECtHR, 6 July 2005).

Jaloud v the Netherlands [2014] ECHR 1292.

Jankauskas v Lithuania App no 59304/00 (ECtHR, 16 December 2003).

Joaquín David Herrera Rubio v Colombia 2 Selected Decisions of the Human Rights Committee 192.

Jones v Ministry of Interior Al-Mamlaka Al-Arabiya AS Saudiya (the Kingdom of Saudi Arabia) [2006] UKHL 26.

Jones and Others v UK ECHR 2014.

José Vicente and Amado Villafañe Chaparro, Dioselina Torres Crespo, Hermes Enrique Torres Solis and Vicencio Chaparro Izquierdo v Colombia 6 Selected Decisions of the Human Rights Committee 135.

Jurisdictional Immunities of the State (Germany v Italy: Greece intervening) (Diss Op Trindade) [2012] ICJ Rep 179.

Jurisdictional Immunities of the State (Germany v Italy: Greece intervening) (Judgement) [2012] ICJ Rep 99.

Kalogeropoulou and Others v Greece and Germany (Admissibility) EHCR 2002-X.

Kasumaj v Greece (Admissibility) App no 6974/05 (ECtHR, 5 July 2007).

Kaya v Turkey ECHR 1998-I.

Kelly and Others v UK App no 30054/96 (ECtHR, 4 May 2001).

Kemal Kiliç v Turkey ECHR 2000-III.

Khilal Avadanov v Azerbaijan Communication no 1633/2007 (Human Rights Committee, 25 October 2010).

Kurt v Turkey ECHR 1998-III.

L C B v UK ECHR 1998-III 1403.

La Palmeras v Colombia Inter-Am Ct HR Series C No 90 (6 December 2001).

Legal Consequences of the Construction of a Wall in the Occupied Palestinian Territory (Advisory Opinion) [2004] ICJ Rep 316.

Legal Status of Eastern Greenland Case (Denmark v Norway) (Judgment) PCIJ Rep Series A/B, No 53, 48.

Loayza-Tamayo v Peru Inter-Am Ct HR Series C No42 (27 November 1998).

Loizidou v Turkey Series A No 310.

Lotus (*France v Turkey*) (Judgment) PCIJ Rep Series A No 10.

M C v Bulgaria ECHR 2003-XII.

M G B and S P v Trinidad and Tobago 3 Selected Decisions of the Human Rights Committee 36.

M & Co v Germany Series A No 64.

Mahmut Kaya v Turkey ECHR 2000-III.

Marcellana and Gumanoy v The Philippines Communication no 1560/2007 (Human Rights Committee, 30 October 2008).

Maria da Penha Maia Fernandes v Brazil 12.051 Inter-Am Com HR Series L No 54/01.

Özgür Gündem v Turkey ECHR 2000-III.

Marija and Dragana Novakovic, on behalf of their son, Zoran Novakovic (deceased) v Serbia Communication no 1556/2007 (Human Rights Committee, 21 October 2010).

Matthews v UK [1999] ECHR 12.

McCann and Others v UK Series A No 324.

McKerr v UK ECHR 2001-III.

McShane v UK App no 43290/98 (ECtHR 28 May 2002).

Mehmet Şentürk and Bekir Şentürk v Turkey App no 13423/09 (ECtHR, 9 April 2013).

Menesheva v Russia App no 59261/00 (ECtHR, 9 March 2006).

Menson and Others v UK ECHR 2003-V.

Messaouda Kimouche v Algeria Communication no 1328/2004 (Human Rights Committee, 10 July 2007).

Mikayil Mammadov v Azerbaijan App no 4762/05 (ECtHR, 17 December 2009).

Mojsiewiew v Poland App no 11818/02 (ECtHR, 24 March 2009).

Mothers of Srebrenica Association v State of the Netherlands Case no 10/04437 EV/AS (Supreme Court of the Netherlands, 13 April 2012), English translation available at: <http://wwwrechtspraaknl/Organisatie/Hoge-Raad/Supreme-court/Summaries-of-some-important-rulings-of-the-Supreme-Court/Pages/Ruling-Dutch-Supreme-Court-Mothers-of-Srebrenicaaspx> Accessed 1 January 2015.

Nguyen-Kropp Postica v Secretary-General of the United Nations Cases no UNDT/NY/2010/107; UNDT/NY/2011/004 Judgment no UNDT/2013/176 (UNDT, 20 December 2013).

North Sea Continental Shelf case (Federal Republic of Germany v Denmark/The Netherlands) [1969] ICJ Rep 3.

Nuclear Tests Case (*Australia v France*) (Merits) [1974] ICJ Rep 253.

Nuhanovic v The State of the Netherlands Case no 265618 HA ZA 06-1672 (Court of Appeal in the Hague, 5 July 2011) English translation available at <http://zoekenrechtspraaknl> Accessed 29 December 2014.

Nuhanovic v The State of the Netherlands Case no 265615/HA ZA 06-1671 (DC Hague, 10 September 2008) English translation available at <http://zoekenrechtspraaknl> Accessed 29 December 2014.

Nydia Erika Bautista de Arellana v Colombia 6 Selected Decisions of the Human Rights Commitee 103.

Ognyanova v Bulgaria App no 46317/99 (ECtHR, 23 February 2006).

Öğur v Turkey ECHR 1999-III.

Öneryildiz v Turkey ECHR 2004-XII.

Osman and Osman v UK ECHR 1998-VIII.

Osmanoglu v Turkey App no 48804/99 (ECtHR, 24 January 2008).

Paniagua-Morales v Guatemala Inter-Am Ct HR Series C No 37 (8 March 1998).

Paul and Audrey Edwards v UK ECHR 2002-II.

Powell v UK ECHR 2000-V.

Prisacariu v Secretary-General of the United Nations Case no UNDT/NY/2012/023, Judgment No UNDT/2014/045 (UNDT, 23 April 2014).

Prosecutor v Akeyasu (Decision on the Motion to Subpoena a Witness) ICTR-96-4-T (19 November 1997).

Prosecutor v Braškić (Decision of Trial Chamber I on Protective Measures of General Phillippe Morillon, Witness of the Trial Chamber) IT-95-14-T (12 May 1999) [2].

Prosecutor v Braškić (Judgment on the request of Croatia for review of the decision of the Trial Chamber II of 18 July 1997) IT-95-14-A (29 October 1997).

Prosecutor v Brima et al. (Decision on Prosecution Appeal Against Decision on Oral Application for Witness TF1-150 to Testify Without Being Compelled to Answer Questions on Grounds of Confidentiality) SCSL-2004-16-AR73 (26 May 2006).

Prosecutor v Brima et al. (Diss Op Donerty on the Prosecution's Oral Application for Leave to Be Granted to Witness TF1-150 to Testify Without Being Compelled to Answer Any Questions on Grounds of Confidentiality) SCSL-04-16-T, TC II (22 September 2005).

Prosecutor v Brima et al. (Sep and Conc Op Robertson, Decision on Prosecution Appeal against Decision on Oral Application for Witness TF1-150 to Testify Without Being Compelled to Answer Questions on Groudns of Confidentiality) SCSL-04-16, AC (26 May 2006).

Prosecutor v Furundzija (Trial Judgement) ICTY-95-17/1-T (10 December 1998).

Questions relating to the Obligation to Prosecute or Extradite (*Belgium v Senegal*) [2012] ICJ Rpt 422.

R (on the application of Al-Jedda) (FC) v Secretary of State for Defence (Sep Op Bingham LJ) [2007] UKHL 58.

R A V N v Argentina 3 Selected Decisions of the Human Rights Committee 20.

Rafael Mojica v Dominican Republic 5 Selected Decisions of the Human Rights Committee 70.

Ramsahai and Others v the Netherlands [2007] ECHR 393.

Reavey v UK App no 34640/04 (ECtHR, 27 November 2007).

Regina v Bow Street Metropolitan Stipendary Magistrate, ex parte Pinochet [1999] UKHL 17, [2000] 1 AC 147.

Reparation for Injuries Suffered in the Service of the United Nations (Advisory Opinion) [1949] ICJ Rep 174.

Rosario Celis Laureano v Peru 6 Selected Decisions of the Human Rights Committee 63.

S E v Argentina 3 Selected Decisions of the Human Rights Committee 41.

Salman v Turkey ECHR 2000-VII.

Shaip Canhasi v UNMIK Case no 004/08 (The Human Rights Advisory Panel, 15 July 2008).

Shanaghan v UK App no 37715/97 (ECtHR, 4 August 2001).

Shefqet Maliqi, against the United Nations Mission in Kosovo (UNMIK) Registration no 361/01, (the Kosovo Ombudsperson, 13 March 2002).

Silih v Slovenia ECHR 2009.

Solomou and Others v Turkey App no 36832/97 (ECtHR, 24 June 2008).

Standard Chartered Bank v ITC and Others [1987] 1 WLR 641, 648 (Bingham J).

Sundara Arachchige Lalith Rajapakse v Sri Lanka Communication no 1250/2004 (Human Rights Committee, 14 July 2006).

Svetlana Jočić v UNMIK Case no 34/09 (Human Rights Advisory Panel, 23 April 2013).

Tanis and Others v Turkey ECHR 2005-VIII.

Tanli v Turkey ECHR 2001-III.

Tanrikulu v Turkey ECHR 1999-IV.

The Legality of the Threat or Use of Nuclear Weapons (Advisory Opinion) [1996] ICJ Rep 238.

The Legality of the Threat or Use of Nuclear Weapons (Declaration of Bedjaoui P) [1996] ICJ Rep 268.

The State of the Netherlands (Ministry of Defence and Ministry of Foreign Affairs) v Hasan Nuhanovic Case no 12/03324 LZ/TT (Judgement of 6 September 2013) Supreme Court of the Netherlands, English translation available at: <http://wwwrechtspraaknl/Organisatie/Hoge-Raad/OverDeHogeRaad/publicaties/Documents/12%2003324pdf> Accessed 10 March 2015.

Tradesman v Colombia Inter-Am Ct HR Series C No 109 (5 July 2004).

US v Coplon et al. US Dist Ct SDNY 10 May 1949, 84 F Supp 472 (SDNY 1949).

Nottebohm case (Lichtenstein v Guatemala) (Second phase) (Judgment of 6 April 1955) [1955] ICJ Rep 4.

US v Melekh US Dist Ct SDNY, 28 November 1960, 190 F Supp 67 (SDNY 1960).

Attorney-General v Eichmann (Israel Sup Ct 1962), 36 Int'l L Rep 277, 1968 (English translation).

US v Rey 663 F 2d 1086 DNM (2009).

Vadivel Sathasivam and Parathesi Saraswathi v Sri Lanka Communication no 1436/2005 (Human Rights Committee, 8 July 2008).

Varnava and Others v Turkey ECHR 2009.

Velásquez Rodríguez v Honduras Inter-Am Ct HR Series C No 4 (29 July 1988).

Westchester County v William Ranollo New Rochelle City Ct, 8 November 1946, 187 Misc 777; 67 NYS 2d 31 (City Ct of New York, New Rochelle 1946); (1946) 13 ILR 168–171.

Wong Sun et al. v US 371 US 471 (1963), 83 S Ct 407; 9 L Ed 2d 441; 1963 US LEXIS 2431.

X and Y v The Netherlands Series A No 91.

Yaşa v Turkey ECHR 1998-VI.

Yasoda Sharma v Nepal Communication no 1469/2006 (Human Rights Committee, 6 November 2008).

Yousuf v Samantar 699 F 3rd 763 (4th Circuit).

Zheikov v Russia Communication No 889/1999 (Human Rights Committee, 17 March 2006).

UN and Other International and Governmental Documents

American Law Institute, *Restatement (Second) Foreign Relations Law of the US* (1965).

American Law Institute, *Restatement (Third) Foreign Relations Law of the United States* (1987).

Deschamps M, Jallow HB and Sooka Y, Taking Action against Sexual Exploitation and Abuse by Peacekeepers – Report of an Independent Review on Sexual Exploitation and Abuse by International Peacekeeping Forces in the Central African Republic (17 December 2015).

ILC, 'Persons falling within the category of "experts on missions for the United Nations"' (1967) 2 IYv 284.

ILC, 'Report of the International Law Commission on the work of its Forty-Eighth Session, 6 May–26 July 1996, Official Records of the General Assembly, Fifty-first session, Supplement no10', (6 May–26 July 1996), UN Doc. A/51/10.

ILC, 'Report of the International Law Commission on the Work of its 53rd Session', (23 April–1 June and 2 July–10 August 2001), UN Doc. 'A/56/10.

ILC, 'Report of the Study Group of the International Law Commission, "Fragmentation of International Law: Difficulties arising from the Diversification and Expansion of Itnernational Law"', (18 July 2006), UN Doc. A/CN.4/L702.

ILC, 'The Obligation to Extradite or Prosecute (*Aut dedere aut judicare*)', (5 March, 30 April, 5 June, 2 and 11 July 2007), UN Doc. A/CN.4/579 and Add. 1–4.

ILC, *The Practice of the United Nations, the Specialized Agencies and the International Atomic Energy Agency concerning their Status, Privileges and Immunities: Study Prepared by the Secretariat* (1967), 2 ILC YB 154.

OSCE Mission in Kosovo, *Kosovo: A Review of the Criminal Justice System 1 September 2000–28 February 2001* (Department of Human Rights and Rule of Law, 2001).

OSCE Mission in Kosovo, *Kosovo Review of the Criminal Justice System, September 2001–February 2002 – Themes: Independence of the Judiciary, Detention, Mental Health Issues* (Department of Human Rights and Rule of Law, 2002).

OSCE Mission in Kosovo, *Kosovo Review of the Criminal Justice System – Themes: Legal Representation, Detention, Trafficking & Sexually Related Crimes, Municipal & Minor Offence Courts* (Department of Human Rights and Rule of Law, October 2001).

Rasmussen J, 'MONUC: Sexual Exploitation and Abuse, End of Assignment Report', (25 February 2005), (on file with author).

The League of Nations, 'From a Letter to the Head of the Federal Political Department of Switzerland', (11 June 1925), UN Doc. LN Document C.66.1925.

UN, 'Accountability Frameworks in the United Nations System', (2011), UN Doc. JIU/REP/2011/5.

UN, 'Amendments to the 100 Series of the Staff Rules (ST/SGB/2002/1)', (1 January 2003), UN Doc. ST/SGB/2003/1.

UN, 'Amendments to the 100 Series of the Staff Rules (ST/SGB/2002/1)', (1 January 2004), UN Doc. ST/SGB/2004/1.

UN, 'Amendments to the 100 Series of the Staff Rules (ST/SGB/2002/1)', (1 January 2005), UN Doc. ST/SGB/2005/1.

UN, 'Amendments to the 100 Series of the Staff Rules (ST/SGB/2002/1)', (1 January 2006), UN Doc. ST/SGB/2006/1.

UN, 'Articles 104 and 105' (1966) Repertory of Practice of United Nations Organs: Supplement I, vol 1–2 217.

UN, 'Code Cable on the Clarification of Roles within Mission Administration with Regard to Conduct and Discipline Issues', (4 June 2007), (on file with author).

UN, 'Code Cable on the Clarification of Conduct and Discipline Issues', (1 February 2006), (on file with author).

UN, 'Code Cable on the Guidance on Cooperation with OIOS on Investigation', (22 November 2005), (on file with author).

UN, 'Comprehensive Review of All Aspects of Boards of Inquiry Report', (2005), (on file with author).

UN, 'Decision of the Secretary-General at the Policy Committee Meeting on Human Rights in Integrated Missions', (26 October 2005), UN Doc. Decision No.2005/24.

UN, *District Court of Haifa, The Government of Israel against Papa Coli Ben Dista Saar: Judgement of 10 May 1979: Question of the Jurisdiction of an Israeli Court Regarding a Member of a National Contingent within UNIFIL, Accused of Smuggling Explosives into Israeli Territory – Claim of Immunity from Territorial Jurisdiction – Question Whether the Accused Could be Considered as a Member of a Foreign Military Force Present in Israel with the Consent and Permission of the State – Extent of the*

Immunity of Jurisdiction of Members of Such Forces in the Absence of a Specific Agreement on the Matter between the Host State and the Country of the Military Forces Origin – Question Whether the Accused Could be Considered as Enjoying Immunity from Jurisdiction as a Member of a United Nations Force (1979), 1979 UN Jurid YB 205.

UN, 'Exchange of Letters Constituting an Agreement between the United Nations and the Government of Cyprus Concerning the Status of the United Nations Peacekeeping Force in Cyprus, 31 March 1964' (1964) YB UJ 40.

UN, 'Exchange of Letters (with General Directive) Constituting an Agreement between the United Nations and the Government of Pakistan Concerning the United Nations Security Force in West New Guinea (West Irian), 6 December 1962 and 18 April 1963' (1964) YB UJ 34.

UN, *Exclusive Authority of the Secretary-General as Regards Permission to Execute the Waivers of Privileges and Immunities Required by a Member State from Staff Members Maintaining or Seeking Permanent Resident Status in that State – Policy of the United Nations in that Respect* (1969), 1969 UN Jurid YB 224.

UN, *Extent of the Immunity from Local Prosecution Enjoyed by United Nations Officials under Existing International Agreements* (1974), 1974 UN Jurid YB 188.

UN, 'Field Administration Handbook', (January 1974), UN Doc. ST/OGS/L.2/Rev.3.

UN, 'Human Rights Due Diligence Policy on UN Support to non-UN Security Forces (HRDDP)', UN Doc.

UN, 'Human Rights Screening of United Nations Personnel', (11 December 2012), (on file with author).

UN, *Immunity from Legal Process of United Nations Officials – Memorandum to the Deputy Chef de Cabinet* (1963), 1963 UN Jurid YB 188.

UN, 'Information Circularon the Reporting of Suspected Misconduct', (24 March 2005), UN Doc. ST/IC/2005/19.

UN, Integrated Assessment and Planning Handbook (UN 2014).

UN, *Legal Status of Certain Categories of United Nations Personnel Serving in Peacekeeping Operations – Civilian Police and Military Observers – Military Members of Military Components (3 May 2002)* (2002), 2002 UN Jurid YB 466.

UN, *Legal Status of Experts Employed by Specialized Agencies – Question whether Salaries and Emoluments of Experts on Mission Should be Accorded Exception from National Taxation in Pursuance of the 1947 Convention on the Privileges and Immunities of the Specialized Agencies – Scope of the Privileges and Immunities Enjoyed by UNIDO Experts and UNDP Volunteers* (1992), 1992 UN Jurid YB.

UN, *Letter to the Acting Chair of the Special Committee on Peacekeeping Operations, United Nations, Regarding Immunities of Civilian Police and Military Personnel* (2004), 2004 UN Jurid YB 323.

UN, *Liability of the Organization for Claims Concerning Loss of or Damage to Personal Property of the Members of the Peacekeeping Contingents – Report of the*

Secretary-General Entitled 'Review of the Background and Development of Reimbursement to Member States Contributing Troops to Peacekeeping Operations' (*A/44/605/Add.l*) *of 12 October 1989 – Financial Arrangements with States Contributing Troops for UNIFIL and UNFICYP – Reimbursability of Extra and Extraordinary Costs as They are Incurred by the States as a Result of their Soldiers' Participation in UNIFIL and UNFICYP – Loss and Damage to Personal Property Fall within the Category of Extra and Extraordinary Costs* (*15 July 1993*) (1993), 1993 UN Jurid YB 346.

UN, *Liability of the United Nations for Claims Involving Off-Duty Acts by Members of Peace-Keeping Forces – Determination of 'Off-Duty' and 'On-Duty' Status* (1986).

UN, 'Revised Disciplinary Measures and Procedures', (2 August 1991), UN Doc. ST/AI/371.

UN, 'Memorandum dated 17 April 1981 from the Assistant Administrator, Bureau for Finance and Administration, to the Field Offices of UNDP and UNDP Headquarters Staff', (17 April 1981), UN Doc. UNDP/ADM/FIELD/762; UNDP/ADM/HQRTS/503.

UN, 'Model Memorandum of Understanding between the United Nations and [participating State] contributing resources to [the United Nations Peacekeeping Operation]', in *Manual on Policies and Procedures Concerning the Reimbursement and Control of Contingent-Owned Equipment of Troop/Police Contributors Participating in Peacekeeping Missions* (*COE Manual*), UN Doc A/51/967, annex A.

UN, 'Model Memorandum of Understanding between the United Nations and [participating State] contributing resources to [the United Nations Peacekeeping Operation]', in *Manual on Policies and Procedures Concerning the Reimbursement and Control of Contingent-Owned Equipment of Troop/Police Contributors Participating in Peacekeeping Missions* (*COE Manual*), (2007), UN Doc. A/C.5/60/26, annex A.

UN, 'Model Memorandum of Understanding between the United Nations and the xxx Contributing Resources to the xxxx', (on file with author).

UN, *Panel Discussion: Sexual exploitation and Abuse in Conflict and Post-Conflict Situations* (Available at <http://wwwunmultimediaorg/tv/webcast/2011/10/panel-discussion-sexual-exploitation-and-abuse-in-conflict-and-post-conflict-situation-shtml> accessed 10 January 2015, 2011).

UN, 'Policy on UN Transitions in the Context of Mission Drawdown or Withdrawal', (4 February 2013), UN Doc.

UN, *Privileges and Immunities of Officials of the United Nations and the Specialized Agencies – Concept of Functional Immunity – Right of the Secretary-General under the International Instruments in Force to Independently Determine, in Case a Staff Member is Being Subjected to Legal Process, Whether an Official Act is Involved – Meaning of the Term 'Officer' in the Conventions on the Privileges and Immunities of the United Nations and of the Specialized Agencies* (1981), 1981 UN Jurid YB 161.

UN, *Proposed Accession by a Member State to the Convention on the Privileges and Immunities of the United Nations Subject to a Reservation Denying to any United Nations*

Official of That State's Nationality any Privilege or Immunity under the Convention – Interpretation Of Articles IV, V and VI of the Convention (1963), 1963 UN Jurid YB 188.

UN, *Question of Privileges and Immunities of the United Nations, of Representatives of Member States and of Officials of the Organization – Statement Made by the Legal Counsel at the 1016th Meeting of the Sixth Committee of the General Assembly on 6 December 1967* (1967), 1967 UN Jurid YB 311.

UN, *Question of Whether Contractors' Personnel Could be Considered as 'Experts on Mission' – Article VI, Section 22, of the 1946 Convention on the Privileges and Immunities of the United Nations – Status of Consultants* (1998), 1998 UN Jurid YB 481.

UN, *Question of Whether United Nations Laissez-Passer Can Be Issued to Individuals Engaged on Special Service Agreements – Article VII. of the Convention on the Privileges and Immunities of the United Nations* (1995), 1995 UN Jurid YB 409.

UN, *Question of Who Can Determine Whether the Acts of United Nations Officials are Performed in their Official Capacity – Section 20 of the Convention on the Privileges and Immunities of the United Nations (24 January 1995)* (1995), 1995 UN Jurid YB 403.

UN, 'Report of the Preparatory Commission of the United Nations', (23 December 1945), UN Doc. PC/20.

UN, 'Report of the Rapporteur of Committee 1V/2 as Approved by the Committee, UNCIO vol 13',(12 June 1945), UN Doc. 933, IV 2/42(2).

UN, 'Report on the Activities of the Office of Internal Oversight Services for the Period from 1 July 2008 to 30 June 2009', (26 August 2009), UN Doc. A/64/326 (Part I)/Add.1.

UN, 'Report Submitted by Subcommittee to Committee IV, UN Conference on International Organization, vol 13', (18 May 1945), UN Doc. 412 IV/2/A/2 (2).

UN, 'Reporting of Inappropriate Use of United Nations Resources and Proposals for Improvement of Programme Delivery', (7 September 1994), UN Doc. ST/AI/397.

UN, *Request by the Government of a Member State that United Nations Technical Assistance Experts Sign a Declaration under an Act on State Security* (1973), 1973 UN Jurid YB 166.

UN, 'Secretary-General's Bulletin on the Establishment of the Office of the Oversight Services', (7 September 1994), UN Doc. ST/SGB/273.

UN, 'Secretary-General's Bulletin on the Financial Regulations and Rules of the United Nations', (9 May 2003), UN Doc. ST/SGB/2003/7.

UN, 'Secretary-General's Bulletin on the Observance by United Nations forces of International Humanitarian Law', UN Doc. ST/SGB/1999/13.

UN, 'Secretary-General's Bulletin on the Protection against Retaliation for Reporting Misconduct and for Cooperating with Duly Authorized Audits or Investigations', (19 December 2005), UN Doc. ST/SGB/2005/21.

UN, 'Secretary-General's Bulletin on the Regulations Governing the Status, Basic Rights and Duties of Officials other than Secretariat Officials, and Experts on Mission (entered into force 1 July 2002)', (18 June 2002), UN Doc. ST/SGB/2002/9.

UN, 'Secretary-General's Bulletin on the Special measures for protection from sexual exploitation and sexual abuse', (9 October 2003), UN Doc. ST/SGB/2003/13.

UN, 'Secretary-General's Bulletin on the Staff Rules, Staff Regulations of the United Nations and Staff Rules I00.1 to 112.8', (1 January 2002), UN Doc. ST/SGB/2002/1.

UN, 'Secretary-General's Bulletin on the Status, Basic Rights and Duties of United Nations Staff Members (entered into force 1 January 1999)', (10 December 1998), UN Doc. ST/SGB/1998/19.

UN, 'Secretary-General's Bulletin on the Status, Basic Rights and Duties of United Nations Staff Members (entered into force on 1 December 2002)', (1 November 2002), UN Doc. ST/SGB/2002/13.

UN, *Status of Military Observers Serving with a United Nations Mission* (1964), 1964 UN Jurid YB 261.

UN, 'Summary Report of the Second Meeting of Committee IV/2', UN Conference on International Organizations, vol 13', (11 May 1945), UN Doc. 228, IV/2/10.

UN, United Nations Police Handbook (2005).

UN CHR, 'Integration of the Human Rights of Women and the Gender Perspective, Violence against Women, Report of the Special Rapporteur on Violence against Women, its Causes and Consequences, Ms. Radhika Coomaraswamy, on Trafficking in Women, Women's Migration and Violence against Women', (24 January 2006), UN Doc. E/CN.4/2000/68.

UN CHR, 'Integration of the Human Rights of Women and the Gender Perspective: Violence against Women, The Due Diligence Standard as a Tool for the Elimination fo Violence against Women, Report of the Special Rapporteur on Violence against Women, its Causes and Consequences, Yakin Ertürk', (20 January 2006), UN Doc. E/CN.4/2006/61.

UN CHR, 'Report of the Special Rapporteur on Violence against Women, its Causes and Consequences, Ms Radhika Coomaraswamy', (23 January 2001), UN Doc. E/CN.4/2001/73.

UN CHR, *Res 1985/33* (13 March 1985).

UN CHR, *Res 1994/45* (4 March 1994).

UN Committee on Economic Social Cultural Rights, *Globalization and Economic, Social and Cultural Rights, Statement by the Committee on Economic, Social and Cultural Rights at the 18th Session (27 April–15 May 1998)* (Available at <http://www20hchrorg/english/bodies/cescr/docs/statements/Globalisation-1998doc> accessed 10 January 2015, 1998).

UN DPA/DPKO/DFS, 'Policy on Accountability for Conduct and Discipline in Field Missions', (1 August 2015), UN Doc. Ref.2015.10.

UN DPKO, 'Directives for Disciplinary Matters Involving Civilian Police Officers and Military Observers', (2003), UN Doc. DPKO/CPD/DDCPO/2003/001; DPKO/MD/03/00994.

UN DPKO, 'Directives for Heads of Police Components in Peacekeeping Operations', (21 November 2006), UN Doc. DPKO/PD/2006/00122.

UN DPKO, 'Functions and Organization of United Nations Formed Police Units', (9 November 2006), UN Doc. DPKO/PD/2006/00060.

UN DPKO, 'Guidelines for Civilian Police Officers on Assignment with the United Nations Assistance Mission in Afghanistan (UNAMA)', (January 2005), (on file with author).

UN DPKO, 'Guidelines for Governments Contributing Special Police Units to UNMIK', (1999), (on file with author).

UN DPKO, 'Guidelines for United Nations Police Officers on Assignment with Peacekeeping Operations', UN Doc. DPKO/PD/2006/00135.

UN DPKO, *Ranking of Military and Police Contributions to UN Operations* (2008).

UN DPKO, 'Standing Operating Procedure on the Assessment of Individual Police Officers for Service in United Nations Peacekeeping Operations and Special Political Missions', UN Doc. Ref 2011/18.

UN DPKO, 'Standing Operating Procedures on the Assessment of Operational Capability of Formed Police Units for Service in United Nations Peacekeeping Operations', UN Doc. Ref.2012.11.

UN DPKO, 'Standard Operating Procedures on the Performance Appraisal of United Nations Police Officers', (19 December 2006), UN Doc. Ref. 2006.29, DPKO/PD/2006/00132.

UN DPKO, 'Ten Rules: Code of Personal Conduct for Blue Helmets', (on file with author).

UN DPKO, 'Undertaking and Declaration by Experts on Mission: UN Police Officer/Corrections Officer/Military Observers/Military Liaison Officer', (on file with author).

UN DPKO, 'We are United Nations Peacekeeping Personnel', (on file with author).

UN DPKO/DFS, 'Formed Police Units in United Nations Peacekeeping Operations', (1 March 2010), UN Doc. 2009.32.

UN DPKO/DFS, 'Guidelines on Police Capacity-Building and Development', (1 April 2015), UN Doc. Ref.2015.08.

UN DPKO/DFS, 'Guidelines on Police Operations in United Nations Peacekeeping Operations and Special Political Missions', (01 January 2016), UN Doc. Ref.2015.15.

UN DPKO/DFS, 'Guidelines on the Police Command in United Nations Peacekeeping Operations and Special Political Missions', (2015), UN Doc. Ref. 2015.14.

UN DPKO/DFS, 'Mission Evaluation Policy', (1 March 2013), UN Doc. Ref.2013.02.

UN DPKO/DFS, 'Policy Directive on the Boards of Inquiry', (27 May 2008), UN Doc. Ref. 2008.23.

UN DPKO/DFS, 'Policy on Internal Evaluations and Inspections of United Nations Police', (1 October 2012), UN Doc. Ref.2012.13.

UN DPKO/DFS, 'Policy on United Nations Police in Peacekeeping Operations and Special Political Missions', (1 February 2014), UN Doc. Ref.2014.01.

UN DPKO/DFS, 'Policy (Revised) on Formed Police Units in United Nations Peacekeeping Operations', (1 March 2013), UN Doc. Ref.2009/32.

UN DPKO/DFS, 'Standing Operating Procedure "Board of Inquiry"', (1 March 2011), UN Doc. Ref.2011.15.

UN DPKO/DFS, 'United Nations Peacekeeping Operations: Principles and Guidelines', (January 2008), (on file with author).

UN ECOSOC, *Res 1989/65* (24 May 1989).

UN ECOSOC, 'Working Paper on the Accountability of International Personnel Taking Part in Peace Support Operations Submitted by Françoise Hampson', (7 July 2005), UN Doc. E/CN.4/Sub.2/2005/42.

UN Human Rights Committee, 'Concluding Observations of the Human Rights Committee: Egypt', (28 November 2002), UN Doc. CCPR/CO/76/EGY.

UN Human Rights Committee, 'Concluding Observations of the Human Rights Committee: India', (4 August 1997), UN Doc. CCPR/C/79/Add.81.

UN Human Rights Committee, 'Concluding Observations of the Human Rights Committee: Jordan', (18 November 2010), UN Doc. CCPR/C/JOR/CO/4.

UN Human Rights Committee, 'Concluding Observations of the Human Rights Committee: Nepal', (10 November 1994), UN Doc. CCPR/C/79/Add.42.

UN Human Rights Committee, 'Concluding Observations of the Human Rights Committee: Nigeria', (24 July 1996), UN Doc. CCPR/C/79/Add.65.

UN Human Rights Committee, 'Concluding Observations of the Human Rights Committee: Rwanda', (7 May 2009), UN Doc. CCPR/C/RWA/CO/3.

UN Human Rights Committee, 'Concluding Observations of the Human Rights Committee: Senegal', (28 December 1992), UN Doc. CCPR/C/79/Add.10.

UN Human Rights Committee, 'Concluding Observations of the Human Rights Committee: Serbia and Montenegro', (12 August 2004), UN Doc. CCPR/CO/81/SEMO.

UN Human Rights Committee, 'Concluding Observations to Italy's Fifth Periodic Report', (24 April 2006), UN Doc. CCPR/C/ITA/CO/5.

UN Human Rights Committee, 'General Comment 6 on Article 6 (The Right to Life)', (30 April 1982), UN Doc. HRI/GEN/1/Rev.1.

UN Human Rights Committee, 'General Comment 20 on the Prohibition of Torture, or Other Cruel, Inhuman or Degrading Treatment or Punishment, Article 7', (30 September 1992), UN Doc. HRI/GEN/1/Rev.1.

UN Human Rights Committee, 'General Comment 29, States of Emergency (Article 4)', (31 August 2001), UN Doc. CCPR/C/21/Rev.1/Add.11.

UN Human Rights Committee, 'General Comment 31 on the Nature of the General Legal Obligation Imposed on States Parties to the Covenant', (29 March 2004), UN Doc. CCPR/C/21/Rev.1/Add.13.

UN Human Rights Council, 'Report of the Special Representative of the Secretary-General on the issue of human rights and transnational corporations and other business enterprises, John Ruggie – Guiding Principles on Business and Human Rights: Implementing the United Nations "Protect, Respect and Remedy" Framework', (21 March 2011), UN Doc. A/HRC/17/31.

UN Human Rights Council, 'Report of the Working Group on the Universal Periodic Review: Bangladesh', (8 July 2013), UN Doc. A/HRC/24/12.

UN Human Rights Council, 'Report of the Working Group on the Universal Periodic Review: Burkina Faso', (8 July 2013), UN Doc. A/HRC/24/4.

UN Human Rights Council, 'Report of the Working Group on the Universal Periodic Review: Pakistan', (26 December 2012), UN Doc. A/HRC/22/12.

UN Human Rights Council, *Res 18/7* (13 October 2011).

UN Human Rights Council, *Res 23/25* (14 June 2013).

UN Human Rights Council, *Res 25/13* (15 April 2014).

UN Human Rights Council, *Res 27/3* (03 October 2014).

UN OCHA, 'Humanitarian Situation Report – Sierra Leone, February 01–28 2002', (on file with author).

UN OHCHR, *Africa Quarterly Report*.

UN OHCHR, *Nepal Conflict Report* (Available at <http://wwwohchrorg/EN/Countries/AsiaRegion/Pages/NepalConflictReportaspx> accessed 10 January 2015, 2012).

UN OHCHR/DPKO/DPA/DFS, 'Policy on Human Rights in United Nations Peace Operations and Political Missions', (1 September 2011), UN Doc. Ref. 2011.20.

UN OIOS, 'Evaluation Report – Programme evaluation of the Standing Police Capacity of the Police Division, DPKO', (12 June 2015), UN Doc. IED-14-002.

UN OIOS, 'Investigation into Allegations of Misconduct, Mismanagement and Corruption in the Engineering and Procurement Section of UNDOF', (5 November 2007).

UN OIOS, *Investigations Manual* (Available at <http://wwwunorg/Depts/oios/pages/id_manual_mar2009pdf> accessed 6 October 2014, March 2009).

UN OIOS, 'Report of the Office of Internal Oversight Services on its Investigation into Allegations of Sexual Exploitation and Abuse in the Ituri Region (Bunia) in the United Nations Organization Mission in the Democratic Republic of the Congo', UN Doc. A/61/841.

UNAT, 'Administrative Tribunal Judgement No1037', (29 November 2001), UN Doc. AT/DEC/1037.

UNAT, 'Administrative Tribunal Judgement No 1266', (31 January 2006), UN Doc. AT/DEC/1266.

UNGA, 'A Comprehensive Strategy to Eliminate Future Sexual Exploitation and Abuse in United Nations Peacekeeping Operations', (24 March 2005), UN Doc. A/59/710.

UNGA, 'A More Secure World: Our Shared Responsibility – Report of the High -level Panel on Threats, Challenges and Change', (2 December 2004), UN Doc. A/59/565.

UNGA, 'Report of the Office of Internal Oversight Services', (27 October 2004), UN Doc. A/59/359.

UNGA, 'Comprehensive Report on All Processes Involved in the Investigation and Prosecution of Crimes Committed against Deployed United Nations Peacekeepers', (9 December 2011), UN Doc. A/66/598.

UNGA, 'Comprehensive Report on the Pilot Project Designated by the General Assembly in Resolution 63/287', (21 February 2013), UN Doc. A/67/751.

UNGA, 'Comprehensive Report Prepared Pursuant to General Assembly Resolution 59/296 on Sexual Exploitation and Sexual Abuse, Including Policy Development, Implementation and Full Justification of Proposed Capacity on Personnel Conduct Issues', (24 May 2006), UN Doc. A/60/862.

UNGA, 'Convention on the Privileges and Immunities of the United Nations – Category of officials to which the provisions of Articles V and VII Shall Apply, Report of the Joint Sub-Committee of the Fifth and Sixth Committees', (28 November 1946), UN Doc. A/C.5/ 99, A/AC.6/97.

UNGA, 'Criminal Accountability of United Nations Officials and Experts on Mission', (11 September 2007), UN Doc. A/62/329.

UNGA, 'Draft Articles on the Responsibility of International Organizations, as appears in International Law Commission Report on the Work of its Sixty-Third Session (26 April to 3 June and 4 July to 12 August 2011), para. 87', (26 April to 3 June and 4 July to 12 August 2011), UN Doc. A/66/10.

UNGA, 'Draft Articles on the Responsibility of International Organizations with Commentaries, as appears in International Law Commission Report on the Work of its Sixty-Third Session (26 April to 3 June and 4 July to 12 August 2011), para. 88', (26 April to 3 June and 4 July to 12 August 2011), UN Doc. A/66/10.

UNGA, 'Draft Articles on Responsibility of States for Internationally Wrongful Acts, with Commentaries, in the Report of the International Law Commission, 53rd Session (23 April–1 June and 2 July–10 August 2001), para. 77', (23 April–1 June and 2 July–10 August 2001), UN Doc. A/56/10.

UNGA, 'Ensuring the Accountability of United Nations Staff and Experts on Mission with Respect to Criminal Acts Committed in Peacekeeping Operations', (16 August 2006), UN Doc. A/60/980.

UNGA, 'Final Act of the United Nations Diplomatic Conference of Plenipotentiaries on the Establishment of an International Criminal Court', (17 July 1998), UN Doc. A/CONF.183/10.

UNGA, 'Fourth Report on the Immunity of State Officials from Foreign Criminal Jurisdiction', (29 May 2015), UN Doc. A/CN.4/686.

UNGA, 'Investigation by the Office of Internal Oversight Services into Allegations of Sexual Exploitation and Abuse in the United Nations Organization Mission in the Democratic Republic of the Congo', (5 January 2005), UN Doc. A/59/661.

UNGA, 'Investigation into Allegations of Fraud at the United Nations Mission in Bosnia and Herzegovina', (20 December 1999), UN Doc. A/54/683.

UNGA, 'Investigation into Sexual Exploitation of Refugees by Aid Workers in West Africa', (11 October 2002), UN Doc. A/57/465.

UNGA, 'Note by the Secretary-General on the Investigations Function in the United Nations System', (13 July 2012), UN Doc. A/67/140.

UNGA, 'Note by the Secretary-General on the Reform of the Procedures for Determining Reimbursement to Member States for Contingent-Owned Equipment', (9 July 1996), UN Doc. A/50/995.

UNGA, 'Privileges and Immunities of the United Nations, Report of the Sixth Committee to the General Assembly', (13 February 1946), UN Doc. A/43/rev.1.

UNGA, 'Promotion and Protection of the rights of Children – Impact of Armed Conflict on Children', (26 August 1996), UN Doc. A/51/306.

UNGA, 'Recommendations Presented by the Secretary-General, Categories of Officials to which the Provisions of Article V and Article VII Shall Apply', (16 October 1946), UN Doc. A/116.

UNGA, 'Recommendations Presented by the Secretary-General, Categories of Officials to which the Provisions of Article V and Article VII Shall Apply – Addendum', (9 Novermber 1946), UN Doc. A/116/Add.1.

UNGA, 'Report of the Ad Hoc Committee on Criminal Accountability of United Nations Officials and Experts on Mission', (15 April 2008), UN Doc. A/63/54.

UNGA, 'Report of the Office of Internal Oversight Services', (11 September 2003), UN Doc. A/58/364.

UNGA, 'Report of the Office of Internal Oversight Services', (19 September 2001), UN Doc. A/56/381.

UNGA, 'Report of the Office of Internal Oversight Services – Part One', (15 August 2006), UN Doc. A/61/264 (Part I).

UNGA, 'Report of the Office of Internal Oversight Services for the Period from 1 July 2001 to 30 June 2002', (4 Oct 2002), UN Doc. A/57/451.

UNGA, 'Report of the Office of Internal Oversight Services on its Investigation into Allegations of Sexual Exploitation and Abuse in the Ituri Region (Bunia) in the United Nations Organization Mission in the Democratic Republic of the Congo', (5 April 2007), UN Doc. A/61/841.

UNGA, 'Report of the Office of Internal Oversight Services on Peacekeeping Operations', (1 March 2011), UN Doc. A/65/271 (Part II).

UNGA, 'Report of the Office of Internal Oversight Services on Peacekeeping Operations', (13 March 2012), UN Doc. A/66/286 (Part II).

UNGA, 'Report of the Office of Internal Oversight Services on Peacekeeping Operations', (23 February 2009), UN Doc. A/63/302 (Part II).

UNGA, 'Report of the Office of Internal Oversight Services on Peacekeeping Operations', (23 February 2010), UN Doc. A/64/326 (Part II).

UNGA, 'Report of the Office of the Internal Oversight Services on the Activities of the Office of Internal Oversight Services on Peace Operations for the Period 1 January to 31 December 2013', (25 February 2014), UN Doc. A/68/337 (Part II).

UNGA, 'Report of the Office of Internal Oversight Services on the Evaluation of the Implementation and Results of Protection of Civilians Mandates in United Nations Peacekeeping Operations', (7 March 2014), UN Doc. A/68/787.

UNGA, 'Report of the Office of Internal Oversight Services on the Global Review of Discipline in Field Missions led by the Department of Peacekeeping Operations', (8 March 2006), UN Doc. A/60/713.

UNGA, 'Report of the Office of Internal Oversight Services on the Activities of the Procurement Task Force for the Period from 1 July 2007 to 31 July 2008', (15 September 2008), UN Doc. A/63/329/Add.1.

UNGA, 'Report of the Office of Internal Oversight Services on the Investigation Conducted by the Investigations Task Force into Fraud and Corruption Allegations at Pristina Airport', (14 March 2006), UN Doc. A/60/720.

UNGA, 'Report of the Office of Internal Oversight Services on the Review of the Reporting by United Nations Peacekeeping Missions on the Protection of Civilians', (15 March 2013), UN Doc. A/67/795.

UNGA, 'Report of the Secretary-General on the Activities of the Office of Internal Oversight Services', (9 September 2005), UN Doc. A/60/346.

UNGA, 'Report of the Secretary-General on the Comprehensive Report of Conduct and Discipline Including Full Justification of All Posts', (20 March 2008), UN Doc. A/62/758.

UNGA, 'Report of the Secretary-General on the Criminal Accountability of United Nations Officials and Experts on Mission', (11 August 2008), UN Doc. A/63/260.

UNGA, 'Report of the Secretary-General on the Criminal Accountability of United Nations Officials and Experts on Mission – Addendum', (26 September 2008), UN Doc. A/63/260/Add.1.

UNGA, 'Report of the Secretary-General on the Criminal Accountability of United Nations Officials and Experts on Mission', (28 July 2009), UN Doc. A/64/183.

UNGA, 'Report of the Secretary-General on the Criminal Accountability of United Nations Officials and Experts on Mission – Addendum', (28 July 2009), UN Doc. A/64/183/Add.1.

UNGA, 'Report of the Secretary-General on the Criminal Accountability of United Nations Officials and Experts on Mission', (29 July 2010), UN Doc. A/65/185.

UNGA, 'Report of the Secretary-General on the Criminal Accountability of United Nations Officials and Experts on Mission', (23 September 2011), UN Doc. A/66/174/Add.1.

UNGA, 'Report of the Secretary-General on the Criminal Accountability of United Nations Officials and Experts on Mission', (31 July 2012), UN Doc. A/67/213.

UNGA, 'Report of the Secretary-General on the Criminal Accountability of United Nations Officials and Experts on Mission', (22 July 2013), UN Doc. A/68/173.

UNGA, 'Report of the Secretary-General on the Criminal Accountability of United Nations Officials and Experts on Mission', (31 July 2014), UN Doc. A/69/210.

UNGA, 'Report of the Secretary-General on the Model Agreement between the United Nations and Member States Contributing Personnel and Equipment to United Nations Peace-Keeping Operations', (23 May 1991), UN Doc. A/46/185.

UNGA, 'Report of the Secretary-General on the Model Status-of-Forces Agreement for Peace-Keeping Operations', (9 October 1990), UN Doc. A/45/594.

UNGA, 'Report of the Secretary-General on the Progress of Training in Peacekeeping', (21 December 2010), UN Doc. A/65/644.

UNGA, 'Report of the Secretary-General on the Proposed United Nations Code of Conduct', (17 October 1997), UN Doc. A/52/488.

UNGA, 'Report of the Secretary-General on the Special Measures for Protection from Sexual Exploitation and Sexual Abuse', (18 February 2011), UN Doc. A/65/742.

UNGA, 'Report of the Secretary-General on the Special Measures for Protection from Sexual Exploitation and Sexual Abuse', (17 February 2012), UN Doc. A/66/699.

UNGA, 'Report of the Secretary-General on the Special on Measures for Protection from Sexual Exploitation and Sexual Abuse', (28 February 2013), UN Doc. A/67/766.

UNGA, 'Report of the Secretary-General on the Special Measures for Protection from Sexual Exploitation and Sexual Abuse', (14 February 2014), UN Doc. A/68/756.

UNGA, 'Report of the Secretary-General on the Special Measures for Protection from Sexual Exploitation and Sexual Abuse',(13 February 2015), UN Doc. A/69/779.

UNGA, 'Report of the Secretary-General on the Strengthening Investigations', (12 December 2007), UN Doc. A/62/582.

UNGA, 'Report of the Secretary-General on the United Nations Emergency Force', (9 October 1957), UN Doc. A/3694.

UNGA, 'Report of the Secretary-General on the United Nations Interim Administration Mission in Kosovo', (12 July 1999), UN Doc. S/1999/779.

UNGA, 'Report of the Secretary-General on the United Nations Police', (15 December 2011), UN Doc. A/66/615.

UNGA, 'Report of the Secretary-General on Special Measures for Protection from Sexual Exploitation and Sexual Abuse', (15 June 2007), UN Doc. A/61/957.

UNGA, 'Report of the Sixth Committee on the Criminal Accountability of United Nations Officials and Experts on Mission',(23 November 2015), UN Doc. A/70/506.

UNGA, 'Report of the Special Committee on Peacekeeping Operations and its Working Group', (GAOR 59th Session Supp no 19, 31 January–25 February 2005; 4–8 April 2005), UN Doc. A/59/19/Rev.1.

UNGA, 'Report of the Special Rapporteur on Violence against Women, its Causes and Consequences, Yakin Ertürk, Mission to the DRC', (28 February 2008), UN Doc. A/HRC/7/6/Add.4.

UNGA, 'Report on the Activities of the Office of Internal Oversight', (23 February 2007), UN Doc. A/61/264 (Part II).

UNGA, 'Report on the Activities of the Office of Internal Oversight Services for the Period from 1 January to 31 December 2007', (25 February 2008), UN Doc. A/62/281 (Part II).

UNGA, 'Report on the Activities of the Office of Internal Oversight on Peacekeeping Operations for the Period from 1 January to 31 December 2012', (12 Mar 2013), UN Doc. A/67/297 (Part II).

UNGA, 'Report on the Activities of the Office of Internal Oversight Services on Peace Operations for the Period from 1 January to 31 December 2014', (23 February 2015), UN Doc. A/69/308 (Part II).

UNGA, 'Report on the Activities of the Office of Internal Oversight Services for the period from 1 July 2014 to 30 June 2015', (13 August 2015), UN Doc. A/70/318 (Part I).

UNGA, *Res 44/49* (8 December 1989).

UNGA, *Res 48/218 B* (12 August 1994).

UNGA, *Res 49/59* (9 December 1994).

UNGA, *Res 50/54* (11 December 1995).

UNGA, Res 51/77 (20 February 1997).

UNGA, *Res 52/12B* (9 January 1998).

UNGA, *Res 56/83* (28 January 2002).

UNGA, *Res 57/306* (22 May 2003).

UNGA, *Res 59/287* (13 April 2005).

UNGA, *Res 59/300* (30 June 2005).

UNGA, *Res 60/251* (3 April 2006).

UNGA, *Res 62/63* (8 January 2008).

UNGA, *Res 62/214* (7 March 2008).

UNGA, *Res 62/247* (24 April 2008).

UNGA, *Res 63/119* (15 January 2009).

UNGA, *Res 63/287* (21 February 2013).

UNGA, *Res 64/110* (15 January 2010).

UNGA, *Res 65/20* (10 January 2011).

UNGA, *Res 66/93* (13 January 2012).

UNGA, *Res 67/88* (14 January 2013).

UNGA, Res 69/114 (18 December 2014).

UNGA, Res 69/157 (3 February 2015).

UNGA, Res 76 (1) (7 December 1946).

UNGA, Res 105 (18 December 2013).

UNGA, Res 114 (18 December 2015).

UNGA, *Res 957 (X)* (8 November 1955).

UNGA, *Res 2840 (XXVI)* (18 December 1971).

UNGA, *Res 3074 (XXVIII)* (3 December 1973).

UNGA, 'Revised Draft Model Memorandum of Understanding, as annexed to UNGA, Report of the Special Committee on Peacekeeping Operations and its Working Group on the 2007 Resumed Session', (12 June 2007), UN Doc. A/61/19 (Part III).

UNGA, 'Second Report on Immunity of State Officials from Foreign Criminal Jurisdiction', (10 June 2010), UN Doc. A/CN.4/631.

UNGA, 'Secretary-General's Report on Special Measures for Protection from Sexual Exploitation and Sexual Abuse', (17 February 2009), UN Doc. A/63/720.

UNGA, 'Summary Study of the Experience Derived from the Establishment and Operation of the Force: Report of the Secretary-General', (9 October 1958), UN Doc. A/3943.

UNGA Fifth Committee, 'Approved Resources for Peacekeeping Operations for the Period from 1 July 2010 to 30 June 2011', (13 July 2010), UN Doc. A/C.5/65/15.

UNGA Fifth Committee, 'Approved Resources for Peacekeeping Operations for the Period from 1 July 2011 to 30 June 2012', (13 January 2011), UN Doc. A/C.5/66/14.

UNGA Fifth Committee, 'Approved Resources for Peacekeeping Operations for the Period from 1 July 2012 to 30 June 2013', (27 June 2012), UN Doc. A/C.5/66/18.

UNGA Fifth Committee, 'Approved Resources for Peacekeeping Operations for the Period from 1 July 2013 to 30 June 2014', (18 July 2013), UN Doc. A/C.5/67/19.

UNGA Fifth Committee, 'Approved Resources for Peacekeeping Operations for the Period from 1 July 2013 to 30 June 2014', (23 January 2014), UN Doc. A/C.5/68/21.

UNGA Sixth Committee, 'Draft Resolution on Criminal Accountability of United Nations Officials and Experts on Mission', (3 November 2014), UN Doc. A/C. 6/69/L.11.

UNGA Sixth Committee, 'Draft Resolution on the Criminal Accountability of United Nations Officials and Experts on Mission', (27 October 2011), UN Doc. A/C.6/66/L.16.

UNGA Sixth Committee 'First Report of the Sub-Committee on Privileges and Immunities', (26 January 1946), UN Doc. A/C.6/17.

UNGA Sixth Committee, 'Report of the Sixth Committee on the Criminal Accountability of United Nations Officials and Experts on Mission', (19 November 2013), UN Doc. A/68/461.

UNGA Sixth Committee, 'Second Report of the Sub-Committee on Privileges and Immunities',(5 February 1946), UN Doc. A/C.6/31.

UNGA Sixth Committee, 'Summary Record of the 8th Meeting, Held at Headquarters, New York, on Friday, 12 October 2012, at 10 a.m.', (5 December 2012), UN Doc. A/C.6/67/SR.8.

UNGA Sixth Committee, '67th Session: Summary Record of the 24th Meeting', (28 December 2012), UN Doc. A/C.6/67/SR24.

UNGA Sixth Committee, '68th Session: 10th & 11th Meetings (AM & PM) – Criminal Acts by United Nations Officials, Experts on Mission Must Not Go Unpunished, Sixth Committee Told as Debate Begins', (16 October 2013), UN Doc. GA/L/3460.

UNGA/SC, 'An Agenda for Peace: Preventive Diplomacy, Peacemaking and Peacekeeping', (17 June 1992), UN Doc. A/47/277 – S/24111.

UNGA/SC, 'Report of the Panel on United Nations Peace Operations', (21 August 2000), UN Doc. A/55/305-S/2000/809.

UNGA/SC, 'Report of the Secretary-General on the Future of the United Nations Peace Operations: Implementation of the Receommendations of the High-Level Indepdent Panel on Peace Operations',(2 September 2015), UN Doc. A/70/357–S/2015/682.

UNGA/SC, 'Supplement to an Agenda for Peace: Position Paper of the Secretary-General on the Occasion of the Fiftieth Anniversary of the United Nations', (January), UN Doc. A/50/60-S/1995/1.

UNGA/SC, 'Uniting Our Strength for Peace – Politics, Partnerships and People – Report of the High-Level Independent Panel on United Nations Peace Operations', (16 June 2015), UN Doc. A/70/95-S/2015/446.

UNHCR and Save the Children-UK, *Note for Implementing and Operational Partners on Sexual Violence & Exploitation: The Experience of Refugee Children in Guinea, Liberia and Sierra Leone based on Initial Findings and Recommendations from Assessment Mission 22 October–30 November 2001* (February 2002).

UNICEF, *Trafficking in Human Beings in Southeastern Europe* (June 2002, 2002).

United Nations Peacekeeping Law Reform Project, 'UN Peacekeeping and The Model Status of Forces Agreement – Background Paper' (Experts' Workshop, London, 26 August 2010).

UNMIL, 'CIVPOL: International Police Service – Standard Operating Procedures', (June 2004), (on file with author).

UNMIT, 'UNMIT Human Rights and Transitional Justice Section Report: Report on Human Rights Developments in Timor Leste, August 2006–August 2007', (on file with author).

UNSC, 'Cable Dated 60/07/12 from the President of the Republic of the Congo and Supreme Commander of the National Army and the Prime minister and Minister of National Defence Addressed to the Secretary-General of the United Nations', (13 July 1960), UN Doc. S/4382.

UNSC, 'Explanatory Statement by the Secretary-General Concerning his Further Report (S/20412) Concerning the Implementation of Security Council Resolutions 435 (1978) and 439 (1978) Concerning the Question of Namibia', (9 February 1989), UN Doc. S/20457.

UNSC, 'First Report by the Secretary-General on the Implementation of Security Council Resolution S/4387 of 14 July 1960', (18 July 1960), UN Doc. S/4389.

UNSC, 'Further Report of the Secretary-General Concerning the Implementation of Security Council Resolutions 435 (1978) and 439 (1978) Concerning the Question of Namibia', (23 January 1989), UN Doc. S/20412.

UNSC, 'Letter Dated 26 May 1989 from the President of the Security Council Addressed to the Secretary-General', (26 May 1989), UN Doc. S/20658.

UNSC, 'Letter Dated 28 September 1989 from the President of the Security Council Addressed to the Secretary-General', (28 September 1989), UN Doc. S/20872.

UNSC, 'Note Verbale Dated 5 August 1960 from the Permanent Representative of Ghana Addressed to the Secretary-General', (6 August 1960), UN Doc. S/4420.

UNSC, 'Report of the Commission of Inquiry Established Pursuant to Security Council Resolution 885 (1993) to Investigate Armed Attacks on UNOSOM II Personnel Which Led to Casualties Among Them', (1 June 1994), UN Doc. S/1994/653.

UNSC, 'Report of the Secretary-General on the Implementation of Security Council Resolution 640 (1989) Concerning the Question of Namibia', (6 October 1989), UN Doc. S/20883.

UNSC, 'Report of the Secretary-General on the Rule of Law and Transitional Justice in Conflict and Post-Conflict Societies', (23 August 2004), UN Doc. S/2004/616.

UNSC, 'Report of the Secretary-General Pursuant to Paragraph 10 of Security Council Resolution 1244 (1999)', (12 June 1999), UN Doc. S/1999/672.

UNSC, *Res 39* (14 January 1948).

UNSC, *Res 47* (21 April 1948).

UNSC, *Res 145* (22 July 1960).

UNSC, *Res 435* (29 September 1978).

UNSC, *Res 629* (16 January 1989).

UNSC, *Res 640* (29 August 1989).

UNSC, *Res 643* (31 October 1989).

UNSC, *Res 827* (25 May 1993).

UNSC, *Res 955* (8 November 1994).

UNSC, *Res 1035* (21 December 1995).

UNSC, *Res 1159* (27 March 1998).

UNSC, *Res 1244* (10 June 1999).

UNSC, *Res 1270* (22 October 1999).

UNSC, *Res 1272* (25 October 1999).

UNSC, *Res 1291* (24 February 2000).

UNSC, *Res 1315* (14 August 2000).

UNSC, *Res 1320* (15 September 2000).

UNSC, *Res 1422* (12 July 2002).

UNSC, *Res 1528* (27 February 2004).

UNSC, *Res 1542* (30 April 2004).

UNSC, *Res 1545* (21 May 2004).

UNSC, *Res 1547* (11 June 2004).

UNSC, *Res 1590* (24 March 2005).

UNSC, *Res 1769* (31 July 2007).

UNSC, *Res 1778* (25 September 2007).

UNSC, Res 1888 (30 September 2009).

UNSC, *Res 1925* (28 May 2010).

UNSC, Res 1990 (27 June 2011).

UNSC, *Res 1996* (8 July 2011).

UNSC, Res 2100 (25 April 2013).

UNSC, Res 2149 (10 April 2014).

UNSC, Res 2185 (20 November 2014).

UNSC, *Res 4387* (14 July 1960).

UNSC, *Res 4405* (1960).

UNSC, Res *4426* (9 August 1960).

UNSC, 'Second Report by the Secretary-General on the Implementation of Security Council Resolutions S/4387 of 14 July 1960 and S/4405 of 22 July 1960', (6 August 1960), UN Doc. S/4417.

UNSC, 'Second Report by the Secretary-General on the Implementation of Security Council Resolutions S/4387 of 14 July 1960 and S/4405 of 22 July 1960 – Addendum No 5', (11 August 1960), UN Doc. S/4417/Add.5.

UNSC, 'Second Report by the Secretary-General on the Implementation of Security Council Resolutions S/4387 of 14 July 1960 and S/4405 of 22 July 1960', (6 August 1960), UN Doc. S/4417.

UNSC, 'Second Report by the Secretary-General on the Implementation of Security Council Resolutions S/4387 of 14 July 1960 and S/4405 of 22 July 1960 – Addendum No 5', (11 August 1960), UN Doc. S/4417/Add.5.

UNSC, 'Second Report by the Secretary-General on the Implementation of Security Council Resolutions S/4387 of 14 July 1960 and S/4405 of 22 July 1960 – Addendum No 10', (20 August 1960), UN Doc. S/4417/Add.10.

UNSC, 'Security Council Official Records, 15th Year: 873rd Meeting, 13/14 July 1960', (1 January 1960), UN Doc. S/PV.873.

UNSC, 'Special Report of the Secretary-General on the United Nations Operation in Côte d'Ivoire', (29 March 2012), UN Doc. S/2012/186.

UNSC, 'Statement by the President of the Security Council', (3 May 1994), UN Doc. S/PRST/1994/22.

US Department of Justice, *Civilian Police and Multinational Peacekeeping – A Workshop Series A: Role for Democratic Policing* (US Department of Justice, Office of Justice Programs, National Institute of Justice, 6 October 1997).

US Dept of State, *The Global Landmine Crisis: 1994 Report to the US Congress on the Problem with Uncleared Landmines and the United States Strategy for Demining and Landmine Control* (Prepared by the Office of International Security and Peacekeeping Operations, 1994).

US House of Representatives, *Peacekeeping and Conflict Resolution in Africa: Hearing before the Subcommittee on Africa of the Committee on Foreign Affairs* (House of Representatives, One Hundred Third Congress, 1st session, March 31, 1993, 1994).

US State Government, *US State Government Report: Liberia – Country Reports on Human Rights Practices, Released by the Bureau of Democracy, HR and Labor* (6 March 2007, 2007).

Books and Articles

The Blue Helmets: A Review of United Nations Peacekeeping (UN, Dept of Public Information 1985).

International peacekeeping (Taylor & Francis 1994).

International Peacekeeping: The Yearbook of International Peace Operations, vol 8 (Martinus Nijhoff 2004).

Abi-Mershed EAH, 'Due Diligence and the Fight against Gender-Based Violence in the Inter-American System' in Benninger-Budel C (ed), *Due Diligence and its Application to Protect Women from Violence*, vol 73 (Brill 2008).

Akehurst M, 'Jurisdiction in International Law' in Reisman M (ed), *Jurisdiction in International Law* (pp. 25–138, Ashgate 1999).

Aksu E, *The United Nations, Intra-State Peacekeeping and Normative Change* (Manchester University Press 2003).

Allan JH, *Peacekeeping: Outspoken Observations by a Field Officer* (Praeger 1996).

Allison GT, Kelley PX and Garwin RL (eds), *Nonlethal Weapons and Capabilities Report of an Independent Task Force Sponsored by the Council on Foreign Relations* (Council on Foreign Relations Press 2004).

Al-Qaq RK, *Managing World Order: United Nations Peace Operations and the Security Agenda* (Tauris Academic Studies 2009).

Alvarez JE, *International Organizations as Law-Makers* (Oxford University Press Oxford 2005).

Amerasinghe CF, *Principles of the Institutional Law of International Organizations* (2nd edn, Cambridge University Press 2005).

Andreas P, *Blue Helmets and Black Markets: The Business of Survival in the Siege of Sarajevo* (Cornell University Press 2008).

Andrew C, Aldrich RJ and Wark WK (eds), *Secret Intelligence: A Reader* (Routledge 2009).

Ashdown P, *United Nations Interventionism, 1991–2004 – Swords and Ploughshares: Bringing Peace to the 21st Century* (Berdal M and Economides S eds, Cambridge University Press 2007).

Aust A, *Handbook of International Law* (Cambridge University Press 2010).

Azimi N (ed) *The Role and Functions of Civilian Police in United Nations Peace-Keeping Operations: Debriefing and Lessons* (Kluwer Law International 1996).

Azimi N and Lin CL (eds), *The Nexus between Peacekeeping and Peace-building: Debriefing and Lessons; Report of the 1999 Singapore Conference* (Kluwer Law International 2000).

Badsey S and Latawski P (eds), *Britain, NATO, and the Lessons of the Balkan Conflicts, 1991–1999* (Frank Cass 2004).

Basch FF, 'The Doctrine of the Inter-American Court of Human Rights Regarding States' Duty to Punish Human Rights Violations and Its Dangers' 23 American University International Law Review 195.

Bayley DH, *Democratizing the Police Abroad: What to Do and How to Do it* (US Department of Justice, Office of Justice Programs, National Institute of Justice 2001).

Bekker PHE, 'Difference Relating to Immunity from Legal Process of a Special Rapporteur of the Commission on Human Rights' (1999) 93 American Journal of International Law 921.

Bekker PHP, *The Legal Position of Intergovernmental Organizations – A Functional Necessity Analysis of Their Legal Status and Immunities*, vol 17 (Martinus Nijhoff Publishers 1994).

Bellamy AJ, *Peace Operations and Global Order* (Routledge 2008).

Bellamy AJ, Williams P and Griffin S, *Understanding Peacekeeping* (1st edn, Polity Press 2004).

Bellamy AJ and Williams PD, *Understanding Peacekeeping* (2nd edn, Polity 2010).

Belloni R, *State Building and International Intervention in Bosnia* (Routledge 2007).

Bentley KA and Southall R, *An African Peace Process: Mandela, South Africa and Burundi* (HSRC Press 2005).

Benton B, *Soldiers for Peace: Fifty Years of United Nations Peacekeeping* (Facts On File 1996).

Bercovitch J and Jackson R, 'Conflict Resolution in the Twenty-First Century: Principles, Methods, and Approaches ' in Adebajo A (ed), *From Global Apartheid to Global Village: Africa and the United Nations* (University of KwaZulu-Natal Press; University of Michigan Press 2009).

Berdal M and Leifer M, 'Cambodia' (1991) 1994 The New Interventionism 25.

Berger U, Mochizuki MM and Tsuchiyama J (eds), *Japan in International Politics: The Foreign Policies of an Adaptive State* (Lynne Rienner Publishers 2007).

Bhatia MV, *War and Intervention Issues for Contemporary Peace Operations* (Kumarian Press 2003).

Bianchi A, 'Immunity Versus Human Rights: The Pinochet Case' (1999) [2] 10 European Journal of International Law 237.

Biermann W and Vadset M (eds), *UN peacekeeping in Trouble: Lessons Learned from the Former Yugoslavia: Peacekeepers' Views on the Limits and Possibilities of the United Nations in a Civil War-Like Conflict* (Ashgate 1998).

Blokker N and Schrijver N, *The Security Council and the Use of Force: Theory and Reality – A Need for Change?* (Martinus Nijhoff Publishers 2005).

Bloom ET, 'Protecting Peacekeepers: The Convention on the Safety of United Nations and Associated Personnel' [1995] American Journal of International Law.

Bloomfield LP and Bowman EH, *International Military Forces: The Question of Peacekeeping in an Armed and Disarming World* (Little, Brown 1964).

Bolkovac K, *The Whistleblower: Sex Trafficking, Military Contractors, and One Woman's Fight for Justice* (Palgrave Macmillan 2011).

Bolton JR, 'The Risks and Weaknesses of the International Criminal Court from America's perspective' [2001] Law and Contemporary Problems 167.

Bothe M and Dörschel T (eds), *UN Peacekeeping: A Documentary Introduction* (Kluwer Law International 1999).

Boulden J (ed) *Dealing with Conflict in Africa: The United Nations and Regional Organizations* (Palgrave Macmillan 2003).

Bourke-Martignoni J, 'The History and Development of the Due Diligence Standard in International Law and Its Role in the Protection of Women against Violence' in Benninger-Budel C (ed), *Due Diligence and its Application to Protect Women from Violence* (Brill 2008).

Boutros-Ghali B, 'Beyond Peacekeeping' (1992) 25 New York University Journal of International Law and Politics.

Boutros-Ghali B, 'Introduction' in UN (ed), *The United Nations and Cambodia, 1991–1995* (UN, 1995).

Bowett DW and Barton GP, *United Nations Forces: A Legal Study* (The Lawbook Exchange 2008).

Brenchley F and Fursdon E, *The Aegean and Cyprus* (Research Institute for the Study of Conflict and Terrorism 1990).

Briscoe N, *Britain and UN Peacekeeping, 1948–67* (Palgrave Macmillan 2003).

Brown G, Barker B and Burke T, *Police as Peacekeepers: The History of the Australian and New Zealand Police Service with the United Nations Force in Cyprus 1964–1984* (UN CIVPOL Victoria 1984).

Brownlie I, *Principles of Public International Law* (3rd edn, Oxford University Press 1979).

Brownlie I, *Principles of Public International Law* (6th edn, Oxford University Press Oxford 1995).

Butler MJ, *International Conflict Management* (Routledge 2009).

Cain K, Postlewait H and Thomson A, *Emergency Sex and Other Desperate Measures: A True Story from Hell on Earth* (Miramax 2004).

Call C and Barnett M, 'Looking for a Few Good Cops: Peacekeeping, Peacebuilding and CIVPOL' (1999) 6 International Peacekeeping 43.

Call C and Barnett M, 'Looking for a Few Good Cops: Peacekeeping, Peacebuilding and CIVPOL' in Holm TT and Eide EB (eds), *Peacebuilding and Police Reform* (Frank Cass 2000).

Cameron I, *The Protective Principle of International Criminal Jurisdiction* (Dartmouth 1994).

Caplan R, *International Governance of War-Torn Territories Rule and Reconstruction* [Electronic reproduction. Oxford : Oxford University Press, 2004 (Oxford Scholarship Online), Oxford University Press 2005].

Caplan R, *International Governance of War-Torn Territories: Rule and Reconstruction* (Oxford University Press 2005).

Carlisle RP, 'Persian Gulf War' in Ikenberry J and Inoguchi T (eds), *Reinventing the alliance US – Japan Security Partnership in an Era of Change* (Palgrave Macmillan 2003).

Cassese A, *International Criminal Law* (Oxford University Press 2003).

Cassese A and Gaeta P, *Cassese's International Criminal Law* (Oxford University Press 2013).

Center for International Cooperation and Security, *International Post-Conflict Policing Operations: Enhancing Co-ordination and Effectiveness* (CICS 2004).

Cerone J, 'Reasonable Measures in Unreasonable Circumstances: A Legal Responsibility Framework for Human Rights Violations in Post-Conflict Territories under UN Administration' in White ND and Klaasen D (eds), *The UN, Human Rights and Post-Conflict Situations* (Manchester University Press 2005).

Cerone J, 'Human Dignity in the Line of Fire: The Application of International Human Rights Law During Armed Conflict, Occupation, and Peace Operations' (2006) 39 Vanderbilt Journal of Transnational Law 1417.

Chappell D and Evans J, 'The Role, Preparation and Performance of Civilian Police in United Nations Peacekeeping Operations' (1998) 24 Commonwealth Law Bulletin 1248.

Chesterman S, *You, the People: the United Nations, Transitional Administration, and State-building* (Oxford University Press 2004).

Chesterman S, 'You, the People: the United Nations, Transitional Administration, and State-Building' in Armstrong D, Farrell T and Maiguashca B (eds), *Force and Legitimacy in World Politics* (Cambridge University Press; Oxford University Press 2005).

Chiyuki A, De Coning C and Thakur R (eds), *Unintended Consequences of Peacekeeping Operations* (United Nations University 2007).

Choi S-W and James P, *Civil-Military Dynamics, Democracy, and International Conflict: A New Quest for International Peace* (Palgrave Macmillan 2005).

Christie N, *Towards an Enhanced United Nations Peacekeeping?* (Peace Research Centre, Australian National University, Research School of Pacific Studies 1993).

Clapham A, *Human Rights Obligations of Non-State Actors* (Oxford University Press 2006).

Cleaver G, 'African Perspectives: Regional Peacekeeping' in Furley O and May R (eds), *Peacekeeping in Africa* (pp. 29–48, Ashgate 1998).

Cohen B and Stamkoski G, *With No Peace to Keep...: United Nations Peacekeeping and the War in the Former Yugoslavia* (Grainpress 1995).

Cohen J, *One-Hundred Days of Silence: America and the Rwanda Genocide* (Rowman & Littlefield Publishers 2007).

Coicaud J-M, *Beyond the National Interest: The Future of UN Peacekeeping and Multilateralism in an Era of US Primacy* (United States Institute of Peace Press 2007).

Coicaud J-M and Heiskanen V (eds), *The Legitimacy of International Organizations* (United Nations University Press 2001).

Coleman KP, *International Organisations and Peace Enforcement: The Politics of International Legitimacy* (Cambridge University Press 2007).

Collins R and White ND, *International Organizations and the Idea of Autonomy: Institutional Independence in the International Legal Order* (Routledge 2011).

Connaughton RM, *Peacekeeping and Military Intervention* (Strategic and Combat Studies Institute 1992).

Cooper AF, Hughes CW and De Lombaerde P, *Regionalisation and Global Governance: The Taming of Globalisation?* (Routledge 2008).

Costa G, 'The United Nations and Reform of the Police in El Salvador' (1995) 2 International Peacekeeping 365.

Costa G, 'The United Nations and the Reform of the Police in El Salvador' in Azimi N (ed), *The Role and Functions of Civilian Police in United Nations Peace-Keeping Operations: Debriefing and Lessons* (Kluwer Law International 1996).

Cottey A and Forster A, *Reshaping Defence Diplomacy: New Roles for Military Cooperation and Assistance* (Oxford University Press for the International Institute for Strategic Studies 2004).

Coulon J, *Soldiers of Diplomacy: The United Nations, Peacekeeping, and the New World Order* (University of Toronto Press 1998).

Council of Europe, *Extraterritorial Criminal Jurisdiction* (1990).

Cox AM, *Prospects for Peacekeeping* (Brookings Institution 1967).

Cryer R, 'International Criminal Law vs State Sovereignty: Another Round?' (2005) 16 European Journal of International Law 979.

Dalgaard-Nielsen A (ed) *Germany, Pacifism and Peace Enforcement* (Manchester University Press 2006).

Dallaire R and Beardsley B, *Shake Hands with the Devil: The Failure of Humanity in Rwanda* (Arrow 2004).

Daniel DC and Hayes BC, *Coercive Inducement and the Containment of International Crises* (US Institute of Peace Press 1999).

Daniel DCF, Taft P and Wiharta S (eds), *Peace Operations Trends, Progress, and Prospects* (Georgetown University Press 2008).

De Brabandere E, 'Immunity as a Guarantee for Institutional Autonomy' in Collins R and White ND (eds), *International Organizations and the Idea of Autonomy: Institutional Independence in the International Legal Order* (Routledge 2011).

De Rossanet B, *Peacemaking and Peacekeeping in Yugoslavia* (Kluwer Law International 1996).

De Wet E, *The Chapter VII Powers of the United Nations Security Council* (Hart 2004).

Defeis EF, 'UN Peacekeepers and Sexual Abuse and Exploitation: An End to Impunity' (2008) 7 Washington University Global Study Law Review 185.

Der S, 'Is More Accountability Needed in Peacekeeping Operations?' (LLM thesis, University of Essex 2002).

Diehl PF, *International Peacekeeping* (Johns Hopkins University Press 1994).

Diehl PF (ed) *The Politics of Global Governance: International Organizations in an Interdependent World* (Lynne Rienner Publishers 1997).

Diehl PF, 'Peace Operations' in Jarstad AK and Sisk TD (eds), *From War to Democracy: Dilemmas of Peacebuilding* (Cambridge University Press; Polity 2008).

Diehl PF, 'Evaluating Peace Oerations' in Charlesworth H and Coicaud J-M (eds), *Fault Lines of International Legitimacy* (Cambridge University Press; Lynne Rienner Publishers 2010).

Diehl PF and Cho YL, 'Passing the Buck in Conflict Management: The Role of Regional Organizations in the Post-Cold War Era' (2006) 12 Brown Journal of World Affairs 191.

Dobbins J, *The UN's Role in Nation-Building from the Congo to Iraq* (RAND Corp 2005).

Dobbins J and et al., *The UN's Role in Nation-Building: From the Congo to Iraq* (RAND Corp 2005).

Dokken K, *African Security Politics Redifined* (Palgrave Macmillan 2008).

Dorman AM, *Blair's Successful War: British Military Intervention in Sierra Leone* (Ashgate 2009).

Doyle MW, *UN Peacekeeping in Cambodia: UNTAC's Civil Mandate* (Lynne Rienner Publishers 1995).

Doyle MW and Sambanis N, *Making War and Building Peace: United Nations Peace Operations* (Princeton University Press 2006).

Duffield MR, *Development, Security and Unending War: Governing the World of Peoples* (Polity 2007).

Dupuy P-M, 'The Constitutional Dimension of the Charter of the United Nations Revisited' (1997) 1 Max Planck Yearbook of United Nations Law 1.

Durch WJ (ed) *The Evolution of UN Peacekeeping: Case Studies and Comparative Analysis* (St Martin's Press 1993).

Durch WJ, *The Evolution of UN Peacekeeping: Case Studies and Comparative Analysis* (Macmillan 1994).

Durch WJ, *UN Peacekeeping, American Politics, and the Uncivil Wars of the 1990s* (Macmillan 1997).

Dwan R, *Executive Policing: Enforcing the Law in Peace Operations* (Oxford University Press 2002).

Dziedzic MJ, 'Policing the New World Disorder: Addressing Gaps in Public Security during Peace Operations' in Manwaring MG and Fishel JT (eds), *Toward Responsibility in the New World Disorder – Challenges and Lessons of Peace Operations* (Frank Cass 1998).

Echle R, 'Passive Personality Principle and the General Principle of Ne Bis In Idem' (2013) 9 Utrecht Law Review 56.

Elliott L and Cheeseman G (eds), *Forces for Good: Cosmopolitan Militaries in the Twenty-First Century* (Manchester University Press 2004).

Engdahl O, 'Protection of Personnel in Peace Operations: The Role of the "Safety Convention" against the Background of General International Law' in Chandler D and Heins V (eds), *Rethinking Ethical Foreign Policy: Pitfalls, Possibilities and Paradoxes* (Martinus Nijhoff 2007).

Fagan A, *The Atlas of Human Rights: Mapping Violations of Freedom Worldwide* (Earthscan 2010).

Fermann G, *Bibliography on International Peacekeeping* (Martinus Nijhoff 1992).

Fetherston AB, *Towards a Theory of United Nations Peacekeeping* (Macmillan 1994).

Findlay M, 'Sign up or Sign off – Asia's Reluctant Engagement with the International Criminal Court' (2013) No. 13/44 Sydney Law School Legal Studies Research Paper.

Findlay T, *Cambodia: The Legacy and Lessons of UNTAC* (Oxford University Press 1995).

Findlay T, *The Use of Force in UN Peace Operations* (Oxford University Press 2002).

Fleck D (ed) *The Handbook of the Law of Visiting Forces* (Oxford University Press 2001).

Forster A, *Armed Forces and Society in Europe* (Palgrave Macmillan 2006).

Fortier P, 'The Evolution of Peacekeeping' in McRae RG and Hubert D (eds), *Human Security and the New Diplomacy: Protecting People, Promoting Peace* (Carleton University Press 2001).

Fortna VP, *Does Peacekeeping Work?: Shaping Belligerents' Choices after Civil War* (Princeton University Press 2008).

Fottrell D, 'How much Due Diligence is Due? The Concept of "Due Diligence" in the context of Human Rights Violations' (LLM thesis, University of Essex 2002).

Francis DJ and et al. (eds), *Dangers of Co-Deployment: UN Co-Operative Peacekeeping in Africa* (Ashgate 2005).

Frantzen H-A, *NATO and Peace Support Operations, 1991–1999: Policies and Doctrines* (Frank Cass 2005).

Frederking B, *The United States and the Security Council: Collective Security since the Cold War* (Routledge 2007).

Friman HR and Reich S (eds), *Human Trafficking, Human Security, and the Balkans* (University of Pittsburgh Press 2007).

Furley O and May R, *Peacekeeping in Africa* (Ashgate 1998).

Furley O and May R (eds), *Ending Africa's Wars: Progressing to Peace* (Ashgate 2006).

Gaeta P, 'Is NATO Authorized or Obliged to Arrest Persons Indicted by the International Criminal Tribunal for the Former Yugoslavia?' (1998) 9 European Journal of International Law 174.

Giegerich B, *European Military Crisis Management: Connecting Ambition and Reality* (Routledge 2008).

Girard PR, *Clinton in Haiti the 1994 US Invasion of Haiti* (Palgrave Macmillan 2004).

Goldman P, 'Abuse of Power: The Law and Violations by United Nations Peacekeeping Forces' (LLM thesis, University of Essex 1996).

Goldman RM and Hardman WM, *Building Trust: An Introduction to Peacekeeping and Arms Control* (Ashgate 1997).

Graça M, *The Impact of War on Children* (Orient Blackswan 2001).

Gray C, *International Law and the Use of Force* (Oxford University Press 2000).

Gray CD, *International Law and the Use of Force* (3rd edn, Oxford University Press 2008).

Greener BK, 'UNPOL: UN Police as Peacekeepers' (2009) 19 Policing & Society 106.

Greener BK, 'The Rise of Policing in Peace Operations' (2011) 18 International Peacekeeping 183.

Greenwood C, 'International Humanitarian Law and United Nations Military Operations' (1998) 1 Yearbook of International Humanitarian Law 3.

Grzyb AF (ed) *The world and Darfur: International Response to Crimes against Humanity in Western Sudan* (McGill-Queen's University Press 2009).

Guehenno JM, 'On the Challenges and Achievements of Reforming UN Peace Operations' (2002) 9 International Peacekeeping.

Guliyev MF, 'The International Criminal Court and its Jurisdiction over Peacekeeping Operations with Specific Reference to the United States of America' (LLM thesis, University of Essex 2002).

Hampson F and Kihara-Hunt A, 'The Accountability of Personnel Associated with Peacekeeping Operations' in Aoi C, De Coning C and Thakur R (eds), *Unintended Consequences of Peacekeeping* (United Nations University 2007).

Hanitzsch T, 'Journalists as Peacekeeping Force?: Peace Journalism and Mass Communication Theory' (2004) 5 Journalism Studies.

Hannum H, 'The Status of the Universal Declaration of Human Rights in National and International Law' (1995) 25 Georgia Journal of International and Comparative Law 287.

Hansen AS, *From Congo to Kosovo: Civilian Police in Peace Operations* (Oxford University Press for the International Institute for Strategic Studies 2002).

Harrington AR, 'Victims of Peace: Current Abuse Allegations Against UN Peacekeepers and the Role of Law in Preventing Them in the Future' (2005) 12 ILSA Journal of International & Comparative Law 125.

Harrington C, *Politicization of Sexual Violence: From Abolitionism to Peacekeeping* (Ashgate 2010).

Harrison SS and Nishihara M (eds), *UN peacekeeping : Japanese and American perspectives* (Carnegie Endowment for International Peace 1995).

Hartz H, 'CIVPOL: The UN Instrument for Police Reform' (1999) 6 International Peacekeeping 27.

Hartz HA, 'Experiences from UNPROFOR – UNCIVPOL' in Biermann W and Vadset M (eds), *UN Peacekeeping in Trouble: Lessons Learned from the Former Yugoslavia* (Ashgate 1998).

Harvard Law School's Reseach on International Law, 'Draft Convention on Jurisdiction with Respect to Crime' (1935) 29 American Journal of International Law 435.

Heininger JE, *Peacekeeping in Transition: The United Nations in Cambodia* (Twentieth Century Fund Press 1994).

Henkin AH (ed) *Honoring Human Rights* (Kluwer Law International 2000).

Hesztera G, *30 Jahre Polizei – Kontingente im UN – Einsatz* (BMI 1994).

Higgins R, *The Development of International Law through the Political Organs of the United Nations* (Oxford University Press 1963).

Higgins R, *United Nations Peacekeeping, 1946–1967: Documents and Commentary* (Issued under the auspices of the Royal Institute of International Affairs by Oxford University Press 1969).

Higgins R, *Problems and Process: International Law and How We Use It* (Oxford University Press 1994).

Higgins R, 'Allocating Competence: Jurisdiction' in Reisman WM (ed), *Jurisdiction in International Law* (Aldershot 1999).

Hilaire M, *Annual Review of Global Peace Operations: United Nations Law and the Security Council* (Lynne Rienner Publishers; Ashgate 2006).

Hill M, *Immunities and Privileges of International Officials: The Experience of the League of Nations* (The Lawbook Exchange 2003).

Hill SM, *United Nations Disarmament Processes in Intra-State Conflict* (Palgrave Macmillan 2004).

Hill SM, *United Nations Disarmament Processes in Intra-State Conflict* (Palgrave Macmillan 2005).

Hill SM and Malik SP, *Peacekeeping and the United Nations* (Dartmouth 1996).

Hills A, 'The Inherent Limits of Military Forces in Policing Peace Operations' (2001) 8 International Peacekeeping 79.

Hirsch JL and Oakley RB, *Somalia and Operation Restore Hope: Reflections on Peacemaking and Peacekeeping* (United States Institute of Peace Press 1995).

Hirst M, *Jurisdiction and the Ambit of the Criminal Law* (Oxford University Press 2003).

Holm TT and Eide EB (eds), *Peacebuilding and Police Reform* (Frank Cass 2000).

Hood L, 'Missed Opportunities: The United Nations, Police Service and Defence Force Development in Timor Leste, 1999–2004' (2006) 8 Civil Wars 143.

Hood L, 'Security Sector Reform in East Timor, 1999–2004' (2006) 13 International Peacekeeping 60.

Houghton RB and Trinka FG (eds), *Multinational Peacekeeping in the Middle East* (Foreign Service Institute, US Dept of State 1990).

Howard J and Oswald B (eds), *The Rule of Law on Peace Operations: A 'Challenge of Peace Operations' Project Conference* (Law School, University of Melbourne 2002).

Howard LM, *UN Peacekeeping in Civil Wars* (Cambridge University Press 2008).

Hughes BW, Hunt CT and Kondoch B (eds), *Making Sense of Peace and Capacity-Building Operations: Rethinking Policing and Beyond* (Martinus Nijhoff Publishers 2010).

Hurst CJ, 'Diplomatic Immunities-Modern Developments' 10 Brit YB Int'l L 1.

Hurwitz A (ed) *Civil War and the Rule of Law* (Lynne Rienner 2008).

Hurwitz AG and Huang R, *Civil War and the Rule of Law: Security, Development, Human Rights* (Lynne Rienner Publishers 2008).

IBA, *Report of the Task Force on Extraterritorial Jurisdiction* (IBA 2009).

Ingram JL, *Criminal Evidence* (Elsevier 2011).

International Peace Academy, *Peacekeeper's Handbook* (Pergamon Press 1984).

Iqbal MA, 'An Overview of the CIVPOL Operations in Angola (UNAVEM)' in Azimi N (ed), *The Role and Functions of Civilian Police in United Nations Peace-Keeping Operations: Debriefing and Lessons* (Kluwer Law International 1996).

Ishizuka K, *Ireland and international peacekeeping operations 1960–2000 : A Study of Irish Motivation* (Frank Cass 2004).

James A, *Peacekeeping in International Politics* (Macmillan in association with the International Institute for Strategic Studies (IISS) 1990).

James A, *Keeping the peace in the Cyprus Crisis of 1963–64* (Palgrave 2002).

Jenks CW, *International Immunities* (Stevens Inst Technol 1961).

Jett DC, *Why Peacekeeping Fails* (Macmillan 2000).

Jett DC, *Why Peacekeeping Fails* (1st ed edn, Palgrave 2000).

Jockel JT, *Canada and International Peacekeeping* (Canadian Institute of Strategic Studies ; Center for Strategic and International Studies 1994).

Johansen K, 'Civilian Police in Former Yugoslavia (UNPROFOR)' in Azimi N (ed), *The Role and Functions of Civilian Police in United Nations Peace-Keeping Operations: Debriefing and Lessons* (Kluwer International 1996).

Jones BD, *Peacemaking in Rwanda: The Dynamics of Failure* (Lynne Rienner 2001).

Jonson L, 'Russia and Peacekeeping in Eurasia' in Jonson L and Archer C (eds), *Peacekeeping and the Role of Russia in Eurasia* (Westview Press 1996).

Jonson L and Archer C (eds), *Peacekeeping and the Role of Russia in Eurasia* (Westview Press 1996).

Joseph S, Schultz J and Castan M, *The International Covenant on Civil and Political Rights*, vol 386 (Oxford University Press 2000).

Kalyuzhnova Y and Lynch D (eds), *The Euro-Asian World a Period of Transition* (St. Martin's Press, in association with the Centre for Euro-Asian Studies 2000).

Katayanagi M, *Human Rights Functions of United Nations Peacekeeping Operations* (Martinus Nijhoff 2002).

Kavalski E, *Extending the European Security Community: Constructing Peace in the Balkans* (Tauris Academic Studies 2008).

Kelly MJ, *Restoring and Maintaining Order in Complex Peace Operations: The Search for a Legal Framework* (Kalyuzhnova Y and Lynch D eds, Kluwer Law International 1999).

Kenny K, *UN Accountability for its Human Rights Impact: Implementation through Participation* (Manchester University Press 2005).

Khan KAA, Buisman C and Cosnel C, *Principles of Evidence in International Criminal Justice* (1st edn, Oxford University Press 2010).

Khan SM, *The Shallow Graves of Rwanda* (IB Tauris Publishers 2000).

Kholov M, 'Accountability for the UNCIVPOL involved in sexual abuse of local population in Peace Support Operations?' (LLM thesis, University of Essex 2005).

Kihara-Hunt A, 'Individual Criminal Accountability of UN Police Personnel' (PhD thesis, University of Essex 2015).

Kihara-Hunt A, 'Mechanisms of Individual Criminal Accountability of Civilian Police in Peace Support Operations' (LLM thesis, University of Essex 2004).

Kihara-Hunt A, 'Why Does the Immunity Afforded to UN Personnel Not Appropriately Reflect the Needs of the Organization?: The Case of the UN Police' (2016) 17 United Nations Studies 205.

Kim L, Cheryl M and Metrikas M, 'Holding a Fragile Peace: The Military and Civilian Components of UNTAC' in Doyle M, Johnstone I and Orr RC (eds), *Keeping the Peace: Multidimensional UN Operations in Cambodia and El Salvador* (Cambridge University Press 1997).

King I and Mason W, *Peace at Any Price: How the World Failed Kosovo* (Hurst 2006).

Kinloch-Pichat S, *A UN 'Legion': Between Utopia and Reality* (Frank Cass 2004).

Klabbers J and Wallendahl A, *Research Handbook on the Law of International Organizations* (Edward Elgar Publishing 2011).

Knight WA (ed) *Adapting the United Nations to a Postmodern Era* (Palgrave 2001).

Komori T and Wellens K (eds), *Public Interest Rules of International Law: Towards Effective Implementation* (Ashgate 2009).

Kondoch B, 'Human Rights Law and UN Peace Operations in Post-Conflict Situations' in White ND and Laasen DK (eds), *The UN, Human Rights and Post-Conflict Situations* (Manchester University Press 2005).

Kondoch B (ed) *International Peacekeeping* (Ashgate 2007).

Krasno JE (ed) *The United Nations: Confronting the Challenges of a Global Society* (Lynne Rienner Publishers 2004).

Ladley A, 'Peacekeeper Abuse, Immunity and Impunity: The Need for Effective Criminal and Civil Accountability on International Peace Operations' (2005) 1 Politics and Ethics Review 81.

Langholtz HJ (ed) *The Psychology of Peacekeeping* (Praeger 1998).

Larsen KM, 'Attribution of Conduct in Peace Operations: The 'Ultimate Authority and Control' Test' (2008) 19 European Journal of International Law 509.

Larsen KM, *The Human Rights Treaty Obligations of Peacekeepers* (Cambridge University Press 2012).

Lau M, 'Islamic Law and the Afghan Legal System' (2001) 2002 Yearbook of Islamic and Middle Eastern Law 27.

Leck C, 'International Responsibility in United Nations Peacekeeping Operations: Command and Control Arrangements and the Attribution of Conduct ' (2009) 10 Melbourne Journal of International Law 346.

Ledgerwood J, *UN Peacekeeping Missions: The Lessons from Cambodia* (PN 1994).

Lehmann IA, *Peacekeeping and Public Information: Caught in the Crossfire* (Frank Cass 1999).

Lewis CJ, *State and Diplomatic Immunity* (3rd edition edn, Lloyd's of London Press 1990).

Ling Y-L, 'A Comparative Study of the Privileges and Immunities of United Nations Member Representatives and Officials with the Traditional Privileges and Immunities of Diplomatic Agents' (1976) 33 Washington & Lee Law Review 91.

Linton S, 'Liability for the Actions of Members of the Armed Forces Involved in United Nations Peacekeeping Operations' (LLM thesis, University of Essex 1997).

Liu FT, *United Nations Peacekeeping and the Non-Use of Force* (L Rienner Publishers 1992).

Llewellyn H, 'The Optional Protocol to the 1994 Convention on the Safety of United Nations and Associated Personnel' (2006) 55 International & Comparative Law Quarterly.

Lowe V, *The United Nations Security Council and War the Evolution of Thought and Practice since 1945* (Oxford University Press 2008).

Lowe V and others (eds), *The United Nations, Security Council and War – The Evolution of Thoughts and Practice Since 1945* (Oxford University Press 2008).

Lynch D, *The Conflict in Abkhazia: Dilemmas in Russian 'Peacekeeping' Policy* (Royal Institute of International Affairs 1998).

Lynch D, *Russian Peacekeeping Strategies in the CIS: The Cases of Moldova, Georgia and Tajikistan* (Macmillan 2000).

MacKinnon MG, *The Evolution of US Peacekeeping Policy under Clinton: A Fairweather Friend?* (Frank Cass 2000).

Macqueen N, *United Nations Peacekeeping in Africa since 1960* (Longman 2002).

Macqueen N, *Peacekeeping and the International System* (Routledge 2006).

Magyar KP and Conteh-Morgan E (eds), *Peacekeeping in Africa: ECOMOG in Liberia* (Macmillan 1998).

Mahmoud A, 'UN Operation in Mozambique (ONUMOZ)' in Azimi N (ed), *The Role and Functions of Civilian Police in United Nations Peace-Keeping Operations: Debriefing and Lessons* (Kluwer Law International 1996).

Maley W, Sampford C and Thakur R (eds), *From Civil Strife to Civil Society: Civil and Military Responsibilities in Disrupted States* (United Nations University Press 2003).

Malone DM, *The International Struggle over Iraq Politics in the UN Security Council 1980–2005* (Oxford University Press 2006).

Mann FA, 'The Doctrine of International Jurisdiction Revisited after Twenty Years' (1964) III Recueil des Cours de l'Académie de Droit International de La Haye.

Mann FA, 'The Doctrine of International Jurisdiction Revised after Twenty Years' in Reisman WM (ed), *Jurisdiction in International Law* (Aldershot 1999).

Mansson K, 'Use of Force and Civilian Protection: Peace Operations in the Congo' (2005) 12 International Peacekeeping.

Manwaring MG and Joes AJ (eds), *Beyond Declaring Victory and Coming Home: The Challenges of Peace and Stability Operations* (Praeger 2000).

Marten KZ, *Enforcing the Peace: Learning from the Imperial Past* (Columbia University Press 2004).

Matheson MJ, *Council Unbound: The Growth of UN Decision Making on Conflict and Postconflict Issues after the Cold War* (United States Institute of Peace Press 2006).

Mays TM, *Historical Dictionary of Multinational Peacekeeping* (Scarecrow Press 1996).

Mays TM, *Africa's First Peacekeeping Operation the OAU in Chad, 1981–1982* (Praeger 2002).

McCLanahan GV, *Diplomatic Immunity* (Hurst & Company 1989).

McCoubrey H and Morris J, *Regional Peacekeeping in the Post-Cold War Era* (Kluwer 2000).

McCoubrey H and White ND, *The Blue Helmets:Legal Regulation of United Nations Military Operations* (Dortmouth).

McGregor L, 'Torture and State Immunity: Deflecting Impunity, Distorting Sovereignty' (2007) 18 European Journal of International Law 903.

McRae R and Hubert D (eds), *Human Security and the New Diplomacy: Protecting People, Promoting Peace* (McGill-Queen's University Press 2001).

McRae RG and Hubert D, *Human Security and the New Diplomacy: Protecting People, Promoting Peace* (McGill-Queen's Press-MQUP 2001).

Mégret F and Hoffman F, 'UN as a Human Rights Violator – Some Reflections on the United Nations Changing Human Rights Responsibilities' (2003) 25 Human Rights Quarterly 314.

Mendelson S, 'US-Russian Military Relations: Between Friend and Foe' (2001) 25 Washington Quartery 161.

Mendelson SE, *Barracks and Brothels: Peacekeepers and Human Trafficking in the Balkans* (Center for Strategic and International Studies 2005).

Merkel W and Grimm S (eds), *War and Democratization* (Routledge 2010).

Merlingen M and Ostrauskaite R, *European Union Peacebuilding and Policing Governance and the European Security and Defence Policy* (Routledge 2006).

Merrills JG, *International Dispute Settlement* (4th edn, Cambridge University Press 2005).

Messineo F, 'The House of Lords in Al-Jedda and Public International Law: Attribution of Conduct to Un-Authorized Forces and the Power of the Security Council to Displace Human Rights' (2009) 56 Netherlands International Law Review 35.

Mettle S, 'Operation in Somalia (UNOSOM)' in Azimi N (ed), *The Role and Functions of Civilian Police in United Nations Peace-Keeping Operations: Debriefing and Lessons* (Kluwer Law International 1996).

Meyer J, 'Vicarious Administration of Justice: An Overlooked Basis of Jurisdiction' (1990) 31 Harvard International Law Journal 108.

Mgbeoji I, *Collective Insecurity the Liberian Crisis, Unilateralism, and Global Order* (UBC Press 2003).

Milanović M and Papić T, 'As Bad as it Gets: The European Court of Human Rights's Behrami and Saramati Decision and General International Law' (2009) 58 International and Comparative Law Quarterly 267.

Miller AJ, 'Legal Aspects of Stopping Sexual Exploitation and Abuse in UN Peacekeeping Operations' (2006) 39 Cornell International Law Journal 71.

Miller AJ, 'Privileges and Immunities of United Nations Officials' [2007] International Organizations Law Review 169.

Miller AJ, 'United Nations Experts on Mission and their Privileges and Immunities' (2007) 4 International Organizations Law Review 11.

Montgomery TS (ed) *Peacemaking and Democratization in the Western Hemisphere* (North-south Center Press, University of Miami 2000).

Morgan PM, *International Security: Problems and Solutions* (CQ Press 2006).

Morrison A, 'Methodology, Contents and Structure of UN Civilian Police Training Programmes' in Azimi N (ed), *The Role and Functions of Civilian Police in United Nations Peace-Keeping Operations: Debriefing and Lessons* (Kluwer Law International 1996).

Morrison A, Blair SA and Anderson D (eds), *Refugees, Resources and Resoluteness* (Canadian Peacekeeping Press 1997).

Morrison A, Tychonick R and McNish S (eds), *Changing Face of Peacekeeping* (Canadian Institute of Strategic Studies 1993).

Mowbray A, *Cases, Materials, and Commentary on the European Convention on Human Rights* (Oxford University Press 2012).

Moxon-Browne E (ed) *A Future for Peacekeeping?* (Macmillan 1998).

Munch W, 'Wrongdoing of International Civil Servants – Referral of Cases to National Authorities for Criminal Prosecution' (2006) 10 Max Planck Yearbook of United Nations Law.

Murphy R, 'Sexual Misconduct by Peacekeeping Personnel' in Murphy R and Mansson K (eds), *Peace Operations and Huma Rights* (Routledge 2008).

Murphy R and Mansson K (eds), *Peace Operations and Human Rights* (Routledge 2008).

Mychajlyszyn N and Shaw TM (eds), *Twisting Arms and Flexing Muscles: Humanitarian Intervention and Peacebuilding in Perspective* (Ashgate 2005).

Nasu H, *International Law on Peacekeeping: A Study of Article 40 of the UN Charter* (Martinus Nijhoff Publishers 2009).

Nasu H, 'Operationalizing the Responsibility to Protect in the Context of Civilian Protection by UN Peacekeepers' (1995) 18 International Peacekeeping 364.

Newman E and Richmond OP (eds), *The United Nations and Human Security* (Palgrave 2001).

Newman E and Schnabel A (eds), *Recovering from Civil Conflict: Reconciliation, Peace, and Development* (Frank Cass 2002).

Nsereko DDN, 'Prosecutorial Discretion before National Courts and International Tribunals' (2005) 3 Journal of International Criminal Justice 124.

Oakley RB, Dziedzic MJ and Goldberg EM (eds), *Policing the New World Disorder: Peace Operations and Public Security* (NDU Press 1998).

Odello M, 'Tackling Criminal Acts in Peacekeeping Operations: The Accountability of Peacekeepers' (2010) 15 Journal of Conflict and Security Law.

O'Flaherty M, *The Human Rights Field Operation: Law, Theory and Practice* (Ashgate Publishing 2007).

Oh KC, 'Singapore Civilian Police Contingent in UNTAC: Observations and Lessons Learned' in Azimi N (ed), *The Role and Functions of Civilian Police in United Nations Peace-Keeping Operations: Debriefing and Lessons* (Kluwer International 1996).

O'Hanlon ME, *Expanding Global Military Capacity for Humanitarian Intervention* (Brookings Institution Press 2003).

Olonisakin F, *Reinventing Peacekeeping in Africa: Conceptual and Legal Issues in ECOMOG Operations* (Kluwer Law International 2000).

Olonisakin F, *Peacekeeping in Sierra Leone: The Story of UNAMSIL* (Lynne Rienner Publishers 2008).

Olsson L, *Gender Equality and United Nations Peace Operations in Timor Leste* (Martinus Nijhoff Publishers 2009).

Olsson L and Tryggestad TL (eds), *Women and International Peacekeeping* (Frank Cass 2001).

Omaar R and De Waal A, *Somalia: Operation Restore Hope: A Preliminary Assessment* (African Rights 1993).

O'Neil WG, 'UN Peacekeeping Operations and Rule of Law Programs' in Hurwitz A (ed), *Civil War and the Rule of Law* (Lynne Rienner 2008).

Orakhelashvili A, 'The Legal Basis of the United Nations Peace-Keeping Operations' [2003] Virginia Journal of International Law 485.

Orentlicher DF, 'Settling Accounts: The Duty to Prosecute Human Rights Violations of a Prior Regime' (1991) 100 Yale Law Journal 2537.

Orler A-M, 'Professionalism: UN Policing 2012' (2011) 8 UN Police Magazine 3.

Osman MA, *The United Nations and Peace Enforcement: Wars, Terrorism, and Democracy* (Ashgate 2002).

Oswald B, 'Peacekeeping and Legal Immunities' (1997) 126 Australian Defence Force Journal 19.

Oswald B, *Documents on the Law of UN Peace Operations* (Oxford University Press 2010).

Oswald B and Bates A, 'Privileges and Immunities of United Nations Police' in Hughes BW, Hunt CT and Kondoch B (eds), *Making Sense of Peace and Capacity-Building Operations: Rethinking Policing and Beyond* (Martinus Nijhoff 2010).

Oswald B and Finnin SJ, 'Combating the Trafficking of Persons on Peace Operations' (2006) 10 International Peacekeeping: The Yearbook of International Peace Operations 1.

Perito RM, *Where is the Lone Ranger When We Need Him?: America's Search for a Postconflict Stability Force* (United States Institute of Peace Press 2004).

Phal KS, 'The Lessons of the UNTAC Experience and the Ongoing Responsibilities of the International Community for Peacebuilding and Development in Cambodia' (1995) 7 Global Change, Peace & Security 129.

Polman L, *We Did Nothing: Why the Truth Doesn't Always Come out When the UN Goes in* (Penguin 2004).

Pouligny B, *Peace Operations Seen from Below: UN Missions and Local People* (C. Hurst & Co. 2006).

Pugh M (ed) *Maritime Security and Peacekeeping: A Framework for United Nations Operations* (Manchester University Press 1994).

Raevsky A and Vorob'ev IN, *Russian Approaches to Peacekeeping Operations* (United Nations 1994).

Rainey B, Wicks E and Ovey C, *Jacobs, White and Ovey: The European Convention on Human Rights* (Oxford University Press 2014).

Ramcharan BG (ed) *Human Rights Protection in the Field* (Martinus Nijhoff 2006).

Ramsbotham O and Woodhouse T, *Encyclopedia of International Peacekeeping Operations* (ABC-CLIO 1999).

Rathbun BC, *Partisan Interventions: European Party Politics and Peace Enforcement in the Balkans* (Cornell University Press 2004).

Ratner SR, *The New UN Peacekeeping: Building Peace in Lands of Conflict after the Cold War* (Macmillan 1996).

Ravo LM, 'The Role of the Principle of Effective Judicial Protection in the EU and its Impact on National Jurisdictions' (2012) 1 Sources of Law and Legal Protection 101.

Rawski F, 'To Waive or Not to Waive: Immunity and Accountability in UN Peacekeeping Operations' (2002) 18 Connecticut Journal of international law 103.

Razack S, *Dark Threats and White Knights: The Somalia Affair, Peacekeeping, and the New Imperialism* (University of Toronto Press 2004).

Rees E, 'Security-Sector Reform and Transitional Administrations' (2002) 2 Conflict, Security and Development 151.

Reese WLM, 'Legislative Jurisdiction' [1978] Columbia Law Review 1587.

Regan PM, *Civil Wars and Foreign Powers: Outside Intervention in Intrastate Conflict* (University of Michigan Press 2002).

Reimann J, 'Debriefing on CIVPOL Experiences: United Nations Mission for the Referendum in Western Sahara (MINURSO)' in Azimi N (ed), *The Role and Functions of Civilian Police in United Nations Peace-Keeping Operations: Debriefing and Lessons* (Kluwer International 1996).

Reinisch A, *International Organizations Before National Courts* (Cambridge University Press 2000).

Reinisch A, 'Securing the Accountability of International Organizations' (2001) 7 Global Governance 131.

Reinisch A, 'Privileges and immunities' in Klabbers J and Wallendahl A (eds), *Research Handbook on the Law of International Organizations* (Edward Elgar Publishing 2011).

Ricci A, *From Early Warning to Early Action?: The Debate on the Enhancement of the EU's Crisis Response Capability Continues* (European Commission 2008).

Ricci A (ed) *From Early Warning to Early Action?: The Debate on the Enhancement of the EU's Crisis Response Capability Continues* (Office for Official Publications of the European Communities 2008).

Rifkind M, ' UN Peacekeeping: Past Lessons and Future Prospects' in (David Hume Institute 1995).

Rikhye IJ, *The Theory and Practice of Peacekeeping* (St Martin's 1984).

Rikhye IJ, *Military Adviser to the Secretary-General: UN Peacekeeping and the Congo Crisis* (Hurst 1993).

Rikhye IJ, Harbottle M and Egge B, 'The Thin Blue Line: International Peacekeeping and its Future' in (Yale University Press 1974).

Rikhye IJ and Skjelsbaek K (eds), *The United Nations and Peacekeeping: Results, Limitations and Prospects – The Lessons of 40 Years of Experience* (Macmillan in association with the International Peace Academy 1990).

Roberts A, 'The Crisis in UN Peacekeeping' (1994) 36 Survival 93.

Roos KC, 'Debriefing of Civilian Police Components: UN Transitional Authority in Cambodia (UNTAC)' in Azimi N (ed), *The Role and Functions of Civilian Police in United Nations Peace-Keeping Operations: Debriefing and Lessons* (Kluwer Law International 1996).

Roper J and et al., *Keeping the Peace in the Post-Cold War Era: Strengthening Multilateral Peacekeeping – A Report to the Trilateral Commission* (Trilateral Commission 1993).

Rubinstein RA, *Peacekeeping under Fire: Culture and Intervention* (Paradigm Publishers 2008).

Ruiz CA, 'Role and Functions of the Civilian Police in Human Rights Verification Missions' in Azimi N (ed), *The Role and Functions of Civilian Police in United Nations Peace-Keeping Operations* (Kluwer Law International 1996).

Ryngaert C, *Jurisdiction in International Law* (Oxford University Press 2008).

Sari A, 'Jurisdiction and International Responsibility in Peace Support Operations: The Behrami and Saramati Cases' (2008) 8 Human Rights Law Review 151.

Sari A, 'UN Peacekeeping Operations and Article 7 ARIO: The Missing Link' (2012) 9 International Organizations Law Review 77.

Sarooshi D, *The United Nations and the Development of Collective Security: The delegation by the UN Security Council of its Chapter VII Powers* (Clarendon Press 1999).

Satow E, 'Satow's Guide to Diplomatic Practice, 5th edn' Lord Gore-Booth (London and New York: Longman, 1979) 41.

Schmalenbach K, 'Third Party Liability of International Organizations – A Study on Claim Settlement in the Course of Military Operations and International Administrations' (2006) 19 Journal of International Peacekeeping 33.

Schmidl EA, *Peace Operations between War and Peace* (Frank Cass 2000).

Schnabel A and Ehrhart H-G (eds), *Security Sector Reform and Post-Conflict Peacebuilding* (United Nations University Press 2005).

Schöndorf E, 'Against the Odds – The Ill-Structured Conditions, Organizational Pathologies, and Coping Strategies of United Nations Transitioanl Administrations' (Dr rer soc thesis, Universität Konstanz 2009).

Seidl-Hohenveldern I, 'Failure of Controls in the Sixth International Tin Agreement' in Blokker N and Muller S (eds), *Towards More Effective Supervision by International Organizations, Essays in Honour of Henry G Schermers*, vol I (Multinus Nijhoff 1994).

Shatzmiller M, *Islam and Bosnia Conflict Resolution and Foreign Policy in Multi-Ethnic States* (McGill-Queen's University Press 2002).

Shaw MN, *International Law* (6th edn, CUP 2008).

Sheeran SP, 'A Constitutional Moment?: United Nations Peacekeeping in the Democratic Republic of Congo' (2011) 8 International Organizations Law Review 55.

Shelton D, 'Private Violence, Public Wrongs and the Responsibilities of States' (1989) 13 Fordham International Law Journal 1.

Shope VC, *Peacekeeping: A Selected Bibliography* (US Army War College Library 1995).

Shope VC, *Peacekeeping: A Selected Bibliography* (3rd revised edn, US Army War College Library 1996).

Shotton A, 'A Strategy to Address Sexual Exploitation by UN Peacekeeping Personnel' (2006) 39 Cornell International Law Journal 103.

Simm G, *Sex in Peace Operations* (Cambridge University Press 2013).

Simma B and others, *The Charter of the United Nations: A Commentary*, vol 2 (Oxford University Press Oxford 2002).

Sitkowski A, *UN Peacekeeping: Myth and Reality* (Praeger Security International 2006).

Sklansky DA, 'Hearsay's Last Hurrah' (2009) 1 Supreme Court Review 1.

Skold N, *United Nations Peacekeeping after the Suez War: UNEF I – The Swedish Involvement* (Hurst 1996).

Smith D, 'Managing CIVPOL – The Potential of Performance Management in International Public Services' in Dijkzeul D and Beigbeder Y (eds), *Rethinking International Organizations* (Berghahn Books 2003).

Smith JDD, *Canada in Croatia, Peacekeeping & UN Reform – The View from the Ground* (Strategic and Combat Studies Institute 1995).

Smith MG and Dee M, *Peacekeeping in East Timor: The Path to Independence* (Lynne Rienner Publishers 2003).

Smith SS, *Afghanistan's Troubled Transition Politics, Peacekeeping and the 2004 Presidential Election* (First Forum Press 2011).

Snow DM, *Peacekeeping, Peacemaking and Peace-enforcement: The US Role in the New International Order* (Strategic Studies Institute, US Army War College 1993).

Stahn C, 'The United Nations Transitional Administrations in Kosovo and East Timor: A First Analysis' (2001) 5 Max Planck Yearbook of United Nations Law 105.

Stahn C, *The Law and Practice of International Territorial Administration: Versailles to Iraq and Beyond*, vol 57 (Cambridge University Press 2008).

Staley RS, *The Wave of the Future: The United Nations and Naval Peacekeeping* (Lynne Rienner Publishers 1992).

Stavrinides Z, 'Human Rights Obligations under the United Nations Charter' (1999) 3 The International Journal of Human Rights 38.

Steiner HJ, Alston P and Goodman R, *International Human Rights in Context* (Clarendon Press Oxford 1996).

Stewart C, 'What Limitations Exist, or Should Exist, on a UN-Mandated Transformative Peacekeeping Operation?' (LLM thesis, University of Essex 2006).

Stjernfelt B, *The Sinai Peace Front: UN Peacekeeping Operations in the Middle East, 1973–1980* (Nihlen S tr, Hurst 1992).

Stodiek T, 'International Police Forces in Peace Operations' in Langholtz H, Kondoch B and Wells A (eds), *International Peacekeeping: The Yearbook of International Peace Operations*, vol 9 (Koninklijke Brill N V 2004).

Sugget N, *See the Road Well Shaping East Timor's Frontier* (Pandanus Books 2005).

Synge R, *Mozambique : UN Peacekeeping in Action, 1992–94* (United States Institute of Peace Press 1997).

Taibo FJ, *Uruguayos en el Congo: La Primera Guerra Mundial Africana* (La Republica 2003).

Tarassenko S and Zacklin R, 'Independence of International Civil Servants (Privileges and Immunities)' in De Cooker C (ed), *International Administration: Law and Management Practices in International Organizations* (1990).

Taylor AM, Cox D and Granatstein JL, *Peacekeeping: International Challenge and Canadian Response* (Canadian Institute of International Affairs 1968).

Taylor I, *China's New Role in Africa* (Lynne Rienner Publishers 2009).

Teixeira P, *The Security Council at the Dawn of the Twenty-First Century to What Extent is it Willing and Able to Maintain International Peace and Security?* (UNIDIR 2003).

Thakur R and Schnabel A (eds), *United Nations Peacekeeping Operations Ad Hoc Missions, Permanent Engagement* (United Nations University Press 2001).

Thakur RC, *Peacekeeping in Vietnam: Canada, India, Poland, and the International Commission* (University of Alberta Press 1984).

Thakur RC and Schnabel A, *United Nations Peacekeeping Operations: Ad Hoc Missions, Permanent Engagement* (United Nations University Press 2001).

Thomas EM, *The Old Way: A Story of the First People* (Farrar, Straus and Giroux 2006).

Thornberry C, *Peacekeeping, Peacemaking and Human Rights* (INCORE 1995).

Tillett G, *Peacekeeping: Conflict Resolution Training for Military Peacekeepers: Paper Presented at the INCORE Conference on the Training and Preparation of Military and Civilian Peacekeepers* (Conflict resolution training for military p ed, INCORE 1997).

Tomuschat C, *International Law: Ensuring the Survival of Mankind on the Eve of a New Century: General Course on Public International Law*, vol 281 (Martinus Nijhoff 2001).

UN, *Annual Report of the Secretary General on the Work of the Organization 16 June 1962–15 June 1963* (UN 1963).

UN, *The Blue Helmets: A Review of United Nations Peacekeeping*, vol 5 (UN 1990).

UN, *The Blue Helmets: A Review of United Nations Peacekeeping* (2 edn, UN 1990).

UN, *Peace-Keeping Information Notes*, vol 1995 (UN 1995).

UN, *United Nations Civilian Police Handbook* (UN 1995).

UN, *The Blue Helmets: A Review of United Nations Peace-Keeping* (3 edn, UN 1996).

UN DPKO, *Selection Standard and Training Guidelines for UNCIVPOL* (UN 1997).

UN DPKO, *Handbook on United Nations Multidimensional Peacekeeping Operations* (UN 2003).

UN DPKO, 'Brief History' [2011] UN Police Magazine 6.

UN DPKO, *UN Police Magazine* (6 edn, 2011).

UN DPKO, 'Recruitment: Member States' [2012] UN Police Magazine 22.

UN DPKO, '"Police Week" Brings the UN's Top Cops to New York' (2014) 12th Edition UNPOL Magazine 7.

UN DPKO, *UNPOL Magazine* (9 edn, UN July 2012).

UN DPKO, *UN Police Magazine* (2nd edn, UN June 2007).

UNITAR and IPS, *The United Nations Transitional Authority in Cambodia (UNTAC: Debriefing and Lessons: Report and Recommendations of the International Conference, Singapore, August 1994)* (Azimi N ed, Martinus Nijhoff Publishers 1995).

UNITAR and IPS, *United Nations as Peacekeeper and Nation-Builder: Continuity and Change: What Lies Ahead? – Report of the 2005 Hiroshima Conference* (Azimi N and Chang LL eds, Martinus Nijhoff Publishers 2006).

UNITAR, IPS and JIIA, *The Reform Process of United Nations Peace Operations: Debriefing and Lessons – Report of the 2001 Singapore Conference* (Azimi N and Chang LL eds, Kluwer Law International 2001).

UNITAR, IPS and JIIA, *From Civil Strife to Civil Society: Civil and Military Responsibilities in Disrupted States – The United Nations Transitional Administration in East Timor (UNTAET): Debriefing and Lessons – Report of the 2002 Tokyo Conference* (Maley W, Sampford C and Thakur R eds, United Nations University Press; Martinus Nijhoff 2003).

Urscheler M, 'Accountability of Non-Military Personnel in PSOs' (LLM thesis, University of Essex 2005).

US Congress Senate Committee on Foreign Relations, *Reform of United Nations Peacekeeping Operations: A Mandate for Change* (Senate. Committee on Foreign Relations US GPO 1993).

US Senate, *US Participation in Somalia Peacekeeping: Hearing before the Committee on Foreign Relations, United States Senate, One Hundred Third Congress, 1st session, October 19 and 20, 1993* (US GPO 1993).

Utley RE (ed) *Major Powers and Peacekeeping: Perspectives, Priorities and the Challenges of Military Intervention* (Ashgate 2006).

Van Dervort TR, *International Law and Organization: An Introduction* (Sage Thousand Oaks 1998).

Van Steenberghe R, 'The Obligation to Extradite or Prosecute Clarifying its Nature' (2011) 9 Journal of International Criminal Justice 1089.

Verdirame G, 'UN Accountability for Human Rights Violations in Post-Conflict Situations' in White ND and Klaasen D (eds), *The UN, Human Rights and Post-Conflict Situations* (Manchester University Press 2005).

Verdirame G, *The UN and Human Rights: Who Guards the Guardians?* (Cambridge University Press 2011).

Verrier A, *International Peacekeeping: United Nations Forces in a Troubled World* (Penguin 1981).

Verrier A, *The Future Pattern of Pacekeeping* (Department of Government, University of Essex 1999).

Virally M, 'Review Essay: Good Faith in Public International Law' (1983) 77 American Journal of International Law 130.

Vogel FE, *Islamic Law and the Legal System of Saudi: Studies of Saudi Arabia*, vol 8 (Brill 2000).

Wainhouse DW, *International Peacekeeping at the Crossroads: National Support – Experience and Prospects* (Johns Hopkins University Press 1973).

Warner D (ed) *New Dimensions of Peacekeeping* (Martinus Nijhoff 1995).

Weiss TG and Daws S (eds), *The Oxford Handbook on the United Nations* (Oxford University Press 2007).

Wellens KC, *Remedies against International Organisations* (Cambridge University Press 2002).

Weller M, *Law Enforcement within the Framework of Peace Support Operations – Peace Lost: The Failure of Conflict Prevention in Kosovo* (Arnold R ed, Martinus Nijhoff 2008).

White ND, *Keeping the Peace – The United Nations and the Maintenance of International Peace and Security* (Manchester University Press 1993).

White ND, 'The UN Charter and Peacekeeping Forces: Constitutional Issues' (1996) 3 International Peacekeeping 43.

White ND, *Democracy Goes to War: British Military Deployments under International Law* (Oxford University Press 2009).

White ND and Klaasen D (eds), *The UN, HR and Post-Conflict Situations* (Manchester University Press 2005).

Whiteman MM, *Digest of International Law*, vol 8 (US Government Printing Office 1967).

Whitfield T, *Friends Indeed?: The United Nations, Groups of Friends, and the Resolution of Conflict* (US Institute of Peace Press 2007).

Whitman J, *Peacekeeping and the UN Agencies* (Frank Cass 1999).

Whitworth S, *Men, Militarism and UN Peacekeeping: A Gendered Analysis* (Lynn Rienner 2004).

Wilde R and Schrijver N, 'The Complex Role of the Legal Adviser When International Organizations Administer Territory' (2001) 95 Proceedings of the Annual Meeting (American Society of International Law) 251.

Williams GH, *Engineering Peace: The Military Role in Postconflict Reconstruction* (United States Institute of Peace Press 2005).

Williams MC, *Civil-Military relations and peacekeeping* (Oxford University Press for the International Institute for Strategic Studies 1998).

Williams P and Scharf MP, 'The Letter of the Law' in Cohen B and Stamkoski G (eds), *With No Peace to Keep: United Nations Peacekeeping and the War in the Former Yugoslavia* (Grainpress 1995).

Williams S and Sherif L, 'The Arrest Warrant for President Al-Bashir: Immunities of Incumbent Heads of State and the International Criminal Court – Immunities of Incumbent Heads of State and the ICC' (2009) 14 Journal of Conflict and Security Law.

Wills S, 'The 'Responsibility to Protect'by Peace Support Forces under International Human Rights Law' (2006) 13 International Peacekeeping 477.

Wills S, 'The "Responsibility to Protect" by Peace Support Forces under International Human Rights Law' in Murphy R and Mansson K (eds), *Peace Operations and Human Rights* (Routledge 2008).

Wills S, *Protecting civilians : the obligations of peacekeepers* (Oxford University Press 2009).

Wilson W, *Criminal Law: Doctrine and Theory* (2nd edn, Pearson Education 2003).

Winckler JG, 'Protectionism within the Organization of United Nations Peacekeeping: Assessing the Disconnection between Headquarters and Mission Perspectives' (2014) 5 Journal of International Organizations Studies 71.

Woodhouse T and Ramsbotham O, *Peacekeeping: Terra Incognita – Here Be Dragons – Peacekeeping and Conflict Resolution in Contemporary Conflict: Some Relationships Considered* (INCORE 1996).

Woodhouse T and Ramsbotham O (eds), *Peacekeeping and Conflict Resolution* (Frank Cass 2000).

Woodhouse T and Ramsbotham O, *Peacekeeping in the 21st Century: Cosmopolitanism and the Globalization of Security* (Routledge 2008).

Woods JL, 'Mozambique: The CIVPOL Operation' in Oakley RB, Dziedzic MJ and Goldberg EM (eds), *Policing the New World Disorder: Peace Operations and Public Security* (DIANE Publishing 1998).

Wulf H, *Internationalizing and Privatizing War and Peace* (Palgrave Macmillan 2005).

Yew GCK, 'Prosecutorial Discretion and the legal limits in Singapore' (2013) 25 Singapore Academy of Law Journal 15.

Zacarias A, *The United Nations and International Peacekeeping* (IB Tauris 1996).

Zacarias A, *The United Nations and International Peacekeeping* (Tauris Academic Studies 1996).

Zacklin R, 'Diplomatic Relations: Status, Privileges and Immunities' in Dupuy RJ (ed), *A Handbook on International Organizations* (1988).

Zacklin R, 'Managing Peacekeeping from a Legal Perspective' in Warner D (ed), *New Dimensions of Peacekeeping* (Martinus Nijhoff 1995).

Zacklin R, 'United Nations Management of Legal Issues' in Howard J and Oswald CSC B (eds), *The Rule of Law on Peace Operations, 'Challenges of Peace Operations' Project Conference* (Law School, University of Melbourne, 11–13 November 2002, Kluwer Law International 2002).

Zwanenburg M, 'The Secretary-General's Bulletin on Observance by United Nations Forces of International Humanitarian Law: A Pyrrhic Victory?' (2000) XXXIX The Military Law and Law of War Review 15.

Zwanenburg M, *Accountability of Peace Support Operations* (Martinus Nijhoff 2005).

Miscellaneous, NGO Documents and Reports by Other Organizations

NGO Reports and Reports by Other Organizations

ACCORD, *South Africa's Peacekeeping Role in Burundi: Challenges and Oppportunities for Future Peace Missions* (Occasional Paper Series vol 2, no 2, 2000).

Advocacy Forum – Nepal, *Vetting in Nepal: Challenges and Issues* (July 2014, 2014).

Akandji-Kombe J-F, *Positive Obligations under the European Convention on Human Rights* (Council of Europe, Human Rights Handbooks No 7, 2007).

Amnesty International, *East Timor: Justice Past Present and Future* (ASA 57/001/2001, 27 July 2001).

Amnesty International, *Peace-keeping and Human Rights 13* (IOR 40/001/1994, 1994).

Amnesty International, *Setting the Standard? UNMIK and KFOR's Response to the Violence in Mitrovica* (EUR 70/013/2000, 2000).

Amnesty International, *Asia Pacific Report* (2003).

Amnesty International, *The Apparent Lack of Accountability of International Peace-Keeping Forces in Kosovo and Bosnia-Hercegovina* (EUR 05/002/2004, 31 March 2004, 2004).

Amnesty International, *Kosovo (Serbia and Montenegro): So Does It Mean That We Have the Rights? – Protecting the Human Rights of Women and Girls Trafficked for Forced Prostitution in Kosovo* (EUR 70/010/2004, 2004).

Amnesty International, *Serbia and Montenegro (Kosovo): The Legacy of Past Human Rights Abuses* (EUR 70/009/2004, 31 March 2004, 2004).

Amnesty International, *Serbia (Kosovo): UNMIK Legacy – The Failure to Deliver Justice and Reparations to the Relatives of the Abducted* (EUR 70/009/2013, 2013).

Amnesty International, *Kosovo (Serbia) The UN in Kosovo – a Legacy of Impunity* (EUR 70/015/2006 November 2006).

Call C, *Challenges in Police Reform: Promoting Effectiveness and Accountability* (IPA Policy Report, 2003).

Carlson SN, *Legal and Judicial Rule of Law Work in Multi-Dimensional Peacekeeping Operations: Lessons-Learned Study* (UN DPKO, 2006).

Chappell D and Evans J, *The Role, Preparation and Performance of Civilian Police in United Nations Peacekeeping Operations* (1997).

Council of Europe, *Accountability of International Organisations for Human Rights Violations* (Committee on Legal Affairs and Human Rights, Doc 13370, 2013).

Csáky C, *No One to Turn to – The Under-Reporting of Child Sexual Exploitation and Abuse by Aid Workers and Peacekeepers* (Save the Children – UK, 2008).

Durch WJ et al., *Improving Criminal Accountability in United Nations Peace Operations* (Stimson Center Report, 2009).

Durch WJ, *United Nations Police Evolution, Present Capacity and Future Tasks* (The Henry L Stimson Center, Discussion Paper, 2010).

Durch WJ and England ML, *Ending Impunity: New tools for Criminal Accountability in UN Peace Operations by William J. Durch and Madeline L. England* (Stimson Center, Accountability Issue Brief September 2009, 2009).

Durch WJ and England ML, *Enhancing United Nations Capacity to Support Post-Conflict Policing and Rule of Law: Revised and Updated* (Stimson Centre Report No 63 Rev 1, 2010).

Durch WJ and Ket M, *Police in UN Peacekeeping: Improving Selection, Recruitment, and Deployment* (Providing for Peacekeepning, 2013).

Dziedzic M and Stark C, *Bridging the Public Security Gap* (United States Institute of Peace Briefing, June, 2006).

Fleshman M, *Tough UN Line on Peacekeeper Abuses* (Africa Survival, April 2005, 2005).

Geneva Academy of International Humanitarian Law and Human Rights, *Counterpiracy under International Law* (Academy Briefing No 1, August 2012).

Government of Canada, *Toward a Rapid Reaction Capability for the United Nations* (Prepared for the 50th session of the UNGA, September 1995, 1995).

Grimstad E, *Final Report, Review of the OIOS Investigations Division, United Nations* (Submitted to the Under-Secretary-General of Office of Internal Oversight Services, 2007).

Hansen AS, *Policing the Peace: The Rise of United Nations Formed Police Units* (ZIF Center for International Peace Operations-Policy Briefing vol 2, 2011).

Human Rights Watch, *Killings in Kiwanja: The UN's Inability to Protect Civilians* (December 2008).

Human Rights Watch, *Somalia: Beyond the Warlords; the Need for a Verdict on Human Rights Abuses* (7 March 1993, vol 2, 1993).

Human Rights Watch, *Bosnia-Herzegovina: The Fall of Srebrenica and the Failure of UN Peacekeeping* (October 1995, vol 7, no 13, 1995).

Human Rights Watch, *Hopes Betrayed – Trafficking of Women and Girls To Post-Conflict Bosnia and Herzegovina for Forced Prostitution* (November 2002, vol 14, no 9 (D), 2002).

Human Rights Watch, *Iraq: Hearts and Minds – Post-War Civilian Deaths in Baghdad Caused by US Forces* (October 2003, vol 15, no 9 (E), 2003).

Human Rights Watch, *'We'll Kill You If You Cry' – Sexual Violence in Sierra Leone Conflict* (Vol 15, No 1 (A) – January 2003, 2003).

Human Rights Watch, *Imperatives for Immediate Change: The African Union Mission in Sudan* (January 2006, vol 18, no 1 (A), 2006).

Human Rights Watch, *Darfur 2007: Chaos by Design – Peacekeeping Challenges for AMIS and UNAMID* (September 2007, vol 19, no 15 (A), 2010).

Independent Police Complaints Commission, *Misconduct Sanctions Imposed on Officers 2007/08* (2008).

Independent Police Complaints Commission, *Misconduct Sanctions Imposed on Officers 2008/9* (2009).

Independent Police Complaints Commission, *Police Complaints: Statistics 2011/12* (IPCC Research and Statistics Series: Paper 25, 2012).

International Alert, *Gender Mainstreaming in Peace Support Operations: Moving beyond Rhetoric to Practice* (July 2002).

International Law Association, *Report of the Seventy-First Conference, Accountability of International Organizations: First Report* (2004).

International Peace Institute, *Being a Peacekeeper: The Challenges and Opportunities of 21st-Century Peace Operations* (February 2011).

IRIN-HOA, *Horn of Africa IRIN-HOA* (Weekly Round-up #53, 1–7 September 2001, 2001).

Jan A, Orr RCO and Wilkins TA, 'Peacemaking and Peacekeeping for the Next Century' (25th Vienna Seminar, Co-sponsored by the Government of Austria & International Peace Academy, 2–4 March 1995).

Lattu K, *To Complain or Not to Complain: Still the Question, Consultations with Humanitarian Aid Beneficiaries on Their Perceptions of Efforts to Prevent and Respond to Sexual Exploitation and Abuse* (Humanitarian Accountability Partnership, 2007).

Lin T and Law P, 'Objective-Based Policing Typology' (The Oceanic Conference on International Studies, 2–4 July 2008).

Lutz C, Gutmann M and Brown K, *Conduct and Discipline in UN Peacekeeping Operations:Culture, Political Economy and Gender – Report submitted to the Conduct and Discipline Unit, Department of Peacekeeping Operations United Nations* (Watson Institute for International Studies, Brown University, 19 October 2009).

Marcus BBR and Powers-Steves T, (Report No3).

Marks RT and Denham T, *Roundtable Report: A Roundtable on Police and Gendarmerie Women in Peace Operations – West African Solutions to Gender Mainstreaming Challenges* (Pearson Peacekeeping Centre, The Canadian Peacekeeping Press, West African Police Project, 2006).

Martin S, *Must Boys be Boys? Ending Sexual Exploitation and Abuse in UN Peacekeeping Missions* (Refugees International, October 2005).

McFarlane J and Maley W, *Civilian Police in United Nations Peace Operations* (Australian Defence Studies Centre Working Paper, vol 64, 2001).

Mobekk E, *Identifying Lessons in United Nations International Policing Missions* (Geneva Centre for the Democratic Control of Armed Forces (DCAF) Policy Paper vol 9, November 2005).

Omaar R and Waal AD, *Somalia – Human Rights Abuses by the United Nations Forces* (African Rights, July 1993).

Ombudsperson Institution of Kosovo, *On Certain Aspects of UNMIK Regulation No 2000/59 Amending UNMIK Regulation 1999/24 on the Law Applicable in Kosovo (27 Oct 2000)* (Special Report no 2 2000).

Palwankar U, *Symposium on Humanitarian Action and Peace-Keeping Operations* (ICRC Legal Division, 1994).

Pearson Peacekeeping Center, *Roundtable Report UNSCR 1820: A Roundtable Discussion with Female UN Police Officers Deployed in Peacekeeping Operations* (Pearson Peacekeeping Center, 6 August 2009).

Ramsbotham D, *The Changing Nature of Intervention: The Role of UN Peacekeeping* (Research Institute for the Study of Conflict and Terrorism, 1995).

REDRESS/FIDH, *Extraterritorial Jurisdiction in the European Union – A Study of the Laws and Practice in the 27 Member States of the European Union* (December 2010).

Save the Children, *From Camp to Community: Liberia Study on Exploitation of Children* (2006).

Schaefer BD, *The UN Should Stop Ignoring Its Financial Regulations and Pay its Debts to the Member States* (Backgrounder, The Heritage Foundation no 2484, 2010).

Schmidl EA, *Police in Peace Operations* (Militärwiss Büro d Bundesministeriums für Landesverteidigung, Informationen zur Sicherheitspolitik, Issue 10, 1998).

Serafino NM, *Policing in Peacekeeping and Related Stability Operations: Problems and Proposed Solutions* (Library of Congress, CRS Report for Congress, 30 March 2004).

Sismanidis RDV, *Police Functions in Peace Operations – Report from a Workshop organized by the United States Institute of Peace* (United States Institute of Peace, 1996).

Smith JG, Holt VK and Durch WJ, *Enhancing United Nations Capacity for Post-Conflict Police Operations* (The Henry L Stimson Center, 2007).

Smith JG, Holt VK and Durch WJ, *From Timor-Leste to Darfur: New Initiatives for Enhancing UN Civilian Policing Capacity* (The Henry L Stimson Center, Future of Peace Operations Programe Issue Brief, August 2007, 2007).

Smith JG, Holt VK and Durch WJ, *From Timor-Leste to Darfur: New Initiatives for Enhancing UN Civilian Policing Capacity* (The Henry Stimson Center Issue Brief August 2007, 2007).

South Asia Human Rights Documentation Centre, *Human Rights Features* (Volume 6(3), 31 March–6 April 2003, 2003).

St-Pierre K, *Then and Now: Understanding the Spectrum of Complex Peace Operations* (Pearson Peacekeeping Centre, 2008).

Xefina Consulting, *Preventing Sexual Exploitation and Abuse (PSEA) Project: KAPB Survey Results* (Report to International Rescue Committee, September 2007).

Media Reports

CNN (19 September 2000) <http://www.cnn.com/2000/us/09/19/ussoldiers.kosovo.ap/> accessed 8 September 2006.

Der Spiegel (1 February) <http://www.balkanpeace.org/hed/archive/feb01/hed2555.shtml> accessed 21 August 2007.

Inter-Press Service (24 July 1995) <www.ips.org> accessed 6 June 2008.

South China Morning Post (Hong Kong) (Hong Kong, 28 December 1992) <www.scmp.com/> accessed 22 June 2010.

The Associated Press (6 December 1993).

The Associated Press (13 December 1993).

The Associated Press (24 November 2004).

The Gazette (Montreal) (25 April 1997).

The Globe and Mail <http://www.haiti-news.com/article.php3?id_article=2876> accessed 29 August 2008.

The Times (27 August 1993).

USA Survival <www.usasurvival.org/ck052804.shtml> accessed 6 August 2008.

Washington Post (29 October 1993).

'A police officer and divorced mother of three, Kathryn Bolkovac was looking for a fresh start when she signed up as a UN peacekeeper in Bosnia' *The Guardian Weekend* (London, 22 January 2011) 19.

'African Refugees Condemn Sex Abuses' *BBC* (London, 28 February 2002) <http://news.bbc.co.uk/2/hi/africa/1847483.stm> accessed 15 August 2015.

'Aid-for-Sex Children Speak Out' *BBC* (27 February 2002) <http://news.bbc.co.uk/2/hi/africa/1843930.stm> accessed 28 August 2015.

'An Open Letter to Yasushi Akashi' *The Phnom Penh Post* (Phnom Penh, 22 August 2014) <http://www.phnompenhpost.com/national/open-letter-yasushi-akashi> accessed 25 August 2015.

'Britons in Sex-for-Aid Scandal' *BBC* (18 March 2002) <http://news.bbc.co.uk/2/hi/africa/1878063.stm> accessed 12 August 2015.

'Burundi: UN Mission Sets Up Units to Check Sexual Abuse' *IRIN* (15 November 2004) <http://www.globalpolicy.org/security/peacekpg/general/2004/1115checkabuse.htm> accessed 9 July 2008.

'Burundi: UN Peacekeepers Suspended for Sexual Misconduct' *IRIN* (21 December 2004) <http://list.web.net/archives/women-peace-and-security/2004-December/001261.html> accessed 15 July 2006.

'Canadian troops did not visit Serb brothels Federal official says' *The Vancouver Sun* (Vancouver, 2 November 1993).

'Child Refugee Sex Scandal' *BBC* (26 February 2002) <http://news.bbc.co.uk/2/hi/africa/1842512.stm> accessed 15 July 2005.

'Eritrea Arrests UN Staff' *Reuters* (2006) <http://www/redorbit.com/news/international/639859/eritrea_arrests_un_staff_on_people_smuggling_charge/index.html> accessed 10 September 2008.

'Eritrea Arrests UN Staff on People Smuggling Charge' *Reuters* (31 August 2006) <http://www.redorbit.com/news/international/639859/eritrea_arrests_un_staff_on_people_smuggling_charge/index.html> accessed 2 September 2007.

'Eritrea Expels Five UN Staff over Episonage' *AFP* (5 September 2006) <http://www.reliefweb.int/rw/rwb.nsf/db900sid/HMYT-6TCR4P?OpenDocument&query=unmee> accessed 20 August 2015.

'Eritrea Expels Five UN Staff Over Espionage' *AFP* (5 September 2006) <http://www.reliefweb.int/node/434798> accessed 26 August 2008.

'Great Lakes: Focus on Sexual Misconduct by UN Personnel' *Irinnews* (23 July 2004) <http://www.irinnews.org/report.asp?ReportID=42343&SelectRegion=Africa&SelectCountry=GREAT%20LAKES> accessed 25 August 2015.

'Haiti: Poor Residents of Capital Describe a State of Siege' *Inter Press Service* (28 February 2007) <http://www.ipsnews.net/2007/02/haiti-poor-residents-of-capital-describe-a-state-of-siege/> accessed 29 August 2015.

'Horn-Eritrea-Italy: Eritrean Govt Probing Allegations of Child Prostitution Ring' *AFP* (30 August 2001) <http://www.aegis.com/news/afp/2001/af010883.html> accessed 10 August 2005.

'Human Development: UNMIS Spokesperson: No Evidence that Supports Akhir Lahza Allegations' *Sudan Vision Daily* (19 May 2007) <http://www.sudanvisiondaily.com/modules.php?name=News&file=article&sid=21319> accessed 7 July 2008.

'Iraq Expels Five UN Staff' *CNN* (5 September 2001) <http://archives.cnn.com/2001/WORLD/meast/09/05/iraq.un/index.html> accessed 8 August 2008.

'Jaque Grinberg – an Apology' *The Independent* (28 April 2005) <http://www.independent.co.uk/news/world/politics/jaque-grinberg--an-apology-6147266.html> accessed 15 August 2006.

'Justice Minister Investigates UNMIS Rape Allegations' *Sudan Vision Daily* (13 September 2007) <http://www.sudanvisiondaily.com/modules.php?name=News&file=article&sid=25518> accessed 9 September 2010.

'Kosovo Peacekeepers Accused of Theft' *BBC* (26 June 2000) <http://news.bbc.co.uk/1/hi/world/europe/806408> accessed 2 August 2007.

'Kosovo UN Troops "Fuel Sex Trade"' *BBC* (London, 6 May 2004) <http://news.bbc.co.uk/2/hi/europe/3686173.stm> accessed 27 August 2015.

'Liberia: Gambian Peacekeepers Flog Lawmaker' *All Africa* (17 May 2004) <http://allafrica.com/stories/200405170740.html> accessed 30 August 2015.

'Morroco Soldiers Face Sexual Abuse Charge' *CNN* (13 February 2005) <http://www.cnn.com/2005/WORLD/africa/02/13/morroco.abuse.reut/> accessed 26 August 2006.

'Over Allegations of Abusing Duty Free Privilege: Unmil Boss Demands Evidence Or Apology' *All Africa* (26 February 2004) <http://allafrica.com/stories/200402270636.html> accessed 29 August 2015.

'Pakistan UN Peacekeeping Role at Risk after 3 Punished in Haiti Sexual Abuse Case' *The Express Tribune* (14 March 2012) <http://tribune.com.pk/story/349652/pakistan-risks-un-peacekeeping-role-after-3-found-guilty-of-sexual-abuse-in-haiti/> accessed 12 August 2015.

'Peacekeeper Kills E Timor Refugee' *BBC* (23 February 2007) <http://news.bbc.co.uk/2/hi/asia-pacific/6388741.stm> accessed 1 August 2010.

'Peacekeepers "Abusing Children"' *BBC* (London, 27 May 2008) <http://news.bbc.co.uk/2/hi/7420798.stm> accessed 2 May 2010.

'Peacekeepers Die in Clash over Iraq' *The Telegraph* (19 April 2004) <http://www.telegraph.co.uk/news/main.jhtml?xml=/news/2004/04/19/wkos19.xml> accessed 25 August 2006.

'Peacekeepers Held for Sex Crimes' *CBS News* (15 February 2005) <http://www.cbsnews.com/stories/2005/02/15/world/main674173.shtml> accessed 15 August 2006.

'Probe into MONUC Gold, Arms Trafficking "Well Advanced"' *IRIN* (25 May 2007) <http://www.irinnews.org/Report.aspx?ReportId=72373> accessed 15 August 2006.

'Push to Make Dads of "Peacekeeper Babies" Pay' *The Weekend Australian* (26 May 2005).

'S Lanka Troops "Abused Haitians"' *BBC* (2 November 2007) <http://news.bbc.co.uk/2/hi/south_asia/7075866.stm> accessed 15 September 2009.

'Sexual Assault Inquiry into Peace Troops' *The Australian* (26 June 2001).

'Seven UN Uruguayan Peacekeepers Probed for Stealing Sacred Objects in DRCongo' *BBC* (London, 12 September 2003).

'Sex-for-Aid Under UN Spotlight' *BBC* (8 March 2002) <http://news.bbc.co.uk/2/hi/africa/1861763.stm> accessed 20 August 2015.

'Sri Lanka to Probe UN Sex Claims' *BBC* (3 November 2007) <http://news.bbc.co.uk/2/hi/south_asia/7076284.stm> accessed 11 August 2012.

'Three Army Officers Facing Rape Allegations' *Tha Indian News* (18 March 2008) <http://www.thaindian.com/newsportal/lifestyle/three-army-officers-facing-rape-allegations_10028631.html> accessed 5 September 2010.

'UN Acts to Halt Abuses' *BBC* (18 October 2005) <http://news.bbc.co.uk/2/hi/americas/4354934.stm> accessed 24 August 2007.

'UN Haiti Troops Accused of Rape' *BBC* (30 November 2006) <http://www.bbc.co.uk/carribian/news/story/2006/11/061130_unrapehaiti.shtml> accessed 30 August 2008.

'UN Investigating Allegation of Rape in Haiti by Three UN Pakistani Peacekeepers' *Reuters* (23 Feburuary 2005) <http://www2.webster.edu/~corbetre/haiti-archive-new/msg24640.html> accessed 25 July 2008.

'UN Peace Missions in Fraud Probe' *BBC* (19 December 2007) <http://news.bbc.co.uk/2/hi/africa/7151558.stm> accessed 20 August 2009.

'UN Peacekeeper Charged with Rape' *BBC* (London, 24 August 2001) <http://news.bbc.co.uk/2/hi/asia-pacific/1508473.stm> accessed 25 August 2006.

'UN Peacekeepers in Haiti Cleared or Rape' *Jamaica Observer* (25 February 2005) <http://www.jamaicaobserver.com/news/html/20050224T200000-0500_75738_OBS_UN_PEACEKEEPERS_IN_HAITI_CLEARED_OF_RAPE.asp> accessed 2 September 2008.

'UN Peacekeepers in Timor Face Possible Sex Charges' *Reuters* (3 August 2001).

'UN Says Scores Of Peacekeepers Ousted for Abuse' *Washington Post* (1 December 2006) <http://www.washingtonpost.com/wp-dyn/content/article/2006/11/30/AR2006113001388.html> accessed 20 August 2009.

'UN Says 10 Withdrawn from Iraq' *BBC* (7 September 2001) <http://news.bbc.co.uk/1/hi/world/americas/1531854.stm> accessed 18 September 2015.

'UN Sends Home Sri Lankan Peacekeepers on Sex Misconduct Charges' *DPA News* (2 November 2007) <http://www.digitaljournal.com/article/244922> accessed 15 August 2010.

'UN Sends Porn Peacekeeper Home' *Breaking News* (20 December 2002) <http://archives.tcm.ie/breakingnews/2002/12/20/story81564.asp> accessed 10 July 2014.

'UN Sex Abuse Sackings in Burundi' *BBC* (19 July 2005) <http://news.bbc.co.uk/2/hi/africa/4697465.stm> accessed 25 August 2008.

'UN Soldiers Arrested for Alleged Sexual Abuse' *China Daily* (16 February 2005) <http://china.org.cn/english/international/120416.htm> accessed 16 May 2007.

'UN Soldiers Arrested in DR Congo' *BBC* (London, 13 February 2005) <http://www.news.bbc.co.uk/1/hi/world/africa/4262743.stm> accessed 24 August 2005.

'UN Suspends Soldiers in Burundi Over Sex Abuse' *Afrol News* (17 December 2004) <http://www.afrol.com/articles/15055> accessed 25 August 2015.

'UN Takes Step to Prevent Sex Abuse in East Timor' *ABC PM* (30 August 2006) <http://www.abc.net.au/pm/content/2006/s1728448.htm> accessed 28 August 2015.

'UN to Probe Alleged Sexual Abuse by Danish Peacekeepers' *AP* (28 February 2001).

'UN to Probe Sudan Sex Abuse Claim' *BBC* (3 January 2007) <http://news.bbc.co.uk/2/hi/africa/6226829.stm> accessed 10 September 2009.

'UN Tribunal Overturns Ruling Backing Whistleblower' *The New Zealand Herald* (4 September 2014) <http://www.nzherald.co.nz/world/news/article.cfm?c_id=2&objectid=11320116> accessed 6 October 2014.

'UN Troops Held Over Sex Crimes' *CNN* (15 February 2005) <http://www.cnn.com/2005/WORLD/africa/02/15/un.congo.peacekeepers/> accessed 25 August 2006.

'UN Wants Charges against Sri Lanka Troops for Misconduct in Haiti' *Tamil Week* (30 March 2008) <http://tamilweek.com/news-features/archives/1243> accessed 3 July 2010.

'Uruguay Apologises' *BBC* (7 September 2011) <http://www.bbc.co.uk/news/world-latin-america-14817191> accessed 30 August 2015.

'Uruguay Marines Charged over Haiti Abuse' *BBC* (24 September 2012) <http://www.bbc.com/news/world-latin-america-19708878> accessed 1 August 2014.

'US Servicemen Beat Kosovo Civilians' *BBC* (16 September 2000) <http://news.bbc.co.uk/2/hi/americas/927323.stm> accessed 8 August 2008.

Bernstein D, 'Answers needed to charges of UN misconduct in Bosnia' *Pacific News Service* (6 April 1993) <http://politicsforum.org/forum/viewtopic.php?f=42&t=31398> accessed 5 September 2005.

Bonzio R, 'Establising an International Framework for the Elimination of Trafficking in Persons Especially Women and Children' *Reuters* (28 August 2001) <http://www.protectionproject.org/human_rights/countryreport/ethiopia.htm> accessed 29 August 2005.

Borger J, 'UN Tribunal Finds Ethics Office Failed to Protect Whistleblower' *The Guardian* (London, 27 June 2012) <http://www.theguardian.com/world/2012/jun/27/un-tribunal-whistleblower-james-wasserstrom > accessed 6 October 2014.

Bowcott O, 'Nepalese Colonel Faces Torture Trial in UK ' *The Guardian* (London, 27 February 2015) <http://www.theguardian.com/law/2015/feb/27/nepalese-colonel-faces-torture-trial-in-uk> accessed 2 April 2015.

Bowcott O, 'Report Reveals Shame of UN Peacekeepers' *The Guardian* (London, 25 March 2005) <http://www.guardian.co.uk/world/2005/mar/25/unitednations> accessed 30 November 2014.

Clayton J and Bone J, 'Sex Scandal in Congo Threatens to Engulf UN's Peacekeepers' *The Times* (23 December 2004) <http://www.thetimes.co.uk/tto/news/world/article1975210.ece> accessed 15 July 2006.

Correspondence, 'Behaviour of UNTAC Troops in Cambodia and Thailand, Lieutenant General John Sanderson' *Sanderson Papers, MS 359, Box 31, Folder 181* (29 June 1992).

Deen T, 'Rights: UN Targets Sexual Exploitation by Peacekeepers' *Inter Press Service* (25 July 2002) <http://www.ipsnews.net/2002/07/rights-un-targets-sexual-exploitation-by-peacekeepers/> accessed 28 August 2015.

Dodd M, 'Hushed Rape of Timor' *The Weekend Australian* (26 March 2005) <http://www.etan.org/et2005/march/20/26hushed.htm> accessed 25 August 2005.

Doualy A, *Fraternite Matin* <http://fratmat.net/content/detail.php?cid=185T4Y955V1> accessed 19 August 2008.

Editorial, 'UN Boss Faces Harassment Charge' *BBC News* (London, 31 March 2005) <http://news.bbc.co.uk/1/hi/world/americas/4396577.stm> accessed 12 August 2015.

Gerstenfeld M, 'The UN's Own Abuses' *Jerusalem Post* (Jerusalem, 30 August 2001) <http://www.jpost.com/editions/2001/08/30/opinion/opinion.33735.html> accessed 20 July 2005.

Henao LA, 'Uruguay Apologizes over Alleged Rape by UN Peacekeepers' *Reuters* (6 September 2011) <http://www.reuters.com/article/2011/09/07/us-haiti-uruguay-un-idUSTRE78603I20110907> accessed 20 August 2014.

Holt K, 'DR Congo's Shameful Sex Secret' *BBC* (03 June 2004) <http://news.bbc.co.uk/go/pr/fr/-/2/hi/africa/3769469.stm> accessed 25 August 2006.

Holt K and Hughes S, 'Sex and Death in the Heart of Africa' *The Independent* (25 May 2004) <http://www.independent.co.uk/news/world/africa/sex-and-death-in-the-heart-of-africa-6169265.html> accessed 14 August 2008.

Holt K and Hughes S, 'Sex and the UN: When Peacemakers Become Predators' *Independent* (11 January 2005) <http://www.independent.co.uk/news/world/africa/sex-and-the-un-when-peacemakers-become-predators-6155183.html> accessed 5 January 2015.

Holt K and Hughes S, 'UN Staff Accused of Raping Children in Sudan' *The Telegraph* (2 Jan 2007) <http://www.telegraph.co.uk/news/worldnews/1538476/UN-staff-accused-of-raping-children-in-Sudan.html> accessed 10 October 2012.

Last A, 'Porn Scandal Rocks Eritrean Peace Force' *BBC* (Asmara, 20 December 2002) <http://news.bbc.co.uk/2/hi/africa/2595003.stm> accessed 3 August 2006.

Lewis D, 'Sexual Abuse in Congo' *Reuters* (10 May 2004) <www.peacewomen.org/un/pkwatch/news/04/sexabusecongo.html> accessed 26 August 2006.

Lingsay R, 'UN Effort Dogged by Sex Claims Peacekeepers Based in Haiti the Latest Accused of Abuse' *San Francisco Chronicle* (22 December 2006) <http://www.sfgate

.com/cgi-bin/article.cgi?f=/c/a/2006/12/22/MNGRLN47IA1.DTL> accessed 28 August 2009.

Loconte J, 'The UN Sex Scandal' *The Magazine* (3 January 2005) <http://www.weeklystandard.com/Content/Public/Articles/000/000/005/081zxelz.asp> accessed 15 August 2012.

Lyall S, 'Aid Workers Are Said to Abuse Girls' *The New York Times* (9 May 2006) <http://www.nytimes.com/2006/05/09/world/africa/09liberia.html?_r=0> accessed 29 August 2009.

Lynch C, 'Misconduct, Corruption by US Police Mar Bosnian Mission' *Washington Post* (Washington, 29 May 2001) <http://www.balkanpeace.org/index.php?index=article&articleid=11668> accessed 12 August 2014.

Lynch C, 'UN Cites Misconduct in Firing Elections Chief' *Washington Post* (7 December 2005) 21 <http://www.washingtonpost.com/wp-dyn/content/article/2005/12/06/AR2005120601515.html> accessed 12 August 2015.

Lynch C, 'UN Faces More Accusations of Sexual Misconduct' *Washington Post* (13 March 2005) <http://www.washingtonpost.com/wp-dyn/articles/A30286-2005Mar12.html> accessed 25 August 2015.

Lynch C, 'UN Says Its Workers Abuse Women in Congo' *Wathington Post* (27 November 2004) <http://www.washingtonpost.com/wp-dyn/articles/A15363-2004Nov26.html> accessed 22 July 2007.

Lynch C, 'UN Sexual Abuse Alleged in Congo' *The Washington Post* (16 December 2004) <http://www.washingtonpost.com/wp-dyn/articles/A3145-2004Dec15.html> accessed 24 August 2007.

MacFarquhar N, 'Peacekeepers' Sex Scandals Linger, On Screen and Off' *New York Times* (New york, 7 September 2011).

Milmo C, 'UN Troops Buy Sex from Teenage Refugees in Congo Camp' *The Independent* (25 May 2005) <http://www.africaspeaks.com/reasoning/index.php?topic=1834.0;wap2> accessed 29 August 2015.

Murdoch L, 'UN Under Fire for Turning a Blind Eye to Peacekeepers Misconduct' *The Sydney Morning Herald* (7 May 2007) <http://www.smh.com.au/news/world/un-under-fire-for-turning-a-blind-eye-to-peacekeepers-misconduct/2007/05/06/1178390145310.html> accessed 30 August 2015.

Payne T, 'Brothel-Running, Child Abuse Images, and Selling Firearms Among Nearly 200 Crimes Committed by Police in Last Three Years' *Independent* (16 January 2014) <http://www.independent.co.uk/news/uk/crime/sex-drugs-and-evenin-all--the-police-officers-that-break-the-law-9065376.html> accessed 1 January 2015.

Plaut M, 'UN Troops "Traded Gold for Guns"' *BBC* (23 May 2007) <http://news.bbc.co.uk/2/hi/africa/6681457.stm> accessed 22 August 2008.

Price S, 'Annan Sacks UN Head of Elections' *BBC News* (London, 7 December 2005) <http://news.bbc.co.uk/1/hi/world/americas/4505436.stm> accessed 12 August 2015.

Proudman CR, 'Charitable Rape: Peacekeepers' Dirty Little Secrets' *The Independent Blogs* (22 May 2012) <http://blogs.independent.co.uk/2012/05/22/charitable-rape-peacekeepers-dirty-little-secrets/> accessed 24 May 2012.

Saloomey K, 'Panel Says UN Failed to Protect Whistleblower' *Al Jazeera* (23 June 2012) <http://www.aljazeera.com/video/americas/2012/06/201262322950126228.html> accessed 6 October 2014.

Sengupta S and Gladsone R, 'Panel Urges Changes in Using UN Soldiers' *The New York Times* (New York, 16 June 2015) <www.nytimes.com/2015/06/17/world/html?smid> accessed 26 June 2015.

Stuart J, 'Dark Side of Peacekeeping' *The Independent* (10 July 2003) <http://www.peacewomen.org/news/SierraLeone/newsarchive03/darksidepk.html> accessed 10 September 2006.

Tekle B, 'UN Peacekeeping Watch – Learning from Others' Experiences: Human Rights Violations Committed by Peacekeepers' *Dehai News* (9 May 2004) <http://www.dehai.org/archives/dehai_news_archive/0163.html> accessed 8 August 2008.

Travis A, 'Police Numbers Fall by Further 3,488 Officers' *The Guardian* (London, 29 January 2014) <http://www.theguardian.com/uk-news/2014/jan/29/police-numbers-fall-by-3488-officers> accessed 21 August 2014.

UN, 'Letter dated 1 April 2009 from UN Office of Legal Affairs to the UN Department of Peacekeeping Operations, available in "UN Army Told Not to Join Congo Army in Operation"' *New York Times* (New York, 9 December 2009) <http://www.nytimes.com/2009/12/10/world/africa/10congo.html> accessed 3 January 2015.

Wallis W, 'UN Staff in Congo Face Child Sex Claims' *Financial Times* (Nairobi, 15 May 2004) <http://www.freerepublic.com/focus/f-news/1137380/posts> accessed 14 November 2014.

Walsh D, 'Peacekeeper Jailed for Porn Films' *Scotsman* (23 January 2003) <http://www.peacewomen.org/un/pkwatch/News/03/Irishpeacekeeper.html> accessed 28 August 2006.

Walsh D and Byrne N, 'UN Peacekeepers Criticized' *The Scotsman* (22 December 2002) <https://www.globalpolicy.org/component/content/article/199/40816.html> accessed 22 August 2014.

Watkins T, 'Ban Ki-Moon Backs UN Use of Fiji Soldiers' *Fairfax News NZ* (7 September 2011) <http://www.stuff.co.nz/national/politics/5577793/Ban-Ki-moon-backs-UN-use-of-Fiji-soldiers> accessed 24 August 2014.

Watson I and Vaccarello J, 'UN Sued for "Bringing Cholera to Haiti", Causing Outbreak that Killed Thousands' *CNN* (New York, 10 October 2013) <http://edition.cnn.com/2013/10/09/world/americas/haiti-un-cholera-lawsuit/> accessed 6 October 2014.

Weisbrot M, 'Is This Minustah's "Abu Ghraib Moment" in Haiti?' *The Guardian* (3 September 2011) <http://www.theguardian.com/commentisfree/cifamerica/2011/sep/03/minustah-un-haiti-abuse> accessed 2 September 2014.

Wilson J and Maguire K, 'American Firm in Bosnia Sex Trade Row Poised to Win MoD Contract ' *The Guardian* (London, 29 November 2002) <http://www.theguardian.com/uk/2002/nov/29/military.politics> accessed 6 October 2014.

Web Sources

(*Social Council Research Council*) <http://www.ssrc.org/programs/gsc/gsc_quarterly/newsletter5/content/graybill.page/> accessed 15 August 2006.

'Briefing Deboutcongolais' <http://www.deboutcongolais.info/weblogs/briefing> accessed 15 August 2006.

'Canadian Armed Forces: Peacekeepers Brief Performance sheet' <http://www.geocities.com/famous_bosniaks/english/general_lewis_mackenzie.html> accessed 3 August 2005.

'Global Policy Forum' <www.globalpolicy.org> accessed 25 August 2006.

'Heritiers de la Justice' <www.heritiers.org/> accessed 15 August 2006.

'M2 Presswire' <http://www.m2.com/m2/web/page.php/home> accessed 5 September 2005.

'Somalia: Atrocities Committed by UN Troops' (*OZ*) <http://www.oz.net/~vvawai/sw/sw35/somalia.html> accessed 15 August 2005.

'UN Atrocities in Somalia' (*Shire*) <http://www.shire.net/big.brother/unatroc.htm> accessed 25 August 2006.

'UNMEE to Investigate Misconduct of Peacekeepers' (*Intellnet*, 1 March 2001) <http://www.intellnet.org/news/2001/03/01/3048-1.phtml> accessed 1 February 2006.

'Millennials Writing for Social Change: MINUSTAH Soldiers: Personae Non Gratae' (5 February 2015) <https://w4socialchange2015.wordpress.com/2015/02/05/minustah-soldiers-personae-non-gratae/> accessed 30 March 2015.

'UN Peacekeepers Sweep into Violent Haitian Shanty Town' (*ReliefWeb*, 14 December 2004) <http://www.reliefweb.int/w/rwb.nsf/6686f45896f15dbc852567ae00530132/bf3b6ea11a76e78f85256f6a0076ee82?OpenDocument> accessed 22 July 2008.

'Sexual Exploitation in Liberia: Are the Conditions Ripe for Another Scandal?' (*SOS*, 20 August 2004) <http://www.sos-sexisme.org/English/Sexual_Exploitation.htm> accessed 30 August 2015.

'UN in Haiti Accused of Second Massacre' (*Haiti Information Project*, 21 January 2007) <http://www.haitiaction.net/News/HIP/1_21_7/1_21_7.html> accessed 30 August 2015.

'US Embassy in Haiti Acknowledges Excessive Force by UN' (*Haiti Information Project*, 24 January 2007) <http://www.haitiaction.net/News/HIP/1_23_7/1_23_7.html> accessed 29 August 2015.

'B-info' (27 October 1993) <www.b-info.com/places/macedonia/republic/news/93-10/93-10-27.mic> accessed 15 September 2005.

'News from Africa: War and Peace' (January 2002) <http://www.newsfromafrica.org/newsfromafrica/articles/art_614.html> accessed 14 August 2006.

'UN Peacekeeper Accused of Assaulting Congo Girl' (*Paksearch*, January 2002) <http://www.pakseach.com/br2002/jan/3/un%20peacekeeper%20accused%20of%20assaulting%20congo%20girl.htm> accessed 29 August 2005.

ABC, 'Allegations against Jordanian Peacekeepers' (*AM Archive*, 25 June 2001) <http://www.abc.net.au/am/stories/s317953.htm> accessed 28 August 2015.

AFLANZ, 'Armed Forces Law Association of New Zealand' <http://www.aflanz.org/news.htm> accessed 2 September 2005.

AFP, 'UN Says It Has Insufficient Evidence of Sexual Exploitation by Staff' (*Reliefweb*, 1 March 2002) <http://www.reliefweb.int/w/RWB.NSF/s/1D842B6723EC082BC1256B6F005D68CC> accessed 30 August 2015.

Amnesty International, 'News' <http://news.amnesty.org/library/index/engeur700052002?open&of=eng-2eu> accessed 23 August 2005.

Amnesty International, 'Nepal: Bar Human Rights Violators from UN Peacekeeping Missions' (17 December 2009) <http://www.amnesty.org.au/news/comments/22304/> accessed 2 April 2015.

AU, 'African Commission on Human and People's Rights' <http://www.achpr.org> accessed 27 December 2014.

AU, 'African Court of Human and People's Rights' <http://www.african-court.org/en/> accessed 27 December 2014.

Australian Federal Police, 'Peace Support Operations and Policing – An Explosive Human Skills Mix' (2000) <http://www.afp.gov.au/media-centre/publications/platypus/previous-editions/2000/september-2000/3penrose.aspx> accessed 26 July 2011.

Australian Federal Police, 'International Policing Conference 2011 – Australian Federal Police' (2001) <http://www.afp.gov.au/media-centre/publications/platypus/previous-editions/2001/june-2001/unmills.aspx> accessed 26 July 2011.

Ben and Alexis, 'Ben and Lexi: Regarding MINUSTAH' (29 July 2011) <http://blexi.blogspot.it/2011/07/regarding-minustah.html> accessed 30 August 2015.

Brodeur J-P, 'C & C' (2002) <http://conflits.org/article.php3?id_article=496> accessed 2 September 2005.

Burke L, 'UN Peacekeepers Traded Food For Sex' (*The World Post-WikiLeaks*, 9 January 2011) <http://www.huffingtonpost.com/2011/09/01/wikileaks-un-peacekeepers_n_944917.html> accessed 12 August 2015.

Capps R, 'Sex-Slave Whistle-Blowers Vindicated ' (*Salon*, 7 August 2002) <http://www.salon.com/2002/08/06/dyncorp/> accessed 16 October 2012.

Clarin, 'Acusan a Cascos Azules de Uruguay por Torturas en Africa' (21 September 2003) <http://old.clarin.com/diario/2003/09/21/i-02201.htm> accessed 15 August 2006.

Council of Europe, 'European Court of Human Rights, ' <http://www.echr.coe.int/Pages/home.aspx?p=court&c=#n1354801701084_pointer> accessed 27 December 2014.

Danto E, 'Statement of Haitian Mother of Five, Raped and Sodomized by Jordanian Soldier "Peacekeeping" in Haiti' (28 November 2005) <http://www.margueritelaurent.com/campaigns/campaignone/testimonies/jordanrape.html> accessed 22 August 2008.

East Timor Action Network (ETAN), 'UN Peacekeepers in Timor Face Possible Sex Charges' (3 August 2001) <http://www.etan.org/et2001c/august/01-4/03unpeac.htm> accessed 24 August 2005.

East Timor Action Network (ETAN), 'UN Policeman Charged with Rape in East Timor' (19–25 August 2001) <http://www.etan.org/et2001c/august/19-25/24unpolc.htm> accessed 3 September 2005.

Ely-Raphel N, 'The UN and the Sex Slave Trade in Bosnia: Isolated Case or Larger Problem in the UN system' (*US Government, Office to Monitor and Combat Trafficking*, 24 April 2002) <http://www.state.gov/p/io/rls/rm/2002/9777.htm> accessed 20 July 2007.

European Parliament, 'Sitting on Thursday 4 Oct 2001' (4 October 2001) <http://www3.europarl.eu.int/omk/omnsapir.so/debatsl5?file=20011004en&langue=en&questid=h-0745_01&level=annex_quest_doc> accessed 31 August 2006.

European Parliament, 'Resolution on the Involvement of UN Forces in Sexual Abuse in Liberia and Haiti' (14 December 2006) <http://www.europarl.europa.eu/sides/getDoc.do?Type=TA&Reference=P6-TA-2006-0606&language=RO> accessed 8 October 2014.

FOK, 'Lawsuit against the UN and Other International Organizations' (5 May 2006) <http://www.un-follies.blogspot.com/> accessed 29 August 2015.

Geevon-Smith W, 'The Grand Gedeh: Advocacy Group Expresses Concerns About Sexual Exploitation by Aid Staff' (17 March) <http://www.grandgedeh.com/gg-en0504.htm> accessed 22 August 2010.

Grigg WN, 'Beasts in Blue Berets' (*The New American*, 1997) <http://whatreallyhappened.com/RANCHO/POLITICS/UN/peace.html> accessed 28 August 2015.

Human Rights Watch, 'Mozambique' <http://www.hrw.org/reports/1995/WR95/AFRICA-06.htm> accessed 28 August 2006.

Human Rights Watch, 'EU Should Ensure International Mission is Accountable' (10 March 2008) <https://www.hrw.org/news/2008/03/09/kosovo-eu-should-ensure-international-mission-accountable> accessed 29 August 2015.

ICC, 'The States Parties to the Rome Statute' <http://www.icc-cpi.int/en_menus/asp/states%20parties/Pages/the%20states%20parties%20to%20the%20rome%20statute.aspx> accessed 19 October 2014.

Institute for Justice and Democracy in Haiti, 'Soldiers in Uruguay Released from Charges of Sexual Assault in Haiti' (*Canada Haiti Action Network*, 9 January 2012)

<<http://www.canadahaitiaction.ca/content/soldiers-uruguay-released-charges-sexual-assault-haiti>> accessed 30 August 2015.

IRIN, 'Eritrea: UN Protests at Staff Expulsions' (*Reliefweb*, 7 September 2006) <http://www.reliefweb.int/rw/rwb.nsf/db900sid/LSGZ-6TED8W?OpenDocument&query=unmee> accessed 29 August 2015.

IRIN, 'DRC' (*Peacewomen*, 11 January 2004) <www.peacewomen.org/un/pkwatch/press.html#drc> accessed 25 August 2005.

JJ, 'Home Planet' <http://home.planet.nl/~kempe103/> accessed 23 August 2005.

Jones K, 'International Workers Bulletin: Canadian Government Defends Military over Atrocities in Somalia' (*World Socialist Website*, 28 July 1997) <http://www.wsws.org/public_html/iwb7-28/canada.htm> accessed 22 August 2006.

Judicial System Monitoring Programme, 'JSMP' (6 November 2002) <http://66.102.9.104/search?q=cache:oVvw99PcDQIJ:www.jsmp.minihub.org/News/Summary%25201-8%2520November.pdf+rape+Police+Jordan&hl=ja> accessed 28 July 2005.

JuriGlobe, 'Muslim Law Systems and Mixed Systems with a Muslim Law Tradition' <http://www.juriglobe.ca/eng/sys-juri/class-poli/droit-muslman.php> accessed 26 June 2015.

Khaleeli J, 'Addressing the Sexual Misconduct by Peacekeepers' (*Refugees International*, 23 September 2004) <http://www.globalpolicy.org/security/peacekpg/general/2004/0923misconduct.htm> accessed 25 August 2006.

Mackay A, 'Sex and the Peacekeeping Soldier: The New UN Resolution' (*Peace News*, June–August 2001) <http://peacenews.info/node/3602/sex-and-peacekeeping-soldier-new-un-resolution> accessed 22 August 2014.

Martin S, 'Sexual Exploitation in Liberia: Are the Conditions Ripe for Another Scandal?' (*Refugees International*, 20 April 2004) <http://www.refugeesinternational.org/cgi-bin/ri/bulletin> accessed 22 September 2008.

McKenna M, 'Sins of the Peacekeepers' (*Sunday Herald*, 30 June 2002) <http://www.sundayherald.com/25914> accessed 30 August 2005.

MONUC, 'MONUC News' <http://www.monuc.org/news.aspx?newsID=9167> accessed 15 August 2006.

MONUC, 'Press Release: United Nations Investigates Allegations of Gold Trafficking in Ituri' (23 May 2007) <http://www.monuc.org/News.aspx?newsID=14640> accessed 22 April 2009.

Muindi M, 'Sex scandal threatens UN peace mission' (*Peacelink*, September 2001) accessed 22 August 2005.

Munyaneza J, 'Rwanda Insists on Probe into MONUC Misconduct' (*Allafrica*, 15 July 2007) <http://allafrica.com/stories/200707161302.html> accessed 15 August 2008.

Nadin P, 'Peace Support: A New Concept for UN Peacekeeping?' (*United Nations University*, 29 May 2013) <http://unu.edu/publications/articles/peace-support-a-new-concept-for-un-peacekeeping.html> accessed 22 August 2014.

NATO, 'NATO Ends SFOR Mission' (2 December 2004) <http://www.nato.int/docu/update/2004/12-december/e1202a.htm> accessed 22 August 2014.

NATO, 'NATO's Role in Kosovo' (10 June 2010) <http://web.archive.org/web/20100611233430/http://www.nato.int/cps/en/natolive/topics_48818.htm> accessed 28 August 2015.

Ngowi R, 'CNews' (*CANOE*, 11 May 2004) <http://cnews.canoe.ca/cnews/world/2004/05/11/455562-ap.html> accessed 24 August 2005.

Norwegian Refugee Council, <www.nrc.no/engindex.htm> accessed 18 August 2006.

OAS, 'Inter-American Commission on Human Rights' <http://www.oas.org/en/iachr/> accessed 27 December 2014.

OAS, 'Inter-American Court of Human Rights' <http://www.corteidh.or.cr/index.php/en> accessed 27 December 2014.

OIOS U, 'About Us' <http://www.un.org/Depts/oios/pages/about_us.html> accessed 8 October 2014.

O'Meara KP, 'US: DynCorp Disgrace' (*Insight Magazine*, 14 January 2002) <http://www.corpwatch.org/article.php?id=1119> accessed 22 August 2014.

ONUB, 'Press Release: Heeding Annan's Zero-Tolerance on Sex Abuse, UN Suspends Two Solders in Burundi' (17 December 2004) <http://www.un.org/Depts/dpko/missions/onub/pr45e.pdf> accessed 10 August 2008.

Payne T, 'Brothel-Running, Child Abuse Images, and Selling Firearms Among Nearly 200 Crimes Committed by Police in Last Three Years' (*The Independent*, 16 January 2014) <http://www.independent.co.uk/news/uk/crime/sex-drugs-and-evenin-all--the-police-officers-that-break-the-law-9065376.html> accessed 21 August 2014.

Peacewomen, 'Peacewomen' <www.peacewomen.org/> accessed 25 August 2005.

Peacewomen, 'Liberia: UNMIL Investigating Alleged Sexual Misconduct by Peacekeepers in Four Incidents' (3 May 2005) <http://www.peacewomen.org/un/pkwatch/News/05/UNMILinvestigating.html> accessed 22 August 2008.

Peacewomen, 'Nigeria Recalls UN Peacekeepers' (19 September 2005) <http://www.isn.ethz.ch/news/sw/details.cfm?id=12877> accessed 2 September 2007.

Peacewomen, 'Sexual Abuse in Congo' (2004) <www.peacewomen.org/un/pkwatch/news/04/sexabusecongo.html> accessed 26 August 2005.

Peacewomen, 'UN Sex Abuse Sackings in Burundi' (July 2005) <www.peacewomen.org/news/Burundi/July05/UNSexAbuse.htm> accessed 22 July 2006.

PSEA Task Force, 'Protection from Sexual Exploitation and Abuse by Our Own Staff' <http://www.pseataskforce.org/> accessed 28 September 2016.

Refugees International, 'Haiti: Sexual Exploitation by Peacekeepers Likely to Be a Problem' (7 March 2005) <www.refworld.org/docid/47a6eeb40.html> accessed 3 September 2014.

Reliefweb, 'Four Ethiopian Peacekeepers Suspected of Sex Crimes in Burundi' (10 March 2005) <http://www.reliefweb.int/rw/rwb.nsf/db900sid/RMOI-6AD37F?OpenDocument&query=onub%20sexual> accessed 30 August 2008.

Scoop, 'UN-Arrest of 6 Peacekeepers for Sexual Abuse' (16 February 2005) <http://www.scoop.co.nz/stories/WO0502/S00429.htm> accessed 23 August 2006.

Survival International, <www.survival-international.org/> accessed 15 August 2006.

UN, 'Kosovo News' <http://www.un.org/peace/kosovo/news/kosovo2.htm> accessed 23 August 2006.

UN, 'Protection from Sexual Exploitation and Abuse by UN and Related Personnel' <http://www.un.org/en/pseataskforce/tools_engage.shtml> accessed 12 December 2012.

UN, 'SEA Task Force "Statement of Commitment on Eliminating Sexual Exploitation and Abuse by UN and Non-UN Personnel"' <http://www.un.org/en/pseataskforce/docs/statement_of_commitment_on_eliminating_sexual%20_exploitation.doc> accessed 6 October 2014.

UN, 'Serve with Pride' <http://www.un.org/en/pseataskforce/video_english.shtml> accessed 6 October 2014.

UN, 'United Nations Treaty Collection' <https://treaties.un.org/> accessed 7 November 2014.

UN, 'UN-SAAT[1] UN Selection Assistance Assessment Team' <http://womenspolicenetwork.org/wp-content/uploads/2013/04/UN-SAAT.pdf.> accessed 12 October 2014.

UN, 'Special Committee on Peacekeeping Operations Begins Review of Report on Sexual Exploitation' (4 April 2005) <http://www.un.org/press/en/2005/gapk186.doc.htm> accessed 16 December 2014.

UN, 'Press Statement on Establishment of Board of Inquiry on Allegations of Misconduct' (5 September 2001) <http://www.un.org/depts/dpko/unmee/st050901.htm> accessed 22 August 2006.

UN, 'UN Electoral Chief Receives Letter of Dismissal' (6 December 2005) <http://www.un.org/News/ossg/hilites/hilites_arch_view.asp?HighID=443> accessed 12 August 2015.

UN, 'Police Officers Suspected of Rape Will Enjoy No Immunity UN Official Says' (6 July 2001) <http://www.un.org/peace/etimor/news/01jul06.htm> accessed 22 August 2005.

UN, 'UN News: As Eritrea Decides to Expel 5 UN Personnel, Annan Decries "Pattern of Hostility"' (6 September 2006) <http://www.un.org/apps/news/story.asp?NewsID=19735&Cr=eritrea&Cr1=#> accessed 20 August 2015.

UN, 'Task-Force on Sexual Exploitation and Abuse, "Draft Guidelines on the Community-Based Complaints Mechanisms Regarding Sexual Exploitation and Abuse by UN and non-UN Personnel"' (15 September 2009) accessed 1 January 2015.

UN, 'Probe Closed of Police Officers Connected to Deadly Shootings in Kosovo' (19 May 2004) <http://www.un.org/apps/news/story.asp?NewsID=10794&Cr=kosovo&Cr1=&Kw1=unmik&Kw2=misconduct&Kw3=> accessed 26 August 2006.

UN, 'UN Spokesperson's Noon Briefing' (21 March 2007) <http://www.un.org/News/briefings/docs/2007/db070321.doc.htm> accessed 20 August 2008.

UN, 'Spokesperson's Daily Highlights' (23 January 2012) <http://un.mofat.go.kr/webmodule/htsboard/template/read/legengreadboard.jsp?typeID=16&boardid=10470&seqno=671694&c=&t=&pagenum=1&tableName=TYPE_ENGLEGATIO&pc=&dc=&wc=&lu=&vu=&iu=&du=> accessed 30 August 2015.

UN, 'Jordanian Civilian Police Indicted on Rape Charges' (24 August 2001) <http://www.un.org/en/peacekeeping/missions/past/etimor/DB/db240801.htm> accessed 8 October 2014.

UN, 'Police Officer Serving with UN Mission in East Timor Charged with Rape' (24 August 2001) <http://www.un.org/peace/etimor/news/01aug24.htm> accessed 22 August 2005.

UN, 'Press Conference on Peacekeeping Misconduct Allegations' (25 July 2007) <http://www.un.org/press/en/2007/070725_Lute.doc.htm> accessed 12 August 2015.

UN, 'Press Conference on Peacekeeping Misconduct Allegations' (25 July 2007) <http://www.un.org/press/en/2007/070725_Lute.doc.htm> accessed 22 August 2008.

UN, 'Member of UN Mission in DR of Congo Accused of Sexual Abuse Sent Home for Trial' (26 May 2004) <http://www.un.org/apps/news/story.asp?NewsID=10882&Cr=congo> accessed 26 August 2006.

UN, 'Security Council Condemns "In the Strongest Terms" All Acts of Sexual Abuse, Exploitation by UN Peacekeeping Personnel' (31 May 2005) <http://www.un.org/press/en/2005/sc8400.doc.htm> accessed 16 December 2014.

UN, 'UN Force Link' <https://cc.unlb.org/default.aspx> accessed 18 September 2016.

UN, 'United Nations Criminal Justice Standards for Peacekeeping Police' (1994) <http://www.uncjin.org/Documents/BlueBook/BlueBook/english/bbeforeword.html> accessed 26 August 2013.

UN CDU, 'Conduct and Discipline Teams' <http://cdu.unlb.org/AboutCDU/ConductandDisciplineTeams.aspx> accessed 3 June 2014.

UN CDU, 'Conduct and Discipline Unit' <https://cdu.unlb.org/> accessed 6 October 2014.

UN CDU, 'Statistics' <https://cdu.unlb.org/Statistics/OverviewofStatistics.aspx> accessed 28 September 2016.

UN DFS, 'Standard Training Module 2: Combating Sexual Exploitation and Abuse, Role of Mid-Level Managers and Commanders' <www.un.org/en/pseataskforce/docs/dpko_dfs_standard_training_module_2_role_of_mid_level_manager_ppt> accessed 6 October 2014.

UN DPKO, 'Angola – UNAVEM I Facts and Figures' <http://www.un.org/depts/DPKO/Missions/unavem1/UnavemIF.html> accessed 22 August 2014.

UN DPKO, 'Angola – UNAVEM II Facts and Figures' <http://www.un.org/en/peacekeeping/missions/past/Unavem2/UnavemIIF.html> accessed 22 August 2014.

UN DPKO, 'Angola – UNAVEM III' <http://www.un.org/Depts/DPKO/Missions/unavem_f.htm> accessed 22 August 2014.

UN DPKO, 'Angola – United Nations Angola Verification Mission II' <http://www.un.org/en/peacekeeping/missions/past/Unavem2/Unavem2.htm> accessed 8 December 2014.

UN DPKO, 'Bosnia and Herzegovina – UNMIBH Facts and Figures' <http://www.un.org/en/peacekeeping/missions/past/unmibh/facts.html> accessed 10 August 2014.

UN DPKO, 'Burundi – ONUB – Facts and Figures' <http://www.un.org/en/peacekeeping/missions/past/onub/facts.html> accessed 16 August 2014.

UN DPKO, 'Cambodia – UNTAC Facts and Figures' <http://www.un.org/en/peacekeeping/missions/past/untacfacts.html> accessed 10 August 2014.

UN DPKO, 'Department of Peacekeeping Operations' <https://www.un.org/en/peacekeeping/about/dpko/> accessed 7 August 2014.

UN DPKO, 'Department of Peacekeeping Operations' <http://www.un.org/en/peacekeeping/about/dpko/> accessed 14 February 2013.

UN DPKO, 'East Timor – UNMISET – Facts and Figures' <http://www.un.org/en/peacekeeping/missions/past/unmiset/facts.html> accessed 16 August 2014.

UN DPKO, 'East Timor – UNTAET Facts and Figures' <http://www.un.org/en/peacekeeping/missions/past/etimor/UntaetF.htm> accessed 10 August 2014.

UN DPKO, 'El Salvador – ONUSAL Facts and Figures' <http://www.un.org/en/peacekeeping/missions/past/onusalfacts.html> accessed 22 August 2014.

UN DPKO, 'Ethiopia and Eritrea – UNMEE – Facts and Figures' <http://www.un.org/en/peacekeeping/missions/past/unmee/facts.html> accessed 29 August 2015.

UN DPKO, 'First United Nations Emergency Force: UNEF I (November 1956–June 1967)' <http://www.un.org/en/peacekeeping/missions/past/unefi.htm> accessed 30 November 2014.

UN DPKO, 'Formed Police Units' <http://www.un.org/en/peacekeeping/sites/police/units.shtml> accessed 30 June 2011.

UN DPKO, 'Former Yugoslavia – UNPROFOR' <http://www.un.org/en/peacekeeping/missions/past/unprof_p.htm> accessed 10 August 2014.

UN DPKO, 'Getting Involved' <http://www.un.org/en/peacekeeping/sites/police/recruitment.shtml> accessed 10 January 2015.

UN DPKO, 'Haiti Facts and Figures' <http://www.un.org/en/peacekeeping/missions/past/unmihfacts.html> accessed 10 August 2014.

UN DPKO, 'History of United Nations Police' <http://www.un.org/en/peacekeeping/sites/police/history.shtml> accessed 19 September 2016.

UN DPKO, 'MINURCAT Facts and Figures' <http://www.un.org/en/peacekeeping/missions/past/minurcat/facts.shtml> accessed 16 August 2014.

UN DPKO, 'MINURSO – United Nations Mission for the Referendum in Western Sahara' <http://www.un.org/en/peacekeeping/missions/minurso/> accessed 8 December 2014.

UN DPKO, 'MINUSTAH Facts and Figures' <http://www.un.org/en/peacekeeping/missions/minustah/facts.shtml> accessed 16 August 2014.

UN DPKO, 'MONUC Facts and Figures' <http://www.un.org/en/peacekeeping/missions/past/monuc/facts.shtml> accessed 29 August 2015.

UN DPKO, 'MONUSCO Facts and Figures' <http://www.un.org/en/peacekeeping/missions/monusco/facts.shtml> accessed 16 August 2014.

UN DPKO, 'Mozambique – ONUMOZ Facts and Figures' <http://www.un.org/en/peacekeeping/missions/past/onumozF.html> accessed 10 August 2014.

UN DPKO, 'Namibia – UNTAG' <http://www.un.org/en/peacekeeping/missions/past/untagFT.htm> accessed 27 June 2013.

UN DPKO, 'Peacekeeping Fact Sheet Archive' <http://www.un.org/en/peacekeeping/resources/statistics/factsheet_archive.shtml> accessed 28 February 2015.

UN DPKO, 'Peacekeeping Resource Hub' <http://peacekeepingresourcehub.unlb.org/PBPS/Pages/Public/Home.aspx> accessed 6 October 2014.

UN DPKO, 'Republic of the Congo – ONUC Facts and Figures' <http://www.un.org/en/peacekeeping/missions/past/onucF.html> accessed 10 August 2014.

UN DPKO, 'Sierra Leone – UNAMSIL – Facts and Figures' <http://www.un.org/en/peacekeeping/missions/past/unamsil/facts.html> accessed 29 August 2015.

UN DPKO, 'Sierra Leone – UNOMSIL Facts and Figures' <http://www.un.org/en/peacekeeping/missions/past/unomsil/UnomsilF.html> accessed 22 August 2014.

UN DPKO, 'Somalia – UNOSOM I Facts and Figures' <http://www.un.org/en/peacekeeping/missions/past/unosom1facts.html> accessed 22 August 2014.

UN DPKO, 'Somalia – UNOSOM II Facts and Figures' <http://www.un.org/en/peacekeeping/missions/past/unosom2facts.html> accessed 22 August 2014.

UN DPKO, 'Somalia: United Nations Operation in Somalia I ' <http://www.un.org/en/peacekeeping/missions/past/unosomi.htm> accessed 2 January 2015.

UN DPKO, 'Specialized Training Materials for Formed Police Units' <http://research.un.org/FPUPackage> accessed 29 September 2016.

UN DPKO, 'Standing Police Capacity' <http://www.un.org/en/peacekeeping/sites/police/capacity.shtml> accessed 9 December 2014.

UN DPKO, 'Troop and Police Contributors' <http://www.un.org/en/peacekeeping/resources/statistics/contributors.shtml> accessed 18 February 2016.

UN DPKO, 'UN Police Division Minimum Recruitment Requirements' <http://www.un.org/en/peacekeeping/sites/police/requirements.shtml> accessed 12 August 2014.

UN DPKO, 'UNAMID Facts and Figures' <http://www.un.org/en/peacekeeping/missions/unamid/facts.shtml> accessed 16 August 2014.

UN DPKO, 'UNFICYP Background' <http://www.un.org/en/peacekeeping/missions/unficyp/background.shtml> accessed 24 August 2014.

UN DPKO, 'UNFICYP Fact Sheet' <http://www.unficyp.org/nqcontent.cfm?a_id=1593> accessed 2 January 2015.

UN DPKO, 'UNMIBH' <http://www.un.org/en/peacekeeping/missions/past/unmibh/> accessed 16 August 2014.

UN DPKO, 'UNMIK Facts and Figures' <http://www.un.org/en/peacekeeping/missions/unmik/facts.shtml> accessed 10 August 2014.

UN DPKO, 'UNMIL Facts and Figures' <http://www.un.org/en/peacekeeping/missions/unmil/facts.shtml> accessed 16 August 2014.

UN DPKO, 'UNMIS Facts and Figures' <http://www.un.org/en/peacekeeping/missions/past/unmis/facts.shtml> accessed 16 August 2014.

UN DPKO, 'UNMIT Facts and Figures' <http://www.un.org/en/peacekeeping/missions/past/unmit/facts.shtml> accessed 16 August 2014.

UN DPKO, 'UNOCI Facts and Figures' <http://www.un.org/en/peacekeeping/missions/unoci/facts.shtml> accessed 16 August 2014.

UN DPKO, 'UNPOL' <http://www.un.org/en/peacekeeping/sites/police/division.shtml > accessed 12 December 2014.

UN DPKO, 'UNTSO United Nations Truce Supervision Organization' <http://www.un.org/en/peacekeeping/missions/untso/> accessed 3 August 2014.

UN DPKO, 'Women in Peacekeeping' <http://www.un.org/en/peacekeeping/issues/women/womeninpk.shtml> accessed 23 September 2014.

UN DPKO, 'Jordanian Civilian Police Indicted on Rape Charges' (24 August 2001) <http://www.un.org/en/peacekeeping/missions/past/etimor/DB/db240801.htm> accessed 16 December 2014.

UN DPKO, 'Gender Statistics' (November 2014) <http://www.un.org/en/peacekeeping/contributors/gender/2014gender/nov14.pdf> accessed 31 December 2014.

UN Jobs, 'Investigator, Vienna' (18 January 2012) <http://unjobs.org/vacancies/1326958725958> accessed 6 October 2014.

UN MINUGUA, 'Press Release' (4 June 1997) accessed 22 August 2005.

UN MINUGUA, 'Press Release' (7 August 1997) accessed 22 August 2005.

UN MINUGUA, 'Press Release' (25 June 1998) accessed 20 August 2005.

UN MINUGUA, 'Press Release' (28 May 1997) accessed 22 August 2005.

UN News Center, 'UN Probe Finds Peacekeepers in DR Congo Used Excessive Force' (11 June 2007) <http://www.un.org/apps/news/story.asp?NewsID=22862> accessed 22 August 2008.

UN News Center, 'Haiti – Three UN Peacekeepers Repatriated for Sexual Abuse' (13 March 2012) <http://www.un.org/apps/news/story.asp?NewsID=41538#.VUJL-mZzdWo> accessed 2 August 2014.

UN News Center, 'Heeding Annan's Zero-Tolerance on Sex Abuse, UN Suspends Two Soldiers in Burundi' (17 December 2004) <http://www.un.org/apps/news/story.asp?NewsID=12853&Cr=sex&Cr1> accessed 7 September 2008.

UN News Center, 'UN Will Not Turn "Blind Eye" to Peacekeepers' Misconduct, Vows UN Official' (25 July 2007) <http://www.un.org/apps/news/story.asp?NewsID=23333> accessed 22 August 2009.

UN News Centre, 'UN Mission Expresses Shock That Eritrea Alledges Old and New Offenses' (10 May 2004).

UN Office of Administration of Justice, 'UN Appeals Tribunal' <http://www.un.org/en/oaj/appeals/jurisdiction.shtml> accessed 6 October 2014.

UN Office of Administration of Justice, 'UN Dispute Tribunal' <http://www.un.org/en/oaj/dispute/> accessed 6 October 2014.

UN OHCHR, 'Monitoring the Core International Human Rights Treaties' <http://www.ohchr.org/EN/HRBodies/Pages/TreatyBodies.aspx> accessed 27 December 2014.

UN OHCHR, 'Special Procedures of the Human Rights Council' <http://www.ohchr.org/EN/HRBodies/SP/Pages/Welcomepage.aspx> accessed 27 December 2014.

UN OIOS, 'Frequently Asked Questions' <https://oios.un.org/page?slug=frequently-asked-questions> accessed 3 June 2015.

UN OIOS, 'Investigation Division' <http://www.un.org/Depts/oios/pages/id.html> accessed 13 December 2012.

UN OIOS, 'Office of Internal Oversight Services: Annual Reports' <http://www.un.org/Depts/oios/pages/annual_reports.html> accessed 22 December 2014.

UN OIOS, 'Overview of Investigations; How to Report Misconduct' (November 2008) <http://www.un.org/Depts/oios/pages/id_brochure.pdf> accessed 8 October 2014.

UN Press Release, 'Special Committee on Peacekeeping Operations Begins (New York)' (4 April 2005) <www.un.org/News/Press/docs/2005/gapk186.doc.htm> accessed 8 October 2014.

UN Radio, 'UN Is Investigating Allegations of Peacekeepers Trafficking in Arms and Gold in the Democratic Republic of the Congo' (23 May 2007) <http://www.un.org/radio/detail/7017.html> accessed 10 August 2010.

UN Wire, 'UN to Investigate Alledged Sex Abuse by Peacekeepers' (2 March 2001) <http://www.unwire.org/unwire/20010302/13293_story.asp> accessed 10 October 2005.

UN Wire, 'Survey Finds UN Staff Fear Retribution for Reporting Misconduct' (10 June 2004) <http://www.unwire.org/UNWire/20040610/449_24749.asp> accessed 5 June 2006.

UN Wire, (20 April 2004) <http://unwire.org/UNWire/20040420/Current_Print.asp> accessed 26 August 2005.

UN Wire, (27 May 2004) <http://www.unwire.org/unwire/20040527/449_24314.asp> accessed 25 August 2005.

UNGA Sixth Committee, '68th Session and Previous Sessions: Criminal Accountability of United Nations Officials and Experts on Mission' <http://www.un.org/en/ga/sixth/68/CrimAcc.shtml> accessed 1 October 2014.

UNGA Sixth Committee, '69th Session: Criminal Accountability of United Nations Officials and Experts on Mission (Agenda Item 75)' (2014) <http://www.un.org/en/ga/sixth/69/criminal_accountability.shtml> accessed 30 November 2014.

UNGA Sixth Committee, 'Seventieth session: Criminal Accountability of United Nations Officials and Experts on Mission (Agenda Item 80)' (2015) <http://www.un.org/en/ga/sixth/70/criminal_accountability.shtml> accessed 19 September 2016.

United States Institute for Peace, 'Guide for Participants in Peace, Stability, and Relief Operations' <http://www.usip.org/node/5545> accessed 9 November 2014.

University of Lille, 'UNMEE' <http://www.univ-lille1.fr/pfeda/ethiop/docs01/0831unmee.htm> accessed 30 July 2005.

UNMEE, 'Statement on Allegations against UNMEE Staff' (25 September 2006) <http://www.unmeeonline.org/index.php?option=com_content&task=view&id=419&Itemid=53> accessed 26 August 2015.

UNMEE, 'UN Mission in Ethiopia to Probe Misconduct Charges against Former Peacekeeper' (*Reliefweb*, 28 Feb 2001) <http://www.reliefweb.int/w/rwb.nsf/0/5ee44b3a66b9466685256a01006bfdf0?opendocument> accessed 22 August 2006.

UNMEE, 'SG Annan Responds to Eritrean Allegations against UNMEE' (May 2004) <http://www.unmeeonline.org/index.php?option=com_content&task=view&id=935&Itemid=53> accessed 15 July 2008.

UNMEE Military Officers, 'Military Officers Raise Questions on Force Commander' (*UN Forum*, 15 December 2005) <http://www.unforum.com/UNheadlines290.htm> accessed 29 August 2015.

UNMIK, 'UNMIK Online' (13 August 2001) <http://www.unmikonline.org/press/2001/trans/tr130801.html> accessed 24 August 2005.

UNMIK, 'UNMIK Online' (May 2004) <http://www.unmikonline.org/pub/focuskos/may04/focuskchron.htm> accessed 23 August 2006.

UNMIL, 'Press Release' (7 June 2006) <www.un.org/Depts/dpko/missions/unmil/pr7june.pdf> accessed 20 August 2008.

UNOCI, 'Press Release' (31 October 2004) <http://www.un.org/french/peace/peace/cu_mission/onuci/pr83.pdf> accessed 20 August 2006.

UNPOL, 'Towards a New UN Police: Revised Procedures for Assessment of Individual Police Officers' (2013) <http://www.womenspolicenetwork.org/wp-content/uploads/2013/08/II.1.B-Importance-of-new-assessment-procedure.pdf> accessed 10 December 2014.

UNPOL, 'UN Selection Assistance and Assessment Team (SAAT)' (2013) <www.womenspolicenetwork.org/wp-content/uploads/2013/04/UN-SAAT.pdf> accessed 15 December 2014.

UNTAET, 'Media Release' (3 August 2001) <http://www.un.org/peace/etimor/DB/db030801.htm> accessed 25 July 2005.

UNTAET, 'Media Release' (6 August 2001) <http://www.un.org/peace/etimor/DB/db060801.htm> accessed 29 August 2005.

UNTAET, 'Media Release' (6 July 2001) <http://www.un.org/peace/etimor/DB/db060701.htm> accessed 22 August 2005.

UNTAET, 'Media Release' (10 August 2001) <http://www.un.org/peace/etimor/DB/db100801.htm> accessed 23 August 2005.

UNTAET, 'Media Release: Jordanian Civilian Police Indicted on Rape Charges' (24 August 2001) <http://www.un.org/en/peacekeeping/missions/past/etimor/DB/db240801.htm> accessed 28 August 2015.

US Department of State, 'Italy Human Rights Practices, 1995' (March 1996) <http://dosfan.lib.uic.edu/ERC/democracy/1995_hrp_report/95hrp_report_eur/Italy.html> accessed 3 September 2014.

US Office, 'US Office Pristina' <http://www.usofficepristina.rpo.at/hrkos2.htm> accessed 22 August 2005.

US Senate, 'Debate in US senate' (*The Library of Congress*, 05 November 1993) <http://thomas.loc.gov/cgi-bin/query/z?r103:S05NO3-1112> accessed 29 August 2005.

Wada H, 'Houjin Dansei-ni UNTAET ga Syazai Wakai Seiritsu Hutou Taiho Meguru Teiso Jiken' (*Asia Kisya Club*,, 1 February 2002) <http://apc.cup.com/?no=93.1.0.0.33.0.0.0.0.0.> accessed 3 September 2005.

Wallis W, 'UN Staff in Congo Face Child Sex Claims' (*Peacewomen*, 17 May 2004) <www.peacewomen.org/un/pkwatch/news/04/sexclaims.html> accessed 25 August 2006.

Wilson R, 'Violent Truths: the Politics of Memory in Guatemala' <http://www.c-r.org/accord/guat/accord2/wilson.shtml> accessed 22 August 2005.

Xinhua, 'English News' <www.xinhuanet.com/english/> accessed 28 August 2006.

Index

Accountability 197–198, 285–286, 341
Importance of 2, 66, 144, 341
Lack of 1, 67, 341
Perception 1, 15, 115, 144, 205
African Union (AU)
Joint operation 40
Agenda for Peace 3, 29
Supplement to 3–4, 22–23, 30, 35

BINUB 156
BOI (Board of Inquiry) 89–90, 123–128, 129, 130, 159–162, 172–175, 184, 343
Boutros-Ghali 30
Brahimi report 35, 37

Capacity building 21, 28, 47–48
Training 19, 21, 26, 27, 28, 29
Capstone Doctrine 198–199
Case referral 172–176, 181–183, 186, 200, 351
CDU/T 70, 95–96, 100–103, 104–105, 107, 108, 114, 116, 118, 130–131, 139, 145, 147–148, 155–158, 168, 174–176, 179, 184, 343–344
Child Protection Advisor 139
Civil Claims/Redress 9, 114, 117, 269, 324
Civilian Police (CIVPOL) 13, 20, 37, 273
Code of Conduct 98, 138, 146, 149, 195, 200, 343
COE (Contingent-Owned Equipment) system 58, 197
Command
Military 17–18, 19
Outside 20, 24–25
Cold War, The
The end of 4, 18, 22, 25, 38
Conflict
Changed nature of 4, 22
Criminal Jurisdiction 6, 10, 188–192, 197, 198, 202–208, 212–219, 220–222, 226–229, 238, 286, 347–348
Active Personality/Active Nationality 204, 206–208, 215, 216, 227
Double Criminality 207, 209, 216, 221–222, 223, 225–226
Enforcement 188–190, 202–203, 213, 280
Extra-territorial 213–222
Draft convention 221–222
Obligatory 202
Passive Nationality 204, 208–210, 223–224
Permissive 189, 202, 349
Prescriptive 188–189, 202–203
Protective 204, 212
Territoriality 204–206, 213, 227
Universal 210–212, 224–225, 227
Criminal Law 189–191, 198–199, 201, 202, 222, 224, 228–229
Obligation to respect 192, 194, 196–199, 228
Criminal Proceeding 10, 133–134, 202, 211, 213, 269, 286, 302, 344
Political will 8, 11, 14, 286–287, 349
Criminal Prosecution 116–118, 172, 174, 176, 177, 186, 188, 200, 201, 213, 228, 230–231, 249, 263, 283, 285, 343, 345, 346
Data 10, 92–94, 102–103
Prosecutorial discretion 308–310, 324, 338–339
Criminal Sanctions
Appropriate 307
As deterrent 3, 117–118

Data
Author's 10, 69–94, 95, 96, 102, 104, 109, 111, 117, 184–185
Lack of 14, 65–71, 95- 97, 107–109, 114, 342
Disciplinary accountability 5, 7–9, 124–131, 140, 154, 164, 172, 175
Due process 92, 121, 133, 206, 226, 271–272, 282–286, 349

Effective investigation 3, 120–134, 158–172, 177–178, 185, 290, 303, 335–336, 338–340, 350
European Court of Human Rights (ECtHR) 253–254, 290–293, 294, 297–298, 300–301, 303–308, 311, 313–316, 324
Jones case 253, 258
Al-Adsani case 253, 324
Al-Skeini case 293, 306

Evidence
  Chain of custody 122
  Generating 10, 119, 121–134, 161–172, 185–187, 205, 208–209, 304, 335, 344, 346
  Lack of 309–310, 346
  Standard 133, 161–162, 174, 185–186
Ex Gratia payment 9

Firearms 48–50
Follow up with sending States 116, 118, 178–179, 182–183, 186–187

Gender Advisor 139
General Assembly 1, 14 199, 205, 220, 253, 256, 343
  Sixth Committee 206–207, 214, 215, 219, 222, 234, 236, 238–240, 244, 255–256
Ghana 17, 18, 19, 33–34, 38

HIPPO Report 12, 56, 222, 273
  Response to 53

ICJ 202–203, 238, 241–242, 253–255, 264, 266–267, 276, 280, 315, 324, 348
  Arrest Warrant case 253–254, 258, 276
  Cumaraswamy case 241, 250, 255, 264, 266–267, 276, 349
  Genocide case 3
  Mazilu case 241, 255, 276
  Reparations case 233, 310, 318, 325, 327, 333
Immunity 10, 94, 115, 119, 121, 123, 132, 172–177, 183, 191, 196, 198–200, 206, 217, 230–286, 323–325, 335, 339, 348–349
  Diplomatic 232, 238, 240, 245, 247–249, 258–261, 279
  From arrest and detention 247–249, 254, 258–261, 263, 269, 272–275, 278, 280–281
  From legal proceedings 247–249, 254, 258–259, 261, 269, 271, 274–275, 278, 280–281
  Functional 232–234, 246–249, 254, 262, 264, 273, 280
  General Convention 183, 231, 233–234, 236–240, 242–243, 245–249, 255–262, 268, 270, 276, 279–281, 347
  Official functions 119, 234, 246–248, 250–252, 257, 260, 262, 268, 272–274, 278, 279–280, 282, 342, 349
  Rationale 231–234, 258, 261, 279
  Waiver 176, 249–250, 253, 256, 263–264, 266–267, 268–272, 274–275, 277–281, 323–324, 348
Inter-American Court of Human Rights 290, 292, 293, 295, 298, 299, 301, 306–307
  Velasquez Rodriquez case 292
International crime 211, 212, 253–254, 270–271, 278
International Criminal Law 191
International Human Rights Law 11, 120–121, 133, 162, 183, 199, 288, 292–294, 322, 328–329, 331, 337–338, 349
  Legal obligation of States 11, 286, 287–288, 290, 314, 315–317, 349–350
  Mechanisms 288–290, 308
    Human Rights Committee 284–286, 288–289, 291–292, 294–297, 299, 301–303, 307, 308, 309, 311, 316
      General Comment 6 294
      General Comment 31 296, 299
      Herrera Rubio case 294, 299, 308
  Obligation to investigate 290, 301–307, 315–317, 324–335, 338–340, 349–350
    Control 315, 339
  Obligation to prosecute 287, 290, 307–315–317, 322–324, 324–334, 335–337, 339–340, 349–350
  UN's obligation 11, 288, 324–337, 339–340, 350
International Law Commission (ILC) 239–240, 252, 318
IPTF 28, 29, 98

KFOR 31, 34, 76
KLA 31

Legal obstacles 10, 188, 202, 227, 229, 230, 272, 286–287
Lotus case 188–189, 192, 202, 208, 209

Military Police 20
MINUGUA 46, 74, 161
MINURCAT 36, 87, 156, 193, 236
MINURSO 24, 25, 26, 111, 156
MINUSCA 36, 87
MINUSMA 36, 87
MINUSTAH 36, 40, 83, 85–86, 87, 89, 91, 93, 103, 105, 136, 156, 193–194, 206

MIPONUH 31, 36
Misconduct
  Category I 96, 100, 101, 103, 156, 162, 184–185
  Category II 100, 156, 162
  Complaint 6, 12, 66–70, 92, 96–98, 101–102, 109–110, 112–113, 118, 119–120, 123–126, 131, 134–143
    Retaliation 141–142
  Criminal 10
    Nature and scale of 10, 68, 69-
      Link with functions 89–91, 92, 94, 96–97, 106, 110, 111, 112, 117, 251
    Serious 12, 100, 188, 271
      Evidence of 65–114
    Visibility of 15, 16, 26–27, 32, 38, 96, 104, 106, 107, 112, 117, 125
  Data of 6–7, 70 (for author's data, see *Data – author's*)
    Sources 6
    Lack of information 65, 70–71, 95–97, 107–109, 178–182, 185, 345
  Negative effect of 62–63, 104, 106, 117
  Reporting 6, 68, 70, 95–97, 113–114, 125, 134–142, 144–149, 154
    Retaliation 142, 150–154
  Serious 1
  Unpunished 5
      Adverse effect of 5, 65
MONUC 29, 77–79, 80, 82, 83, 103, 105, 126, 145, 147, 156, 160, 193, 206
MONUSCO 36, 87, 93, 103, 105, 136
MOU (Memorandum of Understanding) 58, 115–116, 133, 179, 180–182, 197, 220, 222, 226, 314–315, 336, 346–347
  Model 197–198, 220, 228

Namibia 37, 38
NATO 31, 38
Nigeria 18, 19, 33–34, 38

OIOS 70–71, 91, 95–96, 99–100, 101–103, 108, 114, 127, 128–132, 139–140, 143–144, 146–148, 151–158, 162–170, 175–178, 180–181, 184–185, 228, 343–344
OLA (Office of Legal Affairs) 124, 126, 173, 175–176, 228, 238, 251, 265, 272–273, 328, 330
ONUB 36, 83, 86, 193, 206
ONUC 17, 18, 21, 27, 33, 38
ONUMOZ 24, 26, 38, 74, 115
ONUSAL 24, 28, 71, 110, 111
OROLSI 36

Peace Enforcement 24
Peacekeeping Operations
  Traditional 25
Peacekeeping Principles 17–18, 23
  Consent 22, 23–24
  Non-use of force 23
Peacekeeping Capability Readiness System (PCRS) 53
Peace Operations
  Definition of 11–12
  Environment 10, 15, 16, 21–22, 343
  Establishment of 3–4
  Evolution of 3–5, 124–125, 341
  Mandates 4, 23, 28
Peace Support Operations 11, 31
Pinochet case 253
POC (Protection of Civilians) 87
Preliminary investigation 149

Role models 32, 51, 62
Rwanda
  Genocide 30

SAAT (Selection Assessment and Assistance Team) 54
SAT (Selection Assistance Team) 54
Secretary-General (SG) 12, 17, 18, 19, 23, 30, 35, 37, 39, 95, 109, 128, 129, 163, 168, 173–177, 186, 192, 195, 241–242, 244–245, 250, 253–254, 257, 259, 263–268, 270, 274, 277, 280, 283, 310, 327, 348
Security Council 30, 237, 244, 250, 265, 269
  Resolution 4, 21, 22, 23, 24
Security gap 32–33
Sexual exploitation and abuse (SEA) 67, 70–71, 74, 79–80, 83, 89, 95–96, 99, 104–106, 108, 111–114, 116, 118, 128, 130- 131, 133, 135–141, 143–146, 148–149, 156, 166, 179, 180, 184–185, 196–198, 200, 202, 220, 222
SFOR 34, 38, 73
SMART concept 25

SOFA/SOMA 126, 192–194, 234–237, 243, 246, 250, 252, 255, 257–259, 261–262, 267–269, 279, 281, 283, 347
  Model SOFA 192–194, 234, 236–237, 243, 246, 260
SOP 146, 150, 161
Srebrenica 30
State Responsibility 9
Suspect
  Nationality of 91–92, 180–182, 345, 352

The Rule of Law 4, 5, 29–30, 34, 35, 41, 62, 205, 271, 285, 341
Transitional Administration(s) 117–118
Transparency 66, 118, 178–182, 351

United Nations, The
  As government 4–5, 75, 92, 113, 115, 314, 325
  Charter 233–234, 238–240, 258, 285, 288, 324–329, 331, 336
  Criminal Tribunal 189–190
  DFS (Department of Field Services) 149, 175
  DPKO (Department of Peacekeeping Operations) 23, 28, 37, 52, 56, 108, 130, 175–176, 184, 195
    Police Division 37, 52, 56, 175, 176
    Police Unit 37
  Expert on Mission 133, 153, 195, 221, 228, 231, 234–235, 237, 239–244, 246, 248, 256, 264, 265, 270, 276
  Its role in instituting criminal prosecution 7–8, 10, 177, 183, 186–187, 220–223, 283, 285–286, 335–336, 339, 350
  Obligation of 11, 177
  Official 239–241, 243, 244, 246, 249, 256, 260, 262
  Machinery 8, 10, 119–187
  Internal Code 167, 183, 185, 195–198, 200, 228, 343
    Evolution of 8, 123–134
    Effectiveness 10, 134–187
  Responsibility of 9, 14
    Draft Articles on the Responsibility of International Organizations (DARIO) 317–322
      Effective Control 318–322
  Vacarious liability of 9
United Nations Police (UNPOL) 12–13
  Creation of 16–22, 37
  Expertise 42–45, 241–242
    Link with criminal behaviour 42
  Formed Police Unit (FPU) 5, 12–13, 20, 32–34, 41, 42, 50, 52, 58–61, 63, 93, 103, 115–116, 121, 133–134, 146, 150–151, 171, 176, 177, 180, 182–183, 186–187, 197, 217–220, 223, 226, 228, 242, 243–244, 287, 314, 317–322, 336, 341, 346
  Function of 10
    Executive Policing 29, 31, 112
    Evolution of 14, 15, 16–38, 341
      Link with criminal misconduct 15, 341
    Increase of 15, 16, 38
      Link with visibility 16, 38
    Monitoring 25, 26
    Police reform 26, 28, 36, 41
  Individual Police Officer (IPO) 5, 12–13, 33, 41, 52, 53, 93, 177, 180, 182, 183, 186–187, 197, 220, 226, 228, 242, 336, 341, 347
  Individual Undertaking 140, 145, 149, 194, 200, 228, 287
  National units 20
  Number 15
  Police Advisor 41
  Police Commissioner 24, 45, 47, 125, 132, 176, 235–237, 244–246, 254, 259–263, 268–269, 274, 276, 279, 280–281
  Role of 5, 10
    Evolution of 14–38
  Selection of 16, 52–59, 341–342, 352
    Reference to functions 16, 42–43
    Required standards (selection criteria) 43–51
      Exclusion 51–52, 55–58
        human rights violation 52, 56, 59
        violation of international humanitarian law 52, 56, 59
  Skills and qualities of 15, 52, 63
    Lack of 15, 42–43, 45–46
    Operational skills 47
      Specific 48–50
    Personal qualities 50–52, 63, 118
      Integrity 50, 51, 58
  Standing Police Capacity (SPC) 37

Special Police Unit (SPU) 31, 33–34
Specialized Police Teams (SPTS) 53
Training of 61, 63, 145–146, 201, 342
Visibility of 26, 62
SRSG 132, 172, 177, 244, 267–269, 283, 346, 349
UNAMA 156, 160, 252
UNAMI 41, 156
UNAMID 36, 40, 87, 103, 156, 193–194, 236
UNAMIR 24
UNAMSIL 77, 80, 82, 193, 206
UNAVEM 46, 74–75, 110–111, 115
UNAVEM II 24, 25, 26, 30, 74–75, 110–111
UNAVEM III 38, 74–75, 110–111
UNDOF 192–193
UNEF I 17, 283
UNFICYP 18, 20, 21, 27, 38, 49
UNIFIL 71, 156
UNIFSA 87
UNIIMOG 23
UNISFA 36
UNITAF 74
UNMEE 34, 77, 80, 82, 193, 236
UNMIBH 28, 39–40, 72, 98
UNMIH 24, 28, 36, 38
UNMIK 4, 31–32, 40, 75, 83, 89, 91, 92, 93, 94, 112, 113, 115, 126, 132, 156, 273, 275, 278, 312, 324, 327
UNMIL 36, 40, 45, 83, 87, 103, 105, 136, 145, 156, 174, 175
UNMIS 29, 36, 83, 86, 87, 103, 105, 136, 156, 193–194, 236, 283
UNMISET 36, 40, 48
UNMISS 36, 87, 194
UNMIT 36, 40, 83, 86, 87, 91, 105, 156
UNMOGIP 17
UNOCI 36, 40, 48, 83, 98, 103, 105, 136, 156, 193, 206
UNOMIG 194
UNOMUR 194
UNOMSIL 111, 112
UNOSOM II 24, 38, 98
UNPROFOR 24, 38, 45, 46, 73, 83, 110, 115
UNSAS (UN Standby Arrangements System) 53
UNSF 18, 21
UNSMIS 34, 87
UNTEA 21
UNTAES 48, 194
UNTAET 4, 31–32, 34, 40, 48, 75–77, 83, 92, 93, 112, 113, 132, 192, 273
UNTAC 24, 26, 27, 38, 43, 46, 47, 48, 71–72, 82–83, 89, 91, 98, 101, 110, 111, 117, 159
UNTAG 24, 25, 27, 38
UNTSO 13, 17

Whistleblower(s) 98, 114, 147, 150–154, 185

Zeid Report 8, 101, 104, 108, 115, 127–129, 133, 136, 139, 143, 144, 145, 160, 174, 181, 250, 283, 343

www.ingramcontent.com/pod-product-compliance
Lightning Source LLC
LaVergne TN
LVHW010623300926
849162LV00001B/45